American Law and Legal Systems

American Law and Legal Systems ...ophy of law within a political, social, and economic frame... ...eat clarity and insight. Readers are introduced to operative legal c...epts, everyday law practices, substantive procedures, and the intricacies of the American legal system. Eliminating confusing legalese, the authors skillfully explain the basics, from how a lawsuit is filed to the final appeal. This new edition provides essential updates to forensic and scientific evidence, contract law, family law, and includes new text boxes and tables to help students understand, remember, and apply central concepts.

New to the Eighth Edition

- Updates the coverage of environmental law, especially in relation to climate change.

- Updates the coverage of family law, especially in relation to gay marriage and abortion rights.

- Includes new coverage of challenges to the Voting Rights Act, campaign finance, and cybersecurity.

- Covers the effects of social media on judicial procedure.

- Includes 16 new cases including *Obergefell v. Hodges*.

- Adds new text boxes on intriguing subjects throughout.

- Accompanied by an author-written Instructor's Manual that includes Learning Objectives, Chapter Summaries, Chapter Outlines, Key Terms and Concepts, as well as Test Questions for each chapter.

James V. Calvi is Professor of Political Science at West Texas A&M University.

Susan Coleman is the retired Director of the Criminal Justice Program at West Texas A&M University.

In this excellent eighth edition of *American Law and Legal Systems*, Calvi and Coleman go beyond describing the legal doctrines at issue to more fully identify, summarize, and apply them; they write at a level that undergraduate students can comprehend without being condescending, and empower students to determine what a particular statute means. It is ideal for students of the American judicial process, and particularly for those considering law school – I will certainly be assigning it again.

Kathleen Waggoner, *Iowa State University*

With topics matching an undergraduate course introducing the American legal system, Calvi and Coleman's new edition introduces the essential vocabulary and concepts in an accessible way. The work is particularly useful for students considering further law study or preparing for citizenship.

William A. Eagles, *University of North Carolina-Greensboro*

American Law and Legal Systems

Eighth Edition

JAMES V. **CALVI**

West Texas A&M University

SUSAN **COLEMAN**

Attorney at Law

Routledge
Taylor & Francis Group

NEW YORK AND LONDON

Eighth edition published 2017
by Routledge
711 Third Avenue, New York, NY 10017

and by Routledge
2 Park Square, Milton Park, Abingdon, Oxon OX14 4RN

Routledge is an imprint of the Taylor & Francis Group, an informa business

Fifth edition published by Pearson Education, Inc., 2004
Sixth edition published by Pearson Education, Inc., 2008
Seventh edition published by Pearson Education, Inc. 2012, and Routledge, 2016

Library of Congress Cataloging in Publication Data
Names: Calvi, James V., 1949- author. | Coleman, Susan L., author.
Title: American law and legal systems / James V. Calvi, West Texas A&M
University, a member of the Texas A&M University system,
Susan Coleman, attorney at law.
Description: Eighth edition. | Milton Park, Abingdon, Oxon ; New York, NY :
Routledge, 2017. | Includes bibliographical references and index.
Identifiers: LCCN 2016011952| ISBN 9781138654389 (hardback) |
ISBN 9781138654396 (pbk.) | ISBN 9781315623276 (ebook)
Subjects: LCSH: Law–United States.
Classification: LCC KF387 .C28 2017 | DDC 349.73–dc23
LC record available at http://lccn.loc.gov/2016011952

ISBN: 9781138654389 (hbk)
ISBN: 9781138654396 (pbk)
ISBN: 9781315623276 (ebk)

Typeset in Sabon
by Cenveo Publisher Services

Printed and bound in the United States of America by
Edwards Brothers Malloy on sustainably sourced paper

Dedication

For my friends and colleagues in the Law Related Education Section of the State Bar of Texas—Jim

and

For my family and friends who have so enriched my life—Susan

BRIEF CONTENTS

CONTENTS

PREFACE

More than one commentator on the nature of the law has noted the glacial pace at which the law appears to move. Certainly, as one views areas of the law such as property and contracts, it is easy to see why concepts rooted in the Middle Ages make the law appear stagnant and sluggish. Yet, since the first publication of *American Law and Legal Systems* in 1988, we have seen tremendous change take place in the law. This current edition reflects some of the dynamic changes law has undergone since that first edition. Perhaps the starkest change has been in the area of family law with the Supreme Court's landmark decision to legalize same-sex marriages in the United States. Not only questions about the institution of marriage itself but also questions of adoption, child-rearing, insurance, entitlements, and medical care will continue to come before the courts because of the *Obergefell* decision. To continue the analogy, we have only seen the tip of the iceberg.

But other areas of the law have also undergone dramatic change. The ability to transform and to copy vast amounts of information into electronic and digital forms has shaken traditional approaches to intellectual property. In criminal law the proliferation of electronic devices presents new challenges to the reasonableness of searches and seizures under the Fourth Amendment. The enactment of open and concealed carry laws portend an increase in civil suits surrounding the use of handguns in society. As we write, an unexpected vacancy on the U.S. Supreme Court could result in an ideological shift in the makeup of the Court that could last a generation.

As with any new edition, we have tried to include the developments in the law that have occurred since the last edition was published in 2012. At the same time we hope we have retained the concepts and features that appealed to our readers in the past. We have also tried to keep the language of the text as clear, precise, and accurate as possible. As teachers, our major goal has always been to explain the abstract concepts of the law in a manner that our readers can understand. Only our readers can judge whether we have succeeded.

NEW TO THE EIGHTH EDITION

It is always challenging when writing a revision of a book to decide what should remain and what should be deleted. For example, the 1983 case of *Bob Jones University v. United States* seemed to be a natural candidate for deletion until the *Obergefell v. Hodges* case made *Bob Jones* very relevant once again. In law, as in many other areas of life, the more things change the more they stay the same. We have made a conscious attempt not to become too attached to the examples and explanations used in previous editions but if, after reflection, we concluded that previous examples had not lost their relevancy, we did not hesitate to keep them.

This is not to say that the new edition is not without major revisions. The most significant change, of course, has to be in the area of family law (Chapter 13) and the effects that *Obergefell v. Hodges* has had and will have on marriage, adoption, divorce, credit, home buying, and health care just to name a few areas. Increased interest in world events encouraged the expansion of our comparative law coverage of Shariah and Chinese law (Chapter 2). We have updated the chapter on judicial selection with more recent examples and replaced *Republican Party of Minnesota v. White* with a 2015 Supreme Court decision on judicial campaign financing (Chapter 3). In Chapter 6, the section on the legislative veto has been replaced with the more recent conflict between the President and Congress over recess appointments by the President. Chapter 4 was revised to note the effects of social media such as Facebook or Twitter upon judicial procedure, especially when jurors misuse social media.

Chapter 7, which covers criminal law, notes recent changes in Fourth Amendment cases involving the seizure of information on a defendant's cell phone. New developments in the interpretation of the *Miranda* warnings were also included. The problems of litigating issues such as global warming have been explored in the chapter on environmental law (Chapter 9). Again, the challenges likely to face courts in the future concerning the ownership and willing of property in same-sex marriages have been outlined in Chapter 12. Throughout all the chapters updated examples and additional clarification have been added.

We hope most of the features that adopters valued in the previous seven editions of *American Law and Legal Systems* have remained intact. Our text boxes that illustrate unusual and "quirky" aspects of the law have been retained in the Eighth Edition. We hope readers find them as interesting as we do. Finally, we hope that we have kept our own views of law and politics to a minimum. However, as has been observed so often, if people did not disagree about the law there would not be so many case books on the shelves.

ACKNOWLEDGMENTS

The publication of any book is, by definition, a collaborative effort. We wish to thank our colleagues in the Department of Political Science and Criminal Justice at West Texas A&M University for their support over the years. Our special thanks go to those who reviewed our revision plan and offered helpful suggestions: Adam Abelkop, Indiana University; William A. Eagles, University of North Carolina at Greensboro; Marie Palladini, California State University Dominguez Hills; and Kathleen M. Waggoner, Iowa State University.

Finally, we wish to thank the people at Routledge for their help in making this new edition possible. Our thanks go to Jennifer Knerr and Ze'ev Sudry for ensuring the continued publication and success of our book. Also, many thanks to the copyeditor Ann King and the production editor Carrie Bell at Routledge.

Introduction

In order to understand the American legal system one must first come to terms with the question: What is law? Americans have always had ambivalent feelings about law. Our rhetoric is full of noble ideals such as "equal justice under law" and the "rule of law." We pride ourselves on having a "government of laws, not men," and on the assertion that "no one is above the law." At the same time, disregard for the rule of law has been part of our political tradition. We are a nation born of violent revolution, and during our frontier period, vigilante groups sometimes took the law into their own hands.[1] Between the time the first organized vigilante group made its appearance in South Carolina in the 1760s and the early 1900s, 729 people were executed by such groups.[2] *Civil disobedience* is the belief that a person has a moral right to disregard an unjust law. Recent history has seen Americans debate the role of civil disobedience in the civil rights, animal rights, abortion, and anti-nuclear movements. In the 1960s, some elements of the radical left believed that ending the war in Vietnam or achieving civil rights for African Americans justified the use of violence. More recently, the more extreme members of the radical right have used similar arguments to justify violence against abortion clinics. A recent manifestation of vigilantism is the border militia groups' anger and frustration at the U.S. government's inability to stem the tide of illegal immigration into the country.

In many ways, the questions we ask ourselves about the nature of law are the same ones we ask about our political system and about society at large. How do we account for the conflicting attitudes Americans have toward law? How can persons who are law-abiding one day turn into a lynch mob the next? How can a nation founded on the basis of its citizens' "inalienable rights" systematically deny those rights to African Americans and other minorities? How can we explain these contradictions? The answers to these questions are not easy, but we can begin to understand the paradox by understanding the nature of law both in general terms and in American society specifically.

In this chapter we will focus on several aspects of law in the United States. First, we will examine the functions of law in society. Second, we will discuss the source of law in society in order to help us understand why people do or do not obey the law. Next, we will define the different kinds of law in our legal system, with examples of the various forms the law takes. Finally, we will conclude with a case study of *Bob Jones University v. United States*, which illustrates a number of the chapter's major points.

FUNCTIONS OF LAW IN SOCIETY

People tend to place far too much emphasis on the negative aspects of law. Many view the law as a list of things they are forbidden to do. Perhaps this attitude is only natural given our socialization. As children we were often told, "Don't do this" and "Don't touch that," so it is understandable that our first contact with authority has negative connotations. Law, like the restrictions placed on us by our parents, defines the boundaries of acceptable and unacceptable behavior. But law is more than just a list of forbidden activities; it touches every aspect of our lives and should be viewed as a positive force. The following are some of the functions of law in our society.

Law Bestows Benefits on People

One of the positive aspects of law which perhaps we seldom consider is that it bestows benefits on people. Government, no matter what its form, uses its lawmaking power to determine who receives certain benefits and who does not. Laws deciding eligibility for programs like Social Security, family assistance benefits, unemployment compensation, and student loans are just a few examples; laws determining who may operate an automobile, practice law, sell real estate, or receive tax deductions are some others. Law is thus closely connected to the political system because it is government that determines "who gets what, when, and how."[3] The law becomes a major focus of interest groups that try to secure the passage of laws beneficial to them while blocking the passage of those that harm their interests. Finally, it is the government's ability to meet the demands of interest groups and its fairness in allocating benefits that provide an important measure of governmental effectiveness.

Law Creates New Programs

The next function of law is closely related to the previous one. Government, by passing laws that bestow benefits, must create both new programs and the bureaucracies to administer them. Programs such as flood control, crop insurance, student loans, and highway construction by their very nature benefit people in varying degrees. Some programs, like highway construction and flood control, are seemingly for the general welfare but also bestow benefits (big profits) on highway contractors and insurance companies. Battles between the president and Congress over the nation's budget are actually struggles over the funding levels of new and existing programs that have been created by the government.

I CAN'T BELIEVE IT'S NOT BUTTER®

An early example of an interest group using the law to promote its own economic interests came before the Supreme Court in *McCray v. United States,* 195 U.S. 27 (1904). The dairy industry, fearing competition from the production of cheaper oleomargarine, succeeded in getting Congress to place a 10¢ per pound tax on oleomargarine that had been colored to look like butter. Meanwhile, the tax on uncolored oleomargarine was only a fourth of a penny. In other words, the tax on colored oleomargarine was 40 times the rate on the uncolored one. In upholding the law, the Supreme Court said it was not empowered to question the motives of Congress in enacting the different rates. Clearly the dairy industry's lobbyists were more politically influential than those of the oleomargarine industry.

Law Reflects Society's Values

Interest groups do not use the law just to promote their selfish economic interests. Law also has important symbolic value in our society. Interest groups, like pro-life and pro-choice groups, want the law to promote (others say impose) certain values that they cherish in society. This is why some people and groups are willing to work to promote school prayers, ban flag desecration, and prohibit same-sex marriages. It is why others are equally willing to push for separation of church and state, freedom of expression, and tolerance of individual lifestyles. People on both sides of a controversial issue believe it is important for the law to reflect the correct view—which, of course, means *their* view of public policy. This eagerness of groups to see their views reflected in the nation's laws occupies the major portion of political debate in a country.

Law Proscribes Certain Activities

As we have noted, much of our thinking about law centers around what we may not do. Law forbids behavior that causes harm to other people or to their property. Some behavior is termed *malum in se,* or "wrong in itself." Consequently, the law forbids homicide, sexual assault, arson, theft, and other forms of anti-social behavior. There are also laws banning activities that, while not harmful in themselves, are forbidden simply because society disapproves of them. Neither parking in a "no-parking" zone nor letting the parking meter expire is really wrong in itself, but both are against the law. These are examples of *malum prohibitum*—acts that are wrong merely because they have been prohibited by government. Some forms of behavior—such as prostitution and physician-assisted suicide—are debatable as to whether they are wrong in themselves or simply wrong because a majority in society thinks they should be prohibited. Finally, not all proscribed activities are criminal in nature. Law proscribes how an individual may use his or her property if by using it they cause harm to others. For example, a property owner whose land use produces offensive waste, water pollution from practices such as fracking, or animal odors may be ordered to stop whatever is causing the problem. In any case, it is only by banning and punishing certain activities that people can live together in society in relative harmony.

Law Provides Predictability

One final function of law is to provide a measure of predictability so that we can conduct our affairs with some certainty. Contract law is a good example of law fulfilling the need for predictability; without contracts enforceable in courts, businesspersons could not conduct their affairs. We also seek predictability because we want some assurance that those in power will not act toward us arbitrarily. For example, due process is the requirement that a criminal law cannot be "void for vagueness."[4] Some Supreme Court justices, for example, have expressed concern over upholding pornography laws when the Court itself has such difficulty defining pornography.[5] They argue that it is unfair for the law to punish a person unless it can clearly define the prohibited behavior. Lawyers want some assurance that the law governing the outcome of yesterday's cases will serve as guideposts for today's decisions and tomorrow's cases. That assurance is why lawyers so eagerly look for *precedents* (i.e., cases previously decided) when presenting cases. Lawyers hope that such precedents will help guide the judge's decision and make the outcome more predictable.

Despite the comforting assurances of predictability that we seek in the law, there is, paradoxically, unpredictability as well. Professor Lief Carter reminds us that if law always predicted the outcome of disputes, people would never go to court. When the law fails to predict the outcome of a dispute and both sides believe they have a chance to win, lawsuits follow.[6] Carter notes that the use of ambiguous wording in statutes and court opinions is one reason for the unpredictability of law. Phrases such as "due process of law" and "beyond a reasonable doubt" illustrate the ambiguity of the language of law.[7]

These functions of law give us some clues about the nature of law by making us aware of its purpose for a society. Law may be seen as a battle for scarce resources, as a way of organizing society, or as a source of predictability and stability. But understanding the functions of law in society is not enough. Another important aspect of law is the *source* of law in a society. We now turn our attention toward understanding why people obey the law.

SOURCES OF LAW IN SOCIETY

It is because law performs such important functions that it becomes necessary to examine the source of law in society. The source of law concerns not only the legitimacy of the law in the eyes of the people but also the legitimacy of the lawmaker. In an absolute monarchy, the will of a single individual and the law are one and the same. In the film *The Ten Commandments*, the Pharaoh had only to say, "So let it be written, so let it be done," and his word became law. How can the will of a single person be so readily accepted by others as binding? In other words, from where did the Pharaoh derive his power, and why did his people obey him?

The answer to why humans obey can be as varied as humans themselves, but generally the reasons can be reduced to two, people obey either because they believe that they should or because they are afraid not to. Compliance with the law is much easier to effect if the lawmaker can convince the people that he or she has the right to make the law. In some societies (e.g., ancient Egypt and pre-World War II Japan), the lawmaker was seen as a god. Thus, people obeyed the Pharaoh and the Japanese emperor out of both religious respect and fear. During the Age of Absolutism in Europe, the theory of the *divine right of kings* governed people's thinking about the source of the king's power. In Roman Catholic theology, the Pope was chosen by God to be the "Vicar of Christ" on earth and was considered to be infallible in matters of Church doctrine. Similarly, people believed that the king was chosen by God to rule over them in secular matters. Just as the Pope was infallible in Church matters, the belief that "the king can do no wrong" was based on the belief that God had chosen the king and guided him. But what if the king should suffer the misfortune of being dethroned? Did this disprove the theory that the king was king "by the grace of God"? No, because in the Bible, as everyone knew, God replaced Saul as king of Israel with David when Saul displeased Him.[8] As a result, all law, spiritual and temporal, was inspired by God, and to disobey God's earthly representative was to disobey God Himself; the punishment was eternal damnation, a powerful penalty in the minds of medieval people.

Law, as understood by medieval thinkers, came from God and was considered to be eternal and immutable. During the Age of the Enlightenment, however, both religious and political thinkers began to challenge the absolutism of popes and kings. The idea developed that the lawmaker received his authority not from God by virtue of his fortunate birth but from the consent of the governed. Thomas Jefferson incorporated the concept of natural law into the Declaration of Independence when he invoked the notion that persons are endowed by their Creator with certain "inalienable rights." But he also emphatically stated that governments are instituted among men to protect those natural rights and that when a government no longer does so, it is the right of the people to alter or abolish it. Jefferson then chronicled a long list of abuses of power by George III to justify the drastic step the colonies were about to take.

The Declaration of Independence and the philosophy behind it added a new wrinkle to the relationship between the people and their government.

Government derived its power from the consent of the governed, not by some accident of royal birth. Implicit in the concept of government by consent is the idea of majority rule. American democracy, of course, links majority rule with representative government, wherein elected representatives of the people make the laws that bind all members of society. The legitimacy of both the law and the lawmaker rests on what we refer to simply as the democratic process. As long as laws are passed in accordance with the democratic "rules of the game," people are likely to obey them willingly.

The Declaration of Independence also speaks of persons possessing "inalienable rights." Law recognizes that individuals possess rights that are not subject to the whim of the majority. Therefore, in a democratic society law reflects two important values. First, laws must be passed by acceptable procedures such as adherence to majority rule. It is extremely important that these procedures be viewed as fair by all, especially political or other minorities. Second, the laws themselves must be viewed as fundamentally fair. An unfair law, even if enacted by a majority vote, is unfair nevertheless. Again, it is very important that individuals and minorities perceive a law as inherently fair. For example, states that have the death penalty theoretically apply it to everyone convicted of a capital offense. However, minority groups, such as African Americans, Hispanics, and the poor, assert that a disproportionate number of minority defendants actually receive death sentences while non-minority defendants do not. In this case, it is the application of the law and not the law itself that is viewed as unfair. Nevertheless, if minorities conclude that the death penalty as applied is unfair, it can breed discontent and contempt for the law.

Why have we discussed the question of legitimacy at such length? At the beginning of this chapter we stated a paradox of law in America: We are a nation born of revolution, yet we strongly believe in the rule of law. How do we reconcile these two apparently contradictory ideas? To do so, we must look at three approaches to the nature of law.[9]

Natural Law Approach

Natural law theorists believe that the laws that govern relationships among people, like the laws that govern the physical universe, are sown in nature. These laws are eternal and immutable, just as God, the source of all law, is eternal. Natural law is often referred to as a form of "higher law" to distinguish it from lesser—that is, human-made—law. Natural law has moral overtones, and those who invoke it often call it "God's law." Ascertaining just what is and is not God's law can be risky business, but its advocates echo the belief of Justice Potter Stewart that "I know it when I see it."[10]

Appeal to natural, or higher, law provides a justification for civil disobedience. For example, if one's conscience tells one that war is morally wrong, then one has a moral obligation not only to resist induction into the military but also to commit overt acts of civil disobedience in order to raise the consciousness of the community about the evils of war. It was by appealing to the conscience of society that Mahatma Gandhi and Martin Luther King, Jr. were able to make both those in authority and the general public see the immorality of colonialism and segregation.[11] Proponents of animal rights have attempted to make the question of treatment of animals, especially during laboratory tests for drugs and cosmetics, into a moral issue that justifies admittedly illegal behavior such as sit-ins and breaking into facilities to release animals. Invoking this higher law is one way in which a minority can hope to convince the majority to change its mind by appealing to the majority's sense of morality.

A discussion of natural law inevitably leads to the question of whether it is possible to "legislate morality." If by legislating morality it is meant that law can change a person's values, then law obviously cannot legislate morality. A law prohibiting gambling is unlikely to prevent someone who sees nothing wrong with it from betting on the Super Bowl. In such a case the law has altered neither the person's values nor his or her behavior. Among those persons who choose not to gamble are those who refrain from doing so out of fear of punishment rather than a conviction that gambling is "immoral."

It would be wrong, however, to conclude that law has no impact on morality. A generation or two ago, many Americans thought it was perfectly acceptable to use the law to force African Americans to attend separate public schools, drink at separate water fountains, and eat at separate restaurants. But most younger Americans today are surprised to learn that such laws ever even existed. Undoubtedly, years of civil rights and anti-discrimination laws have changed the views of many Americans about the morality of racial segregation. It is in this sense that law can indeed legislate morality.

Positive Law Approach

A second approach, *positive law*, is the belief that law should simply reflect the will of the majority. Law is stripped of any moral overtones and boils down to the old adage, "Might makes right." Despite the immorality of segregation or colonialism, if a majority wishes to have a segregated society or a colonial policy, then it may have it. Those who disagree with the law can certainly work within the democratic process to change it (albeit an unlikely occurrence), but they must accept it as the legitimate reflection of the will of the majority. Under no circumstances, so this argument goes, may the minority resort to unlawful methods to effect change. The law, then, becomes whatever a majority wants at a particular point in time.

Sociological Approach

The *sociological theory of law* holds that law represents a reflection of the values, mores, and culture of the society that produces it and that, as the society changes, the law will also change. For example, we have seen tremendous change in our own society as a result of the women's movement. As traditional views of the role of women have changed, laws dealing with the rights of women in employment, pension plans, credit, and child support have changed to keep pace. Although the law may lag behind a bit, it eventually catches up and reflects society's prevalent views.

The sociological approach is even more evident in our view of criminal behavior. Criminal law, you will recall, defines what type of behavior is anti-social and therefore proscribed. Some behavior is wrong in itself and is almost universally condemned. Other acts are wrong merely because they have been prohibited. At one time, the manufacture and sale of alcoholic beverages were against the law, but after some experience with Prohibition the measure was finally repealed. Similarly, gambling was once restricted to a few states, but today virtually every state permits lotteries, pari-mutuel betting, or casino gambling. While the debate continues over the morality of state-sanctioned gambling, people now view it as acceptable entertainment and not as an unlawful act.

How would each of the three approaches just described deal with an issue such as same-sex marriages? Prior to the Supreme Court's decision in *Obergefell v. Hodges*, natural law theorists argued that such marriages were a sin against God, violated natural law, and should never be legalized. The positive law theorist argued that the morality of same-sex marriages is irrelevant; unless legislative bodies change the positive law governing marriage, such marriages should remain illegal. Advocates of the sociological approach argued, as did the majority of the justices of the Supreme Court, that society's attitude toward same-sex marriages has changed and so the law must change as well. Chapter 13, which deals with Family Law, will explore the implications of same-sex marriages in more detail.

In a sense, American law encompasses all three of these approaches. The resulting paradox is the same one that is inherent in our political system and in society in general. On the one hand, we believe that law should reflect the will of the majority; on the other hand, we accept the notion that minorities also have rights under the law. It is a source of frustration to many who wonder why we permit flag burning if a majority of Americans oppose it, and why we do not have prayers in the schools when a majority favors it. Is the law a manifestation of the majority's will or isn't it? Reconciling this paradox is never easy and seldom satisfying.

KINDS OF LAW

It should be clear by now that one's feelings about the origins of law and the functions it performs in society are crucial to understanding the legal system itself. One final obstacle remains: understanding the kinds of law that exist in the legal environment. This section will introduce the various kinds of law, and the final section will use a case study of *Bob Jones University v. United States* to illustrate them. We will begin by distinguishing substantive law from procedural law.

Substantive versus Procedural Law

It is important at the outset to differentiate between the substance of the law and the process or procedures of the law. The former—that is, *substantive law*—is concerned with the content, or substance, of the law. In criminal law, for example, the substantive law will define what kind of behavior is considered to be anti-social and prescribe the kind of punishment that will be imposed for engaging in it. The substantive law will clearly define the elements of the crime (e.g., the necessary evil intent) and the range of punishment (five to ten years' imprisonment) that may be handed out upon conviction. As previously discussed, the determination of what behavior is forbidden and what punishment is appropriate is made by elected representative bodies such as the Congress and the state legislatures. Likewise, in civil law, the legislature of each state is free to specify the legal grounds for a civil action, such as a *divorce* proceeding. Mental cruelty, adultery, irreconcilable differences, and incompatibility are common substantive grounds for a divorce.

Procedural law governs the *process* of the law. In a political system such as ours, we are as much concerned about *how* the law is applied as about the substance of the law itself. Terms like "kangaroo court" and "railroading a defendant" indicate that our system of law is also concerned about fundamental fairness. Consequently, we guarantee everyone, especially those charged with criminal offenses, *due process of law*. We make this guarantee because our system of constitutional government is based on the idea that there are limits to governmental power and that even those in authority must adhere to the rule of law. We wish to prevent government from acting toward us in an arbitrary fashion, and so we believe that even a person charged with the most heinous crime is entitled to "have his or her day in court" governed by a set of preordained rules of fairness. Thus, we guarantee the accused the right to remain silent before his or her accusers, the right to a trial by jury, and the right to counsel. Even after a conviction, the Constitution protects the condemned person from cruel and unusual punishment.

Of the two types, namely substantive and procedural, the latter tends to generate more controversy. Although debate continues over such questions as whether gambling should be a crime or whether the punishment for marijuana possession is too severe, people generally defer to their elected representatives on these issues. However, procedural due process comes under attack because it provides the "loopholes" through which criminals are sometimes allowed to slip. All of us are aware of cases in which a criminal has been set free because the police failed to comply with certain "technicalities" in the law. Astounded citizens want to know the justice in allowing a factually guilty person to go free because "the constable blunders."[12]

There is no satisfactory answer to the question: What about the rights of the victim? But we should understand that the Framers of our Constitution had firsthand experience of a tyrannical government and believed that in the long run it was better to risk allowing the guilty to go free than to risk tolerating an arbitrary and tyrannical government. Our political will and political commitment to the provisions of the Bill of Rights are being challenged even today. In the aftermath of the September 11, 2001 attacks on the World Trade Center and the Pentagon, some Americans were tempted to ignore provisions of the Constitution dealing with the rights of accused terrorists and enemy combatants.[13] In times of crisis, it is easy to succumb to the temptation to suspend rights in the name of security. Whether we do succumb or stay true to the principle of the rule of law is the real test of the strength of our political system.

In the discussion of the other types of law which follows, it is important to keep in mind that each type has both substantive and procedural aspects. For example, in administrative law, the Social Security Administration has regulations (laws) that determine who is *eligible* for Social Security benefits. However, it has separate regulations which set forth the *procedures* that must be followed when applying for benefits. It should also be noted that substantive rules and procedural rules influence each other. For example, a person who is denied benefits may be turned down because he or she failed to follow the proper application procedures, not because of ineligibility.

Criminal and Civil Law

Several references have already been made to criminal and civil law, but now we want to define them more clearly. *Criminal law*, as we have indicated, deals with activities that have been formally forbidden by a society's government. The range of crimes extends from parking violations to homicide. As we have seen, some crimes are "wrong in themselves," and some are merely wrong because society has seen fit to prohibit them. We have also seen that the Constitution provides a number of procedural safeguards for those accused of crime.

The importance of the role of government in criminal law cannot be overestimated. Of course, government is responsible for detecting and preventing crime, as well as for seeing that criminals are caught and punished. But more importantly, government prosecutes criminals. This statement, while hardly revealing, is significant because of its implications. At one time, perhaps in philosopher John Locke's "state of nature," each person was individually responsible for his or her own protection, or else relied on a family or clan for protection. When someone was injured, it was the duty of the individual to seek revenge; if the victim was unable to do so, the responsibility fell on the family or clan.

In our civilized society, we consider a crime to be an injury not only to a particular individual but also to society as a whole, and it is society's responsibility to seek retribution on behalf of the victim. While the victim's family may find forgiveness in their hearts, the state does not forgive so easily. Instead of permitting blood feuds and vendettas to disrupt society, the government assumes the responsibility for prosecuting and punishing persons charged with crimes. Thus, criminal cases are typically entitled *People v. Jones, State v. Jones*, or *The State of Texas v. Jones* to indicate the state's active role as prosecutor. It was a significant step in the advancement of law in society when people began to permit government to seek retribution on their behalf. It is because of this awesome power government has over our lives and liberties that we impose the procedural safeguards discussed in the previous section. Without significant checks on the power of government, our freedom would soon be lost.

Civil law governs the relationships between individuals in the course of their private affairs. It deals with such matters as contracts, property, wills,

FEUDIN', FIGHTIN', AND FUSSIN'

The ancient tradition of engaging in feuds illustrates the importance of having the rule of law. When families or clans disregard the rule of law and use violence to settle disputes, feuds are the result. Anthropologist Keith Otterbein has identified three essential elements of a feud. First, kin groups emerge and killings occur as revenge for some perceived injustice. Second, Otterbein believes a minimum of three killings or acts of violence must occur. Third, the killings must occur within an overall political authority. The last element means that the political authority has been unable to end the violence by lawful means.

Source: Keith F. Otterbein, "Five Feuds: An Analysis of Homicides in Eastern Kentucky in the Late Nineteenth Century," *American Anthropologist, New Series* 102, 2 (June, 2000), pp. 231–232.

and torts. When two or more persons have a dispute, it is in the best interests of society as a whole to ensure that the dispute is resolved peacefully. Unlike criminal prosecutions, in which the government is an active participant, the government's main interest in civil cases is to provide a forum, a court of law, in which to resolve the dispute. In most cases the government itself does not care who wins the dispute as long as it is settled peacefully. Although the cost of providing courts to resolve these essentially private disputes is considerable, it is justified on the grounds of maintaining harmony in society. The fact that citizens are willing to submit their disputes to the courts and abide by the court's decision is in itself a tribute to the legitimacy of a society's judicial system.

One final point about criminal and civil law should be made. It is possible for both a criminal *and* a civil action to arise out of the same set of facts or the same incident. Two examples should clarify this point. Suppose Wilson runs a red light and collides with Johnson's car, causing considerable damage to it. The police will issue a traffic ticket to Wilson for running the light and he will be punished, probably by having to pay a fine. The state's interest is limited to punishing Wilson for disregarding one of its traffic laws. There is still the matter of Johnson's car, however. Wilson has damaged her property—which, in legal terminology, is called a *tort*. A tort is a legal injury one person has caused another. Let us further suppose that Wilson has no liability insurance (itself a crime in many states) to cover the damages, so Johnson decides to sue him in order to force him to pay for the damage he has caused. This suit is a *civil action*, and if Wilson loses the suit he will be made to pay the cost of repairing the car. Thus, two legal actions, one criminal and one civil, arose from a single automobile accident.

Our second example is similar but a rather more complicated one. Anderson starts a fight with Cooper. Anderson hits Cooper, breaking the latter's jaw. Anderson is arrested for assault, convicted, and given a year in prison as his punishment. Cooper has suffered a broken jaw, however, and has had to pay his own medical expenses. He decides to sue Anderson in order to force him to pay his medical bills. Again, the latter suit is civil in nature, and if Cooper wins, Anderson can be forced to pay. Someone might suggest that Anderson is being subjected to "double jeopardy" as he is being hauled into court twice for the same offense. But the prohibition against double jeopardy limits the number of times the *government* can prosecute a person for a *criminal offense* and does not protect Anderson from a civil action started by the person he has injured.

Constitutional Law

In the United States and in each of the 50 states, the most basic fundamental law is a constitution. The national Constitution declares, "This Constitution, and the Laws of the United States which shall be made in Pursuance thereof; and all Treaties made, or which shall be made, under the Authority of the United States, shall be the supreme Law of the Land."[14] The Constitution adds that state judges must take an oath to uphold it and that state constitutions and state laws may not conflict with the national Constitution.[15]

Noted constitutional scholar C. Herman Pritchett asserted that a good constitution should do four things. It should provide for the structure of government, place limitations on government, list the powers of government, and provide for an amending process.[16] The U.S. Constitution does all four, but with one small problem. The Framers had a tendency to write as if everyone understood exactly what they meant. The Eighth Amendment, for example, prohibits "cruel and unusual punishment" for criminal offenses, but we are given no clue as to just what is to be considered cruel or unusual. The executive power is vested in the president, but no attempt is made to define the scope of the executive power. The Framers probably figured that they had done the hard part, and it was up to future generations to do the rest.

Because the Constitution is so ambiguous and because it serves as our fundamental law, courts—especially the U.S. Supreme Court—have played an important role in our political as well as legal system. The Supreme Court has an opportunity to expand the meaning of the Constitution each time it interprets it. With its power of *judicial review*—the power to determine whether laws or actions are contrary to the Constitution—the Supreme Court effects changes never dreamed of by the Framers. Whether the Court is settling the outcome of a presidential election, defining the meaning of "interstate commerce," or interpreting the Establishment Clause, the Court breathes life into the words of the Constitution. *Constitutional law*, then, represents the sum of thousands of Supreme Court and lower court decisions that have been settled in over 200 years of constitutional development. We will say much more about the role of the Supreme Court in subsequent chapters.

Statutory Law

We have already noted that statutes passed by elected representative bodies are a major source of positive law. Congress and state legislatures pass statutes on the national and state levels, while city and county governments pass ordinances on the local level. In most cases, statutes are passed by a simple majority vote of the legislative body, subject to a veto by the chief executive. The content of *statutory law* may serve any number of purposes. Statutes may be passed to create or abolish government programs, increase the penalty for a crime, make an appropriation from the treasury, or raise the salaries of government workers. Statutes can regulate business activities, create new judgeships, impose a new tax, or proclaim a new holiday. In short, statutes can do anything that does not conflict with the Constitution—including making everyone rise an hour earlier each morning during the summer months.

LOONY LAWS, LOONY LAWMAKERS

Numerous websites list so-called "loony laws" allegedly passed by cities and states that outlaw silly, if not downright ridiculous, conduct. One that appears on virtually every list of loony laws is "It is illegal to hunt camels in the state of Arizona." As silly as it sounds, there may be basis in fact. Just before the Civil War, the U.S. Army imported camels into Arizona with the intent of using them as pack animals in the arid Southwest. When the war came, the plans were abandoned but herds of camels still roamed the area. Although there is no evidence that such a law was actually passed, its existence is not entirely implausible.

Source: "Arizona Defense," Snopes.com, http://www.snopes.com/legal/arizona.asp (visited June 23, 2015).

You will recall from our earlier discussion of natural law and positive law that there is an inherent conflict between constitutional and statutory law. Constitutional law deals with fundamental principles of government and fundamental rights of citizens. The Framers believed that these fundamental rights and principles should only be changed through the process of constitutional amendment. Today's majority may wish to limit the terms of members of Congress, but the terms and qualifications for election of members of Congress are fixed in the Constitution.[17] Likewise, the Framers believed that the rights of citizens, such as freedom of speech and press, are "natural rights" which no government, not even one based on the principle of majority rule, may infringe. Statutory law, on the other hand, reflects the collective will of the majority (at least insofar as we have faith in representative government) at a particular point in time. In exercising its power of judicial review, the Supreme Court must decide whether to adhere to the fundamental law or to a law that reflects current opinion on a particular subject. By their very nature, the kinds of issues the Court is asked to resolve (abortion, capital punishment, and so on) are ones that require tough choices to be made between two or more conflicting sets of values. We will have more to say about judicial review in Chapter 6 because understanding this inherent conflict is crucial to understanding not only our legal system but our political system as well.

Administrative Law

Under the U.S. Constitution, it is Congress that has the power to regulate various activities that affect our lives on a daily basis. Thus, it is within congressional power to regulate the Internet, telecommunications, labor activities, airlines, and many other aspects of business and industry. Given the structure and makeup of Congress, it is impossible for this body to have the expertise needed to regulate highly technical industries like broadcasting or nuclear energy. Consequently, Congress has seen fit to delegate its authority to regulate business and industry to more specialized bodies it has created within the executive branch of government. Over the years, it has created numerous executive departments (such as the Department of Transportation) and so-called independent regulatory agencies (such as the Federal Trade Commission) to perform the tasks Congress is incapable of doing itself. These executive agencies have been empowered to promulgate rules and regulations that have the force of law. For example, the Transportation Security Administration in the Department of Homeland Security may promulgate rules prohibiting carrying certain items, such as knives, pepper spray, and scissors, on airplanes. The Food and Drug Administration (FDA) may specify the procedures with which drug manufacturers must comply before they may market a new drug. Failure to comply with an agency's regulations may lead to a heavy fine or other penalty.

Professors Lief Carter and Christine Harrington, noted experts on administrative law, have pointed out that administrative law is often confused with regulatory law. What we have discussed thus far is technically *regulatory law*. *Administrative law*, by contrast, is the law that controls those whom Congress has empowered to regulate on its behalf. As Carter and Harrington have noted, "Regulatory law governs the citizenry; administrative law governs the government."[18] Administrative agencies are not directly accountable to the people, and yet, as we have seen, the rules they promulgate are just as binding as any statute passed by a legislative body. We have also seen that our political system seeks to reduce the potential for the official abuse of power. Administrative law governs the bureaucrats to ensure that they will not act in an arbitrary manner or abuse their power. Although administrative law is of increasing importance, it receives relatively little attention from scholars.

Case Law

There is an old maxim that says, "I will let you write the law if you will let me interpret it." The implication of this statement, of course, is that while a law may appear to be clear and unequivocal when written, it may be subjected to many different interpretations. In Mosaic law the command "Thou shalt not kill" is precise and to the point. Yet questions about its meaning still arise.

What about killing in self-defense or during combat? What about an accidental killing? Shouldn't the word "kill" actually be interpreted as "murder"? *Case law* develops when judges interpret the meaning of constitutions, statutes, or other forms of written law. It may also include interpretations of other cases that have previously been decided under the law. Instead of trying to write laws that attempt to cover every conceivable contingency, lawmakers prefer to write general laws subject to judicial interpretation. Then, as circumstances and real cases or controversies arise, the judge may interpret the law to resolve the conflict in question.

Whenever judges interpret a law in a particular way they create a precedent, or rule of law. As we have seen with constitutional law, each time the Supreme Court interprets the Constitution, it breathes new meaning into it and may create a new precedent. In the classic case *Miranda v. Arizona*,[19] the Supreme Court ruled that persons accused of a crime must be given information about their constitutional rights to remain silent and to consult with an attorney. This case created a precedent that in future cases, not just in Miranda's case, any person subject to a custodial arrest must be given these same "*Miranda* warnings." The Court, in effect, created a new rule of law where one had previously not existed. Although the justices claim only to "find" law, it is decisions like *Miranda* that leave the Court open to charges that the justices are really "making law." We will have more to say about judicial lawmaking in Chapter 6.

Common Law

It is customary to save the best for last. Anglo-American law is rooted in the tradition of the *common law*. In 1881, Justice Oliver Wendell Holmes, Jr. wrote, "The life of the law has not been logic: It has been experience."[20] What Holmes meant is that law is not so much a function of our ability to logically deduce solutions to every conceivable conflict as it is a response to what he called "the felt necessities of the time."[21] Common law developed as a response to the need to find solutions to the pressing issues of the time. But common law is "not a stagnant pool, but a moving stream. It seeks to purify itself as it flows through time. The common law is our responsibility; the child of the courts. We are responsible for its direction."[22]

Common law originated during the period of English history when there were very few written laws. Beginning about the time of Henry II, English kings sent their judges throughout the country to dispense the king's justice with little or no statutory law to guide their decisions. When conflicts arose and no statute applied, judges still had to resolve them somehow. As a result, decisions were based on rules of law, which in turn were based on an individual judge's sense of equity or fairness. Like King Solomon, who had to decide which of the two women should be given the baby,[23] English judges had to make on-the-spot decisions to resolve pressing disputes. Once a rule of law thus formulated was recognized as just and reasonable, other judges in other jurisdictions would adopt it and apply it in their own, similar cases. Eventually, the rule

COMMON LAW AND COMMON SENSE

The common law doctrine—*cujus est solum est usque ad coelom*—is an ancient one that translates as "Whoever has the land possesses all the space upward indefinitely." Shortly after World War II, the Supreme Court was faced with the question whether this doctrine was still feasible in the age of the airplane. A North Carolina farmer claimed that low-flying military aircraft landing at an airfield near his farm were killing his chickens. The issue was whether the government was liable under the Takings Clause of the Fifth Amendment. In his majority opinion, Justice William O. Douglas wrote, "But that doctrine has no place in the modern world. The air is a public highway, as Congress has declared. Were that not true, every transcontinental flight would subject the operator to countless trespass suits. Common sense revolts at the idea. To recognize such private claims to the airspace would clog these highways, seriously interfere with their control and development in the public interest, and transfer into private ownership that to which only the public has a just claim."

Source: United States v. Causby, 328 U.S. 256 (1946) at 261–262.

would be written down and used by all judges in the realm. A rule of law became "common," not in the sense of being ordinary, but in the sense of being common to all parts of England.

The reader should note the close relationship between common law and case law. Both rely heavily on the rule of precedence and both allow the judge discretion in interpreting the law. Common law, like case law, is often described as "judge made." One important difference exists. Unlike case law, which is a court's interpretation of an existing constitution or statute, common law rules developed in the absence of any positive law. In addition, a common law rule may be set aside by the enactment of a statute. For example, under the common law doctrine of *caveat emptor* ("let the buyer beware"), the purchaser of an item was expected to examine the merchandise before buying it in order to avoid being cheated by the merchant. If the purchaser failed to do so, he or she was partly to blame for not being careful; that is, one should have taken care so that he or she would not be cheated. Today, most states have laws to protect consumers from fraudulent business practices, and the common law doctrine of *caveat emptor* is no longer applicable. Thus, the common law doctrine may be superseded by the enactment of positive law.

Law in a Federal System. One of the complications of the American legal system is the influence of federalism on law, so we should briefly mention its important effect on our legal system. In Chapter 3 (Court Organization) we explain that we have a dual court system in which the state's court system exists alongside the federal court system. However, the importance of this dual system goes far beyond mere court organizational structure. For example, states have their own constitutions so that each state's constitutional law is unique. State supreme courts are free to interpret their state constitutions just as the U.S. Supreme Court interprets the national Constitution. Each state's statutes on criminal and civil law are unique to that state. It follows then that each state's case law will also be particular to the individual state. State administrative agencies promulgate rules and regulations under the state's regulatory laws and, again, will be unique to that state. Court procedures and rules of evidence will also vary from state to state. While U.S. Supreme Court decisions, especially in the area of criminal justice, tend to make procedural safeguards more uniform, there is still quite a variety in criminal procedures. Coming to understand a legal system within a federal framework is one of the more fascinating challenges of studying American law and legal systems.

BOB JONES UNIVERSITY V. UNITED STATES

Our approach to the discussion of the functions, sources, and kinds of law may lead one to believe that law can be neatly categorized. In reality, it is a bit more complicated. The following Supreme Court decision, *Bob Jones University v. United States*, illustrates how a single case may involve several kinds of law and incorporates a number of the points made in this chapter.

Background of the Case[24]

Section 501(C)(3) of the Internal Revenue Code contains a description of organizations that are granted tax-exempt status by the national government. Section 170 of the Code specifies that individual contributions to these organizations may qualify as charitable deductions on individual tax returns. Until 1970, Bob Jones University was granted tax-exempt status under § 501(C)(3) by the Internal Revenue Service (IRS). Due to its interpretation of a lower federal court ruling,[25] however, the IRS notified the University in November 1970 that it could no longer grant tax-exempt status to "private schools which practice racial discrimination," nor could contributions made to them be charitable deductions under § 170. The IRS formalized this policy by promulgating Revenue Ruling 71–447.

Bob Jones University is an institution dedicated to teaching fundamentalist Christian beliefs. Up until 1971 it had completely excluded African Americans. From 1971 to 1975 it accepted applications from African Americans who were married within their own race. The university permitted the enrollment of unmarried blacks in 1975 but also enforced a strict policy banning interracial dating and marriage, and expelling any student who espoused the idea. According to the IRS interpretation, an organization qualifies for tax-exempt status only if it is a "charitable" institution within the common law meaning of that term. Under the common law, an institution that pursues activities contrary to public policy is not charitable. The IRS ruled that by practicing racial discrimination, Bob Jones University was acting contrary to a clear "national policy to discourage racial discrimination in education."[26]

Ruling in the Case

Bob Jones University challenged the revocation of its tax-exempt status on three grounds. First, it asserted that the IRS had no authority to promulgate Revenue Ruling 71–447. Second, the university challenged the IRS's interpretation of § 501(C)(3). According to the university's interpretation, the section grants tax-exempt status to organizations that operate exclusively for "religious, charitable, scientific ... *or educational* purposes."[27] Because the word "or" separates "charitable" from "educational" purposes, the IRS's application of the common law definition of "charitable" was inappropriate. Because the university is clearly organized for educational purposes, it should have qualified for the exemption. Finally, the university argued that the IRS's construction of § 501(C)(3) and § 170 violated the Free Exercise Clause of the First Amendment because the university's racial policy was based on sincerely held religious beliefs.

In an 8 to 1 decision, the Supreme Court rejected all three of the university's challenges in an opinion written by Chief Justice Warren E. Burger. The Court rejected the university's contention that the IRS had no authority to promulgate Revenue Ruling 71–447 without specific congressional authorization. Chief Justice Burger noted that since the inception of the tax code, Congress had granted broad authority to the IRS to interpret the tax laws. He wrote, "In an area as complex as the tax system, the agency Congress vests with administrative responsibility must be able to exercise its authority to meet changing conditions and new problems."[28] The Chief Justice then proceeded to note that any time after the promulgation of Revenue Ruling 71–447, Congress could have modified it; Congress had chosen not to do so however, indicating tacit approval of the policy. Thus, if Congress felt that the IRS's ruling was arbitrary or constituted an abuse of its authority, Congress could have done something about it during the ensuing ten years and did not.

The Court also rejected the university's contention that the IRS misapplied the term "charitable" and that it should qualify for tax-exempt status solely because of its educational purposes. The Chief Justice stated that it was clearly the intent of Congress to exempt "charitable" organizations—that is, organizations that serve a public purpose, and not purposes contrary to established public policy. In a footnote to the opinion,[29] Chief Justice Burger pointed out that if the university's interpretation was accepted, then a school for training terrorists (clearly "educational" in purpose) would qualify for an exemption. He concluded that Congress surely did not intend for that to happen.

Finally, the Court rejected the university's First Amendment claim that the revocation of the tax exemption constituted a violation of the Free Exercise Clause. In previous cases[30] interpreting that clause, the Court has ruled that the government may justify a limitation on religious liberty by demonstrating "an overriding governmental interest." Chief Justice Burger concluded that the government's interest in eradicating racial discrimination in education was "compelling" and that it justified the burden on religious liberty. He noted that although the denial of tax benefits would have an impact on the university, it would not prevent the university from observing the tenets of its religion.[31]

Analysis of the Case

The *Bob Jones University* case illustrates several of the points previously made in this chapter. First, it involves several kinds of law: constitutional, statutory, regulatory, administrative, case, and common law. The constitutional question raised was the free exercise claim made by the university. Statutory law was involved when the Court was called upon to interpret § 501(C)(3) and § 170. The common law definition of "charitable" adopted by the IRS was a major issue in the case. The question of whether or not the IRS had the authority to promulgate Revenue Ruling 71–447 was one of the administrative law while the IRS's use of "charitable" in promulgating the Ruling was one of regulatory law. Finally, the Court cited numerous precedents, not included in our analysis, to substantiate its decision, thus illustrating the use of case law.

Second, *Bob Jones University* demonstrates the conflict between minority rights and majority rule. There is no reason to doubt that the officials of the university were sincere in their racial viewpoint or that their views were grounded in their religious beliefs. In following the course that they chose, these officials undoubtedly believed that they were obeying a higher law, superior to the laws of the IRS or even the U.S. government. But the Supreme Court's opinion made it clear that the racial views of Bob Jones University were incompatible with a public policy endorsed by all three branches of the national government. The conflict was between the university's right to act upon its sincerely held religious beliefs and the majority's right to eradicate racial discrimination in the field of education.

Third, the case demonstrates the role of courts in supervising the government bureaucracy. The Supreme Court had to decide whether the IRS's application of the term "charitable" to the university was reasonable and within the IRS's power. A ruling either that the IRS's application was unwarranted or that it had exceeded its authority would have resulted in a victory for the university.

BOB JONES AS PRECEDENT?

At first blush one may not readily see the connection between the *Bob Jones Case* and the Supreme Court's same-sex marriage ruling in *Obergefell v. Hodges*. But Chief Justice John Roberts' dissent in *Obergefell* raises the specter of *Bob Jones*. The Chief Justice wonders whether a religiously affiliated university that offers married student housing to heterosexual couples must now extend that benefit to same-sex couples. More to the point, could the IRS deny tax-exempt status to a university that refused to do so? Roberts fears that these questions and others like them will someday have to be resolved by the Supreme Court.

Source: Obergefell v. Hodges, 576 U.S. _____ (2015), Roberts, dissenting at 28 (Slip Opinion)

Finally, the case illustrates how judges make decisions. Attorneys for the university offered some sound arguments that Congress intended to exempt organizations that are "charitable *or* educational" rather than "charitable *and* educational." Courts must often ascertain the intent of Congress when interpreting an ambiguous statute. Even when one or more interpretations are reasonable, courts must choose one over the other. In cases of far-reaching importance, such as *Bob Jones University*, the interpretation chosen will have a broad impact as a precedent in future cases. In this manner, we see that law is an evolving concept that appears to be static but is actually constantly changing.

CONCLUSION

We began this chapter by asserting that there is a paradox of law in the United States. Americans possess ambivalent feelings about law. These feelings result from the fact that people disagree over what law is, where it comes from, and what it should do. We said that our ambivalence about law is related to the ambivalence we have about our society in general. We may all believe in "equality of opportunity" in principle but disagree over the propriety of affirmative action programs. Likewise, we may agree with the ideal of the rule of law without agreeing on just what that means. There is no right or wrong or even single answer to the question: What is law? Our view of the law depends on what we consider to be the functions of law and the source of law. In the final analysis, we must decide for ourselves what law really is.

Understanding the major ideas in this chapter is important to understanding what will follow. Without a firm grasp of these basic concepts, it will be more difficult to fully appreciate much of the discussion of the material covered in the remaining chapters.

NOTES

1. Richard White, *"It's Your Misfortune and None of My Own": A New History of the American West* (Norman: University of Oklahoma Press, 1991), pp. 332–334.
2. Craig B. Little and Christopher P. Sheffield, "Frontiers and Criminal Justice: English Private Prosecution Societies and American Vigilantism in the Eighteenth and Nineteenth Centuries," *American Sociological Review* 48, 6 (December 1983): 803.
3. Harold Lasswell, *Politics: Who Gets What, When, How?* (New York: McGraw-Hill, 1936).
4. Anthony G. Amsterdam, "The Void-for-Vagueness Doctrine in the Supreme Court," 109 U. Pa. L. Rev. 67 (1960).
5. *Ginzburg v. United States*, 383 U.S. 463 (1966) (Black, J., dissenting).
6. Lief H. Carter and Thomas F. Burke, *Reason in Law*, 6th edn (New York: Longman, 2002), p. 23.
7. Ibid.
8. I Samuel 15:10 and I Samuel 16:1, New International Bible.
9. cf. David Eliot Brody, *The American Legal System: Concepts and Principles* (Lexington, MA: Heath, 1978), pp. 4–7.

10. *Jacobellis v. Ohio*, 378 U.S. 184 (1964), at 197 (Stewart, concurring).
11. Martin Luther King, Jr., "Letter from Birmingham Jail," in Fred R. Harris, *America's Democracy*, 2nd edn (Glenview, IL: Scott, Foresman, 1983), pp. 117–118.
12. *People v. DeFore*, 242 N.Y. 13, 150 N.E. 585 (1926) (Cardozo, J.).
13. *Hamdi v. Rumsfeld*, 542 U.S. 507 (2004) and *Hamdan v. Rumsfeld*, 548 U.S. 557 (2006).
14. U.S. Constitution, Art. VI, cl.2.
15. Ibid.
16. C. Herman Pritchett, *The American Constitutional System*, 5th edn (New York: McGraw-Hill, 1981), p. 2.
17. *U.S. Term Limits, Inc. v. Thornton*, 514 U.S. 779 (1995).
18. Lief H. Carter and Christine Harrington, *Administrative Law and Politics: Cases and Comments*, 3rd edn (New York: Addison Wesley Longman, Inc., 2000), p. 55.
19. *Miranda v. Arizona*, 384 U.S. 436 (1966).
20. Oliver Wendell Holmes, Jr., *The Common Law* (Boston, MA: Little, Brown, 1881), pp. 1–2.
21. Ibid.
22. *Hilen v. Hays*, 673 S.W.2d 713 (Ky., 1984) at 717 (Leibson, J.)
23. I Kings 3:16–28, New International Bible.
24. The facts of this case are summarized from the majority opinion of Chief Justice Warren E. Burger, *Bob Jones University v. United States*, 461 U.S. 574 (1983).
25. *Green v. Kennedy*, 309 F.Supp. 1127 (D.D.C., 1970).
26. *Bob Jones University v. United States*, 461 U.S. 574 (1983), at 579.
27. Ibid., p. 585.
28. Ibid., p. 596.
29. Ibid., fn. 18, pp. 591–592.
30. *Prince v. Massachusetts*, 321 U.S. 158 (1944); *United States v. O'Brien*, 391 U.S. 367 (1968); *Goldman v. Weinberger*, 475 U.S. 503 (1986).
31. *Bob Jones University v. United States*, 461 U.S. 574 (1983), at 603–604.

History and the Law

The law embodies the story of a nation's development through many centuries and it cannot be dealt with as if it contained only the axioms and corollaries of a book of mathematics. In order to know what it is, we must know what it has been, and what it tends to become.[1]

A ll societies develop methods of resolving conflicts among their members. Some are formally organized, such as the court systems in the United States, while others are much more primitive; but it is imperative that the rules governing a society be enforced if chaos is to be prevented. The need to maintain order in society is not recent. Ancient civilizations created laws and legal systems to control their members and to resolve conflicts. Remnants of these legal systems linger, and many of today's theories and practices may be traced to them. Cases such as *Roe v. Wade,* commonly known as the abortion case, are replete with historical references to other, older systems of legal doctrine.

The history of law and legal systems is not neatly striated by chronology but blends together as societies have both borrowed from other systems and created laws to reflect their own experiences and times.

The main criterion [for borrowing from other systems] is accessibility. An outsider's system of law is accessible above all when it is (a) in writing, (b) in a form that makes it relatively easy to find and understand (and this includes the language in which it is written), and (c) readily available …

Once a system becomes used as a quarry, it will ... be borrowed from again, and the more it is borrowed from, the more the right thing to do is to borrow from that system.[2]

LAW THROUGH THE AGES

One of the earliest extant sets of laws is the Code of Hammurabi, developed by King Hammurabi of Babylon about 2000 BCE. It set forth the rules of human behavior demanded by the gods as supplemented by the ruler's edicts. The Code was frequently harsh; for example, adulterers and a person accusing another of murder who could not prove it were punished by death. A wife who "has not been careful but has gadded about, neglecting her house and belittling her husband" shall be thrown into the water, but, on the other hand, if the husband is found to have wrongfully belittled her, she could take her dowry and return to her father's home. A wife could be set aside for not providing her husband with children, but the husband had to give her the marriage price and give her the dowry her father had provided. In addition, the wife's property rights were protected from her children. Thus, women were at least partially protected and were not treated solely as the property of the husband.[3] Hammurabi's Code of nearly 300 laws covered such diverse topics as administration of justice, property, irrigation, loans and interest, regulation of trade, slavery, marriage and the family, adoption, personal injury, and building and wage regulations.[4]

In addition to a well-developed system of criminal law, ancient Mesopotamians developed strict patterns in drafting contracts that are still employed today. First, the object of the transaction (e.g., a marriage contract or lease of real property) was clearly indicated. Second, all parties to the transaction were listed with a clear identification of their roles in relation to each other; for example, seller and buyer. Third, other clauses delineating details such as price or the obligations undertaken were added. Fourth, the witnesses present at the time of transaction were identified in the document. To prevent fraudulent alteration, the Mesopotamians sealed the actual documents in clay cases that were inscribed with the same information. In case of a dispute, the judge would compare the writings of the two documents to see if they matched.[5]

Egyptian law, like the civilization itself, was highly developed. From the time of the Old Empire (3000–2500 BCE), the administration of justice was centralized with judges being chosen from the aristocrats and from one of six great law courts, and later judges were also priests.[6] Some records of criminal trials still exist. For example, in 1100 BCE, during the reign of Ramses IX, bands of thieves were charged with robbing the tombs of the Pharaohs as well as those of private individuals for the gold and other valuables.[7] Although the death penalty existed, it was often commuted to penal servitude or slavery.[8]

In civil matters, the plaintiff proceeded first and presented his case while standing in front of a seated court (the practice followed today in federal courts). The defendant was then summoned to present an answer. After the court had rendered its decision, both parties orally accepted the judgment of the tribunal.[9] The right of inheritance was primarily through maternal, rather than paternal, lines.[10] Egyptologists have located written contracts setting out obligations of the parties.[11]

Hebrew law has coexisted with various legal traditions discussed here, and, employing the terms of the earlier analogy, it has been both the quarry and the borrower. It is based on the premise that law is of divine origin; that is, God is the source of all law, and justice is administered in the name of God. Customs approving or disapproving appropriate behavior were eventually codified and, along with Pentateuch (the first five books of the Old Testament), form the basis of the Talmud—the collection of laws, traditions, customs, and interpretations—that governs many aspects of Jewish life.[12] Ancient Hebrew law incorporated the idea of private vengeance—"an eye for an eye"—but certain offenders had to undergo public punishment including the death penalty for crimes such as premeditated murder, kidnapping a free person and selling him or her into slavery, flogging for assault and some first offenses, and fines and restitution for violation of property rights.[13] The Hebrew system had two striking features: (1) there were no advocates or lawyers involved, and the witnesses were the accusers and prosecutors; and (2) most courts had more than one judge—three at the lowest level, 23 at the next, and 71 at the highest court in Jerusalem.[14]

The Greeks also made major contributions to legal philosophy. The laws of Greece in the fourth and fifth centuries BCE were flexible and could be tailored to fit the dispute when it was brought before the king, who relied on the gods for help in making his decisions. This individualization probably stemmed from the fact that Greek citizens could participate in government and were therefore influential.

Several prominent philosophers considered the role of law in society. Plato and Aristotle struggled with the question of whether the required conduct was fair and just by nature or merely required by convention or legislative enactment. For them, law was primarily a method of maintaining the status quo and the social order. A later commentator, Draco, felt that all crimes were equal and should be punished alike; it was the violation of the law, the act against society, that was critical and not the harm done to the individual.[15]

Later, the Romans became the dominant force in the development of law. The Roman Empire covered an immense geographic area from England to Turkey and Northern Africa. A Roman citizen in London had the same legal rights as he or she did in Rome. Administration of such an empire required a highly developed administrative apparatus that mirrored the development of the law and the eventual creation of the world's primary legal system.

The Twelve Tables, written around 450 BCE, are often cited as the beginning of the Roman law. The Tables, the product of a formal deliberative process between "those of high rank and those of lower rank," contained "some very elementary principles on how to resolve disputes."[16] Disputes were to be decided by patricians or members of the nobility, not by professional judges. Access to the process was controlled by the praetor, a government official, who also formulated the issues that were to be decided in the matter. Eventually, courts became more open and accessible, and the initial screening was abolished.

With no legislation to draw upon and with no training in the field, these amateur judges needed help in resolving complex legal issues; they relied on the College of Pontiffs for assistance. These juris-consults could not decide the cases but did provide the patricians with indispensable expertise. From this process came the "entire idea of law as learning, in written form and according to rigorous requirements of reasoning. The writing started on papyrus rolls, during the time of the empire; the rolls then became leaves, eventually bound into volume (codex) form."[17]

Romans, like the Greeks, had philosophers who thought deeply about the nature of the law. For example, Cicero, the noted Roman lawyer, examined the idea of natural law, a single law or scheme of laws that governs the entire universe and to which all natural things conform. Inanimate objects were bound to such laws by natural necessity but people discerned the law of nature through reason, and all people were equal in their capacity to discern the natural law. Natural law was the foundation for all actual laws and customs; it was the supreme and permanent law to which all human order must conform if it was to have any truth or validity. The Church Fathers, early Christian writers from the first through seventh centuries, viewed this supreme law as the universal and eternal law of God, and St. Augustine, by criticizing the emperors who persecuted early Christians, indicated that states, not just individuals, could commit injustices when they transgressed against God's law. The idea that breaking a secular law was the same as sinning against God dominated European thinking in the Dark Ages and into the Middle Ages, times when the Catholic Church was the predominant unifying social institution.[18] However, by the thirteenth century, religion and morality were viewed as separate and apart from civil order and law. Secular law was given an autonomous role of its own, although canon law or church law continued to develop.[19]

Cicero also defined three elements of law: legislation, administrative edicts, and judicial reasoning on the basis of legal tradition. Today, these same three elements dominate U.S. law. *Roman law* was highly developed, and it was spread throughout the far reaches of present-day Europe and northern Africa under the empire's superb administrative system. Even after the fall of the Western Empire in 476 CE, the Eastern Empire, led by the emperor at Constantinople, continued to develop the concepts of Roman law. In 528 CE, the emperor Justinian collected the laws of the vast empire and published them as the Code of Justinian, or *Corpus Juris Civilis*. The authority and power of this collection are immense. Justinian's Code is a cornerstone of today's so-called *civil law* systems. Much of the *canon law* developed by the Catholic Church is based on Justinian's Codes, and its precepts may be found in common law countries as well. Although the Code essentially disappeared for a time, it was revived during the twelfth century by professors at the Italian universities, especially at Bologna. This initiated the growth of new law and the system of legal science; however, the process was a long and complex one, spurred on by changes in both the political and commercial spheres that accompanied the revitalization of trade and the emergence of Europe from the Dark Ages.[20]

René David and John E.C. Brierley in their comparative study of legal systems and jurisprudence describe Romano-Germanic law or civil law as "rules of conduct intimately linked to ideas of justice and morality."[21] Ascertaining and formulating these rules are primarily done by legal scholars in university settings rather than by courts and practitioners. In describing the civil law as the predominant legal system in the world, we are not speaking of a particular set of laws or statutes but instead of the methodology and philosophy used to resolve various legal issues. It is distinct from any set of local laws or the study of the actual laws governing property, venue, crime, or inheritance, to name a few. Although Swedish universities began teaching national law as early as 1620 at Uppsala, most European universities did not initiate national law courses until the eighteenth century: 1707 at Wittenberg, 1741 in Spain, 1758 at Oxford, and 1800 at Cambridge. Before that time, only Romano-Germanic and canon law were taught at the universities.[22] Law was studied not to provide the solution in a particular trial or to give students mastery of legal technique but rather to tell "judges how they should decide in justice."[23] The universities were not entrusted with application of the law but instead stated how the law was to be viewed and how knowledge of law might be attained.[24] The rules themselves were "woven from many strands: existing customs and practices, the customs of merchants, canon law, the revived Roman law, and, at a later stage, natural-law philosophies."[25]

Historically, Romano-Germanic law governs relationships among individuals rather than the relationship between individuals and government.[26] However, during the seventeenth and eighteenth centuries, the Natural Law School, or movement, became the dominant paradigm at the universities. This school of thought blended the idea of a universal, unchanging law, common for all time and for all nations, with the approach to legal reasoning established by the civil law. The two were not contradictory in the area of private law. The Natural Law movement is noted for two major changes in the civil law system. First, accompanied by transformations in the political and religious systems of the time, law was also modified to reflect the natural rights of persons and to guarantee the liberties of the individual.[27] Under traditional Roman law, the public law dealing with the relations between those who govern and those who are governed was left to persons other than jurists, but this arrangement was forever changed by the Natural Law movement and the public law is now an integral part of the civil law system.

Second, the Natural Law school spurred extensive codifications that led to the fusion of theoretical and practical law.[28] Justinian had not been the only ruler to order compilations of the laws. Various Germanic leaders also initiated written collections of various legal customs, including the Salic Law that was compiled under Clovis toward the end of the fifth century. These codes primarily concerned the amount of fines for various offenses and contained relatively few civil provisions, although the Salic Law did provide that no woman could inherit property. Women were not left without other protections, however; there were heavy fines for insulting women, and the killing of a woman resulted in the most extreme penalties.[29]

From the fifth century forward, Europe depended increasingly on codes, but it was not until the Natural Law school that national codes achieved their preeminent status. In civil law countries the law is extensively codified, and decisions are based on the code as designed by the legislature rather than on binding judicial precedent. The premise is that each case should be decided on its own merits within the parameters prescribed by the codes. "From the Anglo-American point of view, French legal reasoning appears to start with a highly generalized proposition of law to which the facts are then fitted, rather than to begin with a detailed examination of the facts followed by application of a narrowly formulated rule."[30] Or, as another legal scholar explained,

> For their point of departure, civil law judges search the legislation for the controlling principle and the rules which govern the subject; this principle or rule is then applied or interpreted according to the particular facts of the case in dispute. The reasoning process is to go from the general principle to the special case. ... [C]ommon-law judges search in the previous decisions for a similar case, and are guided accordingly. If a statute is involved and the text is clear, the judge abides by its provisions; but if doubt or ambiguity can avoid the statute's applicability, there is again resort to a search of previous decisions for common-law authority as a basis of decision.[31]

These systems employ an inquisitorial process of trial. The judge, rather than being a passive party, is an active participant in the trial. The judge's assigned task is to ascertain the truth, and the entire process revolves around him or her. A judge directs the investigation or the fact-gathering process. There are fewer technical rules of evidence and procedure, and trials are often rather informal, more closely resembling an administrative hearing than a full-blown trial. Judges, however, are rigidly bound by the code and the description of their judicial duties, and conformity is required.[32] The same transactions and activities are governed or barred by the civil codes as by common law jurisdictions; it is the approach taken in legal reasoning and methodology that distinguishes them. Generally, judges in these systems are specially trained for their role; they are not elevated from among practicing lawyers. In France, virtually anyone can give legal advice or prepare legal documents, but specialists must be hired for litigation and presentation of oral arguments which are rare. Generally, the facts and legal arguments are submitted by the attorneys in writing, and oral advocacy plays little role.[33]

> Another point of interest is that the common-law jury trial in civil cases left the determination of facts to the jury, so that the judicial technique of reducing the power of the jury was to broaden the scope of "matters of law" which fell within the judge's power. In the civil law, a jury in civil cases is either very rare or nonexistent, so the judge is in complete control of all phases of the trial.[34]

Today, the civil law tradition dominates throughout the world in such diverse locales and nations as Europe, South America, Scotland, Quebec,

TABLE 2.1

Comparison of Common Law and Civil Law (Romano-Germanic) Traditions

	Common Law	Civil Law
Major Source of Law	Judicial decisions	Legislation
Reliance on Precedent	Yes (Strong)	No (Weak)
Role of Legal Scholarship	Peripheral	Extensive and influential
Trials	Adversarial	Inquisitorial
Role of Lawyers during Trial	Active advocates	Secondary
Function of Lawyers	Frame and present case	Advise and inform
Role of Judges during Trial	Referee	Active participant who directs trial and examines facts
Selection of Judges	Usually elevated from among practicing attorneys	Specialized training for career as judge
Citizen Participation at Trial	Jury	Members of judicial panels
Evidentiary Rules	Formal and restrictive, e.g., exclusionary rule	None
Trial Emphasis	Procedures	Substantive law and factual certainty

Source: Edward Wells, http://my.ilstu.edu/~ewells/cjs102/CommonvsCivilLaw-Chart.pdf (visited November 9, 2015); William Tetley, "Mixed Jurisdictions: Common Law v. Civil Law (Codified and Uncodified)," 60 La. L. Rev. 677 (2000).

Louisiana in North America, Russia, the Vatican City, Vietnam, Iceland, and Central Africa. Many nations adapted the Napoleonic Code or one of its progeny such as the 1896 Germanic Code and grafted it onto tribal and customary law such as Swaziland, or into religious systems such as Islam in Morocco and Iran. The Napoleonic Code of France, adopted in 1804, provided a unified system of law for the country as a whole, replacing a system of localized laws, and is the basis of most civil law jurisdictions today. The 1896 Germanic Code was later adopted by Japan and by pre-communist China. Thus, the widespread use of the civil system has extended far beyond the boundaries of Europe.[35]

Nearly 100 years after Justinian codified the Roman law, a new religion developed in the Middle East, the teachings of which have expanded into a major legal system with worldwide influence. "The sacred law of Islam is an all-embracing body of religious duties, the totality of Allah's commands that regulate the life of every Muslim in all its aspects ... Islamic law is the epitome of Islamic thought."[36] Before Islam, the law in the area for both the Bedouins and the sedentary populations was the law of the ancient Arabian tribal systems, and the pattern of adhering to tradition and precedent continues. Islam supplied a uniform system of precepts, a system that was not limited by national boundaries but encompassed all of the followers of Allah. The schism among Muslim sects affected the interpretation of the law, but many of the basic precepts are adopted by all.[37] Modern Islamic nations often seek to synthesize Islamic laws with other systems, especially the Roman-Germanic traditions. The religious law usually prevails with regard to family, inheritance, and criminal matters, while the civil law influence is frequently stronger in the area of commercial matters. The "most potent" civil law source is the Napoleonic Code that is modified to meet the unique requirements of Islam.[38] One of the most obvious influences of Islamic law in the United States is the prisoners' rights cases in which incarcerated Black Muslims claimed the protection of the First Amendment's Free Exercise Clause.

Americans are known for their insular approach to many things, not the least of which is law. The English common law has so dominated our jurisprudence that we tend to overlook other systems; but that system was not created in a vacuum, nor was it the only highly developed one. For example, treatises describing the Chinese codes that were developed as early as 220 BCE are extant. In his work *Law and Society in Traditional China*, T'ung-Tsu Ch'u argues that Chinese society remained essentially static until the twentieth century and that both the prominent elements of the system—status by kinship and by social stratification—and the laws remained remarkably unaltered from the law codes of the Ch'in (221–207 BCE) until the last century.[39]

Today, the categorization of dominant legal systems or amalgamations thereof varies, but includes the common law systems, the Romano-Germanic (civil) law systems, the socialist systems, customary law and the religious systems such as Islamic, Hindu, and Jewish. Recent political changes have diminished the role of socialism, and the Lenin-Marxist theories have frequently been altered to incorporate market-oriented and globalization-driven reforms.[40] Customary law often arises from indigenous or ethnic groups who recognize that behaving in accordance with established rules and traditions of the group is both beneficial and necessary for governing that group. It

> derives its binding force not through written agreements, but through sustained, established conduct that arises over time and which parties (states, in the case of international law, or individuals, in the case of domestic law) follow out of a sense of legal obligation or *opinio juris* . . . [It] exists distinct from agreements, recognized principles of law.[41]

Identifying the appropriate equilibrium between the national or international laws and the customary law is often quite difficult and, while sometimes accomplished through treaties or agreements, it may require legislative or judicial action.

The religious systems primarily emphasize the religious duties of the person regardless of nationality, but some nations are theocracies governed by religious leaders. Islam is primarily a religion that espouses a specific moral code and, like

Judaism and Christianity, is considered as one of the Abrahamic faiths. Islamic laws, the Shariah, are autonomous and are based primarily on the *Quran*, the written text of the messages given to Muhammad by God through the angel Gabriel; the *Sunna,* a compilation of the statements of Muhammad and his actual deeds; the actions and sayings of the Companions of the Prophet; and the interpretations of Muslim scholars. Experts differ over the number of verses of the *Quran* that deal with legal issues; appraisals range from 350 to 500 of the 6342 verses, and many of those deal with religious duties and obligations. Just as Christianity is divided between Catholicism and the many Protestant denominations, Muslims are split primarily between the Sunni and Shia (Shiite) and the subdivisions within each. The initial division arose over the issue of leadership following Muhammed's death, as he did not name a successor and had no living sons. The Shia Muslims believe that the leader must be a descendant of the Prophet Muhammad's cousin and son-in-law, Ali ibn Abi Talib, while the Sunni, the majority branch, do not. Both adhere to the principal tenets of Islam, including recognition of God as the sole source of authority and the lawgiver and the emphasis on individual and collective moral duties, but there are disagreements about dogma, governance, and the law.[42] For example, the Sunni inheritance laws allow the widow a proportionate share in all her deceased husband's property while the Shiite laws permit her to receive a portion of her husband's movable assets but not the land. A Sunni daughter or her descendants will be excluded in favor of her brothers, uncles, or other male relatives, while under Shia law she and her children would prevail over the collaterals.[43] It is important to note that

> a common misunderstanding about Islamic law is that it is a single unified system of law which is the same the world over ... [but though] there exists a set of common historical sources and methods, the modern expressions of Islamic law vary immensely from country to country.[44]

Classic socialist systems of law traditionally have three purposes: (1) to provide for national security; (2) to regulate economics on the basis of socialist principles; and (3) to educate the general population as well as any lawbreaker about the law. The system flourishes in the People's Republic of China (PRC), Vietnam, Cuba, and North Korea, and remnants remain in the former Soviet bloc nations.[45] The legal system of the PRC exhibits the typical characteristics of the socialist systems. Its constitution establishes the PRC as a "socialist country under the people's democratic dictatorship and led by the proletariat on the basis of a worker–peasant alliance. Socialism is the political system of the country where all power belongs to the people."[46] Furthermore, the Constitution provides that the state's economic system is one of "socialist public ownership," that is, one of collective and national ownership of the means of production, although private enterprise is now an important component of the economic reforms.[47]

The basis of the law is legislation as in the Romano-Germanic system, although it is embedded in the ancient traditions and philosophy of Asia, especially the PRC.[48] The National People's Congress (NPC) is the sole authority for the creation of laws and regulations as well as the enforcement and adjudication of such; there is no doctrine of separation of powers.[49] The NPC and its Standing Committee alone have the right to enact and revise basic statutes and laws, although local ordinances may be created within the provinces, municipalities, and autonomous regions. However, all power and authority stem from the NPC.[50] The primary purpose of the judiciary is to maintain social order and to reduce criminality through the principle of prevention first. The goal is to "mobilize all citizens in an effort to eliminate the root causes of the crime and eliminate the social and economic causes within the environment which creates it."[51] Criminal penalties stress ideological reform through education and productive labor.[52] One interesting aspect of Chinese criminal law is that confessions are to be discounted. It is the role of the court to investigate, to seek the truth from the facts, and to apply the law.[53]

To maintain social order, the Chinese rely heavily on programs disseminating basic legal knowledge to the public at all levels of the educational system, from elementary schools through universities and through a variety of other programs such as those at workplaces and at various locations. Because China was a feudal state for thousands of years, many citizens lack basic familiarity with the law and a legal system; therefore, intensive efforts by the state have been mounted to overcome this unfamiliarity.[54] However, one aspect of prior Chinese jurisprudence that has been maintained and incorporated into the socialist system is mediation. "From the time of antiquity, the common people have formed the habit of asking prestigious persons to mediate settlements in clans, villages, and neighborhoods."[55] This tradition has been systematized with local mediation committees elected by the people with the goal of allowing the "quarreling parties to treat each other in a spirit of mutual understanding and accommodation, so as to solve misunderstanding," and provisions for both court and private mediation as well as arbitration are found in the Constitution and statutes such as the Arbitration Law and the Laws of Civil Procedure. Mediation is also employed in minor criminal actions.[56] As we will discuss in Chapter 3, this tradition of mediation is becoming more important in the West, with courts in the United States following the pattern of requiring mediation between litigants before conducting full-blown court proceedings.

The internal changing social, political, cultural, and economic structure in a number of countries such as South Africa, Russia, and Iraq is requiring the transformation of the legal systems within each of these nations.[57] Obviously, such alterations have created chaos and uncertainty as well as exhilaration for all those affected by the changes. Basic notions of authority, legitimacy, property, individual and commercial relationships, and procedures must be rethought and reconceptualized. For example, the creation of the European Union has led to the "growing convergence within the Union between Europe's two major legal traditions, the civil law of the continental countries and the common law of England, Wales, and Ireland."[58] However, a number of nations including those as diverse as Scotland and Zimbabwe or subdivisions thereof (e.g., Louisiana in the United States and Quebec in Canada) have successfully melded both.[59]

Each of these systems or branches of law derives from common origins, and each system serves the same purposes. They cannot be wholly separated from one another in tracing the sources and effects, nor should they be, especially in today's global community and economy.

THE ENGLISH HERITAGE

Following the collapse of the Roman Empire, anarchy and confusion predominated. No one source of authority had the might to enforce order. Any restraints on antisocial behavior developed within tribes or within local areas, and most conflicts were resolved by violence. As society emerged from that period, the demand for order increased, and the primary source was the Roman civil law, especially Justinian's Code, although the canon law of the Catholic Church was pervasive.

Development of the Common Law

In England, however, the pattern was broken. The earliest extant code of that country was a succinct collection of laws created by Æthelbert, Christian King of Kentings, about 600 CE. These laws essentially set the fines for injury to the person or damage to the property of another. For example, if an ear was cut off, the fine was 12 shillings; if the ear was pierced, the fine was 3 shillings; and if hearing was lost, the fine was 25 shillings. There was no provision relating to commercial transactions and very little relating to other relationships; however, a widow who had borne a living child was entitled to receive one-half of her husband's estate. A woman who left her husband with her children could have half the goods; if the husband kept the children, she was entitled to a share of the goods equal to a child's share.[60]

This code was expanded by Canute, who ruled England, Norway, and Denmark from 1017 to 1035 and whose laws were written in English.[61] The Danes had conquered not only England but also northern France (which came to be known as Normandy), sections of Ireland and Scotland, and the Orkney, Shetland, and Hebrides Islands. Their legacy included a type of grand jury proceeding, property transactions in which land could freely be bought and sold, and flourishing borough institutions.[62] The word *law* itself is Norse, not English.[63]

By the early twelfth century, Anglo-Saxon England differed from other European realms in having an organized system of justice. The country was divided into vills, or townships, a number of which composed the hundred, while several hundreds formed the shire. The administration of justice was primarily local. There were public courts at both the hundred and shire levels, and there were courts headed by the lord of the manor, who resolved disputes among his own tenants.

Court procedure was fairly uniform. Each party appeared in court. The plaintiff would allege the improper activity in the form of an oath, and the defendant would enter a denial in the form of an oath. Generally, the defendant would then present a requisite number of character witnesses (frequently 12) who would swear that the defendant was telling the truth; these witnesses did not testify on the facts of the case but merely on the veracity of the defendant. The communities were small, and all the trial participants were known to each other. Those who swore falsely were subject not only to distrust from their peers but also to punishment imposed by God.

In criminal cases, 12 freemen served as the accusers before the court and presented the names of those they believed to have committed crimes. Guilt or innocence would then be proven either by compurgation (the process, just described, of clearing a person by oaths of others as to his veracity) or by ordeal. Trial by ordeal frequently involved burning a person's hand or arm, binding the wound, and examining it after a short period. If the wound was clean, the accused was cleared of the crime. Another creative method of trial was to toss a bound person into a stream. If she sank, she was innocent; if she floated, she was guilty.[64] Either result was quite unfortunate. The Anglo-Saxons also employed fines or a system of reparation for those found guilty. They used the system even for homicides; each person's life had a value, set according to his or her station, with the king's being the most valuable. The *wergild,* the fine, was divided among the king for the loss of a subject, the lord for the loss of a vassal, and the deceased's family. The Normans added the possibility of trial by combat, wherein one could either compete for oneself or hire a champion to engage in battle. Although the methods were crude, these courts provided a forum for grievances to be heard.

The Normans greatly strengthened the administrative organization of the country and tightened the control of the government in the hands of the monarch. In addition, feudalism, which had just begun to flourish in England, became the dominant social order. William the Conqueror assumed ownership of land for himself as monarch, but he allowed his followers dominion over great tracts of it in exchange for certain services and goods, including military service or agricultural products. In turn, William's tenants subdivided the land and responsibilities until they had established an entire chain of reciprocal duties, reaching from the monarch to the lowliest serf.

William also maintained his own tribunal, the King's Court, both for the protection of royal interests and as an appellate court for those litigants who could travel to the royal court; however, the vast majority of cases were resolved in the hundred or shire courts or in the seignorial courts of the barons. It was a time of establishing new patterns in resolving conflicts, of turning from self-help methods of revenge to a quasi-formal means of adjudication; nevertheless, much of Anglo-Saxon law and customs continued relatively unchanged. William and his successors did not overturn the laws that they found but instead supplemented them with a strong centralized judiciary and uniformity of decisions.

Henry II, the first Plantagenet, who ruled from 1154 until 1189, had a major influence on the development of English law and the centralization of the judicial system. His goals were twofold. The first was to ensure that the fees paid by litigants flowed into the royal coffers and not to the barons, and the second was to consolidate royal control. Crimes became wrongs against the king as well as against the individual, and more serious criminal matters came before the Curia Regis, an advisory body of the king's counselors who carried out judicial, executive, and administrative functions. Juries were employed in trial, supplanting the older systems of trial by compurgation, ordeal, and combat.

Henry II bolstered his control over local courts by vigorously applying the royal executive writ that directed his subjects to perform or to refrain from certain actions; failure to obey the writ could result in punishment. A writ might very well order judges of the shire, hundred, or seignorial courts to find for a particular plaintiff, a usurpation of authority that contributed to the demise of the local courts. In addition, Henry II revived the practice, instituted by Henry I, of sending judges from the Curia Regis into the countryside to settle disputes, although their primary task was revenue collection. It was Edward I who, by the Statute of Westminster in 1285, institutionalized the practice of sending itinerant judges on circuits to render justice.

As these changes were occurring, other developments were also taking place. By the end of the thirteenth century, there were three law courts in the secular realm and a firmly entrenched system of ecclesiastical courts. The latter enforced canon law as handed down by the Catholic Church and had sole jurisdiction over matters of marital relationships and inheritance. The canon law was composed of papal decrees, writings of church scholars, and scripture; it was heavily influenced by Italian law and by the training that the priests received in the traditions of Roman law. The domination of the ecclesiastical courts over marriages lasted until the mid-nineteenth century, although the Catholic Church was supplanted by the Church of England.

The three law courts were distinguished by function, although their jurisdictions often overlapped. The Court of Common Pleas, located in London, dealt with disputes that were essentially civil in nature. The Court of the King's Bench was mobile; it initially followed the king on his journeys across the countryside. It exercised appellate jurisdiction over the Court of Common Pleas and over matters, including criminal matters, involving the king. The third court, the Exchequer, dealt primarily with matters of revenue and taxation.

The outcome of the monarchs' centralization of the judicial system is the rejection of the civil law tradition in England and the substitution of the common law. Strong kings who consolidated judicial power in their own hands, and who imposed a uniform system of tribunals over the entire country rather than allowing the local courts to remain viable, contributed mightily to the development of the common law, often termed *judge-made law*. Because of the paucity of statutes, the judges formalized the customs and mores of the times into court decisions and applied the same rules in whatever corner of the realm they happened to be. Consistency was facilitated by written reports of judicial decisions kept by the king's courts, collected by such authors as Henry of Bracton, and used as authority or precedent by subsequent judges.[65] Common law "describes that part of the law that is enacted, non-statutory, that is common to the whole land and to all Englishmen."[66] It became the basis for the legal systems of the English-speaking nations of the world.

Development of Equity

The business of government in England during the thirteenth century was carried out by two governmental departments: the Exchequer, which handled fiscal matters, and the Chancery, which was the secretarial department. The Chancery was headed by an official called a chancellor, usually a cleric, who was responsible for handling the government's paperwork, including the writs for courts. The writs served three purposes: (1) as the document giving the plaintiff access to the courts in exchange for the payment of a fee; (2) as a method of designating which court would decide the case; and (3) as a tool for directing the sheriff to summon the defendant for the court appearance. The Chancery eventually developed standard writs for various legal wrongs, but by statute (the second Statute of Westminster in 1285), the Chancery was empowered to "let a writ be made by those learned in the law so that for the future it shall not befall that the court shall delay over-long in doing justice to complaints."[67]

Although the common law courts were initially creative and flexible, they soon petrified, adopting rigid, harsh procedures. In addition, the courts could provide only one remedy: damages. The reservoir of justice remained the king, who was God's secular representative on earth. In those situations in which the remedy provided by the common law courts was inadequate, or when the plaintiffs were impoverished and could not afford the court fees (or their opponents were influential and wealthy), the complainants petitioned the king to consider their causes. The king, in turn, transferred to the chancellor the laborious task of reading the numerous petitions, and soon the petitions were filed directly with the Chancery rather than with the monarch. But the plea remained the same: "to do what is right for the love of God and in the way of charity."[68] Remember that the chancellors were ecclesiastics who were trained in Roman and canon law, with its foundation of natural law. The appeal was to the conscience of the chancellor and a higher system of justice.[69] If the chancellor agreed with the petition, the defendant would be ordered to appear before the chancellor to respond to the allegations. At that time, the defendant would be placed under oath and questioned by the chancellor, who determined questions of both law and fact and then shaped a remedy.

It is for the formation of extraordinary relief that the Chancery achieved its greatest fame in jurisprudence. As pointed out earlier, the sole remedy in common law courts was monetary damages; however, that is not always an adequate solution. Suppose that there is a building of substantial historic significance in your community, but over the years it has deteriorated; now the new owner of the property is determined to tear it down. The payment of monetary damages will neither reconstruct the building nor pay the community for the loss of a symbol of its past. Preservationists would seek an injunction to prevent the destruction of the building. The *injunction,* a court order directing a person to refrain from carrying out certain acts, could halt demolition of the building. If the property owner defied the injunction, he or she would be subject to certain legal penalties, such as fines and possibly even a jail sentence. The injunction is an example of the remedies created by the courts of *equity;* the common law courts, on the other hand, as originally structured, would not intervene and would wait until the injury had occurred to award damages—a patent absurdity. Other equitable remedies included specific performance and trusts, both of which will be discussed in later chapters. The result of the chancellor's activities was to forge parallel court systems, each with different remedies.

Thus, for some 400 years, England had two types of courts: the historic common law courts and the more flexible courts of equity; in the late nineteenth century the two were merged, and all courts were to apply the rules of both, with equity being dominant in case of conflict. The remedies fashioned by the English jurists during these centuries are basically the same as those used by courts today. The remedies provided for particular types of legal wrongs are discussed in connection with particular theories, but it is appropriate to describe the traditional forms of redress here also. Judges, whether in common law or equity courts, adhered to the principle that "for every wrong there is a remedy"—even if the remedy is to seek legislative aid—and they struggled to create the forms of judicial relief available today.

One approach to the study of remedies is to examine them from the perspective of both the plaintiff and the defendant. A court may award specific relief and substitutionary relief to a successful plaintiff. *Specific relief,* such as an injunction or an order for the defendant to perform his or her portion of a contract, is an equitable remedy and is directed to individuals and their activities. It has limited application and is not always the most appropriate or the most desirable remedy. *Substitutionary relief,* the basic common law remedy, generally refers to the award of money as compensation for a loss. The losing defendant may be imprisoned (e.g., for contempt of court), required to pay either compensatory or punitive damages, or mandated to transfer property to the plaintiff.

A second approach is to identify the type of legal wrong and the related remedial goals. Tort law deals with injuries sustained by individuals and with their lawsuits against those who injure them. There are three general remedial goals in tort law: restoration to the status quo, compensation or indemnification, and punishment. For example, assume that there has been an automobile accident with injuries sustained by the drivers and property damage to the cars. The repair work done to the vehicles to remove the dents and replace the headlights is an example of restoration to the status quo, or to the pre-accident condition. The money paid to the injured party for his or her hospital bills and lost wages illustrates the principle of compensation or indemnification, whereby the party is reimbursed for pecuniary losses stemming from the accident. A monetary award may be assessed by the jury to punish the wrongdoer for egregious acts, such as driving while intoxicated and injuring a child. By contrast, the goals of contract remedies include the following: (1) putting the party in the position he or she would have been in if the contract had been fulfilled; (2) restoring the parties to their original positions; (3) compensating the plaintiff for any detriment incurred in reliance on the contract (such as a painter purchasing paint in expectation of the homeowner fulfilling his portion of the contract); and (4) punishing the party breaching the contract. Obviously, some of the goals are similar in both areas (restoration of the plaintiff to his or her original position and punishment of the wrongdoer), but other remedies are tailored to rectify specific legal wrongs.[70]

OLLEY OXEN FREE!!

Olley Mattison, by his own account, was "addicted to habits of intemperance, [and] was married to the defendant, in the Spring of 1840 while in a fit of *delirium tremens.*" Five years later, he filed a suit in equity to prevent Mary Mattison, also known as Mary Clements, from "passing as his wife, and harassing him with groundless actions and suits for alimony, maintenance, &c." and to declare the marriage null and void. South Carolina courts denied his motion for nullification on the grounds that the state legislature had not given the power to terminate the marriage by divorce or other means to the judiciary but noted that the courts did have the power to protect the person or property under equity.

Source: Mattison v. Mattison, 20 S.C. Eq. 387, 1847 WL 2210 (S.C.App.Eq.)

Equity provided the flexibility to tailor remedies to situations in which the legal remedies were not adequate. It added a sense of fairness, of an appeal to the conscience of the purveyors of justice that greatly strengthened the system. Frederic Maitland, one of the greatest English legal scholars and a noted expert on equity, described its place in jurisprudence:

> We ought to think of equity as supplementary law, a sort of appendix added on to our code, or a sort of gloss written round our code, an appendix, a gloss ... The language which equity held to law, if we may personify the two, was not "No, that is not so, you make a mistake, your rule is an absurd, an obsolete one"; but "Yes, of course that is so, but it is not the whole truth." ... We ought not to think of common law and equity as of two rival systems. Equity was not a self-sufficient system, at every point it presupposed the existence of common law. Common law was a self-sufficient system. [I] do not think that any one has expounded or ever will expound equity as a single, consistent system, an articulate body of law. It is a collection of appendixes between which there is no very close connexion. If we suppose all our law put into a systematic order, we shall find that some chapters of it have been copiously glossed by equity, while others are quite free from equitable glosses.[71]

THE AMERICAN EXPERIENCE

The colonists who moved to the New World brought with them the legal traditions of their homelands. Vestiges of each system—Dutch, English, French, and Spanish—may be found in the laws of the various states.

> History of a system of law is largely a history of borrowings of legal materials from other legal systems and of assimilation of materials from outside the law. In the history of Anglo-American law there are successive borrowings and adaptations from Roman law (e.g., the rules as to title by occupation), from the canon law (e.g., our law and practice as to marriage and divorce and probate and administration), from the modern Roman law and Continental codes (e.g., in our law of riparian rights), and from the commercial law of Continental Europe.[72]

The dominant scheme was the common law system of England. Formalistic in tenor and designed to deal with a highly structured society, it was inadequate for the demands of the colonists. They tempered the system and forged new precepts that more accurately reflected the social and economic realities of the New World. One hallmark of the new system was the merger of law and equity, and the power of a single judge to render both types of remedies in the appropriate cases (as opposed to the English scheme of parallel court systems). A second characteristic of the new system was the abolition of the common law power of judges to define crimes and the substitution of the legislature as the body to identify criminal activity and to determine the appropriate range of punishment. In the settlements, there was increased emphasis on the individual, because of both religious beliefs and the need to be self-sufficient in opening up new territory. The colonists adopted those portions of the common law that were appropriate and modified others, and each colony developed innovative approaches to conflict resolution. In sum, there was no abandonment of important principles or abrupt break with the English system, although adjustments were made to suit the new environment.

> Those who formed the Constitution struck out anew free of previous shackles in an effort to obtain a better order of government more congenial to human liberty and welfare. It cannot be seriously claimed that they intended to adopt the common law wholesale. They accepted those portions of it which were adapted to this country and conformed to the ideals of its citizens and rejected the remainder. In truth there was widespread hostility to the common law in general and profound opposition to its adoption into our jurisprudence from the commencement of the Revolutionary War until long after the Constitution was ratified.[73]

To illustrate the adaptation process, consider the incorporation of established elements of citizens' rights against government into the fundamental laws of the United States. The Magna Carta, sealed by King John in 1215 and regarded as one of the most important documents in the history of the English-speaking world, constituted formal recognition by the monarch of certain rights held by citizens. It contains several provisions that were adopted into the U.S. Constitution. For example, the section of the Magna Carta which stated that there should be no criminal "trial upon … simple accusation without producing credible witnesses to the truth therein" was the foundation of the rights guaranteed to criminal defendants in the Fifth and Sixth Amendments. Similarly, Section 39, which provided that "no freeman shall be taken, imprisoned or disseised [dispossessed], or outlawed, or banished, or in any other way destroyed, nor will we go upon him, nor send upon him, except by legal judgment of his peers or the law of the land," was the basis of the constitutional provisions preventing deprivation of life, liberty, or property without due process of law. Other basic guarantees found in the English Bill of Rights of 1689, such as the ones preventing the suspension of laws without the consent of Parliament and protecting the freedom of speech that "ought not to be impeached or questioned," were wholly adopted by the writers of the U.S. Constitution. Fundamental liberties available to the English were identified and guaranteed to the former colonists, but the influence of the English pattern extends to both substantive and procedural laws as well.

Following the Revolution, legislatures representing the will of the sovereign people came to supplant judges and governors as the primary lawmakers. This was due, in part, to several factors. First, the absolute governments in Europe had been successfully challenged by legislative bodies, as indicated by the victory of Parliament and Oliver Cromwell over the absolute monarchs in the English Revolution of 1688. Second, these entities represented the will of the sovereign people to have a democratic and representative government. Third, the Founding Fathers were familiar with the law on the Continent, with its strong tradition of the legislature as absolute lawgiver; in addition, English law and the king's judges were in some disrepute in this nation following the Revolution. Fourth, the legislature was the dominant branch of government during these formative days. Fifth, the Constitution of the United States, unlike that of Great Britain, carefully prescribes the responsibilities of each governmental branch; however, judges retain the option to approve new theories of recovery and to demand new procedures in accordance with their assigned constitutional duties.[74]

In addition, the legislatures began in the early 1800s to codify the various statutes within the states. Unfortunately, legislatures pass laws in a haphazard order and amend them at later dates, again with no particular attention paid to organization. The purpose of the codification movement in the United States was to collect the related statutes and arrange them coherently in order to facilitate their use. Although some advocates anticipated that these codes would be used as the Continental codes were, that has not been the result; instead, courts retained much of their power to determine the constitutionality of the codes, and judges still rely more on precedent than on the code provisions. Today's practitioners, laypersons, and judges routinely use codes, such as the Internal Revenue Code or the Penal Code, but they use them primarily as references or collections of statutes; the interpretation of the statutes is left to the judicial and administrative branches. Some of the codes are merely re-enactments of judicially established rules, such as the various codes of criminal or civil procedures. Both the uniform laws that are adopted by individual states and the Restatements (standard compilations of laws in various substantive areas) have contributed to the consistency of laws within a nation composed of 51 sovereign entities invested with the power to make law.

Nevertheless, judges remain a potent and powerful component of the American legal systems. It is they who work daily with the law and who give it a unique twist to fit the situations confronting the courts. The reliance of judges on precedent and the doctrine of *stare decisis* remains as strong and viable as it was in the day of Henry II. *Stare decisis* refers to the policy of courts to follow the rules laid down in previous judicial decisions and to refrain from disturbing established points of law. The purpose is to ensure stability and certainty in the legal system. Litigants are aware of the results in similar prior cases and make their decisions in regard to the lawsuit accordingly; *stare decisis* enhances predictability. Judges are entrusted with great power and authority, not only in deciding specific cases but also as lawgivers.

Yet, the Anglo-American judicial system is based on the adversarial system, a system that is lawyer-centered in many ways. There is enormous responsibility and emphasis placed on the attorneys because the lawsuit is directed by the lawyers and the parties who control and shape the litigation. "The traditional view is that the judge sits solely to decide disputed questions, most commonly questions of law and procedure. Issues not raised, objections not mentioned, and points not made are, with very few exceptions, waived."[75]

THE AMERICAN LEGAL PROFESSION

As will be discussed in Chapter 3 on court organization, most American judges—although not all—are practicing attorneys at the time they assume the bench. Americans have a love–hate relationship with lawyers. On the one hand, lawyers are highly regarded and respected; on the other, many citizens share the feelings of Plato, William Shakespeare, and others who have launched scathing attacks on the legal profession and its practitioners. For instance, the explorer Vasco Núñez de Balboa entreated King Ferdinand of Spain in 1513 that "no Bachelor of Law … may pass to these parts under a heavy penalty [for] they even contrive and possess methods how to bring about a thousand lawsuits and villainies."[76] Americans both appreciate and resent lawyers' specialized knowledge and the power that information carries. Attacks on the legal profession have become even more virulent as politicians and the public attempt to blame every social woe on attorneys, especially trial lawyers, while conveniently overlooking the fact that juries decide cases and set policy, not lawyers.

Most lawyers in the United States today have at least a baccalaureate degree in addition to three years of law school. They must also be licensed by the state in which they practice and by the federal courts in which they try cases. This was not historically the case. Attorneys lacked formal legal education; instead, they trained as apprentices by "reading" law with established practitioners. In fact, reading the learned treatises about the law, especially William Blackstone's *Commentaries on the Laws of England,* was the major method of legal education.

Few reports of court cases were available, and Blackstone's comprehensive restatement of the law served as the principal collection for students for many years. His work was eventually supplemented by American scholarly writings, published reports of court cases, and formal legal training.

Modern legal education centers around universities, as has always been the case in civil law countries. The usual educational model is for students to read cases, extract the general principles, and then submit to classroom interrogation by professors. Law classes rarely involve lectures; instead, they are conducted along the lines recommended by Socrates; that is, a continuous series of challenging questions to be answered by the students. The students are to apply to hypothetical situations the reasoning and rules of law they have abstracted from assigned cases. The procedure resembles that used by a judge in examining the pertinent precedent and applying it to the case at bar.

This format enables students to think in terms of plaintiffs and defendants, and to consider only those facts relevant to the guiding principle of the case. It is an impersonal analysis. It obscures the reality that the cases involve real people with real injuries, a fact that has been frequently criticized. In his book *Persons and Masks of the Law,* John T. Noonan examines the treatment of one of the most famous of all tort cases, *Palsgraf v. Long Island Railroad Company.* In part, his purpose is to challenge the impersonal, detached treatment and to advance the argument that scholars and lawyers "should be concerned with law not as a set of technical skills which may be put to any use but as a human activity affecting both those acting and those enduring their action."[77] The facts of the *Palsgraf* case, as described in the opinion, were that a railroad passenger carrying some fireworks was jostled by railroad employees who were trying to assist him. The passenger dropped the fireworks, which exploded, and the shock of the explosion knocked down some scales that struck and injured the plaintiff. She sued the railroad company.

For law students, this meager description raises the question of whether the railroad should be held liable for damages as neither it nor its employees directly caused the injury. For Noonan, the description of the facts obscures as much as it reveals. The opinion does reveal that the plaintiff is a woman, but it says nothing about "her age, marital status, maternal responsibilities, employment or income. What injuries she had suffered, whether she had been almost decapitated or whether she had been mildly bruised .... What compensation she had sought or what compensation she had been awarded."[78] (As an aside, Mrs. Palsgraf, aged 43, had three children, two of whom were with her at the time of the accident. She was a janitor in the apartment building in which she lived and earned about $8 a week. She was struck on the arm, hip, and thigh, but the lingering effect was a stammer that her physicians attributed to the trauma of the accident. She was awarded $6000 from a company with assets valued at $1,700,000 in 1924, the year in which the accident occurred. In addition, the railroad industry had a dismal safety record, with 6617 people killed and 143,739 injured that year.)[79]

Interesting though these parenthetical facts may be, they are irrelevant to the law student because they do not add to the understanding of the legal principles of the case. Both the ability to sort through the various accounts in order to reduce the event to its barest legal bones and the resulting detachment are valued skills for most lawyers. They actively pursue detachment from the parties and their misery. The reason advanced is that the advocate must be able to accurately assess the situation and choose the appropriate legal tactics, a task hampered by the involvement of emotions. Yet Noonan challenges the accuracy of that premise:

> Focusing on the rules, [the professors] instilled in students a sense that the legal system was not the creature of individual caprice or the expression of raw power, but tradition constantly refined by reason ... Their purpose, as is mine, was to increase the sense of responsibility of those who by their thought and action make the system exist. But, for me, the responsibility comes in the response to other persons.[80]

Litigants, who are emotionally involved with their lawsuits and usually care passionately about the outcomes, often have difficulty dealing with the impersonality of their attorneys and of the legal system and may very well agree with Noonan. They seek revenge or justification and are frustrated with their advocates' lack of involvement. Watching the opposing lawyers talking and laughing together in the halls during breaks, they suspect collusion. Laypersons not familiar with courthouse proceedings fail to recognize the norms that bind the court personnel. "Courts are not an occasional assemblage of strangers who resolve a particular conflict and then dissolve, never to work together again. Courts are permanent organizations."[81] The judge, clerk, court reporter, and bailiff are a fairly static group. Attorneys work together and oppose each other on a fairly regular basis. Thus, group norms promote the establishment of friendly relations among the work group participants.

These same norms characterize every legal system. In the United States, the bench and bar are closely connected, not only as officers of the court but also by training. In the United States, as contrasted with Continental nations, there is no specialized track for those who aspire to judicial positions; nor are there formal divisions between those who argue cases in court and those who do not, such as is found in France and Great Britain. The English distinguish between barristers, who are courtroom advocates, and solicitors, who are general practitioners who do not generally appear in higher courts. Barristers are specialists who seldom have the right of direct access to the lay client and whose referrals come from solicitors. Each of the branches is governed by professional organizations—the Law Society for solicitors and the four Inns of Court for barristers—that control membership and the discipline of its members. Again, the group is essentially closed, tied together by professional norms and education.

Bar associations at the local, state, and national levels help unify the legal profession in the United States. The American Bar Association (ABA), a voluntary organization, plays an active role in the selection of federal judges, especially Supreme Court justices. State bar associations may be integrated; that is, all practitioners of law within the state must belong to the association.

Integrated bars often govern the conduct of the lawyers within the state; otherwise, a state commission or court considers grievances against lawyers. A code of ethics governs the professional behavior of attorneys. Violation of the code may lead to reprimands, temporary suspensions, or permanent disbarment of erring lawyers, depending on the severity of the breach.

Lawyers are both cursed and praised. They are criticized for their detachment and applauded for their honed analytical skills. They are reviled for feeding upon the sorrows of others and acclaimed for representing the downtrodden of our society. They are denounced as too powerful and too influential in government, but they are frequently elected to office. The bar is not a monolithic group, however. Its members represent a wide spectrum of political philosophies and interests, as indicated by the varying approaches to their profession and its practice.

CONCLUSION

The American legal system is a hodgepodge of borrowed principles and home-grown theories. An adaptable system, it changes to meet the needs of the times. Its origins may be traced over 4000 tumultuous years, and it owes an indelible debt of gratitude to the lawmakers (and lawbreakers) who have gone before. It represents the sometimes controversial efforts of society to provide justice and fair treatment in the resolution of conflicts and in the prescription of appropriate behavior.

NOTES

1. Oliver Wendell Holmes, Jr., *The Common Law* (Boston, MA: Little, Brown, 1881), p. 1.
2. Alan Watson, *Legal Transplants: An Approach to Comparative Law*, 2nd edn (Athens, GA: University of Georgia, 1993), p. 113.
3. Nels M. Bailkey and Richard Lim, eds, *Readings in Ancient History*, 6th edn (Boston, MA: Houghton Mifflin, 2002), pp. 24–25, 29.
4. Ibid., pp. 25–32.
5. A. Leo Oppenheim, *Ancient Mesopotamia*, 2nd edn, rev. Erica Reiner (Chicago, IL: University of Chicago Press, 1977), pp. 280–282.
6. Adolf Erman, *Life in Ancient Egypt*, trans. H.M. Tirard (reprint, New York: Benjamin Blom, 1969), p. 87.
7. Ibid., pp. 130–137.
8. Robert W. Ferguson and Allen N. Stokke, *Concepts of Criminal Law* (Boston, MA: Holbrook Press, 1976), p. 29.
9. Erman, pp. 140–141.
10. Ibid., p. 156.
11. Ibid., pp. 145–147.
12. Ze'ev W. Falk, *Hebrew Law in Biblical Times*, 2nd edn (Provo, UT: Brigham Young University Press, 2001), pp. 4–8.
13. Ibid., pp. 67–77.

14. Walter M. Chandler, *The Trial of Jesus from a Lawyer's Standpoint* (Norcross, GA: Harrison, 1976), pp. 35–87.
15. Ferguson and Stokke, p. 29.
16. H. Patrick Glenn, *Legal Traditions of the World*, 2nd edn (Oxford: Oxford University Press, 2004), p. 127.
17. Ibid., p. 129.
18. William Seal Carpenter, *Foundations of Modern Jurisprudence* (New York: Appleton-Century-Crofts, 1958), pp. 29–35.
19. René David and John E.C. Brierley, *Major Legal Systems in the World Today*, 3rd edn (London: Stevens & Sons, 1985), p. 39.
20. Arthur T. von Mehren, "The Civil Law System: An Historical Introduction," in John Honnold, ed., *The Life of the Law* (London: Free Press, 1964), pp. 486–493.
21. David and Brierley, p. 22.
22. Ibid., p. 43.
23. Ibid., p. 41.
24. Ibid., p. 52.
25. von Mehren, p. 489.
26. David and Brierley, p. 22.
27. Ibid., p. 49.
28. Ibid., p. 63.
29. Carpenter, pp. 91–98.
30. René David and Henry D. deVries, "French Legal Tradition," in John Honnold, ed., *The Life of the Law* (London: Free Press, 1964), p. 520.
31. Joseph Dainow, "The Civil Law and the Common Law: Some Points of Comparison," 15 Am. J. Comp. L. 419 (1966), p. 431.
32. Stephen Landsman, *Readings in Adversarial Justice: The American Approach to Adjudication* (St. Paul, MN: West, 1988), pp. 38–39.
33. David and deVries, pp. 519–525; "French Law," http://www.frenchlaw.com/french_litigation.htm (visited November 9, 2015).
34. Dainow, pp. 431–432.
35. Rudolf B. Schlesinger, "The Code Systems," in John Honnold, ed., *The Life of the Law* (London: Free Press, 1964), pp. 494–509; University of Ottawa, "Civil Law Systems and Mixed Systems with a Civil Law Tradition," http://www.ju riglobe.ca/eng/sys-juri/class-poli/droit-civil.php (visited November 9, 2015).
36. Joseph Schacht, *An Introduction to Islamic Law* (Oxford: Clarendon Press, 1964), p. 1.
37. Ibid., pp. 1–99.
38. Schlesinger, pp. 506–507.
39. T'ung-Tsu Ch'u, *Law and Society in Traditional China* (Paris: Mouton & Co., 1965).
40. David and Brierley, pp. 22–30; University of Ottawa, "Introductory Remarks," http://www.juriglobe.ca/eng/sys-juri/class-poli/droit-civil.php (visited November 9, 2015).
41. Carissa Michelle Wong and Wu Guo, "Water for Whom? Improving Water Governance in Yunnan China Through Environmental Customary Law," 15 Vt. J. Entvl. L. 291 (2014) at p. 305.
42. Deborah Dennison, "Islamic Legal Research," Judge Ben C. Green Law Library at Case Western Reserve University, http://lawlibrary.case.edu/research-guides/islamic-law-research/ (visited November 9, 2015); Richard J. Terrill, *World*

Criminal Justice Systems; A Comparative Survey (Waltham, MA; Anderson Publishing, 2013), pp. 529–638.

43. Shahbaz Ahmad Cheema, "Shia and Sunni Laws of Inheritance: A Comparative Analysis," *Pakistan Journal of Islamic Review* 10 (2012): 269.
44. Ian Edge, *Islamic Thought and Legal Theory* (New York: New York University Press, 1996), p. xv.
45. Steven Vago, *Law and Society*, 8th edn (Upper Saddle River, NJ: Pearson Prentice Hall, 2006), pp. 12–14.
46. Du Xichuan and Zhang Lingyuan, *China's Legal System* (Beijing: New World Press, 1990), p. 214.
47. Ibid., p. 216.
48. David and Brierley, p. 18; Werner Menski, *Comparative Law in a Global Context: The Legal Systems of Asia and Africa* (Cambridge: Cambridge University Press, 2006), pp. 569–593.
49. Xichuan and Lingyuan, p. 30; Glenn, pp. 330–337.
50. Xichuan and Lingyuan, p. 32.
51. Ibid., p. 81.
52. Ibid., p. 105.
53. Ibid., p. 107.
54. Ibid., p. 146.
55. Ibid., p. 200; Glenn, p. 150.
56. Xichuan and Lingyuan, p. 200; Peking University, "Legal System of China," http://en.pkulaw.cn/Legal/index., visited (November 19, 2015).
57. Vago, pp. 14–15.
58. William Tetley, "Mixed Jurisdictions: Common Law v. Civil Law (Codified and Uncodified)," 60 La. L. Rev. 677 (2000), p. 678.
59. Ibid.
60. F. L. Attenborough, ed., *The Laws of the Earliest English Kings* (New York: Russell & Russell, 1963), pp. 2–17.
61. F.W. Maitland, "History of English Law," in Helen M. Cam, comp., ed., *Selected Historical Essays of F.W. Maitland* (Cambridge: Cambridge University Press, 1957), pp. 97–98.
62. Theodore F.T. Plunkett, *A Concise History of the Common Law*, 5th edn (Boston, MA: Little, Brown, 1956), pp. 9–10.
63. *Webster's New International Dictionary of the English Language*, 2nd edn (Springfield, MA: G. & C. Merriam, 1937), p. 1401.
64. In 2006, Governor Timothy M. Kaine of Virginia issued a pardon to Grace Sherwood 300 years after she survived trial by water on a charge of witchcraft. She was bound with her thumbs tied to her feet and weighted down with a 13-pound Bible before being dropped into the Lynnhaven River. After her survival, she was imprisoned for seven years before being released. Ian Shapira, "After Toil and Trouble, 'Witch' Is Cleared," *Washington Post*, July 12, 2006, p. B–1.
65. C. Gordon Post, *An Introduction to the Law* (Englewood Cliffs, NJ: Prentice-Hall, 1963), pp. 18–61.
66. F.W. Maitland, *Equity: A Course in Lectures*, rev. John Brunyate (Cambridge: Cambridge University Press, 1969), p. 2.
67. Post, p. 40.
68. Maitland, *Equity,* p. 5.
69. S.F.C. Milsom, *Historical Foundations of the Common Law*, 2nd edn (London: Butterworths, 1981), pp. 82–89.

70. Kenneth H. York and John A. Bauman, *Cases and Materials on Remedies*, 2nd edn (St. Paul, MN: West, 1973), pp. 1–10.
71. Maitland, *Equity,* pp. 18–19.
72. Roscoe Pound, *The Formative Era of American Law* (Boston, MA: Little, Brown, 1938), pp. 94–95.
73. *Green v. United States,* 356 U.S. 165 (1958), at 212.
74. Pound, pp. 52–79.
75. Jack H. Friedenthal, Mary Kay Kane, and Arthur R. Miller, *Civil Procedure*, 4th edn (St. Paul, MN: Thomson/West, 2005), p. 2.
76. Vasco Núñez de Balboa to King Ferdinand, January 20, 1513, as quoted in Charles L.G. Anderson, *Life and Letters of Vasco Núñez de Balboa* (Fleming H. Revell, 1941; reprint, Westport, CT: Greenwood Press, 1970), p. 125.
77. John T. Noonan, *Persons and Masks of the Law* (New York: Farrar, Straus & Giroux, 1976), p. xi.
78. Ibid., p. 113.
79. Ibid., pp. 113–139.
80. Ibid., p. xi.
81. James Eisenstein and Herbert Jacob, *Felony Justice: An Organizational Analysis of Criminal Courts* (Boston, MA: Little, Brown, 1977), p. 20.

Court Organization

Court organization in the United States is complicated by our form of government, *federalism.* Instead of a single, unified court system such as exists in Great Britain or France, the United States actually has 51 court systems: the federal courts and the courts of the 50 individual states. This situation results in two very different consequences for the American legal system. First, Congress and the state legislatures are free to organize their respective court systems to meet their own needs. The results are that not only is the federal court structure different from those in the states but there is also tremendous diversity among the individual states. A trial court might be called a district court in one state, a superior court in another, and a supreme court in yet another. Most states have a single supreme court; two states, Oklahoma and Texas, have two courts of last resort: one for civil appeals and one for criminal appeals. Such diversity makes it difficult to generalize about the "typical" state court system.

A second consequence of our federal form of government is its impact on substantive and procedural law. As will be seen in Chapter 7, each state is free to determine for itself what behavior is forbidden, and each is free to establish reasonable punishment for defined crimes. Consequently, two states may have different definitions of the same criminal act and two different penalties for it. Likewise, in the case of civil law, different states may have different laws of incorporation for businesses and other organizations, different tax laws, and different marriage and divorce requirements. Federalism also impacts the role of precedent in the law. Because each state's substantive law is unique to that state, it follows that interpretations of state laws by state judges will also be unique. What is true for substantive law is also true for procedural law. Although rulings of the U.S. Supreme Court have tended to make criminal procedural law more uniform throughout the country, rules of civil procedure may vary slightly from state to state. As a result, a lawyer trained in the law of one state sometimes finds it necessary, upon moving to another state, to seek additional training in the substantive and procedural law of the new state. Indeed, many states require lawyers from other states to pass their own bar exams, even though they were licensed to practice in their home states.

Such problems notwithstanding, this chapter will try to describe court organization in the United States. Because any attempt to describe all 50 state systems would be tedious and repetitious, no such attempt will be made. Although there are enough similarities among state court systems to allow for some generalization, the reader should keep in mind that each state's system is truly unique. Because the federal court system offers a relatively simple introduction to court structure, we will begin with this system and return to state systems later in the chapter.

THE FEDERAL COURT SYSTEM

The federal court system is characterized by two types of courts: constitutional and legislative. *Constitutional courts* are sometimes referred to as Article III courts because they are created under Article III of the Constitution, which authorizes Congress to "ordain and establish" courts inferior to the Supreme Court.[1] The Constitution also states that judges of both the supreme and inferior courts "shall hold their Offices during good Behaviour,"[2] which is tantamount to a lifetime appointment, subject to removal only through the impeachment process. Finally, Congress may not reduce the salaries of constitutional court judges "during their Continuance in Office."[3] U.S. district courts, U.S. courts of appeal, and the U.S. Supreme Court are examples of constitutional courts. *Legislative courts* are also created by Congress, pursuant to one of its other legislative powers. For example, Article I empowers Congress to make all laws "for organizing, arming, and disciplining the Militia."[4] Under that authority, Congress may establish military tribunals for the purpose of disciplining soldiers. Similarly, Article IV empowers Congress to make rules and regulations for U.S. territories.[5] Judges who serve in the legislative courts do not have lifetime appointments, nor are their salaries protected as are those of Article III judges. However, most federal judges are appointed by the president, subject to confirmation by the Senate. While it should be noted that these and other differences[6] between constitutional and legislative courts exist, the line is not always a clear one. For example, in 1956, Congress changed the status of the U.S. Customs Court from a legislative to a constitutional court.[7] Ultimately, Congress determines the status of federal courts. Let us now proceed to discuss each of the two types of federal courts separately.

Constitutional Courts

Constitutional courts may be classified as courts of either general or specialized *jurisdiction*. Article III of the Constitution establishes federal jurisdiction over certain parties to a case and over certain subjects. For example, the federal judicial power extends "to all Cases affecting Ambassadors, other public Ministers and Consuls" and "to Controversies between two or more States."[8] Thus, if a foreign ambassador is a party to a case, federal courts have jurisdiction regardless of the subject matter of the case. Similarly, Article III gives federal courts jurisdiction over "Cases of admiralty and maritime Jurisdiction."[9] Consequently, if the subject matter of the case is admiralty or maritime, the federal courts have jurisdiction regardless of who the parties are. Finally, Article III states that "The judicial Power shall extend to all Cases, in Law and Equity, arising under this Constitution, the Laws of the United States, and Treaties made, or which shall be made, under their Authority."[10] This means that if a case raises what is called a *federal question*—an interpretation of the Constitution, a federal statute, or a U.S. treaty—federal courts may hear the case. Generally speaking, it is a constitutional court of general jurisdiction that will hear these kinds of cases.

Under its delegated powers Congress may make uniform laws on the subject of bankruptcies,[11] may lay and collect taxes, and may impose duties on goods coming from foreign countries into the United States.[12] Because of the specialized subject matter of some areas of the law, Congress has created specialized courts with jurisdiction limited to specialized subject matter; these are the constitutional courts of specialized jurisdiction. As most readers will be more familiar with the courts of general jurisdiction, we will begin our discussion of constitutional courts with them. The federal courts of general jurisdiction are organized into three tiers, or levels. The first tier consists of the U.S. district courts. When Congress first created the lower federal courts in 1789, it merely created one for each state, or 13 federal district courts. As the nation grew, it became apparent that some states needed more than one federal court, so Congress created new ones while maintaining the tradition that district courts should not cross state lines.[13] Today there are 89 federal district courts in the 50 states and one each in the District of Columbia, Guam, the Virgin Islands, the Northern Mariana Islands, and Puerto Rico for a total of 94 federal district courts. States that have more than one federal district court use geographical designations to distinguish among them. For example, a court may be named the U.S. District Court for Eastern Kentucky to distinguish it from the U.S. District Court for Western Kentucky. The number of federal judges assigned to each federal district varies. The U.S. District Court for Northern New York has five judgeships assigned to it, while the Southern District of New York has 28 judgeships authorized. It is common for each major city within the federal district to have at least one judge assigned to it. Currently, Congress has authorized 667 regular and ten temporary federal district court judges in the United States.[14] Partisan wrangling in recent years has delayed the nomination of federal judges at all levels, but it appears now that some progress is being made. In mid-2010 there were as many as 100 vacancies in federal judgeships but in late June 2015 the number of vacancies in all constitutional courts was down to 62.[15]

In addition to active federal judges there are retired judges, called senior judges, who hear cases on a part-time basis. Finally, there are magistrate judges who issue search and arrest warrants and handle arraignments, preliminary hearings, the civil consent docket, and misdemeanors for the federal courts.

The U.S. district courts, the main trial courts for the United States, have both criminal and civil jurisdiction. When our Constitution came into existence the states

TABLE 3.1

Cases Filed, U.S. District Courts, 2013–2014

Type of Case	2013	2014	Percent Change
Civil Cases	292,912	290,358	−0.88
Criminal Cases	80,073	70,919	−12.9
Total Civil and Criminal	372,985	361,277	−3.24

Source: http://uscourts.gov/statistics/table/na/federal-court-management-statistics/2014/12/31-2 (visited June 26, 2015).

already had fully functioning state court systems, and opponents of the Constitution feared that the newly created federal courts would supplant state courts. This concern was alleviated by limiting the judicial power of the federal courts so that most legal controversies would continue to be settled by state courts. Table 3.1 illustrates the caseload of federal courts in two recent years.

U.S. district courts function like other trial courts in the country. A single judge presides, and a jury hears the evidence. Federal courts have their own unique rules of evidence, but evidence is submitted and a verdict is reached in the same manner as in state trial courts. Federal courts are no better or worse than state courts in many ways; they are just different because of the different jurisdiction, organization, and procedures. Nor are state courts necessarily inferior to federal courts. Unless a state case raises a federal question or otherwise falls within the jurisdiction of the federal courts, the decisions of state courts are not reviewable by federal courts. Indeed, federal judges are required to respect the interpretations of state laws by state courts if there is not a federal question raised.

The second tier of federal courts with general appellate jurisdiction consists of the U.S. courts of appeals. There are currently 13 permanent U.S. courts of appeals. Eleven of the courts of appeals are designated by number. For example, the U.S. Court of Appeals for the Fifth Circuit includes Texas, Louisiana, and Mississippi, and any appeal from one of the nine U.S. district courts located in one of those states is heard by it. The twelfth court of appeals, the U.S. Court of Appeals for the District of Columbia, mainly hears appeals from District of Columbia government and various departments assigned by Congress. The thirteenth court of appeals is the U.S. Court of Appeals for the Federal Circuit, which hears appeals from several Article III courts and a few commissions and agencies. Because U.S. courts of appeals hear only cases on appeal from U.S. district courts or federal regulatory agencies, they naturally have the same substantive jurisdiction. In the year ending December 31, 2014, a total of 53,799 cases were filed in the federal courts of appeal.[16]

As of 2014, the number of appeals court judges totaled 179, with the number of judges assigned to individual circuits varying from six for the First Circuit to 29 for the Ninth Circuit.[17] Normally, appeals are heard by groups of three judges, called *panels*. When an appeal reaches the court, three judges are assigned to hear it, and the decision of a majority decides the case. Occasionally, the court of appeals will decide to hear a case *en banc,* which simply means that all the judges assigned to that circuit will hear the case.[18] In a majority of federal cases, the court of appeals is the last stop. For a variety of reasons, including time, money, and the unlikely chance of Supreme Court review, the parties will abandon their fight, resulting in the decision of the court of appeals being the final one.

The third and highest tier is, of course, the U.S. Supreme Court, consisting of the Chief Justice of the United States and eight associate justices. Unlike the other federal courts discussed in this chapter, the Supreme Court was created by the Constitution. However, the Constitution is silent about the number of justices and other aspects of the Court's organization. For example, the first Supreme Court had only six members, and immediately following the Civil War it had ten members. In 1869, Congress set the number at nine, where it remains today. President Franklin D. Roosevelt's famous court packing attempt in 1937 has been the only serious attempt to alter the Court's membership since 1869. Roosevelt tried to expand the number of justices to as many as 15, but the attempt failed. It appears that the number will remain at nine for some time to come.

As previously noted, Congress has created some constitutional courts that have specialized jurisdiction. Among these are the Court of International Trade and the U.S. Court of Appeals for the Federal Circuit. The Court of International Trade was created by Congress in 1980 to be the successor of the old U.S. Customs Court. Its jurisdiction covers disputes over goods imported into and exported out of the United States. Such disputes include controversies over the admissibility of goods and the duties owed on them.[19] A second specialized constitutional court is the U.S. Court of Appeals for the Federal Circuit, created in 1982, from a merger of the U.S. Court of Claims and the U.S. Court of Customs and Patent Appeals. Table 3.2 lists the lower federal courts and administrative agencies over which the Court of Appeals for the Federal Circuit

TABLE 3.2

Jurisdiction of U.S. Court of Appeals for the Federal Circuit

Other Federal Courts	Administrative Agencies
All U.S. District Courts	U.S. Merit Systems Protection Board
U.S. Court of Federal Claims	Boards of Contract Appeal
U.S. Court of International Trade	Patent Trial and Appeal Board
U.S. Court of Appeals for Veterans Claims	Trademark Trial and Appeals Board
	Department of Justice Bureau of Justice Assistance
	International Trade Commission
	Government Accountability Office Personnel Appeals Board

Source: http://uscourts.gov/statistics/table/na/federal-court-management-statistics/2014/12/31-2 (visited July 2, 2015).

has appellate jurisdiction. On average, 55 percent of the court's caseload is administrative jurisdiction while 31 percent are intellectual property cases and 11 percent are for money damages against the U.S. government.[20]

Other courts of questionable constitutional status are the Alien Terrorist Removal Court, the Foreign Intelligence Surveillance Court (FISC), and the Foreign Surveillance Court of Review. The Alien Terrorist Removal Court, which has "jurisdiction to conduct all removal proceedings"[21] of aliens in the United States, is a good example because its judges are assigned by the Chief Justice of the United States from the judicial districts but serve fixed, staggered terms of office on the court.[22]

Similarly, the FISC has judges chosen from among the ranks of the federal courts and has "jurisdiction to hear applications for and grant orders approving electronic surveillance anywhere within the United States."[23] In the aftermath of the World Trade Center and Pentagon bombings, Congress increased the size of the FISC from 7 to 11 members.[24] Since its creation in 1978, the FISC had never turned down a request from the Justice Department for a wiretap application. However, in August 2002 the FISC refused to grant the Attorney General John Ashcroft's request for wiretaps under the USA Patriot Act. This prompted an appeal to the Foreign Intelligence Surveillance Court of Review, the first in that court's 25-year history.[25] The FISC also received some notoriety when one of its members openly broke with the George W. Bush administration over its eavesdropping program.[26]

It should be apparent by now that the federal court system is a hodgepodge of courts created by Congress in a piecemeal fashion to deal with cases arising under federal jurisdiction. As two noted experts on the federal court system have observed, "the distinction between a constitutional and a legislative court is of the type that would have delighted those meticulous medieval scholastics who argued about how many angels would fit on the head of a pin."[27] With that caveat in mind, we now turn our attention to the legislative, or Article I, courts.

Legislative Courts

As discussed earlier, Article I courts are created by Congress to implement one of its enumerated powers. Although confusion exists about the exact status of some federal courts, two major distinctions generally differentiate legislative courts from constitutional courts. First, judges of legislative courts do not have lifetime appointments but instead serve fixed terms of office. The length of the term designated by Congress is often a long one in order to ensure judicial independence, but it is a fixed term nonetheless. The second distinction is that a legislative court judge's salary is not protected, as in the case of constitutional court judges. The Constitution stipulates that the compensation of Article III judges "shall not be diminished during their Continuance in Office."[28] Congress has occasionally tried to clarify the status of individual federal courts by designating whether they are to be legislative or constitutional, but, as we have seen, it has not been entirely successful.

Three courts that bridge the legislative-constitutional court gap are the U.S. District Courts in three American territories: Guam, the Virgin Islands, and the Northern Marianas.[29] These courts hear the same kinds of cases heard in regular federal district courts, but they also hear cases involving local laws.[30] This would be analogous to a single court being authorized to hear cases involving both state and federal law. Congress governs the territories of the United States under Article IV of the Constitution and may make laws for them much the same as a state legislature does for a state. The judges on these courts do not enjoy life tenure but serve ten-year terms.[31] Congress made one former territorial court, the U.S. District Court for Puerto Rico, an Article III court, and its judges serve for life during good behavior.

Another example of a legislative court is the U.S. Court of Federal Claims (formerly the U.S. Court of Claims). The judges serving on this court are appointed by the president and confirmed by the Senate for 15-year terms of office.[32] This court primarily hears money claims against the U.S. government such as disputes over federal contracts and federal takings of private property.[33] The U.S. Tax Court, created by Congress in 1924, is also a legislative court. It consists of 19 judges who serve 15-year terms. Although the U.S. Court of Federal Claims and the regular district courts exercise concurrent jurisdiction over tax cases, the Tax Court is the only court the taxpayer can appeal to before the payment of the disputed tax. In the Claims Court and district courts, the taxpayer must first pay the tax and then try to recover it later.[34] Finally, bankruptcy court judges serve as adjuncts to the district courts. Until 1978, bankruptcy court judges served six-year terms and were appointed by the district court judge. That year Congress lengthened their terms to 14 years and made them presidential appointees. When the Bankruptcy Reform Act of 1978 was declared unconstitutional by the Supreme Court,[35] Congress passed new legislation retaining the 14-year term but leaving the selection of bankruptcy judges to the courts of appeals.[36] As of September 2012, there were 350 bankruptcy judges.[37] There were 911,086 petitions for bankruptcy filed during a 12-month period ending March 31, 2015, a decrease of 12.3 percent from 2014.[38]

President Ronald Reagan signed the law creating the Court of Veterans' Appeals in November 1988. In March 1999 its name was changed to the Court of Appeals for Veterans Claims.[39] This seven-judge court hears appeals on all veterans' and survivors' benefits, including loans and educational benefits, from the Board of Veterans' Appeals. An appeal from the Court of Appeals for Veterans may be taken to the Court of Appeals for the Federal Circuit.[40]

The final legislative court is the U.S. Court of Appeals for the Armed Forces. This court consists of five civilian judges who are appointed for staggered 15-year terms. As its name implies, the Court reviews the decisions of courts martial. Its caseload consists mainly of cases involving military personnel discharged for bad conduct or sentenced to prison under the Uniform Code of Military Justice. Only about 10 percent of the decisions of the Court of Appeals for the Armed Services are reviewable by the Supreme Court.[41]

In conclusion, the federal court system is composed of courts created by Congress under either its Article I or Article III powers. The federal courts are not "superior" to state courts; rather, they exist alongside state courts. The vast majority of cases are tried in state courts, and it follows that they will resolve many important cases. Nevertheless, the federal courts remain an alternative forum to which citizens can turn for relief if state courts prove unresponsive. Despite the confusion caused by federalism, a dual-court system provides additional guarantees that justice will eventually prevail.

STATE COURT SYSTEMS

As we have noted, there is no "typical" state court system because federalism allows each state to adopt a court system fitted to its individual needs. Consequently, the most that can be done is to describe state courts in general without being too specific about any particular state's courts. In addition to the traditional specialized forums such as probate and domestic relations courts, many states are employing other innovative approaches to docket overcrowding, such as the creation of specialty courts, especially in criminal cases, often with the corollary goal of diverting offenders, frequently those with special needs such as mental health issues or unique problems, away from the criminal justice system. Drug courts and teen courts have proliferated in the past few years to offer alternatives. Among the newest courts are those aimed at veterans who are first-time, nonviolent offenders and who may be experiencing difficulty readjusting after combat and the courts seek to prevent them from getting a stained criminal record leading to a downward spiral. The following section describes the structure and jurisdiction of courts that are found in some form or fashion in each of the 50 states.

Courts of Limited Jurisdiction

All state courts have their jurisdiction limited in some way. The jurisdiction of any court comes from the state constitution or from statutes passed by the state legislature, or both. Some state constitutions spell out the jurisdiction of the courts in great detail, while others leave the details of court jurisdiction to the discretion of the legislature. In either case, courts are dependent on others for the source of their jurisdiction. Similarly, the organization and number of state courts will also be determined by the state constitution or by state statutes. Courts of limited jurisdiction, as their name implies, are created to handle cases of a limited or specialized nature. In this section, we will examine some of the more common courts of limited jurisdiction found in the states.

One of the most common courts of limited jurisdiction is the *municipal court*. Municipal courts are often, although not always, limited to minor offenses or misdemeanors. Municipal courts are often referred to as "traffic courts" because their main function is to hear cases involving traffic violations within the city limits. In 2012, for example, traffic cases represented 54 percent of the caseload of state courts, both criminal and civil cases.[42] Municipal courts frequently have jurisdiction over cases involving violations of city ordinances. Cities possess *ordinance power*; that is, the power to enact laws enforceable within the city limits. Such laws include prohibitions against discharging fire-arms, burning trash, and letting animals run loose within the city limits. Persons who receive traffic citations or citations for other offenses may have their cases heard in municipal court.

The phrase "You can't fight city hall" must have been coined by someone after an experience in municipal court. Typically, the defendant's cause is a lost one. That is because it is usually the defendant's word against the word of the arresting officer, and judges and juries tend to believe the latter. That is also why most people simply pay the fine and save themselves the trouble of going to court even if they believe themselves to be innocent. Those who do choose to fight a ticket often discover that municipal court is not what they expected. First, attorneys are infrequently used in municipal court because their fees often exceed the fine. The defendant normally opts to "tell it to the judge" in his or her own words without benefit of counsel. A second difference is that there is often no jury. Although some states give the defendant the right to a jury trial, most of the matters that come before a municipal court are relatively trivial, and most defendants prefer a bench trial, in which the judge decides the outcome. A third, and somewhat surprising, difference is that in some cases the judge may not even be a lawyer. Although many municipal court judges are lawyers, some states allow city officials, such as the mayor, to double as municipal court judge, especially in small towns. Finally, although appeals are allowed, like jury trials they do not occur very often. Again, considering the fine involved, the time and trouble associated with an appeal are seldom worth the effort. If the average citizen ever encounters a courtroom situation as a party to a case, however, it is quite likely to be in a municipal court.

A second common type of court of limited jurisdiction is the justice of the peace court. JP courts, as they are commonly called, have a variety of functions, not all of which are judicial in nature. Justices of the peace in some states perform marriages, and in some states they serve as coroner in cases in which foul play or accidental death is suspected in someone's death. Most justices of the peace also have minor administrative duties, such as preparing the court's yearly budget and hiring court personnel.

JP courts usually have both criminal and civil jurisdiction. Their criminal jurisdiction extends to misdemeanor offenses that occur within the limits of their geographic boundaries. Crimes such as petty theft and simple battery are the kinds that are most likely to be tried in JP court. Most states limit the amount of punishment a JP court can impose. For example, a JP court's criminal jurisdiction may be limited to offenses in which the maximum penalty is six months in the county jail or a $500 fine. In addition to hearing trials, justices of the peace often conduct arraignments for persons accused of more serious crimes.

The civil jurisdiction of a JP court is limited to small monetary amounts (e.g., $2000). That is, the amount involved in the lawsuit cannot exceed $2000 if the JP court is to have jurisdiction. This is why JP courts are frequently called *small claims courts*. Although lawyers are allowed to appear in JP courts in most states, the litigants often just represent themselves and let the judge decide the case without a jury. Popular daytime television shows like *The People's*

Court and *Judge Judy* do much to familiarize the general public with the operation of small claims courts.

As may be seen, the kinds of cases handled by the typical JP court are more varied than those of a municipal court. However, many states still do not require justices of the peace to be licensed attorneys, a common criticism of the JP system. The JP system is a holdover from an era when people believed that anyone with a little common sense could fairly apply the law in simple cases. Whether that remains true today is debatable. However, justices of the peace, through strong and effective lobbying of state legislatures, have retained their essential functions and character despite repeated attempts to reorganize them out of existence. It appears that the office, though accused of being antiquated, will be with us for some time to come.

A third category of courts of limited jurisdiction includes county courts. Like municipal courts, that are limited to exercising their jurisdiction within city limits, county courts' jurisdiction is limited to county lines. County courts typically have a greater expanse of jurisdiction than either municipal or JP courts. In criminal cases, for example, county courts may have jurisdiction over offenses with penalties as great as one year in jail and relatively high fines. For civil cases, the amount in controversy may be as high as several thousand dollars. County courts may also function as courts of appeal for lower courts of limited jurisdiction. County courts are frequently **courts of record** (which means that a transcript is made of the proceedings), whereas municipal and JP courts usually are not. When an appeal is made to a county court from a lower court, it is not an "appeal" in the usual sense of the word. In actuality, as no record exists in the lower court, the county court conducts a **trial de novo**. A *trial de novo* is, in effect, an entirely new trial, or a trial from the beginning.

Like other judges in courts of limited jurisdiction, the judges of county courts are not required to be licensed attorneys in some states. However, states that have attempted to modernize their judicial systems are requiring judges at all levels to have law degrees. Many states retain the tradition of the county judge as the political leader of the county. In such states, county judges are as much administrative officials as judicial ones. A county judge may be responsible for duties such as budget preparation and the county welfare system. County judges probate wills, take responsibility for wards of the county, commit persons to mental institutions, and serve as juvenile court judges in some states. It is at this level that we see a fusion of judicial, executive, and legislative functions that is not so evident at the national level, with its stricter adherence to the system of separation of powers. For this reason, characterizing the office of county judge as a purely judicial one is misleading.

Courts of General Jurisdiction

A second level of courts in most state judicial systems consists of courts of general jurisdiction. A **court of general jurisdiction** has the power to hear any case that falls within the general judicial power of the state. That is, a court of general jurisdiction has the authority to render a verdict in any case capable of judicial resolution under the constitution and laws of the state. Cases involving the state's criminal laws, civil code, or state constitution fall within the judicial power of the state. Laws regulating marriage, *corporations*, real estate, insurance, and education are just a few of the categories of law within the state's authority. It will be recalled that the Framers of the Constitution intended that most lawsuits would fall within the judicial power of the states, thus ensuring the continued importance of state courts.

THE PLAYMATE AND THE OILMAN

The case of former Playboy Playmate, Anna Nicole Smith, and her husband, Houston oil billionaire J. Howard Marshall II, illustrates the importance of state courts in the American legal system. After Marshall's death in 1995 a twenty-year battle over his estate began. Marshall's son, E. Pierce Marshall, challenged Smith's right to any inheritance from his father's estate. Disputes over the inheritance, stock transfers, and bankruptcy filings, and IRS attempts to recover back taxes have involved hundreds of millions of dollars. Although Pierce died in 2006 and Anna Nicole in 2007, Pierce's widow and Anna Nicole's minor daughter have kept the battle raging. The case has even been heard twice by the United States Supreme Court. The case illustrates that monetarily the stakes can be as high in a state court as any court in the land.

Source: Daniel Fisher, "The Oilman, the Playmate, and the Tangled Affairs of the Billionaire Marshall Family," http://www.forbes.com/sites/danielfisher/2013/03/04/the-billionaire-the-playboy-bunny-and-the-tangled-affairs-of-the-marshall-family/print/. Visited July 3, 2015.

Courts of general jurisdiction are the major trial courts of the state. As noted in the chapter's introduction, they may be called superior courts, district courts, circuit courts, or, as in the case of New York, supreme courts.[43] For the sake of simplicity, we will refer to this type of court as a district court. Despite the general nature of district courts' jurisdiction, they too are limited by geography. The state legislature typically divides the state into well-defined and numbered judicial districts that have definite boundaries. These boundaries may coincide with county lines, consist of several counties, or even overlap and disregard county lines. Although most judicial districts will have only a single judge assigned to each, others will be multi-judge districts. Finally, the boundaries of the districts may overlap, in which case two or more judges will exercise concurrent jurisdiction over suits. In these instances, the judges may agree to specialize by allowing one judge to hear exclusively criminal cases while the other hears only civil cases. Such informal, or even formal, specialization is common in large metropolitan areas because of the workload faced by urban courts.

Courts of general jurisdiction have both criminal and civil jurisdiction but may, as just noted, specialize out of necessity. Some judges may prefer to handle family law matters, while others concentrate on juvenile cases. The criminal jurisdiction of these courts includes felony offenses. Most states adhere to the definition of a felony as any offense for which the penalty exceeds one year of imprisonment or imprisonment at the state penitentiary as opposed to a county jail. Felony cases, then, include more serious crimes, such as robbery and murder. The civil jurisdiction of district courts has no upper limit as to the amount in controversy. Lawsuits may run into millions or hundreds of millions of dollars. The kinds of cases range from the uncontested divorce case to multi-million-dollar tort or breach of contract cases. This point illustrates again the importance of state courts. When the stakes are high, state courts do not play second fiddle to federal courts. The operation of trial courts will be examined more closely in Chapter 4.

Appellate Courts

All states have some kind of appeals mechanism available for litigants who were unsuccessful at the trial-court level. Most states have created an intermediate appeals court between the trial courts and the state's highest court of appeal. Like the U.S. courts of appeals, the purpose of intermediate appeals courts is to guarantee the litigants the right to at least one appeal while preventing the state's highest court from having to hear "routine" appeals. These intermediate *appellate courts* screen out the routine cases so that only the most important cases reach the state's highest court. However, this screening process does not mean that intermediate appellate courts are totally lacking in discretion in selecting cases. Like all appellate courts, intermediate courts of appeals are limited to deciding questions of laws raised during the trial, decide cases in panels or *en banc,* and rely on written decisions in making their rulings.

Every state has a *court of last resort,* usually called the state supreme court. As the name implies, a court of last resort is a litigant's last chance to have his or her case decided favorably once the case has exhausted all other appellate avenues. Most states have a single court of last resort that handles both civil and criminal appeals, but two states, Oklahoma and Texas, have two courts of last resort. For example, the Texas Supreme Court hears only civil cases, while criminal cases are handled by the Texas Court of Criminal Appeals. Many states have chosen to pattern their state's highest court after the U.S. Supreme Court in the number of justices, procedures, and so forth. But, as we have seen, states have shown considerable independence in creating their court systems, and state supreme courts should not be viewed as merely "little Supreme Courts." The duties of state supreme courts are identical to those of other appellate courts except that their decisions are final unless an appeal is made to the U.S. Supreme Court. As previously noted, when a state's highest court makes a ruling involving the interpretation of the state constitution, a state statute, or a precedent in an earlier state case, that ruling is final. The exception is when the case raises a federal question; such a matter may be taken to the U.S. Supreme Court. Another duty of state supreme courts includes ruling on opinions of the state's attorney general. Some states permit the attorney general to make preliminary interpretations of state laws that are binding unless overturned by a state court.

Finally, state supreme court justices, especially the chief justice, are often given additional duties by the state. For example, the state's chief justice is usually given the task of presiding over impeachment trials. In addition, other justices may have to serve on various state boards or commissions dealing with the judiciary. A common practice is to have several supreme court justices serve on the state's judicial conduct board.

A MAN AND A WOMAN

Some states permit the state's attorney general to issue opinions that have the force of law until otherwise overruled by a court. The El Paso, Texas county clerk had quite a problem one day when two persons, both clearly women, applied for a marriage license. Here was the clerk's dilemma: Texas law does not permit same-sex marriages but it also says that a person's gender is whatever is indicated on his or her birth certificate. One of the women had been born a man but had undergone a sex-change operation and produced a birth certificate so indicating. Because the county clerk was unsure whether to issue the license, she requested the El Paso county attorney to seek an opinion from the Texas attorney general. In mid-2010, the Texas Attorney General's Office announced it would not make a ruling on the case. A federal court's decision earlier in the year that the California ban on same-sex marriages is unconstitutional undoubtedly encouraged the attorney general to take a wait-and-see attitude pending review by the U.S. Supreme Court. The issue became moot once the U.S. Supreme Court ruled in *Obergefell v. Hodges,* 576 U.S. _____ (2015) that states may not refuse to issue licenses to same-sex couples.

Source: Brandi Grissom, "Some Gay Marriages Legal in Texas," *The Texas Tribune,* May 14, 2010. http://www.texastribune.org/stories/2010/may/14/some-gay-marriages-legal-texas/ (visited March 31, 2016)

The coexistence of state and federal court systems adds an element of complexity not present in nations without federalism. Nevertheless, it is the possibility that each state may approach court organization in its own unique fashion that makes federalism an attractive form of government. There is much to criticize about state courts. There are too many judges and courts, delays in coming to trial are too long, the procedures are antiquated and overly complex, and so forth. Lawyers, like most of us, are loath to change a system with which they have become familiar, and judges see plans to unify, modernize, or reorganize the court structure as threats to their power and prestige. But change does come, albeit slowly, to court systems, just as it does to all areas of the law. As in most cases, those with patience will eventually prevail.

JUDICIAL SELECTION

Once when New York Yankee manager Casey Stengel was reminiscing about his own career as a major league ballplayer, Mickey Mantle expressed surprise that Stengel had once been a major leaguer. Stengel reportedly replied, "Do you think I was born 60 years old and manager of the New York Yankees?" Although this story may be apocryphal, it does serve to remind us that judges are not born judges at any age. The selection of judges at both the state and federal level is a complex and political process. The selection method as well as the criteria for selection will have much to do with the kinds of persons chosen for the bench. The selection process is not only political; it is also highly partisan and heavily influenced by the organized bar. In this section we will examine in detail the selection of federal judges of the three major constitutional courts and then describe the process used to select judges in the states.

Selection of Federal Judges

The selection of federal judges is a deceptively simple process. The Constitution authorizes the president to appoint Supreme Court justices with the consent of the Senate, and Congress has extended the practice by statute to other federal judges. Surprisingly, there are no constitutional or legal qualifications for appointment to the federal bench. Theoretically, the president could appoint anyone reading this book to a federal judgeship as long as the Senate concurs. In reality, of course, there are informal professional and political qualifications to be met, and each president may add to or subtract from the list of qualifications. An example of a professional qualification is that the nominee be a lawyer, preferably a graduate of one of the nation's prestigious law schools.[44] The nominee need not have previous judicial experience, but some presidents prefer that their nominees for U.S. district courts have prior experience on a state court or perhaps as a federal bankruptcy judge. Some presidents require a certain number of years of legal experience, a minimum or maximum age limit, and even a clean bill of health before they will consider a person for nomination. In recent years, every president, both Democrat and Republican, has made a conscious effort to include women and minorities in his appointments, as Table 3.3 illustrates.

Although most presidents are reluctant to admit it, they also consider political factors such as gender, race, religion, ethnicity, and even geography when choosing nominees. For simplicity, in Table 3.3 judicial nominees were divided by race and gender. Although individual presidents have done a better job of improving diversity on the federal bench, the overwhelming majority of judicial nominees were still men (81 percent) and white (83 percent) by the end of George W. Bush's administration. White males constituted over 68 percent of

TABLE 3.3

Article III Appointments by Race and Gender from Carter to G.W. Bush

Category	Males	Females	Total
White	1022 (68.5%)	223 (14.95%)	1245 (83.44%)
African American	107 (7.17%)	33 (2.21%)	140 (9.38%)
Hispanic	69 (4.62%)	22 (1.47%)	91 (6.1%)
Others	14 (0.94%)	2 (0.013%)	16 (1.07%)
Total	1212 (81.23%)	280 (18.77%)	1492 (100%)

Source: Jennifer Segal Diascro and Rorie Spill Solbert, "George W. Bush's Legacy on the Federal Bench: Policy in the Face of Diversity," *Judicature* 92, 6 (May–June, 2009), p. 292.

the total nominations while white women made up nearly 15 percent of the nominations. During his first term, nearly 53 percent of President Bill Clinton's appointees were either nonwhite or female (or both) compared with only 27 percent of President George H.W. Bush's nominees and less than 15 percent of President Ronald Reagan's.[45] During his eight years in office, President George W. Bush continued diversifying the federal judiciary by appointing minority female candidates at a slightly higher rate (6.52 percent of his nominations) than his predecessors. In terms of minority male candidates, Bush appointed a higher percentage than his immediate Republican predecessors but fewer than his Democratic predecessors.[46] President Barack Obama has accelerated the gender diversity of the federal courts during his presidency. In the 113th Congress (2013–2014), Obama nominated 152 persons to various federal courts of whom 43.4 percent were women.[47] Partisan politics also come into play, as evidenced by the fact that approximately 90 percent of all federal judges belong to the same political party as the president who appointed them.

Finally, a president may require some general ideological qualifications of his nominees. For example, it is no secret that President Reagan chose to appoint only persons of conservative ideology to the federal bench.[48] More recently, President Bush's appointees to the lower federal courts have proven to be nearly as conservative as those of his father and Reagan.[49] The extent to which a president weighs professional competence, past judicial experience, age, ideology, and partisanship will vary with each president. A president normally determines the general criteria for his nominees and then allows the other significant actors in the process—members of the White House staff, the attorney general or deputy attorney general, and the relevant U.S. senators—to recruit candidates who conform to his standards. Just how the process of choosing particular individuals occurs will be discussed later in this chapter. At this point, it is preferable to have a general overview of the entire selection process.

Once a candidate for the federal bench has been identified, the Federal Bureau of Investigation (FBI) is called upon to do a background check. Formerly, FBI background investigations were conducted only on the nominee actually selected, but since the Nixon administration background checks have been run on all serious contenders.[50] The purpose of the background check is to ensure that there is nothing in the candidate's background that may prove embarrassing to the president or to the senator sponsoring the nominee. It would not do if the president's nominee turned out to be a spouse abuser or to have a history of drunken driving. Even past and present political and social affiliations are checked out; membership in a racially segregated club, a restrictive covenant in a property deed, or some ill-considered posts on a private social media page may come back to haunt a candidate for the federal bench. Even thorough investigations can fall short of the mark, as evidenced by President Reagan's withdrawal of the nomination of Douglas H. Ginsburg to the Supreme Court. Ginsburg's admission that he used illegal drugs in his younger days embarrassed Reagan, who was known for his anti-drug stance.

The next part of the process is the informal rating of the nominee's qualifications by the American Bar Association (ABA) Standing Committee on the Federal Judiciary. The ABA created the Standing Committee on the Federal Judiciary to serve as a kind of watchdog over the federal judiciary. The Committee is composed of 15 prominent attorneys representing each of the federal circuits. Their job is to review the qualifications of the president's nominee according to "integrity, professional competence and judicial temperament."[51] Once evaluated, the nominee is rated "well-qualified," "qualified," or "not qualified." Although every president would like nominees to receive the highest rating, the weight given to the ABA rating will depend on the individual president. In general, Republican presidents have placed greater emphasis on ABA ratings. During the Eisenhower administration, for example, the president refused to appoint anyone rated "not qualified." This, in effect, gave the ABA a virtual veto over nominations to the federal bench. President Richard Nixon followed a similar policy early in his administration but later began the practice of submitting his nominees' names to the ABA only after he had announced them publicly.[52] Neither President Reagan nor President George H.W. Bush nominated persons rated "not qualified." By contrast, Democratic Presidents John F. Kennedy, Lyndon B. Johnson, and Clinton nominated persons despite a "not qualified rating."[53]

In the past, except as noted in the Nixon administration, the names of nominees were submitted to the Committee in advance for its rating, but in March 2001 President George W. Bush announced that his administration would no longer submit the nominee's name in advance. The stated reason for the policy change was that President Bush believed it gave a single interest group (the ABA) too much influence in the selection of federal judges. In early 2009, President Obama announced that his administration would return to the practice of submitting names of lower federal court nominees to the ABA before the nominations were made public.[54]

Now the nomination is ready for confirmation hearings by the Senate Judiciary Committee. The Judiciary Committee handles judicial nominations in much the same way as it handles regular legislation within its jurisdiction. That is, formal hearings are held on the nomination and testimony is taken.

The nominee is "invited" to testify, of course, but it is really a command performance. In general, the committee hearings are fairly routine. If a nominee for district judge who has the blessing of the home state's senators is being considered, few members of the Judiciary Committee are interested in the nomination. After all, even if the nominee is incompetent, the damage will be confined to a single federal district court in someone else's home state. As we shall see, however, nominees for the courts of appeals and the Supreme Court are subject to much greater scrutiny.

If the nominee, regardless of the court level, is noncontroversial, the witnesses before the Judiciary Committee are usually a parade of supporters who have come to sing the praises of the nominee. On the other hand, a nominee who is controversial because of past judicial decisions, public statements, or political philosophy may come under fire from interest groups. Interest group opposition, especially when the Supreme Court is involved, can be intense. Civil rights groups, women's groups, labor organizations, and pro-abortion and anti-abortion groups may all wish to testify for or against the nominee. Coalitions of civil rights groups, civil liberties groups, and labor and pro-choice groups successfully defeated President Reagan's nomination of Robert Bork in 1987. Similar groups came very close to defeating President George H.W. Bush's nominee, Clarence Thomas, in 1991. Thomas was approved by a 52 to 48 vote in the Senate.[55] Ironically, it was members of President George W. Bush's own Republican Party who derailed the nomination of his White House Counsel Harriet Miers to the Supreme Court in October 2005. President Obama has avoided serious controversy over his Supreme Court nominees with the successful confirmations of Sonia Sotomayor in 2009 and Elena Kagan in 2010. However, partisanship re-emerged in early 2016 following the untimely death of Justice Antonin Scalia when Republican Senate leaders and presidential candidates announced their belief that the appointment of Scalia's replacement should wait until after the 2016 presidential election. Interest groups may uncover information about the nominee's background that was overlooked or ignored by the FBI and the ABA. Interest group activity, even if ineffective, serves to remind us of the political nature of the judicial selection process.[56]

In recent years, there has been growing concern about the role of the Senate Judiciary Committee in the selection process, especially at the Supreme Court level. As mentioned, interest groups opposed to Robert Bork successfully defeated his nomination, although by all accounts he was well qualified to serve on the Supreme Court. Critics allege that Bork was subjected to stricter and harsher scrutiny regarding his views of the Constitution than had previous nominees appearing before the Senate Judiciary Committee. However, one study of 23 Supreme Court nomination hearings indicates that Bork's experience was not unique.[57] The researchers classified questions of the Senate Judiciary Committee members as "character," "competence," or "constitutional philosophy" questions. The study discovered that in 15 of the 23 hearings, questions concerning the constitutional views of the nominee exceeded 75 percent of the questions asked and in eight hearings the percentage exceeded 80 percent. The researchers also found that in the three nomination hearings immediately following Bork's (Anthony Kennedy, David Souter, and Clarence Thomas), the percentage of constitutional philosophy questions exceeded 75 percent of the questions asked.[58] Paul A. Freund and Stephen Carter argue in separate articles that nominees to the Court historically have been required to defend their constitutional views before the Senate.[59] Despite the highly charged partisan nature of the confirmation process, the fact remains that, with the exception of the Miers nomination, recent presidents have been able to name who they want to the Supreme Court.

Finally, after all the testimony has been given and all the witnesses heard, the Judiciary Committee votes to recommend approval or rejection of the nomination to the full Senate. If the nomination is approved by the Committee, approval by the Senate is almost assured. Very little, if any, debate takes place unless the nominee is controversial. A vote is taken, and if it is approved by a simple majority the nominee is confirmed. Upon being sworn in, the president's nominee is a federal judge for life during good behavior.

Although the process of FBI investigation, ABA scrutiny, Judiciary Committee hearings, and Senate confirmation is the same for the appointment of all federal judges, the process by which the selection is narrowed from a large pool of candidates to a single individual differs according to the level of federal court involved. Selection of district court judges is heavily influenced by state politics and the state's U.S. senators. Selection of court of appeals and Supreme Court judges tends to be influenced more by the president and national politics. We shall examine the selection process at each level and compare all three. There is an old saying that a federal judge is just a lawyer who knows a president. At the district court level, however, it is more accurate to say that a federal judge is a lawyer who knows a U.S. senator. That is because at the district court level the selection process is heavily influenced by the state's senators. It will be recalled that the boundaries of U.S. district courts are entirely within the boundaries of a single state. U.S. senators have traditionally felt that the appointment of federal officials within their states should be their prerogative; that is, the president should clear any federal appointment in a state with the senators of the president's party. This tradition is known as *senatorial courtesy*. Should a president attempt to nominate someone to the federal bench without the senator's blessing, the senator in question would merely ask his or her colleagues in the Senate to defeat the nomination. In the past, a senator merely had to state that the president's nominee was "personally obnoxious" to him or her, and that was sufficient justification. Today, senators are expected to provide more substantive grounds for invoking senatorial courtesy.[60]

Because of senatorial courtesy, the actual selection process works like this. Let us assume that there is a Republican president in the White House. When a vacancy occurs on a U.S. district court, the attorney general will contact the Republican senators in which the federal court lies for input into the selection. If the state has no Republican senators, the attorney general may consult with state Republican officials, party leaders, or Republican members of the House of Representatives. Under these circumstances, the president is freer to choose whomever he pleases for the judgeship.

In some cases, the senator may have in mind a specific candidate who generally meets the president's criteria for nomination. In such a case, if the person is not totally objectionable to the president (and in some cases even if he or she is), the president will nominate the senator's candidate. Senators often use federal judgeships to reward political supporters in their home states for past political support. Another possibility is that the senator may have several qualified candidates for the position but is reluctant to alienate the others by actively promoting one over the others. In that case, the senator may merely send a list of acceptable candidates to the attorney general and let the president make the final choice. This strategy removes the onus from the senator of offending the persons not selected. A variation of this approach is for the senator to establish his or her own merit selection process. The senator may ask a committee of judges, lawyers, law professors, and the like to screen the applicants and select the person best qualified. This approach also takes the pressure off the senator who does not want to offend his or her supporters. Finally, a senator may choose to stay out of the process by allowing the president to make the choice. The senator would merely retain the option of exercising a veto over the final choice in the event that the president selects a Democrat or someone from a rival faction of the party. This latter strategy keeps the senator from being obligated to the president.

Senatorial courtesy has undergone a change in recent years for a number of reasons. In the past, senatorial courtesy dictated that senators of the same party as the president would virtually name federal judges in their states in the manner described above, and it is still true that nominees from states of the president's party are confirmed more quickly.[61] Recent presidents are more likely to consult both of the state's senators regardless of political party. One reason for this is that the Senate has been closely divided in recent years. President George W. Bush, for example, had a narrow Republican majority in the Senate through the middle of his second term in office. In that atmosphere, every senator's vote becomes crucial in winning confirmation. Another reason is that the confirmation process, even at the district court level, has become increasingly controversial. Candidates who in the past would have been easily confirmed are now having their nominations delayed and even defeated. So today the president must find support for his judicial candidates wherever he can. Approval of the Chair of the Senate Judiciary Committee, especially if the opposition party controls the Senate, is almost as important as support by the nominee's home state senator.[62] It seems that consultation of the opposition senators is just good politics.

The selection of persons to fill vacancies on the courts of appeals is less sensitive to the pressures of senatorial courtesy than is selection at the district court level, for two reasons. First, the federal circuits consist of several states, unlike district courts that are located entirely within a single state. Because, by tradition, the president is free to nominate anyone from the circuit, no single senator can claim the appointment as a personal prerogative. Custom dictates that court of appeals judgeships be fairly evenly divided among the states within the circuit so that all of the judges do not come from the same state. For example, if a judge from Texas retires from the U.S. Court of Appeals for the Fifth Circuit, the expectation is that another Texan will be named to the bench and that the state's senators will be consulted. However, the senators from Texas are not in a position to force a particular candidate on the president, as they are at the district court level. If they try to "muscle" the president with the threat of senatorial courtesy, he can merely nominate a candidate from either Louisiana or Mississippi, the two other states in the Fifth Circuit. Still, the president may need the support of the senators from Texas and may therefore allow them considerable influence over the nomination.

A second reason for the decreased influence of senatorial courtesy at the court of appeals level is the perception that these positions are more important than district court judgeships. A district court judge's influence is confined to a single state or part of a state. If a district court judge is lazy, incompetent, or corrupt, the damage is limited to one court. However, the decisions of appeals court judges serve as precedents for every district court in the circuit. Because only a small fraction of federal cases move on to the Supreme Court, the decisions of the courts of appeals are often final. The decisions of a court of appeals may never be reviewed or overturned by the Supreme Court, so the precedents set by them are the law within that circuit. Consequently, more emphasis is placed on the professional competence of candidates for the courts of appeals. For these reasons, politics is not allowed to play as great a role as in the selection of federal district judges.

Senatorial courtesy is virtually nonexistent where the nomination of a Supreme Court justice is involved. This does not mean, of course, that a president may totally disregard the Senate when making a nomination. Historically, approximately 20 percent of the presidents' nominees have been rejected by the Senate, which indicates that its members do not take their obligation to give "advice and consent" lightly. A Supreme Court justice is in a position to influence public policy in America for many years; the nominee must therefore be chosen carefully. Every president knows that the person named may have an impact on constitutional law in the United States long after he has left the White House. Justice John Paul Stevens, appointed by President Gerald Ford in 1975, served until 2010, 34 years after Ford's presidency ended. For this reason, presidents are keenly aware of the importance of each nomination to the Court.

Despite the importance of nominations of the Supreme Court, it does not necessarily follow that politics plays no role in the selection process. Indeed, it is because the stakes are so high that we might guess that politics plays an even greater role in the selection of Supreme Court justices. Generally speaking, nominees are chosen for their ideology, their representational qualities, and their professional competence, in roughly that order of importance. Let us examine all three areas in order to ascertain how each influences the president's decision to select a particular individual to serve on the Supreme Court.

As will be discussed in Chapter 6, the Constitution, like the Bible, is open to a variety of interpretations. This means that two individuals can read the same section of the Constitution and arrive at two totally different interpretations. And because judges, like major league managers, are not born 60-year-old judges, each person who comes to the Supreme Court arrives with his or her "bags packed." That is, each justice comes to the Court with preconceived ideas about such issues as same-sex marriage, the death penalty, law and order, ownership of guns, and civil liberties. Although it is not uncommon for a justice to change views once on the Court, a majority come with their views set. In making a nomination to the Supreme Court, a president seeks to nominate a person whose views are similar to his own. Whether a liberal or a conservative, a loose or strict constructionist, pro-abortion or anti-abortion, the president wants a nominee who will decide constitutional issues as he would if he were on the Court. Presidents have had their share of disappointments. Theodore Roosevelt was disappointed with Oliver Wendell Holmes, Jr., and Dwight D. Eisenhower regretted his nomination of Earl Warren as Chief Justice. Consequently, the better informed he is about the political and judicial philosophies of his nominee, the less likely it is that a president will be stuck with a justice whom he does not like.

Even more revealing of the political nature of the Supreme Court selection process are the representational qualities that presidents seek in their nominees. Presidents are reluctant to admit that politics influences their choices for the Court, but that is indeed the case. This is because the judiciary is supposed to be "above" politics. In a nation that stresses equality before the law, it is incongruent to admit that political considerations influence the selection process. But just as the nominee's political philosophy is taken into consideration, so are the nominee's representational qualities. The Supreme Court is a very important political symbol in our system of government. Because of the significance of the Court's symbolism, it is important to certain groups in our society that they be represented on the Supreme Court. As a result, there has developed the tradition of reserving certain "seats" on the Supreme Court for representatives of prominent groups. For example, early in our nation's history, many Catholics believed that as a significant religious minority they were entitled to have at least one Catholic on the Court. Chief Justice Roger B. Taney became the Court's first Catholic justice, thus creating the "Catholic seat" on the Court. President Woodrow Wilson named the first Jewish justice, Louis Brandeis, in 1916. Interestingly, for the first time in its history, the Supreme Court no longer has a Protestant sitting on the Court. With the confirmations of Justices Sotomayor and Kagan, there are six Catholic and three Jewish members.

President Lyndon Johnson made Thurgood Marshall the first African American to sit on the Court; Marshall was succeeded by Clarence Thomas in 1991. President Reagan broke the gender barrier with the nomination of Sandra Day O'Connor to the Court in 1981. President Clinton created a second woman's seat with the appointment of Ruth Bader Ginsburg in 1993. With President Obama's nomination of two women to the Court, there is hope that women will someday achieve parity of representation. Some Court watchers believe that another significant barrier was broken with the confirmation of Sotomayor as the nation's first Latina justice to the Court. Although presidents profess to seek the best-qualified person regardless of race, religion, or gender, the reality of the process is that these political factors cannot be ignored.

The influence of representational qualities on a Supreme Court nomination may be illustrated with a few examples. In one situation, a president may wish to use a Supreme Court nomination to reward a group that has helped him politically. When President Johnson nominated Thurgood Marshall, he did so in part to show his appreciation for the support of African American voters in the 1964 election and in anticipation of their continued support in 1968 (although Johnson ultimately did not seek re-election). Another group important to Democratic presidential candidates is Jewish voters. Only two Jewish candidates have been nominated to the Supreme Court by Republican presidents, and one, the nomination of Douglas H. Ginsburg by President Reagan, was unsuccessful. Every other Jewish Supreme Court justice has been nominated by a Democratic president. This is because Jewish voters constitute a consistently loyal part of the Democratic coalition. Therefore, when Jewish justice Abe Fortas resigned from the Court in 1969, President Nixon, a Republican, felt no obligation to nominate a Jewish replacement. As a result, the "Jewish seat" remained vacant until the nomination of Ruth Bader Ginsburg by President Clinton in 1993. However, with the appointments of two additional Jewish justices—Stephen Breyer in 1994 and Elena Kagan in 2010—the discussion of a "Jewish" seat on the Court is moot.

A second instance in which the president might use a nomination to the Supreme Court for political purposes is when he is trying to curry the favor of an important political group. In 1968, Nixon had devised his so-called Southern Strategy for winning the presidency. The Southern Strategy called on Republicans to appeal to disgruntled conservative Democrats in the South who were opposed to the liberal policies of the national Democratic Party. As part of the Southern Strategy, Nixon promised to nominate a southerner to the Supreme Court. Thus, when Justice Fortas resigned, Nixon chose not a Jewish nominee but a southerner, Clement Haynesworth of South Carolina. When the Senate rejected the Haynesworth nomination, Nixon nominated another southerner, G. Harrold Carswell of Florida. After the Senate rejected Carswell, Nixon accused the Senate of prejudice against southerners. Even in defeat Nixon won: he could point out to southern voters that he had twice tried to place one of their own on the High Court but had been thwarted in his attempts by the northern liberal Democrats in the Senate.

Finally, a president might nominate a particular person to the Supreme Court as a means of bolstering his support among a key political group. Voting studies indicated that in the election of 1980, President Reagan had not done as well among women voters as among men voters. This was probably in part the result of Reagan's opposition to the Equal Rights Amendment (ERA). When Justice Potter Stewart announced his resignation in 1981, it gave Reagan an opportunity to mend his fences with an important bloc of voters. Reagan's nomination of Sandra Day O'Connor helped lay to rest criticisms that he was "anti-women." Similarly, President Clinton, a favorite among women voters, showed his appreciation for their electoral support by naming a second woman, Ruth Bader Ginsburg, to the Court in 1993, as has President Obama with his two nominations of women.

The final area of qualifications to be discussed that presidents consider in their choice of Supreme Court nominees is professional competence. As previously noted, presidents would like their nominees to receive the highest possible ABA approval rating and overwhelming Senate approval. Naturally, the president seeks persons of high intellect, character, and integrity for the Court. The public expects and the Senate demands that Supreme Court justices be of the highest caliber. What, then, does the president seek by way of professional competence? Recent presidents of both parties have valued prior judicial experience on appellate courts over candidates with political experience such as a former senator or governor. Indeed, service on the U.S. Court of Appeals for the District of Columbia has become almost a requirement for appointment to the Supreme Court.

Some presidents consider prominence in the legal profession an important qualification for a Supreme Court nomination. Lewis Powell was a former president of the ABA when he was named to the Court by President Nixon. Before becoming Obama's solicitor general, Kagan was dean of the Harvard Law School. Overall, judicial experience and professional competence, although important, take a back seat to ideological and representational qualifications. That is because there are enough outstanding judges and lawyers in the country to give the president the luxury of basing the choice on nonprofessional criteria.

Selection of State Judges

The selection of judges for state courts varies according to several factors. First, because of federalism, states may vary the selection method according to their individual wishes and needs. Basically, there are three selection methods from which to choose: election, appointment, and merit selection. States may use a combination of selection methods; they may choose, for example, to elect lower court judges and to appoint appellate and supreme court judges. Another factor is the influence of the state bar association. State bars have promoted merit selection in the past because it is believed to increase their influence in the selection of judges. Still another factor is the political environment of the state. Some states look upon judgeships as just another political office, to be controlled by election or patronage. Other "reform" states have tried to remove the judiciary from politics as much as possible. In this section, we will examine each of the three methods of judicial selection used by the states, indicating the strengths and weaknesses of each.

One method, used in approximately half of the states, is to elect judges by a popular vote of the people. Candidates for judgeships run on either a partisan or a nonpartisan basis. If the state has partisan elections, the judicial candidate vies for the nomination in the primary, campaigns just as any other candidate would, and wins if he or she receives a majority (or plurality) of the vote. The election method became popular in the states during the period known as Jacksonian Democracy. Jacksonian Democracy held that if it was a good idea to elect some officials to government office it was a good idea to elect all of them, including judges. Judges, after all, make political decisions (e.g., abortion or same-sex marriage), so the people should be able to hold them accountable for those decisions. The election of judges would guarantee that judges would not become judicial tyrants. The fact that a judge must periodically face the voters and run on his or her record ensures that the judge will not stray too far from local community standards when applying the law. It also guarantees that judges will not abuse their power as federal judges are often accused of doing.

Those who oppose the election method do so for several reasons. First, elections undermine judicial independence. If we are to have a nation of laws, not men, we must allow judges to apply the law as they see it without fear of political reprisals at the next election. Subjecting them to election tempts judges to make rulings that are popular but not necessarily legally or even morally correct. Second, the election method does not guarantee that the most qualified person will be elected to the bench. Studies indicate that elections favor white, male, middle-class, and professional candidates. The possibility of qualified minorities becoming judges is reduced with the election method. A third criticism is that most voters are not qualified to evaluate candidates for judicial office. The average voter is simply not equipped to assess the professional competence or judicial temperament of candidates for the bench.[63] Even if there is an incumbent who has a record on which to run, the average voter is unfamiliar with the decisions a judge has made. The exception, of course, is when the judge has made a controversial ruling resulting in a move to unseat the judge at the next election. The voters may never hear of the many good rulings the judge has made but may hear of only the controversial one. Finally, critics of judicial elections argue that the election method demeans the judicial system by forcing candidates for the bench to campaign for office. Candidates must often solicit campaign contributions from the same lawyers who will later come before them in court. It is unreasonable, critics argue, to assume that a judge will be able to treat impartially the lawyer who contributed $5,000 during the previous campaign. Similarly, a judge may be biased against a lawyer who supported the judge's opponent in the last election. For these reasons, critics argue that election injects politics into the judicial system in ways that undermine the integrity of the process.

Regardless of the relative merits of electing judges, a little-known phenomenon occurs in some states that use elections, and that is the practice of appointing persons to fill the unexpired term of retiring or resigning judges. The process works like this. An incumbent judge who is ready to resign or retire announces his intentions a year or so before his term expires. This allows the governor to name a replacement to serve out the rest of the unexpired term. The newly appointed judge now has the advantage of seeking re-election as the incumbent. In most cases, any other lawyer who was considering making a bid for the judgeship will back off for fear of offending the new judge whom he or she may later have to face in court. Because most incumbents are re-elected, challengers are difficult to find and the incumbent usually runs unopposed. The voters, instead of choosing from among several qualified candidates, find that they have little choice but to ratify the governor's preselected candidate. In Texas, for example, a survey revealed that nearly half of the state-level judges had initially reached the bench by appointment and not by winning an election.[64] In such cases, judges are lawyers who know a governor.

The second method of judicial selection used in the states is the appointment method. The appointment of state judges often parallels that of federal judges. Candidates are nominated by the governor with the consent of the state senate or perhaps with the consent of both the senate and the house of representatives. Confirmation by one or more chambers of the state legislature prevents the governor from merely appointing his or her friends to office.

Its supporters argue that the appointment method allows the governor to choose judges on the basis of their qualifications. As previously noted, the average voter is unqualified to evaluate the qualifications of judges. The governor and his or her advisers, on the other hand, are in a better position to make such evaluations. The governor, with the advice of the state bar association and other judges, is better able to ensure that the most qualified persons are chosen. Another argument is that well-qualified persons are more willing to serve if appointed rather than elected. This argument asserts that the onerous task of running a political campaign for election discourages otherwise qualified applicants from seeking judicial office. A third argument is that the appointment process allows a governor to name well-qualified minority group members to the bench. Proponents of the appointment method argue that minority representation on the bench influences how other minority members perceive the judicial system. Finally, supporters of the appointment method point to the high caliber of federal judges who were selected by appointment.

Opponents of the appointment method make an equally strong case against it. They argue that lifetime appointments encourage arbitrariness in the courts. Judges should be held accountable for their decisions to the people. Second, the appointment process leads to cronyism. The governor is inclined to use judicial appointments to reward friends with public office, regardless of their qualifications; this injects an element of partisan politics into the selection process as well. Finally, while it is true that the quality of federal judges is high, it is not the appointment method that has produced that quality. Federal judgeships pay more and are more prestigious than many state judgeships; hence, the federal bench attracts a higher quality of applicants from the outset.[65]

The third method of judicial selection is merit selection, often called the *Missouri Plan* because the state of Missouri pioneered its use. Merit selection is an attempt to combine the best features of the election and appointment methods. One of the key features of merit selection is the presence of a judicial nominating committee. The judicial nominating committee is usually composed of a combination of lawyers, laypersons, and incumbent judges. When a vacancy occurs in a judicial post, it is the job of the judicial nominating committee to serve as a screening committee. Persons wishing to be considered for the judgeship may submit their own credentials or they may be nominated by someone else. The judicial nominating committee screens the applications and reduces the choices to three candidates. The names of the three candidates are then submitted to the governor, who must appoint one of the three candidates to the judgeship. The person appointed then begins his or her tenure on the court.

A second key feature of the Missouri Plan is the use of a retention election. After the newly appointed judge has served a probationary period of at least one year, he or she must go before the voters for their approval. The judge has no opponents, however. The voters are simply asked, "Shall Judge X of the state [Supreme Court] court be retained in office?" The voter votes either yes or no. If the voters approve, the judge begins a full term of office. Terms of office for judges under the Missouri Plan are generally long—from 8 to 12 years—in order to ensure judicial independence. At the end of the term a judge must stand for retention again, with the voters asked the same question. If the voters approve once again, the judge serves another full term. A judge may continue to serve as long as he or she wishes and as long as the people vote to keep the judge in office. If a judge loses the retention election, the position is declared vacant and the judicial nominating committee must begin the process of filling it.

Supporters of merit selection are generally enthusiastic about the method. The Missouri Plan, like the appointment method, gives a greater role to those who are most knowledgeable about judicial qualifications. As is the case with the election method, judges are periodically held accountable to the voters; judicial tyranny is thereby discouraged. At the same time, lengthy terms of office offer the judge a certain amount of judicial independence. A judge may make a controversial ruling with less fear that the voters will punish him or her for it at the next election, especially if the ruling is made early in the judge's term. Supporters argue that merit selection combines the positive features of the election and appointment methods with few, if any, of their drawbacks.

Critics of merit selection are not convinced that the method is as effective as its supporters claim. First, they point out that merit selection gives inordinate influence to the organized bar. The lawyer-members of the judicial nominating committee are usually chosen by the state bar, and the judge-members are also lawyers. This means that even if there are non-lawyers on the committee, they are outnumbered by the lawyers. Another problem is that the lay members are at a disadvantage in evaluating judicial qualifications. They may allow the lawyers on the committee to unduly influence them in the screening process. Another criticism is that merit selection does not eliminate politics from judicial selection as its supporters claim. The political struggle shifts from partisan politics to the politics of the state bar. State bars usually have factions that try to control the selection of lawyer-members to the judicial nominating committee. Partisan politics may also enter the picture; a Republican governor who is given the choice of two Democrats and one Republican by the judicial nominating committee may conclude that the lone Republican is the "best" candidate. Even after a judge has reached the bench, partisan politics may enter into the retention election. Finally, critics of merit selection argue that there is simply no conclusive evidence that merit selection actually produces a higher caliber of judges than either election or appointment. Given the subjective nature of evaluating judicial qualifications, it is unlikely to be proven that merit selection provides better judges. However, data collected from a study of the judicial system of New York City found that "elected judges are significantly more likely to be disciplined for judicial misconduct than their appointed counterparts."[66]

REMOVAL OF JUDGES

The office of judge is one of the most prestigious in American society; yet judges, like other humans, are susceptible to the vices of corruption, abuse of power, alcoholism, and so on. Consequently, we hear every year of cases of judges removed from the bench for various offenses.[67] Judicial removal involves three very different kinds of situations. The first is the case of a judge who has committed an illegal act either before or after taking office. Judges have been accused of soliciting murder, accepting bribes, and committing perjury, among other crimes. In a sense, the case of a judge who commits a crime is the easiest to deal with because the judge is treated like any other criminal defendant and is therefore entitled to due process of law.

The second kind of situation occurs when a judge has abused his or her power but has not necessarily committed a crime or an impeachable offense. For example, a district court judge in Suffolk County, New York had a coffee vendor brought before him in handcuffs so that he could berate the vendor for selling him a bad cup of coffee.[68] Similarly, a Louisiana judge found a defendant guilty after taking a poll in his courtroom. Although many of the courtroom spectators failed to stand when asked to vote, a verdict of guilty was rendered and the appearance of impropriety was undeniable. Finally, a Michigan judge flipped a coin to ascertain with which parent two children should be allowed to spend the Christmas holidays. Both of the latter judges were subsequently censured.[69]

The third situation occurs when a judge is either incompetent or senile. In some ways, this is the most difficult of the three situations with which to deal. For example, a judge who may have served with distinction for many years may simply have stayed too long on the bench. Most states have mandatory retirement for judges at age 70, but senility does not always wait until then to strike. A judge, regardless of age, may simply be incompetent. Because there is no formal training for judges in the United States, virtually every lawyer is a potential judge. Yet lawyers have different talents and temperaments, so it is possible that a well-meaning judge may just be in over his or her head. Removal of the senile or incompetent judge must be handled carefully. Friends of the judge will usually suggest privately that it is time to resign or retire, but if the judge refuses, forced removal may be necessary.

Removal of Federal Judges

There is only one formal method of removing Article III judges, and that, of course, is by impeachment. The Constitution specifies that impeachment is by a majority vote of the House of Representatives, followed by a trial in the Senate. Conviction is by a two-thirds vote of the Senate, and the penalty may not extend beyond removal from office and disqualification from holding further offices under the authority of the United States. Like other thorny constitutional provisions, impeachment has raised some serious issues. Foremost among those issues is the relationship between impeachment and judicial independence. The case of the impeachment of Justice Samuel Chase, the only Supreme Court justice to ever be impeached, illustrates the problem. By most accounts, Chase exhibited "clearly intemperate and political conduct as a judge."[70] Chase, a Federalist, was an outspoken critic of the Jefferson administration. In addition, critics accused him of abusing lawyers in his court and showing bias against Republican litigants. But at the heart of the controversy was whether a judge's decisions could be the basis for removal from office. Happily for judicial independence, even some Republican senators who believed Chase was a disgrace to the Court were unwilling to vote for his removal on those grounds. The late Chief Justice William H. Rehnquist, writing about the controversy, concluded that several Republican senators put statesmanship above partisanship and voted to acquit Chase. Rehnquist asserted that Federalist senators would have voted to acquit Chase regardless of the evidence but that some Republican senators would have removed him "only if it could have been accomplished consistently with the maintenance of an independent judiciary."[71]

There have been 15 impeachment proceedings against federal judges: Four were acquitted by the Senate, eight were convicted, and three resigned before a Senate vote (Table 3.4). The last federal judge to be impeached—G. Thomas Porteous, Jr. of Louisiana—was impeached by the House on March 11, 2010 for participation in "a pattern of corrupt conduct for years."[72] In December 2010 the Senate found Porteous guilty on four articles of impeachment, disqualified him from holding federal office in the future, and stripped him of his yearly federal pension of $174,000.[73] The procedurally most interesting modern-day impeachment involved Walter L. Nixon, Jr., who was convicted of perjury in February 1986 but refused to resign from the bench and still collected his (then) salary of $89,500 while in prison. The House impeached Judge Nixon in May 1989 by a vote of 417 to 0, and the Senate convicted him on November 3, 1989 by a vote of 89 to 8.[74] In Judge Nixon's case, the Senate used a select committee to hear the evidence. The full Senate, after receiving briefs and hearing oral arguments, voted to convict. Judge Nixon, arguing that use of the select committee violated the constitutional requirement that the Senate "try" all impeachments, appealed to the Supreme Court. The Court, however, ruled that Nixon's case raised a non-justiciable political question and dismissed his suit.[75]

The federal removal process illustrates the problem with impeachment as the only means of removing federal judges. First, the impeachment process is cumbersome, especially the trial stage in the Senate. The Senate, in effect, may be forced to delay other legislative matters pending the outcome of the impeachment trial. A second problem is that impeachment must cover a variety of judicial removal situations. John Pickering, the judge impeached for insanity and alcoholism, undoubtedly deserved to be removed from the bench, but he probably did not deserve the ignominious distinction of being the first federal judge to be removed from office. George W. English was impeached by the House in 1926 for "partiality, tyranny, and oppression."[76] The question raised by English's impeachment (he resigned before conviction by the Senate) was whether "partiality, tyranny, and oppression" constitute "Treason, Bribery, or other high crimes and misdemeanors," the grounds for impeachment specified

TABLE 3.4

Impeached Federal Judges

Name	Court	Charges	Result
John Pickering	District Court, NH	Alcoholism, Insanity	Removed
Samuel Chase	U.S. Supreme Court	Favoritism, Partisanship	Acquitted
James H. Peck	District Court, MO	Misuse of Contempt Power	Acquitted
West H. Humphreys	District Court, TN	Support of Confederacy	Removed
Mark H. Delahay	District Court, KS	Corruption, Alcoholism	Resigned prior to trial
Charles Swayne	District Court, FL	Misuse of Contempt Power	Acquitted
George W. English	District Court, IL	Abusive Treatment	Resigned prior to trial
Robert W. Archbald	Commerce Court	Misconduct in Office	Removed
Harold Louderback	District Court, CA	Allowing Excessive Fees	Acquitted
Halsted L. Ritter	District Court, FL	Tax Evasion	Removed
Harry E. Claiborne	District Court, NV	Tax Evasion	Removed
Alcee Hastings	District Court, FL	Bribery, Perjury	Removed
Walter L. Nixon	District Court, MS	Corruption, Perjury	Removed
Samuel B. Kent	District Court, TX	Sexual Harassment	Resigned prior to trial
G. Thomas Porteous, Jr.	District Court, LA	Corruption, Bribery	Removed

Sources: Data compiled from Henry J. Abraham, *The Judicial Process,* 7th edn (New York: Oxford University Press, 1998), pp. 45–51; "Impeachment of Federal Officials," http://www. Infoplease.com/ipa/A0194049.html; "House Votes to Impeach Federal Judge From Louisiana," http://www.cnn.com/2010/POLITICS/03/11/louisiana.judge.impeached/index.html; and "Federal Judiciary," http://www.justicelearning.org/justice_timeline/ArticlesTimeline.aspx?id=4&Section=19&TimelineID=68&TimelineEventID=1696 (visited August 3, 2010).

by the Constitution. The impeachment process must cover activities ranging from "partiality" to murder, with the same punishment for both. Or, as then Michigan Representative Gerald Ford stated, "An impeachable offense is whatever a majority of the House of Representatives considers it to be at a given moment of history."[77] Finally, as the case of Walter Nixon illustrates, even a judge who has been convicted of a felony may continue to draw his or her salary until the long impeachment process has run its course. In recognition of this problem, Congress passed the Judicial Councils Reform and Judicial Conduct and Disability Act in 1980. The Act establishes a procedure for investigating complaints against federal judges. If the allegations merit action, a committee composed of federal judges may investigate. Possible disciplinary actions for Article III judges include "private or public reprimand or censure, certification of disability, request for voluntary resignation, or prohibition against further case assignments," while bankruptcy and magistrate judges are also subject to removal by the Judicial Council.[78]

Removal of State Judges

Just as in other areas of court organization, the states have addressed the problems of judicial removal in a variety of ways. Forty-five states allow their state legislatures to impeach state judges.[79] The impeachment process in the states parallels the federal model, with some modifications, such as the size of the majority needed to impeach in the House or to convict in the Senate. For example, Justice Rolf Larsen was removed from the Pennsylvania Supreme Court, the first judge to be impeached and convicted in the state in nearly 200 years. The basis of the removal was improperly meeting with an attorney to review two of the attorney's pending cases. The House vote was 199 to 0 to impeach Larsen, and the Senate vote was 44 to 4 for conviction; he was acquitted on six other charges.[80] The New Hampshire House of Representatives impeached the chief justice of the state supreme court, David A. Brock, for allegedly interfering in the divorce case of another judge.[81]

Another method of removal is *legislative address.* Legislative address, unlike impeachment, is not reserved for high crimes and misdemeanors but may be used in cases of incompetency, senility, or partiality. The judge in question does not have to commit an indictable offense to warrant removal. Under legislative address, the unfortunate Pickering could have been spared the indignity of impeachment.

A third method of removal that is popular in some states is *recall.* Recall is a method of removing officials, not only judges, from public office before the expiration of the official's term. Recall begins with the circulation of a recall petition. Suppose a judge was deemed deserving of removal from office. A group of citizens could start a recall campaign by securing a specified number of signatures on a recall petition. In some states the petition must be signed by a specified percentage (e.g., 5 or 10 percent) of the registered voters. If enough valid signatures are collected, the judge in question must face a retention election similar to that used under the Missouri Plan. However, the question before the voters would be, "Shall Judge X of the [state supreme] court be removed from office?" The voters answer either yes or no. Other states allow alternative candidates to run against the incumbent judge in the recall election. This permits the voters to show their discontent with the incumbent by electing someone else to the position. Wisconsin judge Archie Simonson made some inappropriate remarks about the "provocative clothing" worn by the young victim during a rape trial he was conducting. The remarks so angered women's groups in Madison that they mounted a successful recall campaign against Simonson.[82]

Finally, a fourth device used by some states to discipline judges is the *judicial conduct board/commission*. As we have seen, the severity of alleged offenses against judges ranges from the trivial to the very serious. Some allegations made against judges prove to be no more than the unfounded complaints of disgruntled litigants who lost a case over which the judge presided. Still other complaints are more serious and deserve some disciplinary action. Similarly, the punishment should fit the offense. For this reason, some states have created judicial conduct boards to investigate allegations made against judges to determine whether disciplinary action is warranted. If a judge is found guilty of misconduct, the board is empowered to discipline the offender. Such discipline could be a private or public reprimand, censure, suspension, or a recommendation of removal from office by impeachment or legislative address. State judicial conduct boards thus possess a variety of punishments that are appropriate to the seriousness of the offense.

WILLIAMS-YULEE V. FLORIDA BAR

The selection of judges can create a clash of democratic values. In *Williams-Yulee v. Florida Bar* the U.S. Supreme Court was confronted with a dilemma about the role of free speech in a democratic society and the role of elected judges in a democracy.

Background of the Case[83]

Canon 7C(1) of the Florida Code of Judicial Conduct prohibits a candidate for any judicial office in the state from personally soliciting funds for his or her election campaign. In September 2009 Lanell Williams-Yulee (hereafter Yulee) ran for a seat on the county court of Hillsborough County. Yulee admitted that she had mailed a letter to local voters soliciting campaign contributions and posted the letter on her campaign website, but argued that her actions were protected under the First Amendment. After a hearing, the Florida Supreme Court upheld a finding of guilty that carried with it a public reprimand and a payment of $1860 to cover the cost of the proceeding.

Ruling in the Case

In a 5 to 4 decision the U.S. Supreme Court held that Canon 7C(1) does not violate the First Amendment. In an opinion written by Chief Justice John Roberts, the majority applied "strict scrutiny" and ruled that the ban on personal solicitations was narrowly drawn to serve a compelling state interest, namely the state's interest in preserving public confidence in the fairness and independence of the state's judiciary. The Court was mindful that in other cases it had held, campaign contributions are a form of free speech protected by the First Amendment. However, the Court also noted that even though judges are elected in 39 states they are not "politicians" in the usual sense of the word. Although voters expect candidates for legislative and executive positions to favor the interests of their supporters, judges are expected to be impartial.

Analysis of the Case

In upholding the ban on the personal solicitation of campaign contributions, the Court applied what is called "strict" or "exacting" scrutiny. Under normal judicial review the Court assumes that a law passed by Congress or a state is constitutional, thus putting the burden of showing that it is unconstitutional on the party challenging the law. However, strict scrutiny does the opposite: it assumes that any law which infringes a constitutionally protected right, such as freedom of speech, is *unconstitutional*, thus shifting the burden to the state to show that it is constitutional. In order to survive strict scrutiny, the state must show, first, that the law is necessary to further a "compelling state interest" and that, second, it has been narrowly drawn so as to infringe the constitutional right as little as possible. Often, but not always, the level of scrutiny which the Court adopts will decide the fate of the law. Nevertheless, strict scrutiny sets a very high bar for the state to meet in defending the constitutionality of its law.

On the question of whether Canon 7C (1) furthers a compelling state interest, the Court held that unquestionably the state's interest in maintaining the integrity of its judicial system meets that standard. The Court notes that the idea of an impartial judiciary dates back to Magna Carta (1215). The people must have absolute confidence in the fairness and impartiality of the courts and in those chosen to administer justice. Even the appearance of impropriety undermines the state's interest in maintaining the integrity of the judicial process. The fact that lawyers and other parties likely to have business before the court are also most likely to contribute to judicial candidates is another reason to limit personal solicitations. Indeed, a litigant may fear that failure to make a contribution to the winning candidate would prejudice the judge against him or her. Therefore, the majority found that Canon 7C (1) sufficiently furthers a compelling state interest.

The second requirement of strict scrutiny is that the statute be narrowly drawn in order to limit the burden placed on a fundamental right, in this case freedom of speech. Candidates for judicial office in Florida may form campaign committees that may, in turn, solicit funds on behalf of their campaigns. Yulee argued that judicial candidates may legally write thank-you notes to contributors and therefore may learn the identities of those who have contributed. But the Court notes the ban on solicitation addresses the issue most likely to undermine public confidence in the judiciary: personal solicitation. The fact that other forms of contact with contributors are not banned only supports the fact that the law was narrowly written to minimize the infringement on free speech.

As indicated in the introduction to this case study, *Williams-Yulee v. Florida Bar* represents a clash of democratic values. Democratic theory is based on the accountability of elected officials to the voters. On the other hand, due process of law dictates that the parties bringing a case before a presumably impartial judge should not have the deck stacked against them. As noted in Chapter 1, the legitimacy of the judicial system rests in part on the assumption that judges will administer justice impartially. It was also noted that law is a struggle between groups with different values. Certainly, some people will place more value in holding judges accountable, while others will prefer both the appearance and the reality of impartial justice. Finally, in such matters as these, there can be no right or wrong answer.

CONCLUSION

In this chapter, we have examined court organization in the United States. Because of our federal form of government, we have a federal court system superimposed on the 50 state court systems. In addition, federalism results in considerable variation among the states in the organization of their courts as well as in their substantive and procedural law. Federalism has resulted in different approaches to the selection and removal of judges. In short, our federal form of government adds complexity to our courts, but it also adds an element of diversity so that each state may deal with judicial organization, selection, and removal in its own way. For better or for worse, federalism has had a remarkable impact on our judicial system.

NOTES

1. U.S. Constitution, Art. III, § 1.
2. Ibid.
3. Ibid.
4. Ibid., Art. I, § 8, cl. 16.
5. Ibid., Art. IV, § 3, cl. 2.
6. See Henry J. Abraham, *The Judiciary: The Supreme Court in the Governmental Process*, 7th edn (Boston, MA: Allyn & Bacon, 1987), pp. 8–9.
7. Ibid., p. 11.
8. U.S. Constitution, Art. III, § 2.
9. Ibid.
10. Ibid.
11. Ibid., Art. I, § 8, cl. 4.
12. Ibid., cl. 1.
13. The one exception to this rule today is the District Court for Wyoming, which covers the Montana and Idaho parts of Yellowstone National Park. See Stephen L. Wasby, *The Supreme Court in the Federal Judicial System*, 4th edn (Chicago, IL: Nelson-Hall, 1993), p. 43.
14. http://www.uscourts.gov/judges-judgeships/authorized-judgeships (visited June 26, 2015).
15. http://www.uscourts.gov/judges-judgeships/judicial-vacancies (visited July 1, 2015).
16. http://www.uscourts.gov/statistics-reports/caseload-statistics-data-tables (visited June 26, 2015).
17. http://www.uscourts.gov/judges-judgeships/authorized-judgeships (visited June 20, 2016).
18. Because of its size (29 judgeships), not all of the judges of the Ninth Circuit sit *en banc*. See Wasby, pp. 42–43.

19. United States Court of International Trade, www.cit.uscourts.gov/AboutTheCourt. html (visited June 26, 2015).
20. http://uscourts.gov/statistics/table/na/federal-court-management-statistics/2014/ 12/31-2 (visited July 2, 2015).
21. 8 U.S.C. § 1532 (a).
22. 8 U.S.C. § 1532 (b).
23. 50 U.S.C. § 1803 (a).
24. "An Interview with Judge Royce C. Lamberth," *The Third Branch* 34, 6 (June 2002), p. 10.
25. Vanessa Blum, "Little-known Appeals Panel Meets for First Time to Determine Justice Department's Reach in War Against Terrorism," *Broward Daily Business Review*, September 5, 2002, p. A9.
26. Eric Lichtblau, "Judges on Secretive Panel Speak Out on Spy Program," *The New York Times*, March 29, 2006.
27. Sheldon Goldman and Thomas P. Jahnige, *The Federal Courts as a Political System*, 3rd edn (New York: Harper & Row, 1985), p. 18.
28. U.S. Constitution, Art. III, § 1.
29. Until 1982, the federal district court for the Canal Zone was included in this group, but that court was abolished after the ratification of the Panama Canal Treaty.
30. "Territorial Courts," *Federal Judicial Center*, http://www.fjc.gov/history/home.nsf/ page/courts_special_ter.html (visited July 2, 2015).
31. Ibid.
32. Ibid.
33. "U.S. Court of Federal Claims, 1982–Present," *Federal Judicial Center*, http:// www.fjc.gov/history/home.nsf/page/courts_special_cfc.html (visited July 2, 2015).
34. Wasby, pp. 52–53.
35. *Northern Pipeline Construction Co. v. Marathon Pipe Line Co.*, 458 U.S. 50 (1982).
36. Robert A. Carp and Ronald Stidham, *The Federal Courts*, 4th edn (Washington, DC: Congressional Quarterly Press, 1998), p. 52.
37. http://www.fjc.gov/history/home.nsf/page/judges_bank.html (visited July 2, 2015).
38. http://uscourts.gov/statistics/table/f/bankruptcy-filings/2015/03/31 (visited June 29, 2015).
39. "About the Court," *U.S. Courts of Veterans Claims*, http://www.uscourts.cavc.gov/ court_process.php (visited July 3, 2015).
40. Ibid.
41. *U.S. Court of Appeals for the Armed Forces*, http://www.armfor.uscourts.gov/ newcaaf/home.htm (visited July 3, 2015).
42. "Caseload Composition" (National Center for State Courts, 2012), http:// www.courtstatistics.org/~/media/Microsites/Files/CSP/NCSC_EWSC_WEB_ NOV_25_14.ashx (visited July 3, 2015).
43. In New York, trial courts are called supreme courts; therefore, the highest appellate court is simply called the Court of Appeals. See Lawrence Baum, *American Courts: Process and Policy*, 4th edn (Boston, MA: Houghton Mifflin, 1998), p. 47.
44. At the start of the 2014 Term, six members of the U.S. Supreme Court were from Harvard Law School and three from Yale.
45. G. Alan Tarr, *Judicial Process and Policymaking*, 2nd edn (Belmont, CA: West/ Wadsworth, 1999), p. 78.
46. Ibid.

47. "Ratings," ABA Standing Committee on the Federal Judiciary, http://www.americanbar.org/content/dam/aba/uncategorized/GAO/WebRatingChart.authcheckdam.pdf (visited July 3, 2015).

48. David M. O'Brien, "The Reagan Judges: His Most Enduring Legacy?," in Charles O. Jones, ed., *The Reagan Legacy: Promise and Performance* (Chatham, NJ: Chatham House, 1988), pp. 60–101.

49. Robert A. Carp, Kenneth L. Manning, and Ronald Stidham, "The Decision-making Behavior of George W. Bush's Judicial Appointees: Far-right, Conservative, or Moderate?," in Elliot E. Slotnik, ed., *Judicial Politics: Readings from Judicature*, 3rd edn (Washington, DC: CQ Press, 2005), p. 117.

50. Wasby, p. 75.

51. American Bar Association, "Standing Committee on the Federal Judiciary," http://www.americanbar.org/content/dam/aba/uncategorized/GAO/Backgrounder.authcheckdam.pdf (visited July 3, 2015).

52. Carp and Stidham, p. 228.

53. Tarr, p. 77.

54. Statement of H. Thomas Wells, Jr., http://www.abanet.org/abanet/media/statement/statement.cfm?releaseid=574 (visited June 1, 2010).

55. Wasby, p. 126.

56. See, for example, Nancy Scherer, "The Judicial Confirmation Process: Mobilizing Elites, Mobilizing Masses," in Elliot E. Slotnik, ed., *Judicial Politics: Readings from Judicature*, 3rd edn (Washington, DC: CQ Press, 2005), pp. 73–85.

57. Frank Guiliuzza III, Daniel J. Reagan, and David M. Barrett, "The Senate Judiciary Committee and Supreme Court Nominees: Measuring the Dynamics of Confirmation Criteria," *Journal of Politics* 56 (August 1994), p. 776.

58. Ibid., pp. 776–777.

59. Paul A. Freund, "Appointment of Justices: Some Historical Perspectives," 101 Harv. L. Rev. 1146 (April 1988); Stephen Carter, "The Confirmation Mess," 101 Harv. L. Rev. 1185 (April 1988).

60. Wasby, p. 77.

61. Sarah A. Binder and Forrest Maltzman, "The Limits of Senatorial Courtesy," *Legislative Quarterly* 29, 1 (February 2004), p. 14.

62. Ibid., p. 15.

63. In 1976, Texas voters elected Don Yarbrough, who was later accused of soliciting to commit murder and convicted of aggravated perjury, to the state supreme court. In 1994, the same state's voters elected Republican Stephen Mansfield to the statewide Court of Criminal Appeals despite "his admissions that he lied about his legal experience and details of his personal background, including his birthplace and prior political experience." "The Greatest Challenge of My Life," *Texas Lawyer*, November 21, 1994, p. 8.

64. Texas Office of Court Administration, *Texas Judicial System Annual Report* (Austin, TX: Office of Court Administration, 1997), p. 2.

65. Robert S. Lorch, *State and Local Politics: The Great Entanglement*, 5th edn (Englewood Cliffs, NJ: Prentice-Hall, 1995), pp. 207–210.

66. Steven Zeidman, "To Elect or Not to Elect: A Case Study of Judicial Selection in New York City, 1977–2002," 37 U. Mich. J.L. Reform 791 (spring 2004), p. 835.

67. For a list of examples, see Geoffrey P. Miller, "Bad Judges," 83 Tex. L. Rev. 431 (December 2004).

68. Max H. Seigel, "Judge Loses Job over Reaction to 'Terrible Coffee,'" *New York Times,* July 10, 1976, p. 24.

69. Carl E. Stewart, "Abuse of Power & Judicial Misconduct: A Reflection on Contemporary Ethical Issues Facing Judges," 1 U. St. Thomas L.J. 464 (fall 2003).

70. Jonathan Turley, "Senate Trials and Factional Disputes: Impeachment as a Madisonian Device," 49 Duke L.J. 1 (October 1999), p. 60.

71. William H. Rehnquist, *Grand Inquests: The Historic Impeachments of Justice Samuel Chase and President Andrew Johnson* (New York: William Morrow and Company, Inc., 1992), p. 113.

72. "House Votes to Impeach Federal Judge from Louisiana," http://www.cnn.com/2010/POLITICS/03/11/louisiana.judge.impeached/index.html (visited August 3, 2010).

73. Jennifer Steinhauer, "Senate, for Just the 8th Time, Votes to Oust a Federal Judge," *New York Times,* December 9, 2015, p. A–27.

74. "Senate Convicts Judge Nixon, Removes Him from Bench," *Congressional Quarterly* 47, 44 (November 4, 1989), p. 2955.

75. *Nixon v. United States,* 506 U.S. 224 (1993).

76. Abraham, p. 46.

77. Ibid., p. 49.

78. Carp and Stidham, p. 252.

79. Richard D. Bingham, *State and Local Government in an Urban Society* (New York: Random House, 1986), p. 223.

80. "Senate Removes Justice Larsen," *The Legal Intelligencer,* October 5, 1994, p. 1.

81. Carey Goldberg, "New Hampshire's House Impeaches Chief Justice," *New York Times,* July 13, 2000, p. A–16.

82. "Ousted Judge in Rape Case Says Feminists Will 'Stoop' to Any Low," *New York Times,* January 4, 1978, p. B4.

83. The facts of the case are summarized from the majority opinion of Chief Justice John Roberts, *Williams-Yulee v. Florida Bar,* 575 U.S. _____ (2015), Slip Opinion.

Procedure and Evidence

The difference between substantive and procedural law was first introduced in Chapter 1. Substantive law was defined as that which is concerned with the content or substance of the law. Legal definitions of crimes are examples of the law's substantive content. Procedural law was defined as governing the *process* of the law. Later chapters will deal with civil and criminal substantive law in greater detail. In this chapter we will elaborate on procedural law by examining it in both civil and criminal contexts. Before we begin the discussion of the actual civil procedure, it is important to review the reasons for our insistence on strict rules of procedure. In Chapter 1 we stated that most Americans want to prevent government from acting toward them in an arbitrary manner. We are so concerned with the problem of arbitrary government that we have adopted an elaborate system of criminal procedural safeguards to ensure that the innocent person is not wrongfully convicted of a crime. We even accept the inevitability that some guilty persons will go free if "the constable blunders." That is the price we pay to protect our civil liberties.

Our desire to check government capriciousness in criminal cases does not tell us why we also have such elaborate procedural requirements in civil cases, in which, by definition, the government is generally unconcerned about the outcome. The answer lies in the fact that government, by passing laws, sets up the "rules of the game." No one would even begin to play a board game without some prior knowledge of its rules; likewise, before people will risk their time, energy, and money in a lawsuit, they want to know the rules that govern the process. Common sense, therefore, dictates that the rules of civil procedure be known beforehand.

There is, however, another important reason for studying the rules of procedure in civil cases that does directly involve the government. It was an extremely important step in the advancement of civilization when people began relying on government or some other societal institution to resolve disputes. In prehistoric times, it may have been a clan or tribal leader who was responsible for settling disputes among people. In later times, it may have been a king or a council. Regardless of who the dispute settler was, the willingness of individuals to submit their disputes to some neutral third party was a vital characteristic of an advanced society. One important aspect of the willingness to submit disputes for peaceful resolution is the perception by all parties that the dispute settler is fair. Two teams willingly allow a neutral umpire to apply neutral rules of play to their game of baseball if both teams perceive the umpire and the rules to be fair. Then, if a call should go against them, they accept it, even if they do not agree with it. Similarly, if courts of law designated to settle disputes among citizens are perceived by all to apply neutral rules of procedure fairly, the losing party will more readily accept the bitter pill he or she must swallow. In societies in which courts are not perceived as fair and just, people will often resort to illegal or extralegal means to ensure that they receive justice.[1] Consequently, the government has a tremendous stake in maintaining the appearance (and the reality) of its system of justice, even though it seldom cares about the outcome of a particular case. Rule One of the Federal Rules of Civil Procedure emphasizes that both the courts and the parties are required "to secure the just, speedy, and inexpensive determination of every action and proceeding." The government's main interest is in ensuring that the appearance of justice is preserved.

ALTERNATIVE DISPUTE RESOLUTION

Abraham Lincoln, that practical lawyer, once offered a piece of advice to law students: "Discourage litigation. Persuade your neighbors to compromise whenever you can. Point out to them how the nominal winner is often a real loser—in fees, expenses and waste of time."[2] In the years since, little has changed on the American legal scene, and Lincoln's advice is as pertinent today as it was then. When wronged or cheated, people stampede to the courthouse to file civil lawsuits, seeking both retribution and omnipotent judges to ratify their certain belief that they are right. However, there are several roadblocks in their path—overcrowded dockets with very long delays in hearing civil cases; very high expenditures in the form of attorney's fees, court costs, and discovery; no assurance of winning in the end or recouping their costs; further estranged relations with the opposing party with whom they may have an ongoing relationship, such as a former spouse; and perhaps most importantly, the "stress, trauma, and sagging spirits" as well as the incredible investment of time and effort involved in a lawsuit.[3]

Disillusionment and disgruntlement with the civil justice system has led to the burgeoning attention given to alternatives for resolving disputes. The need for timely and affordable justice has provided the impetus for the creation of a multidimensional approach to public justice—involving both formal and informal means. States and the national government have hopped on the bandwagon and have made provisions for some type of alternative dispute resolution (ADR), either through the private sector, or through administrative agencies or the courts. These programs cover the gamut in terms of organization, from the so-called "rent-a-judge" program in which the neutral party (often a retired judge) hears the evidence that would be presented in court before reaching a decision, to neighborhood justice centers where a trained (the term is used advisedly) mediator assists the parties in reconciling their differences in a much more informal setting which encourages participation of the parties and discourages the participation of lawyers.

In evaluating cases to be referred to ADR, attorneys often consider the following:

- the nature of the relationships between the parties
- the business environment
- the issues involved
- the present posture of the case
- the further costs of resolving the dispute through litigation
- the concern for privacy
- the relationship with outside attorneys
- the likelihood of settlement
- if settlement is not achieved, will the procedure affect subsequent litigation?[4]

For example, the desire for privacy led actor Tom Cruise to pursue mediation in divorces from his three former wives—Mimi Rogers, Nicole Kidman, and Katie Holmes—as did country music star Trace Adkins and his wife in their 2015 divorce.[5] Celebrities Brad Pitt and Jennifer Aniston employed a private judge to preside over their divorce.[6]

Utilizing neutral third parties to settle disputes without resorting to litigation is a commonly mandated practice in contracts, especially those relating to labor, employment, and construction contracts. *Mediation* is the intervention of a neutral third party between two contending parties "with a view to reconcile them or persuade them to adjust or settle their dispute."[7] When the parties agree in advance to be bound by the decision of the mediator, then it is called *arbitration.* Arbitration has been an integral part of the legal systems for years and is codified on the federal level in the Arbitration Act, Title 9 of the United States Code.

One trend in ADR is court-annexed arbitration. Courts have had the power to refer cases to arbitration for centuries, but there is a new emphasis on its use at both the state and national levels. Congress has mandated that:

> Each district court shall provide litigants in all civil cases with at least one alternative dispute resolution process, including, but not limited to, mediation, early neutral evaluation, mini-trial, and arbitration ... Any district court that elects to require the use of alternative dispute resolution in certain cases may do so only with respect to mediation, early neutral evaluation, and, if the parties consent, arbitration.[8]

Cases that cannot be referred to arbitration without the consent of the parties are those that involve a violation of the Constitution, a civil rights claim under 42 U.S.C. § 1985 (conspiracy to interfere with civil rights), violations of equal protection including voting rights, or if the amount in controversy is in excess of $150,000.[9] The arbitrator has the power to conduct the hearing, to administer oaths, to issue subpoenas, and to make awards. Once the arbitrator has rendered a decision under this statute, it is final and binding on the parties unless a motion for a *trial de novo* or new trial is filed with the district court within 30 days; otherwise there is no appeal from the decision.

Former Justice Sandra Day O'Connor stated, "The courts of this country should not be the places where the resolution of disputes begins. They should be the places where the disputes end—after alternative methods of resolving disputes have been considered and tried.[10] Proponents argue that not only does ADR relieve the burden on the courts but it also provides expeditious and swifter public justice in many instances. However, not all see neighborhood justice as a panacea. They point out that the wealthy will still have access to the courts while poor people will be forced into lesser forums and that it promotes uncertainty—while one of the legal system's goals is predictability—because ADR is a somewhat *ad hoc* system of justice in that the case outcome may not follow legal norms.[11] Despite the criticisms, it appears likely that ADR will continue to flourish and grow as an alternative to full-blown litigation. For example, the official California judicial branch website touts the benefits of ADR for litigants, including saving time and money, maintaining and increasing control over the process and outcome, preserving relationships, and improving satisfaction of the resolution.[12]

With this background in mind, we turn our attention to the discussion of the rules of civil procedure. In order to avoid confusion and for the purposes of instruction, we have simplified the process as much as possible. In addition, because there are several types of civil actions, we have chosen to use a case of *negligence*, a type of tort case, to illustrate the civil legal process. We hope this overview will help the reader to become generally familiar with civil procedure.

CIVIL PROCEDURE

Every civil case begins with a dispute or controversy that cannot be resolved in a less formal manner. A person who feels that he has been injured by another may begin a civil action against that person. The person filing the suit is called the *plaintiff*, and the person against whom the suit has been filed is called the *defendant*. Prior to actually filing a suit, the plaintiff will usually consult a lawyer, who will advise him about the soundness of his case. If the lawyer feels her prospective client has a good case, she may either agree to handle it personally or refer him to someone else who specializes in the kind of case in question. Lawyers sometimes agree to work on the basis of a *contingency fee*, which means the lawyer is paid only if the client's claim is successful. The contingency fee is typically from 30 to 40 percent of the award. Should he lose, the client pays only for court fees and other expenses involved in pursuing the case.

Often the plaintiff's lawyer will initially suggest an informal resolution of the conflict. She may call or write to the defendant to convey her client's intent to sue, in the hope that the defendant will see that the plaintiff "means business" and will thus be persuaded to settle out of court. The defendant, in turn, may have retained his own lawyer in anticipation of the plaintiff's action. It is quite possible that after the lawyers for both sides confer, an informal agreement can be worked out, thus avoiding the formal legal process. A majority of cases are resolved after some informal negotiation by the lawyers involved or after referral to some ADR program.

Initial Formal Process

When informal methods fail, the next step is the filing of the *complaint.* In the complaint, the plaintiff relates the injury he has received at the hands of the defendant, alleges negligence and liability on the defendant's part, and states what remedy he seeks from the court. In the case of negligence, for example, the complaint will describe the injury; allege that the defendant's negligence caused the injury, thus making him liable; and seek relief, usually in the form of a monetary award for damages. The plaintiff may seek *general damages* to cover items like hospital bills, lost income, and damage to his property. The purpose of general damages is to compensate the plaintiff and to return him, as nearly as possible, to his condition prior to the alleged injury. In addition, if the defendant's behavior has been especially wanton, reckless, or reprehensible, the plaintiff may seek *punitive damages.* Punitive damages are designed to impose monetary punishment upon persons who act in a reckless manner toward their fellow human beings. Its purpose is to make an example of the defendant and warn others that society will not tolerate that type of behavior. Celebrities frequently ask for punitive damages against newspaper tabloids that exhibit "reckless disregard for the truth" when publishing stories about their private lives. After the complaint has been filed in the court with the appropriate jurisdiction, the next step is to notify the defendant formally that a legal action has been brought against him by the plaintiff. This is called the *service.* The defendant is served a copy of the complaint listing the allegations made against him by the plaintiff. Along with the copy of the complaint, the court clerk also issues a *summons* to the defendant. The summons directs the defendant to submit what is called an *answer* within a certain number of days. The answer is the defendant's written account of what happened. The defendant's answer, prepared by his attorney, will deny the facts as alleged in the complaint or deny liability, or both. Often the defendant will file a *demurrer,* or motion to dismiss the complaint; however, the motion is infrequently granted. It is extremely important that the defendant respond to the summons because failure to do so could result in a *default judgment* being given to the plaintiff. Failure to respond is tantamount to an admission of liability, and the plaintiff would become entitled to the damages sought in his complaint. For example, Wisconsin plaintiffs obtained default judgment in the amount of $12.6 billion when PepsiCo failed to file an answer.[13]

Discovery

After the pleadings have been completed, the process known as *discovery* begins. Despite the tendency of movie and television scriptwriters to create situations in which a surprise witness drops a bombshell, real-life court cases seldom happen that way. In fact, the general tendency is for both sides to lay all their cards on the table. This is done for a number of reasons. First, going through the formal trial process is expensive and time consuming. Second, putting the decision in the hands of a jury may be risky. A case may seem airtight to everyone but the jurors, and strange verdicts and awards are possible. A third reason for laying the cards on the table is to determine whether some facts of the dispute can be agreed upon beforehand, thus saving the need to establish them at the trial. Fourth, once the cards are on the table, one side or the other may decide it cannot win, and serious negotiations about a settlement may begin. Lawyers often find that their clients have not been totally candid with them. As a result, certain facts left out of the client's version of the events may come to the lawyer's attention during discovery. Either lawyer may then advise the client to settle the case out of court. Finally, both sides will know exactly what they are up against and can plan their courtroom strategies accordingly.

The Federal Rules of Civil Procedure mandate automatic disclosure of the following: (1) names, telephone numbers, and addresses of all individuals likely to have discoverable information relevant to the disputed facts or are likely to testify; (2) copies or descriptions by category and location of all documents, electronically stored information, and tangible things under the possession, custody, or control of the parties that may be used; (3) materials that are not privileged that relate to the computation of damages; and (4) any liability insurance agreements. Experts must also be identified, and those who are hired for litigation purposes only must provide written reports to all parties. The rules encourage discovery, even if the information sought cannot be used as evidence, if it is reasonable that the information could lead to the discovery of admissible evidence.[14] Most states adhere to the same philosophy and promote openness.

Discovery can take a number of forms. One of the more common ones is a *deposition* that may be taken in either of two ways. One way is to have a *witness* and/or one or more of the *parties* appear at the office of one of the lawyers in the case and answer questions put to him or her by the lawyer. The witness is under oath, and a stenographer records the questions and responses verbatim, or the interview is videotaped or otherwise electronically recorded. Alternatively, a witness may be questioned in the presence of both lawyers and subjected to direct questioning by one and cross-examination by the other. As in the first instance, everything said is recorded. Like all forms of discovery, a witness's testimony may be so devastating to one party's case that the lawyer may urge him to reach a settlement with the other party. Depositions may also be taken upon written questions submitted to either witnesses or litigants.[15]

An *interrogatory* is a second form of discovery. An interrogatory is a written question directed to one of the parties to the case by the other party. Unless questions are answered, the person may be cited for contempt. For example, if the case involved an automobile accident, a lawyer may ask, "Had you been drinking?", "How much?", "How fast were you driving?". As with depositions, the party must be truthful as he or she is under oath. In addition, if the party later gives contradictory testimony at trial, the answers given to the interrogatory may be used to impeach his or her credibility. Another form of written discovery is requests for admission. These are directed to the other party and relate to statements or opinions of fact or the application of law to fact. For example, the opposing party may admit that the document is the original contract or that the weather on the day of the accident was clear and sunny. The effect is that the matter is conclusively established at trial and thus expedites the trial proceedings.[16]

The last form of discovery involves the production of physical evidence, including electronic records, in the possession of one of the parties. The judge may issue a *subpoena duces tecum,* a court order requiring a person to appear in court or at deposition and to produce specified documents pertinent to the case. In a debt collection case, for example, the defendant may be required to produce a receipt or a canceled check as proof of payment of the debt. In a personal injury case, the plaintiff may have to produce copies of a medical exam report and of hospital and doctors' bills to establish the extent of the injury.

Discovery is designed to expedite the legal process. If certain facts can be agreed upon by both parties before the trial, these facts will only need to be recorded as having been stipulated as true by both sides. In a personal injury case, for example, the extent of the plaintiff's injury may be agreed upon by both sides because the real issue is not whether the plaintiff was injured or how badly injured, but whether the defendant was liable for the injury. This simplifies the case for the jury, thus enabling them to concentrate solely on the issue of liability.

Discovery can be extremely costly in terms of hours of preparation as well as money. Therefore, courts have adopted limitations on the number of depositions to be taken or the number of questions in interrogatories and requests for admissions, although the judge may grant exceptions. Failure to disclose information, to cooperate in discovery, or to supplement the disclosures and responses may result in the court holding the person in contempt, striking the pleadings, establishing the matter in contention as true for the purposes of trial, or dismissing the case.[17] To illustrate, a dispute involving the nonpayment of a life insurance policy on National Association for Stock Car Auto Racing (NASCAR) racing legend Dale Earnhardt resulted in a verdict for the plaintiff, Richard Childress Racing, when United of Omaha withheld 18 pages of documents that should have been produced, even though it had produced nearly 1400 pages of other materials.[18]

Remainder of the Pretrial Process

The parties may make a pretrial motion requesting a judgment on the pleadings that is treated as a motion for *summary judgment.*[19] In a personal injury suit, for example, if there is no dispute over the facts but only over the legal question of liability, the plaintiff may request that the judge grant a summary judgment in his or her favor; that is, the plaintiff is asking the judge to settle the legal question of the defendant's liability in favor of the plaintiff. If it is clear that the defendant's negligence caused the injury, the judge will grant the plaintiff's motion. In most cases, however, the defendant's negligence is not clear-cut, and the plaintiff's motion is denied. The defendant may also request a summary judgment. The plaintiff must make what is called a *prima facie case* in the pleadings. This term means that at first glance, or "first face," the plaintiff's version of the facts and legal theories is credible. If the plaintiff has failed to make a *prima facie* case, the defendant may ask the judge to rule that he was not negligent and to dismiss the plaintiff's case. As already noted, most cases are not easily settled if they have gone this far, and the motion is usually denied.

Other pretrial motions may also be filed. For example, parties may seek to limit the material considered by the jury because the evidence was seized improperly in criminal cases or because it is prejudicial, such as the fact that the defendant's insurance company would actually pay the judgment. An interpreter may be needed for someone who is deaf or whose first language is not English. An effort may be mounted to recuse the judge because of bias toward the issue or the litigants. There may have been extensive pretrial publicity that could affect the outcome of the trial, and the parties seek a change of venue.

Selection of the Jury

Once the preliminary maneuvering is over, the focus turns to the actual resolution of the conflict at trial. The first order of business is the selection of the jury, if a jury is to be used. The parties may choose to have a *bench trial,* in which the judge becomes the *trier of fact* while simultaneously acting as the interpreter of the law. After submission of the evidence, the judge alone will decide the outcome of the case. In highly complex or technical cases, the parties often prefer to let the judge decide the case because laypersons who comprise juries frequently lack the expertise to make a learned decision. In other cases (e.g., personal injury cases), the parties prefer to let the judge decide simply because juries are unpredictable, sometimes allowing irrelevant factors, such as the wealth of the defendant, to be considered in awarding damages.

If a jury is used, its members are selected from a pool of prospective persons, called a *venire.* Although we generally think of juries as comprising 12 persons, the number can be less than 12 (even as few as six) in civil cases if the parties agree, although individual states may set different rules.[20] Each prospective juror, or *venireman,* may be asked a few questions by each attorney and perhaps the judge. The initial questions are generally simple ones, designed more to put the person at ease than to elicit information. Then, lawyers seek to determine if the prospective juror has any prejudices concerning the client's case. For example, a lawyer representing an insurance company will try to ascertain the venireman's attitude toward insurance companies. If the venireman appears hostile to insurance companies, the lawyer will try to prevent that person's selection.

A venireman may be struck from a jury in two ways: challenge for cause and peremptory challenge. If, as we have seen, the lawyer's questioning reveals prejudice on the part of the venireman, the lawyer may cite that as a reason for excluding that person. This is known as a ***challenge for cause,*** and the judge must agree that the reason given is sufficient to exclude that person. The number of challenges for cause is unlimited. The second type of challenge is called a ***peremptory challenge;*** if a lawyer feels that a venireman's presence on the jury would harm her client's chances of winning but she cannot specify a reason sufficient to satisfy the judge, the lawyer may strike that person without giving any reason. Lawyers may not use the peremptory challenges to exclude jurors solely on the basis of race.[21] The Rules of Civil Procedure limit the number of peremptory challenges for each side to a specified number, three, while state requirements vary. This process of questioning prospective jurors and striking some from the jury is called ***voir dire***, which means "to speak truth."

CHAIN GANG

A 19-year-old college freshman was hauled into a Texas courtroom in ankle and wrist restraints by U.S. Marshals. The reason for her arrest? Failure to appear for jury duty. Although she could have claimed a student exemption, she chose not to do so. Her incensed father proclaimed, "Don't treat her like she murdered 25 people along the freeway. She's 19, she's ignorant, she's a kid." However, the federal judge who had her arrested demanded, "I'm going to hear exactly what your problem is with jury duty and what your problem is with how our country operates." Upon hearing the student's apology later in the week, the judge gave her a copy of the Constitution and advised her to discuss Articles III (the court system) and VII (guarantee to jury) with her attorney rather than holding her in contempt of court.

Source: Mary Flood, "Teen Who Skipped Jury Duty Apologizes to Judge," *Houston Chronicle*, April 29, 2010.

After the jurors have been selected they are sworn in and said to be ***impanelled.*** The jury's major function is to serve as the trier of fact. Jurors are to listen to the evidence presented in the case and decide who is telling the truth and which party deserves to win. In a sense, the jury serves as the conscience of the community. Although the jurors are not personally concerned with the outcome of the case, they are interested in seeing that the case is resolved in a peaceful, fair manner. For that reason, it is important that the jury be selected from a representative cross-section of the community. The parties to the case are more inclined to accept the final verdict if they perceive the jury to be fair and impartial. As we have noted, this acceptance by the parties is crucial to the acceptance of the legitimacy of the entire judicial system.

Submission of Evidence

After the jury has been impanelled, the trial begins. Each lawyer is allowed to make an ***opening statement*** to the jury, in which she outlines her case.

Generally speaking, the opening statement will inform the jury as to exactly what the lawyer intends to prove and how she plans to prove it. After both lawyers have made their opening statements, the plaintiff's lawyer calls her first witness. In civil law, because the plaintiff is the complaining party—that is, the one who initiated the lawsuit—he or she bears the burden of proof. The standard proof in civil law is the *preponderance of the evidence* standard; that is, a preponderance, or a majority, of the evidence must support the plaintiff's allegations against the defendant. If the plaintiff fails to meet this standard, the defendant will win the case. As noted earlier, the plaintiff bears the burden of establishing a *prima facie* case. Therefore, the plaintiff begins the trial by presenting his case to the jury.

The plaintiff's lawyer calls her first witness and proceeds to question him. This is known as *direct examination.* When the plaintiff's lawyer has finished, the defendant's lawyer may *cross-examine* the plaintiff's witness. On cross-examination, the defendant's lawyer is free either to limit her questions to topics raised by the plaintiff's lawyer or to open a new line of questioning. When the defendant's lawyer has finished, the plaintiff's lawyer may *redirect*, or ask additional questions of the same witness. On redirect examination, however, the plaintiff's lawyer may ask only questions raised by the defendant's lawyer on cross-examination; she may not open a new line of questioning. Upon completion of redirect, the defendant's lawyer may *re-cross-examine* but also is limited to questions raised on redirect. When both lawyers have asked all of their questions, the witness is excused.

Strict rules of procedure govern the questioning of witnesses and the admission of evidence. The *hearsay rule*, for example, forbids witnesses from testifying about facts of which they have no direct knowledge or information. Lawyers are forbidden to ask *leading questions* of their own witness. A question such as "Did you see the defendant strike the plaintiff on the evening of May 1?" would be improper. However, the question "What did you see on or about 6 p.m. on the evening of May 1?" would be acceptable. During the questioning of a witness, a lawyer may note an objection to either the other lawyer's question or the witness's response. The judge must make a ruling to either sustain the objection as valid or overrule it as invalid. These objections, and the judge's subsequent rulings, may provide the losing party with the legal grounds on which to base a future appeal. Objections to a judge's ruling must be timely; after-the-fact objections when the trial is over usually do not provide grounds for an appeal.

During the examination of witnesses, the lawyers will submit physical evidence to substantiate their cases. For example, while questioning the attending physician in a personal injury suit, the lawyer may introduce into evidence a copy of the written medical report on the plaintiff's injury. As with testimony, the defendant's lawyer may object to the introduction of the medical report, forcing the judge to make a ruling on its admissibility. The judge's ruling may also serve as grounds for an appeal if the ruling is incorrect. Any incorrect ruling may be considered a reversible error by an appeals court at some later date. Reversible error may result in a new trial for the losing party.

As we can easily see, the presentation of evidence is the heart of the trial. Because the evidentiary stage of the trial proceeding is so important, we will return to it later in this chapter in order to examine in greater depth the rules of evidence as they apply to both civil and criminal cases. For now, let us continue with our overview of civil procedure.

After the plaintiff's lawyer has called all of her witnesses and submitted all of her physical evidence, the defense may present its side of the case. The defense calls its rebuttal witnesses and the same procedure of questioning is followed, except this time it is the defendant's lawyer who conducts direct examination and the plaintiff's lawyer who cross-examines. The main strategy of the defense is to rebut as much of the plaintiff's damaging evidence or to employ legal defenses. One way to rebut a plaintiff's negligence case is to discuss the plaintiff's role in his injury. If the defendant's lawyer can show that the plaintiff was wholly or partially responsible for his own injuries, the defendant is not wholly liable. The theory is that the plaintiff should come before the whole court with clean hands; that is, he should be able to show that he did not contribute to his own injury through his own negligence. Another defense strategy is to claim *voluntary assumption of risk*; that is, that the person attending the baseball game assumes the risk of being hit by the baseball.

Following the submission of all the oral and physical evidence, the two lawyers will address the jury a final time in their *closing statements*. The plaintiff's lawyer will summarize her case to the jury with the assertion that a preponderance of the evidence supports her client's claims against the defendant. The defendant's lawyer will summarize her own rebuttal evidence and ask the jury to rule in favor of her client.

Final Actions

Once the evidentiary stage of the trial is complete, some additional legal maneuvering is possible before the case is actually submitted to the jury. Either side may request a *directed verdict.* A motion for a directed verdict is a lawyer's request that the judge direct the jury to bring in a verdict favorable to her client. If, for example, the plaintiff has failed to carry the burden of proof in the case, the judge may well grant the defense lawyer's motion for a directed verdict. Similarly, if the defendant has failed to rebut successfully the plaintiff's allegations and evidence, the judge may grant the plaintiff's motion. Generally, however, few judges are willing to take the decision out of the hands of the jury, and so these motions are routinely denied. Like all denied motions, the judge's refusal to order a directed verdict can be appealed.

Once all the formal proceedings have completed with the attorney's closing statements, the judge charges the jury. In her *charge to the jury,* the judge explains the applicable law as it relates to the case and describes what the jury must decide if they are to rule in favor of the plaintiff. The judge also explains what the jury must find if they are to rule for the defendant. Great emphasis is placed on the instructions to the jury, and many decisions, especially in criminal cases, are reversed solely because of flawed jury charges; the result is that judges and the attorneys preparing the charge rely heavily on pattern jury instructions that have been approved in prior litigation. After the charge has been completed, the case is formally submitted to the jury.

JUROR MADE TO "FACE" THE MUSIC

Facebook postings often are seeking guidance and advice from friends, including one inquiry that read, "I don't know which way to go, so I'm holding a poll." What made this solicitation different was that it was posted by an English juror who provided details of the child abduction and sexual assault case on the website in defiance of instructions not to discuss the case with anyone and asked her mates for their opinion. Upon receiving an anonymous tip, the judge immediately dismissed the juror, who faced contempt charges, and the trial proceeded with only 11 jurors. The attorney general eventually declined to prosecute her.

Source: Guy Patrick, "Juror Axed for Verdict Poll on Net," *The Sun*, November 24, 2008; Sean O'Grady, "Trial Juror not Punished for Facebook Postings," *The Independent*, December 17, 2008.

Jury Conduct, Deliberation, and Verdict

From capital murder cases to federal corruption trials, "[t]he explosive growth of social networking has placed enormous pressure on one of the most fundamental of American institutions: the impartial jury. Through social networking services like Facebook and Twitter, jurors have committed significant and often high-profile acts of misconduct." [22] One *potential* juror in a murder trial tweeted, "[g]uilty, guilty ... I will not be swayed. Practicing for jury duty," [23] while a person actually selected stated that the defendant was "presumed guilty." It was this same juror who posted that another juror's knuckle-cracking was so annoying that she wanted to "punch" the other juror. The posts were made from the courthouse. [24]

In a widely reported and particularly egregious case in Illinois, a juror frequently, after leaving the courtroom, "logged into her blog and wrote an entry describing the dialogue that took place in the jury room that day." Her blog posts included information about the demographics of the jury, the identity of the witnesses at trial, and the weight of the evidence at trial. [25]

Judges strive to forestall jury misconduct by issuing expanded instructions from the beginning to both potential jurors and those selected in an attempt to combat any potential bias or prejudice. Most states and the federal courts use a version of the model instructions crafted by the United States Judicial Conference Committee on Court Administration and Case Management (CACM). The instructions given at the beginning and conclusion of trials (and perhaps in the middle of long trials) include the following prohibitions. Jurors may not use any of the following to obtain information about the case, about case processes or legal terms, or to conduct any research about the case: any electronic device or media, such as a telephone, cell phone, smart phone, or computer; the Internet, any Internet service, or any text or instant messaging service, RSS feed, or other automatic alert that may transmit information regarding the case to the juror; or any Internet chat room, blog, or website.[26] Judges and lawyers are generally also not permitted to comment about the ongoing trial through social media or other electronic devices; however, it is common for lawyers and litigants to gather information on judges, parties, clients, opposing counsel, and potential jurors through the use of social media.

The jurors have the case; the fate of both parties is in their hands.[27] In a negligence case, such as the one we have been discussing, the jury is called upon to render one of two types of verdicts. The first type is called a *general verdict*. Under a general verdict, the jury could find the defendant liable and award the plaintiff the monetary damages he sought, less than what he sought, or more than what he sought. The jury could also find that the defendant was not liable; the plaintiff would then not be entitled to damages. A second type of verdict, called a *special issues verdict*, presents the jury with a series of questions that it must answer. For example, in a comparative negligence case, the first question might be, "Do you find the defendant liable for the plaintiff's injury?" If the answer is "Yes," the next question might be, "Do you find the defendant 10 percent liable?" The percentage—20 percent, 30 percent, and so forth—is increased incrementally until the jury reaches the appropriate degree of comparative liability for each party. Damages would then be awarded to the plaintiff on the basis of the percentage of comparative liability. If, for example, the total amount of damages sought by the plaintiff was $50,000 but the jury found the defendant only 60 percent liable, then the defendant would pay the plaintiff only $30,000 in damages. Of course, should the jury rule that the defendant was not liable for the plaintiff's injuries, there is no other decision to be made and the jury's job is done.

After the jury has reached its verdict, the foreperson informs the bailiff, who, in turn, notifies the judge. Court is reconvened, and the jury's verdict is formally read. On the federal level, if the parties agree, verdicts in civil cases need not be unanimous; each state sets its own rules on unanimity of verdicts.[28] The judge may poll each individual juror to make sure there is no mistake about the decision. The judge then thanks the jurors for their service and dismisses them. The trial stage of this particular civil case is now complete.

Appellate Procedure

The person who loses the case at trial has the right to appeal the decision. The grounds for the appeal may vary but generally fall into two categories. The first alleges that the judge made an error or errors regarding questions of law. Recall our previous discussion of the need for attorneys to make timely objections to the judge's rulings on points of law. When an attorney makes such an objection and the judge overrules it, there is a disagreement over a point of law. That disagreement provides the legal grounds upon which the appeal may be based.

The appellate court must first decide whether the trial judge was correct in his or her ruling. If the trial judge is ruled to have been incorrect, the appellate court must next determine whether the error was serious enough to warrant a new trial. In the case of a *reversible error,* the appellate court concludes that the error was so serious that it may have adversely affected the outcome of the trial. In that instance, a new trial will generally be ordered. If the error is found to be a *harmless error,* however, the judgment of the trial court will be affirmed. An appellate court will frequently refuse to overrule the trial judge if the alleged error falls into an area committed to the trial judge's discretion. In such an instance, the trial judge is presumed to be correct and the appellate court is precluded from overruling her.

The second category of appeals, known as *remittitur,* occurs in cases in which monetary damages have been awarded. Such appeals are often based on the grounds that the award was excessive. Juries find it difficult to determine the proper monetary damages to be awarded. In a libel suit, for example, how much is a person's reputation worth, and how can money compensate the victim for damage to his reputation? These are difficult questions to answer, and juries sometimes get carried away and award more in damages than is warranted. An appellate court may reduce the award if, in its judgment, the award was excessive. For example, the Florida Supreme Court upheld the reduction of a $144.8 billion class action verdict against tobacco companies to $7,000,000 for two members of the class while allowing some other class members to pursue further claims and precluding others.[29]

BASEBALL, REVERSIBLE AND HARMLESS ERRORS

The concept of reversible and harmless errors can easily be explained using a baseball analogy. Suppose the Yankees are leading the Red Sox 9 to 0 in the bottom of the ninth inning. With two runners in scoring position, the Yankee shortstop makes a wild throw to first base, and both runners score to make it 9 to 2. The rest of the batters in the ninth make outs and the final score is 9 to 2. The shortstop's error is considered a harmless one, because it did not change the outcome of the game, only the final score. However, assume the Yankees are only ahead 3 to 2. Now suppose the same play occurs with the shortstop making an error and allowing the two runners to score, with a resulting loss of 4 to 3 for the Yankees. The shortstop's error reversed the outcome of the game, turning a potential win into a loss. Likewise, in a court case, a reversible error is one in which the outcome, without the error, may have been different.

As a general rule, litigants have the "right" to one appeal of a trial court decision. The right to an appeal must be based on a statute or it may be granted with the permission of the court. The person requesting the appeal is called the *appellant,* and the person against whom an appeal is made is called the *appellee.* Because state appellate procedures vary, the following discussion summarizes the federal appellate process for a civil case as outlined in *The Federal Rules of Appellate Procedure.*[30] Federal courts generally accept or require electronic filing of the many documents necessary in the appellate process; the trend is to mandate all filings be done electronically.

The first step in the appeals process in a civil case is for the appellant to file a notice of appeal. The appellant (normally the losing party at trial) must file a notice of appeal with the clerk of the U.S. district court within 30 days of the date of the district court's judgment. If the United States, one of its officials, or one of its agencies is a party to the case, 60 days are allowed to file a notice of appeal. The district court may, for good cause or excusable neglect, extend the time allowed for filing an appeal. The notice of appeal must specify the party making the appeal and designate the judgment (or part thereof) appealed from and the court to which the appeal is made. The district court clerk must mail a copy of the notice of appeal to the counsel of record for the appellee and another copy to the clerk of the court of appeals. The appellant must also pay the appropriate fees to the district court clerk, who also receives the docket fee on behalf of the court of appeals.[31]

Within 14 days of filing the notice of appeal, the appellant must order a copy of the transcript of the lower court proceeding from the court reporter. Transcripts need cover only those parts of the trial actually under appeal. Fourteen days after the transcript is ordered, the appellant must file a statement of the issues to be appealed unless the entire transcript is to be ordered. If not, the appellant must send the appellee a copy of the statement of the issues and a copy of the appellant's transcript order. Within 14 days of receiving the copy, the appellee may request a copy of the appellant's transcript and any additional pages of the transcript the appellee may need. Each party pays the cost of the respective transcript requests. Alternatively, at this point the two parties may agree to a statement on how the issues under appeal arose.[32]

Whenever either party takes certain actions concerning the appeal, it is required to notify the other party of the action taken by the process, called *service*. For example, the appellant is required to serve the statement of issues to the appellee. Service may be *personal service,* service by mail, service by a third-party commercial carrier for delivery within three calendar days, or service by electronic means if the party being served agrees in writing. Personal service would include delivery of the notice to the appellee's attorney including a responsible party at the counsel's office. Whatever the method, proof of service is required.[33]

Once the notice of appeal, docket entries, and other forms have been properly filed, the clerk of the court of appeals enters the appeal on the court of appeals court docket. The clerk also notifies the parties of the date on which the record was filed. Within 40 days after the date on which the record is filed, the appellant must file a written *brief* called the *principal brief.* The appellant's principal brief must contain a table of contents, corporate disclosure statement if applicable, table of authorities (a form of bibliography), jurisdictional statement, statement of the issues being appealed, statement of the case including the nature of the case and the disposition below, statement of the facts relevant to the review of the case, legal arguments with citations, a short conclusion stating the precise relief sought, and a certificate of compliance regarding the font–volume limitation. For instance, the appellant's principal brief may not exceed 30 pages; it cannot contain more than 14,000 words or more than 1300 lines of text in a mono-spaced font of no more than 10.5 characters per inch.[34] The appellant must provide 25 copies of the principal brief to the court and two copies to counsel for each party. If the appellant fails to file a brief, the appellee may move for a dismissal of the appeal.[35]

The appellee has 30 days after receiving the appellant's principal brief to submit a brief.[36] The appellee's brief must generally follow the same format as the appellant's, although certain elements such as the jurisdictional statement may be omitted if there is not disagreement; the page limit may not exceed 30 pages in length.[37] The appellee must also submit 25 copies of the brief to the court and two copies to each appellant. If the appellee fails to file a brief, the court may deny him the right to be heard at oral argument. Fourteen days after receiving the appellee's brief, the appellant may file a *reply brief*. The reply brief may not exceed 15 pages, and the same requirements about the number of copies apply.[38]

The next stage of the appellate process is an optional one; that is, the court *may* direct the parties to participate in a prehearing conference. The prehearing conference is an attempt to simplify the issues being appealed and any other matters under dispute. The prehearing conference tries to win a consensus on possible areas of agreement in order to expedite the proceedings.[39]

The court of appeals is finally ready to hear the case. The clerk schedules *oral argument* and notifies the parties of the date, time, place, and amount of time allotted for the hearing. Oral argument is the part of the procedure where the lawyers for the parties appear before the judges to argue their sides of the case. The appellant's lawyer is permitted to open and conclude oral argument. Lawyers are not permitted to read extensively from their briefs and are expected to be prepared to answer questions the judges may ask. If either side should fail to appear at oral argument, the court will hear the arguments of the side that is represented. If neither side appears, the court will decide the case on the basis of the written briefs. The court must schedule oral arguments unless a three-judge panel has unanimously agreed

> that the appeal is frivolous; that the dispositive facts or issues have been authoritatively decided; or that facts and legal arguments are adequately presented in the briefs and record and that the decisional process would not be significantly aided by oral argument.[40]

Occasionally, a court of appeals will be asked to hear a case *en banc*. This means that the entire court, not just a panel of three judges, will hear the case. Generally, the court will agree to an *en banc* hearing if the case raises a question of exceptional importance or when an *en banc* hearing is necessary to ensure uniformity of the court's decisions. For example, two separate panels could rule differently on essentially the same point of law. An *en banc* hearing can provide a definitive ruling binding on all members of the court.[41]

Decisions of the court of appeals are by majority vote. Upon receipt of the court's judgment, the clerk makes a notation in the court docket, which constitutes the entry of judgment. Written opinions are frequent but not required. Dissenting and concurring opinions may also be filed by the judges. The clerk then serves copies of the judgment and any opinions to all parties.[42] Within 14 days after the entry of judgment, unless the United States is a party, in which case the time is extended to 45 days, the losing party may file a petition for rehearing. The petition for rehearing may not exceed 15 pages and is filed and served just like the briefs. There is no oral argument about the petition for rehearing.[43] If the petition for rehearing is granted, the court may make final disposition of the case without reargument, restore the case to the calendar for reargument, or issue other appropriate orders. However, in most cases, petitions for rehearing are denied, and the judgment of the court of appeals is final.

If the appellant wins his appeal, the trial court's judgment is usually altered in some fashion. The court of appeals may order a new trial to be held or simply remand the case with orders to correct the lower court's judgment. If the appellant wins, the appellee must bear the cost of the appeal unless the court orders otherwise. The appellee, however, may choose to appeal the appellate court's ruling to the Supreme Court. If that is done, the appellee is now the appellant. If the appellant loses the appeal, the judgment of the trial court is affirmed and he generally pays the cost of the appeal. The appellant may also choose to appeal to the Supreme Court; however, as noted in Chapter 3, access to the Supreme Court is limited, and for most litigants the decision of the court of appeals ends the case.

The Supreme Court has both original and appellate jurisdiction, but as a practical matter it functions almost entirely as an appellate court. For example, in the 2013 Term, there were 8850 cases filed with the Court, of which only five were cases coming to it under its original jurisdiction.[44] There are three ways in which a case may reach the Supreme Court under its appellate jurisdiction. The first is an appeal as a matter of right. Congress has stipulated that under certain conditions a party has an absolute right to have a case heard by the Court. For example, if a state law has been declared unconstitutional because it conflicts with a U.S. statute or treaty or with the Constitution itself, the State may appeal to the Supreme Court. In reality however, the Court may refuse further considerations of the merits of the case by dismissing it for "lack of a substantial federal question." Just what constitutes a "substantial" federal question is simply left to the discretion of the justices.

The second avenue of appeal is through the **_writ of certiorari_**. A _writ of certiorari_ is an order from a higher court to a lower court to send up the record of a case so that the higher court may review it. Since 1925, the Supreme Court has had complete discretion in deciding whether or not to issue _certiorari_ in specific cases. The Court operates under the **_rule of four_**, which states at least four of the nine justices must agree that a case merits the Court's attention before it will issue the writ.

The final way in which a case may reach the Supreme Court is through **_certification_**. Certification is used when a lower court seeks clarification on a question of law before it can make a ruling in a case. For example, President Franklin D. Roosevelt once dismissed a man named William E. Humphrey from the Federal Trade Commission (FTC). Humphrey sued the government for lost wages. The lower court, before it could decide whether Humphrey was entitled to his lost wages, first had to decide whether his dismissal had been legal. In *Humphrey's Executor v. United States*,[45] the Supreme Court ruled that the dismissal was not legal. Cases that reach the Court through certification are relatively rare because the Court seems to prefer that the lower court make a ruling, which it may then later review if it chooses to do so.

Once the Supreme Court has agreed to hear a case, both parties are required to submit written briefs stating the exact nature of the controversy, their side's position, the legal precedents upon which they are relying, and arguments justifying why the Court should rule in their favor. In addition, all transcripts and other court papers from the proceedings of the lower courts are submitted to the Court. *Oral argument* is next; here the attorneys for both parties appear in person before the justices to argue the case. Each side is given 30 minutes to present its case, with the understanding that any justice may interrupt to question the lawyers. Oral argument is not just a rehash of the written briefs; it is designed to allow the justices to clarify issues presented by the case before the Court.

The actual outcome of the case is decided during the Supreme Court's conference. By tradition, each justice shakes the hand of the other eight justices upon entering the conference room. This is to ensure that the conference begins on a friendly note. The Chief Justice presides over the discussion of the case, and then a tentative vote is taken. At least six of the nine justices must participate in order to decide a case, and a simple majority determines the outcome. If, for example, one justice fails to participate in a case and the others are deadlocked four to four, the decision of the highest court below the Supreme Court will stand. In such instances, a similar case that raises the same issue will have to come before the Court before there will be resolution.

After the case has been discussed and voted upon in conference, the next stage is the opinion writing. If the Chief Justice is in the majority, he assigns the task of writing the *majority opinion* to one of the justices in the majority that includes, of course, himself. If the Chief Justice is not in the majority, the job of assigning the majority opinion goes to the senior associate justice in the majority. The majority opinion is important for several reasons. First, it explains to the parties directly involved in the case why each side won or lost. Second, it establishes a precedent for future cases that raise the same substantive issue. Third, it provides cues for court watchers about how the Court might decide similar issues in future cases.

Although there is no official "minority opinion," the justices in the minority may informally decide that one of them should write the main *dissenting opinion* setting forth the reasons for the minority's disagreement with the majority. However, any of the justices in the minority is free to write a separate dissent or to join another's dissent, or both. In addition to being critical of the majority's legal reasoning or analysis of a case, dissenting opinions can provide the opponents of a particular decision with powerful arguments for opposing that decision. In addition, a well-argued dissent may even convince enough members of the majority to change their minds, turning a minority into a majority; a justice may change his or her mind at any time prior to the actual announcement of the decision in the case.

There are instances in which a majority of the Court may agree on the outcome of a case—that is, on who should win the case—but cannot agree on the reasons why the party should win. For example, a justice may agree that one side should prevail but cannot agree with the legal reasoning given in the majority opinion. In such instances a justice may choose to write a separate *concurring opinion.* A concurring opinion is one in which the justice agrees with the outcome of the case but not entirely with the legal grounds relied upon by the majority. In a concurring opinion, a justice sets forth his or her own rationale for reaching the same result as the majority. Concurring opinions often do little more than provide alternate grounds for reaching the Court's decision. However, there are situations in which the consequences of a concurrence could be significant. Suppose, for example, the Court were divided five to four in a particular case and one of the justices in the majority refused to sign the majority opinion, preferring to write a separate concurring opinion. In this case there would be no majority opinion. Instead, the opinion of the four remaining justices in the majority becomes what is known as a *plurality opinion.* The outcome of the case would not be changed in this situation, but the case would have no value as a precedent because a majority of the Court could not agree on the legal grounds for the case. This is another situation in which the issue will probably have to come before the Court again for final resolution.

Written opinions of the Court are products of much compromise. The justice assigned to write the majority opinion drafts a copy of the opinion and circulates it among the other eight justices for comment and criticism. At the same time, any justice writing a separate dissenting or concurring opinion does the same. In this manner, each justice knows exactly what arguments the others plan to use in their opinions and may use that information in writing subsequent drafts of his or her own opinion. A justice may incorporate any comments suggested by another justice in the final draft of the opinion. The author of the majority opinion must be especially careful in drafting that opinion, because failure to take into account the suggestions of the other justices in the majority could lead to one or more concurring opinions—a situation that should be avoided if possible. Obviously, authors of dissenting and concurring opinions, while sensitive to the criticisms of the other justices, do not have to worry about keeping a majority together. Consequently, they are freer to express their own views in their opinions.

When all of the opinions have been written and rewritten, the Court is ready to announce its decision. The justices assemble in the courtroom, and the Chief Justice announces that the Court's decision has been made. The author of the majority opinion summarizes the Court's decision, and any other justices who have written separately may summarize their opinions. The process of Supreme Court decision making is now complete.

Once all appeals have been exhausted and a final judgment entered, the civil case is over except for the execution of the trial court's decision. In a negligence case such as we have been using to illustrate the civil process, the defendant will have to pay the damages awarded at the trial. This may require the defendant to sell his property or to borrow the needed money, but it usually means the defendant's insurance company will pay. Should a defendant refuse to pay the damages, the plaintiff may resort to two alternatives to get what is due to him. First, the plaintiff may ask the court for a *writ of execution.* This writ authorizes a sheriff or other law enforcement officer to seize the property or bank accounts of the defendant. If property is seized, the sheriff may sell it at auction. The plaintiff's award plus any additional expenses are deducted from the proceeds, and the remainder is returned to the defendant. The second course of action is *garnishment.* In some states, the defendant's salary may be garnished to pay the plaintiff. This means that a certain percentage of the defendant's salary is withheld from his paycheck until the plaintiff's award is paid in full. The drastic measures described here are necessary to enforce the court's authority. The victorious party, in this case the plaintiff, must be able to rely on the power of government to enforce the judgment. Otherwise, as suggested at the beginning of this chapter, few persons would be willing to go through the trouble of bringing a lawsuit, and many would resort to extralegal or illegal methods to resolve conflicts.

CRIMINAL PROCEDURE

Criminal and civil processes are similar enough that it is unnecessary to repeat every step of the procedure in detail. However, the reader should keep in mind the major difference between the two procedures. The defendant who loses a civil suit may be forced, as we have just seen, to pay damages to the plaintiff and perhaps even have his property confiscated in the process. As serious as that penalty may be, it hardly compares to the loss of life or liberty the criminal defendant faces upon conviction for a crime. It is because the consequences of a criminal conviction are so serious that the U.S. system of justice goes to great (some say excessive) lengths to ensure that the innocent go free and only the guilty are punished.

Another important distinction about the criminal justice system must also be understood. A person who is *factually* guilty—that is, one who really committed the crime of which he or she is accused—must be found to be *legally* guilty as well.[46] Unless the determination of legal guilt is accompanied by strict adherence to the rules of criminal procedure, there is denial of due process of law. No matter how firmly convinced we may be that the accused actually committed the crime, the full coercive power of the State cannot be imposed until legal guilt has been proven "beyond a reasonable doubt." Our belief that a person is innocent until proven guilty reflects the difference between factual and legal guilt. With these two distinctions in mind, we begin our discussion of criminal procedure with the reminder that the details of the process vary from state to state as well as on the national level; however, there is a minimal level of due process required in all forums.

Pretrial Procedures

The process of criminal justice begins with the arrest of the defendant. The defendant's arrest may result from a complaint sworn out by the victim, a witness, or a police officer, who is called the *complaining witness.* The complaint is sworn out before a magistrate, who then issues an *arrest warrant.* If the crime was committed in the presence of a police officer, he or she is the complaining witness and will secure the arrest warrant from the magistrate if the defendant is not already in custody. The arrest warrant authorizes the police to take the accused into custody and to bring the accused before the magistrate. Codes of criminal procedure authorize warrantless arrests in limited circumstances as, for example, when the officer observes the commission of a felony; nevertheless, the preference is always for a warrant to conduct a search or to make an arrest.

When the accused is taken into custody, he is brought before the magistrate "without undue delay" for what is termed the *initial appearance.* Prior to the famous *Miranda v. Arizona*[47] decision, the major purpose of the initial appearance was to allow the magistrate to inform the accused of his constitutional rights to remain silent and to have the assistance of counsel. At one time, the police, in their eagerness to secure confessions, unfortunately often delayed presenting the accused before a magistrate until after he had been subjected to the lengthy periods of questioning. In *Mallory v. United States*,[48] the accused, Andrew Mallory, was arrested in the early afternoon and was questioned throughout the day until he confessed. Mallory was not brought before a magistrate and informed of his constitutional right to remain silent until the next day. The Supreme Court overturned Mallory's conviction on the grounds that the police had acted improperly in delaying Mallory's initial appearance. In addition, according to the Court, the fact that Mallory was of fairly low intelligence made it even more imperative that he have the assistance of counsel.

As a result of the *Mallory* and *Miranda* decisions the police are obliged to inform the accused of his constitutional rights whenever a custodial arrest is made, thus lessening the importance of the initial appearance. The initial appearance remains significant, however, because the magistrate will inform the accused of his right to a *preliminary hearing* and will set *bond* for him. Bond is money or property left as security to ensure that the accused will not flee from the jurisdiction of the court. If the magistrate feels that the accused is reliable, has ties to the community, or is unlikely to flee, he may release the accused on his own *recognizance.*

Unless the accused waives it, the next step may be the preliminary hearing. The purpose of the preliminary hearing is to determine whether there is *probable cause* to believe that a crime has been committed and whether there exists sufficient evidence that the accused committed it. The preliminary hearing is largely one-sided, with the prosecutor offering enough evidence to convince the judge that there is sufficient probable cause to continue proceedings against the accused. Should the judge decide that sufficient probable cause exists, the accused is ***bound over*** for trial. If probable cause is insufficient, the accused is released but may be rearrested and recharged at some future time. As indicated, accused persons often waive their right to a preliminary hearing on the advice of counsel because the police have enough evidence to have the accused bound over for trial.

The next stage of the criminal justice process is the formal accusation, called the ***indictment***. About half of the states and the federal government have indictment by ***grand jury***. A grand jury is a body of between 12 and 23 persons who decide whether the accused should be tried for a crime. The grand jury passes a ***true bill***, a declaration that there is sufficient evidence to require the accused to stand trial. The passage of the true bill by a majority of the grand jury constitutes the indictment. If the grand jurors decide that there is insufficient evidence, they return a ***no bill***. Critics of the grand jury maintain that it is little more than a rubber stamp for the prosecutor because a grand jury rarely fails to follow the prosecutor's recommendation in a case.[49] Defenders of the grand jury system maintain that it serves to protect accused persons from malicious prosecution and harassment by unscrupulous prosecutors. As is often the case, one's perspective is based on one's view of the criminal justice system.

The remaining states have chosen to use what is called indictment by ***information***. Under this method the indictment is made at the discretion of the prosecuting attorney. Indictment by information is preferred by those who seek greater efficiency in criminal justice because it is less troublesome than the grand jury system. Although subject to possible abuse by overzealous prosecutors, the states that use indictment by information seem to be satisfied with it.

Following the indictment the accused is brought before a judge for ***arraignment***. At the arraignment the accused is formally notified of the charges and is asked to enter a plea. The accused may plead not guilty, in which case a trial will be scheduled. A second option is for the accused to plead guilty. If the defendant's lawyer and the prosecutor have worked out a ***plea bargain*** the defendant may agree to plead guilty in exchange for leniency or some other consideration on the part of the judge. Plea bargains, therefore, are arrangements by which the defendant exchanges a guilty plea for a reduced sentence, a lesser offense, or dismissal of other charges.[50]

Finally, the defendant may choose to plead ***nolo contendere*** to the charges, which literally means "no contest." A *nolo contendere* plea is tantamount to a plea of guilty, and the judge is free to impose any sentence allowable after either a guilty plea or a conviction at trial. The major difference is that a *nolo* plea is a denial of ***culpability*** on the part of the defendant. In effect, the defendant denies any moral wrongdoing. A *nolo* plea also serves as a "face-saving" device for a person like Spiro T. Agnew, who was allowed to plead *nolo contendere* to bribery and corruption charges in Maryland in exchange for his resignation from the vice presidency in October 1973. If for any reason the defendant should refuse to enter a plea, the judge will merely enter a not-guilty plea on his or her behalf.

The discovery process in the criminal process is different from the one we saw in the civil process. Recall that in a civil proceeding either party may request a deposition or send questions, in the form of interrogatories, to the other party. In a criminal case on the other hand, the accused may not be forced to answer interrogatories or give a deposition because the Fifth Amendment protects him against self-incrimination. The accused does not have to prove his innocence, nor may he be forced to assist the State in proving its case against him. The accused is entitled to know what evidence of his guilt the prosecutor has however, so that his lawyer can prepare an adequate defense. This is another example of how the rules of criminal procedure are tilted in favor of the defendant. Given the resources that the State may bring to bear to secure the defendant's conviction, this small advantage is somewhat justified.

The pretrial conference in a criminal case is similar to that in a civil suit. The defendant's lawyer and the prosecutor hammer out with the judge the basic issues of the case and any facts that can be agreed upon beforehand. If, for example, the defendant is pleading not guilty by reason of insanity in a murder case, the defense may be willing to stipulate that the accused killed the victim. The real issue is the question of the defendant's sanity, and the trial will revolve primarily around that issue. Once these ground rules have been agreed upon, the trial stage begins.

Criminal Trial Stage

The trial process for civil and criminal cases is very similar, so we will highlight only significant differences between the two. One such difference is in jury selection. Criminal procedure usually allows more peremptory challenges than are allowed in civil cases. In Texas, for example, each side is allowed 15 peremptory challenges in a capital case and ten in a noncapital felony case.[51] Once the *voir dire* process is completed and the jury is impanelled, the defendant is said to be in *jeopardy.* The significance of being placed in jeopardy is that the Fifth Amendment to the U.S. Constitution declares that no person shall "be twice put in jeopardy of life or limb." In other words, if the defendant is acquitted or the charges are subsequently dropped, she may not be tried again for the same offense. However, a person who is accused of an act that is both a state and federal crime, such as the assassination of a federal judge, may be tried at both levels.

Another important difference between a civil trial and a criminal trial is the standard of proof required for each. Under the rules of civil procedure, in order for the plaintiff to prevail, he must show that the weight, or preponderance, of evidence favors his version of the facts. In a criminal case however, the State, as the plaintiff, must meet a higher standard—beyond a reasonable doubt. One way to think of the beyond-a-reasonable-doubt standard is to consider and then reject all other possible explanations for the crime except the conclusion that the defendant did indeed commit the crime for which she is being tried. All alternative or feasible explanations of who may have committed the crime other than the defendant are considered and discarded. In presenting evidence, the prosecutor seeks to establish that the conclusion that the defendant is guilty of committing the crime is the only conclusion a reasonable person could reach. The job of the defendant's lawyer is to create a reasonable doubt in the minds of the jurors in order to avoid a guilty verdict. If state law requires a unanimous verdict, a single juror may cause a *hung jury.* In the event of a hung jury, the State retains the right to either retry the defendant on the same charge or on a lesser (but not greater) charge without violating the double jeopardy clause. Finally, the prosecutor may decide that a new trial will not result in a conviction and drop the charges against the defendant.

A third difference between the civil and criminal processes involves the directed verdict. After each side has presented its case, the defense may request a directed verdict from the judge. While the defense may ask the judge to direct the jury to return a not-guilty verdict, the State may not request a directed guilty verdict. The defense's argument is that the State has failed to make a *prima facie* case against the defendant. This is another example of how the rules of criminal procedure tend to favor the defendant. The presumption is that the defendant, who is without the vast resources possessed by the State, must be given some advantages to offset the power that the State is capable of marshaling against him.

After the closing statements and the charge, the men and women of the jury begin their deliberations. In routine cases, the jury will reach a verdict in a relatively short period of time. In highly publicized cases, the judge may order the jury *sequestered* from the time the first juror is selected or when the jury panel is complete. The jurors are then isolated until they either reach a verdict or inform the judge that they are hopelessly deadlocked. The judge must be very careful about how long she allows a deadlocked jury to deliberate. Naturally, the judge (and perhaps the parties) would prefer a definite verdict in order to avoid another trial. However, the jury may not be pressured to bring in a verdict, especially if it turns out to be a guilty verdict. The defendant, on appeal, could argue that the lengthy deliberation indicated reasonable doubt among some of the jurors and that these "holdouts" were pressured to change their votes to "guilty" in order to avoid prolonging their ordeal. Such undue pressure could constitute reversible error, resulting in a new trial for the defendant.

"HIT ME WITH YOUR BEST SHOT, FIRE AWAY!"©

Pat Benatar's hit song "Hit Me With Your Best Shot" illustrates the reason for the prohibition against double jeopardy and why the State cannot appeal a conviction. The prosecution represents the power of the State and the individual is David to the State's Goliath. Notwithstanding how that biblical battle ended, the fact is the State is the giant in the criminal justice process. Therefore, society has determined that the State had better hit the defendant with its "best shot" because it is not going to have another shot at depriving the defendant of his life or liberty. In other words, the State had better do it right the first time because it won't get another chance.

A final way in which criminal and civil cases differ is in the right of appeal. The defendant, of course, is free to appeal her conviction based on errors made during the trial. The State, however, can appeal an acquittal only on rare occasions. Generally speaking, the State may appeal an acquittal only to clarify a matter of law. That is, if the prosecutor believes that the judge has rendered an incorrect legal ruling, the State may appeal the ruling to clarify the point of law for future reference. The defendant actually tried in the case involving the disputed ruling cannot be retried without violating the double jeopardy clause.

The appellate process in a criminal case can be long and arduous if the defendant is willing to pursue it. Conviction for a crime in a state court allows the defendant to avail himself of the state's appellate procedure. If unsuccessful at the state level, the defendant may seek further review in a federal court under federal *habeas corpus* procedures. *Habeas corpus* review, in effect, allows federal courts to reopen a case on the grounds that a right secured by the U.S. Constitution has been abridged by the State. The Rehnquist Court was reluctant to allow lower federal courts to review allegations of violations of constitutional rights if the allegations had already been reviewed extensively by state courts.[52] There is no real indication that the Roberts Court has moved from that practice.

The states and Congress have sharply curtailed death row inmates' use of the *habeas* proceedings. The favored plan is seemingly one that would limit the prisoner to one *habeas* petition that would be considered simultaneously as the direct appeal. These *habeas* petitions challenge the constitutionality of the conviction rather than the issue of guilt or innocence that is the subject of the direct appeal.[53] The federal courts, under the Supreme Court's direction, have conducted their own review and made suggestions for streamlining the policy. The message that the Supreme Court wants to limit its involvement in death penalty matters is bolstered by holdings in cases such as *Herrera v. Collins*.[54] There the Court held that while executing someone with a truly persuasive claim of actual innocence would be unconstitutional, federal *habeas* relief would be available only if there were no state avenues open to process such a claim. Justices Antonin Scalia and Clarence Thomas's concurring opinion declared that if the innocence claim were truly persuasive, then the state's governor would issue a pardon and the matter would not be in the courts at all.

RULES OF EVIDENCE

As previously noted, the submission of evidence is the most crucial part of a legal proceeding. In this section we will examine the rules of evidence in greater detail, providing examples from both civil and criminal cases. Specifically, we will discuss the types and forms of evidence, the hearsay rule, and the exclusionary rule. We begin our discussion with some general observations about evidence.

Trials are perhaps the ultimate contests in our competitive society. Even the names of cases, such as *Smith v. Jones*, reflect the adversarial nature of our judicial system. Each party bears the responsibility of persuading the trier of fact, whether judge or jury, to accept its version of the case, in much the same manner that it is the responsibility of a baseball team to move the batters around the bases in order to score runs and win. Each party is charged with structuring the facts it presents to persuade the fact-finder, although certain "rules of the game" govern the introduction of evidence in legal proceedings.

The umpire of the match is the judge. He or she decides whether a particular piece of evidence is relevant—that is, whether it tends to establish a material fact in the case—and decides questions of law.[55] The parties involved in the trial elect to have either a judge alone or a jury act as the fact-finder and render the decision in the case. The fact-finder hears the statements of the witnesses, observes their demeanor, and examines the physical evidence. The fact-finder decides the credibility of each witness and assesses the weight of the evidence. Suppose that Hope testifies that she saw the accused assault Marion Walker, but the defense produces other witnesses who say that Hope was not present at the scene. The jury may choose to disbelieve Hope and, therefore, not rely on her testimony, while giving full weight to the testimony of the defense witnesses. In other words, the "weight" of the evidence depends on the credibility of the statement in the fact-finder's mind as well as on the amount of influence the evidence has on the final verdict.[56]

Everyone is familiar with the concept of evidence, whether the exposure comes from television dramas, media coverage of sensational trials, or actual involvement in a hearing. Evidence introduced at trials includes not only physical evidence but also the statements of witnesses who testify on the stand. It ranges from simple declarations, such as "I saw the yellow car run the light and smash into the other car," to sophisticated scientific evidence relating to design weaknesses in *product liability* cases. Evidence that was once considered exotic—bite marks, DNA, various body fluids (blood, saliva, semen), and fabric fibers—is becoming commonplace in criminal trials and often forms the basis for a conviction.

Direct and Circumstantial Evidence

Evidence may be classified as either direct or circumstantial, depending on the nature of the facts. *Direct evidence* is derived from one's five senses: taste, touch, smell, sight, and hearing. The following statements are examples of direct evidence: "I smelled alcohol on her breath," or "I saw the accident." Direct evidence proves the facts without the introduction of additional testimony. Although direct evidence may stand alone as proof, the fact-finder may decide to give little weight to it for a variety of reasons, such as the unreliability of the witness or contradictory testimony from another witness.

By contrast, *circumstantial evidence* requires the fact-finder to fit pieces of evidence together to complete the picture, just as one might fit a jigsaw puzzle together. The lawyer carefully provides the necessary pieces of evidence to construct a credible and viable case.[57] To illustrate, suppose the State presents a series of witnesses who testify to the following: (1) Sebastian and Osborn had a disagreement at a party; (2) the two of them went alone into a windowless room with only one exit and locked the door behind them; (3) eavesdroppers loitering outside the room heard a loud bang and decided to investigate; and (4) upon breaking down the door, they found Sebastian holding a revolver and Osborn stretched out on the floor with a neat, circular wound in his arm. Although none of the witnesses actually saw Sebastian shoot Osborn, the fact-finder at Sebastian's trial can easily use the building blocks of testimony provided by the State to infer Sebastian's guilt and convict him.

> [U]nder appropriate circumstances, circumstantial evidence may be given the same weight as direct evidence. In criminal and civil cases, issues may be established by, and verdicts founded on, circumstantial evidence—that is, by inferences from established facts—when no direct evidence is available, so long as there exists a logical and convincing connection between the facts established and the conclusion concurred.[58]

Forms of Evidence

Evidence may be presented in the form of *tangible evidence* (physical exhibits such as weapons or charts), evidence that comes under *judicial notice* (facts that are commonly known or are verifiable by referring to some widely accepted reference book), or *oral testimony*. First, tangible evidence is evidence that the fact-finder can touch or observe in the courtroom. This category is subdivided into two groups: real evidence and demonstrative evidence. Real evidence is a physical object that is involved in the case, such as a murder weapon or the cocaine allegedly sold by the defendant to an undercover police officer. Demonstrative evidence is a visual or audiovisual aid, such as a chart of the intersection where an automobile accident occurred, a skeleton in a personal injury case, or a cellphone photo or video of the incident.[59] Lawyers are becoming increasingly creative in the use of these visual aids. For example, a fairly common practice is to present a video of an average day in the life of a person who is paralyzed because of a defendant's negligence; this strategy is designed to raise the jury's sympathy and thus the amount of damages awarded. Prosecutors and the police have also adopted video technology. Police routinely video allegedly intoxicated drivers taking sobriety tests of various kinds, and then those videos are introduced at trial. In *Pennsylvania v. Muniz*, the Supreme Court ratified the admission of such videos taken before the *Miranda* warnings were given to the accused, although they held that the warnings should be given before asking questions which go beyond routine booking queries.[60]

A second form of evidence is judicial notice, which allows the judge to recognize that certain facts are commonly known within the community or can be ascertained by reference to a highly reliable source such as a calendar. The parties are then relieved of the obligation to provide formal proof through witnesses or exhibits.[61]

I KNOW THAT!

- "[H]igh tides occur twice every day." *Mefer S.A.R.L. of Paris, France v. Naviagro Maritime Corp.*, 533 F.Supp. 337 (D.C.N.Y., 1982), at 347.
- "[M]embers of the New York Police Department are often portrayed as Irish, smokers, drinkers, and third or fourth generation police officers." *Walker v. Time Life Films, Inc.*, 615 F.Supp. 430 (D.C.N.Y., 1985), at 438.
- "It is common knowledge that professional baseball players are trained and coached to knock the ball over the fence for a home run and that such a feat is not at all unusual." *Louisville Baseball Club v. Hill*, 291 Ky. 333, 164 S.W.2d 398 (Ky. Ct. App. 1942), at 400.
- "The traditional features of a snowman are known generally and thus appropriate for judicial notice." *Eden Toys, Inc. v. Marshall Field & Co.*, 675 F.2d 498 (2d Cir., 1982), at 500, note 1.
- "[A] high school principal is a part of the teaching profession, albeit he (or she) may not teach a class. Teacher assignments, curriculum, and handling major student learning or disciplinary problems are all part of the principal's job and very much a part of the teaching profession." *Crawley v. Board of Ed. of Marion County, Ky.*, 658 F.2d 450 (6th Cir., 1981), at 453.

Judicial notice is particularly useful when the case involves the law of several jurisdictions. For example, several states may claim an extremely wealthy person as a resident of their states upon her death in order to enrich their state treasuries through the inheritance tax. The crux of the case is the interpretation of the laws of the various states regarding the definition of legal residency. In such a case, the court could accept the statutes into evidence by judicial notice without calling the state official who is charged with publishing the official version of the laws to testify. This applies to foreign law as well. For example, as early as 1820, Pennsylvania courts accepted as evidence the printed statutes of Ireland, accompanied by an affidavit of an Irish barrister that he received them from the king's printer and that the statutes were evidence in Ireland "without any proof of their having been compared with the original rolls."[62]

The third and most common form of evidence is oral testimony which is given by a witness on the stand in open court or in a deposition under oath. Each party has the opportunity to question the witness and to test his veracity, either on direct examination or on cross-examination. This right to observe the witnesses and their demeanor is guaranteed in criminal trials by the Sixth Amendment to the U.S. Constitution which states, "the accused shall enjoy the right ... to be confronted with the witnesses against him; to have compulsory process for obtaining witnesses in his favor." The opportunity to cross-examine opposing witnesses and to present one's own witnesses is entrenched as firmly in the civil law as in the criminal law, but face-to-face confrontation of the witnesses is not an absolute rule. For example, the Supreme Court has permitted the use of one-way closed-circuit television in child abuse cases in which the victim and the defendant were in separate rooms but the child was subject to cross-examination.[63] A *subpoena,* a written order from the court, may be served on a prospective witness demanding that he or she either appear in court to testify or be subject to a penalty, often contempt of court. As previously noted, a *subpoena duces tecum* requires the witness to bring to court any records in his or her possession related to the case. These legal tools are available in civil and criminal cases to both parties in order to enable them to command the presence of witnesses. A party may not compel an out-of-state witness to appear in the absence of a statute, but states have acted to create procedures to allow the service of subpoenas on out-of-state residents.[64]

Presentation of Evidence

Evidence is presented to the fact-finder through the testimony of witnesses. Generally, one of the first orders of business in a trial is to segregate the witnesses from the courtroom proceedings in order to prevent them from tailoring their testimony to fit the evidence that has already been presented. Obviously, this procedure is not followed for witnesses who are also parties to the lawsuit, because they have a right to be present throughout the proceedings.[65] Witnesses may also be sequestered for the duration of the trial, although this is rather rare. During the trial, the attorney identifies the person to be called to testify and the oath or affirmation is administered. Although oaths were initially founded on religion and often ended with the phrase "so help me, God," current rules have abandoned that, and instead the oath must be "in a form calculated to awaken the witness' conscience and impress the witness' mind with the duty" to testify truthfully.[66]

Information is elicited from the witness through a series of questions and answers. The lawyer calling the witness first questions the person in direct examination, and then the opposing lawyer cross-examines the same witness. The process continues until one or the other counsel informs the judge that there are no more questions for this witness. The successive questions are limited to topics in the previous statements and thus are narrowed on each round of questioning.[67]

As previously noted, an attorney generally may not lead her own witness. However, the Federal Rules of Evidence have altered the traditional rule to allow leading questions on direct examination as "necessary to develop the witness's testimony" while continuing to accept their use for *adverse witnesses* or parties.[68]

Even tangible evidence is introduced into the trial through oral testimony. In other words, a witness on the stand must identify the tangible evidence and explain its significance to the case. However, the parties may agree on certain evidence by stipulation beforehand, and it is then presented to the fact-finder by the attorneys. To present tangible evidence of all types requires that *foundation,* or basic information, be provided about the item before the court will admit it into evidence; this is called *laying a predicate.*[69] Assume, for example, that a contract case involves the records of the XYZ Corporation and that these records are essential to the plaintiff's case. The custodian of the corporation's records is called to the stand and is required to testify to the following before the records are admissible: (1) that the record was made during the regular course of business; (2) that the record was made at or near the time of the event in question; and (3) that the record was made by an employee with personal knowledge or as a regular part of business activities based on information from someone who did have personal knowledge.[70] Different requirements are set forth for items such as photographs, weapons, and other pieces of tangible evidence.

The judge is the umpire who decides on the admissibility of evidence. The opposing party has the opportunity to object to the testimony or tangible evidence as it is introduced, and the party who introduced the evidence then has to explain why the evidence should be admitted. Failure to enter a timely objection to the admission of either tangible or testimonial evidence constitutes a waiver of the objection for purposes of appeal.[71] Evidence that may be inflammatory, such as gory pictures of a murder victim, or otherwise prejudicial, may be the subject of a *motion in limine*. Such a motion is filed and considered before trial or outside the presence of the jury. The judge may forbid the introduction of such evidence and even prevent the attorneys from referring to such evidence.[72] Such exclusions include evidence that the defendant's insurance company will actually pay the damages if the defendant is found to be at fault, that the defendant subsequently repaired the instrumentality that allegedly caused the injury, or that there were discussions of compromise. The obvious intent is to prevent juries from assessing heavier or lighter damages because of the ultimate source of funds or from assuming that the defendant was legally at fault if there is a repair or offer to compromise.[73]

The Witness

One of the main issues at any trial is the credibility of the witnesses. In other words, can and will the trier of fact believe the witness's statements? The chief method of presenting a case in our adversarial system is through the witnesses. The party calling the witness to the stand claims the witness as his or her own. It is imperative that the attorneys have an accurate picture of what the witness will say before calling him to the stand.

People who observe the same event do not always perceive it in the same way. A fan of one football team may deem an interception by his team as a great defensive play, while the other team's fans may call it a horrible offensive play. A husband and wife are both parties to the same marriage and the same events. When each is called to the witness stand in a divorce action however, the testimony often sounds as if they are talking about two different marriages and totally different people. The spouses are not intentionally distorting the truth, but one's perceptions color the testimony given. Police reports abound with examples of eyewitnesses giving conflicting information about a crime. It is the responsibility of the fact-finder to sort through the information in order to arrive at an accurate assessment of the situation.

The first question about any witness is his or her competency to testify. Adults are presumed to have the necessary attributes of competency: the ability to perceive and understand what they are testifying about, the ability to remember the event, and the ability to communicate their knowledge to the fact-finder. This presumption may be challenged for a variety of reasons such as the witness being intoxicated at the time of the event or having difficulty hearing. Even a witness who has been adjudged insane may be a competent witness if the court finds that he or she is able to give an accurate description of the event and that he or she understands the consequences of lying on the stand. The latter requirement is the same for infant witnesses. The question for children is whether they understand the difference between right and wrong and whether they know what it means to lie. The trial judge has a great deal of discretion in deciding whether a child is competent to testify.[74]

An issue similar to competency is that of qualifying someone as an expert witness. The general rule prevents the opinions and conclusions of laypersons from being admitted as evidence, although opinions that are not based on specialized knowledge, that are helpful to a clear understanding, and that are rationally based on the perception of the witness may be admitted.[75] The thought is that the jurors themselves, given the same facts, can form a conclusion just as well as the witness can (and, indeed, it is their job to do so). On the other hand, experts are permitted, and even encouraged, to testify as to their conclusions. Qualification as an expert does not require formal training; an expert is one who has special "knowledge, skill, experience, training, or education" that is not within the ordinary experiences of jurors. For example, a mechanic who has worked in his field for 20 years may be qualified as an expert just as easily as would a mechanical engineer. The opinion is admissible "(1) if the testimony is based on sufficient facts or data, (2) the testimony is the product of reliable principles and methods, and (3) the witness has applied the principles and methods reliably to the facts of the case."[76]

Although a witness may be competent, she may not be credible. The judge or the jury has the opportunity to observe the witness to detect any telltale signs that she is lying. They are assisted in this task by the opposing counsel, who may try to impeach the other party's witnesses. Four primary tactics are used in impeaching witnesses: (1) showing bias or prejudice, (2) using prior inconsistent statements, (3) proving a sensory deficiency, and (4) providing evidence of prior behavior that casts doubt on the witness's veracity.

A lawyer can show a witness to be biased by eliciting information that the other party is paying him for his testimony or that his expenses are being paid during the trial (a frequent and proper arrangement for expert witnesses). A second method of impeachment is through the use of prior inconsistent statements. Suppose that Tanaka testifies on the stand that it was foggy on the day of the accident, but she had said in her deposition that it was clear. Another method is to challenge the witness's ability to perceive the event. For example, Pasternacki testifies that his glasses were broken but that he clearly saw the accident from two blocks away, while his optometrist testifies that Pasternacki's vision would have been blurry and that he could not possibly have seen the accident clearly.[77] A fourth way to cast doubt on veracity is to show prior felony convictions or a bad reputation in the community for truthfulness. Frequently, states delineate both the types of crimes and the time period since the conviction before allowing admission of such evidence. The federal system will generally not permit impeachment through use of a conviction more than ten years old and requires that the crime was one that could result in imprisonment of at least one year or if the crime was one that involved dishonesty of false statements on the part of the witness. In addition, the probative value of the evidence must outweigh the prejudice.[78] Parties may also challenge the witness's reputation in the community for truthfulness or untruthfulness, and evidence to support the evidence of a truthful character is admissible only after untruthfulness has been alleged. Specific instances of conduct regarding the witness's truthfulness are generally inadmissible except on cross-examination and then only with the court's permission, just as other acts or wrongs are not generally admissible to show that the person acted in conformity with those traits on the occasion in question.[79]

Privileges

Certain communications are considered privileged; that is, the witness does not have to reveal the contents of the conversation. The *privilege* is based on the relationship of those having the discussion. As a society, we have decided that maintaining confidentiality in certain relationships is more important than having the relevant information in a particular trial. Examples of privileges are those between attorneys and clients, physicians and patients, and clergy and penitents. The states are split with regard to the marital privilege; some states treat it as a privilege of one spouse not to have the other testify against him or her, while other states treat it as a privilege of the spouse not to give testimony against the other. In other words, some states treat it as a privilege belonging to the defendant to prevent the spouse from testifying against him, while others treat it as a privilege of the witness-spouse to elect not to testify. Obviously, government officials do not have to reveal military or state secrets if they can show that disclosure would be harmful to national defense; there is also a privilege that allows police officers to refuse to reveal the name of an informer. Some states have enacted *shield laws* that allow journalists to protect the identity of their sources from being disclosed without fear of being held in contempt themselves.[80]

Rule against Hearsay

When a witness is testifying about information based on his or her own sensory perceptions, the jury and the parties to the lawsuit have the opportunity to observe the witness's demeanor. This is not the case when the witness quotes someone else, however. For example, statements like "I know he forged the check because he told me he did," or "Dick said that the defendant admitted it was all his fault" are deemed *hearsay* because the person who initially made the statement is not in the courtroom and cannot be cross-examined. Courts have therefore developed the *rule against hearsay* that prevents such statements from being admitted as evidence.

Hearsay includes not only spoken and written comments but also conduct. To illustrate, suppose that a police officer testifies that she conducted a lineup of suspects and that the victim pointed out the defendant as the perpetrator of the crime. The victim did not orally identify the defendant, but the officer is relaying his nonverbal assertion that the defendant is the one who committed the crime. The definition of hearsay is three-pronged: (1) it is an assertion (by verbal, written, or assertive conduct), (2) it is made by someone other than the testifying witness, that (3) is offered to prove the truth of the matter stated. If an assertion meets all three of these conditions it is hearsay, and *must be excluded from trial.*[81] Not all out-of-court statements are offered to prove the truth of the matter stated, however. For example, an ambulance driver's testimony that "Henry told me that the driver of the green car ran the light and was at fault" is not admissible to show which driver was at fault, but it is admissible to show that Henry was conscious following the accident.

The most celebrated case of a conviction based on hearsay, and one that contributed to the development of the rule against hearsay, is that of Sir Walter Raleigh. Raleigh, founder of the American colony of Roanoke, is famous for swirling his cloak to the ground to prevent Queen Elizabeth I from stepping into the mud. He was later charged with treason on the basis of two out-of-court statements. A ship's pilot told the court that a Portuguese gentleman reported to him that Raleigh had expressed an intention of cutting the queen's throat. Lord Cobham declared in his sworn statement that Raleigh and he had plotted to dethrone Elizabeth and put Arabella Stuart in her place. Although Cobham was imprisoned only a few feet away from the site of the trial, he did not appear in person at the proceedings. Thus, Raleigh was convicted on the accusations of two people who did not appear in court and whose veracity was never questioned by the trier of fact. In fact, Cobham later recanted his allegations. Public disgust with the decision and others of the same ilk spurred the development of a new rule of law—hearsay evidence should be excluded from trials.[82]

There are three primary reasons for the exclusion of hearsay evidence. First, it is very possible that the statement has not been repeated accurately. A popular party game called "Gossip" illustrates this possibility. The first person whispers a comment to the next person and so on until everyone in the group has heard the statement. The final statement often does not even resemble the beginning comment. The same may be true for a statement that is being offered as evidence. Second, the person who has made the statement is not in court and therefore is not subject to cross-examination. As we have already discussed, the right to confront witnesses is one of the mainstays of our legal tradition. In addition, the trier of fact, whether judge or jury, is not given the opportunity to observe the declarant and his demeanor in order to determine his veracity. Nor can the fact-finder determine the basis of the declarant's information, whether personal observation or casual rumor. The third reason for excluding hearsay, and perhaps the most obvious, is that the declarant was not under oath when he or she made the original statement and was therefore not compelled to tell the truth.[83]

Over the years, the courts have backed away from the absolute stand that hearsay is never admissible, and certain exceptions have developed. An example is the exception that permits dying declarations to be admitted as evidence on the questionable theory that people who are dying will be truthful because they will soon be facing their Maker. Three basic requirements must be met before such a statement will be admitted: (1) the declarant was aware of his pending death; (2) the declarant had direct and accurate knowledge; and (3) the statement contains facts, not opinions or guesses, about the cause or circumstances of the declarant's death. Traditionally, there has also been a requirement that the person must actually be deceased at the time of trial; however, that has been abandoned by some jurisdictions, including the federal courts.[84]

The Federal Rules of Evidence approach the problem of hearsay and the various exceptions by creating three categories of such statements; many states follow the same pattern, so the discussion will focus on the Federal Rules. First, the rules declare that prior statements by the witness that were given under oath and were subject to cross-examination are not hearsay and neither are admissions by the party opponent. If the statements are not hearsay, then obviously the rule against hearsay does not apply. Second, the rules list a set of circumstances when hearsay can be admitted even when the declarant is available and could be called to testify himself or herself. The 23 exceptions (see Table 4.1) include the following: (1) contemporaneous statements made while under the stress of a startling event or of one's impressions about the event; (2) statements made about the then existing mental, emotional, or physical condition of the declarant or for purposes of medical diagnosis; (3) records of regularly conducted activities or the absence of such entries; (4) various public and religious organization records; (5) widely published and accepted market reports and learned treatises; (6) statement of personal or family history; and (7) reputation as to character or judgment of previous conviction (there are additional rules limiting the admissibility of both). Third, the rules provide for admission of hearsay for former testimony, for statements under belief of impending death, for statements concerning one's own personal or family history, for statements offered against a party who wrongfully contributed to the unavailability of the witness, and for statements against one's pecuniary or proprietary interest or when the declarant intentionally made himself or herself unavailable. The unavailability of the declarant may stem from death, from a refusal to testify despite a court order to do so, from the witness's testimony as to lack of memory of events, from mental or physical illness, or from absence from the proceedings after a showing by the party that he tried to locate the declarant and could not do so.[85] There is also a residual exception that permits the admission of statements regarding a material fact if there are indicia of trustworthiness that are the equivalent of the other hearsay exceptions.[86]

TABLE 4.1

Exceptions to the Rule Against Hearsay

Rule 803. The following are not excluded by the rule against hearsay, regardless of whether the declarant is available as a witness:

(1) *Present Sense Impression.*
(2) *Excited Utterance.*
(3) *Then-Existing Mental, Emotional, or Physical Condition.*
(4) *Statement Made for Medical Diagnosis or Treatment.*
(5) *Recorded Recollection.*
(6) *Records of a Regularly Conducted Activity.*
(7) *Absence of a Record of a Regularly Conducted Activity.*
(8) *Public Records.*
(9) *Public Records of Vital Statistics.*
(10) *Absence of a Public Record.*
(11) *Records of Religious Organizations Concerning Personal or Family History.*
(12) *Certificates of Marriage, Baptism, and Similar Ceremonies.*
(13) *Family Records.*
(14) *Records of Documents That Affect an Interest in Property.*
(15) *Statements in Documents That Affect an Interest in Property.*
(16) *Statements in Ancient Documents.*
(17) *Market Reports and Similar Commercial Publications.*
(18) *Statements in Learned Treatises, Periodicals, or Pamphlets.*
(19) *Reputation Concerning Personal or Family History.*
(20) *Reputation Concerning Boundaries or General History.*
(21) *Reputation Concerning Character.*
(22) *Judgment of a Previous Conviction.*
(23) *Judgments Involving Personal, Family, or General History, or a Boundary.*

Rule 804. The following may be admitted if the declarant is unavailable:

(1) Former Testimony.
(2) Statement Under the Belief of Imminent Death.
(3) Statement Against Interest.
(4) Statement of Personal or Family History.
(5) Statement Offered Against a Party That Wrongfully Caused the Declarant's Unavailability.

Rule 807. Residual Exemption

Under the following circumstances, a hearsay statement is not excluded by the rule against hearsay even if the statement is not specifically covered by a hearsay exception and the adverse party has been provided reasonable notice of its potential use.

(1) the statement has equivalent circumstantial guarantees of trustworthiness;
(2) it is offered as evidence of a material fact;
(3) it is more probative on the point for which it is offered than any other evidence that the proponent can obtain through reasonable efforts; and
(4) admitting it will best serve the purposes of these rules and the interests of justice.

The Exclusionary Rule

As we repeatedly discuss, our legal system places a premium on due process and the fairness of the procedures used for conviction. The courts have outlined procedures to be followed in the course of gathering evidence and preparing for trial. Just as we are aware of the rules we must obey in order to avoid entanglement in the legal system, so the police are aware of the rules that govern the gathering of evidence. When the police violate those rules, the courts decline to accept the improperly collected evidence into the trial. This refusal to accept such "tainted" evidence is called the *exclusionary rule.*

The exclusionary rule was established in the case of *Weeks v. United States*,[87] wherein the Supreme Court argued that if there were no exclusionary rule, "the protection of the Fourth Amendment ... might as well be stricken from the Constitution." Although the *Weeks* rule initially applied only to cases in federal courts, the Supreme Court extended the rule to state cases in *Mapp v. Ohio*.[88] Evidence uncovered as a result of improper police conduct, called "the fruit of the poisonous tree," is inadmissible at trial. The Supreme Court has somewhat eroded the strong protection of the rule through the enunciation of limited exceptions in recent cases. The exclusionary rule continues to be controversial, and we will say more about it in Chapter 7.

Scientific Evidence in Trials

Technological and scientific advances have been made in every societal endeavor and have affected litigation in a variety of areas, including the availability of new types of scientific evidence. For years, courts have accepted the results of certain types of scientific tests. Thanks in part to the popularity of *CSI* and similar shows, most people are familiar with the use of this type of evidence—firearms identifications through ballistics tests, chemical tests for intoxication, fingerprints, and DNA, to name just a few—in criminal cases, and many jurors have come to expect that such evidence will be collected at every crime scene and will be produced at each trial. However, the reality is that lack of resources dictates that very few crime scenes and the resulting evidence are processed with the expertise and technology found in television dramas.

Courts do not rush to endorse scientific or technological advances because of the concerns about validity and reliability. Trial judges who are not experts in the matter are placed in the difficult position of deciding which scientific tests are admissible. Current rules and case law provide little guidance for judges by merely stating that expert testimony about the matter is admissible if it is relevant and rests upon a reliable foundation;[89] this is a shift from the previous standard that the evidence was admissible only if it was "sufficiently established to have gained general acceptance in the particular field in which it belongs."[90] Jurists must balance the need for the most probative evidence to be considered while preventing so-called "junk science" from forming the foundation of a verdict.

Scientific evidence is routinely introduced in both civil and criminal cases. Forensic science is truly the proverbial two-edged sword. On the one hand, the Innocence Project, a national litigation and public policy organization that seeks to clear the wrongfully convicted, cites the exoneration of more than 300 people through post-conviction DNA testing alone and attributes wrongful convictions to a variety of sources, including eyewitness misidentification, false confessions and incriminating statements, testimony of informants, government misconduct, bad lawyering, and invalidated or improper forensic science.[91] On the other hand, the myriad problems such as the lack of standardization and development of best practices, absence of accreditation of personnel and laboratories with standardized procedures, and failure to determine and assure accuracy is extremely troublesome, as recognized by a congressional mandate to the National Academy of Science to review the nation's forensic science system.

Following a two-year study, the Academy produced a damning report, *Strengthening Forensic Science in the United States.* The report examined forensic methods and technologies such as the collection and analysis of data, accuracy and error rates of analyses, sources of potential bias and error in interpretation, and proficiency testing of experts; current training and education in forensics; coroner and medical examiner systems; and the accreditation, certification, and licensing of private and public forensic operations. In addition, specific forensic science practices were examined; the report classified these into three groups: (1) pattern or experience evidence that requires interpretation by an expert (fingerprints, firearms, tool marks, bite marks, impressions of items such as tires and footwear, bloodstain pattern analysis, handwriting, and hair); (2) analytical evidence that is examined in a lab under recognized protocols (DNA, coatings such as paint, chemicals including drugs, materials including fibers, fluids, and serology); and (3) digital evidence such as computers, e-mails, cell phones, and digital cameras.[92] Even such venerable items as fingerprints and the Automated Fingerprint Identification System (AFIS) did not escape criticism, and while the laboratory-based analyses were deemed more credible, the possibility of misinterpretation remained.

Furthermore, the report noted that:

the "forensic science community," in turn, consists of a host of practitioners, including scientists (some with advanced degrees) in the fields of chemistry, biochemistry, biology, and medicine; laboratory technicians; crime scene investigators; and law enforcement officers. There are very important differences, however, between forensic laboratory work and crime scene investigations. There are also sharp distinctions between forensic practitioners who have been trained in chemistry, biochemistry, biology, and medicine (and who bring these disciplines to bear in their work) and technicians who lend support to forensic science enterprises.[93]

Obviously, each group brings a different level of expertise to the investigation. As Kathy Reichs, forensic anthropologist and bestselling author, wrote in the epilogue of one of her novels, "Each 'forensic science' has its own methodologies, technologies, practices and standards. There is significant variability with regard to reliability and potential for error ... Most jurisdictions do not require forensic practitioners to be certified by reliable legitimizing organizations."[94] As someone who "selected forensic science as my life work," Reichs is an adamant advocate of professional competence among all who work in the field, including attaining a specified education level, rigorous examinations, ongoing professional training and activities, and adhering to specified ethical standards. In other words, these scientists, technicians, and investigators should meet minimum standards just as lawyers are required to be licensed and held to certain professional behaviors.[95]

The report also addressed the interpretation of forensic evidence, noting that only nuclear DNA analysis had been "rigorously shown to have the capacity to consistently, and with a high degree of certainty, demonstrate a connection between evidence and a specific individual or source," although even that is not infallible because of other issues such as secondary or tertiary transfer among individuals, failure to follow the proper protocol, or somehow tainting the evidence.[96] In addition, scientists have recently demonstrated that not only can they construct blood and saliva samples from someone other than the original donor but they can also create a DNA sample to match a profile in a database without possessing any tissue from that person. This obviously raises substantial concerns about planting false evidence at a crime scene, but perhaps the more overwhelming concern is the privacy issue when anyone could collect DNA from a discarded drinking cup, an unfinished piece of pizza, or other sources.[97]

A well-publicized arrest in a serial murder case based on familial DNA has heightened discussions about privacy, ethics, and protection of the rights of both the accused and his or her family members. Investigators searching the California database found a near match between DNA samples from an inmate and those found at the murder scenes. They then focused on the inmate's father as the possible perpetrator, gathered his DNA from his discarded pizza, and made an arrest. The benefits of such procedures are readily apparent; yet there are concerns about the use of such searches. The first is the lack of individualized probable cause for suspicion, a basic concept in our criminal justice system. All of us are genetically related to substantial numbers of other people and could be caught up in an investigation simply because some distant family member is in a DNA database. Not all DNA databases are based on criminal activity but may include those who have served in the military, have genetic diseases that are being medically tracked, or simply have investigated their ancestry. The second is that we all leave our DNA scattered everywhere we go, but are we silently giving consent to the police to seize that DNA? There is certainly no intent or conscious choice to abandon the DNA as one might make about physical possessions or even fingerprints. The third is encouraging the use of DNA dragnets. For example, in an effort to solve the same case, California police had conducted a number of arrests in prostitution cases (many of the victims were prostitutes) in order to obtain the DNA of the male offenders. California law permits the collection of DNA from anyone suspected of a felony.[98]

The Academy also examined the admission of evidence during litigation. It noted, as mentioned earlier, that trial courts have "great discretion" in the admission of expert testimony about science, that "their judgments are subject only to a highly deferential 'abuse of discretion' standard of review," and that case law "offers appellate courts no clear substantive standard by which to review decisions by trial courts."[99] In criminal cases, the prosecution nearly always has the advantage of offering expert testimony in comparison with the defendants, who are often impoverished and without the same level of resources as the State, while in civil cases the parties are more likely to be equal in terms of access to experts. However, appellate courts (whose opinions are more likely to be published than those of trial courts) seemingly overturn trial courts' decisions about admissibility of purported scientific evidence more frequently in civil cases than in criminal cases.[100]

Each party in a lawsuit has the responsibility to convince either the judge or the jury to accept its version of the case. They do so through the presentation of evidence. Evidence is classified by types: real evidence, evidence admitted by judicial notice, and oral testimony. All evidence is presented by witnesses who testify under oath either in open court or in depositions about the matters within their personal knowledge or by stipulation by the parties. Statements that fall under the hearsay rule or improperly seized evidence in criminal trials will not be admitted at trial.

CONCLUSION

Procedural due process of law, whether civil or criminal, is fundamental to American law. As we have seen, the rules of civil procedure provide the standard by which essentially private disputes are settled in a just and orderly fashion. Before people are willing to put their cases before a court of law for resolution, they must believe that the ground rules are fair to both sides and that the dispute settler will be impartial. The rules must be spelled out clearly and in advance. All of this is necessary so that citizens will accept the legitimacy of the judicial process.

Procedural due process in the area of criminal law presents an additional problem. There is little doubt that government possesses awesome power to deprive individuals of life, liberty, or property. Consequently, due process places strict procedural requirements on government to ensure that public officials do not abuse their power. Although sometimes criticized for favoring the accused, procedural due process is necessary for liberty in a free society. The requirement that government obtain the deprivation of a person's life or liberty "by the book" is considered by many to be an essential safeguard of freedom. Even a cursory examination of repressive and totalitarian governments reveals that denial of fundamental principles of due process is a common element. In a democratic society, *how* the government deprives a person of life, liberty, or property is every bit as important as *why* it does so.

NOTES

1. The opening scene in the film *The Godfather* illustrates this point. The undertaker, whose daughter has been brutally beaten, seeks "justice" from the Godfather when his daughter's attackers receive only a suspended sentence.
2. Edward J. Kemp, *Abraham Lincoln's Philosophy of Common Sense*, vol. 1 (New York: New York Academy of Sciences, 1965), p. 346.
3. Fletcher Knebel and Gerald S. Clay, *Before You Sue: How to Get Justice Without Going to Court* (New York: William Morrow, 1987), p. 15.
4. 4 Am. Jur. 2d *Alternative Dispute Resolution* § 4.
5. "Why Celebrities Choose Divorce Mediation, http://www.mediation.com/articles/why-celebrities-choose-divorce-mediation.aspx, May 20, 2013 (visited July 21, 2015); Brown Laurel, "Trace Adkins Settles Divorce with Estranged Wife Rhonda through Private Mediation after Fight over $20m Fortune," *Daily Mail*, June 17, 2015, http://www.dailymail.co.uk/tvshowbiz/article-3128520/Trace-Adkins-settles-divorce-estranged-wife-Rhonda-private-mediation-fight-20m-fortune.html (visited July 21, 2015).
6. Mary Alice Robbins, "Rent-A-Judge," *Texas Lawyer*, June 19, 2006, p. 1.
7. Henry C. Black, *Black's Law Dictionary*, 4th edn (St. Paul, MN: West, 1968), p. 1133.
8. 28 U.S.C. § 652(a).
9. 28 U.S.C. § 654.
10. Janice Roehl and Larry Ray, "Toward the Multi-Door Courthouse—Dispute Resolution Intake and Referral," *NIJ Reports SNI* 198 (July 1987), pp. 2–7.
11. Jonathan B. Marks, Earl Johnson, Jr., and Peter L. Szanton, *Dispute Resolution in America: Processes in Evolution* (Washington, DC: National Institute for Dispute Resolution, 1985), pp. 51–56.
12. "Alternative Dispute Resolution (ADR)," *California Courts: The Judicial Branch of California*, http://www.courts.ca.gov/3074.htm#tab4538 (visited July 21, 2015).
13. "$1.26 Billion Default Judgment Entered against Pepsi," *Wisconsin Law Journal*, November 2, 2009; Bruce Vielmetti, "Judge Scraps $12.6 Billion Judgment against Pepsi," *Journal Sentinel*, November 6, 2009.
14. Fed. R. Civ. P. 26.
15. Fed. R. Civ. P. 31.
16. Fed. R. Civ. P. 36.
17. Fed. R. Civ. P. 37.
18. Bob Pockrass, "RCR Wins Case against United of Omaha," *NASCAR Scene*, June 16, 2005.
19. Fed. R. Civ. P. 12, 56.
20. Fed. R. Civ. P. 48.
21. *Batson v. Kentucky*, 476 U.S. 79 (1986).
22. Amy J. St. Eve and Michael Zuckerman, "Ensuring an Impartial Jury in the Age of Social Media," 11 Duke L. & Tech. Rev. 1 (2012).
23. "Prospective Juror Tweets Self Out of Levy Murder Trial," *NBC Washington*, October 22, 2010, http://www.nbcwashington.com/news/local/Prospective-Juror-Tweets-Self-Out-of-Levy-Murder-Trial-105553253.html (visited July 21, 2015).
24. Michael Santo, "'Facebooking' Juror Dismissed after Posting about Murder Trial," examiner.com, December 4, 2010, http://www.examiner.com/article/facebooking-juror-dismissed-after-posting-about-murder-trial (visited July 21, 2015).
25. St. Eve and Zuckerman, pp. 14–15.

26. *Handbook for Jurors Serving in the United States District Courts*, http://www.vaed. uscourts.gov/jury/jurortrialhandbook.pdf (visited July 21, 2015).
27. In rare instances, the disputing parties may be able to work out a last-minute negotiated settlement before the jury returns its verdict. However, such a settlement is rather unlikely.
28. Fed. R. Civ. P. 48.
29. Myron Levin and Molly Selvin, "Fla. High Court Won't Reinstate Tobacco Verdict," *Los Angeles Times*, July 7, 2006, p. A–17.
30. Fed. R. App. P.
31. Fed. R. App. P. 3, 4.
32. Fed. R. App. P. 10.
33. Fed. R. App. P. 25.
34. Fed. R. App. P. 28, 31, 32.
35. Fed. R. App. P. 31.
36. Fed. R. App. P. 31.
37. Fed. R. App. P. 32.
38. Fed. R. App. P. 31, 32.
39. Fed. R. App. P. 33.
40. Fed. R. App. P. 34.
41. Fed. R. App. P. 35.
42. Fed. R. App. P. 36.
43. Fed. R. App. P. 40.
44. "Supreme Court of the United States—Cases on Docket, Disposed of, and Remaining on Docket at Conclusion of October Terms, 2009 Through 2013," http://www. uscourts.gov/statistics/table/1/judicial-business/2014/09/30 (visited February 4, 2016).
45. *Humphrey's Executor v. United States*, 295 U.S. 602 (1935).
46. Herbert L. Packer, "Two Models of the Criminal Process," in George F. Cole, ed., *Criminal Justice: Law and Politics*, 4th edn (Monterey, CA: Brooks/Cole, 1984), pp. 15–29.
47. *Miranda v. Arizona*, 384 U.S. 436 (1966).
48. *Mallory v. United States*, 354 U.S. 449 (1957).
49. Herbert Jacob, *Justice in America: Courts, Lawyers, and the Judicial Process*, 4th edn (Boston, MA: Little, Brown, 1984), p. 188.
50. James V. Calvi, "Plea Bargaining: An Empirical Study of Participant Perspectives" (unpublished Ph.D. dissertation, University of Missouri, 1977), pp. 2–3.
51. Tex. Code Crim. Proc., Art. 35.15.
52. *Stone v. Powell*, 482 U.S. 465 (1976).
53. Mark Ballard, "Fast-Moving Habeas Bill Sets Up Quicker Executions, Counsel Pay," *Texas Lawyer*, April 10, 1995, p. 6.
54. *Herrera v. Collins*, 506 U.S. 390 (1993).
55. Jack H. Friedenthal, Mary Kay Kane, and Arthur R. Miller, *Civil Procedure*, 4th edn (St. Paul, MN: Thomson/West, 2005), p. 2.
56. Milton D. Green, *Basic Civil Procedures* (Mineola, NY: Foundation Press, 1972), pp. 164–165.
57. 29 Am. Jur. 2d *Evidence* § 4.
58. 29 Am. Jur. 2d *Evidence* § 1434.
59. 29 Am. Jur. 2d *Evidence* §§ 934–1022.
60. *Pennsylvania v. Muniz*, 496 U.S. 582 (1990).
61. Fed. R. Evid. 201; Kenneth J. Broun, ed., *McCormick on Evidence*, 6th edn, vol. II (St. Paul, MN: Thomson/West, 2006), pp. 428–468.

62. *Jones v. Maffet*, 1820 WL 1799 (Pa. 1820), at 6.
63. *Maryland v. Craig*, 497 U.S. 836 (1990).
64. 81 Am. Jur. 2d *Witnesses* § 15.
65. Fed. R. Evid. 615.
66. Fed. R. Evid. 603.
67. Fed. R. Evid. 611.
68. Ibid.
69. Kenneth J. Broun, ed., *McCormick on Evidence*, 6th edn, vol. I (St. Paul, MN: Thomson/West, 2006), p. 247.
70. Fed. R. Evid. 803 (6) and (7).
71. 75 Am. Jur. 2d *Trial* § 405.
72. Fed. R. Evid. 403.
73. Fed. R. Evid. 407, 408, 411.
74. Broun, vol. I, pp. 302–306.
75. Fed. R. Evid. 602, 701.
76. Fed. R. Evid. 702.
77. Broun, vol. I, pp. 146–177.
78. Fed. R. Evid. 609.
79. Fed R. Evid. 404, 608.
80. Broun, vol. I, pp. 338–503.
81. Broun, vol. II, pp. 128–131.
82. Sir Walter Raleigh's Case as cited in David W. Louisell, John Kaplan, and Jon R. Waltz, *Cases and Materials on Evidence* (Mineola, NY: Foundation Press, 1972), pp. 51–52.
83. Broun, vol. II, pp.125–128.
84. Fed. R. Evid. 804.
85. Fed. R. Evid. 801–804.
86. Fed. R. Evid. 807.
87. *Weeks v. United States*, 232 U.S. 383 (1914).
88. *Mapp v. Ohio*, 367 U.S. 643 (1961).
89. Fed. R. Evid. 702; *Daubert v. Merrell Dow Pharmaceuticals, Inc.*, 509 U.S. 579 (1993).
90. *Frye v. United States*, 293 Fed. 1013 (D.C. Cir. 1923), at 1014.
91. Innocence Project, "Our Work: Exonerating the Innocent," http://www.innocenceproject.org/exonerate/ (visited July 21, 2015).
92. National Academy of Science, *Strengthening Forensic Science in the United States* (Washington, DC: National Academies Press, 2009), pp. 3, 179, http://www.nap.edu/read/12589/chapter/1 (visited December 28, 2015).
93. Ibid., p. 7.
94. Kathy Reichs, *206 Bones* (New York: Scribner, 2009), pp. 306–307.
95. Ibid., p. 308.
96. National Academy of Science, p. 7.
97. Andrew Pollack, "DNA Evidence Can be Fabricated, Scientists Show," *New York Times*, August 18, 2009.
98. Elizabeth Joh, "The Grim Sleeper and DNA: There's Much to be Concerned About," *Los Angeles Times*, July 10, 2010.
99. National Academy of Science, p. 11.
100. Ibid.

Limitations

The judicial branch of government, although immensely influential, is not unrestrained. The powers of courts and judges are circumscribed by barriers emanating from a variety of sources, including the judicial system itself. The doctrine of *stare decisis*, or following the precedent of prior court decisions, evolved through judicial custom. Courts are confined by constitutional provisions and the procedural guarantees of the Bill of Rights. Although statutes are often merely legislative enactments of established court procedure, they serve to delineate boundaries for courts. The procedure for selecting judges, particularly election, also acts to constrain the power of the judicial branch. This chapter will further describe some of the limitations on the power of courts; other limitations, both substantive and procedural, will be discussed elsewhere in this book.

JUDICIAL RESTRAINT

Despite the widely held belief that judges, like fools, rush in "where angels fear to tread," courts have established rules of procedure which allow them to avoid many of the hard cases that lawyers claim make bad law. Courts, especially appellate courts, have considerable discretion over the cases they hear, and use that discretion to engage in what is often referred to as judicial gatekeeping. As Alexis de Toqueville observed in *Democracy in America*, virtually every issue of public policy comes before the courts sooner or later. The reason usually given for this propensity to litigate is the legalistic nature of the American people. Americans tend to have strong feelings about their rights, and courts of law are the logical forums for vindicating those rights. Consequently, every schoolchild dismissed from the football team or from the cheerleading squad seeks judicial protection of what is perceived to be, at the very least, a God-given right.

While there is much disagreement among judges, lawyers, and legal schol-ars about the degree to which courts should intervene in such disputes, the heart of the debate centers around the question of *access* to courts as appropri-ate forums for the resolution of societal conflict. One school of thought holds that the formal adjudication of conflict should be limited to those issues that are important and worthy of a court's time. Issues such as those raised by our football player and cheerleader may seem to some to be too trivial to warrant a court's time and are a waste of taxpayers' money.[1] Other issues are viewed by this school of thought as inappropriate for judicial resolution. This argument holds that courts are ill-equipped to resolve some issues and that other politi-cal bodies, usually legislatures, should handle them. Finally, some believe that courts should not allow themselves to become embroiled in issues that might bring the stature of the courts into disrepute. Those who take the positions just listed wish to close the judicial gates—that is, to limit access to the courts as forums for the resolution of certain conflicts.

Another school of thought would prefer to see the judicial gates opened wider. Proponents of this position argue that the courts are often the last resort for persons whose rights have been violated. Courts are frequently the last hope of the poor, the elderly, or any other group unable to achieve its goals in the larger political system. If courts are established to ensure that justice is done, then every issue, no matter how seemingly trivial, is worthy of judicial reso-lution. Proponents of opening the judicial gates concede that there are limits to the courts' ability to resolve every societal conflict. They also concede that certain issues are best resolved by the more traditionally political branches of our government. However, proponents of greater judicial involvement argue that courts have a constitutional duty "to say what the law is" and that to avoid thorny issues entirely is a dereliction of judicial duty.

In this section, we will examine a number of judicial doctrines relied upon by courts to either open or close their judicial gates to conflict. Although there are numerous examples illustrating both of these doctrines, we will focus on those aspects of each doctrine that reveal the *political* nature of *judicial gatekeeping*. Let us begin our discussion with the issue of standing.

Standing

The term *standing* refers to the right of a litigant to "stand" before a court. In general, standing refers to the litigant's right to bring a cause of action before a court for judicial resolution. Issues of standing often turn on whether or not the party bringing the case before the court is the appropriate one to do so. For example, in most cases one cannot sue to protect the rights of another because only the party who has actually been injured may bring a lawsuit.[2] A court may close the judicial gates by denying standing to persons wishing to raise issues that the court would prefer to avoid.

Standing is the major bar to so-called *taxpayers' suits*. A taxpayer's suit is a suit filed by someone claiming standing solely on the basis of status as a taxpayer. Taxpayer's suits often involve government programs or policies that a taxpayer, or even a group of taxpayers, disapproves of as a waste of money. In other words, the taxpayer claims that a continuation of the government program being challenged is injurious to the taxpayer because it increases the tax burden. Someone might conclude, for example, that the space program is a waste of taxpayers' money and ask a court to enjoin the government from continuing to finance it. Because there is hardly a government program that does not offend someone, acceptance of the right of a taxpayer *qua* taxpayer to sue would open a big can of worms, requiring courts to review virtually every government program enacted. Such a prospect has caused courts to bar taxpayers' suits in all but a few limited instances.

The first case to raise the issue of taxpayer's suits was *Frothingham v. Mellon*.[3] Congress had enacted the Maternity Act of 1921, which encouraged states to create special health programs for mothers and infants in an attempt to reduce the infant mortality rate. The act provided federal funds as an incentive to states that created such programs. Harriet A. Frothingham, a taxpayer, claimed that the act increased her tax burden and deprived her of her property without due process of law. The Supreme Court ruled against Mrs. Frothingham, stating that the amount of tax an individual taxpayer contributes to the program is so small that it is indeterminable. In addition, the Court realized that to permit Frothingham to challenge the expenditures under the Maternity Act would conceivably allow every disgruntled taxpayer to challenge every program of which he or she disapproved. Because the injury to the individual was so slight and the consequences so potentially damaging, *Frothingham* barred most taxpayer's suits for over 40 years.

In 1968, however, the Supreme Court opened the judicial gates to taxpayer's suits just a crack in the case of *Flast v. Cohen*.[4] Conventional wisdom held that *Frothingham* served as an absolute bar to taxpayer's suits; in *Flast* however, the Court held that although a taxpayer could not challenge federal spending solely on the basis of status as a taxpayer, neither could a taxpayer be barred from showing sufficient personal stake in the outcome of a case to meet the requirement of adversariness that courts demand. If such a showing could be demonstrated, standing could be granted.[5] *Flast* held that the taxpayer must first establish a link, or nexus, between taxpayer's status and exercises of congressional taxing and spending powers *only*. Second, the taxpayer must establish a link between taxpayer's status and a specific constitutional limitation on the taxing and spending powers of Congress. In *Flast,* the petitioners filed suit to enjoin the expenditure of federal funds for parochial schools as a violation of the Establishment Clause of the First Amendment. Consequently, the Court ruled that the petitioners in *Flast* had met both conditions. Mrs. Frothingham had met only the first condition; she merely alleged that the Maternity Act exceeded the general powers of the national government without linking the act and expenditures to a specific constitutional limitation, thus failing to meet the second condition set forth in *Flast*.

Subsequent cases[6] involving the war in Vietnam, the secret budget of the Central Intelligence Agency, and other controversial government spending programs have retreated from *Flast* somewhat, leaving the exact status of taxpayer's suits in limbo. Such a situation does illustrate the political nature of the standing issue, however. If a court, especially the Supreme Court, wishes to open the gates to litigants or their claims, *Flast* may serve as a precedent for granting standing. If, on the other hand, a court wishes to dodge a controversial issue, it can merely rule that the litigants have not demonstrated the links outlined in *Flast*. As mentioned at the beginning of this section, this leaves the courts free to exercise their discretion to open or close the judicial gates on issues of standing.

Mootness and Ripeness

Two judicial doctrines that also permit courts to avoid controversial issues, at least in the short run, are **mootness** and **ripeness**. One requirement American courts insist upon is that a case be a "real case or controversy" within the meaning of Article III of the Constitution. Because American law is based on the adversary system, courts will refuse to hear cases in which one party lacks a personal stake in the outcome or in which the controversy originally at issue has somehow resolved itself. The question of mootness involves both situations. If a situation that gave rise to the lawsuit in the first place somehow resolves itself, then a court will rule that the issue is moot. A case is rendered moot not only because the problem is no longer a problem but also because the party who brought the suit has lost the personal stake in the outcome that the adversary system demands.

Perhaps the best illustration of the Supreme Court's use of mootness to avoid a controversial issue is *DeFunis v. Odegaard*,[7] an early affirmative action case. Marco DeFunis applied to law school in the state of Washington but was denied admission. The law school to which DeFunis applied had an affirmative action program that admitted members of certain minority groups, some of whom had lower grades and Law School Admission Test (LSAT) scores than did DeFunis. DeFunis brought suit, alleging "reverse discrimination," and won in the lower court. The trial court granted DeFunis temporary admission to the law school pending the outcome of the school's appeal. By the time the case reached the Supreme Court, DeFunis was enrolled in his last quarter of law school. Officials of the law school indicated that regardless of the Court's decision, DeFunis would be allowed to finish the current quarter in which he was enrolled. The Court ruled that, inasmuch as DeFunis had won what he had set out to win and because whatever the Court ruled would have no bearing on DeFunis's rights, the case was now moot. Interestingly, if DeFunis had filed his suit as a class action suit, the case would not have become moot because other persons "similarly situated" would still have an interest in the outcome of the case.

The dissenting justices in *DeFunis* argued that the case should not have been declared moot. They pointed out that even though DeFunis was in his last quarter he could become ill, fail courses, or otherwise fail to complete his final quarter. Should that happen, DeFunis might be barred from re-enrolling and completing his law degree. More importantly, the dissenters believed that the Court should address the issue of affirmative action raised by the case. They argued that it was inevitable that the Court would have to rule on the constitutionality of affirmative action programs and that to delay resolution of the issue would only result in a further waste of time and money. In fact, the dissenters proved to be correct. Four years later, the Supreme Court faced the issue again in *Regents of the University of California v. Bakke*.[8] As the dissenters had predicted, the *DeFunis* Court had merely succeeded in postponing the inevitable. On the other hand, the Court had four more years to reflect on one of the most controversial issues to come before it in recent years. Use of doctrines like mootness can provide the Court with the time it needs to prepare itself for difficult and controversial issues.

The Supreme Court cannot always demand strict adherence to the mootness requirement. One brief example will illustrate why. Except under the most unusual circumstances it takes about three years for a case to reach the Supreme Court. Recall that DeFunis was in his third year of law school before his case reached the High Court. A pregnant woman wishing to challenge the constitutionality of a state's abortion law would be unable to do so because the gestation period of humans is only nine months; the issue would thus be moot before it could ever reach the Court. Naturally, the Court could not be expected to adhere to the mootness doctrine because the woman would either have to have the baby or have an illegal abortion. In *Roe v. Wade*,[9] the Court said as much by agreeing to hear the case notwithstanding the issue of mootness. The doctrine employed by the Court is the "capable of repetition, yet evading review" standard.[10] This doctrine is most useful in class-action suits where the actual person filing the suit may no longer have a personal stake in the outcome as in *Roe*.

Whereas mootness involves a situation in which an issue has waited too long before reaching a court, ripeness involves a situation in which an issue reaches a court too soon. A case is said to be "not ripe for review" when a court feels that judicial resolution of the controversy would be premature. In administrative law, for example, the Supreme Court requires litigants to exhaust all of their administrative remedies before bringing a case before it. If the issue is at all capable of being resolved either by lower federal or state courts, or by an administrative agency, the Court wants it to be so resolved. Because the nine justices can review only a small percentage of the total number of cases the Court is asked to review, it wishes to handle only those difficult questions incapable of being resolved by the lower courts.

As with the case of mootness, the Supreme Court will make exceptions to the ripeness doctrine. One aspect of the case the Court looks at is whether a case is "fit" for review. By fitness the Court means that there are no factual issues that still need to be developed. In addition, the Court looks at whether its failure to grant review would impose undue hardship on one of the parties.[11] In *Abbott Laboratories v. Gardner*,[12] the Food and Drug Administration had proposed a rule requiring drug companies to include a drug's generic name on all their labeling and advertising materials. Because the rule was not final, Abbott Laboratories would either have to risk violating the rule or incur the expense of changing all its labels and advertisements. The Court held that this would impose undue hardship on the company and held that the case was ripe for review by a lower federal court.[13]

The requirement for ripeness can postpone the necessity of resolving a difficult issue for the Court. The Court can sit back, wait, and hope that, in effect, the problem will go away. Although we saw with the case of affirmative action that some issues just will not go away, the requirement that an issue be ripe for review may, like mootness did in *DeFunis,* buy the Court enough time to reflect on how to resolve a difficult issue.

Political Questions

Perhaps the clearest indication of the unwillingness of courts to become embroiled in controversial issues is the ***political question*** doctrine. The exact nature of what constitutes a legitimate political question is open to debate. For example, the Supreme Court has agreed to hear cases involving such highly charged issues as abortion, affirmative action, the 2000 presidential election, and the Affordable Care Act. These are certainly "political" questions within any ordinary meaning of that word. Why, then, does the Court choose to label some issues "political questions," thereby avoiding them, while agreeing to hear cases involving some of the most politically charged issues imaginable? The answer, as we have already suggested, is that the "political question" label is a convenient way for courts to avoid issues they would rather not address. Unlike standing, mootness, and ripeness, however, political questions tend to put courts on a collision course with one of the other branches of government, and those are confrontations that courts have a tendency to lose. Consequently, courts, preferring discretion over valor, defer (some say surrender) the resolution of controversial issues to Congress or the president.

An early example of the use of the political question doctrine is *Luther v. Borden.*[14] In that case, Chief Justice Roger B. Taney refused to decide which of two competing governments in Rhode Island—the Charter government or the Dorr government—was the legitimate one. Participants in the so-called Dorr Rebellion wanted the Court to decide whether under the old Charter government Rhode Island had a "republican form of government." Taney ruled that either Congress or the president, but certainly not the courts, should decide whether a state has a "republican form of government" within the meaning of Article IV, § 4 of the Constitution. In *Luther,* because Congress had not refused to seat the members of the House elected from Rhode Island under the Charter government and because President John Tyler had promised to send federal troops to support the Charter government, the Supreme Court did not believe that its decision could or should countermand the decisions of the two political branches of government.

In reaching its decision in *Luther,* the Court did not necessarily remain neutral. Indeed, by refusing to decide the issue, the Court implicitly backed the Charter government. By adopting a hands-off policy, the Court may actually be supporting the status quo, as the case of *Colegrove v. Green*[15] demonstrates. After many years of failure to redraw the lines of congressional districts, Illinois was severely malapportioned. Some Illinois congressional districts had as much as eight times as many people as others. This left the people in the large districts severely underrepresented. Kenneth W. Colegrove, living in one of the disfavored districts, sought an injunction against further congressional elections in Illinois until the district lines had been redrawn to reflect equal populations. The Supreme Court ruled against Colegrove for several reasons. First, the Court was unsure about whether it could provide an appropriate judicial remedy. If the Court did rule that the existing lines were unconstitutional, it could do nothing if the state still refused to redraw them. Second, if the Illinois delegation was elected in violation of the Constitution, Congress could refuse to seat the state's representatives. In other words, should Congress decide that Illinois' method of selecting representatives to Congress was not in line with a "republican form of government," Congress could refuse to seat the state's representatives. Third, if malapportionment was a problem in Illinois, it was not for the Court, but for the people—through the ballot box—to correct it. Finally, the Court took note of the highly partisan nature of reapportionment and ruled that courts ought not to enter this "political thicket."

Colegrove did not put an end to the issue of reapportionment as a political question. In 1962 the Court was faced with the issue again, except that this time the case involved the malapportionment of *state* legislative districts. In *Baker v. Carr*,[16] the Supreme Court ruled that federal courts could take jurisdiction in reapportionment cases. In reversing itself on whether reapportionment was a "political question," the Court outlined six criteria for determining whether an issue raises a political question. The Court ruled that a case raises a political question: (1) if the issue has clearly been left to a coequal branch of the national government by the Constitution; (2) if a judicial decision would embarrass the nation in its foreign relations; (3) if the Court lacks manageable judicial standards by which to decide the case; (4) if the Court's decision would demonstrate a lack of respect for a coequal branch of government; (5) if there is a need to adhere to a decision already made; or (6) if the issue involves a policy determination clearly left to non-judicial policymakers.[17] In ruling that reapportionment cases were not political questions, the Court opened the door to numerous challenges of legislative and non-legislative districts that did not conform to the "one person, one vote" standard of equal population.

Other applications of the political question doctrine have involved one of the most controversial cases in American history. In *United States v. Nixon*,[18] lawyers for former President Richard Nixon argued that the use of "executive privilege" was a political question left to the president's discretion. The Supreme Court disagreed and ordered the Watergate Tapes released, resulting in the first presidential resignation. In *Massachusetts v. Laird*,[19] the Court refused to hear a case on the constitutionality of the war in Vietnam. In *Powell v. McCormack*,[20] the Court was asked to decide whether the refusal by Congress to seat a member of the House of Representatives was a political question. The Court agreed to hear the case despite arguments that the decision to seat members was clearly left to Congress by the Constitution. Finally, in *Nixon v. United States* (not to be confused with the above-mentioned Watergate Case), the Supreme Court held that the Senate's procedure in convicting federal judge Walter Nixon on impeachment charges was within the discretion of the Senate and therefore a political question.[21] Table 5.1 provides a brief summary of some of the criteria and cases illustrating the political question doctrine.

TABLE 5.1

The Political Question Doctrine: Criteria and Cases

Criteria	Representative Case	Reasoning
Constitution clearly gives the power to another branch	*Nixon v. United States*[a]	The Senate has the "sole" power to try impeachments, so the decision is clearly theirs
A judicial decision would embarrass the government with a foreign nation	*Massachusetts v. Laird*[b]	Both presidents and Congress had committed the United States to the defense of South Vietnam
Courts lack manageable judicial standards to apply	*Luther v. Borden*[c]	No clear judicial meaning of the term "republican form of government"
Judicial decision would show lack of respect for a coequal branch of government	*Nixon v. United States*	Would permit the judiciary to interfere with the internal rules of the Senate
Need to adhere to a decision already made	*Luther v. Borden*	President Tyler had already verbally committed to helping one of the disputed parties involved
Decision is one involving a policy clearly left to nonjudicial policymakers	*Massachusetts v. Laird*	The decision to go to war is one that is clearly left to the political branches of government

[a] *Nixon v. United States,* 506 U.S. 224 (1993).
[b] *Massachusetts v. Laird,* 400 U.S. 886 (1970).
[c] *Luther v. Borden,* 48 U.S. 1 (1849).

In this section we have attempted to demonstrate how courts can use doctrines such as standing, mootness, ripeness, and political questions as tools of judicial policymaking. If the Supreme Court wishes to enter a particular "political thicket," it seldom has trouble finding a way to do so. On the other hand, these doctrines serve as convenient excuses for the Court if it wishes to avoid controversy. An important point to remember is that the decision *not* to get involved in a controversy can have as many policy implications as the decision *to* get involved. By not involving itself, the Court supports the status quo. Similarly, a decision to rush in where angels fear to tread can put the Court in the forefront of policymaking in the United States. The decision about which road to take is itself a highly charged political question.

LEGAL LIMITATIONS

The previous section dealt with political limitations that are invoked by judges to avoid having to resolve certain questions. Those same limitations may also be regarded as legalistic in nature. To illustrate, standing may be employed to restrict access to courts, but it may also be used to prevent those without a stake in the matter from meddling in a lawsuit while allowing those with an interest to participate in the proceedings. For example, you cannot intercede in a lawsuit brought by a creditor against your best friend merely because the debtor is such a good person and you think it is harsh that she must pay the debt. On the other hand, a statute may grant standing to grandparents to intervene in their child's divorce (a lawsuit in which the grandparents otherwise would not have standing) in order to protect visitation rights with their grandchildren. Just because these limitations on judicial power are characterized here as either political or legalistic does not imply that they are exclusively one or the other.

Jurisdiction

The threshold question in any lawsuit is to determine which court or courts have jurisdiction in the matter. Judicial *jurisdiction* may be defined as the power or authority of a court to decide a particular case. As discussed in Chapter 3, jurisdiction stems from constitutional or legislative provisions, and the boundaries of each court's jurisdiction are carefully delineated. The concept of jurisdiction appears fairly simple in its initial definition but is infinitely complex in its application.

Jurisdiction has three facets: (1) geographic limitations, (2) subject matter limitations, and (3) personal or *in rem* jurisdiction. All three requirements must be met before a court may decide a case. Every tribunal in the United States is limited by geographic boundaries. Decisions of the U.S. Supreme Court are operative everywhere in the United States, but they are both irrelevant and ineffective in Brazil. The same principle holds true for state and local courts as well; municipal courts lack the power to decide cases that arise outside the city boundaries and that do not involve city ordinances. The Supreme Court succinctly explained the principle in the following excerpt:

> The authority of every tribunal is necessarily restricted by the territorial limits of the State in which it is established. Any attempt to exercise authority beyond those limits would be deemed in every other forum ... an illegitimate assumption of power.[22]

In addition, jurisdiction is defined topically. Courts are assigned particular types of lawsuits to handle. Misdemeanors are generally heard by courts of limited jurisdiction, while felonies are heard by trial courts of general jurisdiction in the state systems. In civil matters such as tort or contract litigation, jurisdiction is commonly determined by the amount in controversy or the monetary damages sought by the parties. Cases involving relatively smaller amounts, perhaps less than $5000, can be heard by county or justice of the peace courts, while suits involving $10,000 or more can be heard in superior courts. "Federal courts have jurisdiction in civil cases, called *diversity of citizenship suits,* involving citizens of different states when the amount in controversy exceeds $ 75,000."[23]

The third element is that the court must have either *in personum* or *in rem* jurisdiction. "[E]very state possesses exclusive jurisdiction and sovereignty over persons and property within its territory."[24] ***In rem jurisdiction*** arises in suits affecting property interests and stems from the physical location of the property inside state boundaries and under the control of the court. Technically, suits *in rem* are filed against the property itself (for example, a suit to seize an obscene film or to determine ownership of an abandoned cache of jewels) but the term is also used generically to describe suits affecting the property interests of the parties. Probate proceedings or suits to partition land would fall into this category.[25]

In personum jurisdiction is the power of the court to "determine the personal rights and obligations of the defendants."[26] Personal jurisdiction may be founded on presence, domicile, consent, and certain activities within the state. Those who reside in a state or who are physically present within the territorial limits of a state are subject to the *in personum* jurisdiction of the state's courts; however, a caveat must be added in that the other prerequisites must be met for a court to have jurisdiction to render an effective decree. Out-of-state residents come under the jurisdiction of the court either by voluntarily consenting to be sued in that state (a common provision in contracts) or because of jurisdictional statutes. Specific legislative enactments, commonly referred to as ***long-arm statutes,*** extend the power of state courts over nonresident parties. The long-arm statutes are based on a form of implied consent; that is, if one is doing business in the state or commits a tort therein, one is deemed to have consented to be sued in the state courts.

> Due process requires only that in order to subject a defendant to a judgment in personum, if he be not present within the territory of the forum, he have certain *minimum contacts* [emphasis added] with it such that the maintenance of the suit does not offend "traditional notions of fair play and substantial justice."[27]

Remember that the defendant, whether a natural person or a corporation, must receive adequate notice of the proceedings and an opportunity to be heard. That notice may be in the form of either personal or substituted service. ***Personal service*** occurs when the party is officially notified of the pending litigation in accordance with the statutory requirements, generally by mail or by personal delivery of the petition by the process server. ***Substituted service*** frequently occurs through publication in the local newspaper. Personal service is the preferred method of advising the defendant of the pending litigation, and substituted service is ineffective in certain instances. These are rather technical rules, and reference to applicable state and federal rules would be needed to determine whether substituted service is acceptable in a given lawsuit.[28]

Quasi-in-rem jurisdiction allows the court to exercise judicial jurisdiction over land, chattels, and intangibles to satisfy a personal obligation such as a debt of the owner, even if the owner is not personally subject to the court's jurisdiction.[29] This hybrid may form the basis for jurisdiction when a plaintiff is attempting to secure a pre-existing claim to property (or to extinguish others' claims) or when the plaintiff (a South Carolina resident) attaches local property (a valuable collection of antique books stored in Charleston) that the nonresident defendant (a Pennsylvania resident) owns in order to litigate a personal claim unrelated to the property (a debt owed in Pennsylvania for the purchase of baseball trading cards). The drawback is that the recovery is limited to the value of the property under the court's control, which may be less than the debt.[30]

A defendant who wishes to challenge the jurisdiction of the court must generally either do so in the initial pleading or forfeit the right to question the authority of the court. Similarly, any effort to change the location of a trial must be filed as a pretrial motion.[31]

Venue

Venue must be distinguished from jurisdiction, or the power to adjudicate. *Venue* refers to the site or geographic location where a trial takes place. A court may have jurisdiction to hear a particular case, but venue may not be proper with the particular court. District courts may have the prerequisites of jurisdiction to hear felony cases, but the venue statute will limit the venue to the county in which the crime occurred. Venue is thus a further limitation on the power of the court.[32]

Venue provisions are deemed so important that they appear in the U.S. Constitution: "The trial of all crimes ... shall be held in the State where the said crimes shall have been committed."[33] The social policy is that the parties to a lawsuit, whether civil or criminal in nature, should not be hauled to far-distant forums and forced to defend lawsuits in a place inconvenient for them and for their witnesses. Such inconvenience may seriously prejudice the case in that the witnesses may be unable to travel to the new location; in addition, transporting and lodging the necessary personnel can be expensive. A particular concern in criminal cases is that the defendant be tried in the community in which the crime was committed for at least two reasons: (1) the defendant is entitled to be tried before peers who are applying contemporary community standards and (2) the community has a vested interest in the trials of those accused of committing crimes in their neighborhoods.

Venue is generally governed by statutory provisions and may be based on the issues involved in the lawsuit. In litigation concerning land, for example, venue is proper in the county in which the land is located. Litigants have a limited opportunity to modify the venue of the proceeding, but such a move requires court approval. The most common ground for transfer in a civil case is *forum non conveniens*, a doctrine that allows the court to decline jurisdiction if in the interest of justice and for the convenience of the parties the case should be moved.[34] Better known, however, is the motion in a criminal case to change venue because of prejudice and bias in the community that would prevent a fair trial. This perceived prejudice or bias is often attributed to *pretrial publicity* in a particularly newsworthy case.[35] The issue for the court and potential jurors is not whether they have heard about the case, but rather whether they have already formed an opinion about the matter to the extent that they would be unable to listen to the evidence and render a fair and impartial verdict. In other words, the jurors do not have to be recluses who know nothing about community events, but they must have open minds about the guilt or innocence of the accused, despite having heard the pretrial publicity.[36] Courts are hesitant to grant motions to move trials because of the community's interest in resolving local matters and because it may be a very expensive proposition. Moving the trial may be especially costly in criminal cases, in which the original forum has to pay all travel and lodging expenses for court personnel, attorneys, and witnesses.

Statutes of Limitation

An additional legislative restriction on the court's power to hear a particular matter is statutes of limitation. *Statutes of limitation* are temporal in nature and prescribe the time periods in which actions must be brought. The plaintiff must file within the time limit or be forever barred from seeking relief; violation of the statutes of limitation is a defense to the suit.[37] The purpose is to ensure that the action is brought within a reasonable time and while the evidence is still fresh. As time proceeds, valuable information could be lost or destroyed, and witnesses' memories of the event fade.[38]

Again, statutes of limitation vary according to the type of lawsuit. The basic rule in civil cases is that the statute begins to run when the cause of action accrues—at the time of injury, for example.[39] However, determining the time of injury is not always as easy as it may first appear. A medical condition caused by an automobile accident or by malpractice may not manifest itself immediately; similarly, a psychological problem caused by a traumatic event such as child molestation may surface years after the event. Some statutes allow tort victims leeway by extending the limit from the date of injury to the date that the injury was discovered or should have been discovered; the latter provision protects a defendant from perennial potential for suit. Criminal laws also include statutes of limitation. The limits for misdemeanors are usually shorter than those for felonies, and there is rarely a statute of limitations for the crime of murder.

STATUTES OF LIMITATION

Such statutes are designed to promote justice by preventing the revival of hoary claims that have been allowed to slumber until evidence has been lost, memories have faded, and witnesses have disappeared. "The theory is that even if one has a just claim it is unjust not to put the adversary on notice to defend within the period of limitation and that the right to be free of stale claims in time comes to prevail over the right to prosecute them."[40]

Mitigation of the possible harshness of the statutes of limitation is brought about by provisions allowing the statute to be tolled, or suspended.[41] Conditions such as infancy or insanity may cause the statute to be tolled. It is the time of filing the petition, and not the time of judgment, which is critical. In other words, the statute is tolled with the initiation of the legal action.

Conflict of Laws

Americans live in a mobile and interconnected society. For business or for pleasure, we frequently cross state lines or even cross the country, and we think nothing of entering into contracts with companies located across the continent from us. We often change our domiciles from one state to another. We seek assistance from experts in cities and institutions far from home. We purchase goods produced in factories in other regions of the country or complete transactions online. We do all of these things without fully appreciating the ease with which we do them and the legal safeguards that are afforded to us.

This mobility poses special legal problems. If our extraordinary communications and transportation systems failed and we were isolated within our own states, an entire subfield of law would be eradicated. But we are not confined and unable to communicate, and conflict of laws is therefore a flourishing branch of law. The area of conflict of laws involves three subsidiary issues: (1) selection of the court with the correct jurisdiction; (2) choice-of-law questions; and (3) effect of judgments under the Full Faith and Credit Clause of the U.S. Constitution. The former was discussed in the section on jurisdiction, and the latter two are the topics discussed here.

Each of the 50 states and the national government is a sovereign entity with its own unique laws and procedures. Plaintiffs naturally gravitate to the forum in which the laws are likely to be most beneficial and in which they are likely to be most successful. Jurisdiction and choice-of-law rules limit plaintiffs' ability to "forum shop" in order to find the best deal. *Choice-of-law questions* arise in ascertaining which law the forum will apply when some or all of the operative events occurred in a jurisdiction other than the forum state. To illustrate, assume that Buchanan and McNair, both South Carolina residents, are involved in an automobile accident in Santa Fe. The other driver, George, is from Rhode Island. Because of diversity jurisdiction, Buchanan and McNair could file suit in their home state of South Carolina, in New Mexico, in George's home state of Rhode Island, or in the federal court in any of the three states if the amount of controversy exceeds $75,000. It would certainly be more convenient for the pair to pursue the lawsuit on their home ground, but George can make the same argument about Rhode Island. The witnesses are in New Mexico. (This may be the ideal time for using the discovery techniques discussed in Chapter 4.) It appears, then, that there is no one place that is truly convenient for all.

The choice of the forum in which to pursue this matter is very important. Like all good bargain hunters, the plaintiffs are seeking the best deal. Such situations also generate "races to the courthouse" because as long as all other prerequisites are met, the party who files first (and, in our example, it could be George) typically determines the location. If the plaintiff seeks relief in federal courts, the federal court is obligated to enforce the law of the state in which it is located, unless the matter is governed by the U.S. Constitution or by federal statutes.[42] Our accident case involves neither, and the applicable law will be that of one of the states.

If the suit is filed in either South Carolina or Rhode Island, we have the classical choice-of-law problem, in which the operative facts occurred elsewhere. Generally, when a state applies the law of a sister state (foreign law), it applies the *internal* law, or the law that the sister state would use if there were no conflicts issues. The theory that would allow the use of the sister state's *whole* law, including choice-of-law rules, is **renvoi**; renvoi is seldom used in this country because it often exacerbates the problem of determining which law applies. Procedural matters, such as pleading and venue, are normally governed by the local law of the forum, whereas substantive matters, loosely interpreted to mean any matter determinative of outcome, are governed by the appropriate foreign law. Again however, classifying a particular aspect of a case as one or the other can be rather complex.[43] Foreign law must be proven at trial, and in the absence of proof it is presumed to be the same as the law of the forum.[44] Most states allow judicial notice of foreign law or provide some method to facilitate its introduction and proof.

There are fairly standard rules for determining which state law will be applied in choice-of-law questions; like many other legal standards, however, they are riddled with exceptions. In a tort case the place of injury usually determines the applicable law, although many courts are applying a more flexible significant relationship rule; that is, the court determines which state has the most significant contacts and then applies that state's rule.[45] Questions involving title or interest in land are governed by the laws of the state in which the land is located.[46] The most confused area is that of contract law, and a number of approaches have been used by the courts. These include the place of making; the place of performance; the intention of the parties that may be expressed in a specific contractual clause; and the balancing approach of applying the law of the state with which the parties and the contract have the greatest relationship or most significant contacts.[47]

The concept of *domicile* is important because the law to be applied in many controversies is the law of the party's domicile, or home. Domicile involves more than mere physical presence; it requires intent to retain permanent ties with the locale. Nonresident college students living in dormitories are classic examples of those whose residence may not coincide with their domicile. Domicile is likely to be the controlling factor in the following areas: (1) probate matters; (2) divorce, including child custody and property matters; (3) political rights and privileges such as voting; (4) federal diversity jurisdiction; and (5) *in personum jurisdiction* that automatically accrues to the state courts of the party's domicile.

The mobility of our society and the complexity of our transactions complicate the courts' job of resolving conflicts. The Framers of the Constitution were concerned about the orderly flow of commerce and business among the various states and about state courts discriminating against residents of other states, as exemplified by the inclusion of diversity jurisdiction that provides a neutral forum in federal courts. In addition, Article IV, § 1 provides that "Full faith and credit shall be given in each State to the public acts, records, and judicial proceedings of every other state." Remember that state law, standing alone, has no force outside the state's geographic boundaries, but the Full Faith and Credit Clause expands the effective reach of state law. This does not mandate automatic and immediate acceptance. Before it will be recognized by the receiving state,[48] the party wishing to enforce the court order must file suit in the new state and prove the foreign judgment which is presumed to be valid and final. Equity decrees apparently do not fall under the Full Faith and Credit Clause, but they may be recognized on a *comity,* or courtesy, basis. The same holds true for international judgments and decrees, although there may be special treaty provisions relating to the reciprocal recognition of court judgments among sovereign nations.

Stare Decisis

Another precept that limits the judges' power in resolving cases is *stare decisis*, which, as you will remember, is the doctrine of applying precedents from previous case law to the case at bar. Precedent is developed from examining the facts and applying the appropriate law to reach the decision. It adds stability and predictability, in that cases are decided in the same way when the material facts are the same.[49] In part, it is a result of the itinerant justices who traveled around England and employed the same principles to decide similar cases, thereby developing the common law.

The general rule is that *stare decisis* is mandatory, and judges are bound to follow precedent. However, the same judicial innovators who developed the doctrine also determined how to circumvent it. One of those ways is to distinguish the present case from the prior one. This is usually done on the basis that the material facts in the current case are not the same as those in the preceding case. To illustrate, let us examine two dog-bite cases. The first case, or the precedent, occurred when a casual passerby was bitten by a dog, and the owner was held fully responsible and ordered to pay all damages. The second situation varies in that the person who was bitten had been beating the dog. The injuries are the same. The dog, under the control of his owner, bit the stranger. Employing the legal formula of precedent, the results should also be the same; that is, the owner should pay in both instances. In the second case however, the court could consider that the provocation offered to the dog was a material fact, differentiate the two cases on that basis, and relieve the owner of all or partial liability.

Decisions rendered by the highest courts within the same state are binding on lower courts; that is, the lower court must follow the precedent. In order to avoid that obligation however, the court may determine that the relevant section of the precedent was *obiter dictum*—statements by the judge that were not essential to the resolution of the particular case and are therefore ineffective as precedent. Those points and the reasoning critical to the case are known as *ratio decidendi*, which is binding.[50] In addition, a certain hierarchy exists in the organization of U.S. court systems, and judges are exempt from complying with orders of courts not in their particular hierarchy. Every court must generally follow the decisions of the Supreme Court and their own state's highest courts. In regard to intermediate courts of appeals that generally have only regional jurisdiction, judges are bound only by the decisions of their own regional courts, and opinions of other courts are only persuasive, not mandatory.[51]

CONCLUSION

Courts are extremely powerful institutions, but they are not unencumbered by restrictions. Some of these restraints are judicially created and serve to protect the integrity of the judicial branch by providing mechanisms for the court to avoid confrontations with the more "political" branches. Others stem from constitutional provisions or statutes ratifying long-standing judicial practices and are rather technical in application. Both the "gatekeeping" aspects and the legalistic rules affect access to the courts and the availability of relief for those seeking assistance from the judicial branch.

NOTES

1. We caution the reader to remember that although cases may seem trivial on the surface, even cases such as those described here may involve serious issues of racial or gender discrimination beyond what a cursory look may reveal.
2. As is the case with most rules there are exceptions, such as those for minors and the mentally incompetent.
3. *Frothingham v. Mellon*, 262 U.S. 447 (1923).
4. *Flast v. Cohen*, 392 U.S. 83 (1968).
5. Peter Woll, *Constitutional Law: Cases and Comments* (Englewood Cliffs, NJ: Prentice-Hall, 1981), pp. 40–42.
6. See *United States v. Richardson*, 418 U.S. 166 (1974); *Schlesinger v. Reservists' Committee to Stop the War*, 418 U.S. 208 (1974); *Warth v. Seldin*, 422 U.S. 490 (1975); and *Simon v. Eastern Kentucky Welfare Rights Organization*, 426 U.S. 26 (1976).
7. *DeFunis v. Odegaard*, 416 U.S. 312 (1974).
8. *Regents of University of California v. Bakke*, 438 U.S. 265 (1978).
9. *Roe v. Wade*, 410 U.S. 113 (1973).
10. See *Southern Pacific Terminal Co. v. ICC*, 219 U.S. 498 (1910), p. 515.
11. David Floren, "Pre-Enforcement Ripeness Doctrine: The Fitness of Hardship," 80 Or. L. Rev. 1107 (Fall 2001), pp. 1108–1112.
12. *Abbott Laboratories v. Gardner*, 387 U.S. 136 (1967).
13. Floren, p. 1109.
14. *Luther v. Borden*, 48 U.S. 1 (1849).
15. *Colegrove v. Green*, 328 U.S. 549 (1946).
16. *Baker v. Carr*, 369 U.S. 186 (1962).
17. Otis H. Stephens and Gregory J. Rathjen, *The Supreme Court and the Allocation of Constitutional Power: Introductory Essays and Selected Cases* (San Francisco, CA: W.H. Freeman, 1980), p. 90.

18. *United States v. Nixon*, 418 U.S. 683 (1974).
19. *Massachusetts v. Laird*, 400 U.S. 886 (1970).
20. *Powell v. McCormack*, 395 U.S. 486 (1969).
21. *Nixon v. United States*, 506 U.S. 224 (1993).
22. *Pennoyer v. Neff*, 95 U.S. 714 (1877), at 720.
23. 28 U.S.C. § 1332.
24. *Pennoyer v. Neff*, at 722.
25. Jack H. Friedenthal, Mary Kay Kane, and Arthur R. Miller, *Civil Procedure*, 4th edn (St. Paul, MN: Thomson/West, 2005), pp. 110, 116–117.
26. *Pennoyer v. Neff*, at 727.
27. *International Shoe Co. v. Washington*, 326 U.S. 310 (1945), at 316.
28. Fed. R. Civ. P. 4, 4.1, 5.
29. *Freeman v. Alderson*, 119 U.S. 185 (1886).
30. Friedenthal, Kane, and Miller, pp. 116–121.
31. Fed. R. Civ. P. 12.
32. Friedenthal, Kane, and Miller, pp. 10–11.
33. U.S. Constitution, Art. III, § 2.
34. Friedenthal, Kane, and Miller, pp. 89–97.
35. *Sheppard v. Maxwell*, 384 U.S. 333 (1966).
36. *Murphy v. Florida*, 421 U.S. 794 (1975).
37. *Christmas v. Russell*, 5 Wall. 290 (1866).
38. *Weber v. State Harbor Commissioners*, 18 Wall. 57 (1873).
39. *Maytin v. Vela*, 216 U.S. 598 (1909).
40. *Liberty Mutual Insurance Co. v. Fales*, 505 P.2d 213 (Cal. 1973), at 217.
41. *Amy v. Watertown*, 130 U.S. 320 (1889).
42. *Erie R. Co. v. Tompkins*, 304 U.S. 64 (1938).
43. 16 Am. Jur. 2d *Conflict of Laws* §§ 4–5.
44. *Loebig v. Larucci*, 572 F.2d 81 (2nd Cir. 1978).
45. *Guillory on Behalf of Guillory v. United States*, 699 F.2d 781 (5th Cir. 1983).
46. *Sunderland v. United States*, 266 U.S. 226 (1924).
47. *Duncan v. Cessna Aircraft Co.*, 665 S.W.2d 414 (Tex. 1984).
48. *Christmas v. Russell*, 5 Wall. 290 (1866).
49. Lief H. Carter and Thomas F. Burke, *Reason in Law*, 8th edn (New York: Pearson Education, 2010), pp. 26–30.
50. Mark W. Cannon and David M. O'Brien, eds., *Views from the Bench* (Chatham, NJ: Chatham House, 1985), pp. 123–124.
51. Carter and Burke, pp. 30–31.

Constitutional Law

In Chapter 1 we introduced constitutional law, along with case law, statutory law, and several others, as one of the many kinds of law comprised by the American legal system. We noted that the U.S. Constitution and the laws and treaties of the United States are the supreme law of the land. However, we also noted in Chapter 1 that the language of the Constitution tends to be ambiguous, employing such phrases as "due process of law," "equal protection of the law," and "cruel and unusual punishment" without clearly defining them. This ambiguity presents a problem: How can the Constitution be our supreme law if we don't know what it means? Also, how can we ever learn the meaning of the Constitution when those who wrote it have long since died? The answer lies in judicial interpretation of the Constitution, which is the main but not exclusive responsibility of the U.S. Supreme Court. As Chief Justice John Marshall wrote in the famous case of *Marbury v. Madison,* "It is emphatically the province and duty of the judicial department to say what the law is."[1] Chief Justice Charles Evans Hughes, in the same vein, remarked, "We are under a constitution but the constitution is what the judges say it is."[2]

This ability to be the final arbiter of the meaning of the Constitution has given the Supreme Court tremendous power to affect not only the laws of the nation but its politics and policies as well. This point was vividly illustrated when the Supreme Court decided the outcome of the 2000 election with its ruling in *Bush v. Gore*[3] and again in 2012 when it upheld the constitutionality of the Affordable Care Act.[4] As the final interpreter of the Constitution, the Supreme Court has the ability to rule on the constitutionality of the actions of the other two branches of government as well as those of the states and other governmental entities. Through judicial elaboration of the meaning of the Constitution, the Court can broaden or limit the powers of the president and Congress. In so doing, the Court breathes life into the Constitution, making it a "living" document that changes as the nation changes, and giving it as much relevance in the twenty-first century as it had when it was written in 1787.

The study of constitutional law, then, becomes a study of the development of a nation. In a sense, constitutional law is a political history of the United States. While it is not possible in an introductory text to afford extensive coverage to any kind of law, we will attempt to provide our readers with sufficient background to acquaint them with at least some of the major areas of interest to constitutional law scholars. In this chapter we will examine several facets of constitutional law. First, we will discuss the doctrine of judicial review and its origin and significance. Next, we will analyze several approaches to constitutional interpretation. Finally, we will look at some major constitutional doctrines, such as federalism, separation of powers, and equal protection to provide a better understanding of our constitutional system.

JUDICIAL REVIEW

Judicial review is the power of a court to review the actions of other government bodies in order to determine whether or not those actions are consistent with the Constitution. If, in the opinion of a majority of the court, an act is not consistent with the Constitution, the court will declare the act invalid. Judicial review is usually associated with the court's determination that a law passed by Congress or a state legislature is unconstitutional, but judicial review is much broader than that. It extends to actions taken by the president, administrative agencies, or any other government body. Another overlooked aspect of judicial review is that it often upholds the actions of governmental bodies. Judicial review is not always negative; it sometimes gives judicial legitimacy to the actions of government officials. Justice Owen Roberts, in *United States v. Butler*, wrote the following famous passage describing judicial review:

> The Constitution is the supreme law of the land ordained and established by the people. All legislation must conform to the principles it lays down. When an act of Congress is appropriately challenged in the courts as not conforming to the constitutional mandate the judicial branch of the Government has only one duty—to lay the article of the Constitution which is invoked beside the statute which is challenged and to decide whether the latter squares with the former.[5]

Although many constitutional scholars view Justice Roberts' description of the process as overly simplistic, it does capture the essence of judicial review.

Having defined judicial review as a court's ability to rule on the constitutionality of actions of governmental bodies, we need to understand how the courts acquired this important power. To do so, we must understand the case of *Marbury v. Madison,* in which the Supreme Court, in effect, gave itself the power of judicial review.

Marbury v. Madison

Constitutional scholar Craig R. Ducat has written, "There is scarcely a case-book on constitutional law that does not begin with *Marbury v. Madison*."[6] Ducat's observation underscores the importance of *Marbury*, since without the power of judicial review the Supreme Court would be unable to transform the Constitution into a living document. Understanding *Marbury* is therefore essential to understanding not only judicial review but also our entire consti-tutional development. We will begin our discussion of this important case with some historical background.

Marbury v. Madison really begins with the election of 1800. The two dominant political parties of that era were the Federalists, led by President John Adams and Alexander Hamilton, and the Democratic-Republicans, led by Thomas Jefferson and James Madison. In the election of 1800, the Federal-ists suffered a tremendous defeat. Jefferson, in an election that was eventually decided by the House of Representatives, defeated Adams for the presidency. At the same time the Jeffersonians, as the Democratic-Republicans were called, had also won control of both houses of Congress. The Jeffersonians had dealt the Federalists a defeat from which the latter would never recover. In those days however, a new president was not inaugurated until March 4 of the following year, so Adams remained in office as a "lame duck" president from late 1800, when the election was held, until March 4, 1801, when Jefferson was inaugu-rated.[7] During the same period, the "lame duck" Congress was still controlled by the Federalists.

The Federalists realized that they were on the ropes politically, but they did not intend to take their defeat lying down. Instead, they devised a plan to entrench themselves in the one branch of government they still controlled: the federal judiciary. On February 3, 1801, the Federalist Congress passed a law creating 16 new circuit court judgeships, and a few weeks later it passed another law creating 42 new justice-of-the-peace positions for Washington, DC. President Adams promptly nominated, and the Federalist-controlled Senate confirmed, the individuals chosen to fill the positions. The Jeffersonians were outraged at this blatant attempt by the Federalists to entrench themselves in the judicial branch, but there was nothing they could do about it until they came to power.

At this point, the events that led to the *Marbury* case began to unfold. Because of the hurried manner in which the judgeships were created and in which the judges were nominated and confirmed, the Adams administration was actually still trying to complete the appointment process late on the evening of March 3, 1801.[8] The person responsible for delivering the judicial commis-sions to the appointees was Adams's secretary of state, John Marshall. Because Secretary Marshall was too busy to deliver the commissions personally, he asked his brother James to deliver them for him. James was unable to deliver 12 of the commissions, so he merely placed the undelivered commissions (including William Marbury's) on the secretary of state's desk. In May of that year however, Jefferson's secretary of state, James Madison, took office, and the undelivered commissions came into his possession. Because of the blatantly partisan way in which the judgeships had been created and because he believed the positions were unnecessary, President Jefferson ordered Secretary Madison to deliver some but not all of the 12 commissions. The stage was now set for a dramatic confrontation between Jefferson and the Federalist-dominated Supreme Court.

William Marbury and three others decided to sue to recover their commissions. In 1789, Congress had passed the Judiciary Act, which established the federal court system for the United States. Section 13 of the act authorized the Supreme Court "to issue writs of *mandamus* in cases warranted by the principles and usages of law, to any courts appointed or persons holding office under the authority of the United States."[9] A writ of *mandamus* is a court order directing a government official to perform a nondiscretionary act. Therefore, under § 13 of the Judiciary Act of 1789, Marbury had the right to bring an original action in the Supreme Court against James Madison. Marbury's suit asked the Supreme Court to order Madison to deliver his commission because Madison had no legal authority to withhold it from him. Because of some retaliatory legislation on the part of the Jeffersonians once they took power, the case was not decided until the 1803 Term of the Court.

The Chief Justice of the United States in 1803 was none other than John Marshall. The *Marbury* case presented Chief Justice Marshall with a number of problems. First, as the person responsible for the failure of Marbury to receive his commission, Marshall probably should have recused (disqualified) himself in the case. Second, Marshall's own appointment to the Supreme Court was under a cloud. As part of the Federalist "court-packing" scheme, the previous chief justice, Oliver Ellsworth, had been persuaded to resign so that President Adams could appoint the younger Marshall to be Chief Justice. Third, the highly partisan case threatened the integrity of the Supreme Court itself. If the Court denied the writ, the public might question the validity of all the Federalist appointments to the federal bench. If the Court ruled in favor of Marbury, it would leave itself open to charges that it had based its decision solely on partisan issues. Finally, President Jefferson had made it clear that he would not comply with a writ of *mandamus* coming from the High Court. He would instead defy a direct order from the Supreme Court, and, given Jefferson's popularity, the Chief Justice knew that the Court would be unable to do anything about the defiance. Marshall appeared to be in a classic no-win situation, which is why *Marbury v. Madison* is a masterpiece of judicial decision making.

Chief Justice Marshall's decision revolved around the answers to three questions posed by the Court. The first question was, "Has Marbury a legal right to the commission he demands?" Marshall answered that Marbury was indeed entitled to the commission because the positions had been legally created by Congress and Marbury had been nominated by the president and confirmed by the Senate in accordance with the law. Marbury, the Chief Justice ruled, unquestionably had a legal right to the commission.

The second question was, "If Marbury has a legal right to the commission and if that right has been violated, does the law afford him a legal remedy?" Again, Marshall answered affirmatively by indicating that a legal right is useless if it is without a legal remedy. Marshall proceeded to discuss the writ of *mandamus* and concluded that the delivery of a judicial commission was not a discretionary power of the secretary of state; that is, the secretary had no authority to refuse to perform what is essentially a ministerial or clerical task. Therefore, the writ of *mandamus* was the appropriate legal remedy in this case.

It was with the third question however that Chief Justice Marshall dropped his bombshell. The question was, "If the law affords Marbury a legal remedy, is it a *mandamus issuing from the Supreme Court?*" (emphasis added). To this, Marshall answered no. The key to Marshall's negative answer is the phrase "issuing from the Supreme Court." Marshall, in effect, threw out Marbury's suit on a technicality. The Supreme Court, according to Marshall, lacked jurisdiction to hear Marbury's case. But did not § 13 of the Judiciary Act of 1789 specifically authorize the Supreme Court to issue writs of *mandamus* to persons holding office under the authority of the United States? Yes, Marshall conceded, but § 13 was unconstitutional and therefore invalid. According to the Constitution, the Supreme Court has only two types of jurisdiction: original and appellate. Any case that comes before the Court must do so under either its original or its appellate jurisdiction. But the Constitution limits the Supreme Court's original jurisdiction to cases involving foreign ambassadors and cases involving states. By enacting § 13, Congress had created, whether intentionally or not, a third category of original jurisdiction; that is, suits involving the writ of *mandamus*. This, Marshall ruled, Congress could not do. The only way to either increase or reduce the *original* jurisdiction of the Supreme Court was to amend the Constitution in the manner prescribed in the Constitution itself. To allow Congress to change the Court's original jurisdiction by ordinary statute (as § 13 was) would defeat the purpose of having a written constitution as fundamental law. Because the law under which Marbury brought his suit was invalid, the Supreme Court had no authority to hear the case, and Marbury's suit was dismissed.

With the decision in *Marbury v. Madison,* Chief Justice Marshall appropriated for the Supreme Court (and all courts) the power of judicial review. We must remember that there is no specific reference to judicial review in the Constitution. Marshall used a logical reasoning process, first, to deduce that the power to invalidate unconstitutional legislation actually exists, and second, to conclude that the power to decide when and if legislation conflicts with the Constitution belongs to the judiciary. Marshall accomplished his first goal by arguing that a written constitution must be considered to be superior to ordinary legislative acts; otherwise, having a written constitution would be senseless. What is the point of having a written constitution if its provisions can be altered by ordinary legislation passed by simple majorities? Next, he argued that the Constitution implicitly recognizes that Congress could inadvertently pass a law that conflicts with the Constitution. Article VI declares that the Constitution and the laws of the United States *made in pursuance of the Constitution* are the supreme law of the land. Marshall argued that laws *not* made in pursuance of the Constitution were *not* the supreme law of the land. Someone or some group, then, must determine which laws are and which laws are not made in pursuance of the Constitution.

Having established the fact that laws passed in opposition to the Constitution were invalid, Marshall next appropriated the power to determine their invalidity for the judiciary. With a sweep of the pen, Marshall declared, "It is emphatically the province and duty of the judicial department to say what the law is." Marshall argued that it was not uncommon for cases to arise where two laws conflict, and it was part of the job of the judiciary to resolve such conflicts. Finally, Marshall argued that judges take an oath to uphold the Constitution and that it was their duty, when confronted with a law that clearly violated the Constitution, to declare that law null and void.

Chief Justice Marshall accomplished a number of goals with his decision in *Marbury*. First, he extricated himself from a serious dilemma that he, through his failure to deliver the commissions personally, had created. The Federalist Supreme Court could not be accused of partisan politics because it had not ruled in Marbury's favor. (Many people incorrectly interpret the decision as a victory for Madison but, in reality, by holding that the Supreme Court lacked jurisdiction in the case, neither side "won" even though William Marbury never received his commission.) In addition, the Court had avoided a potentially dangerous confrontation with President Jefferson. The president could hardly refuse to obey an order the Court had declined to issue; thus, the president had no need to openly defy the Court's authority. Second, Marshall, in answering the first two questions he posed, scolded the president for refusing to deliver to Marbury that which was legally his. Third, the Court increased its own prestige by showing that it was "above politics." Fourth, and most importantly, Marshall secured for his Court and future courts the power of judicial review. Because the federal judiciary was heavily dominated by the Federalists, the Jeffersonians were put on notice that laws passed by them in Congress might someday be subjected to Federalist scrutiny. Despite this veiled threat, having once acquired the power of judicial review, the Supreme Court would not use it again to invalidate a congressional statute for another 54 years.[10]

Judicial Review and Constitutional Law

The Supreme Court's power of judicial review enables it to interpret the meaning of the Constitution and, in so doing, give substance to the Constitution's ambiguous phrases. But the Supreme Court is not free to roam at will, handing down constitutional decisions like some self-proclaimed prophet interpreting the meaning of the stars. There are real limits to the Court's use of judicial review, some of which are self-imposed[11] and some of which are political.[12] Our primary concern, however, is in understanding how the Supreme Court has used its power to interpret the Constitution and has thereby shaped what we have called constitutional law.

As we have noted, the Supreme Court is not free to issue constitutional pronouncements on its own. It cannot, in other words, issue what are commonly called "advisory opinions." If the president proposed to take an action of dubious constitutionality and wanted to clear it with the Court first, the justices would simply refuse to do so. That is because the Court will rule on the constitutionality of acts only if there is a real "case or controversy." If the president proceeded to take the same action, and if his action were later challenged in court by a person with proper standing, the Court could properly hear the case. Other reasons that the Court might refuse to hear certain cases are because they raise "political questions," because a controversy has become moot, or because the Court feels that the issue is not "ripe" for judicial review.[13] Finally, the power of juridical review is checked by the role that precedents play in constitutional interpretation. Courts seldom write on a "clean slate," meaning they cannot ignore interpretations of constitutional provisions that were made by earlier courts. It is important to remember that the availability of judicial review does not mean that the justices will always use their power "to say what the Constitution is."

A second important aspect of constitutional law is that it tends to be evolutionary. Recall that in Chapter 1 we defined case law as law that develops when judges make interpretations of the meaning of constitutions, statutes, or other forms of written law. Case law develops over a long period of time and tends to be an ongoing process. Let us look at the right to counsel as an example.

The right to counsel was included in the Bill of Rights because of the British practice of refusing the accused the right to have an attorney in certain cases, even if the accused could afford one.[14] So despised was this practice that Massachusetts declared in 1641 that "Every man that findeth himselfe unfit to plead his owne cause in any Court shall have liberty to imploy any man against whom the Court doth not except, to help him."[15] As a result, throughout most of our constitutional history, the Sixth Amendment's guarantee of the right to counsel meant only that the accused was entitled to an attorney *if he could pay for one*. The exception to this practice was capital cases because all states provided counsel to indigent defendants. Beginning in 1932, the Supreme Court began to change the meaning of the right. In the Scottsboro Boys Case (*Powell v. Alabama*),[16] a number of African-American youths were accused of raping two white women near Scottsboro, Alabama in March 1931. Because of what the Court termed an atmosphere of "great hostility," the local sheriff had to call in the state militia to protect the defendants. At the trial, the judge appointed the entire Scottsboro bar as the defendants' counsel, and, to no one's surprise, all but one of the youths were convicted. The Supreme Court overturned the convictions on the grounds that the defendants had been denied effective counsel. In addition, because of their youth, their illiteracy, and the hostile environment, the defendants had been denied due process of law as a result of their lack of effective counsel. With the Scottsboro Boys Case the Supreme Court began the "special circumstances" rule, which stated that when special circumstances were present (youth, illiteracy, low IQ) the state had an affirmative duty to provide effective counsel for persons accused of serious crimes.

For the next ten years, the Supreme Court wrestled with the problem of which "special circumstances" required the state to appoint counsel for indigent defendants in noncapital cases. In 1942, the Court ruled that indigence alone was insufficient grounds for requiring court-appointed counsel. In that case, *Betts v.* Brady,[17] an indigent defendant named Betts was forced to defend himself and was convicted. The Supreme Court said that Betts was a man of average education and intelligence, capable of understanding the proceedings and protecting his own interests. They allowed Betts's conviction to stand, ruling that indigence alone did not constitute a "special circumstance."

The next major step in the development of the right to counsel was the *Gideon v. Wainwright*[18] case. Clarence Earl Gideon was charged with a felony in Florida, and because he was indigent he asked for court-appointed counsel. Under Florida law, a judge was permitted to appoint counsel for indigent defendants only in capital cases, so the trial judge denied Gideon's request. Gideon proceeded to defend himself but was convicted and sent to prison. Gideon appealed his case to the U.S. Supreme Court *in forma pauperis* and, in a rare occurrence, the Court agreed to hear his case. The Court ruled 9 to 0 that the Due Process Clause of the Fourteenth Amendment requires states to provide free counsel to indigent defendants in all noncapital felony cases. At his new trial, this time with the assistance of court-appointed counsel, Gideon was found not guilty. A few years later, the Court extended its ruling to include misdemeanor cases in which the possibility of a jail term exists.[19] By its interpretation of the meaning of the Sixth Amendment and due process of law, the Supreme Court changed the meaning of the right to counsel. Instead of merely assuring a defendant who can afford to hire a lawyer the right to have that lawyer with him in court, the state now had an affirmative duty to provide counsel to those who cannot afford to hire their own. Later cases, such as the *Escobedo*[20] and *Miranda*[21] decisions, addressed the question of when a person accused of a crime has the right to consult with an attorney, and even today the Supreme Court continues to struggle with the problem of right to counsel.[22]

The final aspect of the nature of constitutional law is related to the one just discussed. If constitutional law has an evolutionary character, then it is also true that the resolution of constitutional issues is seldom final. Recall that in Chapter 1 we discussed the sociological theory of law, which holds that law changes as a society changes. As a society's view of what constitutes fairness or justice changes, those views will slowly be incorporated into its system of law. The previously discussed issue of the right to counsel illustrates this point. Prior to the 1963 *Gideon* decision, many well-intentioned people saw nothing unfair about requiring an indigent defendant to argue his own case without the assistance of a lawyer. But today, a majority of people would probably agree with Justice Hugo Black, author of the *Gideon* decision, who wrote that "lawyers in criminal courts are necessities, not luxuries."[23] Yet, as our society continues to change and the makeup of the Supreme Court changes, "settled" issues such as the right to counsel are raised again and again. Although unlikely, it is possible that a future generation will return to the pre-*Gideon* view of the right to counsel. As unfortunate as that may be, that is a fundamental characteristic of the American legal system.

The changing face of constitutional law is apparent in virtually every aspect of the field. In the next section, we will see how the way in which the Supreme Court interprets the Constitution influences its evolution over time. Then, in the following section, we will examine five major areas of constitutional law in order to increase our understanding of this important field.

CONSTITUTIONAL INTERPRETATION

Constitutional law provokes a tremendous amount of controversy in our political system. This is, in part, because constitutional law is a struggle over which values shall predominate in our society.

> Judges given stewardship of a constitutional provision—such as the first amendment—whose core is known but whose outer reach and contours are ill-defined, face the never-ending task of discerning the meaning of the provision from one case to the next. There would be little need for judges—and certainly no office for a philosophy of judging—if the boundaries of every constitutional provision were self-evident. They are not . . . [I]t is the... task of the judge in this generation to discern how the framers' values, defined in the context of the world they knew, apply to the world we know. The world changes in which unchanging values find their applications.[24]

Legal battles over gun control, same-sex marriages, abortion, and the death penalty are, in reality, battles over whose sets of values shall govern our law. Everyone who gives law any thought would like to see the law reflect his or her value system as much as possible. Because constitutional law is the supreme law of the land, it follows that the values it embodies are also supreme. The stakes being so high, it is small wonder that so much has been written about the proper way to interpret the Constitution.

Constitutional interpretation may be viewed in terms of both *who* and *how*. In Chapter 3 we discussed judicial selection, which focused on how a person becomes a Supreme Court justice. Just as important is *who* the person interpreting the Constitution will be. For example, when President Ronald Reagan nominated Robert Bork to the Supreme Court in 1987, liberals were very concerned about how he would interpret, if confirmed, the right of privacy. Bork's defeat was due less to *who* he was as a person than *how* he would rule as a Supreme Court justice, but both factors were present in the Senate's decision to reject his nomination.

How to properly interpret the Constitution leads us to consider another side of judicial review. Because judicial review permits judges to say what the law is, it has become an object of controversy. Critics of the Supreme Court claim that judicial review permits judges to inject their own values into the Constitution. The Constitution means what a majority of the Supreme Court at a given point in time wants it to mean. These critics assert that judges should not inject their personal values into the Constitution but should merely interpret the intentions of the Founding Fathers. Another school of thought holds that if the Constitution is to solve contemporary legal problems, it must be interpreted in terms of contemporary values. The thinking of the Framers who accepted slavery can hardly dictate race relations in the twenty-first century.

In the remainder of this section we will examine several of the leading theories or methods of constitutional interpretation. Each theory has its strengths and weaknesses, which we will try to denote. To a certain extent, each theory reflects the values of the persons who espouse it. For example, conservatives like Robert Bork have been accused of favoring reliance on the original intentions of the Framers because it "can consistently be made to support the conservative position."[25] Finally, each will have to be evaluated by the reader who should determine for oneself which is the "proper" way to interpret the Constitution.

Original Intention

The predicament posed by the theory of original intention (or *original intent,* as it is sometimes called) can be revealed by a modern controversy: Did the Framers intend flag burning to be protected by the First Amendment? If your answer is "No," how do you know that? Many of the members of the First Congress who submitted the First Amendment to the states for ratification were also delegates who helped frame the original Constitution. Many were leaders of the American Revolution. Perhaps some were flag burners themselves, although the flag they might have burned was probably the Union Jack, not the Stars and Stripes. If your answer is "Yes," how do you know that? The First Amendment protects freedom of *speech* but flag burning is an action, not speech. Testifying before a congressional committee on why flag burning should be banned, legendary Los Angeles Dodger manager Tommy Lasorda said, "Freedom of speech is when you talk."[26] Perhaps the Framers intended merely to protect words, not the actions that accompany words. To the Supreme Court this is no theoretical debate. In *Texas v. Johnson* (The Flag-Burning Case),[27] the justices had to decide an issue that touches the very soul of our constitutional government. That answer, like previous decisions involving abortion, school prayers, and desegregation, sparked a heated, ongoing debate.

JUDICIAL RESTRAINT AND GORING OXEN

Judicial restraint and its counterpart—judicial activism—are, like beauty, in the eye of the beholder. When constitutional scholars speak of judicial restraint, they generally have in mind two meanings. The first meaning is that judicial restraint requires judges to defer to the elected representatives of the people. In our constitutional system, legislators, not judges, make law. Advocates of judicial restraint, while not denying judicial review, maintain that it should only be exercised in rare cases. The second meaning is that judges should adhere to precedent or *stare decisis.* Again, advocates of judicial restraint do not contend that precedent should never be overturned but, again, only rarely. Political conservatives argue that a judge should always exercise judicial restraint but in truth judicial restraint is neither conservative nor liberal. Throughout American history, conservative courts have struck down liberal legislation passed by Congress and the states and liberal courts have upheld conservative legislation. As the old saying goes, "Your position on goring oxen depends on whose ox is being gored." If you favor the law or precedent being challenged, you advocate judicial restraint whether you are a conservative or a liberal. If you wish to see it struck down, you favor judicial activism whether conservative or liberal. It's whose ox is being gored.

Original intention is the name given to the doctrine which asserts that the only proper way to interpret the Constitution is in conformity to the intentions of the Framers. Its supporters claim that the original intentions of the Framers may be ascertained by either the plain language of the Constitution itself or from the debates and writings of the Framers. James Madison, for example, kept copious notes of the debates of the Constitutional Convention. Extensive historical research has uncovered letters, diaries, and contemporary newspaper accounts written about the Convention by actual participants and observers. *The Federalist Papers* by Madison, Hamilton, and John Jay are yet another valuable source of insight into the thinking of the Founding Fathers.

Supporters of original intention argue that once the meaning of a constitutional provision has been determined, judges should merely rule accordingly. For example, if one wishes to determine if capital punishment is "cruel and unusual punishment," forbidden by the Eighth Amendment, one need only decide the Framers' position. Because all 13 states permitted capital punishment at the time of the Constitution's adoption, it is inconceivable that the Framers thought capital punishment was "cruel," and it was certainly not "unusual."

Proponents of original intention give several reasons for this theory of constitutional interpretation. First, they argue that it just makes common sense to give weight to the intentions of the persons who wrote the Constitution. The Framers could not have intended to forbid capital punishment when it was an acceptable form of punishment at the time. To rule otherwise is simply nonsense. Second, adherence to original intention constrains the abuse of judicial review. Requiring judges to stick to the intent of the Framers limits judicial discretion and prohibits judges from introducing their personal values into the Constitution.[28] Third, reliance on original intention also provides a certain amount of consistency over time.[29] The "true" meaning of the Constitution does not change as the makeup of the Supreme Court changes.

A frequent criticism of original intention is that it often fails to provide answers to contemporary legal issues. For example, while capital punishment per se may be constitutional, is death by electrocution "cruel and unusual punishment"? Because death by electrocution was unknown to the Framers, how can we know their position on its use? Supporters of original intention respond that the solution is simple. The Constitution was never intended to address every conceivable manner of punishment. The Constitution does, however, provide for a Congress and state legislatures composed of the people's representatives to decide contemporary issues. Because the Framers' views cannot be determined, the collective judgment of elected officials should decide the issue. Judges should prohibit death by electrocution only if there is a clear constitutional ban against it.

A variation of original intention is what one author has termed "moderate originalism." This approach states that interpreters should concern themselves with the general purpose of a constitutional provision rather than its exact purpose.[30] Judges should ascertain the underlying purpose of the "cruel and unusual punishment" clause and rule accordingly. If the clause was intended to prohibit inhumane punishment, then the real issue is whether electrocution is inhumane.

Critics find original intention objectionable for a variety of reasons. First, they maintain that it is impossible to discover original intention. They point out that the records of the Constitutional Convention are incomplete and unofficial. Although James Madison took notes on the various positions of the delegates, estimates are that only about one-tenth of what was said was actually recorded.[31] A second problem surrounds the question of who should be included among the "Framers." Should original intention be limited to those who attended the Philadelphia Convention, those who signed the Constitution, or both? Should the delegates who ratified the Constitution in the state ratifying conventions also be included? Only six states had complete records of their deliberations while the remainder had either incomplete or no records.[32] Finally, how can we assume that there was a consensus among the Framers, regardless of how they are identified, on the meaning of a constitutional provision? As the debates at the Convention reveal, there was widespread disagreement on what the Constitution meant. For example, despite assurances from Hamilton in *The Federalist Papers* that a citizen of one state could not sue a state in a federal court, the Supreme Court later ruled just the opposite.[33] This fact led one constitutional scholar to conclude, "So no jurisprudence of original intention is possible, because original intention is undiscoverable."[34]

Critics of original intention also claim that it is too narrow to be the overriding consideration of constitutional interpretation. Society, they argue, changes its attitudes and opinions on subjects such as capital punishment. Are we, they ask, to be bound forever by the opinions of the Framers? Although it is possible to amend the Constitution to reflect the changes in societal values, such an approach is tedious and impractical. Finally, many critics claim that reliance on original intention is merely a smokescreen used by conservatives to implement a conservative agenda now that conservative justices command a majority of the Supreme Court.[35]

Is original intention an honest attempt to return to our constitutional roots, or is it a covert attempt to activate a conservative agenda? As noted earlier in this chapter, constitutional issues are seldom final in their resolution, so it should come as no surprise that the extent to which judges should rely on the intentions of the Framers will probably never be conclusive.

Interpretivism

Closely related to original intention is the doctrine of *interpretivism*. This doctrine holds that the persons who wrote and ratified the Constitution selected certain principles they deemed fundamental and incorporated them into a written Constitution.[36] These principles, such as the Bill of Rights, were regarded as so fundamental that they were even to be protected from majority rule. Freedom of speech, being so essential to the maintenance of democratic government, was not to be abridged by laws passed at the whim of a mere majority. Only through the passage of constitutional amendments, which require extraordinary majorities, could these fundamental principles be altered.

Interpretivism, then, holds that the task of the judge is to apply new facts to these fixed and binding principles recognized by the Framers.[37] A jurist adopting this approach can disclaim injecting his or her own values into the Constitution. Instead, the values being upheld are those of the Founding Fathers. For example, in his concurring opinion in The Flag-Burning Case, Justice Anthony Kennedy wrote that the invalid Texas flag desecration law had to be "judged against a pure command of the Constitution."[38] Implicit in this statement is the assertion that Justice Kennedy's position reflected not his personal views of flag burning but a directive of the Framers themselves.

Justice Hugo L. Black was one of the foremost proponents of interpretative theory. Justice Black never accepted substituting the term "freedom of expression" for freedom of speech. Black was critical of the notion that certain actions termed "symbolic speech" were protected by the First Amendment. For Justice Black, wearing black armbands to protest the war in Vietnam was not "speech" within the meaning of the First Amendment.[39] Thus, Black would disagree with Justice Kennedy that the decision to permit flag burning was a "pure command" of the Constitution. On the contrary, because flag burning constitutes action, not speech, Black would probably have held that it is unprotected. At the same time, Black often took the words of the Constitution literally. For example, he interpreted the First Amendment's command that "Congress shall make no law" abridging freedom of speech to mean that all speech, even obscene speech, was protected.

Interpretivism differs slightly from original intention. The advocate of interpretivism realizes that the intent of the Framers cannot always be ascertained. However, the interpretivist does not necessarily defer to legislative bodies if original intention cannot be determined. For example, in deciding whether the Eighth Amendment prohibits persons from being electrocuted, proponents of original intent would defer to legislative bodies. The interpretivist would try to determine whether death by electrocution violates the spirit of the provision prohibiting cruel and unusual punishment. In other words, although the interpretivist might agree with the advocate of original intent that capital punishment is constitutional, he or she would not necessarily agree that electrocution as a method of capital punishment is. The interpretivist, consequently, is less willing to relinquish the justices' right to "say what the law is."

One of the major criticisms of judicial review is that it is inherently undemocratic. The nine justices of the Supreme Court can strike down a law passed by the elected representatives of the people. Interpretivism may be viewed as a form of judicial restraint. As we have seen, it is the Framers' values, not the justices' values, that are being respected. As one scholar has noted, "The chief virtue of this view is that it supports judicial review while answering the charge that it is undemocratic."[40]

Non-interpretivism

Non-interpretivism espouses the position that the Framers never intended to create a Constitution frozen forever in the eighteenth century. Instead, they intended to write a "living Constitution" which would endure for all time. The most prominent champion of this position was Chief Justice John Marshall, who wrote in *McCulloch v. Maryland*, "This provision is made in a constitution intended to endure for all ages to come, and, consequently, to be adapted to the various crises of human affairs."[41] Non-interpretivism calls for the Supreme Court to serve as an ongoing constitutional convention, constantly modifying, revising, and reinterpreting the Constitution to meet the needs of the current generation of Americans.

Non-interpretivists claim that their approach is the only one that makes sense. No one, not even the Framers, could have anticipated the changes that have occurred over the past 225 or so years. The Constitution has to be flexible enough to meet the exigencies of modern America. To paraphrase Chief Justice Marshall, as long as the Supreme Court's decisions are consistent with the spirit of the Constitution, they are constitutional.

An example will illustrate the non-interpretivist approach. When the Fourteenth Amendment was added to the Constitution, segregation laws and laws prohibiting interracial marriages were common in the states. Does that fact preclude a modern Court from striking down such laws as violations of equal protection? Of course not, claim the non-interpretivists. The Constitution is full of phrases such as "equal protection," "due process," and "liberty," which are evolutionary, not stagnant, concepts. These concepts must be constantly reassessed to reflect today's morals. Should the public's attitudes about interracial marriages and segregation change, the Constitution must be free to change with them. The Supreme Court, in a sense, acts as both the conscience of the nation and the guardian of its constitutional values.

Critics of non-interpretivism are less concerned about innovative interpretations of existing constitutional provisions than the practice of pulling constitutional rabbits out of a hat. In *Griswold v. Connecticut*,[42] for example, the Court struck down a law banning the use of contraceptives by married couples on the basis of the right to privacy. Similarly, in *Roe v. Wade*[43] the majority based the right to have an abortion on privacy. Although there is an acknowledged common law right to privacy, there is no explicit constitutional reference to privacy. Defenders of the non-interpretivist approach point out that many constitutional doctrines, including executive privilege, federalism, separation of powers, and even judicial review itself, are not specifically mentioned in the Constitution. However, no one would deny that these doctrines are woven into the very fabric of the Constitution.

MAJOR CONSTITUTIONAL DOCTRINES

The field of constitutional law is so immense that it is virtually impossible to cover it in a single textbook, much less in one chapter of an introductory text. Consequently, we have chosen to focus on five major doctrines of constitutional law—federalism, separation of powers, due process of law, equal protection, and civil liberties—that we believe will increase your understanding of constitutional law. Each doctrine will be presented separately with an attempt to identify some of the problems it poses and some of the approaches the Supreme Court has adopted in resolving the issues raised by it.

Federalism

It may come as a surprise to some people that the word "federalism" never appears in the Constitution. That is because the Framers did not deliberately set out to create a federal form of government. The 13 states that comprised the United States each had a viable state government in the summer of 1787. Most of the delegates who met in Philadelphia had one major concern: to strengthen the ineffective national government without unnecessarily weakening the existing state governments. To achieve this goal, they devised a plan that divided governmental powers between the national government and the states. A typical textbook definition of federalism defines it as a "Constitutional arrangement whereby power is divided by a constitution between a national government and constituent governments, called states in the U.S."[44]

Under our federal system the Constitution assigns some powers, like the power to declare war and to regulate interstate commerce, to the national government. The so-called "police power," or the power to regulate health, safety, and morals, is one of the powers reserved to the states. Still other powers, like the taxing power, may be exercised by both levels of government. Although it may appear to be a simple task of assigning a power to one or the other level of government, actually defining the boundaries of the national and state powers has been one of the most perplexing problems in our constitutional history.

The commerce power of the national government and the police power of the states serve to illustrate the problem. Congress may regulate interstate commerce or commerce among the states. Consequently, any commercial activity involving two or more states comes under congressional authority. If, however, the activity is internal to the state, it constitutes *intrastate commerce* and falls within the state's police power.

An early approach to federalism, called dual federalism, was based on the premise that governmental and commercial activities could be placed into neat, discrete categories. The major task of the Supreme Court was to decide whether a particular activity belonged to the national government or to the states. To assist it in deciding to which level of government the power to regulate a given activity belonged, the Court devised certain tests it could apply. For example, the "direct–indirect effect test" held that if the activity had a direct effect on interstate commerce it fell within the power of the national government, but if the effect was only indirect the states were free to regulate the activity. Of course, the determination of whether an effect on interstate commerce was direct or indirect was left to the subjective judgment of a majority of justices.

An example should clarify this dual federalism approach. In 1916, Congress passed the Child Labor Act, which banned goods manufactured with child labor from interstate commerce. Congress considered passage of this act to be a legitimate use of its commerce power. Although states had their own child labor laws, some states, like North Carolina, permitted children as young as 12 to work full time. In striking down the Child Labor Act, the Supreme Court found that child labor practices had only an indirect effect on interstate commerce.[45] The Supreme Court took similar positions when Congress tried to regulate monopolies[46] and set minimum wages and maximum hours for workers.[47] Even though, for all practical purposes, these decisions have been reversed or superseded, they serve to illustrate the rigid, legalistic approach which dual federalism brought to constitutional law.

The modern approach to federalism has been that of cooperative federalism. Unlike dual federalism, which portrays the two levels of government as antagonistic competitors for power, cooperative federalism stresses the need for states to work with the national government to solve the nation's problems. Cooperative federalism also stresses the interplay of politics in our federal system. Instead of the Court serving as a referee of jurisdictional disputes between the two levels of government, it assumes that the states have the political skills to protect their interests both in and out of Congress. The reasoning behind this approach is that members of Congress represent states and they must be presumed to have the states' best interests at heart.

Cases involving the commerce power may again help to illustrate the cooperative federalism approach. By the late 1960s, the Supreme Court had adopted a broad, expansive view of the commerce power permitting Congress to regulate wages and hours of workers,[48] labor relations,[49] farm production,[50] and even race relations.[51] However, these uses of the commerce power were all aimed at regulating the commercial practices of private companies and individuals. A different question of federalism arose about whether the commerce power could be used to regulate the activities of the states themselves. That is, while Congress may unquestionably require the local McDonald's to pay its employees a minimum wage, may it require the states to pay their employees the federal minimum wage?

The Supreme Court has equivocated on the issue of using the commerce power to regulate the activities of states. Initially, the Court ruled that Congress could require public as well as private hospitals to pay their employees the minimum wage.[52] However, when Congress attempted to extend the provisions of the Fair Labor Standards Act to include other state employees, the Supreme Court declared the attempt unconstitutional.[53] Surprisingly, only nine years later the Court reversed itself again, ruling that Congress could require the City of San Antonio to pay its transit authority workers the prevailing minimum wage.[54] However, in 1997, the Court appeared to reverse itself again and ruled that the federal government could not require state law enforcement officials to enforce the provisions of the Brady Handgun Violence Prevention Act.[55]

Since 1937, the Supreme Court has allowed an expansive role for the national government under the Commerce Clause. During the 1994 to 1995 Term however, the Court again faced a dilemma which Justice Anthony Kennedy described as a case that "requires us to consider our place in the design of the Government and to appreciate the significance of federalism in the whole structure of the Constitution."[56] Alfonso Lopez, Jr., a senior at a

San Antonio high school, was sentenced, under the Gun-Free School Zones Act of 1990,[57] to six months' imprisonment and two years' supervised release. The act barred the possession of a firearm on or within 1000 feet of a school or its grounds. He challenged the conviction on the ground that the statute was unconstitutional because Congress had exceeded its authority under the Commerce Clause in enacting the law. The Court conceded that the goal of safe schools was a laudable one but agreed with Lopez. The legislation interfered with the right of states and local authorities to govern education, "a traditional concern of the States,"[58] by regulating an activity that was "in no sense an economic activity that might ... substantially affect any sort of interstate commerce."[59]

Lopez is just one in a series of cases in which it appears that the Supreme Court is returning to the era of dual federalism. In *United States v. Morrison*,[60] the Court struck down the Violence Against Women Act of 1994, in which Congress had relied on its commerce power to make sexual assault a federal offense. Similarly, the Court has resurrected the Eleventh Amendment to curtail Congressional power to allow the use of the federal courts to sue states.[61] The Supreme Court has limited the power of the federal government to compel states to implement federal policies without their permission.[62]

More recent issues of federalism have involved two of the most controversial issues of public policy: legalization of marijuana and illegal immigration. In *Gonzales v. Raich*, the Court held that federal law banning marijuana under the Controlled Substances Act trumps a California law that permits the growing and use of marijuana for medicinal purposes.[63] In the area of immigration the Court invalidated several provisions of an Arizona law that attempted to punish persons who have entered the state illegally. In *Arizona v. United States* the Court ruled that federal law pre-empts state laws in the area of illegal immigration.[64] Undoubtedly, the Supreme Court will continue to rule on cases that will change state–federal relationships. It seems clear that the debate over federal regulation of state activities is entering a new phase. It is equally clear that as we enter a third century of constitutional development the issue of federalism is not dead.

Separation of Powers

Just as the Framers sought to divide power between the national government and the states, they also wanted to prevent the concentration of power into the hands of one individual, or even one group of individuals, within the national government. The Framers reduced all governmental functions to essentially three: legislative, executive, and judicial. They believed that the very root of tyranny was to allow these three essential governmental functions to be exercised by one person or group. Consequently, they deliberately set out to divide the three functions into three separate and distinct institutions. Congress was to exercise the legislative power while the president and his subordinates would exercise the executive power. Finally, the Supreme Court, with any inferior courts created by Congress, would possess the judicial power of the United States.

It is very difficult to discuss *separation of powers* without mentioning the corresponding doctrine of checks and balances. The Framers believed that one branch of government would invariably seek to encroach upon and to usurp the powers of the others. In fact, given the ambiguous language describing the powers of each branch, they almost guaranteed that there would be such attempts. The Framers anticipated that one branch would resist attempted encroachments of its powers, but they also realized that safeguards were needed to help each branch protect its powers against attacks. As James Madison wrote:

> But the great security against a gradual concentration of the several powers in the same department consists in giving to those who administer each department the necessary constitutional means and personal motives to resist encroachments of the others.[65]

The "necessary constitutional means" of which Madison writes form the basis for the doctrine of checks and balances.

The president's veto is the most common example of checks and balances. Ordinarily, we think of the president's veto as a check on legislation which he considers unwise. While this is certainly a valid and frequent reason for using the veto, the Framers also expected the president to use his veto to strike down any law that encroached upon his prerogatives. For example, in 1973 when President Richard Nixon vetoed the War Powers Act, he did so mainly because he believed the law encroached upon his powers as commander-in-chief. Even though Congress passed the War Powers Act over Nixon's veto, all of his successors to date have shared his doubts about its constitutionality. The point is, however, that each branch possesses constitutional weapons to defend itself from the other two.

It is easy to overemphasize the "separateness" of the doctrine of separation of powers. Similarly, it is easy to overemphasize the adversarial nature of checks and balances. But the Framers did not create three separate institutions operating in their different spheres oblivious to one another. Nor did they create circumstances under which the three branches would be constantly battling in a permanent struggle for power. On the contrary, the Framers created a system of interdependency among the three branches and in doing so created one of the greatest paradoxes of American government. That paradox is this: despite the tendency for the three branches to confront one another, in order for our national government to work, they must cooperate with one another. Laws must be passed by Congress, signed and enforced by the president, and upheld by the federal courts. This need for cooperation is especially true if one political party is in control of Congress and the other party controls the White House.

A major source of conflict involving separation of powers is the doctrine of *executive privilege*. Executive privilege is the president's claim to be able to withhold information from Congress.[66] The term "executive privilege" does not appear in the Constitution but is maintained by some to be grounded in the doctrine of separation of powers. George Washington set the precedent for executive privilege when, in 1792, the House sought information about a failed Indian expedition in the Northwest led by General Arthur St. Clair. After discussing whether he should comply with the request with his Cabinet, President Washington gave the House the papers it requested.[67]

Essentially, the issue of executive privilege is over access to information needed by Congress and possessed by the president. Congress claims that the information in the president's hands is needed for its lawmaking function. There are times when the information Congress seeks is politically embarrassing to the administration and Congress wants it exposed for partisan political reasons. Historically, Congress has not insisted that the president reveal information if public disclosure would harm national security or generally not be in the public interest. The main problem, of course, is who—the president, Congress, or the Court—should decide when the president may withhold information that Congress feels it has a legitimate right to see.

The most famous conflict over executive privilege involved the Watergate tapes. A burglary at the headquarters of the National Democratic Party in June 1972 touched off a series of events that led to the resignation of President Nixon. Although President Nixon denied any knowledge of the break-in or subsequent attempt to cover up White House involvement, investigations into the Watergate affair kept getting closer to the Oval Office. When it was discovered that President Nixon had installed a voice-activated taping system in his office to record presidential conversations, the crisis intensified. In the summer of 1973, the Senate Watergate Committee began investigating the 1972 presidential campaign. In the summer of 1974, the House Judiciary Committee began hearings on whether the House should impeach the president. Both committees wanted copies of the tapes containing conversations between the president and key Watergate figures. President Nixon, claiming that the release of the tapes would damage the presidency, invoked executive privilege and refused to surrender the tapes.

Ultimately, however, it was not Congress but a member of the president's own executive branch who succeeded in securing release of the tapes. The Watergate special prosecutor, Leon Jaworski, asked federal judge John Sirica to issue a *subpoena duces tecum* to the president ordering him to produce the tapes as evidence in the criminal prosecution of the Watergate defendants. When Judge Sirica complied, the president challenged the issuance of the subpoena. Jaworski then appealed to the Supreme Court.

The Court ruled unanimously 8 to 0 (Justice William Rehnquist did not participate, having served as an assistant attorney general in the Nixon administration) that the president had to release the tapes.[68] The Court recognized the constitutional basis for executive privilege but held that the president's right to decide when it is invoked is not absolute. The Court found the need to balance the president's admitted right to protect his confidential conversations with the need of the Watergate defendants to have all relevant evidence in their trial. The Court found that absent a compelling national security interest, a president's claim of executive privilege, standing alone, was insufficient to overcome the defendants' right to a fair trial.

The late 1990s saw a revival of sorts in separation of powers issues, beginning with the passage of the Line Item Veto Act in April 1996.[69] The Act, which became effective on January 1, 1997, allowed the president to veto specific appropriations contained in a bill without affecting the remaining sections. Members of Congress who initially tried to have the Act declared unconstitutional were held by the Supreme Court to lack standing.[70] However, when President Bill Clinton actually used the item veto to cancel part of the Balanced Budget Act of 1997, the Supreme Court agreed to consider the matter. In *Clinton v. New York*,[71] the Court ruled 6 to 3 that the Act was unconstitutional. In holding that the act violates the Presentment Clause, Justice John Paul Stevens wrote:

> If the Line Item Veto Act were valid, it would authorize the President to create a different law—one whose text was not voted on by either House of Congress or presented to the President for signature. Something that might be known as "Public Law 105–33 as modified by the President" may or may not be desirable, but it is surely not a document that may "become a law" pursuant to procedures designed by the Framers of Article I, § 7 of the Constitution.[72]

In several cases involving scandals in the Clinton Administration, the Supreme Court ruled that a sitting president is not immune from being sued in a civil suit,[73] that Secret Service agents guarding the president may be required to testify before a federal grand jury about alleged criminal activities,[74] and that an attorney in the Office of the President may invoke neither executive privilege nor the attorney–client relationship in refusing to testify before a grand jury investigating a criminal matter.[75] More recently, a separation of powers conflict between the president and federal courts has centered around the detention of enemy aliens and enemy combatants in the aftermath of the September 11 terrorist attacks.[76]

The same dynamics that foster cooperation also foster friction when government is divided along party lines. During the Obama Administration, for example, disagreement arose with the Republican-controlled Senate over the practice of recess appointments. Article II, § 2 states, "The President shall have Power to fill up all Vacancies that may happen during the Recess of the Senate, by granting Commissions which shall expire at the End of their next Session."[77] This provision was given to enable the president to fill sometimes vital executive offices when, as in the early days of the Republic, the Senate was not in session for months at a time.

Disagreement has arisen in recent years over the meaning of the term "recess." Each Congress has two sessions lasting approximately one year each. One meaning of recess would be that period of time between the end of the First Session and the Second Session. This is known as an "inter-session" recess. However, Congress takes several long breaks during the year usually around major holidays like Easter, July Fourth, and Christmas. These breaks are known as "intra-session" recesses. To maintain the appearance that the Senate is still "in session" during recesses the Senate has used what are termed *pro forma* sessions where in reality few, if any, Senators are actually present. So, the question arose whether the president's power to make recess appointments included making appointments "that happen" during an intra-session recess. Another question arose whether the vacancy must actually occur *during* the recess itself or simply be vacant when the president makes the appointment. For example, a vacancy that occurs near the end of a session would not be one occurring *during* the recess but would become one once the session ends. Some members of the Senate argued that President Obama could only make recess appointments during inter-session recesses and only if the vacancy occurred during the recess.

President Obama made three appointments to the National Labor Relations Board on January 4, 2012 during one of the Senate's *pro forma* recesses. After the NLRB made an adverse ruling against Noel Canning, a Pepsi-Cola distributor, the company challenged the constitutionality of the appointments. In *National Labor Relations Board v. Noel Canning*,[78] the Supreme Court addressed three questions. First, the Court held that the president's power to make a recess appointment extends to both inter-session and intra-session recesses finding that both history and logic support that position. Second, the justices held that the president may fill vacancies "that happen" before a recess begins, such as near the end of a session, and not just those that happen during an actual recess of the Senate. In other words, if the vacancy exists during a recess of the Senate, the president may fill the vacancy. However, on the third question the Court ruled that the president may not make a recess appointment during a *pro forma* session unless the session is longer than ten days. In this case President Obama appointed the Board members during a three-day *pro forma* session. Although the Obama Administration argued that the Senate was not really in session when the appointments were made, the Court ruled it must accept that the Senate is in session when it says it is. Consequently, the Court held that the January 4 appointments were invalid.

This brief discussion of separation of powers illustrates that the concept, like federalism, is neither archaic nor static. Cases like Watergate serve to remind us that constitutional doctrines are both relevant and dynamic concepts. Future disputes over the powers of the three branches will undoubtedly arise simply because of the nature of our constitutional arrangement of shared powers. That is because, as Madison predicted so long ago, such struggles are inherent in the governance of human beings.

Due Process

The U.S. Constitution actually contains two due process of law clauses. The Fifth Amendment reads, "No person shall ... be deprived of life, liberty, or property without due process of law." Due to an early Supreme Court ruling which held that the Bill of Rights restricts only the actions of the national government,[79] a second Due Process Clause was included in the Fourteenth Amendment which was adopted shortly after the Civil War. That Amendment reads, "nor shall any State deprive any person of life, liberty, or property without due process of law." There was widespread belief that another Due Process Clause was needed to protect the newly freed slaves from vindictive actions at the hands of southern state governments.

Due process is one of the most elusive and complex concepts in law. In simple terms, it means that before government can take away a person's life, liberty, or property, certain procedures must be followed. Due process is the individual's major defense against despotic and arbitrary government. It prevents government interference with the basic rights of its citizens. Due process has real significance only in a system of government where the people are truly sovereign, since it means that not even the government itself is above the law. The government itself must respect certain rights and conform to accepted standards of behavior.

It is important to clarify two common misconceptions about due process. Due process does not mean that government may *never* take away one's life, liberty, or property. When the state executes a convicted murderer, it takes life; when it drafts a person into the armed forces, it takes liberty; and when it confiscates land to build a new highway, it takes property. All that is required for due process is that the law be properly followed and the "takings" are not arbitrary or capricious. The second misconception is that due process is reserved for citizens. However, the Fifth and Fourteenth Amendments refer to persons, not just citizens. Everyone, including legal and illegal aliens and even corporations, within the jurisdiction of the United States is entitled to due process. This is because the Framers of these two amendments regarded life, liberty, and property as basic human or natural rights that do not depend on citizenship for protection against government abuse.

Previously, due process was described as an elusive concept. It is certainly one of the most elastic and controversial in American law. Persons attempting to capture the essence of due process frequently resort to such phrases as "fundamental fairness" or "canons of decency." Violations of due process are said to "shock the conscience" or "offend a sense of justice."[80] The major problem with due process is that it is a highly subjective concept: How much process is due? To one person, our legal system provides too many loopholes that allow criminals to elude justice. To another, life, liberty, and property are sacred and every safeguard is essential. As is often the case, where one stands depends on where one sits; due process may have different connotations for a person facing confiscation of his property than for a highway contractor.

Due process of law has two interesting dimensions: procedural and substantive. *Procedural due process* stresses the policies or procedures government must observe when depriving someone of life, liberty, or property. Virtually everyone agrees, for example, that someone should not be imprisoned without first having a trial. But in Anglo-American law we also speak of a "fair trial," which implies that there is more to a trial than mere adherence to a set of procedures. The phrase "fair trial" also implies some subjective evaluation of whether the judge was impartial and the jury unbiased. The evaluation of the fairness of a judicial proceeding or law is the essence of *substantive due process*.

Substantive due process, in effect, permits judges to decide what is "fundamentally unfair," "unreasonable," or "shocking" to the conscience of society.

Substantive due process exposes justices to charges of injecting their personal policy preferences into the Due Process Clause. In the early twentieth century, the Supreme Court was accused of imposing its economic views on the nation by striking down laws regulating the number of hours bakers could work[81] and minimum wages for hospital workers.[82] Although substantive due process is generally conceded to be a discredited constitutional doctrine, modern courts have been accused of resurrecting substantive due process, especially in the area of the right to counsel. Critics of the *Miranda v. Arizona*[83] decision contend that it is a prime example of the Court extending the right to counsel far beyond the original intent of the Framers. It is not always easy to keep procedural and substantive due process separate. The *Miranda* decision outlines a procedure that police must follow when making an arrest, but it also contains a subjective evaluation of the fairness of informing the accused of his or her constitutional rights.

In the remainder of this section, we will focus on the constitutional doctrine known as *incorporation.* Although incorporation has been applied to First Amendment freedoms and other provisions of the Bill of Rights, we will limit our discussion to those provisions concerning the rights of the accused. An understanding of the incorporation process should shed light on the interplay between procedural and substantive due process of law.

As noted at the outset of this section, there are two due process clauses in the Constitution. When the Supreme Court ruled that the Bill of Rights applied only to the national government, it meant that only the national government had to observe due process. Because, as we saw in Chapter 3, the vast majority of criminal cases are tried in state, not federal, courts it meant that for most criminal defendants the Bill of Rights might just as well not exist. Theoretically, at least, each state was free to define the meaning of due process for itself, affording or withholding procedural rights as it saw fit. Although state constitutions contained bills of rights with similar protection, due process often varied from state to state.

As we have seen, the Fourteenth Amendment was passed in part to ensure that southern states would not oppress the newly freed slaves. Consequently, states were also forbidden to deny persons within their jurisdictions due process of law. The problem, of course, is what is meant by due process of law? Is due process whatever is required of the federal government, or could states continue to define due process independently? Does due process require the states to adopt some, all, or none of the provisions of the Bill of Rights? These questions and others complicate the already confusing issue of due process.

Three theories emerged as a result of the debate over which provisions of the Bill of Rights apply to the states. The first theory, known as *total incorporation,* holds that *all* the procedural safeguards in the Bill of Rights were made applicable to the states through the Due Process Clause of the Fourteenth Amendment. This process, also known as *absorption,* maintains that the Fourteenth Amendment's Due Process Clause, like a sponge, absorbs the Bill of Rights. Due process is merely a shorthand summary of the Bill of Rights. Without the right to counsel, protection against self-incrimination, and the other procedural safeguards, due process has no meaning. Advocates of total incorporation would include Supreme Court decisions that interpret procedural safeguards, but they would limit the definition of due process to the Bill of Rights.

A second theory, known as *selective incorporation,* holds that some, perhaps most, but certainly not all the Bill of Rights are applicable to the states through the Fourteenth Amendment. Selective incorporation holds that the Supreme Court should decide on a case-by-case basis whether a particular provision of the Bill of Rights is essential to due process. For example, the Fifth Amendment requires that a person charged with a federal offense be indicted by a grand jury. Selective incorporationists argue that the Due Process Clause of the Fourteenth Amendment does not require states to use grand jury indictment. In our federal system, states should be free to employ other methods of indictment and, in fact, approximately half the states indict by information, not by grand jury.

Over the years, the Supreme Court has favored selective incorporation. By the end of the 1960s, under the late Chief Justice Earl Warren, most of the major provisions of the Bill of Rights had been incorporated. There is still some disagreement over the extent to which the states must follow federal procedural rules. For example, in *Duncan v. Louisiana*, the Court ruled that due process requires a jury trial where the maximum punishment possible is two years' imprisonment. Although Justice Abe Fortas agreed that due process required a jury trial, he did not believe that states should have to observe other federal requirements, such as a unanimous verdict.[84] Later, the Supreme Court did, in fact, rule that unanimous verdicts are not essential to due process in all criminal cases.[85]

The third theory, which we might label "due process plus," holds that due process is not limited to the provisions of the Bill of Rights. Using the language of the non-interpretivists, advocates of this position argue that limiting due process to the Bill of Rights is too restrictive and too narrow. Due process evolves as society evolves and is not limited to how it was conceived by the eighteenth-century Framers or to how it is interpreted by twenty-first-century Supreme Courts.

In this section, we have tried to cover some of the basic ideas behind due process of law. If due process is, in fact, an evolving concept, then it will probably never be fully understood. Another problem is that due process depends heavily on individual notions of fairness and justice. For these reasons, due process will continue to elude a clear definition. We can only hope that this brief exposure to due process will assist the reader in coming to terms with this fascinating concept of law.

Equal Protection

Like the Due Process Clause, the Equal Protection Clause of the Fourteenth Amendment was designed to prevent discrimination against the newly freed slaves. The Fourteenth Amendment reads, "No State shall ... deny to any person within its jurisdiction the equal protection of the laws." The general thrust of the Equal Protection Clause is that government must treat people "similarly situated" alike. This does not mean that government may never classify people or never treat them differently. A state may classify people into those aged 16 years and older for the purpose of issuing driver licenses. Similarly, a state may provide special benefits for farmers, veterans, or low-income people. Depending on the criteria, these benefits may be extended to some people and denied to others without violating the Equal Protection Clause.

If equal protection permits government both to classify and to treat people differently, what then does it mean? The Supreme Court has approached equal protection analysis by weighing two major factors. The first is the nature or basis of the classification. In the past, states have classified people on the basis of race, age, sex, height, and other physical characteristics. States have also classified people according to wealth, IQ or some other test score, occupation, and education. In deciding whether a classification is constitutional or not, the Court determines whether there is a rational basis for the classification and whether the classification has some rational relationship to a legitimate government concern or goal.

Suppose, for example, that a college professor decides to categorize everyone in her class according to eye color, those with brown eyes in one group and those with non-brown eyes in the other group. Suppose further that she decrees that those with brown eyes will be allowed to earn extra credit points but those with non-brown eyes may not. The professor has denied the non-brown-eyed students equal protection because her classification scheme is arbitrary and has no basis in logic or reason. Furthermore, there is no rational relationship between eye color and class performance as reflected in grades.

Suppose, on the other hand, that the same professor decides to permit students to earn extra credit points based on good class attendance. She again divides the students into two groups: attenders and non-attenders. In the first place, this classification is based on objective criteria; that is, the number of absences a student has. Second, it may be reasonably assumed, though not necessarily proven, that good attendance and class performance are related. Although it is possible that someone with perfect attendance will fail the class, it is still sensible to assume that class attendance will help the performance of most of the students in the class. In conclusion, while a classification based on eye color is irrational and subjective, one based on attendance is objective and reasonable.

Over the years, the Supreme Court has developed criteria for determining whether classifications are reasonable. In the process, the Court has created a category containing what it calls *suspect classifications*. Race and alienage are examples of suspect classes. Any law that classifies on the basis of race or alienage is immediately "suspect" and presumed unconstitutional. The Court decides whether a classification is suspect by first determining whether its members constitute a "discrete and insular minority." That is, if the group members are readily identifiable, distinct, and separate from the majority of citizens, it may qualify as a suspect class. Second, the Court ascertains whether there has been a history of past discrimination against the group. Finally, the Court looks at the relative political power of the group. A group possessing relatively little ability to affect the political process may qualify for suspect status. These groups may need judicial protection from the majority that groups with political power do not require.

Race is a good example of a suspect class because it is difficult to justify the use of racial classifications. We do not mean, of course, that government census takers may not ask a person's race or record it on a census form. We do mean that race may not generally be a factor in how a person is treated under the law. Racial classification may be used if the state can suggest a compelling reason why it is justified. For example, affirmative action advocates maintain that the state's interest in overcoming past discrimination against blacks is compelling enough to justify favorable treatment of African Americans. Some people view this as "reverse discrimination" and contend that affirmative action programs are unconstitutional.

The Court has recognized a second category of classes that are commonly called "near-suspect" classes. Near-suspect classes include gender, illegitimacy, disability, and age. These groups, for one reason or another, fail to meet the criteria necessary for suspect status but still deserve some protection from possible discrimination at the hands of the majority. Women are a good example of a near-suspect class because numerically they constitute a majority of Americans. Yet few would deny that there has been a history of discrimination, especially in terms of employment opportunities, based on gender in the United States. On the other hand, since women received the right to vote in 1920, there has been no serious attempt, as in the case of African Americans, to prevent them from exercising voting rights.

Finally, there are classifications based on criteria that the Court considers "non-suspect." As we have already noted, laws that bestow benefits on farmers, veterans, poor people, college students, and other special interest groups are generally considered to be reasonable and will usually survive judicial review. The benefits available to these groups are open to anyone who is qualified to receive them regardless of race, religion, or gender.

Thus far, we have focused entirely on the first major factor of equal protection analysis: the nature of the classification. The second major factor is whether the law or practice being challenged involves a fundamental interest or right. When a state enacts legislation that infringes a fundamental right, the Court considers the nature of the right, the interest of the state, and the hardship to the individual in its analysis. If a constitutional or statutorily created right is involved, the Court is more likely to strike down the law. For example, in *Sherbert v. Verner*, the Court ruled that a Seventh-Day Adventist could not be denied unemployment benefits because her refusal to work on Saturdays (her Sabbath) made her unemployable. The Court found that the denial of benefits placed an unfair burden on her free exercise of religion.[86]

A major problem, of course, is determining exactly what is a fundamental right or interest. Consider the following situations: (1) a state law denies aliens the opportunity to become notaries;[87] (2) a county bar association refuses to allow a noncitizen to take the bar exam even though she is qualified in every other respect;[88] and (3) a state law prohibits the certification of noncitizens as public schoolteachers.[89] In each example, the person involved is a noncitizen and the issue is whether a state may deny access to these occupations to noncitizens. The Court must decide whether a person has a fundamental right to pursue a particular occupation.

As in the case of suspect classifications, a state may overcome an infringement of a fundamental right by showing it has a compelling interest in enacting the law. In addition, if the state can demonstrate that the law is carefully tailored to minimize the burden on a fundamental right, the statute may be constitutional. In our three examples, the Court found no compelling reason to deny noncitizens the opportunity to be notaries and lawyers but did find cause to deny noncitizens certification as public schoolteachers.[90] The Court held that the citizenship requirement "was rationally related to the State's interest in furthering the promotion of civic virtues and understanding."[91] The Court also held that because the law made exceptions for noncitizens who intended to apply for citizenship, it was carefully tailored to serve its purpose without placing an unnecessary burden on noncitizens.[92]

We finally come to the interrelationship between classification schemes and fundamental interests. In determining whether the Equal Protection Clause has been violated, the Supreme Court has employed a two-tier approach. If the law involves a suspect class, a fundamental right, or both, the Court applies "strict scrutiny" to the law. In such instances, the Court presumes that the law is unconstitutional and the state bears the heavy burden of overcoming this presumption. As we have seen, that is done by the state showing a compelling reason to justify the law.

The second tier is when the Court applies its reasonable basis analysis. If a law involves neither a suspect class nor a fundamental right, the Court merely determines whether there is a reasonable or rational basis for the law. The burden is on the person challenging the law to show that it violates equal protection. Earlier, we referred to the minimum age for receiving a driver license. Because persons under the age of 16 are not a suspect class and because most legislatures do not consider driving a fundamental right, the Court would simply determine whether the state had a reasonable or rational basis for setting the age limit at 16. Because driving a car requires a certain degree of maturity, it is easy to see that the law does not violate equal protection to 16-year-olds no matter how unfair they believe it to be.

Some constitutional law scholars and Supreme Court justices have advocated a middle-tier approach to equal protection analysis. This would allow judges to employ more than a reasonable basis analysis but less than strict scrutiny in close cases. For example, the Court could use this middle-tier analysis in cases in which near-suspect classifications are involved. In any case, the degree of scrutiny is a function of the amount of deference the Supreme Court is willing to afford legislative bodies. As our earlier discussion of judicial review indicated, the degree of deference to legislative bodies is critical to understanding the role of the courts in our constitutional system.

Civil Liberties

The field of civil liberties concerns one of the most controversial areas of constitutional law because it involves the fundamental question of the rights of the individual versus the rights of society. Most people agree that order and stability are necessary for personal freedom to exist, and that individuals must sacrifice some freedom for the good of society. However, we do not wish to sacrifice more freedom than is absolutely necessary to achieve the desired level of stability. But how much stability is enough and how much freedom must be sacrificed to achieve it? Unfortunately, there is no easy answer. This is an especially difficult question in a democratic society that simultaneously values individual freedom and majority rule. Nor is the tension between the rights of the individual and the rights of a democratic society easily reconciled. In the American political system, it is the job of the Supreme Court to strike a balance between the two. The times and the circumstances of society will determine the extent of personal liberty. At times we seem to enjoy tremendous freedom and at other times there seems to be a "chilling effect" on the exercise of individual freedom. As a result, civil liberties are in a constant state of fluctuation in which the amount of freedom we enjoy will depend on the willingness of society and the Court to tolerate our exercise of freedom.

Civil liberties are not rights conferred upon citizens by government as they are often misperceived to be. John Brigham has written that liberties "are rights held against authorities" that "limit interference with a variety of activities deemed worthy of special protection."[93] In other words, certain liberties, such as freedom of speech and religion, are considered to be so fundamental that they are protected from majority rule. The field of civil liberties is traditionally divided into First Amendment freedoms, and the rights of the accused. First Amendment freedoms include freedom of religion, speech and assembly, and freedom of the press. Because the rights of the accused, such as the right to counsel, are addressed in other sections of this book, we will limit our discussion here to First Amendment freedoms. We begin with freedom of religion.

There are actually two clauses in the First Amendment that pertain to freedom of religion: the Establishment Clause and the Free Exercise Clause. The Establishment Clause reads, "Congress shall make no law respecting an establishment of religion." One theory of the Establishment Clause is that it was designed to erect a "wall of separation" between church and state. This theory holds that the majority will attempt to use the power of government to promote or advance a particular religion. To prevent that from happening, civil libertarians must be vigilant about any attempt to use state power to promote religion in any manner. In other words, the wall should be kept high. A second theory asserts that erecting a wall of separation results in government hostility toward religion, which was never the intent of the Constitution's Framers. Instead, the Establishment Clause was designed to ensure that all religions received equal treatment from government. As long as government shows no preference for one religion over others, the Establishment Clause is not violated.

Cases involving the Establishment Clause have entailed those in which government financial aid is at issue and those in which some form of religious exercise is challenged. The first category consists of cases in which the government sought to provide financial aid to parochial schools, for example. In the early cases,[94] the Supreme Court was asked to rule on the constitutionality of providing bus transportation, school books, and other forms of assistance to students attending religiously affiliated schools. In some instances the Court allowed such government aid, while in others the aid was denied. The Court formulated the much-criticized *Lemon* test to resolve issues of financial aid. The *Lemon* test states that in order to survive judicial scrutiny, the policy (1) must have a secular legislative purpose, (2) may neither advance nor inhibit religion, and (3) must avoid excessive entanglement between church and state. If any one of these three components is not met, the Establishment Clause is violated.

The second category of establishment cases includes those in which some form of religious exercise involving government is challenged. The prayers-in-school controversy that continues to surface in political debate is such an example. Beginning with *Engel v. Vitale*[95] in 1962, which banned the use of a nondenominational prayer in New York public schools, the Supreme Court has been faced with a multitude of religious exercise cases. The Court has been asked to rule on the posting of the Ten Commandments in public school classrooms,[96] an Alabama law authorizing a period of silence for "silent meditation or prayer,"[97] and prayers at high school commencement ceremonies[98] and football games.[99] To illustrate the complexity of these issues, the Supreme Court held in its 1994 Term that the University of Virginia's refusal to pay for the publication of a Christian student magazine from student fees violated the students' freedom of *speech*. The University had refused to pay for the publication on the grounds that to do so would violate the Establishment Clause. However, the Court ruled 5 to 4 that freedom of speech, not the Establishment Clause, was the critical issue involved.[100]

The second great clause of the First Amendment that deals with religion is, of course, the Free Exercise Clause. After admonishing Congress not to establish a religion, the Constitution forbids it to prohibit "the free exercise thereof." A common thread that runs through the free exercise cases is this fundamental question: Should an individual or group be exempt from some general law or obligation for religious reasons? The Supreme Court confronted this very question in *Reynolds v. United States,* better known as the Mormon Polygamy Case.[101] George Reynolds argued that because polygamy was a tenet of the Mormon religion, he and other Mormons should be exempt from laws that make multiple marriages a crime. The Supreme Court refused to grant the exemption and drew a distinction between holding a religious belief and acting on that religious belief. Mormons were free to believe in polygamy, but the state may punish actions that violate the norms of society. "Suppose," Chief Justice Morrison Waite asked, "one believed that human sacrifices were a necessary part of religious worship, would it be seriously contended that the civil government [could] not interfere to prevent a sacrifice?"[102]

In addition to the polygamy issue, religious groups have sought exemptions from general laws in a variety of other cases. Jehovah's Witnesses have challenged laws that require reciting the Pledge of Allegiance in public schools[103] and that require licenses for religious door-to-door solicitation.[104] In *Wisconsin v. Yoder*, Amish parents successfully challenged compulsory school attendance beyond the eighth grade for their children.[105] Finally, in *Employment Division, Department of Human Resources of Oregon v. Smith*, the Supreme Court ruled against two Native Americans who claimed that their use of peyote was for religious purposes.[106] As in other areas of civil liberties, the Supreme Court fluctuates on its willingness to protect free exercise claims.

Perhaps nothing in recent years has caused more controversy in the free exercise of religion than the debate over government placing "burdens" on the free exercise of religion. In 1993 Congress passed the Religious Freedom Restoration Act (RFRA) in reaction to a Supreme Court decision, *Employment Division, Department of Human Resources of Oregon v. Smith*.[107] The decision reversed a previous Supreme Court interpretation that required government to have a "compelling reason" for placing a burden on the free exercise of religion. The Act made it clear that Congress wanted the compelling reason standard to be reinstated when laws placed a burden on religious free exercise. Many states followed by passing their own versions of the Religious Freedom Restoration Act.[108] Problems arose when critics of the laws argued that they were being used to encourage discrimination against homosexuals and other gender minorities. For example, Indiana's RFRA had to be amended when critics alleged that it "could be used by business owners to deny services to gays and lesbians for religious reasons."[109] Pressure came from businesses and groups, including the NCAA, which threatened to boycott events scheduled for Indianapolis because of the law. In April 2015 the Indiana state legislature amended the law to make clear that its purpose was not to endorse any kind of discrimination against minorities.[110] Indiana's experience demonstrates that the battle over religious freedom and minority rights is far from over.

Using religious freedom to justify florists, photographers, caterers and even health clubs refusing to serve lesbian, gay, bisexual and transgender (LGBT) customers has not been the only problem. In mid-2015 in Kentucky, a county clerk achieved notoriety when, in the aftermath of the Supreme Court decision legalizing same-sex marriages, she refused to issue marriage licenses with her signature. After being jailed and threatened with additional contempt proceedings, the clerk relented. However, the case illustrates the belief by some that religious beliefs should be able to trump the rule of law.

Freedom of speech is the second great area of civil liberties protected by the First Amendment. Although freedom of speech can be defended on the need to protect the dignity of all persons, it is absolutely essential for a democratic society. Justice Oliver Wendell Holmes, Jr. said that free speech in a democratic society was essential to the "marketplace of ideas."[111] Freedom of speech, like other liberties, requires the Supreme Court to balance the rights of the speaker against the rights of society. For our purposes, we will examine the following areas: pure speech, symbolic speech, and speech plus action.

Pure speech is the use of language alone to communicate one's ideas. Pure speech becomes a problem when the speaker urges his or her audience to do something that is illegal. In one sense, the person responding to the speech is responsible for his or her response. For example, if a person is urged to participate in a lynching, each member of the mob is guilty of the crime. On the other hand, the person who exhorts others to illegal actions is equally guilty in the eyes of many people. In an early free-speech case, the Supreme Court formulated the "clear and present danger test" to help determine when government may punish speech.[112] The clear and present danger test held that if a person's speech presented a clear and present danger of bringing about an evil which the government had a right to prevent, then the speaker could be punished. Another area in which pure speech has raised problems is in the category of "fighting words" or "words likely to cause an average addressee to fight."[113] Fighting words would include but are not limited to obscene words that would provoke the average person to engage in a confrontation. In general, the Supreme Court is willing to permit government to impose these and other reasonable "time, place, and manner" restrictions on even pure speech.

A second and even more controversial area of free speech is symbolic speech. Symbolic speech involves the nonverbal conveyance of an idea or opinion, such as burning an American flag. Although not the first case to raise the issue of symbolic speech, *Tinker v. Des Moines Independent School District*[114] is one of the best known. High school students opposed to the war in Vietnam wore black armbands to protest that war in violation of a school policy. The Supreme Court upheld the students' right to engage in non-disruptive protest under the First Amendment. Burning of the American flag has aroused debate over the concept of symbolic speech. The Supreme Court ruled in *Texas v. Johnson*[115] that states could not punish flag burning. The Court reaffirmed its commitment to this form of freedom of expression by declaring the Flag Protection Act of 1989 (passed in response to *Johnson*) unconstitutional in *United States v. Eichman.*[116]

The final type of free-speech constitutional issue is speech plus action, which combines pure speech and symbolic speech. If a person makes a speech while burning a draft card, is the speech protected even if the draft card burning is not? In other words, is it possible to separate a forbidden act (draft card burning) from protected speech? In *Street v. New York*, the Supreme Court overturned Sidney Street's conviction for flag burning on the grounds that it was impossible for the jury to separate the action from his accompanying speech.[117] However, the year before *Street* in *United States v. O'Brien*, the Supreme Court held that David Paul O'Brien could be punished for burning his draft card to protest the war in Vietnam, even though a speech in opposition to the war was protected.[118] In any event, it is difficult for some people to understand why burning a draft card may be punished but burning a flag may not be.

Some of the most intriguing issues of freedom of expression are those developing in the jurisprudence dealing with the nexus of the First Amendment and the Internet. Congress passed a 103-page law, the Telecommunications Act of 1996,[119] that included the provisions commonly known as the Communications Decency Act (CDA) of 1996.[120] In part, the law provided that anyone sending communications that were "obscene or indecent" or "patently offensive as measured by community standards" to anyone under the age of 18 could be imprisoned for two years as well as fined. Consortiums of nearly 50 organizations—private and commercial—filed suit challenging the constitutionality of the statute.

In the case that one commentator referred to as "Internet 101 for Justices,"[121] but officially known as *Reno v. ACLU*,[122] Justice John Paul Stevens lauded the congressional goal of protecting minors from harmful influences in a medium that was used by approximately 40 million people at the time of the trial. He examined the nature of the Internet—that no single organization controls the Internet and that it is incredibly diverse in content. Furthermore, while no one program can block sexually explicit sites, some systems assist parents in controlling content that may come into the home; almost all such sites carry warnings and some providers use various screening devices to determine the age of the recipients. The Internet is less invasive than television or radio, and users must initiate the contact and rarely reach a site accidentally.

After describing the Internet, Stevens turned to the crux of the case:

> The vagueness of the CDA is a matter of special concern for two reasons. First the CDA is a content-based regulation of speech. The vagueness of such a regulation raises special First Amendment concerns because of its obvious chilling effect on free speech. Second, the CDA is a criminal statute. In addition to the opprobrium and stigma of a criminal conviction, the CDA threatens violators with penalties including up to two years in prison for each act of violation. The severity of criminal sanctions may well cause speakers to remain silent rather than communicate even arguably unlawful words, ideas, and images. As a practical matter, this increased deterrent effect, coupled with the "risk of discriminatory enforcement" of vague regulations, poses greater First Amendment concerns than those implicated by the civil regulations [citations omitted].[123]

In addition, the CDA went too far in suppressing the speech that adults have a constitutional right to send and receive, especially because the transmission of child pornography and obscenity, in whatever medium, is already a criminal act under other statutes. Stevens closed with the statement,

> As a matter of constitutional tradition, in the absence of evidence to the contrary, we presume that governmental regulation of the content of speech is more likely to interfere with the free exchange of ideas than to encourage it. The interest in encouraging freedom of expression in a democratic society outweighs any theoretical but unproven benefit of censorship.[124]

The Supreme Court continues to emphasize that the First Amendment guards only against encroachment by the government and does not provide a shield against merely private conduct.[125] For example, a private company "does not have a right under the First Amendment to the United States Constitution ... to send unsolicited e-mail advertisements over the Internet," and Internet service providers may block such attempts.[126]

Freedom of the press is the last great area of civil liberties to be discussed in this section. Freedom of the press is less important to us as individuals than freedom of religion or speech, which are personal liberties. Freedom of the press involves the rights of someone else; that is, the press. In a sense, however, freedom of the press is about a citizen's right to receive information. Just as a speaker has a right to air his or her views, an individual has a right to hear the views of others. This makes a free press vital to a democratic society.

Problems with freedom of the press fall into three general categories: prior restraint, libel, and obscenity. Under a system of *prior restraint,* the government requires the press to submit to a preclearance, a procedure whereby officials can check a publication for problems and eliminate them before the publication can reach its audience. For example, articles for high school newspapers are frequently submitted to the paper's faculty sponsor for such preclearance, and the Supreme Court approved the practice in *Hazelwood School District v. Kuhlmeier.*[127] Issues involving questions of national security is another area where prior restraint is sometimes justified. Libel is the punishment of an author or publisher after something has been printed and distributed. Libel is a form of defamation in which the person libeled seeks damages from the author or publisher for inflicting the alleged harm, usually to a person's reputation. While private persons may avail themselves of the protection from libel, the Supreme Court has held that a higher standard of malice exists for public officials and those who deliberately seek to become public figures, such as movie stars.[128] Finally, in *Roth v. United States,*[129] the Supreme Court ruled that "implicit in the history of the First Amendment is the rejection of obscenity as utterly without redeeming social importance."[130] As a result, it became necessary for the Court to fashion some sort of test to determine which materials were obscene and unprotected and which were protected. Not only the printed word but also motion pictures,[131] radio broadcasts,[132] virtual child pornography,[133] and even nude dancing[134] have sought the protection of the First Amendment. To the consternation of the justices, finding an acceptable definition of obscenity and the scope of freedom of expression have proven elusive.

Civil liberties are important because they reinforce the rule of law in society. There are some activities that are so vital to democratic society that even the government must respect them. Civil liberties are also important because they provide the freedom necessary for individuals to express themselves without government interference. Democracy strives to ensure that each person can reach his or her full potential. Civil liberties are the guarantees the Constitution provides to meet this ideal.

CONCLUSION

This chapter has tried to introduce the field of constitutional law within the limits of an introductory text. We have examined judicial review, introduced several approaches to constitutional interpretation, and analyzed five major constitutional doctrines. Yet we have only covered the tip of the iceberg. Constitutional law is a vast and fascinating area of law because it deals with ideals, hopes, and rights for which some people are willing to die. In a real sense, our Constitution says a lot about who we are as a people and as a nation. The Constitution is the foundation of American law, since in the final analysis all our law must conform to its principles.

NOTES

1. *Marbury v. Madison*, 1 Cranch 137 (1803), at 177.
2. Dexter Perkins, *Charles Evans Hughes and American Democratic Statesmanship* (Westport, CT: Greenwood Press, 1956), p. 32.
3. *Bush v. Gore*, 531 U.S. 98 (2000).
4. *National Federation of Independent Business v. Serbelius*, 567 U.S. _____ (2012).
5. *United States v. Butler*, 297 U.S. 1 (1936), at 62.
6. Craig R. Ducat, *Modes of Constitutional Interpretation* (St. Paul, MN: West, 1978), p. 1.
7. The date of the president's inauguration was not changed to January 20 until the passage of the Twentieth Amendment in 1933.
8. This is the reason that those appointed came to be known as the "Midnight Judges."
9. *Marbury v. Madison*, 1 Cranch 137 (1803), at 173.
10. In 1857, the Supreme Court invalidated the Missouri Compromise in *Dred Scott v. Sanford*, 19 Howard 393 (1857).
11. See, for example, Henry J. Abraham, *The Judicial Process*, 3rd edn (New York: Oxford University Press, 1975), pp. 354–376.
12. See, for example, Sheldon Goldman and Thomas P. Jahnige, *The Federal Courts as a Political System*, 3rd edn (New York: Harper & Row, 1985), pp. 224–229.
13. See Howard Ball, *Courts and Politics: The Federal Judicial System*, 2nd edn (Englewood Cliffs, NJ: Prentice-Hall, 1987), ch. 5.
14. For a brief discussion of the British approach to right to counsel, see Martin Bahl, "The Sixth Amendment as Constitutional Theory: Does Originalism Require That *Massiah* be Abandoned?," 82 J. Crim. L. & Criminology 423 (1991).
15. "The Liberties of the Massachusetts Colonies in New England, 1641," in Neil H. Cogan, ed., *Contexts of the Constitution* (New York: Foundation Press), p. 672.
16. *Powell v. Alabama*, 287 U.S. 45 (1932).
17. *Betts v. Brady*, 316 U.S. 455 (1942).
18. *Gideon v. Wainwright*, 372 U.S. 335 (1963).
19. *Argersinger v. Hamlin*, 407 U.S. 25 (1972).
20. *Escobedo v. Illinois*, 378 U.S. 478 (1964).
21. *Miranda v. Arizona*, 384 U.S. 436 (1966).
22. On the right to effective counsel, see *Bell v. Cone*, 535 U.S. 685 (2002).
23. *Gideon v. Wainwright*, 372 U.S. 335 (1963), at 344.
24. *Ollman v. Evans*, 750 F.2d 970 (1984) (Bork J., concurring), at 995.
25. Judith A. Baer, "The Fruitless Search for Original Intent," in Michael W. McCann and Gerald L. Houseman, eds, *Judging the Constitution: Critical Essays on Judicial Lawmaking* (Boston, MA: Scott, Foresman, 1989), p. 63.
26. "Perspectives," *Newsweek* 132, 3 (July 20, 1998), p. 21.
27. *Texas v. Johnson*, 491 U.S. 397 (1989).
28. Paul Brest, "The Misconceived Quest for the Original Understanding," in John H. Garvey and T. Alexander Aleinikoff, eds, *Modern Constitutional Theory: A Reader* (St. Paul, MN: West, 1989), p. 60.

29. Ibid.
30. Ibid, pp. 60–61.
31. Baer, p. 53.
32. Ibid.
33. *Chisholm v. Georgia*, 2 Dallas 419 (1793).
34. Baer, p. 59.
35. Ibid, p. 62; Lief H. Carter, *Contemporary Constitutional Lawmaking: The Supreme Court and the Art of Politics* (New York: Pergamon Press, 1985), p. 42.
36. Thomas C. Grey, "Do We Have an Unwritten Constitution?," in John H. Garvey and T. Alexander Aleinikoff, eds, *Modern Constitutional Reader* (St. Paul, MN: West, 1989), p. 29.
37. Ibid.
38. *Texas v. Johnson*, 491 U.S. 397 (Kennedy, J., concurring), at 420.
39. *Tinker v. Des Moines Independent Community School District*, 393 U.S. 503 (1969) (Black, J., dissenting).
40. Grey, p. 28.
41. *McCulloch v. Maryland*, 4 Wheaton 316 (1819).
42. *Griswold v. Connecticut*, 351 U.S. 479 (1965).
43. *Roe v. Wade*, 410 U.S. 113 (1973).
44. James MacGregor Burns, J.W. Peltason, and Thomas Cronin, *Government by the People, Texas Edition*, 2nd edn (Englewood Cliffs, NJ: Prentice-Hall, 1998), p. G-3.
45. *Hammer v. Dagenhart*, 247 U.S. 251 (1918).
46. *United States v. E.C. Knight Co.*, 156 U.S. 1 (1895).
47. *Schechter Poultry Corp. v. United States*, 295 U.S. 495 (1935).
48. *United States v. Darby Lumber Co.*, 312 U.S. 100 (1941).
49. *National Labor Relations Board v. Jones & Laughlin Corp.*, 301 U.S. 1 (1937).
50. *Wickard v. Filburn*, 317 U.S. 111 (1942).
51. *Heart of Atlanta Motel v. United States*, 379 U.S. 241 (1964).
52. *Maryland v. Wirtz*, 392 U.S. 183 (1968).
53. *National League of Cities v. Usery*, 426 U.S. 833 (1976).
54. *Garcia v. San Antonio Transit Authority*, 469 U.S. 528 (1985).
55. *Printz v. United States*, 521 U.S. 898 (1997).
56. *United States v. Lopez*, 514 U.S. 549 (1995) (Kennedy J., concurring), at 575.
57. 18 U.S.C.A. § 922(g)(1)(A).
58. *United States v. Lopez*, 514 U.S. 549 (1995) (Kennedy J., concurring), at 580.
59. Ibid., at 567.
60. *United States v. Morrison*, 529 U.S. 598 (2000).
61. See *Seminole Tribe of Florida v. Florida*, 517 U.S. 44 (1996) and *Alden v. Maine*, 527 U.S. 706 (1999).
62. See *New York v. United States*, 504 U.S. 224 (1993) and *Printz v. United States*, 521 U.S. 898 (1997).
63. *Gonzales v. Raich*, 545 U.S. 1 (2005).
64. *Arizona v. United States*, 567 U.S. 1 (2012).
65. James Madison, "Federalist No. 51," in Clinton Rossiter, ed., *The Federalist Papers* (New York: New American Library, 1961), pp. 321–322.
66. Raoul Berger, *Executive Privilege: A Constitutional Myth* (New York: Bantam Books, 1974), p. 1.
67. Arthur M. Schlesinger, Jr., *The Imperial Presidency* (New York: Popular Library, 1973), p. 28.
68. *United States v. Nixon*, 418 U.S. 683 (1974).

69. 2 U.S.C.A. §§ 691 *et seq.*
70. *Raines v. Byrd*, 521 U.S. 811 (1997).
71. *Clinton v. New York*, 524 U.S. 417 (1998).
72. Ibid., at 448–449.
73. *Clinton v. Jones*, 520 U.S. 681 (1997).
74. *In re Sealed Case*, No. 98-3069 (D.C. Cir., 1998).
75. *In re Lindsey*, No. 98-3060 (D.C. Cir., 1998).
76. See, for example, *Rumsfeld v. Padilla*, 542 U.S. 426 (2004) and *Hamdi v. Rumsfeld*, 542 U.S. 507 (2004).
77. U.S. Constitution, Art. II, § 2, cl. 3.
78. *National Labor Relations Board v. Noel Canning*, 573 U.S. ____ (2014).
79. *Barron v. City of Baltimore*, 7 Peters 243 (1833).
80. See, generally, *Rochin v. California*, 342 U.S. 165 (1952) for an excellent discussion of the meaning of due process.
81. *Lochner v. New York*, 198 U.S. 45 (1905).
82. *Adkins v. Children's Hospital*, 261 U.S. 525 (1923).
83. *Miranda v. Arizona*, 384 U.S. 436 (1966).
84. *Duncan v. Louisiana*, 391 U.S. 145 (1968) (Fortas, J., concurring).
85. See *Johnson v. Louisiana*, 406 U.S. 356 (1972) and *Apodaca v. Oregon*, 406 U.S. 404 (1972).
86. *Sherbert v. Verner*, 374 U.S. 398 (1963).
87. *Bernal v. Fainter*, 467 U.S. 216 (1984).
88. *In re Griffiths*, 413 U.S. 717 (1973).
89. *Ambach v. Norwick*, 441 U.S. 68 (1979).
90. Ibid.
91. Ibid., at 80.
92. Ibid.
93. John Brigham, *Civil Liberties and American Democracy* (Washington, DC: Congressional Quarterly Press, 1984), p. 6.
94. See *Everson v. Board of Education*, 330 U.S. 1 (1947); *Board of Education v. Allen*, 392 U.S. 236 (1968); and *Lemon v. Kurzman*, 403 U.S. 602 (1971).
95. *Engel v. Vitale*, 370 U.S. 421 (1962).
96. *Stone v. Graham*, 449 U.S. 39 (1980).
97. *Wallace v. Jaffree*, 472 U.S. 38 (1985).
98. *Lee v. Weisman*, 505 U.S. 577 (1992).
99. *Santa Fe Independent School District v. Doe*, 530 U.S. 290 (2000).
100. *Rosenberger v. Rector and Visitors of University of Virginia*, 513 U.S. 959 (1994).
101. *Reynolds v. United States*, 8 Otto 145 (1879).
102. Ibid., at 166.
103. *Minersville School District v. Gobitis*, 310 U.S. 585 (1940) and *West Virginia State Board of Education v. Barnette*, 319 U.S. 624 (1943).
104. *Murdock v. Pennsylvania*, 319 U.S. 105 (1943) and *Martin v. City of Struthers*, 319 U.S. 141 (1943).
105. *Wisconsin v. Yoder*, 406 U.S. 208 (1972).
106. *Employment Division, Department of Human Resources of Oregon v. Smith*, 494 U.S. 872 (1990).
107. Ibid.
108. Christopher C. Lund, "Religious Liberty after *Gonzales*: A Look at State RFRAS," 55 S.D.L. Rev. 466 (2010 symposium). pp. 466–500.

109. Tony Cook, "Gov. Mike Pence signs 'religious freedom' bill in private," *Indianapolis* Star, April 2, 2015, http://www.indystar.com/story/news/politics/2015/03/25/gov-mike-pence-sign-religious-freedom-bill-thursday/70448858/ (visited December 1, 2015).

110. Ibid.

111. *Abrams v. United States*, 250 U.S. 616 (1919) (Holmes, J., dissenting).

112. *Schenck v. United States*, 249 U.S. 47 (1919).

113. *Chaplinsky v. New Hampshire*, 315 U.S. 568 (1942), at 573.

114. *Tinker v. Des Moines Independent School District*, 393 U.S. 503 (1969).

115. *Texas v. Johnson*, 491 U.S. 397 (1989).

116. *United States v. Eichman*, 496 U.S. 310 (1990).

117. *Street v. New York*, 394 U.S. 576 (1969).

118. *United States v. O'Brien*, 391 U.S. 367 (1968).

119. Telecommunications Act of 1996, Pub. L. 104-104.

120. 47 U.S.C.A. § 223.

121. Donna M. Higgins, "Federal Courts Set a Trend in Rulings on Internet Regulation," *Computer & On-Line Industry Litigation Reporter*, July 1, 1997, p. 24415.

122. *Reno v. ACLU*, 521 U.S. 844 (1997).

123. Ibid., at 871–872.

124. Ibid.

125. *Hurley v. Irish-American Gay Group of Boston*, 515 U.S. 557 (1995).

126. *Cyber Promotions, Inc. v. America On-Line, Inc.*, 948 F.Supp. 436 (E.D. Penn. 1996), at 447.

127. *Hazelwood School District v. Kuhlmeier*, 484 U.S. 260 (1988).

128. See *New York Times Company v. Sullivan*, 376 U.S. 254 (1964) and *Time Inc. v. Firestone*, 424 U.S. 448 (1976).

129. *Roth v. United States*, 354 U.S. 476 (1957).

130. Ibid., p. 484.

131. *Kingsley International Corporation v. Regents of University of New York*, 360 U.S. 684 (1959).

132. *Federal Communications Commission v. Pacifica Foundation*, 438 U.S. 726 (1978).

133. *Ashcroft v. Free Speech Coalition*, 535 U.S. 234 (2002).

134. *Barnes v. Glen Theatre, Inc.*, 501 U.S. 560 (1991).

Criminal Law

O f all the subfields of American law, criminal law is perhaps the most controversial. As we noted in Chapter 1, criminal law deals with activities that have been formally forbidden in a society by its government. The controversy surrounding criminal law centers around both the substance or content of criminal law and the procedures by which we deprive accused persons of their life, liberty, and property. Substantive criminal law asks questions such as what should be made a crime, what is the appropriate punishment for committing a particular crime, and what specific behavior constitutes a crime. The first question focuses on the kinds of activities that may or should be forbidden by government. Certain actions, like murder, are inherently evil and universally condemned as criminal behavior. Other activities, such as gambling, are questionable as "criminal" because there is not universal consensus on their immorality as there is with crimes like murder and rape.

For example, at one time most states imposed long sentences on persons convicted of possessing marijuana. Many people, while still believing that marijuana use should be forbidden, believed that the penalty was excessive for the crime of mere possession of the drug as opposed to the manufacture or sale of it. Indeed some states, like Colorado, have legalized the sale and possession of marijuana, while others still categorize both as crimes. Making the punishment, if any, fit the crime, then, is an important concern of criminal law and one that we will revisit with our case study at the end of the chapter.

As controversial as substantive criminal law is, it pales in comparison with the controversy generated by procedural law. Procedural criminal law is closely associated with the concept of due process of law. Due process of law refers to the process or procedures that must be followed before a person can legally be deprived of "life, liberty, or property." In criminal law, procedural due process sets forth the procedures that government must observe before it can execute, imprison, or fine an individual. Although it is not really a game, procedural due process may be thought of as the "rules of the game" that the State must adhere to before it imposes punishment. Some people argue that government has "gone too far" in protecting the rights of those accused of crimes, while ignoring the rights of their victims. Critics of procedural due process argue that most persons accused of crimes are indeed guilty and that they should not be allowed to escape punishment because of a "technicality" in the law. Justice, after all, requires that persons committing crimes be punished.

Defenders of procedural due process offer a number of rationales for supporting the rights of persons accused of committing crimes. First, our system of justice is based on the assumption that a person is innocent until proven guilty; thus, the State bears the burden of proof in a criminal case. Under our legal system, the accused is not required to assist the State in securing his or her own conviction. Consequently, safeguards, such as protection against self-incrimination, ensure that the State has evidence independent of the accused's own testimony to secure a conviction.

A second reason for procedural safeguards is the possibility of unjustly convicting an innocent person. In recent years, for example, DNA testing has revealed a startling number of wrongful convictions of persons for serious crimes such as murder and rape.[1] Because no system of justice is infallible, most Americans believe that we should take whatever precautions are needed to ensure that, ideally, the innocent person is always freed and the guilty person is always convicted. Overall, most defenders of procedural due process would argue that it is better for ten guilty persons to go free than for one innocent person to be imprisoned.

A final rationale for protecting the rights of the accused is political. Since time immemorial, governments have used their criminal justice systems as a means of repressing certain groups in society. Governments have used the criminal justice system against religious, racial, and political dissidents throughout history. The argument, then, is that if government can use the law against one unpopular group today, it may very well use it against a group to which we belong tomorrow. Therefore, citizens must remain vigilant to ensure that punishment for criminal activity is never used as a pretext for persecuting an individual or a group for its religious or political beliefs. Only by guaranteeing that government obeys the "rules of the game" can we be certain that religious, political, or hysterical prosecutions do not occur under the pretext of law and order.

This chapter will focus on both the substance and procedures of criminal law. First, it will discuss the characteristics of criminal law and the elements of a crime. Second, it will examine three areas of criminal procedures to highlight our previous discussion of this controversial topic. Third, we will briefly focus on the juvenile justice system. Finally, we will look at two case studies, one substantive and one procedural, to illustrate the complexities of criminal law.

CHARACTERISTICS OF CRIMINAL LAW

What is the nature of criminal law? In Chapter 1, we noted that one of the functions of law is to proscribe certain activities. In so doing, a society is defining exactly what is and what is not acceptable behavior. In a democratic society, it is the function of legislative bodies, as the elected representatives of the people, to decide what behavior will be made criminal and what penalties will be attached to violations of the law. In this section, we will attempt to define the nature of criminal behavior more precisely, with an emphasis on how criminal law reflects the society that creates it.

In Chapter 1, we introduced two terms: *malum in se* and *malum prohibitum*. *Malum in se* means "wrong in itself" and is applied to behavior that could be considered inherently wrong or evil. Murder and rape are two examples of acts that are criminal because they are inherently wrong in themselves. Murder (as opposed to killing in self-defense, for example) is inherently wrong because there can be no legitimate justification for it. Rape is another example. What possible justification could exist for a person to force oneself sexually on another? Crimes that are considered *malum in se* have two primary characteristics. They tend to have highly moral overtones, and there is nearly universal consensus that the type of behavior involved cannot be tolerated in a civilized society. The latter characteristic does not mean that every person agrees that rape should be a crime; obviously the rapist may not think so. It means that acts of murder and rape have been universally condemned by most civilized societies throughout history. In a sense, then, crimes that are *malum in se* are the easiest to define because they are so universally condemned.

A much more complex problem surrounds the second category of crimes—those defined as *malum prohibitum*. Some behavior has been labeled "criminal" not so much because it is inherently wrong or universally condemned, but merely because a legislative body has deemed it undesirable. As we noted in Chapter 1, parking in a "No Parking" zone is not the kind of behavior that arouses moral condemnation or social ostracism, but it is a crime, albeit a minor one. It is a crime because a city council has chosen to make it one. Crimes defined as *malum prohibitum* may have rational justifications, such as public safety or traffic control, but they are hardly inherently evil. What, then, makes the classification of *malum prohibitum* so complex? It is the fact that society is sometimes in disagreement over whether an activity is criminal because it is immoral or because it is just undesirable. In this chapter's introduction, we mentioned gambling to illustrate this problem. Why is gambling a crime? Is it because it is a morally reprehensible activity? If so, then why do millions of presumably moral people annually bet on the Super Bowl? Is it because the compulsive gambler may gamble away the family's grocery money? Is it because gambling is an activity that brings the "wrong element" into a community? Any or all of these could be reasons that a legislature might choose to prohibit gambling. However, the success of places like Las Vegas and the legalization of casino gambling in many states indicate that millions of people see no harm in it.

In addition to gambling, activities such as prostitution, the illegal use (as opposed to the illegal sale) of drugs, and even homosexuality have at one time or another been declared criminal partly because they are considered immoral by some and partly because they were once considered offensive by the majority. The prohibition of these activities is sometimes justified on the grounds that while morally debatable, they lead to other serious crimes or create other problems. Prostitution, for example, can spread AIDS and other sexually transmitted diseases, exploit women, lead to drug addiction, and result in violence against women. Drug addiction may lead its victims to commit crimes, such as burglary, to feed their habit. Finally, prohibiting so-called victimless crimes is justified on the grounds that the State has the right to safeguard the quality of life in a community. Prostitution, gambling, and drug addiction rely on baser human needs. The State should uplift the human spirit by prohibiting activities that debase individuals and society. In the final analysis then, activities labeled *malum prohibitum* may be considered immoral or just a nuisance, but either way, in a democratic society, legislatures may make them criminal.

One final aspect of the *malum prohibitum* category is worth mentioning. Given the debatable nature of the morality of such activities as gambling, what is the appropriate penalty? At one time some states allowed sentences of ten or more years for the mere possession of marijuana, regardless of the amount. Many people believed that such penalties were excessive, given the nature of the crime. Still others argued that only a "get-tough" policy would eradicate the undesirable activity. Today, many of the crimes we have been discussing are classified as misdemeanors. Prostitution, possession of small amounts of marijuana, and so forth receive small fines and/or light sentences. Laws dealing with the purveyors of crime are harsher. Selling drugs, particularly in a school zone, will result in a stiffer sentence than mere possession, and acting as a pimp is generally considered more serious than prostitution itself. In attempting to get at the source of the crime, the law has made the drug dealer, the pimp, and the bookmaker more criminally liable and therefore more susceptible to harsher penalties. Whether such tactics are effective in the "war on crime" is another matter.

As may already be apparent from the foregoing discussion of *malum in se* and *malum prohibitum*, criminal law is a reflection of the society that produces it. This does not mean, however, that legislative bodies in the United States are free to criminalize any behavior at will. The Supreme Court has held that it is unconstitutional for states to make marriage to a person of another race or sexual relations between two consenting adults of the same sex a crime.[2] Still, as a general rule in an Islamic theocracy, such as Iran, criminal law will reflect the religious teachings of the Koran, and in a Catholic country it will reflect the tenets of Catholicism. In addition, the law will change to reflect changes in society, especially attitude changes. As noted, the use of marijuana was once considered a serious crime with harsh penalties, whereas today the penalties in most states are either relatively light or non-existent. As public tolerance of marijuana use grew, the severity of the penalties was reduced. As a society advances, its judgments about crime and punishment change. Thomas Gardner has written:

> The criminal punishments used hundreds of years ago in England and Europe were severe. In England alone, more than two hundred offenses were punishable by death. Condemned criminals were usually hanged, although occasionally they were beheaded, quartered, or drawn (dragged along the ground at the tail of a horse).[3]

Obviously, both the number of capital offenses and the penalties have been changed in modern England. The point is that attitudes about what should be made a crime and what penalty should be assessed vary from one society to another and from one historical era to another. In 1850, Justice Robert Grier wrote of lotteries:

> [W]idespread pestilence of lotteries [that] infests the whole community; it enters every dwelling; it reaches every class; it preys upon the hard earnings of the poor; it plunders the ignorant and the simple.[4]

Today, most states have turned to lotteries as a means of relieving their financial problems. Law does and should change with the needs and attitudes of the society it serves.

ELEMENTS OF A CRIME

In this section, we will examine a very important aspect of substantive criminal law: the elements of a crime. Specifically, we will focus upon the type of behavior that an individual must engage in to be guilty of a crime. Obviously, different crimes require different behavior, but there are common elements necessary for proving all crimes, and identifying these common elements will be our primary concern. The first element of a crime is the *actus reus*. Black's Law Dictionary defines *actus* as "an act or action"[5] and *reus* as "a person judicially accused of a crime."[6] Therefore, *actus reus* is literally the action of a person accused of a crime. David W. Neubauer has defined *actus reus* simply as "the guilty act."[7] All this means is that a criminal statute must clearly define exactly what act is deemed "guilty"; that is, the exact behavior that is being prohibited. This is done so that all persons are put on notice that if they perform the guilty act they will be liable for criminal punishment. Courts will occasionally nullify a law that is "void for vagueness." Justice George Sutherland defined an unconstitutionally vague law as "a statute which forbids or requires the doing of an act in terms so vague that men of common intelligence must necessarily guess at its meaning and differ as to its application."[8] Unless the *actus reus* is clearly defined, one may not know whether or not one's behavior is illegal.

In addition to adequate notice of the proscribed behavior, another characteristic of *actus reus* needs clarification. The guilty act may not just be what one does; it may also be what one fails to do. Criminal laws not only prohibit certain behavior; in some cases they require action. That is, a person can be held criminally liable for failure to act. Examples of when failure to act is a crime include failure to come to the aid of a police officer when requested to do so and failure to submit to a breathalyzer test when requested to do so.[9] On May 27, 1998, Judge G. Thomas VanBebber sentenced Michael Fortier to 12 years in prison, imposed a fine of $200,000, and ordered restitution in the amount of $4100 to an Arkansas gun dealer whose weapons had been stolen. Fortier's crime? He failed to warn authorities of the plans of Timothy McVeigh and Terry Nichols to bomb the Alfred P. Murrah Federal Building in Oklahoma City. His silence contributed to the deaths of 168 people and the injury of 500 others on April 19, 1995. Fortier had provided key testimony against both McVeigh and Nichols, a factor that contributed to a lighter sentence.[10] This is but one example of when the failure to act is, or should be, a crime. Such crimes are crimes of omission as opposed to crimes of commission, but both may be considered morally reprehensible under the circumstances.

Finally, *actus reus* should be understood to mean that in order to be guilty of a crime, a person must do or not do something rather than just *be* something. As commonsensical as that may seem, some states have passed laws making a person's status a crime. In *Robinson v. California*,[11] the Supreme Court struck down a California law that made status of narcotics addiction a crime. Under the law, there was no need to provide evidence that Robinson had actually used narcotics in California—only that at some time he had been addicted to narcotics. By contrast, in *Powell v. Texas*,[12] the Court ruled that a chronic alcoholic could be punished even though the alcoholism was a disease. Powell had been convicted for being drunk in public, not for being an alcoholic.

Mens Rea

A second element of a crime is **mens rea**. Black defines *mens rea* as "a guilty mind; a guilty or wrongful purpose; a criminal intent."[13] *Mens rea,* then, refers to an individual's state of mind when a crime is committed. Criminal statutes employ terms such as *knowingly, willfully, intentionally, purposely, recklessly,* or *criminal negligence* to describe the state of mind one must have in order to possess "a guilty mind." While the *actus reus* is proven by physical or eyewitness evidence, *mens rea* is more difficult to ascertain. The jury must determine for itself whether the accused had the necessary intent to commit the act, and that raises a number of difficult problems. Finally, *mens rea* includes an element called **scienter,** which refers to the degree of knowledge a person must have to be guilty of a particular crime. One aspect of *scienter* is simply the knowledge that a certain activity is illegal. People of common intelligence know that murder, burglary, and arson are illegal, but certain crimes require additional knowledge on the part of the accused. In Texas, the murder of a police officer is a capital offense, but the prosecutor must prove that the defendant knew that his or her victim was a police officer. For example, a drug dealer might claim he did not know his murder victim was an undercover narcotics officer. The crime of receiving stolen property requires that the buyer knows that the property has been stolen.[14] These crimes require additional proof beyond the fact that the accused knew his actions were illegal.

The requirement of *mens rea* is one reason that insanity is a legal defense for some persons accused of crimes. In an insanity defense, the accused typically does not deny that he performed the *actus reus* but merely asserts that because of his insanity he was incapable of distinguishing right from wrong. Under U.S. law, persons cannot be punished for a crime unless they are able to distinguish right from wrong. Even if someone is found not guilty by reason of insanity, the law requires that he or she be institutionalized. A similar rationale applies to children below a certain age. The law assumes that children are incapable of understanding that their acts are wrong and therefore they cannot be punished.

The issue of the execution of the mentally retarded is a recurring one. In 1989, in *Penry v. Lynaugh*,[15] the Supreme Court held that the execution of mentally retarded persons did not violate the Eighth Amendment's prohibition against cruel and unusual punishment. However, in 2002 the Court reversed itself, citing a growing national consensus against the execution of the mentally retarded in *Atkins v. Virginia*.[16] Similarly, in 2005 the Supreme Court held that it is unconstitutional for a state to execute a juvenile under the age of 18 at the time the crime was committed.[17] These Court reversals illustrate again that controversial legal issues are seldom, if ever, settled for good.

Causation

The next element of a crime is *causation*. To *cause* an event is to bring it about or to make it happen. Often the phrase "but for" is used to determine whether causation has occurred. For example, we might say "Cain killed Abel," by which we really mean "Cain caused Abel's death." In other words, "But for Cain's act, Abel would still be alive." Causation, then, means that "but for" the actions of A, B would not have been harmed. In criminal law, causation is an element that must be proven beyond a reasonable doubt.

One type of causation is ***direct causation,*** which means that nothing intervenes between cause and effect. In a modern version of the biblical story, let us say that Cain shoots Abel, causing Abel's immediate death. Cain is clearly the direct cause of Abel's death. But suppose that Cain shoots Abel, inflicting what is normally a nonfatal wound. Then Abel is dropped by the ambulance attendants as he is being loaded into the ambulance, receives a fatal infection from an unsterile blood transfusion needle, and ultimately dies. Did Cain kill Abel? May Cain be charged with murder? Certainly Cain caused the bullet wound that necessitated the ambulance call and the blood transfusion that ultimately resulted in Abel's death, but did Cain "cause" Abel's death, or did other factors cause it? What, if any, is the extent of Cain's criminal liability in the death of Abel?

The foregoing example illustrates what is known as ***proximate cause.*** We see a chain of events that leads to Abel's death, but can Cain be held legally responsible? Cain is undoubtedly guilty of *something,* but is it the crime of murder? One might argue that but for the gunshot wound, Abel would not have been taken to the hospital, where he received the fatal blood transfusion. But can Cain be held responsible for the unsterile needle? Obviously, an intervening variable (the needle) has entered the equation contributing to Abel's death.

In order to prove murder or even manslaughter, the prosecution must prove that Cain's actions were the proximate cause of Abel's death; otherwise a lesser offense, such as assault with a deadly weapon, must be charged. The determination of causation under circumstances much more complex than those we have described is one of the most difficult tasks in criminal law.

Culpability

Culpability is related to the concept of responsibility or criminal liability. Responsibility or criminal liability for a crime is related to causation; that is, who is responsible for or who committed the crime. Culpability also involves the issue of who may be punished for a crime. A person other than the perpetrator may be criminally responsible if he or she "solicits, encourages, directs, aids, or attempts to aid the other person to commit the offense."[18] Under the common law, there were four categories of culpability: *principals* of the first and second degrees and *accessories* before and after the fact. Under the common law system, accessories generally could not be prosecuted for a crime until one of the principals had been convicted.[19] Today, most jurisdictions have done away with the distinction between a principal of the first and second degree and an accessory before the fact. Now all three are classified as principals and possess the same degree of culpability. The fourth category, accessory after the fact, is still a separate degree of culpability in most jurisdictions.[20] As the term implies, *an accessory after the fact* is a person who aids the perpetrator after the crime has been committed. For example, a person who knowingly hides someone sought by the police could be charged as an accessory after the fact.

SAMUEL MUDD: ACCESSORY AFTER THE FACT

Perhaps one of the most famous examples of "accessory after the fact" is Dr. Samuel Mudd. Dr. Mudd was the man who set the broken leg of John Wilkes Booth after Booth shot President Abraham Lincoln. Dr. Mudd was tried along with the other conspirators and sentenced to life in prison. Although he maintained his innocence all his life, there was evidence that he knew about Booth's role in the assassination the next day and that he assisted Booth in more than just setting his broken leg.[21] While in prison, Dr. Mudd helped with an outbreak of yellow fever and his sentence was commuted by President Andrew Johnson shortly before Johnson left office. Historians continue to debate whether this famous accessory to the Lincoln murder was guilty or merely in the wrong place at the wrong time.

A person may be held criminally responsible for the acts of another even in the absence of a conspiracy. For example, the owner of a store whose employees sell tobacco or alcohol to underage customers may be punished even if the owner was not present at the time and had not established a policy or custom approving such sales. A number of corporate executives have received rather harsh prison sentences for the wrongdoings of their employees or of the corporation. The corporation itself may be subject to criminal penalties in the form of fines for diverse activities such as violations of securities laws or even for homicide.[22]

Penal codes include statutory defenses or justifications that alleviate or excuse criminal responsibility. Insanity and age, discussed earlier, are examples because they impact an essential element of the crime as does involuntary intoxication. Defenses such as duress, choice of evils, self-defense, or defense of others are essentially justifications that require the defendant to admit the commission of the illegal act but to provide a legally acceptable reason for acting in this way. In defining a crime, the legislature may include the specific defense within the statute as, for example, consent in assault cases. There are other legal defenses including that the statute is unconstitutional because it violates equal protection or is void for vagueness, or that the state has failed to prove all the elements of the crime. Of course, the defendant may present factual defenses such as mistaken identity or alibi to escape criminal responsibility.[23]

Standard of Proof

Under the U.S. system of law, the person who brings the cause of action before the court bears the burden of proof. That is, the plaintiff is responsible for proving the truthfulness of his allegations. Under the rules of civil law, the plaintiff must usually meet only the *preponderance-of-evidence* standard in order to win. Under that standard, the weight of evidence, however slight, must favor the plaintiff's version of the dispute. If the plaintiff fails to meet this standard of proof, the defendant will prevail. In criminal law, a different standard of proof, called *beyond a reasonable doubt,* is required. This standard places a greater burden on the State, which is the plaintiff, in a criminal case. "Beyond a reasonable doubt" essentially means that all possible alternative explanations for what happened have been considered and rejected except one—the one that concludes that the accused committed the crime for which he is charged. Note that the standard means not beyond all doubt, but only beyond "reasonable" doubt. Courts employ the "reasonable person" standard, which holds that if 12 reasonable persons, after hearing the relevant evidence, conclude beyond a reasonable doubt that the accused committed the crime, the burden of proof has been met.

The law requires a higher standard of proof in criminal cases than in civil cases for a number of reasons. One is that the stakes are much higher in a criminal case. A person convicted of a crime may be stripped of his liberty or even his life. The taking of a person's life or liberty is so serious that it may be done only if there is a high degree of certainty that the person committed the crime. Imagine the case of a person wrongfully convicted of a crime who serves five years in prison before the error is discovered. Now consider the mental anguish of such a person, who alone knows that he is innocent. How can such a person or his family ever be compensated for those five years of mental anguish? How can the State give back five years of a person's life? The beyond-a-reasonable-doubt standard seeks to minimize the chances of the innocent person's conviction, but even then we know that some innocent people are convicted.

A second reason for the greater standard of proof in criminal cases is the relative strength of the two parties involved. The criminal defendant is usually David to the State's Goliath. Notwithstanding the outcome of that biblical conflict, the State still has tremendous human and financial resources at its disposal to try to prove the defendant's guilt. Even with the requirement of court-appointed counsel, the poor person is at a distinct disadvantage. Because most defendants are poor, the higher standard of proof evens the odds somewhat.

A third reason for the higher standard is one mentioned earlier in this chapter. Because the criminal justice system is capable of becoming a means of repressing persons who hold unpopular political views, the higher standard of proof guarantees that the State will not use its awesome power to "railroad" an innocent person simply because she holds unpopular views. Although it is impossible to absolutely guarantee that the criminal justice system will not be used as a tool of repression, the higher standard of proof reduces the risk that it will be.

The beyond-a-reasonable-doubt standard places a heavy burden on the State in a criminal case. It is important to remember that the accused does not have to prove anything. The defendant does not have to take the stand in his own defense, to call any witnesses to testify, or to present any evidence in his own behalf. The defendant may do nothing, and if the State has failed to prove its case beyond a reasonable doubt, the defendant must be acquitted. That is why, in the technical sense, an accused is not found "innocent." Innocence implies that the defendant is blameless. The accused may be *factually* guilty of the crime, but unless the State proves its case, the accused is not *legally* guilty. Therefore, a verdict of not guilty may mean that the State was unable to prove its case to the satisfaction of the jury, not that the defendant was innocent or morally blameless.

Let us now summarize the elements of a crime. First, the prohibited behavior designated as criminal must be clearly defined so that a reasonable person can be forewarned that engaging in that behavior is illegal. Each criminal statute has certain elements which distinguish that crime, and the State must prove each element. Second, the accused must be shown to have possessed the requisite intent to commit the crime. Third, the State must prove causation. Fourth, the State must prove culpability or criminal liability. Finally, the State must prove beyond a reasonable doubt that the defendant committed the crime with which he or she is charged. Understanding these essential elements of a crime can provide added insight into the substantive and procedural nature of criminal law discussed later in this chapter.

PROCEDURAL CRIMINAL LAW

In Chapter 4, we discussed criminal procedures primarily from what might be termed a "cookbook" approach; that is, we followed the steps of the criminal process from arrest to appeal, much as one might follow the steps of a recipe. Our purpose in Chapter 4 was to provide the reader with an overview of criminal procedures without getting bogged down in details. In this section, we wish to discuss in greater detail some of the procedural safeguards guaranteed by the Constitution. We will look at three controversial areas of constitutional law: search and seizure, the right to counsel, and the protection against self-incrimination. Our purpose in focusing on these three topics is to provide the reader with an understanding of the history of these procedural safeguards, the philosophical basis of each, and the complexity of the issues involved with each. As noted in the introduction to this chapter, our concern about procedural due process is motivated by our desire to ensure that government "plays by the rules," by our anxiety about convicting the innocent, and by our fear that government may use the criminal justice system to prosecute unpopular individuals or groups. With these considerations in mind, we turn our attention to the first topic: search and seizure.

Search and Seizure

"A man's home is his castle" is a common adage. Although this adage fails to inform us of the status of a *woman's* home, we will proceed on the premise that under the English common law even the humblest home in the realm was to be a haven from the outside world. The lowest of the king's subjects was entitled to the sanctuary of his or her home. It is with this understanding that the Fourth Amendment was included in our Bill of Rights. The Fourth Amendment reads as follows:

> The right of the people to be secure in their persons, houses, papers, and effects, against unreasonable searches and seizures, shall not be violated, and no warrants shall issue, but upon probable cause, supported by oath or affirmation, and particularly describing the place to be searched, and the persons or things to be seized.[24]

Several things should be noted from the text of the Fourth Amendment. First, the Amendment prohibits only "unreasonable" searches and seizures, thus implying that reasonable ones are permitted. What is and what is not reasonable ultimately becomes a question for the courts to decide. Second, search warrants are to be issued only "upon probable cause," another rather vague notion. Decisions of the U.S. Supreme Court indicate a growing willingness to substitute reasonableness for the probable-cause standard of the Constitution. For example, the Court has upheld searches of a public school student's purse,[25] highway sobriety checkpoints,[26] mandatory drug testing of railroad employees following a train accident,[27] and random searches of passengers on interstate buses.[28] Each of these searches failed to meet the probable-cause standard but was permitted without a search warrant anyway because the Court deemed each search reasonable under the Fourth Amendment. Third, the warrant, if issued, must describe the place to be searched and the things to be seized. All three of these stipulations are of sufficient ambiguity to cause problems for the Supreme Court in interpreting the Fourth Amendment.

One might wonder why the Framers of the Constitution, and especially those who wrote the Fourth Amendment, were so concerned about the rights of criminal defendants. Were they a bunch of "knee-jerk" liberals who were "soft on crime"? On the contrary, we sometimes forget that the Framers were revolutionaries who had firsthand experience with a tyrannical government. They knew what can happen when government begins to ignore the rights of its citizens, and they were certainly familiar with the general warrants of George III authorizing British troops to search the homes of suspected patriots for powder and shot that might be used by the rebels. In other words, the Framers were not glassy-eyed idealists who failed to foresee the consequences of their actions. Instead they were pragmatists who, in balancing the rights of individuals against the need for law and order, made an initial determination that, in a free society, the former was more important. But, as noted in Chapter 6, constitutional law is constantly changing to meet the needs of new generations of Americans. The values underlying the protection against unreasonable searches and seizures, although important to our Founding Fathers, may not be shared by Americans in the twenty-first century. Or are they? Perhaps we should ask ourselves that question as we study the Fourth Amendment.

Historically, the items subject to seizure by government in a criminal case fell into three categories: contraband, fruits of the crime, and instrumentalities of the crime. *Contraband* is something the government has forbidden to be in a person's possession, such as illegal drugs, explosives, or obscene materials. *Fruits of the crime* include stolen goods or money. *Instrumentalities of the crime* are tools or weapons used in the commission of a crime. Even a getaway car can be classified as an instrumentality subject to seizure. In 1969, in *Warden v. Hayden,*[29] the Supreme Court created a fourth category it labeled "mere evidence." In *Hayden,* a jacket and a pair of trousers identified as being similar to those worn by the robber of a taxi company were found in Hayden's home after a warrantless search. After first deciding that the search was reasonable, the Court turned to the issue of whether the jacket and trousers were subject to lawful seizure. Rather than continue the legal fiction that the clothes were subject to seizure as "instrumentalities" of the crime, the Court ruled that the clothes, as "mere evidence," were also subject to seizure. The Court ruled that the purpose of the Fourth Amendment is the protection of privacy, not property, and noted, "Privacy is disturbed no more by a search directed to a purely evidentiary object than it is by a search directed to an instrumentality, fruit, or contraband."[30] Besides the question of what may be seized as evidence, another issue is how evidence is obtained by the police. Under the common law, courts did not concern themselves about the methods used to obtain evidence but only with the reliability of that evidence. That is, if the evidence was "good," it mattered not how the police acquired it. That common law rule was changed for federal courts in *Weeks v. United States.*[31] Fremont Weeks was accused of running an illegal lottery through the mails. Local police and, later, a federal marshal conducted an illegal search and seized letters and papers as evidence. Weeks made a motion for the return of his property, which the trial court denied. The Supreme Court, in overturning Weeks's conviction, ruled:

> If letters and private documents can thus be seized and held and used in evidence against a citizen accused of an offense, the protection of the

4th Amendment, declaring his right to be secure against such searches and seizures, is of no value, and, so far as those thus placed are concerned, might as well be stricken from the Constitution.[32]

Thus was born the *exclusionary rule*. The exclusionary rule states that evidence obtained in violation of a person's constitutional rights must be excluded from the trial of the accused person. Because Weeks's papers were seized by an illegal search and seizure, they could not be used as evidence against him. The *Weeks* rule initially applied only to the exclusion of evidence in cases in federal courts, but in 1961 the Supreme Court made the rule applicable to the states in the case of *Mapp v. Ohio*.[33] Although the exclusionary rule developed in the context of search and seizure, it was later extended to include other violations of a defendant's constitutional rights.

There has probably never been a more controversial issue in criminal law than the exclusionary rule. Proponents of the rule argue that there are a number of important justifications for its existence. First, proponents argue that the exclusionary rule preserves the integrity of the judicial system by excluding evidence "tainted" by illegal police activities. Most would agree that a confession extracted through torture is an improper way to obtain evidence even if the person is factually guilty. The argument, then, is that in accepting the "reliable" but coerced confession, the courts are aiding and abetting improper police tactics. Justice Louis Brandeis has written:

> If the Government becomes a lawbreaker, it breeds contempt for law; it invites every man to become a law unto himself; it invites anarchy. To declare that in the administration of the criminal law the end justifies the means—to declare that the Government may commit crimes in order to secure the conviction of a private criminal—would bring terrible retribution. Against that pernicious doctrine this Court should resolutely set its face.[34]

Courts, according to Brandeis, should not close their eyes to the methods used to obtain evidence but should see that law enforcers also obey the law.

A second justification for the exclusionary rule is one mentioned by Justice William Day, author of the *Weeks* opinion. If evidence seized in violation of the Fourth Amendment is admitted, then the amendment has no meaning. Why should a police officer obey the amendment's command to secure a search warrant when it is easier to obtain evidence without one? As long as the courts close their eyes to police methods, the police will continue to collect evidence without warrants.

A third justification is the deterrent effect of the exclusionary rule. The assumption is made that what police want most is to secure convictions. If evidence seized illegally is excluded, resulting in the accused getting off, the police will no longer have an incentive to engage in unconstitutional practices. That is, if an officer knows that the evidence obtained from an illegal search will be excluded from the trial, he or she is less likely to conduct illegal searches. As a practical matter, the officer's work will be for nothing, and the criminal defendant will go free in some cases. Thus, the police will take greater pains to secure proper search warrants rather than risk letting a guilty person go free.

A fourth justification for the exclusionary rule is that it is the only viable solution to the problem of abuses of constitutional rights. Unless the police are to be "above the law," they too must obey the Constitution. According to proponents, the exclusion of illegally obtained evidence is the only realistic solution. Other solutions, such as making the offending officer liable in a civil suit for violating the constitutional rights of the accused, are simply impractical. Suppose, for example, that an officer conducts an illegal search that produces reliable evidence which is then used to secure the defendant's conviction. The defendant may sue the officer for violating his constitutional rights, but what jury is going to rule in favor of a convicted criminal under such circumstances? Suggestions that officers be fined or suspended for violating the rights of accused persons also raise problems. Would the police be afraid to make an arrest or search a car for fear of being fined or suspended later? Proponents argue that the exclusionary rule is the only effective way to deal with violations of constitutional rights.

Finally, proponents of the exclusionary rule argue that it is more important to keep the police in check than to worry about guilty persons being set free. This argument is similar to the "integrity of the judicial system" argument discussed earlier. Police must understand that they too must obey the Constitution, the supreme law of the land. Those in authority must understand that the ends (convictions) do not always justify the means (illegal searches). As Justice Tom Clark wrote in *Mapp,* "The criminal goes free, if he must, but it is the law that sets him free."[35] If we are truly to be a nation of laws, not men, then we must make sure that those who enforce the law also obey the law.

The opponents of the exclusionary rule advance a number of valid counterarguments. First, they reject the "integrity of the judicial system" argument by pointing out that the purpose of a trial is to arrive at the truth. If illegally seized evidence is reliable, then what difference does it make how it was obtained? Only in extreme cases of police overzealousness—cases that "shock the conscience"[36] of the community—should the exclusionary rule be employed.

A second objection is that if the purpose of the Fourth Amendment is to protect privacy, then the exclusionary rule is a totally inadequate solution. The person's privacy has already been violated, so how does excluding the otherwise reliable evidence further any Fourth Amendment privacy values? The damage to privacy interests has been done, so what purpose is served by perhaps letting a factually guilty person go free? Even if the State could get a conviction without the illegally seized evidence, why take the chance?

A third objection questions the deterrent effect of the exclusionary rule. Suppose that a police officer makes what she believes to be a legal search, and the search is later ruled invalid. How could the officer have been deterred in her conduct? She made a "good-faith" error in conducting the search in the first place, so how could she have been deterred in making a search she believed to be valid?

HELLO, DOLLREE!

Although the Supreme Court had applied the exclusionary rule to federal cases, the Court initially declined to apply the rule in state courts. As the Court explained in *Wolf v. Colorado*,[37] the exclusionary rule was not the only way to enforce the Fourth Amendment's prohibition against unreasonable searches and seizures. But in 1961 the Court reversed its position in *Wolf* and held that the exclusionary rule does apply to state as well as to federal courts. Cleveland police invaded the home of Dollree Mapp without a search warrant. Mapp asked to see the warrant and the officers produced a piece of paper that they claimed was a warrant but, in fact, it was not. When the search failed to uncover the evidence the police were actually seeking, they continued searching until they found something with which to charge Mapp. In a trunk in her basement they found some allegedly obscene materials. In *Mapp v. Ohio*,[38] the Court acknowledged that states were not taking effective measures to prevent violations of the Fourth Amendment and held that evidence seized without a warrant or a warrant exception be excluded from state trials as well as federal trials.

A fourth objection is that the exclusionary rule punishes the wrong people. It is society that is being punished by the enforcement of the exclusionary rule because it allows some factually guilty defendants to go free just because "the constable blunders." The offending officers are not punished (except that they lose their "bust"), and the criminal reaps a bonus by getting away with no punishment in some cases.

Finally, opponents of the rule argue that the exclusionary rule itself "breeds contempt for the law." This argument holds that when law-abiding citizens see criminals set free on "technicalities," they become contemptuous of the law. Instead of protecting law-abiding citizens, the law seems to protect the lawless. For these reasons and others, the exclusionary rule continues to be one of the most controversial issues of criminal law. However, opponents of the exclusionary rule have been encouraged by a 2006 decision of the Supreme Court indicating that future questions about the exclusionary rule will focus on the "social costs to be weighed against the deterrence" and that the majority felt that both the threat of civil lawsuits and internal departmental disciplinary actions would adequately discourage inappropriate police behavior.[39]

In the remainder of this section, we will focus on the instances of reasonable and unreasonable searches. We begin by asking: When is a search reasonable? Obviously, a search made pursuant to a valid search warrant falls within this category. The police officer goes before a judge or magistrate with sufficient evidence to establish probable cause and the latter will decide if a search warrant is justified. This allows a neutral third party to independently decide whether the warrant should be issued. A second type of reasonable search is one that is made pursuant to a lawful arrest. The Supreme Court has recognized that searches made pursuant to lawful arrests are valid because of the need for the officer to uncover any weapons the suspect may have that could harm others or aid in his escape. In *Chimel v. California*[40] however, the Court also made it clear that the search could only extend to the area within the immediate reach of the suspect. In *Chimel,* the police, while serving an arrest warrant, searched Chimel's entire house, despite his objections. The Court ruled that because Chimel was already in custody, a warrantless search of the house was not "pursuant" to the arrest and therefore was unreasonable. The police should have secured a warrant and returned later to conduct the search.

A third category of reasonable searches is one in which permission to make the search is granted. This can lead to a number of problem situations. For example, what constitutes an "intelligent waiver" of one's constitutional rights? A police officer's *request,* such as "Do you mind if I look in your trunk?" becomes a *command* to most people. When the teacher says to Johnny, "Will you please go to the blackboard?" no one in the class believes Johnny really has the right to refuse. Similarly, a polite request from a police officer takes on the air of an order one may not refuse. Is "permission" under such circumstances an intelligent waiver of constitutional rights?

Another problem concerns the question of who may give permission to the police to conduct a search. In *Warden v. Hayden,* the "mere evidence" case, the Supreme Court ruled the search valid because Mrs. Hayden had given the police permission to enter her home (although one might question whether her waiver was an intelligent one). The general rule is that "The person giving the consent must have the capacity to consent."[41] The Supreme Court has ruled that if a person has authority over the area to be searched, that person's consent is valid; however, if another person with the same authority, such as a husband or wife, is physically present and refuses consent, then the evidence cannot be used against the objecting party.[42]

A fourth area of controversy is so-called stop-and-frisk searches, which by their nature are warrantless. The leading case in this category is *Terry v. Ohio.*[43] Martin McFadden, a plainclothes police officer with 39 years' experience, observed John W. Terry and two other men acting in a suspicious manner. The men repeatedly walked past a store window, peered in, and then conferred with one another on a street corner. After observing the ritual for approximately ten minutes, McFadden concluded that Terry and the others were "casing" the store for a robbery. McFadden approached the men, identified himself as a police officer, and patted them down. When he discovered a revolver in Terry's coat pocket, he arrested him for carrying a concealed weapon. Terry was convicted and appealed on grounds of an unreasonable search and seizure. The Supreme Court, aware of the potential abuse of stop-and-frisk searches by the police, nevertheless ruled that Officer McFadden had sufficient reasonable suspicion to believe a crime was about to be committed and was therefore justified in conducting his limited "pat-down" search. The Supreme Court has recognized that reasonable suspicion must be more than "a hunch." In *Terry,* the Court ruled that "in justifying the particular intrusion the police officer must be able to point to specific and articulable facts, which taken together with rational inferences from those facts reasonably warrant the intrusion."[44]

Thus, reasonable suspicion requires "specific and articulable facts" along with "rational inferences" before a warrantless search is valid.

Another category of search and seizure that has caused problems is the search of automobiles and other movable vehicles. It is obvious that, in requirements for search warrants, an automobile cannot be treated like a house or a building because an automobile can be moved out of the issuing court's jurisdiction before the warrant can be executed. The Supreme Court first recognized this problem in *Carroll v. United States*.[45] Since *Carroll,* many of the search-and-seizure cases involving automobiles have concerned the questions of whether the police had enough probable cause to stop and search particular automobiles,[46] searches pursuant to an arrest for traffic violations,[47] and inventory searches of automobiles that have been impounded.[48] In 1990, the Supreme Court upheld a Michigan law allowing police officers to set up highway sobriety checkpoints to check for drunk drivers. Every car encountering the checkpoint was stopped. The Court held that given the danger of drunk driving to the public safety and the relatively minor inconvenience to motorists, the "seizure of law abiding citizens is reasonable."[49] Surprisingly however, in *City of Indianapolis v. Edmonds,*[50] the Court held that similar checkpoints to check for illegal drug possession were unconstitutional.

Two final areas of search and seizure are cases involving the plain-view doctrine and wiretaps. The plain-view doctrine holds that the police may seize evidence in plain view without a search warrant if certain conditions are met. First, the police must be on the premises legally or otherwise conducting a legal search. For example, evidence discovered pursuant to a valid arrest is considered in plain view. Second, the nature of the evidence must be immediately apparent to the officer. That is, it must be readily apparent that the items in plain view are either contraband, fruits or instrumentalities of the crime, or "mere evidence." The logic of the plain-view doctrine was enunciated by the Supreme Court in *Harris v. United States*.[51] In that case, the Court reasoned that "the police are not required to close their eyes and need not walk out and leave the article where they saw it. Any other principle might lead to an absurd result and at times perhaps even defeat the ends of justice."[52]

Accessing without permission cellular phone communications, e-mails, and Internet connections illustrates how advances in technology can affect the application of the Fourth Amendment. Is a wiretap a "search" or "seizure" within the meaning of the Fourth Amendment? It is obvious that the Court cannot rely on the intent of the Framers in such cases because telephones did not exist when the Constitution was written. The Supreme Court confronted the issue in *Olmstead v. United States,*[53] in which it ruled that a wiretap was not a "search" because there was no physical invasion of Olmstead's residence. In *Katz v. United States*[54] however, the Supreme Court ruled that a wiretap placed on the outside of a public telephone booth did constitute an illegal search and seizure, thus overruling *Olmstead.*

Technology continues to present the Court with interesting Fourth Amendment issues. In *Kyllo v. United States,* the Court held that the police may not use thermal imagers to detect heat lamps used to grow illegal marijuana.[55] In 2014 the Court made an important ruling regarding cell phones. The Court held that a warrant is necessary to access information on a cell phone seized incident to an arrest.[56] Finally, although the use of drones for search purposes has not yet reached the Supreme Court, it is merely a matter of time. In June 2011 in a North Dakota case a man was convicted when police used a drone to record a stand-off with police.[57]

The above cases raise the question of the underlying purpose of the Fourth Amendment. If one assumes that the amendment protects *property*, then the *Olmstead* position is defensible. If, on the other hand, the purpose of the amendment is to protect people's *privacy*, then the *Katz-Kyllo* position is preferred. As the technology such as that found in *Kyllo* provides new ways to invade our privacy, the courts must be vigilant that law enforcement officers, in their eagerness to fight crime, do not adopt a "Big Brother" mentality. The question of privacy or property continues to be a recurring one, especially in light of the passage of the USA Patriot Act in the wake of the World Trade Center and Pentagon attacks.[58]

Right to Counsel

Much of the background of the right to counsel was discussed in Chapter 6, so only a brief summary is needed here. Suffice it to say that the right to counsel was intended to guarantee the services of a lawyer for those accused who could afford to pay for one. In Chapter 6, we chronicled how the Supreme Court extended the privilege in *Powell v. Alabama, Gideon v. Wainwright*, and *Argersinger v. Hamlin*. As a result of these cases, no person must face a serious criminal offense without the presence of an attorney, either retained or court appointed.

Despite the fact that the right to counsel has been clearly established at trial, a more perplexing problem is *when* the accused has the right to counsel. An early federal case illustrates the problem of what can happen if the accused does not have access to an attorney in the early stages of the criminal justice process. Andrew Mallory was a young man of "limited intelligence" accused of raping a woman in a Washington, D.C. laundromat. Although Mallory was arrested early in the afternoon, he was detained and questioned by the police throughout the rest of the day. During the interrogation, Mallory confessed to the crime. The next day he was taken before a U.S. magistrate for arraignment, at which time he was informed of his right to remain silent and his right to an attorney. But it was too late for Andrew Mallory. Any advice an attorney could have given him was useless in light of his confession. Mallory was convicted of rape and sentenced to die for his crime. Attorneys for Mallory decided to appeal his case however, on the grounds that the police had delayed too long before bringing Mallory before the magistrate. To inform Mallory of his constitutional rights after his confession was a classic case of closing the barn door after the horse is gone. In *Mallory v. United States*,[59] the Supreme Court agreed. The Court noted that the magistrate was located in the same building where Mallory was being interrogated, and it would have been a simple task to bring him before the magistrate before intense questioning began. The Court considered the delay between Mallory's arrest and his arraignment unreasonable and overturned his conviction. In *Mallory,* the Supreme Court recognized that the exercise of constitutional rights, such as the right to counsel, can be critical long before the accused is brought to trial. Knowledge and understanding of one's constitutional rights are needed early in the process, especially in the case of someone like Mallory, who had a limited capacity to understand what was happening to him.

The Supreme Court continued to develop the question of when the accused has the right to counsel in the case of *Escobedo v. Illinois.*[60] Danny Escobedo was accused of murdering his brother-in-law. He was arrested, interrogated, and later released by the police even though he remained the prime suspect. When additional evidence implicating Escobedo turned up, he was arrested again. In the meantime, his family had retained a lawyer who went to the jailhouse to see Escobedo, but the police purposely kept Escobedo from seeing his lawyer. When Escobedo asked to see his lawyer, he was told that his lawyer did not want to see him. At the same time, Escobedo's lawyer was being told that he could not see his client until the police had finished interrogating him. Escobedo subsequently confessed, and his confession was used to convict him of murder. In overturning Escobedo's conviction, the Court stressed the importance of the "guiding hand of counsel,"[61] noting that "The right to counsel would be hollow indeed if it began at a period when few confessions were obtained."[62] In other words, the advice of an attorney is needed most during the period between arrest and arraignment, when most confessions are made. The Court ruled that when the focus had shifted from a general inquiry into an unsolved crime to a particular suspect, that suspect must be informed of his right to remain silent. Otherwise, he has been denied the assistance of counsel guaranteed by the Sixth Amendment.[63]

In the controversial *Miranda v. Arizona*[64] decision, the Warren Court reaffirmed *Escobedo* and explicitly stated what the police must do when making an arrest. The Court ruled that when a person is taken into custody or otherwise denied freedom of movement, the police must inform the accused of his constitutional rights before questioning. These rights include the right to remain silent, the right to an attorney either appointed or retained, and the right to know that anything he says may be used against him in court. The *Miranda* decision is perhaps the most controversial decision in criminal justice since the imposition of the exclusionary rule. The police argued that the decision would make it virtually impossible to gain confessions from criminals and, that because confessions are a major source of evidence, convictions would be more difficult to obtain. Studies have indicated that the worst fears of the police have not been realized.[65] The major reason that the police still obtain confessions from accused persons is plea bargaining. Guilty persons are still willing to trade their confessions for a charge reduction or lighter sentence. Because confessions are seldom the only evidence the police have, criminal defendants prefer to plea bargain rather than take chances at trial. The *Miranda* warnings have become such a part of our legal system that when the Supreme Court was presented with the opportunity to overturn the case in 2000, it declined to do so. Ironically, national police organizations that had roundly condemned *Miranda* when it first came down were among the groups urging that the Court *not* reverse the decision.[66]

The issues surrounding the right to counsel in *Miranda* have focused on when the *Miranda* warnings are required and what constitutes an intelligent waiver of one's rights. One of the first cases to decide when the *Miranda* warnings are required was *Mathis v. United States*.[67] While in prison for an unrelated offense, Robert T. Mathis, Sr. was "routinely" questioned by IRS agents about his 1960 and 1961 tax returns. The agents failed to give Mathis the *Miranda* warnings, and evidence elicited from Mathis was used to convict him of tax fraud. The Supreme Court ruled that because tax investigations can lead to criminal charges the *Miranda* warnings are required.

Similarly, in *Orozco v. Texas*,[68] the Court ruled that suspects must be given the *Miranda* warnings when they are under arrest, even if the questioning is not in a "coercive environment." The police arrested Reyes Arias Orozco at his boarding house and questioned him, without the *Miranda* warnings, while he sat on his bed. The Court ruled that Orozco had been deprived of his freedom of action in a significant way and therefore the warnings were required. In contrast to *Mathis* and *Orozco* however, the Court ruled in *Beckwith v. United States*[69] that an interrogation by IRS agents in the home of the accused was not a custodial arrest requiring the specific *Miranda* warnings. It should be noted, however, that the IRS agents did advise Alvin A. Beckwith of his right to remain silent and his right to an attorney.

In *Oregon v. Mathiason*,[70] the Court ruled that a confession by a person who voluntarily appears at police headquarters and who is not under arrest may be used even though the *Miranda* warnings were not given. Although the interrogation of Carl Mathiason took place in a "coercive environment," the Court ruled that he was not denied his freedom of action in any significant way. Finally, in *Estelle v. Smith*,[71] the Court extended the *Miranda* requirements to include pretrial psychiatric examinations in which the psychiatrist is permitted to testify in the punishment stage of a capital case.

A second area of concern in right-to-counsel cases involves the intelligent waiver of constitutional rights after *Miranda* warnings have been given. Police may not rely on "trickery and deceit," nor do anything to overbear the defendant's will once he has asserted his right to counsel. For example, in *Brewer v. Williams*[72] (one of our case studies at the end of this chapter), the police, after being warned not to question Robert Anthony Williams, made statements designed to elicit incriminating information from him in the absence of his lawyer. The police, knowing of Williams's religious beliefs, talked of allowing the parents of his 10-year-old victim to give her a "Christian burial." The Supreme Court held that the "Christian burial" speech was psychologically calculated to coerce Williams into identifying the location of the girl's body, which he did. The *Brewer v. Williams* case and its aftermath will be examined at greater length at the end of this chapter.

In *North Carolina v. Butler*,[73] the Court again faced the issue of an intelligent waiver. William Thomas Butler was arrested by the FBI on a North Carolina fugitive warrant. After agents determined that Butler had an eleventh-grade education, he was handed an FBI "Advice of Rights" card, which he read. Butler refused to sign the waiver at the bottom of the form but agreed to talk with agents, whereupon he made some incriminating statements. Butler neither requested counsel nor asked to terminate the questioning. The North Carolina Supreme Court ruled that Butler's statement could not be used as evidence without an explicit statement of waiver, but the Supreme Court reversed. The Court ruled that in agreeing to answer questions, Butler had implicitly waived his right to counsel and his protection against self-incrimination. In a similar vein, in 2010 the Supreme Court ruled in *Berghuis v. Thompkins*[74] that a defendant must affirmatively assert his desire to invoke the *Miranda* rights. Thompkins underwent an interrogation lasting almost three hours by refusing to give more than one-word answers to most of the officers' questions. After being asked by one officer if he had sought God's forgiveness for killing the victim, Van Chester Thompkins answered yes and subsequently confessed. The Court held that because Thompkins had not affirmatively expressed a desire to invoke his rights, the officers were under no obligation to terminate the questioning.

Although *Miranda* has become more widely accepted by the law enforcement community, all attempts to circumvent the decision have not ended. The Supreme Court was asked to rule on the constitutionality of a "two-step" approach to interrogations in the absence of counsel. Patrice Seibert was accused of covering up the death of her young son who suffered from cerebral palsy by having her older son and his friend set fire to the trailer where the family lived. Police deliberately interrogated Seibert without giving her the *Miranda* warnings and secured incriminating statements. Then, the police interrogated her again shortly after the first interrogation but this time taping the confession and giving her the *Miranda* warnings. The Court held, in a plurality decision, that giving the warnings at the start of the second interrogation "could not effectively comply with *Miranda's* constitutional requirement" and ruled her incriminating statements inadmissible.[75]

The cases examined here involving the right to counsel indicate an erosion of the *Miranda* decision and illustrate the game, or contest, approach to criminal justice. The police, for their part, try to devise clever ways to elicit incriminating evidence from defendants without violating the letter (but not the spirit) of *Miranda*. Criminal defendants try to devise clever ways to show how the police tricked or otherwise deceived them into offering incriminating evidence. But criminal justice should not be a game of "Trickery and Deceit" or "Catch Us If You Can." Yet, as these cases illustrate, that is what the process often becomes.

Self-Incrimination

The privilege against self-incrimination was already well established at common law when the Bill of Rights was added to the Constitution. Under English law, individuals charged with crimes could not be compelled to testify against themselves at trial. The privilege reflects, in part, a reluctance to force individuals to provide the means of their own destruction. That is, we are opposed to forcing people to condemn themselves to prison or death. It also reflects our accusatory approach to law. The accused does not have to prove her innocence; the State must prove her guilt. Surely, the accused cannot be expected to assist the State in making a case against her. Finally, the privilege reflects concern over the reliability of confessions, especially if any evidence of coercion is involved. Recall that in *Mallory v. United States* the Supreme Court was concerned not only with the failure of the police to arraign Mallory but also with Mallory's inability to make an intelligent confession because of his limited mental capacity. Of course, the Constitution does permit the accused to confess, but there must be an intelligent waiver of the right to remain silent.

Despite some valid arguments for protection against self-incrimination, the privilege is not without its critics. The major criticism centers around this argument: If the accused is innocent, why should he be afraid to take the stand in his own defense? If, the argument runs, the accused has nothing to hide, why should he be afraid to take the stand to deny his guilt or to explain away the State's evidence against him? The problem, of course, is that this argument shifts the burden of proof to the defendant. The defendant is told, in effect, that he must prove his innocence and should therefore be willing to take the stand in his own defense. This argument is valid, and some criminal defendants do take the stand in their own defense, but only voluntarily and only with the advice of counsel.

Until fairly recently, some states allowed a prosecutor to comment on a defendant's failure to take the stand even when state law protected the defendant's right to refuse to testify. In two early cases, *Twining v. New Jersey*[76] and *Adamson v. California*,[77] the Supreme Court ruled that the Constitution did not prohibit a state jury from drawing negative inferences from a defendant's failure to take the stand in his or her own defense. Nor was due process violated if a state judge called the defendant's failure to testify to the attention of the jury, even though federal judges are not allowed to do so. In *Malloy v. Hogan*[78] however, the Court overturned *Twining* and ruled that the same protections against self-incrimination apply to both state and federal prosecutions.

The privilege against self-incrimination is closely related to both the right to counsel and protection against unreasonable searches and seizures. After being placed under arrest, the accused is usually told of his right to remain silent and then informed of his right to have an attorney present during questioning. This is done so that the accused will not inadvertently admit something that incriminates him because, as we have seen, the right to the advice of counsel is useless if the accused has already made incriminating statements. Likewise, the privilege against self-incrimination is related to search-and-seizure issues. In *Boyd v. United States*,[79] for example, the police seized invoices which showed that Boyd had imported cases of plate glass without paying the duties on them. The Supreme Court overturned Boyd's conviction on both Fourth and Fifth Amendment grounds, saying, "we have been unable to perceive that the seizure of a man's private books and papers to be used in evidence against him is substantially different from compelling him to be a witness against himself."[80]

Although *Boyd* has been modified considerably since 1886,[81] private papers, such as diaries, cannot be used to incriminate the accused.

As we have seen with other constitutional rights of the accused, time and technology have forced the courts to reconsider and reinterpret the privilege against self-incrimination. Although it is clear that the accused cannot be forced to admit his guilt, does the privilege extend to nonverbal forms of communication? For example, in *Rochin v. California*,[82] the police saw Antonio Rochin swallow some capsules they believed to be morphine. They took Rochin to a hospital and ordered physicians to pump his stomach against his will. The contents did contain morphine, and Rochin was convicted of its possession, but the Supreme Court reversed. Although it refused to address the self-incrimination issue directly, the Court called the stomach pumping a method "too close to the rack and the screw" and ruled that the actions of the police "shock the conscience." However, in *Breithaupt v. Abram*[83] and *Schmerber v. California*,[84] the Court allowed blood tests to be admitted as evidence of drunk driving. In *Breithaupt*, the accused was unconscious and the test was done under medical supervision. The Court contrasted the relatively painless blood test to the stomach-pumping procedure used in *Rochin*. In *Schmerber*, the Court ruled that a blood test could be required even over the objections of the accused. The Court stated:

> We hold that the privilege protects an accused only from being compelled to testify against himself, or otherwise provide the State with evidence of a testimonial or communicative nature, and that the withdrawal of blood and use of analysis in question in this case did not involve compulsion to these ends.[85]

Nevertheless, in 2013 the Court held that the mere fact that alcohol dissipates in the bloodstream alone is not sufficient to justify a search without a warrant. The Court said that the totality of the circumstances must determine whether exigent circumstances exist to permit a warrantless search in DUI cases.[86]

The "testimonial and communicative nature" requirement has led the Court to permit the admission of a number of types of nonverbal incriminating evidence. The Court has ruled that the accused may be forced to give handwriting samples, fingerprints, voice identifications, dental records, and DNA samples. Although the Court has ruled that the accused must submit to a lineup, it has also ruled that the accused has the right to have counsel present at post-indictment lineups to ensure that no irregularities occur.[87]

PUNISHMENT

Punishment is an integral (and controversial) part of the criminal justice system. We read shrieking headlines that persons committing heinous crimes were on parole or that a death-row killer has been given a stay of execution or a new trial. People become upset at such events, and each person becomes an instant expert on the system. Certainly, no one likes to hear that someone has been injured by a parolee or probationer, but the solution to punishment is not easy. What punishment fits the crime? What modes of punishment are acceptable in a civilized society? What should the treatment of prisoners be like in a society dedicated to human rights? What is the appropriate balance between the rights of the convicted or accused vis-à-vis the victim? These are the questions that the legislative branch must answer in establishing the penalties for crimes and in funding various types of punishment, that the executive branch must answer in operating prisons and probation and parole programs, and that the judicial branch must consider in deciding cases which challenge the conditions and procedures involved in punishment.

Theories of Punishment

There are three primary models of punishment: retribution, deterrence, and rehabilitation. The earliest extant criminal codes—the Code of Hammurabi and the Old Testament—reflect the legal doctrine of *lex talionis* or "an eye for an eye, a tooth for a tooth." Retribution should be distinguished from vengeance; the former is done under authority of the state to enforce the law and maintain social order, whereas the latter is private and personal. Retribution is based on the premise that the perpetrator is a reasonable and rational being who freely made the decision to violate the law. This theory advocates that the wrongdoer be punished in such a way that the punishment fits the crime.

Rehabilitation is the notion that punishment should rehabilitate or reform the behavior of offenders so that they will become law-abiders rather than lawbreakers. This was the dominant theory of punishment in the United States from the 1920s to the 1970s and is based on the premise that treatment programs may change behavior patterns. Many have abandoned the idea of meaningful rehabilitation for our penal institutions for a variety of reasons, including lack of resources (a reflection of lack of public support), and now recognize that prisons and jails are often merely "warehouses" and that while incarceration may be a learning experience, it is rarely a positive one.

Deterrence refers both to discouraging a specific offender from further illegal acts and to deterring others from criminal activity. The underlying theory is that people carefully weigh their actions and the attendant costs and benefits, and that the fear of punishment dissuades them from breaking the law. There has been a resurgence of interest in deterrence theory in the past four decades or so. Scholars and others have examined the deterrent effect in a variety of settings. For example, in the area of capital punishment, the more methodologically sound studies indicate that there is not a deterrent effect on others and may, in fact, encourage similar acts, although most scholars agree that more research needs to be done on this topic. In other areas, such as income tax evasion or fraud, prosecution of offenders does not seem to inhibit criminal activity. It appears that harsher penalties, longer sentences, and promptness of punishment may affect the individual, but unless sentences are well publicized there is little deterrent effect on others who are likely to commit crimes of some magnitude.[88]

Types of Punishment

There are various types of punishment for crimes ranging from the payment of a fine only through the death penalty. Every crime carries with it a penalty that is determined by the appropriate legislative body, and it is an element of due process that individuals are entitled to know the possible range of punishment. The assessment of punishment may come about through plea bargaining, in which the defendant agrees to accept the punishment, or through assessment by judge or jury depending on state law and the defendant's selection of a jury or bench trial (where that option exists).

The punishment defined by statutes is incarceration and/or a fine or the death penalty and fine. Misdemeanors usually carry time at the city or county correctional facility, whereas conviction of felonies usually means incarceration at either the state penitentiary for state crimes or the federal penitentiary for federal crimes. The national government not only has a separate set of laws and courts but it also has a separate program for corrections, including probation and prisons.

The form of punishment most frequently imposed is *probation* or community supervision. Generally, the states impose various limitations on probation and reserve it for less serious crimes. With probation, the defendant is not confined in an institution but remains in the community subject to various conditions such as submitting to drug testing, staying away from certain people or places, and committing no other offenses. The probationer remains under the control of the court, and probation may be revoked for noncompliance with the probation terms as monitored by a probation officer.

Similar to probation is the *suspended sentence*, which is also known as deferred adjudication. Under this, either there is no conviction entered following the plea (suspension of imposition of sentence) or the sentence is prescribed but not carried out (suspension of the execution of the sentence). The result is the same; if the offender successfully meets the court's requirements, such as restitution, completion of a substance-abuse program, or community service, the defendant is unconditionally discharged. With suspension of the imposition of the sentence, there is no conviction on the offender's record. This practice came under attack in driving-while-intoxicated cases. Drivers would be arrested numerous times but would have no convictions on their record because of suspended sentences. To correct that problem, many states adopted laws barring such practices. However, deferred adjudication is still very useful in selected cases for certain offenders (for example, a college honor student who committed a relatively minor criminal indiscretion such as trespass) who have no prior involvement with the law and who are unlikely to err again. This allows the court to impose some punishment without marring the person's record with a conviction.[89]

Parole is release from imprisonment on the condition of good behavior; the terms of parole are similar to those required of probationers to avoid persons and places of bad reputation, participate in treatment programs, and regularly report to a parole officer, to name a few. The state systems vary so widely in terms of organization and in terms of eligibility standards that we can only generalize in the broadest of terms here. One common feature of parole organizations is that they are under the control of the executive or administrative branches of government rather than under the control of the judiciary. Parole is both granted and revoked by administrators rather than by judges. Although these administrators have broad discretion, they are limited by some elements of due process even though the U.S. Supreme Court has determined that not all of the full panoply of procedural rights found in criminal trials must be afforded in parole hearings.[90]

Another common aspect of parole systems is the use of "good time." Good time is a classic example of the carrot–stick approach to control and management. The promise of early release (the carrot) is dangled in front of inmates as a reward for good behavior in prison, and if they do not conform to institutional rules and norms they face the loss of good time (the stick) that results in longer incarceration. Different states take different tacks in regard to the use of good time and even parole. Some states bar parole for those offenders who commit certain crimes such as capital murder; some set minimum time periods (e.g., one-fourth of the sentence) exclusive of good time that must be served for certain offenses; and some use *mandatory release* that provides for automatic release when the calendar time and good time served equal the maximum time for which the inmate was sentenced.[91] Still others have adopted determinate sentencing and abandoned parole. In most *determinate sentencing* schemes, the legislature establishes a flat rate of punishment rather than a range of five to ten years for the crime, which removes judicial and jury discretion in the length of sentences along with abolishing parole.

Prisoners' Rights

Courts have always guarded—sometimes zealously, sometimes not—the rights of prisoners to challenge the basis of their convictions through appeal and writs of *habeas corpus,* but prisoners seeking redress of other grievances have often been faced with closed courthouse doors. They were regarded as slaves of the state who lost all legal rights—regardless of whether they were first offenders for minor offenses or the most heinous of all offenders—and who were totally subject to the arbitrary and capricious (and often brutal) whims of their captors.[92] The courts maintained a "hands-off" policy in regard to prison management, deferring to the expertise of prison administrators.

However, federal courts became more receptive to inmate suits[93] challenging both prison practices and conditions with the advent of the Civil Rights movement and increased interest in all human rights, and by such events as the 1971 Attica (NY) Prison Riot, where armed state troopers killed 29 inmates and ten officer hostages in retaking control of the prison.[94] The vehicle for such suits was the newly rediscovered Civil Rights Act of 1871 (42 U.S.C. § 1983), which gave federal courts jurisdiction to hear civil actions for deprivation of constitutional rights; this meant that a more neutral forum was available than the state courts, which were generally not amenable, if not actively hostile, to this type of litigation.

Prisoner suits have revealed that even within recent years, incarceration in the United States amounted to "banishment from civilized society to a dark and evil world completely alien to the free world."[95] Conditions in both jails and penitentiaries are described by courts as "degrading and disgusting"[96] and as "violating the elemental concepts of decency,"[97] thereby creating cruel and unusual punishment in violation of the Eighth Amendment. Municipal and county jails have not escaped the courts' scrutiny, especially in light of the fact that many of those in jail have not been convicted of the crime for which they are being held and are technically innocent but yet are being subjected to horrible conditions. Courts intervened to mandate that steps be taken to relieve overcrowding and that basic living and sanitary conditions be improved for both the general prison population and those in administrative or punitive segregation.[98]

Inmates also sought protection of the court in arenas other than prison conditions. Courts readily agree that the Eighth Amendment draws "meaning from the evolving standards of decency that mark the progress of a maturing society"[99] and that "prison walls do not form a barrier separating prison inmates from the protections of the Constitution."[100] The difficulty is in balancing the security of the institution and the safety of staff and prisoners against the constitutionally protected interests of the inmates.

Under the First Amendment, courts examine the rights of prisoners in the areas of religious freedom, speech, access to the press, and assembly. Prisoners do maintain some semblance of these rights even though they are circumscribed. For example, prison administrators cannot punish a prisoner or discriminate against him or her on account of the individual's religious faith.[101] They cannot arbitrarily prevent the practice of a religion because it is unpopular but instead must carefully weigh the security interest of the prison versus the prisoner's right to practice his or her religion, and mere speculation as to the danger or dislike of the religion's tenets will not suffice to prohibit a religion.[102]

Although most provisions of the Bill of Rights have been the subject of prisoner litigation, two are particularly noteworthy. One is the issue of access to courts "which is afforded special protection"[103] because "all other rights of an inmate are illusory without it."[104] Prisons are required to provide some system of legal services to inmates to challenge the grounds for their imprisonment.[105] This assistance may take a variety of forms including, but not limited to, state-provided attorneys, law students working in a clinic under supervision, or the assistance of other inmates, the "jailhouse lawyers." In addition, basic materials must be provided for legal research.[106] Prisoners who are perceived to be activists or troublemakers cannot be denied access to their attorneys or subjected to punishment for their activities.[107] Unlike other correspondence, mail to and from attorneys and courts is generally not to be read or even opened.[108]

"COUNTY JAIL BLUES"©

Charles Friedman, a pretrial detainee, filed a *pro se* action against the sheriff of Salt Lake County alleging that his civil rights under 42 U.S.C. § 1983 had been violated. Part of the claim was that the State had hindered his right to access to the courts by not providing him the forms to file against the State in a timely fashion—although this suit was filed within two months of his initial request. Furthermore, he complained that "he is forced to employ 'golf pencils' in the drafting of his pleadings, may purchase only six such pencils per week at the jail commissary, and has access to a pencil sharpener 'every other day.'" The Court noted that this had not impeded him too much as this complaint was 44 pages in length with numerous exhibits and that he had also filed another suit during the same time period. His appeal was dismissed for failure to state a claim on which relief could be granted.

Source: Friedman v. Kennard, 248 Fed. Appx. 918 (10th Circ. 2007), at 922.

Another fertile source of litigation is disciplinary proceedings and due process. Corporal punishment such as flogging or administering electric shocks was long used as the primary disciplinary tool in American penal institutions. However, in the late 1960s, courts recognized that corporal punishment "is easily subject to abuse in the hands of the sadistic and unscrupulous ... generates hatred toward the keepers ... is degrading to the punisher and the punished alike [and] public opinion is obviously adverse."[109] Yet, as recently as 2002, the Court found that a prisoner who had been handcuffed to a hitching post with his hands above his head, who was left shirtless in the sun, who was denied water and bathroom breaks, and who was taunted by a guard about his thirst for a period of seven hours was subjected to cruel and unusual punishment.[110] Today, the use of force (except in emergency situations) to control inmates has been supplanted by the disciplinary hearing as the chief mechanism to maintain order. A hearing must be provided in nonemergency situations before punishment is assessed, whether that punishment is denial of privileges or infringement of a constitutional right such as a prisoner's limited liberty interest in being in the general prison population versus solitary confinement or administrative segregation.

The courts have sought to prevent such hearings from merely being charades. In *Wolff v. McDonnell*,[111] the Supreme Court established minimal due process requirements for such hearings: (1) written notice of the charges at least 24 hours before the hearing, (2) the opportunity to call witnesses and present documentary evidence unless the institutional safety is put in jeopardy by calling such witnesses, (3) impartial hearing board, and (4) written statement of the evidence relied on by the board. While there is no right to an appointed attorney, an inmate who is illiterate or mentally handicapped is entitled to have the assistance of a counsel substitute (another inmate or staff member).[112]

Capital Punishment

Contrary to what many think, the Supreme Court has never held the death penalty to be unconstitutional. Instead, the Court found that the procedures imposing the death penalty were unconstitutional in that they allowed "arbitrary and capricious" actions on the part of the jury in sentencing a person to death[113] but that the defect could be cured by carefully drafted statutes which gave the sentencing authority adequate information and guidance.[114] The courts are concerned that the individual and the circumstances of this particular crime be scrutinized and considered by the jury,[115] and mandatory imposition of the death penalty without that consideration will not pass constitutional muster.[116] The morality and efficacy of the death penalty raise fascinating questions, but our discussion will focus on the legal aspects surrounding this most controversial topic.

Today, the death penalty is generally assessed only when the victim is murdered and then only in limited circumstances. While some states and the federal government do include a few other capital offenses such as treason in their criminal statutes, no one was on death row for the commission of these offenses at the end of 2015.[117] Strange as it may sound, not all murders are treated the same, and statutes define exactly what constitutes capital murder, such as a murder-for-hire scheme or killing a police officer in the line of duty. Although those only tangentially involved in capital murder (such as the driver of the getaway car) may not be given the death sentence,[118] those accessories "with major participation in the felony committed combined with reckless indifference to human life" may receive such punishment.[119] The Court has upheld the various methods of execution including hanging, firing squad, electrocution, and lethal gas, and states that employ the death penalty have adopted the use of lethal injections as the primary method of execution although inmates have challenged both the combination of drugs used and the qualifications of those dispensing the drugs. Both the efficacy of the death "cocktail" and the secrecy surrounding its ingredients and the producers of the drugs have been subjected to judicial scrutiny following a series of botched executions and the decision of several producers to either halt production or require that certain drugs not be used for executions. The Court, however, established a very high burden for prisoners seeking an injunction against the new combination of drugs by requiring that they show, among other things, that there is a "likelihood of success" on the merits at trial.[120] Various aspects of capital punishment—both procedural and substantive—continue to be troublesome for the Court. The manner of jury selection has also provoked appeals. The Supreme Court has denied the state the right to exclude from the jury all those who oppose the death penalty[121] and has barred the racially discriminatory use of peremptory challenges by prosecutors as, for example, eliminating all African-American jurors from a jury when the defendant is African American.[122] Concern still remains that the death penalty is applied disproportionately according to race, particularly when the victim is white and the offender is African American. In *McCleskey v. Kemp*,[123] a sophisticated statistical study was introduced to show that African Americans were more likely to be sentenced to the death penalty than whites in Georgia. The Supreme Court accepted the study and its conclusions but held that Warren McCleskey, who is African American, failed to show that discrimination affected the outcome in his particular case.

In addition to these types of issues, the Court also has practical concerns regarding the death penalty. The seriousness of the punishment and its irreversible nature mandates that the cases be carefully considered, but extensive scrutiny clogs the courts' dockets. The Court is continually examining methods of streamlining the appeals process while maintaining a strict standard of review. It is also worrisome to the Court and others that death row inmates are not receiving adequate legal representation on appeal because many lawyers and law firms are reluctant to take on these cases with their attendant loss of profits because of the attention and resources diverted to such cases.

Several states have placed a moratorium on executions because of concerns that innocent people were being executed, while other states have abolished the death penalty. Illinois Governor George H. Ryan, citing the cases of 13 death row inmates who had been exonerated in his state between 1977 and 2000, stated, "I can't support a system which, in its administration, has proven to be so fraught with error and has come so close to the ultimate nightmare: the state's taking of innocent life … There is no margin of error when it comes to putting a person to death."[124] Former Justice Harry A. Blackmun stated:

> From this day forward, I no longer shall tinker with the machinery of death … I feel morally and intellectually obligated simply to concede that the death penalty experiment has failed. It is virtually self-evident to me now that no combination of procedural rules or substantive regulations ever can save the death penalty from its inherent constitutional deficiencies.[125]

Yet, even as the Supreme Court seemed to narrow the application of the death penalty, several states enacted statutes that would broaden it to include offenders with multiple sexual offenses against children even though the Supreme Court ruled in *Kennedy v. Louisiana*[126] that a state may not assess the death penalty for the rape of a child when the victim did not die—laws that may be challenged.[127] Midway through the second decade of the twenty-first century, 19 states and the District of Columbia did not assess the death penalty by statute; others had moratoriums in place although the federal government and 31 other states retained the death penalty. Today, fewer executions are occurring and fewer death penalties are being assessed as more exonerations are granted which raises the public's awareness of the fallibility of the punishment and as life without parole is substituted as an alternative.[128]

Other Issues

Punishment is one of those areas of the law where everyone sees the problems but no one has the solution. Conviction of the wrongdoer is not the end of the line; he or she does not drop off the face of the earth. Society must decide the appropriate level of punishment as well as the amount of resources it is willing to devote to punitive measures. The financial and human costs of the programs are immense, especially in terms of total institutions. Such costs have encouraged the use of diversionary tools such as electronic monitoring devices, house arrest, boot camps, halfway houses, and other innovative programs, although these programs are not without their critics. The goal of such diversion is not only to limit the economic costs but also the human costs. The vast majority of inmates who are sentenced to prison do not die there but are released back into society after attending the "University of Crime," where their knowledge of crime has been greatly enhanced. Balancing the needs of society for retribution against the costs to society is a difficult and unenviable task for elected officials.

JUVENILE JUSTICE

Criminal law, like all law, reflects the attitudes of the society that produces it, and this may be seen in the legal treatment of children. Under Roman law, for example, children were subject to the complete control of their father under the doctrine of *patria potestas,* or parental authority. The *paterfamilias,* who was sometimes a grandfather, exercised absolute authority, including the power of life and death, over his children. This absolute control was in part a reflection of the reluctance of the state to interfere in the privacy of the home. In keeping with the spirit of the maxim, "A man's home is his castle," the Roman state hesitated to intervene in the private affairs of its citizens. During the Middle Ages, children were often treated as miniature adults who were expected to work when they were able. As part of a feudal society, children were viewed as the property of their parents much as their own serf parents were vassals of the feudal overlord. In our own society, children are not viewed as chattel subject to absolute control of their parents but as individuals with limited rights. Although there is still some reluctance by the state to intervene in family matters, states today have much greater latitude to act "in the best interests of the child."

In this section, we will examine the legal treatment of children in the United States. Like other aspects of criminal law, juvenile law has both procedural and substantive elements. Procedural law concerns the requirements that must be observed before the state denies a person life, liberty, or property. As we shall see, procedural safeguards for juveniles have been equivocal. Substantive law concerns issues such as the age at which juveniles may be punished for criminal behavior. We begin with a look at procedural law and juvenile justice.

Procedural Law

The prevailing philosophy of procedural due process, simply stated, has been that juveniles do not need the same procedural protection our system grants to adults. This is because the state, acting like a concerned parent, is only interested in the welfare of the child and intervenes only to help. The doctrine that permits the state to intervene on behalf of a child is known as *parens patriae.* Originally, this doctrine applied to the king who, as "father of the country," had a paternalistic interest in the well-being of his subjects. In a modern sense, *parens patriae* holds that the state has an obligation to care for its innocents; that is, those who cannot care for themselves. *Parens patriae* imposes an affirmative duty on the state to intervene to protect the life or well-being of a child. This doctrine justifies the removal, if necessary, of the child from the parents' control.

Ironically, the *parens patriae* doctrine has resulted in the ambivalent treatment of children in the area of procedural law:

> From its origins, the juvenile court system denied children procedural rights normally available to adult offenders. Due process rights such as representation by counsel, a jury trial, freedom from self-incrimination, and freedom from unreasonable search and seizure were not considered essential for the juvenile court system because the primary purpose of the system was not punishment but rehabilitation.[129]

Unlike adult criminals who were often viewed as lost causes, many people believe that there is still hope of rehabilitating a child who has committed a crime. Society is less willing to give up on a child who may yet be saved from a life of crime. Oddly enough, this paternalistic approach has had some negative effects. Because the purpose of the juvenile justice system was to save rather than punish the child, the procedural safeguards afforded to adults were denied to children. Supreme Court Justice Abe Fortas explained this rationale in *In re Gault*:

> The right of the state, as *parens patriae,* to deny the child procedural rights available to his elders was elaborated by the assertion that a child, unlike an adult, has a right "not to liberty but to custody." He can be made to attorn to his parents, to go to school, etc. If his parents default in effectively performing their custodial function, that is, if the child is "delinquent"—the state may intervene. In doing so, it does not deprive the child of any rights, *because he has none.* [Emphasis added.] It merely provides the "custody" to which the child is entitled. On this basis, proceedings involving juveniles were described as "civil" not "criminal" and therefore not subject to the requirements which restrict the state when it seeks to deprive a person of his liberty.[130]

Gault and its immediate predecessor, *Kent v. United States*,[131] revealed the disturbing state of juvenile procedural law. Although *Gault* raised several procedural issues including right to counsel, notice of proceedings, and the privilege against self-incrimination, the most egregious issue concerned the penalty which Gerald Gault received. As a delinquent accused of making obscene phone calls, Gault, who was aged 15, was subject to confinement until he reached the age of 21. An adult charged with the same offense would have received a maximum penalty of a $50 fine and/or two months in jail.[132] Although the Supreme Court made it clear that its decision "will not compel the States to abandon or displace any of the substantive benefits of the juvenile process,"[133] many observers heralded *Gault* as the dawn of a due process revolution for juvenile justice.

The Supreme Court extended the procedural rights of juveniles in the years following *Gault*. Three years later, the Court ruled in *In re Winship*[134] that the "beyond a reasonable doubt" standard required for adult convictions also applied to juvenile cases. Before *Winship*, the states applied the "preponderance of the evidence" standard used in civil proceedings. The use of the lesser civil standard in juvenile cases reflected the paternalistic, non-adversarial approach of the criminal justice system. Finally, the Court extended the Constitution's double-jeopardy provision to juveniles in *Breed v. Jones*.[135]

While the Supreme Court made great strides in protecting the constitutional rights of juveniles, the Court clearly does not intend to extend all provisions of the Constitution to juvenile justice. For example, in *McKeiver v. Pennsylvania*[136] the Court held that juveniles are not entitled to a jury trial. Similarly, in *Schall v. Martin*[137] it upheld a New York law that permitted pretrial detention of accused delinquents. Gregory Martin was detained for 15 days, whereas an adult charged with the same offense would have been permitted to post bail.[138] In *New Jersey v. T.L.O.*,[139] the Court upheld the search of T.L.O.'s purse by an assistant principal despite insufficient probable cause. While recognizing student constitutional rights, the Court nevertheless approved such searches under a less stringent standard. A school official need have only a "reasonable suspicion" to search a student's possessions.

After several major advances in procedural due process for juveniles, the Supreme Court has retreated from extending further safeguards. This uncertainty about how to treat juvenile offenders is reflected in substantive juvenile law to which we now turn our attention.

Substantive Law

Procedural law, as we have seen, centers on what procedures the law affords to juveniles. Substantive law raises questions such as when, or even if, a child should be punished for a criminal act. Another important issue is whether a young person should receive the same penalty for a crime as an adult would receive. Substantive juvenile law is like procedural juvenile law in that both raise the fundamental question whether a child should be treated the same as an adult.

Historically, the law has assumed that children below a certain age may not be punished for criminal behavior. Under Roman law, for example, a child under the age of 7 could not be punished for committing a crime. Seven was accepted during the Middle Ages because at that age children made their first confession in the Catholic Church.[140] The American colonies followed the common law rule of the age of 7 as well.[141] Today, most states accept 10 as the age at which children are liable for their criminal actions. This is not to say that children are treated as adults at this age but only that they may be subject to the juvenile justice system.

The principal reason for exempting children from criminal liability is the belief that very young children lack the necessary criminal intent or *mens rea* to commit a crime.[142] The key issue is whether a child can distinguish right from wrong. Similarly, the law recognizes the inability to distinguish right from wrong as an element of an insanity plea.[143] Society has concluded that it is simply wrong to punish a person, adult or child, who is incapable of understanding the consequences of his or her actions.

A second issue of substantive juvenile justice is the punishment a child should receive if convicted. The early practice was to treat a child over the age of 7 as an adult and apply the same penalty. As one legal scholar has noted:

> It was probably not until the time of Spigurnel, Edward II's judge, that it became the practice to ask whether the child could tell good from evil, and children of seven—the crucial age in Roman law—were in danger of being hanged or burned.[144]

In the American colonies, 14 was generally the age at which a person could be sentenced to death.[145] In the twentieth century, the youngest person executed in the United States was by Florida in 1927 at the age of 13.[146]

LIFE WITHOUT PAROLE

A recent example of the differential approach toward juvenile crime is illustrated by *Graham v. Florida*, 130 S. Ct. 2011 (2010), in which the Supreme Court held that states may not sentence a juvenile to prison for life without parole for non-homicide crimes. The Court ruled that sentencing a juvenile to life in prison without parole violates the "cruel and unusual punishment" clause of the Eighth Amendment because the penalty is disproportionate to the crime committed. Terrance Graham committed burglary with two accomplices. He was given parole but committed armed robbery just before his eighteenth birthday. The sentencing judge imposed the maximum sentence of life without parole. The majority found that the traditional arguments for punishment—retribution, deterrence, incapacitation, and rehabilitation—are not applicable in juvenile cases. The Court also held that although 37 states and the District of Columbia permit life without parole for juveniles, in practice the actual imposition of the sentence was rare, supporting its view that the sentence is disproportionate for non-homicide crimes.

Under American law today, the punishment of a child is tied to age and the nature of the offense. For certain crimes, a child may be punished as an adult if he or she is certified as an adult. A recent trend has been to lower the age at which a person may be certified as an adult. For example, in 1994, Congress passed the Omnibus Anti-Crime Bill, which permits a child of 13 to be certified as an adult for such crimes as murder, robbery, and rape.[147] If certified as an adult, the child is subject to the same punishment an adult may receive. The exception is that states may no longer execute persons under the age of 18 when the crime was committed.

As we have seen, the treatment of juveniles under the law has undergone considerable change. The legal treatment of juveniles charged with a crime ebbs and flows with public opinion. Recent events such as the schoolyard massacres by perpetrators as young as 11 highlight the moral and philosophical questions about the difficult balance between the appropriate treatment of very young juvenile offenders and "the pragmatic issue of community protection and the states' rights to wage war on its enemies."[148] In this sense, juvenile justice mirrors society's attitudes about crime in general. Too much reliance on differential treatment of juveniles could result in a return to the pre-*Gault* era. That, in turn, could result in the situation best described by Justice Abe Fortas in *Kent*:

> There is evidence, in fact, that there may be grounds for concern that the child receives the worst of both worlds: that he gets neither the protections accorded to adults nor the solicitous care and regenerative treatment postulated for children.[149]

TWO CASE STUDIES IN CRIMINAL LAW

In the introduction to this chapter, we noted the controversial nature of both substantive and procedural criminal law. In this section, we will examine two Supreme Court cases which illustrate that controversy. The first case, *Rummel v. Estelle*,[150] deals with a question of substantive law—specifically, when does the punishment fit the crime? The second case, *Brewer v. Williams*,[151] raises the difficult question of protecting the constitutional rights of a factually guilty person.

Rummel v. Estelle[152]

Texas, like many other states, had a habitual offender statute that imposed a mandatory life sentence on anyone who was convicted of three felonies. In addition to having been convicted, the defendant must also have actually served time in prison for the first two convictions. In 1964, William Rummel was convicted of fraudulent use of a credit card in the amount of $80 and was sentenced to three years in the state prison. In 1969, he was convicted of passing a forged check for $28.36, for which he received four years in prison. In 1973, Rummel was convicted of receiving $120.75 by false pretenses. The total value of all three of Rummel's crimes was less than $230. At Rummel's 1973 trial, the prosecutor chose to proceed under the Texas habitual offender statute, and Rummel received a life sentence. Rummel challenged the constitutionality of the life sentence on the grounds that it "was so disproportionate to the crimes he committed as to constitute cruel and unusual punishment."[153] The district court rejected Rummel's claim of cruel and unusual punishment, but a panel of the Fifth U.S. Court of Appeals reversed the district court judge. The case was reheard *en banc,* and the full Court of Appeals reversed the panel; that is, it upheld the original judgment of the district court against Rummel's claim. The U.S. Supreme Court, in a 5 to 4 decision, also ruled against Rummel.

Then (later Chief) Justice William Rehnquist authored the Court's majority opinion. Rehnquist began by noting that Rummel was not challenging the Texas recidivist statute per se. Rummel challenged the act only as it applied to him. Nor did Rummel challenge the fact that he could constitutionally have received sentences totaling 25 years for his three crimes. Rummel challenged only the State's ability to impose a life sentence in his particular case. Rummel based his challenge both on *Weems v. United States*,[154] in which the Supreme Court reversed the conviction of a Philippine official imprisoned at hard labor for 12 years for the crime of falsifying public records and on some of the Court's previous decisions in death penalty cases.[155] The Court rejected both in ruling against Rummel.

Justice Rehnquist noted the uniqueness of the *Weems* case. In addition to the lengthy sentence, Paul A. Weems was chained at the ankle and wrist and forced to do hard labor for 12 years. When viewed in its totality—the minor crime of falsifying public records and the harsh sentence—the Court in 1910 found no difficulty in ruling that the sentence was disproportionate to the crime. In Rummel's case, because of the State's liberal "good time" policy, he could be eligible for parole in 12 years. The Court also refused to apply its rationale in death penalty cases to Rummel's situation. Justice Rehnquist noted that the irrevocability of the death sentence gave the death penalty a uniqueness that did not apply to Rummel.

Having stripped Rummel of his precedents, Justice Rehnquist proceeded to explain why the Eighth Amendment was not offended in this case. First, exercising judicial deference, he noted that the length of prison sentences is a legislative prerogative and that the determination of appropriate punishments for various crimes is too subjective for courts to decide. If Rummel's crimes had totaled $5000 instead of a mere $230, would the life sentence be fairer? That, Justice Rehnquist said, is for a legislature, not the courts, to decide. Second, Rehnquist rejected Rummel's argument that the life sentence was excessive because his crimes were nonviolent. The presence or absence of violence has nothing to do with society's interest in deterring crime. Pollution, for example, is nonviolent, but society may impose harsh penalties to deter it. Third, Justice Rehnquist noted that Rummel was *not* being punished just for receiving $120.75 under false pretenses. As a habitual offender, Rummel had shown an inability to conform to the norms of society. Fourth, the penalty imposed by Texas, though severe, is not grossly out of line with recidivist statutes in other states. Finally, the fact that Rummel would be eligible for parole after serving 12 years indicated the unlikelihood of his remaining in prison for the rest of his life. These factors led the majority to conclude that the life sentence did not constitute cruel and unusual punishment.

Justice Lewis Powell, joined by three other justices, wrote a dissenting opinion in *Rummel*. Justice Powell disagreed with the majority's analysis on a number of points. First, in the death penalty cases, the Court ruled that the death sentence is an excessive punishment for certain crimes, such as rape.[156] Powell saw no reason that the disproportionality analysis of death penalty cases should not apply to noncapital cases because there is no basis for such a distinction in Eighth Amendment jurisprudence. Powell also believed that the Court's restriction of *Weems* to its unique facts was not warranted. The *Weems* Court emphasized the number of years Weems received for a minor offense as much as the conditions of hard labor imposed. Nor did Powell accept the notion that society's interest in deterring repeat offenders justified a mandatory life sentence for Rummel's crimes. Powell observed, "A statute that levied a mandatory life sentence for overtime parking might well deter vehicular lawlessness, but it would offend our felt sense of justice."[157] In other words, the fact that Rummel's sentence might meet a societal goal does not make it less offensive to the Eighth Amendment.

Powell attacked the majority's reasoning on another point: the seriousness of Rummel's crimes. It is hard to imagine crimes that pose less danger to the safety of society than Rummel's, Powell argued. Forged checks, misuse of credit cards, and receiving money under false pretenses are hardly on a par with rape and murder. Yet under Texas law, the maximum sentence on a rape conviction was 20 years and the minimum was two years. At the time, the same sentence applied to a person convicted of involuntary manslaughter. The only first-time offense subject to a mandatory life sentence was capital murder. Powell noted that even Texas admitted that Rummel's third offense was not a serious crime because in 1980 the state reduced it to a misdemeanor. Finally, Powell argued that the fact that Rummel might become eligible for parole after 12 years should not be a consideration. Prison inmates have no legal right to parole. Powell noted that in 1979, Governor William Clements of Texas denied parole to 79 percent of the inmates recommended by the state's pardon and parole board.[158] Therefore, Powell argued, the question of the disproportionality of Rummel's sentence should be judged independent of any hypothetical chance of parole.

The *Rummel* case did not end the debate over the practice of imposing life sentences on habitual offenders. Just three years later, in *Solem v. Helm*,[159] the Court reviewed the imposition of a mandatory life sentence on a person convicted of seven felonies. Jerry Helm's offenses, like Rummel's, were nonviolent property crimes, with the last one being the writing of a $100 "no account" check. However, this time the Court reversed its previous position somewhat. This time, with Justice Powell writing for the majority, the Court ruled that the imposition of a life sentence with no chance of parole did violate the Eighth Amendment's prohibition against cruel and unusual punishment. Making many of the same arguments he used in *Rummel,* Justice Powell asserted that the Eighth Amendment does forbid excessive punishment in noncapital as well as capital cases. Powell also argued that objective criteria could be developed to guide courts in determining whether a given penalty was excessive. These criteria include the gravity of the offense versus the harshness of the penalty, whether sentences imposed upon others for more serious crimes are less harsh, and whether sentences imposed for the commission of the same crime in other jurisdictions are less harsh.[160] Applying the criteria to Helm's case, the majority concluded that the life sentence he received was excessive for the crimes he had committed. In addition, Powell emphasized that in *Rummel* the prisoner had a possibility of parole after 12 years, whereas in *Helm* the sentence contained no chance of parole unless the governor commuted the sentence, a possibility the Court considered unlikely.

A more recent pronouncement on the use of the three-strike rule had the Supreme Court reaffirming by implication the constitutionality of the rule. In *Lockyer v. Andrade*,[161] the Court held that two consecutive 25-year sentences imposed by a California court upon Leandro Andrade did not warrant federal *habeas corpus* review of the underlying Eighth Amendment issue of cruel and unusual punishment. The crux in that case was whether the offenses, the latest of which involved only $150-worth of videotapes, clearly violated the *Rummel-Solem* standard of the proportionality of the sentence. The Supreme Court held, again by implication, that it did not.

The *Rummel-Solem-Lockyer* cases raise some of the questions about the nature of substantive criminal law discussed earlier in the chapter. Individuals disagree over the appropriate punishment for habitual offenders. They also disagree, as did the justices of the Supreme Court, over what constitutes excessive or cruel and unusual punishment. It is because reasonable people disagree over the substance of criminal law that one must understand the political nature of the criminal justice system and, as discussed in Chapter 6, the lack of finality of constitutional questions. Suffice it to say that, as *Lockyer* shows, the debate over life sentences for habitual offenders is far from over.

Brewer v. Williams

On Christmas Eve in 1968, a 10-year-old girl named Pamela Powers disappeared while attending a wrestling match at a Des Moines, Iowa, YMCA. A teenager opened the door of the YMCA for Robert Williams, who was carrying a large bundle wrapped in a blanket. When the teenager opened Williams's car door, he noticed two "white and skinny legs" protruding from the bundle. Williams immediately became a suspect in the abduction of Pamela Powers. Later, Williams's car was discovered in Davenport, 160 miles east of Des Moines. A warrant was issued for Williams's arrest.

On December 26, a Des Moines lawyer named Henry McKnight informed police that he had been contacted by Williams from Davenport and that he had advised Williams to turn himself in to the Davenport police, which Williams did. Upon his arrest, Williams was given the *Miranda* warnings. In the presence of the Des Moines chief of police and a police detective named Cleatus M. Leaming, McKnight informed Williams over the telephone that two Des Moines detectives were coming to Davenport to return him to Des Moines. McKnight also told Williams that he was not to discuss Pamela Powers with the detectives during the return trip. Williams was arraigned in Davenport and again given the *Miranda* warnings. Thomas Kelly, a Davenport attorney, also advised Williams not to say anything until he had spoken with McKnight in Des Moines. When Detective Leaming arrived, he again gave Williams the *Miranda* warnings. At one point, Kelly asked Leaming for permission to accompany Williams back to Des Moines but was informed that the police department had a "no passengers" rule.

On the trip back to Des Moines, Detective Leaming made what was later termed "the Christian burial speech." Under the guise of giving Williams "something to think about," Detective Leaming pointed out that the weather was becoming worse and that snow was predicted before the day was over. Leaming pointed out that if it snowed, it might be impossible for anyone, even Williams, to find Pamela's body and that her parents were at least entitled to give their daughter a Christian burial. Williams asked if the police had found the girl's shoes, and when Leaming replied that he was unsure, Williams directed them to a service station where he claimed to have left them. However, a search failed to turn up the shoes. Later Williams inquired about the blanket and directed the detectives to a rest area, but the blanket was not found. Finally, Williams led the detectives to the body of Pamela Powers. Williams was later indicted for first-degree murder, and his motion to suppress all evidence resulting from his statements to Leaming was denied. The trial judge ruled that Williams had waived his right to counsel and his protection against self-incrimination.

The Supreme Court, in a bitterly divided vote, ruled that Williams had not waived his right to counsel and that Detective Leaming's "Christian burial speech" was a form of interrogation forbidden by the Sixth Amendment without the presence of counsel. Justice Potter Stewart, writing for the majority, found that Detective Leaming deliberately set out to elicit incriminatory information from Williams. Leaming, after reading Williams the *Miranda* warnings, said to Williams, "We'll be visiting between here and Des Moines."[162] Although Leaming had been warned not to interrogate Williams, the "Christian burial speech" was designed to appeal to Williams's deep religious beliefs. Moreover, at Williams's trial, Leaming admitted that that was his purpose. In response to a question, Leaming replied, "I was sure hoping to find out where that little girl was, yes, sir."[163] More importantly, the Court ruled, the State bears the burden of proving that a defendant has waived his right to counsel. Williams repeatedly told police that he would tell everything when they reached Des Moines. The Court interpreted that to mean that Williams did not intend to waive his right to counsel until he had a chance to speak with his lawyer, McKnight, in Des Moines. Finally, the fact that Williams had called McKnight in Des Moines and had secured Kelly's services in Davenport provided further proof of his reliance on the assistance of counsel. In light of these factors, Justice Stewart found that the State had failed to meet the burden of proving that Williams had intelligently waived his right to counsel.

In a concurring opinion, Justice Thurgood Marshall shed additional light on Leaming's actions. If, as indicated, Williams promised to tell the whole story back in Des Moines, why didn't the police just wait? If Williams were allowed to tell McKnight the location of the body, McKnight could then have told the police and Williams would not have been forced to incriminate himself directly—that is, by "directly demonstrating his knowledge of the body's location."[164] If finding Pamela Powers's body were truly the main objective, "this scenario would accomplish all that Leaming sought from his investigation except that it would not produce incriminating statements or actions from Williams."[165] In other words, eliciting incriminating statements from Williams, not finding

Pamela's body, was Leaming's real objective. Justice Marshall defended the majority's decision by noting, "The heinous nature of the crime is no excuse, as the dissenters would have it, for condoning knowing and intentional police transgression of the constitutional rights of a defendant."[166] Justice Marshall concluded his opinion by quoting Justice Louis Brandeis's dissent in *Olmstead v. United States*:

> In a government of laws, existence of the government will be imperilled if it fails to observe the law scrupulously. Our Government is the potent, the omnipresent teacher. For good or for ill, it teaches the whole people by example. Crime is contagious. If the Government becomes a lawbreaker, it breeds contempt for law; it invites every man to become a law unto himself; it invites anarchy. To declare that in the administration of the criminal law the end justifies the means—to declare that the Government may commit crimes in order to secure the conviction of a private criminal—would bring terrible retribution. Against that pernicious doctrine this Court should resolutely set its face.[167]

Lawyers like to say that "hard cases make bad law"; *Brewer v. Williams* is undoubtedly a hard case, but whether it made bad law depends on one's perspective. The dissenters in *Williams* saw Leaming's actions as "good police work," while the majority condemned them. There can be no doubt that Williams killed Pamela Powers, but it is important to remember that the Supreme Court does not deal with questions of guilt or innocence per se. The Court is interested in due process of law and in making sure that government obeys its own laws. Although that point may be difficult to understand and to accept, especially when an innocent little girl has been brutally murdered, it may be, to paraphrase Justice Oliver Wendell Holmes, Jr., that due process of law is the price we pay for civilization.

If the reader is still troubled by the decision in *Williams*, there is more to the story. The Supreme Court's decision did not mean that Williams was set free, but only that the State must retry him without using the incriminating evidence secured by Leaming's unlawful interrogation. In 1977, Williams was again tried for first-degree murder and was again found guilty. The prosecution introduced evidence concerning the condition of Pamela Powers's body when it was found, and the defense sought to suppress it as the "fruit" of Leaming's illegal interrogation. The trial court ruled that searchers would have come upon the body eventually even without Williams's help and that it would have been essentially in the same condition. Therefore, the trial judge allowed the evidence. Williams again appealed his case to the Supreme Court, but in *Nix v. Williams*[168] the Court ruled against him and upheld his conviction and life sentence.

These two case studies, *Rummel v. Estelle* and *Brewer v. Williams,* were included in this chapter to illustrate aspects of substantive and procedural criminal law. In a real sense, justice prevailed in both cases. Rummel was paroled just eight months after his appeal was denied by the Supreme Court,[169] and Williams was sentenced to life in prison. However, the questions raised by the two cases are fundamental ones that may never be answered because they deal with our sense of justice and fairness. The debate over these issues will continue, for, as Yogi Berra aptly observed, "It ain't over till it's over."

CONCLUSION

As noted in this chapter's introduction, perhaps no topic in law is as controversial as criminal law. There is perhaps nothing that tells as much about a society as the way it treats those who are accused of crime. In a sense, then, crime is not only a social problem but a political one as well. In this chapter, we have discussed both substantive and procedural criminal law. Substantive criminal law concerns what constitutes criminal behavior, what the elements of a crime are, and what punishment is appropriate for a given criminal act. Procedural criminal law concerns the "rules of the game" by which government must abide before it can deprive one of its citizens of life, liberty, or property. Both topics raise difficult questions that have elusive answers. Perhaps in the final analysis we must determine the answers individually. The one certainty is that the questions will not go away, and it is our hope that we have added to the reader's understanding of an enormously complex area of law.

NOTES

1. For examples of persons cleared of crimes due to DNA testing, see the Innocence Project, http://www.innocenceproject.org/cases-false-imprisonment/front-page#c10= published&b_start=0&c4=Exonerated+by+DNA (visited December 12, 2015).
2. See *Loving v. Virginia*, 388 U.S. 1 (1967) and *Lawrence v. Texas*, 539 U.S. 558 (2003).
3. Thomas J. Gardner and Terry M. Anderson, *Criminal Law: Principles and Cases*, 8th edn (Belmont, CA: Thomson Wadsworth, 2003), p. 165.
4. *Phalen v. Virginia*, 8 Howard 163 (1850), at 168.
5. Henry C. Black, *Black's Law Dictionary*, 4th edn (St. Paul, MN: West, 1968), p. 55.
6. Ibid., p. 1481.
7. David W. Neubauer, *America's Courts and the Criminal Justice System*, 5th edn (Belmont, CA: Wadsworth, 1996), p. 64.
8. *Conally v. General Construction Co.*, 269 U.S. 385 (1926), at 391.
9. Thomas J. Gardner and Terry M. Anderson, *Criminal Law: Principles and Cases*, 8th edn (Belmont, CA: Wadsworth, 2000), p. 10.
10. "Witness Given 12 Years in Prison," *Boston Globe*, May 28, 1998, p. A1.
11. *Robinson v. California*, 370 U.S. 660 (1962).
12. *Powell v. Texas*, 392 U.S. 514 (1968).
13. Black, p. 1137.
14. Gardner and Anderson, 8th edn, pp. 37–38.
15. *Penry v. Lynaugh*, 492 U.S. 302 (1989).
16. *Atkins v. Virginia*, 536 U.S. 304 (2002).
17. *Roper v. Simmons*, 543 U.S. 551 (2005).
18. Tex. Penal Code, § 7.02(a)(2).
19. Gardner and Anderson, 8th edn, p. 68.
20. Ibid.

21. Edward Steers, Jr., "Dr. Mudd and the 'Colored' Witnesses," *Civil War History* 46, 4 (2000), p. 334.
22. Nora A. Uehlein, Annotation, "Corporation's Criminal Liability for Homicide," 45 A.L.R. 4th 1021 (1986).
23. Gardner and Anderson, 8th edn, pp. 127–159.
24. U.S. Constitution, Amendment IV.
25. *New Jersey v. T.L.O.*, 469 U.S. 325 (1985).
26. *Michigan Department of State Police v. Sitz*, 496 U.S. 444 (1990).
27. *Skinner v. Railway Labor Executives' Association*, 489 U.S. 602 (1989).
28. *Florida v. Bostick*, 501 U.S. 429 (1991).
29. *Warden v. Hayden*, 387 U.S. 294 (1967).
30. Ibid., at 301.
31. *Weeks v. United States*, 232 U.S. 383 (1914).
32. Ibid., at 393.
33. *Mapp v. Ohio*, 367 U.S. 643 (1961).
34. *Olmstead v. United States*, 277 U.S. 438 (1928), at 485 (Brandeis J., dissenting).
35. *Mapp v. Ohio*, at 659.
36. *Rochin v. California*, 342 U.S. 165 (1952).
37. *Wolf v. Colorado*, 338 U.S. 25 (1949).
38. *Mapp v. Ohio*, 367 U.S. 643 (1961).
39. *Hudson v. Michigan*, 547 U.S. 586 (2006).
40. *Chimel v. California*, 395 U.S. 752 (1969).
41. John C. Klotter and Jacqueline R. Kanovitz, *Constitutional Law for Police*, 3rd edn (Cincinnati, OH: Anderson, 1977), p. 213.
42. Ibid.; *Georgia v. Randolph*, 547 U.S. 103 (2006).
43. *Terry v. Ohio*, 392 U.S. 1 (1968).
44. Ibid., at 21.
45. *Carroll v. United States*, 267 U.S. 132 (1925).
46. *Chambers v. Maroney*, 399 U.S. 42 (1970).
47. *United States v. Robinson*, 414 U.S. 218 (1973).
48. *South Dakota v. Opperman*, 428 U.S. 364 (1976); *Cady v. Dombrowski*, 413 U.S. 433 (1973).
49. *Michigan Department of State Police v. Sitz*, 496 U.S. 444 (1990).
50. *City of Indianapolis v. Edmonds*, 531 U.S. 32 (2000).
51. *Harris v. United States*, 331 U.S. 145 (1947).
52. Klotter and Kanovitz, p. 226.
53. *Olmstead v. United States*, 277 U.S. 438 (1928).
54. *Katz v. United States*, 389 U.S. 347 (1967).
55. *Kyllo v. United States*, 533 U.S. 27 (2001).
56. *Riley v. California*, 573 U.S. _____ (2014).
57. Scott Bomboy, "A Legal Victory for Drones Warrants a Fourth Amendment Discussion," http://blog.constitutioncenter.org/2014/02/a-court-victory-for-drones-warrants-a-fourth-amendment-discussion/ (visited December 16, 2015).
58. USA Patriot Act, H.R. 3162 (October 24, 2001).
59. *Mallory v. United States*, 354 U.S. 449 (1957).
60. *Escobedo v. Illinois*, 378 U.S. 478 (1964).
61. *Powell v. Alabama*, 287 U.S. 45 (1932), at 69.
62. *Escobedo v. Illinois*, 378 U.S. 478 (1964), at 488.
63. Ibid., pp. 490–491.
64. *Miranda v. Arizona*, 384 U.S. 436 (1966).

65. See Richard H. Seeburger and R. Stanton Wettick, Jr., "*Miranda* in Pittsburgh: A Statistical Study," 29 U. Pitt. L.R. 1 (1967).
66. *Dickerson v. United States*, 530 U.S. 428 (2000).
67. *Mathis v. United States*, 391 U.S. 1 (1968).
68. *Orozco v. Texas*, 394 U.S. 324 (1969).
69. *Beckwith v. United States*, 425 U.S. 341 (1976).
70. *Oregon v. Mathiason*, 429 U.S. 492 (1977).
71. *Estelle v. Smith*, 451 U.S. 454 (1981).
72. *Brewer v. Williams*, 430 U.S. 387 (1977).
73. *North Carolina v. Butler*, 441 U.S. 369 (1979).
74. *Berghuis v. Thompkins*, 560 U.S. 370 (2010).
75. *Missouri v. Seibert*, 542 U.S. 600 (2004).
76. *Twining v. New Jersey*, 211 U.S. 78 (1908).
77. *Adamson v. California*, 332 U.S. 46 (1947).
78. *Malloy v. Hogan*, 378 U.S. 1 (1964).
79. *Boyd v. United States*, 116 U.S. 616 (1886).
80. Ibid., at 633.
81. See *Matter of Grand Jury Empanelled*, 597 F. 2d 851 (3rd Cir., 1979) and *United States v. Payner*, 447 U.S. 727 (1980).
82. *Rochin v. California*, 342 U.S. 165 (1952).
83. *Breithaupt v. Abram*, 352 U.S. 432 (1957).
84. *Schmerber v. California*, 384 U.S. 757 (1966).
85. Klotter and Kanovitz, p. 353.
86. *Missouri v. McNeely*, 569 U.S. _____ (2013).
87. *United States v. Wade*, 388 U.S. 218 (1967).
88. James A. Inciardi, *Criminal Justice*, 7th edn (Fort Worth, TX: Harcourt College Publishers, 2002), pp. 424–426.
89. Ibid., pp. 596–609.
90. *Greenholtz v. Inmates of Nebraska Penal and Correctional Complex*, 422 U.S. 1 (1979).
91. Inciardi, pp. 610–619; see, e.g., Tex. Crim. Proc. Art. 42.18(b).
92. *Ruffin v. Commonwealth*, 62 Va. (21 Gratt.) 790 (1871), at 796.
93. *Inmates of Attica Correctional Facility v. Rockefeller*, 453 F.2d 12 (2d Cir. 1971).
94. Inciardi, p. 558.
95. *Holt v. Sarver*, 309 F. Supp. 362 (E.D. Ark. 1970), at 381, *aff'd* 442 F.2d 304 (8th Cir. 1971).
96. Ibid.
97. *Jordan v. Fitzharris*, 257 F. Supp. 674 (N.D. Cal. 1966), at 679.
98. For further study of prison conditions, see *Holt v. Sarver*, 300 F. Supp. 825 (1969) and 309 F. Supp. 362 (1970); Steve J. Martin and Sheldon Ekland-Olson, *Texas Prisons: The Walls Came Tumbling Down* (Austin, TX: Texas Monthly Press, 1987); Ben M. Crouch and James W. Marquart, *An Appeal to Justice: Litigated Reform of Texas Prisons* (Austin, TX: University of Texas Press, 1989); Roger Morris, *The Devil's Butcher Shop: The New Mexico Prison Uprising* (New York: F. Watts, 1983).
99. *Trop v. Dulles*, 356 U.S. 86 (1958), at 101.
100. *Turner v. Safley*, 482 U.S. 78 (1987), at 84.
101. *Cooper v. Pate*, 382 F.2d 518 (7th Cir. 1967).
102. *Banks v. Havener*, 234 F. Supp. 27 (E.D. Va. 1964).
103. *Taylor v. Sterrett*, 532 F.2d 462 (5th Cir. 1976), at 470.

104. *Adams v. Carlson*, 488 F.2d 619 (7th Cir. 1973), at 630.

105. *Johnson v. Avery*, 393 U.S. 483 (1969).

106. *Younger v. Gilmore*, 404 U.S. 15 (1971).

107. *Cruz v. Beto II*, 603 F.2d 1178 (5th Cir. 1969).

108. *Wolff v. McDonnell*, 418 U.S. 539 (1974); *Thornburgh v. Abbott*, 490 U.S. 401 (1989).

109. *Jackson v. Bishop*, 404 F.2d 571 (8th Cir. 1968), at 579–580.

110. *Hope v. Pelzer*, 536 U.S. 730 (2002).

111. *Wolff v. McDonnell*, 418 U.S. 539 (1974).

112. *Baxter v. Palmigiano*, 425 U.S. 539 (1976).

113. *Furman v. Georgia*, 408 U.S. 238 (1972).

114. *Gregg v. Georgia*, 428 U.S. 153 (1976).

115. *Ring v. Arizona*, 536 U.S. 584 (2002).

116. *Woodson v. North Carolina*, 428 U.S. 280 (1976).

117. *Coker v. Georgia*, 428 U.S. 583 (1977); "Death Penalty for Offenses Other Than Murder," Death Penalty Information Center, http://www.deathpenaltyinfo.org/death-penalty-offenses-other-murder (visited December 12, 2015).

118. *Enmund v. Florida*, 458 U.S. 782 (1982).

119. *Tison v. Arizona*, 481 U.S. 137 (1987), at 158.

120. *Glossip v. Gross*, 574 U.S. ___ (2015); "Lethal Injection," Death Penalty Information Center, http://www.deathpenaltyinfo.org/lethal-injection (visited December 12, 2015).

121. *Witherspoon v. Illinois*, 391 U.S. 510 (1968).

122. *Batson v. Kentucky*, 476 U.S. 79 (1986).

123. *McCleskey v. Kemp*, 481 U.S. 279 (1987).

124. Aaron Chambers, "Ryan Halts all Executions in Illinois," *Chicago Daily Law Bulletin*, January 31, 2000.

125. *Callins v. Collins*, 510 U.S. 1141 (1994), at 1145 (J. Blackmun dissent).

126. *Kennedy v. Louisiana*, 129 S. Ct. 1 (2008).

127. Adam Liptak, "Death Penalty in Some Cases of Child Sex is Widening," *New York Times*, June 10, 2006.

128. "States With and Without the Death Penalty," Death Penalty Resource Center, http://www.deathpenaltyinfo.org/states-and-without-death-penalty (visited December 12, 2015).

129. Larry J. Siegel, Brandon C. Welsh, and Joseph J. Senna, *Juvenile Delinquency: Theory, Practice and Law*, 9th edn (Belmont, CA: Thomson Wadsworth, 2006), pp. 373–374.

130. *In re Gault*, 387 U.S. 1 (1967), at 17.

131. *Kent v. United States*, 383 U.S. 541 (1966).

132. *In re Gault*, 387 U.S. 1 (1967), at 8.

133. Ibid., at 21.

134. *In re Winship*, 397 U.S. 358 (1970).

135. *Breed v. Jones*, 421 U.S. 519 (1975).

136. *McKeiver v. Pennsylvania*, 402 U.S. 528 (1971).

137. *Schall v. Martin*, 467 U.S. 253 (1984).

138. Ibid., p. 259.

139. *New Jersey v. T.L.O.*, 469 U.S. 325 (1985).

140. Nigel Walker, *Crime and Insanity in England* (Edinburgh: Edinburgh University Press, 1968), p. 40.

141. Inciardi, p. 673.

142. Gardner and Anderson, 8th edn, pp. 83–84.

143. Walker, p. 40.

144. Ibid., p. 28.

145. Lamar T. Empey and Marc C. Stafford, *American Delinquency: Its Meaning and Construction*, 3rd edn (Belmont, CA: Wadsworth, 1991), p. 50.

146. Inciardi, p. 697.

147. *Congressional Quarterly* 52, 11 (March 19, 1994), p. 672; *Congressional Quarterly* 52, 34 (August 27, 1994), p. 2490.

148. Inciardi, p. 697.

149. *Kent v. United States*, 383 U.S. 541 (1966), at 556.

150. *Rummel v. Estelle*, 445 U.S. 263 (1980).

151. *Brewer v. Williams*, 430 U.S. 387 (1977).

152. Unless otherwise noted, all facts pertaining to the case are taken from the Supreme Court's written opinions.

153. *Rummel v. Estelle*, 445 U.S. 263 (1980), at 267.

154. *Weems v. United States*, 217 U.S. 349 (1910).

155. See *Furman v. Georgia*, 408 U.S. 238 (1972); *Gregg v. Georgia*, 428 U.S. 153 (1976); and *Coker v. Georgia*, 433 U.S. 584 (1977).

156. *Coker v. Georgia*, 433 U.S. 584 (1977).

157. *Rummel v. Estelle*, 455 U.S. 263 (1980), at 288.

158. Ibid., at 294.

159. *Solem v. Helm*, 463 U.S. 277 (1983).

160. Ibid., at 292.

161. *Lockyer v. Andrade*, 538 U.S. 63 (2003).

162. *Brewer v. Williams*, 430 U.S. 387 (1997), at 391.

163. Ibid., at 399.

164. *Brewer v. Williams*, 430 U.S. 387 (1977), at 408 (Marshall, J., concurring).

165. Ibid.

166. Ibid.

167. *Olmstead v. United States*, 277 U.S. 438 (1928), at 485.

168. *Nix v. Williams*, 467 U.S. 431 (1984).

169. *Solem v. Helm*, 463 U.S. 277 (1983), footnote 25, at 297.

Administrative Law

The twentieth century saw a tremendous growth in the number and power of bureaucratic organizations in the United States. Despite the attempts of the administrations of Ronald Reagan and George H.W. Bush to deregulate the U.S. economy and to shift governmental power from the national government to the states, bureaucracies continue to flourish, seemingly immune from the forces that would weaken them. Indeed, President George W. Bush increased the number of executive departments with the creation of the Department of Homeland Security in late 2002. For better or for worse, bureaucratic government is a political and legal fact of life. The growth of administrative government may be attributed primarily to two of its strongest features: expertise and efficiency.

As the U.S. economy became more complex, there developed a greater need for expertise in the management of our economic system. The victims of the abuse of unchecked economic power by the railroads and other monopolies turned to government for relief. The first federal regulatory agency, the Interstate Commerce Commission (ICC), was created by Congress in 1887 to regulate railroads and to protect farmers from unjust rates and other unfair practices. Similarly, when the labor movement became politically strong enough, workers demanded some form of government protection for the rights of workers. As a result, the National Labor Relations Board (NLRB) was created to regulate labor relations and to prevent such practices as blacklisting, lockouts, and union busting. The Great Depression taught us how damaging the consequences of an unregulated economy can be. The realization developed that government must guarantee the existence of the free enterprise system by regulating banks and the stock market to prevent the recurrence of conditions that led to the Depression. In our own time, the home mortgage and banking crises led to increased demand for closer supervision of large financial institutions allegedly "too big to fail." Indeed, the financial crisis of 2008–2009 may be attributed to too little regulation instead of too much regulation. In each of these areas of economic activity—monopolies, labor relations, banking, and stocks—the issues became so complex that experts were needed to regulate them effectively. These activities, as well as many others, require public administrators with sufficient expertise to handle the myriad problems associated with each. Thus, Congress responded to the demands for more government regulation by establishing agencies staffed by experts who were better qualified than Congress itself to deal with the problems of a modern industrial society. Administrative expertise soon became the justification for leaving major policy decisions to those most familiar with the problems—the administrators themselves.

The need for administrative expertise was paramount due to another aspect of our society. Professor Lief Carter has noted that "We live surrounded by very dangerous things—elevators, cars, airplanes, industrial wastes and chemical products, and recombinant DNA."[1] As technology provided us with new products and inventions, it also provided new ways to injure and kill people. People understandably want guarantees that airplanes, elevators, and even cell phones are safe to use. The private sector, concerned more with profits than with safety, could not be trusted to take the necessary steps to ensure safety. Hence, people again turned to government to guarantee the safety of dangerous products through regulation. Similarly, people wanted guarantees that their food was pure, their prescription drugs effective, their workplaces safe, and their environment clean. Once again government responded to these demands by calling on public administrators who possessed the expertise to handle the problems of our modern society. In short, then, abuses and changes in our economy and technology led to increased demands for government action that, in turn, resulted in the growth of administrative government based on expertise.

A second feature of administrative government that has contributed to its growth is its efficiency. In a sense, efficiency is related to expertise because expertise increases a government agency's efficiency. However, efficiency has another dimension. Because of the growth of the welfare system in the United States, the government receives hundreds of thousands of applications for Social Security benefits, veterans' benefits, Temporary Assistance to Needy Families benefits, and workers' compensation claims each day. In addition, the government issues licenses, ranging from liquor licenses at the state level to licenses for nuclear power reactors at the national level. Each year, thousands of students apply for student loans through state and private colleges and universities. Without highly trained personnel to process these claims and applications, the system would quickly break down. Thus, a bureaucracy must be created to handle the large numbers of applications as expertly and efficiently as possible.

What do the need for expertise and efficiency have to do with administrative law? One often hears of Mussolini's Italy that "at least the trains ran on time." This comment is normally used to illustrate a political system that has sacrificed other values such as freedom, justice, and human dignity for efficiency. While administrative expertise and efficiency are important, we must be careful that they do not outweigh other cherished values such as justice and fundamental fairness. Anglo-American law tends to view justice and fairness in terms of what is called "due process of law." Our Constitution guarantees that "no person shall be denied life, liberty, or property without due process of law."[2] But problems arise, as they often do, with constitutional guarantees. What is a property right? Does a person have a "right" to public employment? Temporary welfare assistance? Housing assistance? Student loans? How much "process" is "due"? How many rights is a person entitled to? What kind of hearing is required before assistance benefits can be denied or terminated? These and other issues are questions of administrative law.

Administrative law concerns itself with the prevention of arbitrary and capricious action at the hands of public administrators. It is concerned with the abuse of official power and the overstepping of official authority. It is also concerned with the rights of citizens in a modern welfare state. In the constitutional language of checks and balances, administrative law deals with how the political system checks the exercise of discretion by public administrators and balances the rights of citizens with the rights of government. Without an understanding of this fundamental aspect of administrative law, we may find ourselves in a bureaucratic state in which the trains run on time, but in which there is little emphasis on human dignity or fundamental fairness.

In this chapter we will examine several facets of administrative law. Specifically, we will examine the legal source of administrative law, some procedural aspects of administrative law, and the role of judicial review. We begin with the legal source of administrative authority.

DELEGATION THEORY

As previously noted, bureaucratic growth has occurred because of the need for expertise and efficiency in handling the problems posed by an increasingly complex economic system, new technology, and the advent of the modern welfare state. Throughout most of American history, the federal bureaucracy was small for a very simple reason: The federal government did not do very much. The New Deal period, as we have seen, sparked increased demands for positive government action in the management of the economy. This resulted in public pressure to create agencies for the regulation of everything from nuclear energy to the safety of the workplace. In so doing, Congress has created what is often termed the "fourth branch of government." The influence of bureaucratic government has become so pervasive that virtually no aspect of the average American's life is unaffected. In order to understand the role of the bureaucracy in our political system, we must first have an understanding of what is known as *delegation* theory.

Under the American Constitution, all sovereignty ultimately resides in the people. In drafting and ratifying the Constitution, the people of the United States have collectively vested their sovereignty in the hands of their government. In so doing, however, the American people have created three distinct branches of the national government—legislative, executive, and judicial—allocating to each certain powers, presumably to be exclusively exercised by each. As we learned in Chapter 6, this doctrine is known as separation of powers.

It was the decision of the people to vest Congress with the lawmaking power. The people, through the Constitution, delegated to Congress the power to make the laws of the nation on their behalf. Congress thus became the agent of the people, exercising only the powers that the people thought proper to give it. At common law there is a maxim, *Delegatus non potest delegare* ("a delegate cannot delegate"). What this means in terms of constitutional law is that Congress may not re-delegate the powers that have been delegated to it by the people. There are some very good reasons for adhering to this doctrine. Suppose that Congress wished to relieve itself of the burden of deciding when a state of war exists between the United States and another nation. Could Congress enact legislation authorizing the president to declare war? Certainly not, because such an act would be a clear violation of the Constitution. If the people had wanted the president to be the one to decide whether to go to war, they would have given the president that power in the Constitution. Instead, the people chose to let Congress make the decisions concerning war and peace. To allow such a law to stand would undermine the doctrine of separation of powers since, theoretically, Congress could transfer all its power to the president, thus achieving a result that the people sought to avoid: the concentration of governmental power in the hands of a single individual.

Despite the theory that Congress may not re-delegate powers delegated to it under the Constitution, the reality of the situation is that Congress is simply incapable of making the countless governmental decisions that must be made on a daily basis. Consequently, Congress has developed the practice of authorizing administrative agencies and executive officials to act on its behalf. Such authorization consists of allowing administrative agencies to "fill in the details" of a general law. Congress will enact legislation setting forth its policy goals in very broad language and allow an administrative agency to deal with specifics. For example, Congress has authorized the Federal Communications Commission (FCC) to regulate the broadcasting industry "in the public interest." The FCC, staffed by professionals familiar with the workings of the broadcasting industry, makes rules governing the licensing of stations as well as numerous other aspects of the industry. Acting as the agent of Congress, the FCC makes rules and regulations that are just as binding on broadcasters as if Congress itself had enacted them. Realistically, then, Congress must either delegate its lawmaking authority to administrative agencies or abandon altogether any attempt to regulate highly complex and technical industries.

If delegation is a political reality, how does our legal system get around the constitutional prohibition against delegation? It does so by simply maintaining the legal fiction that delegation does not occur. In modern constitutional law, the myth of non-delegation is circumvented by the assertion that the Constitution forbids only "excessive delegation." The Supreme Court has ruled that although some delegation is desirable and permissible under the Constitution, there is a line that may not be crossed in delegating power to administrative agencies. Once the line is crossed, delegation is termed "excessive," in violation of the constitutional doctrine of separation of powers. Unfortunately, the line to be crossed is not always a bright one, and Congress can never be sure when it has crossed it.

The Supreme Court, in determining issues of excessive delegation, decides when the line has been crossed on a case-by-case basis. In the 1930s, for example, the Supreme Court ruled in a series of cases[3] that Congress had crossed the line in delegating excessive legislative authority to either the president or his subordinates. In still other cases, the Court has upheld very broad delegations of legislative power to the very same individuals. In the final analysis, the Court's approach to excessive delegation is similar to that of Justice Potter Stewart's view of obscenity; that is, the Court "knows it [excessive delegation] when it sees it."

In the performance of its duties as an agent of Congress, an administrative agency is primarily bound by two legal authorities. First, administrative agencies are subject to the same constitutional restraints as the general government; that is, anything Congress or the president is forbidden to do, an administrative agency is also forbidden to do. Just as Congress may not force people to attend church, neither may a human services agency require church attendance as a condition for receiving public assistance. Similarly, if the national government is forbidden to deny any person "life, liberty, or property without due process of law," neither may a government agency deny due process. As we will learn later, much controversy in administrative law centers around how much process is due.

A second constraint on administrative agencies is their authorization statute, the law that creates and empowers an administrative agency. Although some state administrative agencies are provided for in their state's constitution, federal administrative agencies are the creations of Congress. It is Congress that determines the structure, personnel, and powers of all administrative agencies and executive departments of the federal government. Consequently, an administrative agency may exercise only those powers given to it by Congress. When an agency attempts to exercise powers beyond its statutory authorization, it is said to be acting *ultra vires.* If an agency is allegedly acting *ultra vires,* those wishing to challenge the agency's action may seek judicial review. The court will be asked to decide whether the agency is acting within the limits of its legislative authority. The legislative authority is often vague, resulting in a judicial interpretation that attempts to ascertain the "intent of Congress." Should a court wrongly interpret the intent of Congress, the lawmakers can simply amend the authorization statute in such a way as to clarify their intentions. In addition, despite their dubious constitutionality, Congress has relied on legislative vetoes to ensure administrative adherence to its will. Ultimately, then, Congress possesses the authority to curb *ultra vires* actions of administrative agencies and incorrect judicial interpretations of congressional intent.

Delegation of power to administrative agencies takes three forms. First, as we have already noted, Congress may authorize an agency to promulgate rules and regulations on behalf of Congress by filling in the details of legislation. This is called *rulemaking.* Second, Congress may authorize the employees of the agency to enforce the rules made by the agency. For example, Federal Aviation Administration (FAA) inspectors may make periodic safety checks to ensure that FAA safety regulations are being obeyed by the airlines. This is referred to as *rule enforcement*. Finally, disputes over the promulgation or enforcement of the agency's rules may necessitate *adjudication*. Adjudication may occur, for example, if an airline believes that it has been wrongly fined for violating FAA regulations. Each of the three types of delegation brings into play questions of administrative law. Therefore, let us examine each type separately to see just how each shapes administrative law.

Rulemaking

First, modern administrative law accepts the practice of allowing Congress to delegate its rulemaking authority in general and sweeping terms. The first regulatory agency, the Interstate Commerce Commission (ICC), was authorized to require "reasonable and just rates" for railroads and in 1906 was granted the power to actually set "reasonable and just" rates.[4] Similarly, other agencies are allowed broad delegations of authority. The FCC is charged with reviewing its regulations and "shall repeal or modify any regulation it determines to be no longer necessary in the public interest."[5] The Occupational Safety and Health Administration (OSHA) may protect workers "by providing for the development and promulgation of occupational safety and health standards."[6] Finally, the Consumer Product Safety Commission (CPSC) may make rules "to protect the public against unreasonable risks of injury associated with consumer products."[7] Literally thousands of rules are promulgated each year by myriad administrative agencies. In fact, the number of rules passed by administrative agencies each year far surpasses the number of laws enacted by Congress. As already noted, the rules thus promulgated are just as binding on citizens as if they had been passed by Congress itself.

Administrative law develops in the realm of rulemaking in primarily two ways. First, reviewing courts must ascertain whether the agency has the authority to promulgate the rule in question. That is, was the agency acting *ultra vires* by promulgating a rule that it had no authority to issue? Recall our discussion of *Bob Jones University v. United States*[8] in Chapter 1. Bob Jones University argued that the IRS had no authority to promulgate Revenue Ruling 71-477 without specific authorization from Congress. Although the Supreme Court ruled that 71-477 was valid, *Bob Jones University* illustrates how the authority to issue a rule can be the basis for challenging that rule.

The second way in which administrative law develops in regard to rulemaking centers around the procedures used to promulgate the rule. The question here is: Did the agency follow the statute's procedures for enacting administrative rules? In general, the rules of administrative procedure require (1) that proposed rules be published in advance of their consideration, (2) that interested and affected parties be allowed to comment either orally or in writing on the proposed rule, and (3) that any decision on the rule be based on the findings of the "whole record." These procedural requirements seek to prevent agencies from arbitrarily passing rules without giving opponents of the rules a fair opportunity to be heard. There is a certain "process" that is "due," and it is for the courts to determine whether the procedural rules were followed. It is important not only that the rules themselves be fair but also that the rules be enacted in a fair manner.

In order to facilitate what is known as informal rulemaking, Congress passed the Negotiated Rulemaking Act of 1990.[9] The purpose of the Act is to encourage the promulgation of new rules through negotiation and consensus rather than in an adversarial setting. The act allows the head of an agency to create a negotiated rulemaking committee composed of agency employees and representatives of interested parties. This committee:

> shall consider the matter proposed by the agency for consideration and shall attempt to reach a consensus concerning a proposed rule with respect to such matter and any other matter the committee determines is relevant to the proposed rule.[10]

For example, if an agency proposes a new rule for automobile safety, the negotiated rulemaking committee might be composed of industry representatives, labor union representatives, and consumer group representatives in addition to agency employees. Congress reasoned that if the interested parties could arrive at a consensus on a proposed rule, the persons or industries affected would be less likely to challenge the new rule in court.[11] However, negotiated rulemaking is not without its critics. One author has noted that it blurs the line between the public and private sectors, concluding, "Thus, it creates a context of confusion of status of the respective participants and represented interests at stake, which offers a breeding ground to regulatory capture."[12]

Rule Enforcement

A second way in which administrative agencies exercise authority delegated by Congress is through rule enforcement. Once an administrative agency has promulgated rules that deal with the substantive area within the agency's jurisdiction (e.g., aviation, food and drugs, or broadcasting), the agency may promulgate rules for the enforcement of its substantive rules. For example, OSHA has established regulations designed to ensure the safety of the workplace. OSHA has also established rules of procedures governing the inspection of factories and other workplaces to ensure compliance with its regulations. Failure to comply with OSHA regulations can result in civil penalties for the company involved. Thus, the agency responsible for issuing the original regulations is also responsible for the enforcement of those regulations. The procedures used in the enforcement of agency regulations are concerns of administrative law. As we have noted in relation to rulemaking, procedures employed in rule enforcement must be within the agency's power to enact; otherwise the agency is proceeding *ultra vires*. In addition, the agency's procedures may not violate the Constitution.

Administrative enforcement may take a variety of forms.[13] Some regulatory agencies require their regulatees to keep records for inspection. The FAA, for example, requires airlines to keep maintenance records of their airplanes. The Equal Employment Opportunity Commission (EEOC) requires certain industries to keep employment records for the enforcement of job discrimination laws. Finally, the IRS requires individuals to keep records of income and deductions. Physical inspections constitute another type of administrative enforcement. As previously noted, OSHA inspectors may conduct physical inspections for safety violations, and the Mine Safety and Health Administration (MSHA) inspects mines to ensure safety. At the local level, public health officials may inspect dwellings for potential health hazards, fire inspectors may inspect for fire hazards, and human services workers may investigate the home environment of alleged victims of child abuse. Finally, even such individuals as airline passengers are required to submit to X-ray and metal detector searches.

Rule enforcement by administrative agencies tends to raise the same kinds of constitutional questions common to other fields of law enforcement. In terms of mandatory record keeping, the question of self-incrimination can be raised. That is, does a law that requires a person or company to keep certain records allow them to be used as evidence in an administrative procedure? Suppose, for example, that an airline's maintenance record revealed that the airline was in violation of FAA regulations. Can the maintenance records be used to assess a fine against the airline? Suppose the IRS required persons engaged in illegal gambling to report the earnings from their illegal occupation. Would such persons, by paying the tax, be incriminating themselves by admitting their participation in an illegal activity?

REGULATION AND CORPORATE RESPONSIBILITY

In April 2010, 29 coal-miners were killed in an explosion in a West Virginia coal-mine 30 miles southeast of Charleston in the worst such disaster since 1970. Just the year before, federal regulators had stopped work in a section of the mine owned by Massey Energy for failure to follow safety precautions related to the buildup of methane gas. After the event, President Barack Obama was quoted as saying, "it's clear that more needs to be done" to insure mine safety. In the same month, a drilling rig in the Gulf of Mexico owned by British Petroleum (BP) exploded, killing 11 workers and pouring millions of barrels of crude oil into the Gulf. Fines as a means of regulation appear to be ineffective; a *Newsweek* report states that fines of less than 1 percent of corporate revenue have little effect on corporate behavior.[14] The West Virginia disaster and the oil spill in the Gulf of Mexico by BP are reminders that calls for tougher regulations and larger fines often come after disaster has already struck.[15]

The Supreme Court has ruled that administrative agencies may require record keeping under certain conditions. First, the records must be "of a kind customarily kept." Second, the records must be reasonably related to a public concern.

Third, the records must pertain to a noncriminal area of activity. Thus, in the case of the airlines, because maintenance records are routinely kept, air safety is a public concern, and the records pertain to a noncriminal activity, the airline's maintenance records may be used to uncover violations of FAA regulations.[16] In the case of the gambler however, the Supreme Court ruled in *Marchetti v. United States*[17] that the IRS requirement violates the Fifth Amendment's prohibition against mandatory self-incrimination. James "Totto" Marchetti was being forced to choose between reporting the gambling income, thereby subjecting himself to prosecution for state gambling violations, and not reporting the income, thereby subjecting himself to charges of federal income tax evasion. The Constitution, the Court ruled, forbids forcing a person to make such a draconian choice.

The Fourth Amendment's prohibition against unreasonable searches and seizures is another area of special relevance to administrative enforcement. In regular law enforcement, searches require a search warrant issued by a magistrate on probable cause. The search warrant must describe the places to be searched and the persons or things to be seized. Not all searches require search warrants, however. The Supreme Court has upheld numerous exceptions to the warrant requirement (warrantless searches) when it was shown that a particular search was not "unreasonable" within the meaning of the Fourth Amendment.

There are a number of problems associated with warrantless searches in administrative enforcement. First, it is almost impossible for an administrative agency to meet the probable-cause standard required for search warrants. When OSHA agents go out to check factories for safety violations, they almost never have probable cause to believe that a given factory is in violation of OSHA rules. Similarly, when fire marshals inspect neighborhoods for fire hazards, they have no way of knowing ahead of time which individual residences may constitute a fire hazard. Second, unlike other forms of law enforcement, administrative searches do not always have as their objective the detection of a "crime." OSHA agents and fire marshals are more concerned about correcting a dangerous situation than about punishing the offender. While it is true that civil and even criminal liabilities are possible, administrative enforcement of the type we are discussing is meant to be preventive and corrective rather than punitive. Finally, administrative enforcement often involves issues of public safety. Public health inspections of restaurants and airport inspections are two notable examples. Concern about terrorism has increased the need for inspection of individuals and baggage on airplanes. Because of the grave danger posed by terrorist activities, warrantless searches are deemed "reasonable" even if they do not meet the stricter probable-cause standard necessary for the issuance of a warrant.

The Supreme Court's solution to warrantless administrative searches has been to take a middle-ground approach. The Court recognizes that requiring administrative agencies to meet the probable-cause standard required in criminal cases would defeat the purposes of administrative enforcement. However, the Court has also been aware of the need to protect the privacy rights of businesspeople and individuals. Consequently, the Court's middle-ground approach is to uphold, at least initially, the individual's right to privacy; that is, when a person is first asked to submit his or her home or business to a warrantless search, permission may be denied. After a refusal however, administrative officials may seek a search warrant from a court without meeting the probable-cause standard. If the agency can show that a particular dwelling or business is being searched as part of an overall administrative plan to enforce the agency's regulations, then a search warrant may be issued without probable cause.[18] The practical effect of this approach is that the individual may merely delay a search until a warrant has been secured. In terms of airline security, these searches are considered to be consent searches; that is, a person consents to the search as a condition of boarding the airplane. The Court has ruled that concern over public health and safety outweighs the inconvenience or any absolute right of privacy of an individual.

A final area of Fourth Amendment rights that is somewhat controversial is in the area of protection against child abuse. The following, based on an actual case,[19] illustrates the complexity of protecting parental and child privacy while protecting children from abuse. A female agent of the Child Protective Services was sent to investigate the possibility of sexual abuse of a 6-year-old girl. The agent contacted the mother, explained the situation, and requested a home visit. Although the mother resisted the intrusion at first (even going so far as to ask the agent whether she needed to have her lawyer present), she relented and allowed the agent to photograph her daughter without her top on. When the examination revealed no evidence of harm, the daughter's remaining clothes were removed and additional pictures of her private areas were taken. As a result of the experience, the daughter experienced frequent nightmares and the mother experienced loss of sleep and depression. This example illustrates the troublesome question of whether the need to protect a child from allegations of abuse outweighs the privacy interests of both the parents and the child. In addition, the potential for administrative abuse, whether intentional, is certainly possible.

The problems with administrative enforcement point to a continuing concern of students of administrative government. As more agencies—state, local, and national—are created, there is an increasing number of "faceless bureaucrats" with authority over our lives and happiness. The delicate balance between the rights of individuals and the rights of society is a constant concern of courts responsible for curbing overzealous administrative enforcement.

Administrative Adjudication

The final type of delegation takes the form of what has been termed the "quasi-judicial" function of administrative agencies. In the normal course of an agency's duties, disputes will arise over the application of agency rules to a particular individual. For example, federal statutes and Department of Veterans' Affairs rules set forth the criteria for veterans' benefit eligibility. When an individual applies for veterans' benefits, Department personnel must make an initial determination of the person's eligibility based on statutes and the Department's guidelines. Suppose that the person is denied benefits and wishes to appeal the denial. The Department has a procedure specifying the steps to be followed in appealing a denial of benefits, and the aggrieved person will be required to follow the procedure. This constitutes an adjudicatory procedure. Or suppose that a person who has already been receiving veterans' benefits is informed that she is no longer eligible. If she appeals the loss of benefits, that too is an adjudicatory procedure. Similarly, a loss or denial of a license, loss of public employment, or even a denial of a passport can lead to an adjudicatory procedure.

As in other areas of administrative law, the main thrust of administrative adjudication is the prevention of arbitrary and capricious action at the hands of an administrative agency. Many people believe they have been the victim of an unfair and arbitrary decision made by someone in authority over them. Administrative law seeks to reduce the risk of arbitrary decisions by requiring administrative agencies to observe fair rules of procedure in settling disputes that arise under their jurisdiction. In recent years, administrative law has seen what has been termed a "due process explosion." With increasing frequency, individuals who once meekly accepted the adverse actions of administrative agencies are demanding and receiving hearings on their complaints. Administrators who were once able to make decisions without fear of being questioned now find that their decisions are, in poker parlance, being "called" more frequently. While some observers applaud this more aggressive assertion of rights, others fear that too much emphasis on adjudication will bog down administrative agencies, leaving them unable to perform their functions adequately.

Administrative adjudications run the gamut from a simple disciplinary action in school to egregious violations of safety rules and the awarding of billions of dollars in economic benefits. Formality in adjudication also spans a wide range. At the informal end there is the unilateral decision of a person in authority; the more formal process involves adjudication by an administrative law judge. In this section, we will focus on the more formal aspects of adjudication in order to ascertain how administrative law is brought to bear on this "quasi-judicial" function.

One of the leading cases in administrative adjudication is *Goldberg v. Kelly.*[20] John Kelly, a New York welfare recipient, was notified that his benefits were being terminated. Although several New York welfare administrators reviewed Kelly's eligibility before his benefits were actually terminated, Kelly was given no opportunity to present his side of the issue until *after* his benefits were terminated. At that point Kelly was entitled to a post-termination evidentiary hearing. If he prevailed at the post-termination hearing, his benefits would be restored and he would receive back payments. Pending the hearing however, Kelly's benefits were cut off, and he was practically destitute. Kelly argued that he should be granted a hearing before the termination of benefits, and the Supreme Court agreed. In the process of deciding the case, the Court outlined the "*Goldberg* ingredients" essential for due process of law.

Justice William Brennan, author of the *Goldberg* decision, outlined ten "ingredients" required to meet the minimum standard of due process of law in an administrative procedure.[21] The first *Goldberg* ingredient is (1) *adequate and timely notice.* A person subject to an agency action must be given notice of a change in status. For example, if an agency is preparing to terminate a benefit or suspend a license, the person affected (called the "person aggrieved") has a right to be informed in advance of the nature of the adverse action. Two related *Goldberg* ingredients are (2) the *right to confront adverse witnesses* and (3) the *right to cross-examine adverse witnesses*. Suppose that a liquor retailer has been notified that her license is being suspended for selling liquor to a minor. The retailer has a right to confront the witnesses against her and to cross-examine them concerning their testimony.

The next two *Goldberg* ingredients are also related. The person aggrieved has (4) the *right to present arguments orally* and (5) the *right to present evidence orally*. Under the U.S. legal system, persons aggrieved are not required to stand silently before their accusers. They have the right to present orally any relevant arguments or evidence in their favor. This ensures that those who are entitled to a "hearing" do indeed enjoy the right to be "heard."

(6) *Disclosure of opposing evidence* is the next *Goldberg* ingredient. In Chapter 4, a process called *discovery* was introduced. Discovery is the process whereby each party "discovers" the evidence on which the other party plans to rely in presenting a case. In an administrative procedure, the person aggrieved has the right to know what evidence the agency is using to make its decision. For example, a person faced with the loss of welfare benefits has the right to see the evidence on which the agency is basing its decision to terminate benefits. Perhaps the "evidence" was based on neighborhood gossip or innuendo. Disclosure of opposing evidence places the person aggrieved in a better position to present his or her case to the agency.

The next *Goldberg* ingredient is (7) the *right to retain an attorney*. Although administrative adjudications are not criminal in nature, the loss of a privilege or benefit can cause the person affected a great deal of emotional and financial hardship. Therefore, the person aggrieved has the right to have an attorney present to assist in the presentation of his or her case. This right, however, does not include the appointment of counsel for indigents as required in a criminal case.

The last three *Goldberg* ingredients are (8) the *right to an impartial decision maker*, (9) a *determination on the record*, and (10) an *explanation of the decision*. The requirement of an impartial decision maker may seem self-evident. However, public administrators, like other humans, may prejudge a case or have a conflict of interest. An administrator is guilty of prejudgment if her mind appears to be made up even before the evidence is presented.[22] Conflict of interest means that an administrator has a personal stake in the outcome of a case.[23] Determination on the record is designed to ensure that no extraneous or impermissible evidence is used to make the decision. In criminal cases, for example, lawyers are often concerned that pretrial publicity in a sensational case will influence prospective jurors. That is, lawyers do not want prospective jurors to be influenced by newspaper or television reports containing evidence that is inadmissible in court. The media may report hearsay evidence that is inadmissible at trial. Determination on the record seeks to ensure that only relevant, permissible evidence forms the basis for the decision.

Finally, the person aggrieved is entitled to a written explanation of the reasons for an adverse decision, the evidence on which the decision was based, and the reason that other evidence was not relied on by the decision maker. Basically, this ingredient serves to inform the person aggrieved why he or she lost. The written explanation can serve as the basis of further administrative appeal or even judicial review by an appellate court.

A cautionary note is in order here. The ten *Goldberg* ingredients represent an "ideal" model of administrative due process. A person aggrieved by an administrative agency may find all or none of the *Goldberg* ingredients in place. How is this possible? Professor Carter provides an answer, writing that "the bureaucratic world hardly marches in lockstep with the occasional pronouncements of the Supreme Court."[24] In other words, an administrative agency may continue on its merry way, adjudicating disputes as it has always done, totally oblivious to Supreme Court rulings. Even though *Goldberg v. Kelly* serves as a precedent for future cases, if an agency's procedures go unchallenged, the agency may never have to adopt the *Goldberg* ingredients for its own procedures. This situation serves to remind us that the law is an evolutionary process which sometimes proceeds at an excruciatingly slow pace.

JUDICIAL REVIEW AND ADMINISTRATIVE LAW

In Chapter 6, judicial review was defined as the power of a court to review the actions of other governmental bodies in order to determine whether those actions are consistent with the Constitution. The actions of administrative agencies are, of course, included among those subject to judicial review. However, judicial review of administrative agencies poses problems for courts that may not be present in other areas of the law. First, administrative agencies are highly specialized bodies with highly specialized personnel. Members of the Nuclear Regulatory Commission (NRC), for example, are experts in a highly technical field. It would be presumptuous for a judge to try to second guess the NRC's decisions about nuclear power. Similarly, most judges are not in a position to question the expert judgment of the FAA or the FCC. Second, as noted in the introduction to this chapter, some government agencies process hundreds of thousands of applications for all kinds of government benefits and programs. Excessive judicial meddling in the operations of an agency may paralyze it and undermine its efficiency. In *Goldberg v. Kelly*, for example, the Supreme Court ruled that Kelly must receive an evidentiary hearing prior to the termination of his benefits instead of after termination, as had previously been the welfare agency's practice. Although at first glance it may not seem to make any difference whether the hearing preceded or followed the termination of benefits, consider the possible consequences. If someone is receiving benefits to which he is not entitled, the benefits must continue to be paid until after a hearing is held. If every ineligible recipient chooses to exercise the right to a hearing, it may tax the ability of the welfare agency to conduct timely hearings, resulting in long delays. Meanwhile, recipients who may eventually prove to be ineligible for benefits continue to receive, at the taxpayers' expense, benefits to which they are not entitled. Consequently, the number of termination hearings increases for agency employees, and the government continues to pay benefits to ineligible recipients.

Despite the problems associated with judicial review of administrative agencies, supporters of judicial review in administrative law argue in favor of it. First, supporters argue that public administrators are just as susceptible to abuse of discretion as any other public official. Indeed, because most administrators are not elected, the potential for abuse of discretion may be even greater. The courts should serve as checks on public administrators to guard against arbitrary and capricious actions. Second, supporters of judicial review argue that an administrative agency is frequently "captured" by the agency's clientele group. Capture occurs when an agency begins to place the interests of the regulated industry above the public interest. Critics of the now defunct Civil Aeronautics Board (CAB) complained that air fares were set more to guarantee the airlines a profit than to keep the consumer's traveling costs down. In light of such charges, supporters of judicial review argue that judicial intervention may be necessary to protect the public interest. Finally, supporters of judicial review argue that bureaucrats tend to see problems from a narrow perspective, while judges tend to see the "big picture." In *Goldberg,* for example, Justice Brennan's opinion tended to stress the bigger picture of the role of public assistance in our society, whereas a welfare worker might see only that the decision will increase the number of termination hearings for the agency. In the rest of this section, we will examine some of the limits of judicial review in administrative law.

Preclusion of Judicial Review

There are some areas in which the courts are precluded from reviewing the decisions of administrative agencies. Congress, for whatever reasons, has chosen to take the review of some administrative decisions out of the jurisdiction of the courts. One such area is veterans' benefits, an "especially fertile ground for preclusion controversies."[25] Consider the preclusion language of this statute concerning veterans' benefits that was considered in *Wellman v. Whittier*:[26]

> The decisions of the Administrator of Veterans' Affairs on any question of law or fact concerning a claim of benefits or payments under any Act administered by the Veterans' Administration shall be final and conclusive and no other official or any court of the United States shall have power or jurisdiction to review any such decision.[27]

This section of the statute precludes judicial review of a *denial* of veterans' benefits. However, in *Wellman* and several other cases, appellate courts held that although courts were precluded from reviewing denials of claims, the statute did not preclude judicial review of the *termination* of claims. In other words, a person denied veterans' benefits could not seek judicial review, whereas a person already receiving benefits could appeal a decision to terminate benefits.

As a general rule, a determined Supreme Court can find a way to get around most preclusion language. The Court is able to do this because, as we discussed in Chapter 6, it is the final arbiter of the meaning of the Constitution. For example, Congress amended the above statute on veterans' benefits "[t]o make it perfectly clear that the Congress intends to exclude from judicial review all determinations with respect to noncontractual benefits provided for veterans and their dependents and survivors."[28]

In *Johnson v. Robison*[29] however, William Robert Robison was a conscientious objector who performed alternate service in lieu of his military obligation. Robison sought veterans' education benefits but was denied under a law passed by Congress. Robison challenged the denial of benefits on First Amendment and equal protection grounds, and the Supreme Court agreed to hear the case. As Robison was challenging the *statute* that denied benefits to all conscientious objectors and not the *decision* of the Veterans' Affairs administrator, the Court said that it was not precluded from exercising judicial review. The Court ultimately ruled against Robison's claim for benefits, but, at least, it agreed to hear the case on the merits. *Johnson* makes clear that no statutory language can preclude judicial review of an administrative decision when a constitutional right or issue is at stake.

The Supreme Court again addressed the issue of preclusion in *Traynor v. Turnage*[30] because of a split in federal appeals court decisions. Veterans were entitled to educational benefits only within ten years following their discharge unless the time was extended because of a "physical or mental disability which was not the result of [the veteran's] own willful misconduct." The Veterans' Administration (VA) defined alcoholism unrelated to an underlying psychiatric conduct as "willful misconduct" and refused to pay the benefits. Veterans contested the rule as violating another federal law, the Rehabilitation Act of 1973.[31] The Second Circuit found that such claims were precluded, but the D.C. Circuit held them to be subject to review.[32]

In *Traynor*, Justice Byron White began with the proposition that judicial review of administrative action is favored by Congress unless there is "clear and convincing evidence" otherwise. Here there was no such evidence that Congress intended to preclude a suit claiming that the Rehabilitation Act provisions negated the VA regulations about alcoholism, thus proving once again that courts can and do maneuver around preclusion language. In response to the continuing concern over benefits, Congress created the Court of Veterans' Appeals [now the United States Court of Appeals for Veterans' Claims] and provided for further appeals to the Federal Circuit if a constitutional issue is at stake. More recently, Congress has precluded appeals of certain types of deportation orders and prisoners' rights cases.

Judicial Restraint

Although courts can and do intervene in the administrative process, they are often reluctant to do so and tend to show great deference to administrative expertise when intervention is necessary. Courts have traditionally practiced judicial restraint when exercising the power of judicial review. Requirements of standing, ripeness, and mootness (as discussed in Chapter 5) are just a few of the methods used by courts to avoid the use of their judicial power. In addition to these traditional methods, courts have adopted several other procedural devices to prevent premature judicial intervention into the administrative process. The first of these is the *exhaustion of administrative remedies doctrine.* Courts prefer that formal litigation be looked on only as a last resort for settling disputes. Consequently, courts insist that a person avail himself or herself of all administrative remedies before seeking judicial ones. For example, a person who has had a license revoked must follow the agency's procedure for appealing the revocation before initiating a lawsuit against agency officials. Similarly, a student who has received an unsatisfactory grade must exhaust all university appeals before turning to a court for relief. Courts feel that the individual agency is better equipped to handle these disputes and that judicial intervention should be limited to those few cases that cannot be resolved at the agency level.

A doctrine related to exhaustion of remedies is the *primary jurisdiction doctrine.* Primary jurisdiction holds that litigants should take their disputes to the agency that has primary responsibility for the dispute rather than to a court of law. In *Texas Pacific Railway Co. v. Abilene Cotton Oil Co.,*[33] for example, the cotton oil company sued the railroad to recover $1951.83 in unreasonable overcharges. Even though the Interstate Commerce Act specifically permitted the company either to file a complaint with the ICC or to file a suit in a federal district court, the Supreme Court ruled that the ICC had primary jurisdiction and that the cotton oil company should have filed its complaint with the ICC first. The Court believed that uniformity and fairness could best be achieved by allowing the ICC to make the initial decisions about the reasonableness of rates.[34]

EXHAUSTION OF PATIENCE

The exhaustion of remedies doctrine can lead to an exhaustion of patience on the part of persons who believe administrative agencies are giving them the runaround. But with only a few exceptions, the courts have adhered to the exhaustion doctrine steadfastly. Curtis Dils alleged in his workmen's compensation claim that he had been wrongfully denied benefits by the state Department of Labor and Industries. In addition, the Department seemed to be deliberately delaying making a final ruling that, had it been made, would have permitted Dils to appeal to a state court for judicial review. Instead, Dils decided to forgo the agency's final decision and filed suit in a state superior court seeking declaratory relief. The superior court dismissed the case, and the Court of Appeals affirmed for lack of jurisdiction. Two avenues of which Dils did not avail himself were a request for the Board to reconsider his application and a *writ of mandamus* from a court ordering the Department to make a final decision on his claim. The Court of Appeals felt it had no choice but to affirm the superior court's dismissal of the case for failing to exhaust his administrative remedies.[35]

The difference between primary jurisdiction and exhaustion of administrative remedies is subtle but important. Primary jurisdiction requires a party with a dispute that falls within an agency's jurisdiction to go to the agency before taking the dispute to court. Exhaustion of administrative remedies states that a party already subject to the jurisdiction of a governmental agency must give the agency an opportunity to resolve the dispute before taking it to court.

One final way that courts practice judicial restraint is by observing the *substantial evidence rule.* This rule states that conclusions of fact, if supported by substantial evidence based on the whole record, are to be regarded as final. In other words, an agency's finding of fact is considered final if there is substantial evidence to support it. In *Consolidated Edison v. National Labor Relations Board,*[36] the Supreme Court stated that substantial evidence "means such relevant evidence as a reasonable mind might accept as adequate to support a conclusion."[37] In other words, if there is any plausible evidence to support an agency's conclusion of fact, the court has a duty to defer to the judgment of the agency.

Judicial review of the actions of administrative agencies is still relatively new compared with other areas of the law. It should be recalled that the modern administrative state is a fairly recent development in the United States, so it is not surprising that many areas of administrative law are as yet undeveloped.

CONCLUSION

Administrative law is one of the most fascinating and fastest growing areas of American law. As government gets bigger, the chances for government intrusion in our daily lives increase. If we are to remain "a nation of laws, not men," then we must keep vigilant watch over the rapidly growing government bureaucracy. Administrative law is the law that governs the people in government. We must not let those in government lose sight of the fact that they are the servants of the people, not their masters. Administrative law is one method we use to accomplish this goal.

NOTES

1. Lief H. Carter and Christine Harrington, *Administrative Law and Politics: Cases and Comments*, 3rd edn (New York: Longman, 2000), p. 10.
2. U.S. Constitution, Amendments V and XIV.
3. See *Schechter Poultry Co. v. United States*, 295 U.S. 495 (1935); *Carter v. Carter Coal Co.*, 298 U.S. 238 (1936); and *Panama Refining Co. v. Ryan*, 293 U.S. 388 (1935).
4. Carter and Harrington, p. 8.
5. 47 U.S.C. § 161(b).
6. 29 U.S.C. § 651(b)(9).
7. 15 U.S.C. § 2051(b)(1).
8. *Bob Jones University v. United States*, 461 U.S. 574 (1983).
9. 5 U.S.C. §§ 561 *et seq.*
10. 5 U.S.C. § 566(A).
11. Pub. L. 101-648 § 2(5).

12. Dominique Custos, "The Rulemaking Power of Independent Regulatory Agencies," 54 Am. J. Comp. L. 615 (2006), at p. 638.
13. See Florence Heffron and Neil McFeeley, *The Administrative Regulatory Process* (New York: Longman, 1983), pp. 173–197.
14. "Do Fines Ever Make Corporations Change?," *Newsweek* 156, 11 (September 13, 2010), p. 56.
15. Iba Urbina, "No Survivors Found After West Virginia Mine Disaster," *New York Times*, April 9, 2010.
16. In *Oklahoma Press Publishing Co. v. Walling*, 327 U.S. 186 (1946), the Supreme Court ruled that Fifth Amendment rights do not apply to corporations.
17. *Marchetti v. United States*, 390 U.S. 39 (1968).
18. See *Marshall v. Barlow's Inc.*, 436 U.S. 307 (1978).
19. *Roe v. Texas Department of Protective and Regulatory Services*, 299 F.3d 395 (2002).
20. *Goldberg v. Kelly*, 397 U.S. 254 (1970).
21. For a concise list of the *Goldberg* ingredients, see Carter and Harrington, p. 201.
22. See *Cinderella Career and Finishing School, Inc. v. Federal Trade Commission*, 425 F.2d 583 (D.C. Cir. 1970).
23. See *Gibson v. Berryhill*, 411 U.S. 564 (1973).
24. Carter and Harrington, p. 200.
25. Peter L. Strauss, Todd Rakoff, Roy A. Schotland, and Cynthia R. Farina, *Gellhorn and Byse's Administrative Law: Cases and Comments*, 9th edn (Mineola, NY: Foundation Press, 1995), p. 1205.
26. *Wellman v. Whittier*, 259 F.2d 163 (D.C. Cir. 1958).
27. 38 U.S.C. § 11a-2.
28. Strauss et al., p. 1206.
29. *Johnson v. Robison*, 415 U.S. 361 (1974).
30. *Traynor v. Turnage*, 485 U.S. 535 (1988).
31. 29 U.S.C. § 794.
32. Strauss et al., pp. 1207–1208.
33. *Texas Pacific Railway Co. v. Abilene Cotton Oil Co.*, 204 U.S. 426 (1907).
34. *Dils v. Department of Labor and Industries of the State of Washington*, 752 P.2d 1357 (Wash. App., 1988).
35. Heffron and McFeeley, pp. 308–309.
36. *Consolidated Edison v. National Labor Relations Board*, 305 U.S. 197 (1938).
37. Ibid., at 229.

Environmental Law

Environmental law is a fascinating and fast-growing field of law. It is fascinating because it encompasses so many other areas of law covered in this book. Environmental law deals with property rights and torts as society debates the acceptable uses of the earth's resources. It raises questions of constitutional law under due process and other clauses of both state and federal constitutions. As governmental agencies, most notably the Environmental Protection Agency (EPA), are highly involved in the protection of the environment, it involves administrative law. Even the criminal law may be invoked against persons who deliberately harm the environment.

Environmental law is also a fast-growing field of law. One such area centers on the growing concern about global warming. As a result, Congress and the states have enacted laws requiring among other things "environmental impact statements" that assess the potential effects of new projects on the environment. As these new laws are implemented and because the protection of the environment is not without controversy, litigation is inevitable. Another factor contributing to the growth of environmental law is the fact that, unlike other areas of law, it is not dominated by the legal profession. New advances in science and technology put pressure on the law to keep up with rapid changes in our knowledge of the environment. At the same time, the limitations of science to provide precise answers to the problems of global warming present a serious challenge to those who wish to use the law to protect our environment.

A common misconception is that environmental law is a new area of the law. One author, for example, divides the history of environmental protection in the United States into three periods: Premodern (1840–1891), Conservationist (1891–1969), and Modern (1969 to the present).[1] While it is true that courses in environmental law are relatively new to law school curricula, the idea of using the law to protect the environment dates back at least to the thirteenth century.[2]

For centuries the common law has recognized that a person is not entitled to the unfettered use of his or her land and that society may impose limits on the use of one's property.

Because environmental law touches so many other areas of law, is fast growing, and is a relatively new field of law, it is somewhat difficult to define. For our purposes, *environmental law* may be defined as "a technique of environmental engineering designed to control human and nonhuman objects, in order to preserve a stable environmental system."[3] In this chapter, we will examine three aspects of environmental law. First, we will look at the history of environmental law jurisprudence; that is, we will examine the theories behind laws that protect the environment. Next, we will provide a brief overview of major environmental legislation in the United States, especially those of the Modern period. Finally, we will delve into some major issues, such as the issue of standing, of environmental law.

ENVIRONMENTAL LAW JURISPRUDENCE

Black's Law Dictionary defines jurisprudence as "The philosophy of law, or the science which treats of the principles of positive law and legal relations."[4] In this definition, we confront two aspects of law needed to understand environmental law jurisprudence. The first is the principle of positive law and the second are "legal relations." Relative to environmental law, positive law concerns the authority of the lawmaker to make laws that protect the environment while restricting the use of an individual's or corporation's private property. In addition, as law is about legal relations, a theory of environmental law jurisprudence must address how relationships among members of society are affected by the regulation of property rights.

A theory of environmental law based on positive law might assert that the protection of the environment is within the power of government simply because it is the right thing to do or because it reflects the will of the majority. Still, law does not exist in a vacuum, and environmental law must also take into account human relations and constitutional, political, and historical limitations. In this section, we will examine the foundation of environmental law jurisprudence from a historical and constitutional frame of reference. We begin by looking at the history of environmental law under our common law heritage.

Common Law and the Environment

As noted in this chapter's introductory section, environmental law has been recognized in legal theory since the thirteenth century. Environmental law has its roots at common law in the law of *nuisance*. Nuisance itself is a form of tort or a legal injury one person inflicts on another's property interest. In general, the law of nuisance holds that a person is not permitted to use his or her property in a way that interferes with another's. For example, at common law a person who created air pollution, such as a foul-smelling odor, could be held liable if it interfered with his or her neighbors' enjoyment of their own land. Again at common law, nuisance could be intentional, negligent, or reckless. An intentional nuisance occurs when a person takes an action with full knowledge that it will harm the interests of a neighbor. For example, a person who continues to spray chemicals after being notified that they are blowing onto another's land is guilty of an intentional nuisance.[5] Negligent nuisance is caused by a defendant's action or inaction that harmed the plaintiff inadvertently. For example, a defendant's failure to mend a fence, resulting in animals entering a neighbor's property and causing damage, might be unintentional. Finally, reckless nuisance is caused by the reckless use of property that endangers one's neighbors. Storing dynamite on one's property in an unsafe manner would be an example.[6]

It is important to remember that at common law, nuisance was tied directly to the use of the land and was applicable to persons directly affected by the annoying behavior. Over time however, the common law began to distinguish between private nuisance and public nuisance. As noted, a *private nuisance* is created when a person's behavior affects only his or her immediate neighbors. *Public nuisance* is much broader and may be defined as "an act or omission 'which obstructs or causes inconveniences or damage to the public in exercise of rights common to all Her Majesty's subjects.'"[7] Examples of public nuisances are those things that threaten public health or safety or offend public morals. Thus, the keeping of diseased animals, keeping a bawdy house, or storing explosives would qualify as public nuisances.[8]

The development of the distinction between public and private nuisance was followed by changes in remedies. Like other tort actions at common law, nuisance was a civil action that resulted in money damages awarded to the plaintiff if he or she prevailed. However, because a public nuisance was viewed more as a violation of the "peace of the realm" rather than as a private tort, the wrongful behavior was seen as criminal.

Several interesting issues arise from treating environmental pollution as a public rather than a private nuisance. In one sense, it may be to the defendant's benefit to have the pollution treated as a criminal act rather than as a civil action. For example, it saves the defendant from the possibility of multiple lawsuits. If dozens of neighbors' lands are harmed by the defendant's pollution of a single stream, dozens of lawsuits may be filed. However, by treating the single act of pollution as a public nuisance, judicial time and energy, as well as the defendant's pocketbook, may be spared. Another advantage to the defendant is that labeling an action criminal makes the defendant subject only to the penalties allowed by law. In a civil action, damages paid to multiple plaintiffs, especially punitive damages, may result in large monetary judgments against the defendant. In addition, criminal law requires a standard of proof—beyond a reasonable doubt—that is more stringent than the preponderance of the evidence standard of a civil proceeding. Finally, although the offending polluter is labeled a criminal, the penalty assigned to the act is usually limited to a fine, thus not subjecting the polluting defendant to jail time. As noted in Chapter 1 however, the possibility of a criminal action does not make the defendant immune from a civil action, it merely makes such an action less likely.

Treating environmental pollution as a criminal act also has advantages for the general public. The damage to an individual landowner may be insufficient to justify a single lawsuit. In such circumstances, the pollution may continue unabated. If, however, the pollution is treated as a public nuisance, criminal charges may be filed that, in turn, will put a stop to the pollution much sooner. Finally, treating pollution as a public nuisance allows the power of the state to be invoked against the polluter with greater efficiency than is common in civil lawsuits. Given the delay in civil cases, a private nuisance lawsuit may drag on for years while criminal cases are settled more expeditiously.

As we have seen, the protection of the environment from those who would pollute it has deep roots in common law. Although the United States inherited the common law tradition from Great Britain, the American Constitution has replaced the common law as the supreme law of the land. In the next section, we will examine the effects of the Constitution on environmental law.

Constitutional Law and the Environment

As noted earlier, the ratification of the Constitution made that document the supreme law of the land. The transition from reliance solely on common law to a constitution did not change significantly the common law rulings previously in effect. Thus, the common law rulings affecting private nuisance remained virtually untouched after 1789. However, this is not to say that the Constitution did not affect either the common law or the environmental law. The Constitution created a national government with limited powers, whereas the British monarchy, at least theoretically, was an absolute monarchy. Under the latter, there were few, if any, limits on the exercise of sovereignty. A criminal act, including a public nuisance, was prohibited because it was a violation of the "peace of the realm." Therefore, as we have seen, the pollution of one's own land or the use of one's own land in an offensive manner could be labeled a violation of the "peace of the realm." Later, when Parliament became supreme, the idea remained that there were no limits on the power of government to criminalize or punish environmentally destructive behavior.

The concept of limited powers as embodied in the American Constitution is very different from the British model. While acts of the British Parliament are supreme, the powers of the U.S. government under the Constitution are limited to its delegated powers. Congress may exercise only those powers delegated to it by the Constitution or that may logically be implied from its delegated powers.[9] Therefore, to regulate the use or abuse of the environment there has to be a basis in the Constitution for the exercise of such power. In other words, under the concept of limited government, Congress is not authorized to exercise a power simply because it is wanted or needed by the people. Without constitutional authority, Congress is powerless to act.

Fortunately, it is not difficult to find constitutional authority to regulate the environment. Political scientist Stuart S. Nagel has suggested several constitutional provisions that support environmental protection.[10] For example, Congress is empowered to regulate interstate and foreign commerce. As air pollution seldom respects state lines, it is safe to assume that it moves in interstate commerce. It may also be argued that polluted air harms and even interferes with the free flow of goods in interstate commerce.[11] Nagel argues, for example, that interstate air pollution causes workers to suffer health problems, thereby reducing their productivity.[12] Nagel also suggests that the Taxing and Spending Clause[13] provides constitutional authority for the regulation of the environment. Congress is authorized to tax and spend to promote the general welfare. Laws, such as federal grants to states that reduce their air pollution, may be said to promote the general welfare of all Americans.[14] Finally, even the treaty-making power of the national government may serve as a basis for environmental protection. In the classic case *Missouri v. Holland*,[15] the Supreme Court upheld a federal law made pursuant to a treaty with Great Britain designed to protect migratory birds.

Although the Constitution provides ample positive authority for the passage of laws to protect the environment, it also limits the use of governmental power to control polluters. Three areas of constitutional law will be used to illustrate the limits of constitutional government. The first area that limits governmental power to control polluters is the so-called *Takings Clause*. The Fifth Amendment reads in part, "nor shall private property be taken for public use without just compensation."[16] Opponents of environmental regulation have argued that any denial of the full use of one's property is a "taking" within the meaning of the Fifth Amendment. It follows that if a person's property rights are taken away, he or she must be compensated by the government for the loss. Obviously, if the government has to compensate polluters for their actions, it will be less willing to regulate protection of the environment. Although more will be said about the issue of takings later in this chapter, for constitutional purposes a taking does not occur unless the government actually takes possession of the property and uses it for public purposes.

A second area of constitutional limitation is the provisions of the Bill of Rights that deal with the rights of the accused. When private nuisances were transformed into public nuisances, they essentially became crimes. When they became crimes, the landowner became entitled to all the constitutional safeguards afforded to the accused. For example, the provisions dealing with self-incrimination, double jeopardy, and protections against unreasonable searches and seizures all come into play. In other words, the criminalization of pollution can complicate the process enormously.

A simple case will illustrate the problem. Suppose that a city, to prevent electrical fires, requires that all homes be inspected annually for faulty wiring. Suppose also that there is a heavy fine for having faulty wiring. Must the homeowner submit to the inspection? Will it involve self-incrimination if faulty wiring is discovered? Is a search warrant required? If a search warrant is not issued "on probable cause," does it constitute an unreasonable search and seizure? These and other constitutional issues arise when an act presumed to be administrative or regulatory is made a crime.

The third area of constitutional law that has implications for environmental regulation is the Due Process Clause of the Fourteenth Amendment. That Clause reads, "nor shall any person be denied life, liberty or property without due process of law." At first blush, the Due Process Clause seems to duplicate the Takings Clause, but the two clauses are different. The Takings Clause requires that the government take possession of the property and put it to a public use.[17] The Due Process Clause, on the other hand, may be invoked if a person is merely deprived of the use of the property. For example, if a landowner is forbidden to cut trees for lumber because they contain the nests of golden eagles, has she been deprived of her property without due process of law? Whether an actual deprivation has occurred is a matter that may have to be resolved in a court of law.

MAJOR ENVIRONMENTAL LEGISLATION

The existence of a constitutional basis for the enactment of environmental laws does not mean that such laws will be passed. It is still necessary for the elected representatives of the people to use that constitutional power to pass legislation to effect changes in the ways we interact with our environment. In this section we will examine three of the most important pieces of environmental legislation: the National Environmental Policy Act (NEPA), the Clean Air Act (CAA), and the Endangered Species Act (ESA). We will examine the major provisions of each act, discuss some case law which each has prompted, and assess the politics which each has generated.

The National Environmental Policy Act of 1969

The National Environmental Policy Act of 1969, signed into law by President Richard M. Nixon on January 1, 1970, was the first piece of legislation in the modern era of environmental regulation. According to § 4321 of the act, its purpose is:

> To declare a national policy which will encourage productive and enjoyable harmony between man and his environment; to promote efforts which will prevent or eliminate damage to the environment and biosphere and stimulate the health and welfare of man; to enrich the understanding of the ecological systems and natural resources important to this Nation; and to establish a Council on Environmental Quality.[18]

Unlike subsequent environmental legislation that sought to target pollution in the private sector, the NEPA was created to regulate the actions of federal agencies. Its major purpose is to ensure that federal agencies take into account the environmental impact of their actions. It is also designed to ensure that the public will be made aware of the environmental impact of major federal projects, including federal grants to the states. To help implement its administration, the Act creates a three-person Council on Environmental Quality to advise the president on environmental matters. Later, Reorganization Plan No. 3 of 1970 created the EPA.[19] Many functions of other federal agencies dealing with the environment were transferred to the EPA.

The major impact of the NEPA has been the requirement that federal agencies submit an Environmental Impact Statement (EIS). The NEPA requires all federal agencies to:

(C) include in every recommendation or report for legislation and other major federal actions significantly affecting the quality of human environment, a detailed statement by the responsible official on—

(i)   the environmental impact of the proposed action,
(ii) any adverse environmental effects which cannot be avoided should the proposal be implemented,
(iii) alternatives to the proposed action,
(iv) the relationship between local short-term uses of man's environment and enhancement of long-term productivity, and
(v)   any irreversible and irretrievable commitments of resources which would be involved in the proposed action should it be implemented.[20]

The same section of the Act also requires federal agencies to consult with other federal agencies about the environmental impact of the proposed action.

As often happens with new legislation, the passage of the NEPA left many questions unanswered. A threshold question that is crucial is whether an EIS is necessary at all.[21] That, in turn, requires answers to what is "federal," what is "major," and what is a "significant environmental impact"?[22] Disputes between agencies and environmental interest groups tend to center on the third question more than on the first two. As one critic of NEPA has noted, "the statute is an elaborate catechism requiring years of delay and paperwork—often irrelevant, always self-promoting and at times outright deceitful in its consideration of environmental effects—*before getting on with the job*" (emphasis added).[23] Obviously, what is significant to one group may seem inconsequential to another.

One final area worth discussing is the requirement of § 4332(C)(iii) that agencies consider alternatives. Does the agency have to consider all conceivable alternatives or only those reasonably likely to be implemented? Case law dealing with these issues is not always clear. What is clear, however, is that NEPA does "require that federal agencies take a 'hard look' at the environmental effects of their decisions before acting."[24] Evaluating the effectiveness of NEPA is difficult because no one knows the number of environmentally harmful projects abandoned or never begun because of the obstacles faced under the law.[25] What NEPA clearly does, however, is to provide environmentalists with a tool to obstruct or at least delay environmentally harmful federal projects. It has also served as a model for state laws that require state agencies to assess the environmental impact of their actions. To some, these minor achievements are enough to conclude that NEPA has been a success.

The Clean Air Act

The Clean Air Act (CAA)[26] was first passed in 1963 as a federal grant program designed to encourage states to control air pollution. Since then it has had major amendments added in 1970, 1977, and again in 1990.[27] The basic purpose of the Act is to provide for the establishment of National Ambient Air Quality Standards (NAAQSs) by the EPA. The EPA sets minimum standards for five air pollutants: carbon monoxide, sulfur dioxide, nitrogen dioxide, ozone, and particulate matter. Each state is then required to formulate a State Implementation Plan (SIP) that details how it will meet the minimum NAAQSs. If a state fails to submit an adequate SIP, the EPA is authorized to write a plan for that state called a Federal Implementation Plan (FIP).[28]

Enforcement of the CAA has been strengthened over the years. Under the 1977 amendments, the EPA first had to issue a violator a notice of violation (NOV) and the violator had 30 days in which to correct the problem. If the problem was not corrected, the EPA could either issue an administrative compliance order or sue in a U.S. district court. Under the compliance order, the violation was described and the violator was given a reasonable deadline to correct the problem. If, however, the deadline was not met, the EPA had no power to impose a penalty on the violator. At that point, the EPA could file a civil suit, but as the EPA had no power to enforce the law, the case had to be turned over to the Department of Justice for prosecution. This procedure was cumbersome for minor violations of the Act.[29]

In 1990, Congress amended the CAA to permit a more flexible approach to both major and minor violations. For major violations, after the notice of violation and the 30 days allowed to correct the violation, the EPA may impose penalties of up to $25,000 per day with each day of a continuing violation counting as a separate violation.[30] Persons fined under this procedure are entitled to a formal administrative hearing under the Administrative Procedure Act (APA).[31] EPA field inspectors were authorized to issue citations, not unlike traffic tickets, for minor violations of SIPs. Civil penalties up to $5000 per day may be imposed, and persons fined do not have the right to a formal administrative hearing but need only be given a reasonable opportunity to respond.[32] At the same time that Congress adopted its more flexible approach, it also imposed higher standards. The 1990 amendments identified ten "nonattainment" areas that states were required to adopt as the new standard—best available control measures or BACM—to their SIPs.[33] Surprisingly, the EPA has not always been vigorous in promoting a clean environment. When the state of Massachusetts tried to persuade the EPA to promulgate rules regulating the emission of greenhouse gases, the EPA balked. The EPA argued that scientific evidence on global warming is inconclusive, that the actions of developing nations contribute to global warming, and that EPA action might impair the president's efforts to persuade other nations to attack the problem globally. In *Massachusetts v. EPA* however, the Supreme Court held that, the above arguments notwithstanding, the EPA had abused its discretion by refusing to consider the state's request.[34]

The CAA is a prime example of the power of positive law to effect change in our behavior and environment. Although the United States still has far to go to reduce smog, acid rain, and the deterioration of the ozone layer, there is little doubt that without laws like the CAA little would have been done in the private sector to address the problem of air pollution.

The Endangered Species Act

Few environmental laws have sparked as much controversy as the ESA.[35] Originally passed in 1966, the early version of the law merely authorized the acquisition of land by the federal government for the protection of endangered species. In 1973 the law was amended to include plants as well as animals.[36] In particular, there are three provisions of the act that have sparked controversy. The first, § 1533, authorizes the Secretary of the Interior to promulgate regulations placing species on either the "threatened" or the "endangered" list. The second is § 1531(c)(1), which declares that "all Federal departments and agencies shall seek to conserve endangered species and threatened species and shall utilize their authorities in furtherance of the purposes of this chapter." The third provision forbids taking from an endangered species which the Act defines as "to harass, harm, pursue, hunt, shoot, wound, kill, trap, capture, or collect,"[37] even on private property.

The first provision—the actual listing of threatened and endangered species—has been attacked by critics as both over- and under-inclusive. Critics who claim that the law is over-inclusive say that species that are not really endangered are too easily included in the list. The Act directs the Secretary to make the determination "solely on the basis of the best scientific and commercial data available to him after conducting a review of the status of the species."[38] Critics of the Act maintain that it affords too much protection for too many species and that "failure to apply science rigorously has created unjustified impediments to economic development."[39] Finally, opponents of the Act accuse proponents of using the law to block projects of which they disapprove.[40] Supporters of the ESA concede that there are flaws in the Act but argue that with endangered species it is better to err on the side of caution.

The second area of controversy concerning the ESA is its effect on other federal agencies. The classic example involved the tiny snail darter.[41] In 1967 Congress funded the Tellico Dam and Reservoir Project on the Tennessee River. In 1973 a University of Tennessee ichthyologist discovered a previously unknown species of perch called the snail darter. In October 1975 the Secretary of the Interior added the snail darter to the endangered species list. Throughout this period Congress continued to appropriate funds, which totaled nearly $100 million, for the completion of the Tellico Project. Environmentalists sought an injunction to halt the completion of the dam that, they claimed, would destroy the habitat of the snail darter. The Tennessee Valley Authority (TVA) challenged the injunction on the grounds that Congress never intended the ESA to apply to nearly completed projects. By the time the snail darter was added to the endangered species list, the Tellico Project was nearly ten years into the works. The Supreme Court, however, ruled that the statutory language of the ESA was clear. Congress, ruled the Court, did intend to preserve endangered species even at the risk of halting ongoing projects. Writing for the Court, Chief Justice Warren Burger held:

> One would be hard pressed to find a statutory provision whose terms were any plainer than those in § 7 of the Endangered Species Act. Its very words affirmatively command all federal agencies "to *insure* that actions,

authorized, funded, or *carried out* by them do not *jeopardize* the continued existence of an endangered species," or *"result* in the destruction or modification of habitat of such species" (emphasis in original).[42]

Criticism of *TVA v. Hill,* both in and out of Congress, was sharp and immediate. In response to the decision, Congress amended the ESA by creating an Endangered Species Committee. This committee was empowered to decide whether to grant exemptions to § 1536(a)(2), which was at issue in the *TVA* case.[43] The Snail Darter Case continues to be cited by opponents of environmental law as an example of the excesses of the environmental movement.

The final controversial provision of the ESA concerns the right to "take" a member of an endangered species. (This discussion of the term *take* should not be confused with the taking of property under the Takings Clause discussed later in this chapter.) The Act covers the "dead body or parts thereof" of endangered species and prohibits any commercial activity regarding them.[44] A leading case that illustrates the controversy is *Andrus v. Allard.*[45] Although not technically involving the ESA, the *Andrus* case raises similar issues. The Eagle Protection Act[46] makes it illegal to possess, barter, or offer to sell any part of a bald eagle unless a person is exempt under the statute. Allard sought declaratory relief on the ground that the Act did not apply to the selling of items taken before the passage of the Act as no purpose was served in protecting an animal that is already dead.[47] The Supreme Court, in an opinion by Justice William Brennan, ruled that Congress did intend to prohibit the sale of feathers taken before the ban. Justice Brennan noted that as Congress was aware that "there is no sure means by which to determine the age of bird feathers,"[48] it must have intended the Act to apply to artifacts taken before the passage of the law. The Court's decision, like that in *TVA v. Hill,* illustrates the lengths to which it was willing to go to protect endangered species.

A fundamental characteristic of law is its need to adapt to changes in the political and social environment as well as in the ecological environment. While in the past it has been possible to show direct causation between X (damming a river) and Y (endangered fish and wildlife), new threats to wildlife may be harder to identify. For example, it is possible that new threats, including greenhouse gases and global warming, will not be identifiable by the ESA, which was primarily designed to prevent direct threat to wildlife.[49] As noted throughout this book, the battle over public policy that is reflected in the law is a battle of wills. It remains to be seen whether the American people will continue to have the determination to do what is necessary to protect the environment from harm.

ISSUES OF ENVIRONMENTAL LAW

It would be impossible to explore all the myriad issues involved in the study of environmental law. That is, in part, the result of the extraordinary reliance of environmental law on science and technology. The impact of science and technology on environmental law is far beyond the scope of this book. In this section we will focus on two important legal aspects of environmental law: the issue of standing and the problem of taking. Through these two issues, we hope to introduce the reader to at least some aspects of the legal complexities of regulating the environment.

Standing

In Chapter 5, *standing* was defined as a litigant's right to bring a cause of action before a court for judicial resolution. Standing may be conferred on litigants by a legislative body. That is, Congress may, if it chooses, grant standing to certain parties under conditions or circumstances it prescribes. For example, 5 U.S.C. § 702 provides that:

> A person suffering legal wrong because of agency action, or adversely affected or aggrieved by agency action within the meaning of a relevant statute, is entitled to judicial review thereof.[50]

Thus, § 702 appears to allow environmentalists to challenge the actions of administrative agencies that are harmful to the environment.

A leading case of standing in environmental law is *Sierra Club v. Morton*.[51] The Department of the Interior had approved plans to permit the development of a ski resort in Mineral King Valley in the Sequoia National Forest. The Sierra Club, claiming standing under § 702, sought a preliminary injunction seeking to restrain Interior Department officials from issuing the necessary permits to proceed with the development. Although the District Court granted the preliminary injunction, the Court of Appeals reversed on the issue of standing. The Supreme Court, in an opinion written by Justice Potter Stewart, affirmed the Court of Appeals. The Court held that persons seeking standing under § 702 must show that they were injured or would suffer injury as a result of the agency action. The Court found that the Sierra Club failed to show that any of its members would be adversely affected by the project directly. The Club had failed to show that any of its members had used Mineral King Valley. The Court held that to have standing to challenge an agency action a party must have an "injury in fact." As no member of the Sierra Club had been among those injured by the Department of the Interior's decision, it lacked standing.

However, the setback in *Sierra Club* was short lived. The next year, in *United States v. Students Challenging Regulatory Agency Procedures (SCRAP)*,[52] the Supreme Court granted standing to an environmental group consisting of five law students. When the ICC granted railroads permission to raise their rates by 2.5 percent, SCRAP alleged that the increase would make the transportation of recyclable goods more expensive. This, in turn, would make recycling economically less attractive. SCRAP further alleged that the reduced recycling would increase litter and pollution in the Washington, D.C. area, where its members lived. The Court, again speaking through Justice Stewart, held that SCRAP had shown sufficient "injury in fact" to overcome the objections in *Sierra Club*. A key element in the Court's ruling was the holding that economic harm was not the only type of harm that gave standing. The Court held that loss of aesthetic and recreational value could also provide standing for a litigant.

Standing to challenge environmental cases suffered another setback in *Lujan v. Defenders of Wildlife*.[53] The Endangered Species Act requires agencies to clear federal projects that might jeopardize species on the endangered species list with the Secretary of the Interior. Initially, the Secretary had included projects worldwide where federal money was spent. Later however, the Secretary amended the order to limit its application to the United States and the world's oceans. Two members of the Defenders of Wildlife protested federal dollars not being spent on projects in Sri Lanka and Egypt. They asserted that they planned to visit the sites again at some indefinite time in the future and therefore had standing to challenge the Secretary's reversal of his position.

The Supreme Court, with Justice Antonin Scalia writing a plurality opinion, ruled that the two members did not have standing. The Court held that the members' assertions that they intended to visit the sites again at some indefinite time in the future was not a sufficient "injury in fact" to establish standing. The Court acknowledged that provisions of the ESA seemed to permit "citizen suits" granting standing to challenge governmental action or inaction. However, the Court ruled that the "case and controversy" requirement of Article III still required that a person claiming standing be among those who suffer the injury.

A 1997 Supreme Court decision may have a profound effect on the law of standing in future environmental cases. The case, *Bennett v. Spear*,[54] involved an interpretation of § 1540(g)(1)(A) of the ESA which reads:

> Except as provided in paragraph (2) of this subsection any person may commence a civil suit on his own behalf—(A) to enjoin any person, including the United States and any other governmental instrumentality or agency (to the extent permitted by the eleventh amendment to the Constitution), who is alleged to be in violation of any provision of this Act or regulation issued under the authority thereof.

This provision grants standing to permit individual citizens to act as "private attorneys general." The purpose of the provision is to allow private individuals or representatives of interest groups to file lawsuits to compel the enforcement of the ESA. In *Bennett* however, the petitioner was not seeking to use the "citizen suit" provision of the ESA to protect wildlife. Instead, the petitioner had an economic interest in overturning a decision that would have protected an endangered species. Environmentalists argued that standing only applied to those persons who were seeking to promote the interests of those the statute was written to protect. The Supreme Court, however, ruled that the plain language of the statute included "any person." The majority, through Justice Scalia, noted that in other, similar laws the granting of standing had been limited clearly by statutory language. The conclusion was that if Congress had intended to limit standing to proponents of the statute's goals, it knew how to do so.

The issue of standing took yet another twist in *Massachusetts v. Environmental Protection Agency* mentioned earlier in this chapter. In that case, the EPA alleged that the parties lacked standing to challenge the EPA's decision not to promulgate new rules governing the emission of greenhouse gases. The Supreme

Court held that, as a sovereign state, Massachusetts' "stake in the outcome of this case is sufficiently concrete to warrant the exercise of federal judicial power."[55] In light of the nation's increasing concern about the effects of global warming, *Massachusetts v. EPA* may signal a new trend in granting standing to protect the environment.

Massachusetts v. EPA notwithstanding, there are still considerable obstacles to using the courts to combat global warming. As noted, the primary obstacle is often overcoming the question of standing. For a litigant to meet the requirement of standing, several conditions must be met. First, as noted in *Sierra Club v. Morton*, there must be an "injury in fact." As one author has explained:

> First, the plaintiff must have suffered an "injury in fact"—an invasion of a legally protected interest which is (a) concrete and particularized, and (b) actual or imminent, not "conjectural" or "hypothetical." Second, there must be a causal connection between the injury and the conduct complained of—the injury has to be "fairly … traceable to the challenged action of the defendant, and not … the result [of] the independent action of some third party not before the court." Third, it must be a "likely" as opposed to merely "speculative" that the injury will be redressed by a favorable decision.[56]

Each of the three conditions poses problems for the person wishing to pursue a suit against companies that may be causing global warming. Global warming is a generalized injury rather than one that is "concrete and particularized." In other words, the petitioner must show that she "has an interest distinct from the general population."[57] As we noted in Chapter 5, taxpayers' suits are dismissed on these grounds. Nor is it easy to trace the causes of global warming to a particular defendant. Carbon emissions may cause global warming but so may the effects of farming and ranching, increased paving and building in our cities, destruction of rain forests and even solar activity.[58] The science of global warming is still rather inconclusive in the sense that multiple factors may contribute to global warming, and "that it is safe to say that the science is not settled on this issue, which poses a substantial obstacle to prove legal standing in a federal court."[59] Finally, there is the question of whether a federal court can redress the injury. If the plaintiff can overcome the issues of a concrete and particularized injury and the issue of causation, a federal court may be able to fashion a suitable remedy, but it is highly speculative that it can.

In Chapter 5, the concept of judicial gatekeeping was introduced. Gatekeeping is the process by which certain groups or persons are allowed or forbidden to lay their claims before a court of law. Clearly, the issue of standing is an important one for environmental law. Only the future will tell the extent to which proponents and opponents of environmentalism can lay their claims before a court.

Takings

As mentioned earlier in this chapter, the Takings Clause of the Fifth Amendment forbids the taking of private property by the government for public purposes without "just compensation." The important point to remember is that government *may* take private property for public purposes if the landowner is justly compensated. This is the power of **eminent domain**. A major issue arising under the Takings Clause is determining when a taking has occurred. For example, does a taking occur if the government takes action that diminishes the value of one's property? Or has a taking occurred if the government's action in some way reduces the economic value of the property? As environmental regulation has a tendency both to diminish property values and reduce its economic value, the taking question is an important issue for environmental law.

To understand the application of takings jurisprudence to environmental law, it is necessary to have a general understanding of takings cases. One area that illustrates the problem associated with the Takings Clause is the exercise of the state's police power or the power to regulate health, safety, and morals. Suppose that the state decides that a particular activity, once legal, should be made illegal. Suppose further that a property owner has dedicated his property to the now proscribed activity. Is this a taking within the meaning of the Fifth Amendment? In *Mugler v. Kansas*,[60] the U.S. Supreme Court said no. Peter Mugler had built a beer brewery at a cost of $10,000 in 1877 in Salina, Kansas. In November 1880 the people of Kansas passed a constitutional amendment prohibiting the sale of alcoholic beverages in the state. Mugler was found guilty of illegally selling beer and fined $100. Mugler argued that denying him the right to produce beer, to which the property was dedicated, amounted to a taking requiring state compensation. The Supreme Court disagreed, ruling that the prohibition of alcoholic beverages is within the police power of the state. In its exercise of the police power, Kansas had, in effect, declared the sale of alcohol to be a public nuisance and had every right to prohibit it. Finally, the Court ruled that Mugler had not been deprived of his property without due process of law; nor was he entitled to just compensation. Usually, when the state exercises its police power to regulate a "public nuisance" and that exercise diminishes the economic value of one's property, the person is not entitled to compensation under *Mugler*.

A second area which raises questions of taking is that of zoning. Zoning is the practice whereby a state or municipality limits the use to which property may be put in a defined geographic region. For example, a common form of zoning is commercial zoning, which means that the property in the commercial zone may be used for business or commercial purposes. Unlike *Mugler*, in which the use of the property for the manufacture of alcohol was made illegal, the property owner is not engaged in an illegal activity but is merely barred from using her property in the way she would like to use it.

For most of American history, the zoning of property was nonexistent. However, as cities began to expand and populations began to grow, there was increasing pressure to limit the uses of property in certain parts of the city. People wanted assurances that if they built a beautiful home, a factory spewing noxious odors would not appear next door. Obviously, zoning can have a negative effect on property values and so the issue is whether the diminution of property values is a taking under the Fifth Amendment.

Zoning has been challenged on both due process and takings grounds. The leading zoning case is *Village of Euclid v. Ambler Realty Co.*[61] The Village of Euclid, a suburb of Cleveland, passed an ordinance restricting land owned, including that owned by Ambler Realty, to residential use. The realty company alleged that the value of the property for industrial purposes was $10,000 per acre but was valued at only $2500 per acre for residential use. The Supreme Court upheld the ordinance and in doing so justified the use of zoning by observing that:

> Some of the grounds for this inclusion [i.e., zoning] are—promotion of the health and security from injury of children and others by separating dwelling houses from territory devoted to trade and industry; suppression and prevention of disorder; facilitating the extinguishment of fires, and the enforcement of street traffic regulations and other general welfare ordinances; aiding the health and safety of the community by excluding from residential areas the confusion and danger of fire, contagion and disorder which in greater or lesser degree attach to the location of stores, shops, and factories. Another ground is that the construction and repair of streets may be rendered easier and less expensive by confining the greater part of the heavy traffic to the streets where business is carried on.[62]

In upholding the constitutionality of zoning ordinances, the Supreme Court sent a clear message that individual property rights must sometimes give way to the public good. In addition, the Court ruled that such restrictions on the use of one's property were a valid exercise of the state's police power and not a taking under the Fifth Amendment.

Finally, another area of takings cases involves the issue of historic preservation. Similar to zoning laws in that they restrict the owner's use of property, state and local historic preservation laws may prohibit property owners from destroying or altering their property if it has been designated an historic landmark. The leading case is *Penn Central Transportation Co. v. New York City.*[63] The Grand Central Terminal in New York City had been designated an historic landmark. The Penn Central Transportation Company, owners of the terminal, wished to construct a multistory office building over the terminal. However, the Landmarks Preservation Commission denied its approval. The company claimed that its property had been taken without just compensation and in violation of due process. In addition, it claimed that unlike zoning laws which apply to all classes of property with a specified area, historic preservation laws single out, and therefore discriminate against, property owners in an arbitrary manner.

The Supreme Court conceded that historic preservation laws burden some landowners more than others. The Court also conceded that such laws often prevent the property owner from maximizing the economic value of his or her property. However, the Court held that most government regulations, such as income taxes, affect some citizens more heavily than others. The Court also noted that zoning laws by their nature may reduce any economic benefit the property owner may gain. The Court held that the Penn Central Transportation Company was not denied all economic benefit from its property. Indeed, the company was free to continue to operate the terminal as a railroad station and office complex as it had for the past 65 years. Finally, the Court held that the company was not uniquely burdened by the preservation law, as nearly 400 sites had been designated as landmarks in New York City.[64] The *Penn Central* case is significant because the Court recognized that the state's police power may be used to provide a public benefit and to abate a public nuisance. This distinction is especially relevant for environmental law, as environmental protection is based on the notion that the public good is served by the preservation of our environment.

Takings rulings are relevant to environmental law because, like historic preservation laws, they often restrict how a person may use his or her property. A few examples will illustrate the richness and complexity of takings in environmental law. In an early case, *Barrett v. New York*,[65] the Court of Appeals of New York upheld a state law seeking to protect beavers from extermination. By 1900, beavers were almost extinct in New York. The state legislature passed laws making it illegal to kill beavers and to disturb their natural habitat. In addition, the state released four beavers on the land of the plaintiff, William G. Barrett. The beavers destroyed nearly 200 poplar trees on Barrett's property. Barrett sued the state, claiming it was responsible for releasing the beaver, and sought compensation. The Court of Appeals denied Barrett's claim, stating:

> [T]he general right of government to protect wild animals is too well established to be now called into question. Their ownership is in the state in its sovereign capacity, for the benefit of all the people. Their preservation is a matter of public interest. They are a species of natural wealth which without special protection would be destroyed. Everywhere and at all times governments have assumed the right to prescribe how and when they may be taken or killed.[66]

In *Miller v. Schoene*[67] the Supreme Court upheld a Virginia law that required the destruction of red cedar trees infected with cedar rust disease. Cedar rust disease can infect and destroy apple orchards within a two-mile radius. Dr. C.O. Miller argued that not only were his trees destroyed but also the value of his property was diminished by the loss of the trees and their destruction constituted a taking entitling him to compensation. The Supreme Court, however, ruled that it is within the police power of the state to destroy one class of property to save another. The Court also held that it was the state's choice to decide which class of property was more deserving of protection. Finally, the Court noted that Miller was not denied the complete use of his trees, as they could be sold for lumber or firewood.

Central to takings jurisprudence is the "bundle of rights" concept inherent in ownership of property. Simply put, property carries with it a bundle of different rights, some of which may be diminished by government action, while the remainder are retained by the property owner. In *Miller*, as noted, the property owner was still free to sell the cedar trees even if he had lost their aesthetic value. The property owners in both *Mugler* and *Penn Central* could use their property in other ways for economic gain. If the government's action does not completely destroy all property rights in the bundle, the owner cannot expect compensation under the Takings Clause.

While there may be a consensus in our society that government may restrict the use of private property to abate a public nuisance or to promote the public good, may the state use its police power to extract a public benefit from a property owner without compensation? Two Supreme Court cases have modified the narrow circumstances under which a taking may occur in an environmental context. In the first case, *Lucas v. South Carolina Coastal Council*,[68] South Carolina forbade David H. Lucas from building single-family dwelling units on two beachfront lots he had purchased. A South Carolina trial court had ruled that, as a result, the property owner had been deprived of all economically viable use of his property and awarded Lucas compensation. However, the South Carolina Supreme Court reversed and Lucas appealed. The U.S. Supreme Court distinguished *Lucas* from the *Mugler* line of cases. The *Mugler* line of cases held that property devalued because of the state's exercise of its police power to regulate a public nuisance was not compensable. The Supreme Court held, however, that if the property owner is denied all economically viable use of his or her property, a taking has occurred and compensation is required. The dissenters in *Lucas* argued that Lucas was not deprived of all use of his property. They noted that, as in zoning cases, the fact that Lucas could not use his property in the most profitable way did not mean that there were no economically viable uses for it.

In *Dolan v. City of Tigard*,[69] the Supreme Court found the City's extraction of concessions from Florence Dolan, in exchange for approval to make improvements to her business, to be a taking under the Fifth and Fourteenth Amendments. Dolan wanted to expand her lumber business which bordered Fanno Creek in Tigard. The City, in return for its approval, wanted Dolan to dedicate some of her property to a public greenway and a bicycle/pedestrian pathway. Under the doctrine of "unconstitutional conditions," the government may not extract such concessions from a person in exchange for receiving a benefit. The City of Tigard was, in effect, forcing Dolan to donate part of her property in exchange for the City's permission to expand her business.

Perhaps no better example of the relationship between law and politics exists than in environmental law. Central to politics is the attempt by one group to impose its values on society by the enactment of positive law. Certainly, environmentalists cannot deny that they are using the political system to promote their value system regarding preservation of the environment. Similarly, politics is used by others to promote their own economic interests. Developers, for example, have their economic well-being in mind as they build in the name of progress. Politics, then, is an inevitable clash of interests and values, which is as it should be.

Besides the clash of values and economic interests, the debate over environmental law involves differences over the meaning of what constitutes a taking.

In 1992 the Supreme Court attempted to clarify the distinction between a *physical taking* and a *regulatory taking*. As noted earlier, when the government takes physical possession of property for public use under its power of eminent domain, a physical taking has occurred and just compensation must be provided. However, a regulatory taking occurs when the government uses its regulatory power to restrict or deny use of property but does not take physical possession of it. In *Lucas,* the Court held that when the property owner has been denied "all economically or productive use of land" a taking has occurred and compensation is required.

But does a taking occur when a property owner is denied temporary use of her property? In *Tahoe-Sierra Preservation Council, Inc. v. Tahoe Regional Planning Agency,*[70] the Court said no. The Tahoe Regional Planning Agency had imposed two moratoria on building in the Lake Tahoe area while it developed a comprehensive land use plan for protecting the lake from runoff pollution. During the 32 months of the combined moratoria, property owners who had purchased lots for building retirement or vacation homes were forbidden to build. The Tahoe-Sierra Preservation Council, representing the owners, argued that denial of the use of their property during the moratoria constituted a taking, and they demanded compensation. The Court ruled against the owners and in favor of the government for several reasons. First, it applied the "bundle of rights" concept and held that the owners had not been denied "all economically or productive use" of their land. Second, the Court noted the temporary nature of the building ban that, unlike *Lucas,* would (and did) end. Finally, the Court feared that forcing the government to pay compensation to property owners during the planning process might result in hasty and ill-conceived planning. For these reasons, the Court held that the temporary ban on property owners' use of their land was not a taking under the Constitution.

Another development has occurred which illustrates the ongoing political battle between environmentalists and developers. Almost immediately after becoming the majority party in 1995, Republican members of Congress introduced a bill entitled the Private Property Protection Act of 1995.[71] The purported purpose of the bill was to compensate property owners whose property's value was reduced by 20 percent or more from government regulation. The bill stipulated that if the government regulation diminished any portion of a landowner's property by 20 percent or more, the taking was compensable.[72]

Although it failed to gain congressional approval, if passed, the Private Property Protection Act would have made it easier for a landowner to show a taking and be entitled to compensation. The effect would have been to reverse the case law that, as we have seen, required the government actually to take title to the property or to deny the property owner all economically viable use of the property. The real threat to the environmental movement was not that the law made it easier for the property owner to make a takings claim. The real threat was that the law required any claims against the government as a result of a successful takings claim would come from the offending agency's budget. Historically, Congress has paid both takings judgments and tort claims against the government through the regular appropriations process. After 1956

Congress set up a permanent fund, not unlike the Social Security fund, to pay such claims.[73] Opponents of the bill argued that taking judgments from the operating budgets of the agencies will deter vigorous enforcement of environmental protection law and give property owners unnecessary windfalls.[74] One outspoken critic of such compensation legislation has observed that these bills "are almost certainly intended to undercut environmental protection though of course the text says nothing to that effect."[75]

It is clear that the political battle over the protection of the environment is far from over. As long as law is used by one group to impose either its aesthetic or economic values upon the rest of society, environmental politics will continue.

TWO CASE STUDIES IN ENVIRONMENTAL LAW

In this chapter, we looked at two types of law that affect the environment of the nation: statutory law and constitutional law. In this section, we will examine two Supreme Court environmental law cases requiring statutory and constitutional interpretation. The first case, *Rapanos v. United States*,[76] concerns the interpretation of the Clean Water Act and the second, *Kelo v. City of New London*,[77] is a fairly recent pronouncement by the Court on the Takings Clause of the Fifth Amendment.

Rapanos v. United States[78]

John Rapanos sought to fill in some wetland property he owned in Michigan by bringing in dirt to make it suitable for development. Because the property was classified as "wetlands," he was required by law to obtain a permit from the Army Corps of Engineers under the Clean Water Act (CWA). The CWA,[79] as amended in 1972, gave the Corps rulemaking authority over the "navigable waters" of the United States. Over the years, the Corps has adopted an increasingly expansive definition of the navigable waters to the point that hundreds of millions of acres of land have come under its regulatory authority. When Rapanos failed to apply for the necessary permit and ignored numerous warnings from both the Corps and the EPA, he was charged with civil and criminal proceedings that could have resulted in 63 months in prison and fines of hundreds of thousands of dollars. Rapanos challenged the classification of his property as "wetlands" and the authority of the Army Corps of Engineers to regulate its use. Although the Supreme Court voted 5 to 4 to remand the case to the lower court, there was no majority opinion. The plurality opinion was written by Justice Antonin Scalia with Justice Anthony M. Kennedy writing a separate concurring opinion and supplying the fifth vote for remand.

Justice Scalia began the plurality opinion by noting the expansion of the Corps' authority, the increasing cost of obtaining a permit, and the penalties for failure to comply with the Corps' regulations. He then turned his attention to the Corps' definition of "the waters of the United States." Under the Corps' definition, any body of water, even one separated from a navigable river, lake, or stream by a man-made structure, is considered to be among "the waters of the United States." Petitioner Rapanos argued that the Act is restricted to navigable waters and not to wetlands that are tenuously connected to a navigable body of water. The issue, according to Scalia, is whether the wetlands in this case that will eventually flow into navigable waters are "waters of the United States" under the CWA. Using a standard dictionary, Scalia argued that the placement of the article "the" and the use of the plural "waters" in "the waters of the United States" include "only relatively permanent, standing or flowing bodies of water."[80] As a result, the Corps acted beyond its authority in classifying the wetlands in this case as navigable waters within the meaning of the statute.

Justice John Paul Stevens wrote the principal dissent in this case. Stevens' main argument was that the Corps of Engineers' interpretations of "navigable waters" and "the waters of the United States" were reasonable. In his view, the Court should defer to the reasonable interpretation of an executive agency seeking to fulfill the will of Congress. Stevens argued that Congress clearly intended to cover wetlands in 1977 when it rejected an amendment that would have narrowed the jurisdiction of the Corps.[81] Stevens also accused the plurality of ignoring Court precedents regarding the interpretation of the CWA.

Kelo v. City of New London

Seldom has a case ignited such controversy as *Kelo v. City of New London*. In 2000, city officials of New London, Connecticut approved a development plan that promised to revive the City's downtown and waterfront areas and to revitalize its ailing economy. The City began purchasing the land, but several property owners, including Susette Kelo, refused to sell. The City proposed to use its power of eminent domain to force the sale of the property with just compensation. As the land was, in effect, being taken from its current owners so that private developers could use it to complete the development plan, the issue before the Supreme Court was whether taking property for economic development is a "public use" within the meaning of the Fifth Amendment.

Justice Stevens wrote the opinion in the 5 to 4 decision. After detailing the economic development plans for New London, Justice Stevens described what he called the "polar propositions" at issue. He stated that it is clear that the taking of property from A and transferring it to B for the benefit of B, even with just compensation, is not permitted under the Fifth Amendment. However, it is equally clear that property may be taken for "use by the public" and Stevens cited as an example the taking property for railroad rights-of-way in the nineteenth century. He acknowledged that the condemned land in question will not be used by the general public in the strict sense of the term but asserted that the Court's precedents have long rejected such a narrow interpretation of the term "public use." In evaluating the benefit to be derived for the public, great deference must be given to state legislatures in general, and to the Connecticut statute in particular, when interpreting the Takings Clause. Economic development plans must be executed in their entirety to be effective and it is not for the Court to determine the likelihood that the benefits predicted from the development will actually accrue to the City. Stevens concluded his opinion by noting that states are free to enact laws that place greater restrictions on takings for economic development but that the plan for the City of New London did not violate the Fifth Amendment.

Justice Sandra Day O'Connor wrote the principal dissent in *Kelo*. O'Connor asserted that the taking of private property with just compensation is constitutional in only two instances. The first is when private ownership is transferred to public ownership as in the case of roads, military bases, or hospitals. The second is when the condemnation is to effect the elimination of some harmful condition, such as slum clearance. O'Connor asserted that neither instance applies in this case and that the Court has created a third instance. Now, O'Connor maintained, the government can transfer ownership from one private party to another merely by showing that the property will be more productive under the new ownership. As it is arguable that any property might be better used, the phrase "for public use" may as well be stricken from the Constitution. Finally, O'Connor asserted that petitioners can find little solace in the majority's suggestion that state legislatures be prevailed on to curtail takings for economic development. In her view, the purpose of the Takings Clause was to protect the property of those who may be politically weak and unable to resist the will of the majority.

Rapanos v. United States and *Kelo v. City of New London* illustrate two powerful and often conflicting values in American society: the public good and private ownership of property. Environmental law is often the center of the conflict between what best serves the public welfare while honoring the sanctity of private property. These two cases remind us that law, as often happens, is about the conflict of values in a modern and complex society.

KELO: THE AFTERMATH

Controversial Supreme Court decisions seldom provide people with "the rest of the story." In the case of *Kelo v. City of New London*, the aftermath turns out to be quite interesting. After losing her case before the Supreme Court, Susette Kelo's home was moved to another location to allow for the development hoped for by the City. Unfortunately, the adverse publicity and an economic downturn resulted in Pfizer Pharmaceutical Company scrapping its plans to build the plant for which Kelo's property was needed. The Mayor of New London later apologized and admitted that the decision to exercise the power of eminent domain was ill-advised. In his opinion, Justice John Paul Stevens suggested that if voters were unhappy with the Court's decision they should take it up with their state legislatures, and many did. A number of states revised either their statutes or state constitutions to prevent the kind of taking for economic development that had occurred in New London.

CONCLUSION

Perhaps no other field of law illustrates the interplay of law and politics more than environmental law. Politics enters the decision whether to protect the environment in the first place. Disagreement occurs over the extent to which government should intervene in the protection of the environment. Battles over the enforcement or non-enforcement of existing laws also involve politics. Debate over property rights versus the rights of society is a public policy question as well. Like other fields of law, environmental law concerns the making of value judgments, like deciding the worth of the tiny snail darter. In this chapter we have tried to acquaint the reader with just a few of the many interesting topics in this important field of law.

NOTES

1. Craig Simonsen, ed., *Essentials of Environmental Law* (Dallas, TX: Pearson, 1995), p. 15.
2. William L. Prosser, *Handbook of the Law of Torts* (St. Paul, MN: West, 1971), p. 572.
3. Miguel A. Santos, *Limits and Scope of Environmental Law* (Springfield, IL: Charles C. Thomas, 1996), p. 71.
4. Henry C. Black, *Black's Law Dictionary*, 4th edn (St. Paul, MN: West, 1968), p. 992.
5. Prosser, p. 574.
6. Ibid., p. 575.
7. Ibid., p. 583.
8. Ibid., pp. 583–584.
9. *McCulloch v. Maryland*, 4 Wheat. 316 (1819).
10. Stuart S. Nagel, "Environmental Policy and Constitutional Law," in Stuart S. Nagel, ed., *Environmental Politics* (New York: Praeger, 1974), pp. 254–259.
11. Ibid., p. 254.
12. Ibid.
13. U.S. Constitution, Art. I, § 8.
14. Nagel, p. 254.
15. *Missouri v. Holland*, 252 U.S. 416 (1920).
16. U.S. Constitution, Amendment V.
17. But consider the phrase "public use" in light of *Kelo v. City of New London* discussed at the end of the chapter.
18. 42 U.S.C. § 4321 (1998).
19. 5 C.F.R. § 15623.
20. 42 U.S.C. § 4332(C).
21. Roger W. Findley and Daniel A. Farber, *Environmental Law in a Nutshell*, 3rd edn (St. Paul, MN: West, 1992), p. 27.
22. Ibid.
23. Oliver A. Houck, "Book Review: Is That All? A Review of the National Environmental Policy Act, An Agenda for the Future By Lynton Keith Caldwell," 11 Duke Envtl. L. & Pol'y F. 173 (2000), p. 176.
24. Patricia L. McCarthy, "The National Environmental Policy Act," in Craig Simonsen, ed., *Essentials of Environmental Law* (Dallas, TX: Pearson, 1995), p. 184.
25. Findley and Farber, p. 56.
26. 42 U.S.C. § 7401–7671.
27. Daniel F. O'Connell and Karen L. Hogenboom, "The Clean Air Act," in Craig Simonsen, ed., *Essentials of Environmental Law* (Dallas, TX: Pearson, 1995), pp. 25–26.

28. Ibid., p. 29.
29. Kevin J. Luster, "The Field Citation Program Under the Clean Air Act: Can It Apply to Federal Facilities," 22 Wm. & Mary Envtl. L. & Policy 71 (1997).
30. 42 U.S.C. § 9152(c)(1).
31. Luster, pp. 72–73.
32. Ibid., p. 78.
33. Christopher Raftery, "Annual Review of Environmental and Natural Resources Law: Note: Restoring Webster's Definition of 'Best' Under the Clean Air Act," 37 Ecology L. Q. 595 (2010), p. 596.
34. *Massachusetts v. Environmental Protection Agency*, 549 U.S. 497 (2007).
35. 16 U.S.C. § 1531 (1998).
36. Holly Doremus, "Listing Decisions Under the Endangered Species Act: Why Better Science Isn't Always Better Policy," 75 Wash. U.L.Q. 1029 (1977).
37. 16 U.S.C. § 1532(19).
38. 16 U.S.C. § 1533(b)(1)(A).
39. Doremus, p. 1032.
40. Ibid., pp. 1032–1033.
41. *TVA v. Hill*, 437 U.S. 153 (1978), at 156–163.
42. Ibid., at 173.
43. 16 U.S.C. § 1536(e)(2).
44. 16 U.S.C. § 1532(8) and § 1532(2).
45. *Andrus v. Allard*, 444 U.S. 51 (1979).
46. 16 U.S.C. § 668(a).
47. *Andrus v. Allard*, 444 U.S. 51 (1979), at 56.
48. Ibid., at 58.
49. J. B. Ruth, "Keeping the Endangered Species Act Relevant," 19 Duke Envtl. L. & Pol'y F. 275 (2000), pp. 276–277.
50. 5 U.S.C. § 702.
51. *Sierra Club v. Morton*, 405 U.S. 727 (1972).
52. *United States v. Students Challenging Regulatory Agency Procedures (SCRAP)*, 412 U.S. 669 (1973).
53. *Lujan v. Defenders of Wildlife*, 504 U.S. 555 (1992).
54. *Bennett v. Spear*, 520 U.S. 154 (1997).
55. *Massachusetts v. Environmental Protection Agency*, 549 U.S. 497 (2007), at 519.
56. Blake R. Bertagna, "'Standing' Up for the Environment: The Ability of Plaintiffs to Establish Legal Standing to Redress Injuries Caused by Global Warming," 2006 B.Y.U. L. Rev. 415 (2006), p. 422.
57. Ibid., at p. 434.
58. Ibid., pp. 447–448.
59. Ibid., p. 433.
60. *Mugler v. Kansas*, 123 U.S. 623 (1887).
61. *Village of Euclid v. Ambler Realty Co.*, 272 U.S. 365 (1926).
62. Ibid., at 391.
63. *Penn Central Transportation Co. v. New York City*, 438 U.S. 104 (1978).
64. Ibid., at 130–136.
65. *Barrett v. New York*, 220 N.Y. 423, 116 N.E. 99 (N.Y. 1917).
66. Ibid., at 100.
67. *Miller v. Schoene*, 276 U.S. 272 (1928).
68. *Lucas v. South Carolina Coastal Council*, 505 U.S. 1003 (1992).
69. *Dolan v. City of Tigard*, 512 U.S. 374 (1994).

70. *Tahoe-Sierra Preservation Council, Inc. v. Tahoe Regional Planning Agency*, 535 U.S. 302 (2002).
71. HR 925, 104th Cong., 1st Sess.
72. Charles Tiefer, "Controlling Federal Agencies by Claims on Their Appropriations? The Takings Bill and the Power of the Purse," 13 Yale J. on Reg. 501 (1996).
73. Ibid., pp. 505–506.
74. Ibid., p. 509.
75. Joseph L. Sax, "Using Property Rights to Attack Environmental Protection," 14 Pace Envtl. L. Rev. 1 (1996).
76. *Rapanos v. United States*, 547 U.S. 715 (2006).
77. *Kelo v. City of New London*, 545 U.S. 469 (2005).
78. Unless otherwise noted, all facts pertaining to the case are taken from the Supreme Court's written opinions.
79. 33 U.S.C. § 1251.
80. *Rapanos v. United States*, 547 U.S. 715 (2006), at 732.
81. Ibid., p. 8.

Torts

A tort is a private, or civil, wrong in which the defendant's actions cause injury to a person or to property. Tort law provides redress for wrongs between individuals, while criminal law seeks to punish offenses against the public at large. A tort lawsuit involves only the persons involved in the tort; the state is neutral in regard to the outcome (unless, of course, the state is a party to the lawsuit). There are elementary dissimilarities between torts and crimes: (1) in the civil action of tort the injured person himself or herself initiates and maintains the lawsuit, whereas in criminal trials the State prosecutes, and (2) the goal of each differs. Criminal law seeks to prevent wrongdoing and to punish the miscreant (by incarceration and/or fine), while tort law aims to place the victim in the same position he or she would have been in if the tort had not occurred (by assessment of monetary damages).

The same act often spawns both civil and criminal sanctions. Suppose that you are loitering in the hall before class when, without provocation, Joe suddenly comes up and hits you in the face. Joe is subject to criminal sanctions for this attack. However, you will also wish to file a tort action against Joe to recover money to pay for your new front teeth, your dentist's bill, your pain and suffering, and your mental anguish. The purposes of the two suits, which will be heard separately, are different. Society is punishing Joe for his antisocial behavior in the criminal trial, while you are seeking money from him. The usual remedy for tort liability is monetary reimbursement for the harm suffered.[1]

Tort law is fluid; it changes as society's values shift. Today, new torts are being recognized where no cause of action had previously existed, and the boundaries of tort liability are constantly in flux. One example is the growing recognition of the legal system that animals "have an intrinsic value beyond mere property, because of the bond between pets and their owners. [An] Oregon jury ordered a man who intentionally ran over a neighbor's dog to pay $56,400 in damages, far more than the fair market value of the animal."[2] Generally, only the actor is held civilly liable for the consequences of that act. However, juries have determined that the gun dealers who sell guns and ammunition to intoxicated buyers, underage purchasers, or those exhibiting signs of mental instability violate affirmative common law duties to conduct their business to prevent sales of firearms to high-risk people. This liability has been imposed even without a statutory violation or on the principles of negligence (both of which will be discussed later in this chapter).[3] New causes of action may be created by the people directly acting as jurors in courtrooms or through their elected representatives in various legislative bodies as new statutes are written. The goal in each instance is to provide remedies for perceived wrongs.

Tort law establishes certain legal standards of conduct by which all members of society must abide and then provides a remedy when such a standard is violated. It is primarily designed to protect three types of interests: (1) the person, (2) tangible property, and (3) intangible interests, including relational interests such as business, family, and social relations. The person who breaches the standard of conduct is known as the *tortfeasor*. Generally, the tortfeasor cannot be held liable for damages unless he or she has violated the prescribed standard of conduct.

The plaintiff in the suit decides on the theory of tort recovery and draws the complaint to reflect the theory. Each theory contains certain elements that the plaintiff must prove in order to collect damages from the defendant. It is not unusual for a plaintiff to plead alternative theories of recovery that may contain contradictory elements in the complaint. Then, through discovery, it may be determined which is the strongest, and the plaintiff then proceeds to trial on that theory. The only requirement is that defendants be given adequate notice in the complaint of the possible causes of action in order that they may properly prepare the defense. In our discussion of tort law, we will look at the theories of negligence, intentional torts, strict liability, and product liability.

NEGLIGENCE

Negligence is the reckless or careless failure of the tortfeasor to exercise the degree of care that the law deems appropriate in a particular situation. A common example is that of an automobile accident in which a driver recklessly drives too fast on an icy road, loses control, and slams into another car, causing both personal injuries and property damage. The driver was imprudent and did not exercise the usual standard of care. However, he did not set out to inflict injury; this absence of malicious intent is one of the characteristics of negligence cases. Recovery in negligence cases is not predicated on proving the tortfeasor to be morally at fault. Liability is imposed only for those things that the law requires to be done (commissions) or not to be done (omissions); it is not imposed for "moral" duties that are merely voluntary or are dictated by humane considerations or ethics only.[4] The elements that the plaintiff must prove in order to win at trial are the following: (1) that the defendant owed a duty of care to the plaintiff, (2) that the standard of care was breached, (3) that the defendant's action was the proximate cause of the injury, and (4) that the plaintiff suffered some compensable damage as a result of the defendant's actions. These four elements compose the *prima facie* case in a negligence cause of action; that is, the plaintiff is required to prove each of the elements in order to win the case.[5] The issue of negligence is primarily a question of fact, and is therefore a matter to be decided by the jury.[6]

Duty of Care

The plaintiff must initially show that the defendant owed a legally recognized duty of care. There are two subsidiary issues involved: What is the level of care the defendant must exercise and to whom is the duty of care owed? In most cases the test for the appropriate level of care is whether, under the circumstances of the case, the defendant acted as a "reasonably prudent person" would have acted to prevent the injury. The **reasonably prudent person** is a fictitious individual who has been created by the courts as an objective standard by which to measure a defendant's actions. This cautious and careful person is considered to be of ordinary intelligence and to have a normal memory and normal sensory perceptions. This ubiquitous paragon of virtue has been humorously described by one commentator, A.P. Herbert, in the following manner:

> He is an ideal, a standard, the embodiment of all those qualities which we demand of the good citizen ... He is one who invariably looks where he is going, and is careful to examine the immediate foreground before he executes a leap or bound; who neither star-gazes nor is lost in meditation when approaching trapdoors or the margin of a dock ... who never mounts a moving omnibus and does not alight from any car while the train is in motion ... and will inform himself of the history and habits of a dog before administering a caress ... who never from one year's end to another makes an excessive demand upon his wife, his neighbors, his servants, his ox, or his ass ... who never swears, gambles or loses his temper; who uses nothing except in moderation ... this excellent but odious character stands like a monument in our Courts of Justice vainly appealing to his fellow citizens to order their lives after his own example.[7]

The fact-finder considers the events of the case and decides whether the defendant exhibited the due care that a person of ordinary intelligence would have done. A child is not held to as high a standard of care; each is judged against a child of like age, intelligence, and experience.[8] On the other hand, a person who has a special skill or knowledge is judged by a higher standard of care. For example, architects, engineers, and physicians must exhibit the same skills and care that others in the profession do when carrying out professional activities.[9] Certainly one expects a higher degree of medical knowledge and skill from a physician than one does from a layperson. The physician is required by law to act as a reasonably prudent *physician* would in providing treatment. If the professional does not act in accordance with the standard the usual result is a malpractice suit. Typically, the only way to prove negligence in this type of action is through the use of expert testimony, and professionals are often hesitant to testify against each other.

Another issue in regard to the standard of care is the relationship between the plaintiff and the defendant. It is this relationship that determines just how careful one must be toward another person. Generally, the law does not impose a duty on a person to go to the aid of someone who is in danger, even though there may be a moral duty to do so. However, such a duty may be imposed when there is a special relationship. Although a stranger is not *legally* required to assist a drowning child unless the stranger caused the incident in most instances, the parent may well be expected to do so in the eyes of the law and the lifeguard is obligated to do so.[10] Traditionally, occupiers of land owe different levels of care to trespassers and to business visitors, although there are circumstances when liability accrues regardless of the status of the injured party (for example, when there is willful, wanton, or careless conduct such as the use of a life-threatening device to discourage trespassers). The occupier must extend the greater level of care to business visitors or *invitees*—the duty of ordinary care. Social guests or *licensees* and trespassers, those on the land without the owner's consent, are owed a lesser degree of care—the duty to refrain from willful or wanton misconduct. Many courts have abandoned the rigid classification and apply the duty of ordinary care to all of the groups.[11] Suits involving property owners and their guests are quite common, and most people buy insurance to protect themselves financially in case of such accidents.

Breach of Duty

The second element the plaintiff must establish is that the standard of care owed to him or her was violated by the defendant. There are two prongs to this element of a negligence action. The plaintiff must convince the fact-finder (1) that the act or omission actually occurred, and (2) that such action was a breach of the standard of care owed to this particular plaintiff. Such a breach may be through commission or through omission; that is, through a positive act of the defendant or through a failure of the defendant to act. An example of a positive act is someone dropping a flowerpot from a third-story window without regard for the passerby below; an example of an omission is the failure of a store clerk to pick up banana peel from the floor after seeing it.

Courts have provided short cuts for plaintiffs in proving the lack of ordinary care in limited circumstances. The first of these is *negligence per se*. In a typical case, the legislature passes a statute regulating certain activities in the interest of safety (for example, working conditions in industries or health regulations in restaurants). The plaintiff alleges that the defendant violated such safety standard and that the plaintiff's injury is a result of such violation. If the judge agrees that the defendant violated the safety regulation, the decision is conclusive and the jury is called on only to decide if there is a causal connection to the plaintiff's injuries, and if so, the amount of damages to be awarded.[12]

The second of these short cuts is the doctrine of *res ipsa loquitur*—"the thing speaks for itself." Here, the plaintiff is required to prove that the accident is of a type that ordinarily would not occur without negligence (an airplane crash) *and* that all instrumentalities that would probably cause the accident were under the control of the defendant at the time (the airplane's crew and aircraft maintenance were under the control of the airline). This doctrine resembles circumstantial evidence in that the trier of facts is asked to infer the result from separate pieces of evidence. Again, the jury's task is limited to determining the truth of these allegations rather than actual negligence. If the jury agrees with the plaintiff on these two points, they find for the plaintiff.[13]

Proximate Cause

The plaintiff must also show that the defendant's action was the proximate cause of her injury. In other words, there must be some reasonable connection between the negligent act of the defendant and the plaintiff's injury. Suppose that Sue and her husband have an argument at breakfast; that Sue unjustifiably criticizes her secretary, Davis, during the day, and that Davis is upset and, as a result, is careless while driving home and has an accident. In one sense, it is possible to trace the cause of the accident back to the spat between Sue and her husband because "in a philosophical sense, the consequences of an act go forward to eternity and the causes of an event go back to the discovery of America and beyond."[14] However, courts have declined to enter this hornets' nest and have limited liability to "those causes which are so closely connected with the result and of such significance that the law is justified in imposing liability."[15]

This concept of legal responsibility based on a reasonable connection between the tortfeasor's action and the victim's injury is known as *proximate cause*. The plaintiff must establish not only that the defendant's conduct was *factually* one of the causes of the injury but also that the defendant should be *legally* responsible for his actions. Additional limitations on liability have been developed. If the defendant could not reasonably have foreseen any injury to the plaintiff as a consequence of the act, there is no liability.[16] For instance, a tortfeasor involved in an automobile accident could not reasonably foresee that the sirens of the emergency vehicles would startle someone into dropping a pot of boiling water and scalding herself. In addition, a defendant will be relieved of liability if there is an independent force intervening between the action and the injury.[17] To illustrate, assume that Sanders Gravel constructs a fence around its lake that is adequate to prevent the neighborhood children from straying in; however, a tornado strikes and blows down the fence, and a child drowns in the lake later that day. The tornado is considered to be an independent intervening cause in such a case.

There are often several contributing causes in a single accident which will result in shared liability among the various tortfeasors. Consider a fairly typical automobile accident. Coleman is driving east, is speeding, and is trying to get through the intersection before the light changes to red so he does not slow down. Daniel, who is traveling west on the same street, is obeying all the traffic laws; however, his attention is diverted by his two children, who are squabbling in the back seat. Richard is going north on the intersecting street and is chatting on his cell phone. The three cars collide at the intersection; personal injuries and property damage result. In addition to the foregoing facts, eyewitnesses will testify at the trial that the light was malfunctioning and was showing green on all sides. The trio will sue one another and the city for failing to properly maintain the traffic control device, namely the light. Each of them contributed to the accident, and it will be the jury's responsibility to apportion responsibility for the accident.[18]

Damages

The final element the plaintiff must prove is that of *damages,* a sum of money the law imposes as pecuniary compensation. The plaintiff is required to establish both the nature of the injury and an amount that would fairly recompense him or her for the injury. The emphasis is on placing the plaintiff in the same position, insofar as is possible, as she was in before the accident. Of course, it is difficult to place a monetary value on pain and suffering or on the loss of an arm or a leg, or to predict a person's lifetime earnings; however, juries, utilizing the precedents of previous awards and the evidence adduced at trial, decide these formidable questions each day in rendering verdicts in tort cases.

Plaintiffs' attorneys have been successful in having courts recognize the various ramifications of an injury and in thereby expanding the recovery in tort actions. Assume that John has just signed a multi-million-dollar contract to play professional football when he is paralyzed in an automobile accident. He would likely sue to recover for his pain and suffering, his current and ongoing medical expenses, his present loss of wages, his loss of future earnings, loss of value of his car, and mental anguish (if the state courts have recognized the latter).

Assume that Maria, a university professor, died in the same accident. Her estate would have a common law action for personal injury resulting in death and could recover for her consciousness of impending death, physical pain and suffering, and medical and funeral expenses. Maria's family—spouse, children, and/or parents—could also file a wrongful death suit for damages for the loss of emotional support as well as the loss of economic benefits they could reasonably have expected to receive from Maria if she had not been killed. Wrongful death suits are suits to compensate the survivors and are not derived from the decedent's interests. They are generally founded on statutory enactments that define who may claim such benefits.[19]

The monetary value of these losses is quite troublesome for juries. The easier questions are those involving the loss of value to property such as automobiles, livestock, or buildings. Putting a price tag on someone's pain and suffering or anticipating the amount of future earnings of a child is subjective. Juries rely heavily on the testimony of experts, particularly economists, to assist them. Lawyers work throughout the trial to educate the jurors about the issue of damages; the plaintiff's counsel seeks to demonstrate how horrific the injury is and how only a large sum will adequately recompense the victim, while the defense seeks to minimize the possible award. The same kinds of damages are available for all torts, including intentional torts and those involving product liability.

Defenses

Once the plaintiff has established a *prima facie* case by presenting the four elements, the defendant has the opportunity to present his case and to rebut the plaintiff's arguments.

> Once a man causes harm to another, he has brought himself within the boundaries of the law of tort. It does not follow, however, that he will be found liable in each and every case in which it can be showed that he caused harm, for it may still be possible to escape liability, not by an insistence upon his freedom of action, but upon a specific showing that his conduct was either excused or justified.[20]

Several methods of attack are available to the defendant, including challenging the plaintiff's proof on the four elements of negligence, claiming that the plaintiff was aware of the risk, or establishing that the plaintiff herself was negligent and thereby contributed to her own injury. For instance, a common defensive tactic is to dispute the seriousness of the plaintiff's injury, thereby reducing damages; but the same approach, that of controverting fact questions, may be directed to each prong of the plaintiff's case. In addition, the defendant may also employ the affirmative defenses of voluntary assumption of risk and *contributory negligence*. In utilizing the defense of *voluntary assumption of risk,* the defendant attempts to prove that the plaintiff was cognizant of the danger and voluntarily chose to encounter it. A typical example is a person who, with knowledge that she may be hit by a flying puck, attends an ice hockey game. In other words, the plaintiff, either expressly or impliedly, consented to the risk of possible injury.

In contrast, the defense of contributory negligence alleges that the plaintiff's actions contributed to her own injury. Every person is charged with the legal duty to avoid exposing himself or herself to injury; that is, to exercise as much due care in regard to personal safety as would the reasonable, prudent person in the community. The defendant bears the burden of proof to establish that the plaintiff acted in violation of this standard. The common law rules of *contributory negligence* barred the plaintiff from *any* recovery if she was found to have contributed, even slightly, to her own injury. Modern courts and legislatures have tempered the harshness of this legal precept, however, through the adoption of *comparative negligence*. Under the doctrine of comparative negligence, the negligence is apportioned between the plaintiff and the defendant, with the result that the plaintiff may recover a certain portion of the damages even if she contributed to her own injury. Various jurisdictions have adopted one of the three approaches to comparative negligence. The first, the "pure" approach, allows the plaintiff to recover if she contributed to her own injury, but there is a proportional reduction in the amount of the damages. If she was 30 percent liable, then her award is reduced by 30 percent. The second, the "greater-than" approach, permits recovery so long as the defendant's negligence was greater than the plaintiff's. The third, the "equal-to" rule, bars recovery by the plaintiff if her fault is at least equal to the defendant's fault.[21] Again, the burden rests on the defendant to prove that the plaintiff's own actions caused the injury.

INTENTIONAL TORTS

Unlike torts based on negligence that involve a breach of the standard of care, intentional torts are based on willful and knowing misconduct. The tortfeasor knows or is substantially certain that her actions will result in injury either to a person or to property. To hold the defendant liable for damages, tort law does not require the tortfeasor to harbor a malicious desire to harm someone; instead, courts will imply the requisite intent if the harm suffered was the predictable result of the defendant's actions.

Intentional torts, such as assault and battery and false imprisonment, are often repeated in criminal statutes, and the tortfeasor may also be subject to criminal penalties in a separate lawsuit. Because intentional torts are more culpable than negligence, the defendant faces the possibility of greater liability. Again, the key to distinguishing intentional torts from negligence is that the tortfeasor *intentionally* performed the acts *knowing* that injury would be likely to occur. An intentional tort is considered harmful in and of itself, and the plaintiff is entitled to receive at least nominal damages and often more substantial damages without proof of any other loss than the tortious event.[22] Intentional torts encompass a wide array of actions, and only a few are discussed here.

Assault and Battery

To paraphrase a popular song, assault and battery go together like love and marriage. However, the two are separate and distinct intentional torts. *Battery* is a harmful or offensive contact with another, whereas *assault* is the apprehension of an unwanted contact with another. The former is the actual physical touching; the latter is the mental awareness of the unwanted invasion. A battery may be committed without an assault and vice versa. A person struck in the back of the head may not be aware of the attacker's presence (battery without assault), and someone who throws a punch and misses has committed assault without battery. Technically, one cannot be assaulted by words alone; there must be an accompanying physical act that places one in apprehension of impending contact.

Consent is the primary defense for the torts of assault and battery. A hockey player agrees or consents to have members of the opposing team touch him or her during the game, but it is a limited consent to legal checks and hits within the rules, not criminal assaults. Similarly, you might accept the contact as a caress from one person and yet be highly offended if a stranger touched you in the same manner. Certain persons are deemed to have a privilege to touch another; examples are a police officer making a valid arrest or a physician giving emergency treatment.[23]

False Imprisonment

The social policy underlying the tort of false imprisonment is concern about one of the most treasured of American rights: the freedom to move about freely or, in constitutional terms, one's liberty interest. The plaintiff's *prima facie* case must include proof that the defendant intentionally restrained the plaintiff's freedom against the plaintiff's will and that the plaintiff was aware of such restraint. The victim need not necessarily be incarcerated or locked behind physical barriers; impediments of the freedom to proceed on one's way, including holding one's property, are included. Moral pressure or threats of future action alone are insufficient to create the required restraints. Store security personnel who prevent an alleged shoplifter from leaving the premises are treading a very fine line, although there is some statutory and case law guidance available. Police personnel who exceed their authority in making arrests or who do so maliciously are also subject to suit for false imprisonment, but it is a defense that the defendant had legal authority to restrain the plaintiff.[24]

Infliction of Mental Distress

A person who intentionally or recklessly causes *serious* mental distress to another can be held liable for his or her actions. This tort is limited to cases involving extreme misconduct (for example, telling a mother that her child had been killed when, in fact, the tortfeasor knows the child is fine). It involves more than hurt feelings, disappointment, or worry; there must be actual and severe mental anguish resulting from the actor's outrageous conduct. Although courts traditionally required that mental distress be linked with some other tort and actual physical harm, almost all jurisdictions now recognize the infliction of mental distress as a separate tort.[25]

HOW MUCH IS THAT DOGGIE WORTH?

The plaintiff's 15-year-old poodle was euthanized because of ill-health. She "arranged for an elaborate funeral for the dog, including a headstone, an epitaph, and attendance by the plaintiff's two sisters and a friend. A casket was delivered to the funeral which, upon opening the casket, instead of the dog's body, the plaintiff found the body of a dead cat." The plaintiff filed a lawsuit claiming mental anguish and distress. Noting that "a pet is not an inanimate thing that just receives affection it also returns it" and that "a pet ... occupies a special place somewhere in between a person and a piece of personal property," the court acknowledged her distress and awarded her damages in the amount of $700.

Source: Corso v. Crawford Dog and Cat Hospital, Inc., 97 Misc.2d 530, 415 N.Y.S.2d 182 (N.Y. City Civ. Ct. 1979).

Invasion of Privacy

The concept of privacy is zealously guarded in the United States; it is protected by the courts against invasion from either the government or the private sector. In today's world, in which personal information about all persons is listed on computers that are subject to being hacked, the right to privacy is assuming even more importance. Two related torts deal with the right to be shielded from the public eye and the right to preserve one's reputation. The first, *invasion of privacy*, covers four broad areas: (1) the intentional invasion of a person's privacy, (2) the appropriation of a person's name or likeness without permission, (3) the unwarranted publication of information about an individual's private life that is not a matter of legitimate public concern, and (4) the publication of a matter that put the plaintiff in a false light that the defendant knew was false or acted with reckless disregard as to its truth.

In each instance, the test used to gauge the tortfeasor's actions is whether a reasonable person would find the act to be highly objectionable.[26] Michael Jordan, renowned member of the Basketball Hall of Fame, won a judgment in the amount of $8.9 million from a grocery store chain for using his identity without permission in an advertisement. At trial, Jordan testified that he only signs deals that are worth $10 million or more and that he earned more than $100 million in endorsements in 2014. The defendant's expert had argued that Jordan should receive only $126,900, but the Chicago federal jury disagreed. Jordan declared that "It was all just about protecting my name and my likeness" and that he would donate the net profits to Chicago charities.[27]

"WITH A LITTLE HELP FROM MY FRIENDS"©

Shana and Mia attended the same high school and were on the cheerleading squad together. They were close friends, but the relationship soured for a variety of reasons, including romantic relationships with the same boy. The situation really degenerated when Mia and another classmate painted swastikas on road signs near the home of Shana, who was Jewish. Mia was found guilty of criminal mischief and also agreed to pay damages in a companion civil hate crime case prosecuted by the state's attorney general. In retaliation, Mia's father contracted with a private publishing company to issue a book, *Help Us Get Mia*, which sought to clear his daughter's name and contained information about Shana, including, among other things, that Shana had sought psychological counseling and that she had undergone cosmetic surgery. The book was marketed in a variety of methods, including Amazon.com. Shana filed a lawsuit with several defamation, false light, and invasion of privacy claims. The trial judge held that because Shana herself had revealed on her myspace.com page that she had sought counseling and that the revelation of the plastic surgery was not highly offensive to a reasonable person, the claims should not be sustained. After all, Shana was not a recluse, and people who saw her regularly would probably know that she had undergone the surgery.

Source: Sandler v. Calcagni, 565 F. Supp. 184 (D.Me. 2008).

The second action, *defamation,* also concerns the issue of one's reputation in the community. Defamation is the injury of personal reputation in the community by derogatory or defamatory comments. There are two distinct branches of defamation: *slander,* in which the comment is spoken; and *libel,* in which it is written or is in some permanent form. The underlying public policy is the strong emphasis on protecting people from malicious or untrue attacks on their good name in the community.[28] Hefty damages are frequently requested and sometimes awarded. Clint Eastwood won $150,000 from the *National Enquirer* for the mere, albeit false, suggestion that he agreed to an interview.[29] Donald Trump filed a $5 billion lawsuit against author Timothy L. O'Brien and publisher Warner Books for understating Trump's net worth in a book; Trump lost at both trial and appellate levels.[30]

In order for the plaintiff to recover in a defamation suit, he must establish that the statement was made in the presence of a third party and that it subjected him to ridicule or contempt, lowered him in the esteem of his community, or discouraged people from associating with him. Libel is easier to prove in that the defamation is in writing, pictures, video, or something of a permanent nature. Public figures, those in the public eye, must prove an additional element; namely that the defendant made the statement either with knowledge that it was false or with a careless disregard for its truth. Exactly who is a public figure and whether one can become one involuntarily is an intriguing one; for example, Richard Jewell, the private security guard falsely accused of planting the bomb at the Atlanta Olympics, was held to be a public figure in his libel suit against the *Atlanta Journal-Constitution.*[31] The defendant may rely on one of three primary defenses: (1) that the statement is substantially true; (2) that the defendant was protected by a privilege to speak, such as that given legislators speaking on the floor of the legislature; or (3) that the plaintiff consented to the statement.[32]

Celebrities have become reluctant to file suits because the litigation further publicizes the allegations and subjects them to discovery on the same personal topics—marriage, family life, or health problems—that the story originally targeted.[33] Instead, plaintiffs' suits are claiming that the activities of the news-gathering agency prior to publication were tortious; for example, trespass, fraud, and breach of loyalty.[34]

One of the quirkier defamation cases concerned not damages to a person's reputation but instead that of beef cattle. Bovine spongiform encephalopathy, commonly known as Mad Cow Disease, was the subject of one of the segments of *The Oprah Winfrey Show* entitled "Dangerous Foods." The show featured guests from the U.S. Department of Agriculture and the National Cattleman's Beef Association who stated that U.S. beef is safe, while Howard Lyman, executive director of the Humane Society's Eating with Conscience campaign, asserted that this nation was at risk of the outbreak of the disease.[35] During the course of the segment, Oprah Winfrey exclaimed that this "just stopped me cold from eating another burger!"[36] A group of Texas cattle producers filed suit under the Texas "veggie libel" law and also claimed common law defamation and statutory libel, claiming that these statements caused the cattle market to crash.

In her opinion, U.S. District Judge Mary Lou Robinson wrote that the safety of food is a "matter of legitimate public concern. It would be difficult to conceive of any topic of discussion that could be of greater concern and interest to all Americans than the safety of the food that they eat."[37] However, she also ruled that live cattle are not perishable food as defined in the statute[38] and that as a matter of law the plaintiffs had not proven the statutory requirement that the disparaging statement be "knowingly made." Thus, the issue relating to the constitutionality of the Texas and similar statutes was removed from the suit, leaving the question open. In addition, the other claims were denied. For a defamation suit to succeed, the plaintiff must show injury to his or her personal reputation, but here none of the plaintiffs was named or even referred to by geographic area.

Intentional Torts against Property

Although property damage can and does result from negligence, the law also recognizes intentional torts directed against property interests; among these are conversion, trespass, and nuisance. *Trespass to land* occurs when a person enters the land or building of another without consent. This intrusion must be physical; that is, the trespasser must actually walk on the ground or poke a stick through a fence. But even though the damage may be as minimal as a bent blade of grass, the owner can recover because of the interference with possession of the property.[39]

Nuisance, discussed in the previous chapter, is the use of the *defendant*'s land in such a way that it interferes with the *plaintiff*'s use of his or her land. Suppose, for example, that the defendant owns a quarry where blasting occurs and the shock waves shatter the windows in the plaintiff's home or the defendant runs a chemical plant that produces a noxious odor. Courts must balance each party's right to use his or her own land as he or she chooses against the injury sustained by the other landowner. Factors to be considered in nuisance suits include the frequency of the intrusion, the value to society of the defendant's action, and the plaintiff's knowledge, if any, of the nuisance when he bought the property.[40] Even though nuisance is included here under intentional torts, the nuisance could be caused by the negligent or hazardous activities of the defendant, and therefore the plaintiff could proceed under the theories of negligence or strict liability. In addition to damages, the plaintiff in a nuisance suit may also be awarded the equitable remedy of injunction.

Personal property, as distinguished from real property or land, may also be damaged or lost. *Conversion,* then, is defined as depriving an owner of possession of tangible property. The person who borrows an item without permission or an employee who sells copies of the company's bid on a new construction project to a competitor has interfered with the owner's possession of the property and is subject to tort liability (i.e., damages) as well as criminal penalties.[41] *Trespass to chattel* occurs when the tortfeasor damages a *chattel,* which is an item of tangible, personal property such as jewels, money, or automobiles. For instance, Bill Bully intimidates his classmate Stephen into allowing Bill to ride

Stephen's bicycle by breaking the headlight. Bill has damaged or impaired the bicycle, which is trespass to a chattel, and has also committed conversion by interfering with Stephen's possession of the bicycle.

"LET'S SING A SONG TO GRANDMA"©[a]

Jordan Zeidman sued his mother, Shirley Zeidman, for failure to turn over his Bar Mitzvah gift from his grandmother, Rachel Steinfeld. Neither Steinfeld nor Shirley had been invited to the Bar Mitzvah but attended anyway, and at the celebration Steinfeld, known as Baba to the family, promised her grandson that she would give him $5000 "just like I gave to your brother and sister" in front of Shirley. Jordan moved from his mother's house at approximately the same time because of their "uneasy" relationship and had remained estranged from her. Several years later, he brought suit. While his grandmother denied giving him the money directly or giving it to his mother, her testimony did confirm that she had given money to Jordan's siblings. At trial, bank documents were admitted to evidence that included a handwritten note indicating that the writer owed Jordan for his college fund and that the debt included "+$5000 from Baba." Jordan identified the handwriting as his mother's, and Shirley said it could be her handwriting, but that she had not received any money from her mother to give to Jordan. The judge decided in favor of Jordan and held Shirley liable for both conversion and unjust enrichment. With interest and court costs, the estimated value of the judgment was approximately $12,000.[b]

Sources: [a] Arthur Rubenstein, "The Grandparents Song," American Grandparents Association, http://www.grandparents.com/grandkids/activities-games-and-crafts/the-grandparents-song (visited December 28, 2015).
[b] Andrew Denney, "Mother Owes Son $5000 Bar Mitzvah Gift From 'Baba,' Judge-Says," *New York Law Journal*, http://www.newyorklawjournal.com/id=1202735851686/Mother-Owes-Son-5000-Bar-Mitzvah-Gift-From-Baba-Judge-Says (visited December 28, 2015).

Interestingly, the ancient common law tort of trespass to chattel is being rejuvenated to deal with the most modern technology of the Internet and spamming. *Spamming* is the "practice of sending bulk unsolicited commercial electronic mail (e-mail)."[42] Under the practice of spamming, each user could be subjected to daily inundations of unwanted e-mail. Numerous complaints by consumers have prompted Internet providers to take action against the spammers. CompuServe, a large online service provider, first demanded that Cyber Promotions, a notorious sender of unsolicited advertisements, cease the spamming and even tried to screen out the spam through software programmers. Cyber Promotions evaded these filters and continued to send the unwanted e-mail. CompuServe then filed suit and won an injunction against Cyber Promotions based on the common law tort of trespass to chattel.[43] The Court found that even electronic signals generated and received by computers constituted a trespass or unauthorized interference and use of another's property. Cyber Promotions also unsuccessfully defended itself against litigation based on economic torts, particularly interference with business relations.[44]

Unfair Competition or Interference with Commercial or Economic Relations

This ancient tort dating from Roman law involves interference with contractual relationships or prospects for economic advantage. Courts favor free competition among businesses and individuals; however, there are certain activities that are not legally accepted business practices. These include trademark infringement by using another company's trademark as one's own or by designing one's product container so as to mislead the consumer into believing that one's product is actually that of another, established company. Improperly obtaining trade secrets (items not in the public domain) by industrial espionage or by breach of confidence is also actionable.[45]

This tort may be filed whenever there is intentional and unjustified interference with the business relationships or economic interests of the plaintiff. "The interference torts always involve three persons—the plaintiff, a person with whom he has a valuable economic relationship, and the defendant who disrupts that relationship."[46] For example, a professional New York ballet company that improperly entices a premier ballerina to leave the Salt Lake City ballet company may be liable for the resulting loss of profits because of poor ticket sales. The courts have held that labor is a "property" interest within the constitutional provision of "life, liberty, and property" although there is no constitutional right to have a job. Employers who act improperly in regard to current or past employees may be liable under this tort. To illustrate: an employer who retaliates against an employee who refuses social contact or who is a so-called whistle-blower may be liable for interference with economic relations if there is some particular public policy against discharge; however, most courts reject the claims of at-will employees even though the employer terminated the person in bad faith or with bad motives.[47]

Defenses

There are many other causes of action in tort law—including fraud, malicious prosecution, and alienation of affection—that permit the plaintiff to recover damages for the defendant's intentional infliction of injury. Each theory carries with it specific defenses that are applicable only to it. However, there are defensive tactics that are common to some, if not all, intentional torts. The defendant will initially attack and seek to rebut the plaintiff's *prima facie* case, namely those facts and elements that the plaintiff must prove in order to succeed at trial. The second front on which the defendant will do battle is the presentation of the general defenses; for example, the defendant would allege that the plaintiff consented to the action (that a football player agreed to be struck during the game) or that the defendant had a privilege to take the action (that the firefighter trespassed on the land in order to put out a fire that was threatening other property). The third line of attack is the particular defense that is linked to a specific tort. For example, the defendant in an assault and battery case may counter with the argument that he struck the plaintiff only to protect and defend himself or another against the plaintiff's aggression.

STRICT LIABILITY

We have previously used the concept of fault as one of the distinguishing marks between intentional torts and negligence. In the former, the tortfeasor who knows and intends the consequences of the act is found liable for the injury it causes, and in the latter, the person who fails to exhibit ordinary care or who is reckless toward the welfare of others is required to make good on the damage that was inflicted. However, *fault,* in the eyes of the law, is not synonymous with moral blame. Instead, it implies that the actor has not lived up to the standard of conduct imposed by society.

Originally, the law would not impose liability on the tortfeasor unless it found "fault." However, courts, in the familiar traditions of common law, have developed the doctrine of "strict liability" whereby the tortfeasor may be responsible for the loss or injury of another even if there has been no violation of the reasonable standard of conduct. Legislatures ratified the theory through statutory enactment.

The concept of strict liability was initially applied against the owners of animals such as cattle that escaped and damaged another's property. Owners of cats and dogs were not held liable for trespass but only for personal injuries caused by domestic animals unless the keeper of the animal was aware or should have been aware that the animal is abnormally dangerous, the rule today.[48] Strict liability has been expanded to cover hazardous activities, such as blasting or moving explosive and inflammable liquids. Questions involved in such suits include the locale of the dangerous activity, the likelihood of high risk and substantial harm, the customs of the community regarding the activity, and the fitness of the premises or machinery for these purposes. In these situations in which neither party is at fault, society, through the courts, imposes the costs for the loss on the party who is most able to afford it.[49]

PRODUCT LIABILITY

For the past half century or so, the area of product liability, wherein the manufacturer, seller, or supplier of a defective product or instrumentality is responsible to purchasers, users, and bystanders for any injuries caused by the product, burgeoned. Permitting recovery in tort based on foreseeability of harm to the consumer, rather than founding the recovery in contract only, initially followed the same principles as strict liability. The rationales for imposing liability included that manufacturers would produce safer products if they faced possible litigation; that those who profit from the dangerous product should assume liability for damages sustained by those injured; and that consumers rely on the representations, either explicit or implicit, that the products are safe.[50] The plaintiff must prove that the product was defective as marketed in one of the following ways: (1) there was a defect in the construction of the product; (2) there was a defect in the design of the product and the foreseeable risk of harm could have been reduced by a reasonable alternative design, or (3) there were inherent dangers in the product about which the ultimate purchaser was not warned.[51] A plaintiff who suffered serious injuries as a result of food poisoning because the food was improperly canned might allege the first premise, whereas those suing a tire company because the tires on their SUVs disintegrated causing the vehicles to roll would probably proceed on the second. An example of the third cause of action would be a patient who is suing a pharmaceutical company because the company did not warn that a certain medicine aggravated high blood pressure, even though it was aware of the problem.

Other remedies are also available to a person who is injured because of a malfunction of a product. The first of these is negligence, but there is the practical problem of establishing the failure to exercise the proper standard of care. Another possibility is to proceed on a breach of warranty under contract law. The seller of a product is deemed by the law to have either expressly or impliedly warranted that the product is fit for its intended use. A plaintiff may wish to file suit against the seller for breach of the warranty and against the manufacturer for a defective product under tort law, thereby enhancing the possibility of establishing liability and obtaining damages. Because jurors are consumers too, they have awarded increasingly larger judgments against manufacturers and sellers of defective products.[52] In response, businesses have mounted successful lobbying campaigns in legislatures, and statutes have been created that limit liability and the amount that may be recovered in such litigation. For example, in a case against a pharmaceutical company involving a deceased patient and a prescribed drug, the jury award of $220 million in punitive damages was reduced to the statutory cap of $1.65 million.[53] Today, it appears that "strict liability is retained when it comes to product flaws, but negligence or something very much like it, is the test of liability when it comes to design and warning defects."[54]

GENERAL TORT DEFENSES

Two basic premises of American jurisprudence are that no one is above the law and that one is not liable for someone else's actions. This is not absolutely true in tort law, however. Tort liability may be moved from the actual tortfeasor to another (*factually* innocent) party under the theory of **vicarious liability**; thus, parents are responsible for some torts committed by their children, and employers are responsible for the torts of their employees committed during the course of employment. For example, a Methodist congregation did not have to pay damages to a satellite system repairman who was allegedly locked in a closet by the minister and held for "ransom" until the company refunded the purchase price when the court found that this action was outside the pastor's general scope of authority although the minister remained liable.[55]

The legal theory for shifting the responsibility from the employee to the employer is known as ***respondeat superior***. Vicarious liability is actually a "rule of policy, a deliberate allocation of a risk."[56] It places the monetary punishment on the person or organization with "deep pockets," the one who is profiting from the enterprise or who is able to pay larger judgments. In police misconduct cases, the plaintiff typically sues the city as well as the individual officer because the city has deeper pockets.

One of the largest employers in the country has limited liability for the torts of its employees, however. The U.S. government is subject to suit only for the negligent torts of its employees and not for intentional torts. This is an offshoot of the traditional sovereign immunity of governments, a concept that dates from the absolute monarchies in Europe. Congress and many state legislatures recognize the injustice of this immunity and have passed statutes designed to permit tort actions to be filed against the government. These same legislative bodies may also adopt special legislation allowing a particular plaintiff or class of plaintiffs to petition for redress from the courts even in the face of the immunity laws.[57] However, the U.S. Supreme Court has reinforced the immunity of states in a variety of settings ranging from protection from patent infringement suits[58] and the Americans with Disabilities Act[59] to protection from complaints from private individuals in federal administrative agencies.[60]

Other immunities exist as well. Public officials who are acting in the performance of their duties, such as judges, are also shielded from tort liability. Of course, these officials are not absolved from liability for personal torts or for torts outside the scope of job responsibility. In order to be protected from liability, the official must show that he or she is acting as a public official *and* that the activities fall within his or her job responsibilities.

CONCLUSION

The cry for tort reform has resonated throughout the land and has fallen on receptive ears, both in state legislatures and in Congress. Those who claim that the explosion of tort suits is unwarranted, that Americans are too inclined to sue on frivolous claims, and that all this litigation is too burdensome on business have successfully fought to limit the types of suits brought and to impose ceilings on judgments, particularly on punitive damages. Those plaintiffs who do file the so-called "frivolous" lawsuits essentially are fined by being required to pay the other party's court costs and attorney's fees.

Opponents of such reforms argue that innocent parties, namely the victims, should not be uncompensated for the wrongs done to them and that the wrongdoers should be forced to assume responsibility for their actions. They point to enhanced safety in consumer products that is the direct result of tort litigation as well as protection of personal autonomy in such areas as privacy. Furthermore, businesses also benefit from tort law through recoveries for loss of trade secrets and interference in employee relationships.

Tort law closely resembles criminal law in its effort to avenge the victim. In criminal law, the punishment as set by the state is incarceration or a fine, which is funneled into state coffers; in tort law, however, the money flows to the victim. The social policy that is the foundation for tort law focuses on compensating the innocent victim, in a personal way, for injuries caused by third parties, a goal most find admirable. The public debate centers primarily on who should set that policy—the juries in the courts that are deciding individual cases, or the legislature that is setting broad social policy but is more subject to lobbying by those with vested interests. Some view the trend of tort reform with horror, some with rejoicing, and some with neutrality, regarding it as merely a mid-course adjustment in the fluid field of tort law.

NOTES

1. William P. Statsky, *Torts: Personal Injury Litigation*, 4th edn (Albany, NY: West/ Thomson Learning, 2001), pp. 3–4.
2. Warren St. John, "New Breed of Lawyer Gives Every Dog His Day in Court," *New York Times*, September 3, 2006 § 9, p. 1.
3. Dennis Henigan, "Gun Control Through Tort Law," *Texas Lawyer*, September 9, 1991.
4. Martin Weinstein, *Summary of American Law* (Rochester, NY: The Lawyer's Co-operative/Bancroft-Whitney, 1988), pp. 503–504.
5. Dan B. Dobbs, *The Law of Torts*, vol. I (St. Paul, MN: West Group, 2001), p. 269.
6. Ibid., pp. 353–354.
7. A.P. Herbert, *Uncommon Law* (London: Bibliophile Books, 1986), pp. 2–3.
8. *Rudes v. Gottschalk*, 159 Tex. 552, 324 S.W.2d 201 (Tex. 1959).
9. *Cook Consultants Inc. v. Larson*, 700 S.W.2d 231 (Tex. App.–Dallas, 1985).
10. Dan B. Dobbs, *The Law of Torts*, vol. II (St. Paul, MN: West Group, 2001), pp. 853–876.
11. Dobbs, vol. I, pp. 591–620.
12. *Anderson v. State, Dept. of Natural Resources*, 693 N.W.2d 181 (Minn., 2005).
13. F.M. English, *Annotation, Liability to Patron of Scenic Railway, Roller Coaster, or Miniature Railway*, 66 A.L.R. 689 (1959).
14. William L. Prosser, *Handbook of the Law of Torts*, 4th edn (St. Paul, MN: West, 1971), p. 236.
15. W. Page Keeton, Dan B. Dobbs, Robert E. Keeton, and David G. Owen, *Prosser and Keeton on the Law of Torts* (St. Paul, MN: West, 1984), p. 264.
16. *Palsgraf v. Long Island R. Co.*, 248 N.Y. 339, 162 N.E. 99 (N.Y. 1928).
17. *Garner v. Prescott*, 234 S.W.2d 704 (Tex. Civ. App.–Eastland, 1950).
18. Dobbs, vol. I, pp. 412–430.
19. Dobbs, vol. II, pp. 803–820.
20. Richard A. Epstein, "A Theory of Strict Liability," *Journal of Legal Studies* 2 (1973), p. 204.
21. Dobbs, vol. I, pp. 494–507.
22. Dobbs, vol. II, p. 1047.
23. Dobbs, vol. I, pp. 216–223.
24. William P. Statsky, *Torts: Personal Injury Litigation*, 3rd edn (St. Paul, MN: West, 1995), pp. 407–411.
25. Dobbs, vol. II, pp. 828–829.
26. Dobbs, vol. II, pp. 1197–1212.
27. Kim Janssen, "Jordan Says 'It Was Never About the Money' After $8.9M Jury Award," *Chicago Tribune*, August 21, 2015.
28. Dobbs, vol. II, pp. 1117–1120.
29. Michael P. McDonald, "It's Alive! Libel Law Arises from the Dead," *Texas Lawyer*, June 11, 1990, p. 38.
30. "Trump Sues Writer, Publisher for Misrepresenting Wealth," *The Entertainment Litigation Reporter*, March 29, 2006; *Trump v. O'Brien*, 29 A.3d 109, 422 N.J. Super. 540 (2011).
31. *Atlanta Journal-Constitution v. Jewell*, 555 S.E.2d 175 (Ga. Ct. App., 2001), *cert. denied, Jewell v. Cox Enterprises, Inc.*, 537 U.S. 814 (2002).
32. Dobbs, vol. II, pp. 1147–1186.
33. Michael Higgins, "Public Relief," *ABA Journal* 83 (December 1997), p. 68.

34. Charles C. Sheim, "Trash Tort or Trash TV? *Food Lion, Inc. v. ABC, Inc.* and Tort Liability of the Media for Newsgathering," 72 St. John's L. Rev. 185 (1998).

35. *Texas Beef Group v. Oprah Winfrey,* 11 F. Supp. 2d 858 (N.D. Tex.–Amarillo Div. 1998).

36. "Oprah Sued Again over 1996 Show on Mad Cow Disease," *The Legal Intelligencer,* April 20, 1998, p. 4.

37. *Texas Beef Group,* at 862.

38. "Perishable Food Product Means a Food Product of Agriculture or Aquaculture that is Sold or Distributed in a Form that will Perish or Decay Beyond Marketability Within a Limited Period of Time." False Disparagement of Perishable Food Products Act, Tex. Civ. Prac. & Rem. Code, ch. 96.

39. Dobbs, vol. I, pp. 95–120.

40. *Commerce Oil Refining Corp. v. Miner,* 281 F.2d 465 (1st Cir. 1960).

41. Dobbs, vol. I, pp. 125–154.

42. Anne Hawley, "Taking Spam Out of Your Cyberspace Diet: Common Law Applied to Bulk Unsolicited Advertising Via Electronic Mail," 66 UMKC L. Rev. 381 (1997).

43. *Compuserv v. Cyber Promotions,* 962 F. Supp. 1015 (S.D. Ohio 1997).

44. *Concentric Network Corporation v. Wallace,* No. C-96 (N.D. Cal. Nov. 5, 1996) as cited in Hawley, p. 409.

45. Dobbs, vol. II, pp. 1307–1310.

46. Ibid., p. 1257.

47. Ibid., pp. 1290–1291.

48. Ibid., pp. 942–947.

49. Ibid., pp. 950–951, 964–968.

50. *McPherson v. Buick Motor Co.,* 217 N.Y. 382, 111 N.E. 1050 (N.Y. 1916); Dobbs, vol. II, pp. 977–978.

51. Restatement Third, Products Liability, § 2.

52. Dobbs, vol. II, pp. 977–1037.

53. "Vioxx Judgment," *Texas Lawyer,* July 3, 2006, p. 3.

54. Ibid., p. 977.

55. *Hendricks v. Bauer,* 709 S.W. 2d 774 (Tex. App.—Beaumont, 1986).

56. Prosser, p. 459.

57. Peter H. Schuck, *Suing Government* (New Haven, CT: Yale University Press, 1983), pp. 29–53.

58. *College Sav. Bank v. Fla. Prepaid Postsecondary Ed. Expense Bd.,* 527 U.S. 666 (1999).

59. *Board of Trustees of the University of Alabama v. Garrett,* 531 U.S. 356 (2001).

60. *Federal Maritime Commission v. South Carolina Ports Authority,* 535 U.S. 743 (2002).

Contracts

Contracts are binding agreements that have legal consequences and can be enforced in court. Noted contract scholar Samuel Williston defined a contract as "a promise, or set of promises, for breach of which the law gives a remedy, or the performance of which the law in some way recognizes as a duty."[1] Contracts provide stability and allow society to carry out its transactions in an orderly fashion; however, contracts are not limited to serious business ventures. For example, siblings who enter into bargains to divide the household chores between them are creating contracts. While some contracts are rather elaborate and formal, others are informal and even implied.

Ensuring stability and certainty is the quintessential goal of contracts. Those who enter into these agreements do so with the knowledge that failure to live up to their part of the bargain may result in a court order for specific performance or for monetary damages as well as damage to their reputation in the community. The importance of contract stability is emphasized by Article I, § 10 of the U.S. Constitution, which provides that "No State shall … pass any … Law impairing the Obligation of Contracts." In earlier days, freedom of contract was virtually uncircumscribed by government restrictions; people contracted as they pleased, with the only real restraint being that contracts for illegal purposes were not enforceable by the courts. For example, government contracts secured by bribing a public official cannot be enforced by the corporation offering the bribe. That rule is still valid; however, other restrictions have been added. Consider, for example, employment contracts that are governed by regulations barring discrimination, requiring minimum wages, limiting hours, and providing workers' compensation, to name only a few.

As society becomes more complex and more litigious, legislatures, administrative agencies, and courts at all levels of government are placing greater restrictions on the freedom to contract. Contract law permeates our daily lives in such diverse areas as sales, credit, employment, and various other commercial transactions.

CONTRACTUAL TERMS OF ART

The field of contracts is an area of law in which mysterious terms of art abound. Contracts may be characterized as express or implied; bilateral or unilateral; executory or executed; and *void, voidable,* and unenforceable. It will be helpful for you to have some understanding of these terms as you learn about contracts.

An *express contract* is one in which the terms are stated by the parties; it may be either an oral or a written contract. An example would be your agreement to buy a class ring for the sum of $300 under a written contract. An *implied contract* is one that is inferred from the conduct of the parties. Your conduct in entering a restaurant and ordering a meal gives rise to an implied contract that you will pay the price stated on the menu for the food, even though you may not expressly say so to the waiter when you order. In each case you have entered into a contract, and the only difference is in the type of evidence necessary to establish the contract.[2]

A *bilateral contract* is one in which the parties exchange promises to do some future act. You agree with the car dealer that you will pay for your new Jaguar when you take delivery next week. Each of you has promised to do something in the future: the dealer to deliver the car and you to pay for it. In contrast, a *unilateral contract* is one in which one party acts immediately in response to the *offer.* Assume that you tender a monetary reward for the return of your much-loved, but lost, dog Sebastian. Sterlin finds Sebastian and returns him to you. The response is in the form of immediate action rather than a mutual exchange of promises.[3]

An *executory contract* is one in which some or all of the terms are uncompleted—our car deal, for example. An *executed contract,* then, is one in which all the terms have been completed. You have eaten your meal and paid your bill at the restaurant or paid Sterlin for returning Sebastian to his happy home.[4]

The terms "void, voidable, and unenforceable" are relevant in situations where there is a *breach of contract* or when the one party fails to comply with the terms of the agreement. A *void contract* is a nullity from its beginning, and damages do not result. For example, a contract to murder someone is void, and the person making the "hit" could not successfully maintain a lawsuit to collect his or her salary. On the other hand, a *voidable contract* is one that is binding until it is disaffirmed or canceled by the party with the authority to do so. In many ways, marriage is a contract that either party may rescind by obtaining a divorce.[5] Other contracts are deemed to be unenforceable. *Unenforceable contracts* are those that meet the basic common law elements for contracts but lack some other additional legal requirement such as being signed in front of a notary public; in some instances, the courts will nevertheless enforce the agreement.[6]

FORMATION OF CONTRACTS

The requirements for formulating a contract appear to be relatively uncomplicated. First, there must be two or more parties, each of whom has the legal *capacity* to enter into an agreement. Second, there must be an offer and acceptance, or consent, which reflects a mutual understanding between the parties about the essential elements of the contract. Third, the agreement must be supported by consideration or obligation.[7] Determining the existence of each of these elements is not as simple as it might appear at first glance.

ELEMENTS OF CONTRACTS

- An agreement
- Between two or more parties with capacity
- Based on genuine assent
- Supported by consideration
- Does not contravene principles of law
- In writing if required by the Statute of Frauds

Parties

Two or more parties must be involved in a contract.[8] One cannot enter into a legally enforceable contract with oneself. Parties to such agreements include both natural and *artificial persons* (corporations). The law creates a legal fiction that corporations are persons.[9] This device allows corporations to sue and be sued and to conduct business transactions as entities without involving individual shareholders.

Each party involved in the contract must have the legal capacity to enter into the agreement.[10] Incapacity may result from the age of the individual or from a party's being mentally incapable of understanding the ramifications of the contract. At common law, a person under the age of 21 was considered an infant or a minor. Today, many states establish the *age of majority* at age 18, the age at which citizens may vote. State laws often provide that minors may enter into contracts but that they retain the ability to withdraw from the agreement.[11] Assume that Phillip, aged 17, buys a $750 music system, but on bringing it home and discussing the matter with his parents, he decides to return the stereo to the store. As a minor he may disaffirm the contract, and the store must take the stereo back if there is a timely disclaimer on his part. Minors are under an obligation to return any consideration received under the contract. The fact that minors may avoid contracts causes many people to refuse to contract with them. Minors who contract for necessities such as food, shelter, and clothing are not usually permitted to avoid such agreements after the goods or services have been delivered; however, the minor is liable only for the reasonable value of the goods or services, which may not be the same as the contract price.[12]

Emancipation, or the removal of one's disabilities as a minor, can occur by reaching the statutory age of emancipation, by court order, by entry into the armed forces, or by marriage, according to state law provisions regarding emancipation.

Mental competency is another issue relating to capacity. The mental capacity to contract may be defined as the ability to understand the nature and effects of the business being transacted. Some people, such as the severely mentally infirm, are not capable of understanding the effects and obligations of contracts. They are generally released from any contract they enter.[13] On the other hand, courts are hesitant to intervene in contractual relationships and are reluctant to release people from contracts merely because they were foolish for entering into them. For example, a person who abuses credit cards and charges large amounts that he or she will be unable to pay will not be protected simply because of bad judgment. Adults are presumed to have the legal capacity to contract, and those seeking to be excused from contractual obligations on this ground would be required to prove that they lacked legal capacity. It is incumbent on the competent party to determine the legal capacity of the other party.[14]

Mutual Assent

Cases less frequently turn on the question of whether there are two parties to the contract or whether the parties had legal capacity than on the issue of mutual assent. The question is whether the two parties have a true "meeting of the minds"; that is, the parties must reach an agreement on the same bargain on the same terms.[15] The mutual agreement is generally measured on an objective standard, and the subjective intent of the parties is usually irrelevant. Courts examine the language of the contract and construe it by the usual meanings of the words. A noted jurist, Learned Hand, clearly stated this principle of judicial construction when he wrote:

> If, however, it were proved by twenty bishops that either party, when he used the words, intended something else than the usual meaning which the law imposes upon them, he would still be held, unless there was some mutual mistake, or something else of that sort.[16]

For this reason, complex contracts often contain sections that clearly define certain terms. It is critical that both parties have the same understanding of the terms. Following the collapse of towers at the World Trade Center (WTC) on September 11, 2001, Larry Silverstein, owner of 11 percent of the lease, and the companies insuring the complex disagreed on the interpretation of a single phrase—"per occurrence"—in the insurance binder. Silverstein argued that the attack was really two events because two planes were involved, while the insurance companies argued that the destruction was part of the same terrorist plot. Their position was bolstered because in the binder the term "per occurrence" was defined as "any one loss, disaster or casualty or series of losses, disasters, or casualties arising out of one event ... from the perils of civil commotion ... one event shall be construed to be all losses arising during a continuous period of 72 hours." The difference in the interpretation would be worth $3.55 billion to Silverstein as the buildings were insured for $3.55 billion "per occurrence."[17] One jury considering the matter found for the insurance companies, and another ruled in favor of Silverstein.[18] Property owners along coasts destroyed by hurricanes have fought a similar battle in that many homeowners' insurance policies covered only damage caused by wind, not water, and the insurance companies claimed that the bulk of the destruction was caused by floodwaters, tidal surges, or wind-driven water rather than wind, while the owners, looking at total destruction of their homes, felt that it is impossible to segregate the harm and that the insurance companies should pay.[19] The test used by the courts to measure the party's intention is whether a reasonable person in the position of the other party would also interpret the words and actions in the same light.

The mutual understanding usually follows negotiations in which parties argue back and forth as to the terms of the contract. For example, assume that Charlotte Starr is a nationally known athlete and winner of her sport's highest honor and that she wishes to parlay that recognition into a lucrative professional career. Starr and the team owners may enter into extended talks about the terms of the contract. The team owners may offer a $120 million compensation package, with a yearly salary of $2 million, and the remainder to be paid into a pension plan if Starr plays for the team for a period of five years. Starr may counter with an offer to play for $170 million and a yearly salary of $5 million, with the other terms to remain the same. Such bargaining may continue until a compromise acceptable to both is reached. The final contract could have Starr playing for $150 million with a yearly salary of $3.5 million, a no-cut provision, and a percentage of the team's profits. When one party (the *offeree*) accepts the terms offered by the other (the *offeror*), the negotiations are completed and the contract may then be drafted in final form.

Genuine assent is not present when one party's agreement is based on duress, undue influence, fraud, innocent misrepresentation, or mistake, and generally results in a voidable contract. Duress occurs when a party acts with knowledge and awareness of all the provisions of the contracts but acts because of a high degree of coercion that causes loss of free will, as, for example, when David signs a contract under the threat that he will lose his job or his very substantial inheritance if he does not agree. This goes far beyond the high-pressure tactics from sales personnel.[20] Undue influence takes place when the will of the dominant party is substituted for that of another and creates an unfair bargain.[21] Decades after his death in 1976, comedian Groucho Marx's situation is still employed as an example of undue influence by his companion and caregiver Erin Fleming. Fleming, who had abusive tendencies and was 50 years younger than Marx (who had suffered a debilitating stroke), isolated him from his children and manipulated him with tranquilizers and was the recipient of very expensive gifts and the major beneficiary of his estate.[22]

Similar allegations arose in regard to Harper Lee, author of *To Kill a Mockingbird,* and her attorney Tonja B. Carter. Carter reported that she found the manuscript of an earlier work *Go Set a Watchman* while investigating the contents of Lee's safety deposit box and later negotiated the publication of the work. Before Lee's death in 2016, Carter acted as a gatekeeper for access to the elderly Lee who resided in an assisted living facility because of her various infirmities, including difficulty in seeing and hearing. She also served as Lee's lawyer, spokesperson, and trustee as well as having power of attorney for Lee and controlling her nonprofit organization. Concerns about the relationship even led state officials to investigate whether Lee had been pressured into publishing *Watchman*; they later found the allegations to be unfounded.[23]

Fraud may occur in the execution of the document such as a forged signature or by fraudulent misrepresentations made to induce a person to enter into a contract.[24] To illustrate, the seller has a diamond appraised by a reputable dealer and is advised that it is .75 carat but sells it to Paul as a full carat with full knowledge of the weight of the jewel. Now assume that the same seller follows the same procedure but is advised that the stone is 1 carat and sells it to Paul as such. When Paul has the stone appraised, he is told that it is .75 carat; this is a situation of innocent misrepresentation. A mistake in contract law is a bona fide misunderstanding about some aspect of the contractual terms.[25] Mary and Elizabeth enter into a contract about the purchase of hockey equipment, and the contract specifies that payment is to be in dollars. Elizabeth, the Canadian, interprets the currency to be Canadian dollars while Mary, the American, thinks it is U.S. dollars.

Surprisingly, most newspaper or catalog advertisements which state that goods will be sold for a certain price do not constitute offers in this sense. Instead, they are technically considered to be an invitation for the consumer to offer to pay this price for the goods. The merchant, although not required to have an unlimited supply of the items, is expected to have enough to meet the demand; if he intentionally lacks the needed number and tries to substitute another, he may run afoul of certain consumer protection laws. The language of some advertisements does constitute an offer. An offer from a corporation facing a hostile takeover to buy its own stock at $30 per share is interpreted as an offer. The issue of whether the specific advertisement or circular constitutes an offer depends on the intent of the parties, the specific language, and the circumstances.[26]

Offers are often accompanied by a restriction that the offer will remain open only for a given number of hours or days. When that time has lapsed, the offer is terminated. If no time limit is provided, a reasonable time, as determined by the judge or the jury, will be imposed. Offers may also be terminated by revocation or retraction of the offer, such as when a property owner removes her home from the market. An offer may be rejected by the offeree, and that rejection must be communicated to the offeror directly.[27]

Like rejection, *acceptance* of the offer must be manifested directly to the offeror by words—either oral or written—or by action, such as performance of one's part of the contract. If the offer is to paint a house and the painter does, in fact, paint the house, that performance is considered to be acceptance of the offer. The acceptance must be in the format demanded by the offeror, if any, to be valid.[28] The person accepting the offer must be the one to whom it was directed, but a ***third-party beneficiary*** may be entitled to enforce the contract even though a stranger to the offer and acceptance.[29] A typical third-party bene-ficiary contract is one in which parents agree to pay tuition for a student to a university. The student could sue the university for failing to place her name on the roll if the fees have been paid. The student did not participate in the bargaining process, but it was the clear intent of the parties that she was the intended beneficiary of the contract, and the law therefore provides an avenue of redress for her.

Consideration

Valid contracts are accompanied by *consideration.* Consideration is not limited to money but instead is usually defined in terms of an exchange of benefits or detriments; that is, the parties agree to do something they are not legally obli-gated to do or to refrain from carrying out some activity that they are bound by law to do.[30] This consideration may include the exchange of mutual promises, such as one party agreeing to perform household tasks this week in exchange for a promise that the other party will do so next week, or the exchange of money or goods, such as trading one car for another. The consideration must be the result of the bargaining, and past consideration is not sufficient. The fact that one party did a favor for another last week is not valid consideration for this week's contract. Generally, even economically inadequate considera-tion will be sufficient to support the bargain, but the key is that both parties must suffer a detriment. Again, the courts are very hesitant to correct the fool-ish errors or bad judgment of the parties if there has been no fraud or duress involved in the bargaining.[31]

KEEP YOUR EYE ON THE PRIZE!

A Pennsylvania automobile dealer placed a new Chevrolet on the ninth hole of a golf course along with a sign that read, "HOLE-IN-ONE Wins." Amos made a hole-in-one during tournament play and attempted to claim his prize. The dealer refused to deliver the car on the grounds that the prize was intended for a different charity tournament two days before his success. The judge found for Amos on the grounds that the sign constituted an offer to award the prize and that it was accepted by Amos when he made the hole-in-one. The dealer's failure to limit the offer to the previous tournament or to remove the car and sign did not defeat the contract.[a]

An Indiana tournament sponsor advertised a $10,000 prize for hitting a hole-in-one on the first hole. Joe paid an entry fee to participate and purchased a mulligan or free shot as well; the mulligans were sold to raise additional funds and no limitations were placed on their use. Joe's first tee shot was not a hole-in-one so he used the mulligan and made a hole-in-one on his second effort. The tournament sponsors refused to pay but Joe successfully sued to claim the money because the judge found that a "mulligan" was not a term of the contract but rather a possible means of meeting the contractual term of a hole-in-one.[b]

Mary and Carolyn shared a 35-year-old friendship, and Carolyn invited Mary to join her on a trip to Las Vegas. Carolyn paid all the expenses, including providing the money for gambling. Mary claimed that Carolyn invited her because she thought that Mary was lucky, that Mary had a dream about winning on the slot machines before they ever left Texas, and that she had accepted Carolyn's offer to split the gambling proceeds 50–50. Once they arrived at the casino, Mary, who suffered from advanced arthritis and was in a wheelchair, asked Carolyn to put the money into a machine that looked like the one in her dreams. Carolyn supposedly did as asked, with the comment, "This one's for you, Puddin." The dollar slot machine paid $1908.64. Carolyn then told the casino that she was the sole winner and to pay all the proceeds to her. Unsurprisingly, Mary sued. The court found that the promises, if made, constituted sufficient consideration and ordered the case to trial.[c]

Sources: a. *Cobaugh v. Klick-Lewis, Inc.,* 385 Pa. Super. 587, 561 A. 2d 1248 (Pa. Super. Ct. 1989).
b. *Wright v. Spinks,* 722 N.E.2d 1278 (Ind. Ct. App. 2000).
c. *Iacono v. Lyons,* 16 S.W.3d 92 (Tex App.—Houston [1st Div.] 2000).

In determining the formation of a contract, courts initially look to three factors: the capacity of the parties, the offer and acceptance, and the consideration. These factors are measured by an objective-person standard, which often requires the judge or the jury to reconstruct the negotiations. This is often difficult, particularly in the case of oral contracts. Oral contracts are as valid as written contracts, with a few exceptions, as we will discuss later; and simple contracts are as valid as the most laboriously drawn ones.

Parties often enter into contracts without realizing the full ramifications of their actions; therefore, it is imperative that both parties read the entire written contract and carefully consider all aspects of it. To illustrate, suppose that Katherine buys an automobile from a dealer with the understanding that she is to make monthly payments to him. However, a provision may allow *assignment* (a present transfer of a contractual interest to a third party) of the contract to a financial institution or to someone else without the permission of the obligor. Katherine could owe the bank or some other unknown party; this frequently occurs with notes for consumer goods, which may be considered assets of the business and are often sold. Another example would be hiring a particular carpenter and then discovering that she had assigned the contract to someone else. In order to avoid the possibility of assignment, the contract should clearly state that it is not assignable.[32]

BREACH OF CONTRACT

Defenses

Failure to carry out the terms of one's obligations may result in a lawsuit for a *breach of contract*, defined as any failure to perform a contractual duty. Just as in other areas of law, certain recognized defenses are available that may protect one from liability for breach. Two of these excuses for nonperformance are that the contract contravenes the Statute of Frauds and that the contract is for illegal purposes. In addition, a party may claim *repudiation* or impossibility of performance as protection from legal liability. Repudiation is when one party withdraws from performing the contract based either on his positive statement to the other party that he is unwilling or unable to perform or on a voluntary affirmative act that makes his or her compliance impossible or seemingly impossible. If the act is involuntary and renders contract performance impossible, then the party may be relieved of the contractual obligations without liability. For example, an opera diva who permanently loses her voice due to an accident may repudiate future singing contracts with impunity because the loss of her voice was involuntary rather than voluntary. If the repudiation occurs before the other party has suffered any detriment, there is total protection; however, if the other party has complied or changed positions in reliance on the contract, the court may assess damages. Voluntarily failing to perform under the contract or claiming an impossibility that is the result of one's own acts may result in an award of damages.[33]

Other defenses involve the genuineness of the mutual assent. If there has been an inadvertent, material mistake of fact the contract may be voided, depending on the stage in the transaction at which the mistake is discovered. Recession of the contract will be denied to one who is negligent if the other party is innocent and changed positions in reliance of the contract.[34] The same policy is applied to someone who "having the capacity to understand a written document who reads it, or, without reading it or having it read to him, signs it" is then "bound by his signature." This is known as the duty to read.[35]

Litigation involving computers and software illustrates the issue because of warranties sealed in the carton with the computers or the shrink-wrapped programs on disks or CDs which carry a warning that merely opening the package means that one has consented to the licensing requirements; in each instance, there is no opportunity to read and accept or reject the terms. At least in clicking "I agree" to download a program or game one can make an informed decision. In *ProCD Inc. v. Zeidenberg*,[36] the Seventh Circuit declared that "terms inside a box of software bind consumers who use a box of software after an opportunity to read the terms and to reject them by returning the product."[37] In the subsequent case of *Hill v. Gateway 2000 Inc.*, Rich and Enza Hill telephoned Gateway and placed an order for a computer that was later delivered. Inside the box was a contract that provided for arbitration. The Hills kept the computer for more than 30 days before complaining to the company about the parts and performance and then filed a class action lawsuit against Gateway. The company claimed the suit was barred because the terms in the carton required arbitration first and that the contract went into effect when the Hills did not return the computer within the specified 30 days. The Hills argued that they should not be bound by a contract that they were unaware of until after the computer arrived. The court disagreed and held that the terms of the contract were enforceable; however, other courts have determined that the package terms are not binding, thus leaving the matter unsettled.[38] If fraud or duress is involved in the execution, the courts may nullify the contract, and tort remedies may also be available. However, a contract induced by fraud is void if the misrepresentation is made knowingly.[39] Allegations of this nature allow juries to examine the negotiation process, despite the fact that courts normally do not go behind the contract itself.[40]

Remedies for Breach of Contract

The most common remedy for breach of contract is for the court to assess monetary damages against the wrongdoer. Many contracts provide for liquidated damages; that is, a predetermined sum to be paid in the event of nonperformance. Compensatory damages, as discussed in Chapter 4, are designed to place the aggrieved party in the economic position in which he would have been had the contract been performed; they constitute the most frequent type of award. Punitive damages, those designed to punish intentional or malicious wrongdoers by heaping additional costs on them, are generally not awarded in traditional contract cases.[41] In contract law, the plaintiff may recover those damages that "may fairly and reasonably be considered … arising naturally, i.e., according to the usual course of things, from such breach of contract itself" as well as those damages "such as may reasonably be supposed to have been in the contemplation of both parties, at the time they made the contract, as the probable result of the breach of it."[42]

The result is that damages will be assessed only for the harm that was foreseeable when the contract was made. A corollary legal rule imposes an affirmative duty on the aggrieved party to mitigate damages stemming from the breach and not to sit idly by allowing the damages to mount. Assume that the G.F. Hope Corporation is a wholesale turkey distributor which buys turkeys from locals to sell in New York to a world-renowned restaurant. The restaurant closes unexpectedly and breaches the contract to purchase the turkeys. G.F. Hope must take steps to sell the turkeys elsewhere or to otherwise preserve them rather than intentionally allowing them to sit on the shipping dock and die and then claiming the entire loss. The courts do not look kindly on such procrastination and may reduce the amount of damages awarded; on the other hand, the aggrieved party is required to take only reasonable steps that do not lead to undue expense or humiliation.[43]

Damages are the traditional remedy for contract breaches; however, because damages are not always adequate recompense, equity has stepped in to formulate two additional remedies. The first is *promissory estoppel,* which is applied in cases in which the promisee has substantially changed positions in reliance on a gratuitous promise from the promisor, and the promisor is now claiming inadequate consideration as an excuse for nonperformance. The court will step in to prevent injustice and to force the promisor to comply with the terms of the agreement.[44] To illustrate: Grandfather promises John that if he will return to the family ranch and run it, then Grandfather will give the ranch to John. John abandons his very lucrative career as a software designer to move back to the property, but after a period of ten years Grandfather has failed to deed the ranch to John. John could then initiate a lawsuit under this theory.

Another remedy for breach of contract is specific performance; that is, the court orders the party breaking the contract to comply with its terms. It is particularly appropriate when an item with unique attributes is involved. To illustrate: suppose that you contract to buy the helmet that Richard Petty wore during the race for his last and 200th National Association for Stock Car Automobile Racing victory in 1984. A helmet that Petty wore in another race or one worn by a different driver in the same race is not an acceptable substitute. The remedy for breach is for the court to order the seller to deliver the Petty helmet or to void the contract if compliance is not possible. Specific performance is not the proper remedy for breach of employment contracts. A musical group that declines to honor its contract to perform on a certain date in a certain city because of a more lucrative offer could not be placed under a court order to perform that evening. Such an order would resemble involuntary servitude or slavery, which is prohibited by the Constitution; the court could enter an injunction prohibiting the group from performing elsewhere however, as well as awarding damages to the concert backers.[45]

RULES OF CONSTRUCTION

Despite the well-known need for clarity in contract language, the terms of contracts are frequently disputed. Courts and, to some degree, legislatures have devised tools to deal with these controversies. One of the foremost tools is the Statute of Frauds that requires certain contracts to be in writing in order to be enforceable; this is contrary to the general rule that oral contracts are valid. Depending on state law, a writing is required when the contract involves any of the following: (1) contracts affecting interests in land, such as the sale of real property or the creation of a lien; (2) prenuptial agreements or agreements made in contemplation of marriage; (3) contracts that cannot be performed in one year, such as a construction project that will take three years to complete; (4) agreements involving a surety, such as when the executor of an estate repays the debts of the deceased from her own pocket; and (5) contracts involving the sale of goods valued over a set amount [$500 under the *Uniform Commercial Code* (UCC)]. If such agreements are not written and signed by the parties the contract is generally unenforceable, although equity may step in to provide remedies.[46] However, recognizing the realities of modern commercial activity, Congress passed the Electronic Signatures in Global and National Commerce Act (E-Sign), and most states have adopted the Uniform Electronic Transactions Act whereby electronic records and signatures will satisfy the law's requirements but only for business or commercial transactions.[47]

If the contract is written, the *parol evidence rule* is a critical rule of construction. It provides that only those terms stated in the contract will be considered; that is, the court will look at only what is contained within the four corners of the document. Earlier negotiations or contemporaneous oral agreements are irrelevant. The purpose of the parol evidence rule and the Statute of Frauds is to ensure certainty and stability in contractual relationships.[48]

Courts have developed other rules of construction to help them when the terms of contracts are not clear; an example of such a rule is the requirement that language will be interpreted in its usual meaning or in accordance with previous court decisions if the interpretation cannot be determined from the contract. Courts sometimes strain to interpret conflicting terms as consistent and to give validity to as much of a contract as possible. Courts may even provide missing terms of contracts if they can derive them from the facts of the cases. The policy position is to uphold contracts, and courts are sometimes quite creative in determining the intent of the parties or in dealing with ambiguities in contracts in order to reach that goal.[49] Or, as one judge stated:

> The fact that a contract is incomplete, presents interpretive questions, bristles with unresolved contingencies, and in short has as many holes as a Swiss cheese does not make it unenforceable for indefiniteness. Otherwise there would be few enforceable contracts ... We once decided a case in which the contract exceeded 2,000 pages yet the dispute that gave rise to the suit had not been anticipated (or, if anticipated, provided for) ... If contracting parties had to provide for every contingency that might arise, contract negotiations would be interminable. Contracts can be shorter and simpler and cheaper when courts stand ready to fill gaps and resolve ambiguities in the minority of contracts that get drawn into litigation.[50]

Unfortunately, breach of contracts, with resulting litigation, is a frequent occurrence. Some of these cases are quite complex, requiring years to complete and involving the expenditure of many thousands, if not millions, of dollars on discovery and attorneys' fees. Other contract suits, such as a creditor suing someone for failure to make a car payment, are relatively easy to resolve. Nevertheless, both types of lawsuits exact a toll on the judicial system in terms of the time both of court personnel and of other litigants, whose cases remain on the docket unheard.

UNIFORM COMMERCIAL CODE

Contracts are the core of most business transactions, and the law governing such agreements is primarily case law that has developed over hundreds of years. However, various legislative bodies have entered the fray and codified many of these rules. Congress has approved a treaty, namely the United Nations Convention for International Sale of Goods (CISG), governing international sales.[51] The Uniform Commercial Code (UCC) is an example of a set of laws governing commercial transactions that has been enacted by state legislatures. The initial drafts are proposed by the National Conference of Commissioners on Uniform State Laws and the American Law Institute, but each legislature may modify the provisions when adopting the Code. The goals of the Code are "(1) to simplify, clarify, and modernize the law governing commercial transactions; (2) to permit the continued expansion of commercial practices through custom, usage, and agreement of the parties, and (3) to make uniform the law among the various jurisdictions.[52] In order to facilitate the uniformity of statutes governing commercial transactions, relatively few changes have been enacted by state legislatures. The provisions may be updated such as permitting electronic filing of documents. However, the changes must then be adopted by the individual state legislatures.

The UCC contains 11 substantive articles:

Article 1.	General Provisions
Article 2.	Sales
Article 2A.	Leases
Article 3.	Negotiable Instruments
Article 4.	Bank Deposits
Article 4A.	Funds Transfer
Article 5.	Letters of Credit
Article 6.	Bulk Transfers and Bulk Sales
Article 7.	Warehouse Receipts, Bills of Lading, and Other Documents of Title
Article 8.	Investment Securities
Article 9.	Secured Transactions

Many of the articles deal only with commercial transactions between merchants, but several articles are relevant, in varying degrees, to the average consumer. For instance, the Uniform Law Commissioners describe Article 9 as perhaps "the most important of the eleven" because it governs transactions "(other than finance lease) that couples a debt with a creditor's interest in a debtor's personal property. If the debtor defaults, the creditor may repossess and sell the property (generally called collateral) to satisfy the debt."[53]

However, a note of warning must be issued at this point. The UCC does not cover all commercial transactions, nor does it render contract law obsolete. The UCC is concerned primarily with the sale of goods and does not cover various service and real-estate contracts. Previously developed common law contract principles are codified and not abolished. In addition, there is an ongoing interpretation by the courts of the various provisions. Different courts, in interpreting the provisions and applying them to specific situations, attribute different meanings and constructions to phrases. Thus, while uniformity is a desired goal, it is not automatic.

Many law students spend an entire semester studying the UCC, but our scope here is much more limited. We will briefly examine Article 2 because of its common applications. Article 2 deals with contracts for the sale of goods and applies to sales between consumers and merchants as well as between merchants. Goods are defined in § 2-105 as:

all things (including specially manufactured goods) which are movable at the time of identification to the contract for sale other than the money in which the price is to be paid, investment securities (Article 8) and things in action. "Goods" also includes the unborn young of animals and growing crops and other identified things attached to realty.

Contracts for real property and services are not covered by this provision. Article 2 covers such topics as the formation of the contract and discusses the offer and acceptance. The major differences from the common law are the expansion of the form of acceptance to any "reasonable" manner and to allow the existence of new terms in the acceptance rather than considering it a counteroffer if the sale is between merchants. Again, the policy is to uphold contracts whenever possible.

An important aspect of Article 2 is the warranty provisions it contains. A *warranty* is "an assurance by one party to a contract of the existence of a fact upon which the other party may rely [and] is intended to relieve the other party of any duty to personally ascertain the fact."[54] Under the UCC, the seller automatically warrants that the title is good; that is, he or she warrants that he or she owns the property and has the legal right to transfer ownership. It also guarantees that the goods are being transferred free of a lien or other interest in the property by a third party unless the buyer is notified of the existence of such interest.[55]

Warranties may be either express or implied. *Express warranties* are created by statements or promises made by the seller regarding the durability or other characteristics of the goods or by technical descriptions of goods. No specific language is required to create an express warranty, but the statement must have been a part of the bargaining process and must have become a basic assumption for entering the contract.

The UCC also contains two very important implied warranties. The first is the *Implied Warranty of Merchantability*. This *implied warranty* applies only to sales in which the seller is a merchant and is a rich source for contract actions as well as tort lawsuits. In order to collect, the plaintiff must show the following: (1) that the seller is a merchant; (2) that this merchant sold these goods; (3) that the goods were not merchantable at the time of sale; (4) that the plaintiff or his property was injured; (5) that such injuries were proximately and actually caused by the defective goods; and (6) that notice of the injury was given to the merchant. Merchantable goods are defined as goods that minimally:

- pass without objection in the trade under the contract description;
- in the case of fungible goods, are of fair average quality within the description;
- are fit for the ordinary purposes for which such goods are used;
- run, within variations permitted by the agreement, of even kind, quality, and quantity within each unit and among all units involved;
- are adequately contained, packaged, and labeled as the agreement may require;
- conform to the promises or affirmations of fact made on the container or label if any.[56]

The effect of this provision is to allow the consumer to sue not only the manufacturer but also the middleman or the merchant for injuries sustained because of defective goods. For example, plaintiffs injured because of defective automobiles may sue the car dealer as well as the manufacturer.

The second important implied warranty, the *Implied Warranty of Fitness*,[57] applies to all sellers of goods, be they merchants or not. Here, a seller is warranting that the goods are fit for a particular use, which is a narrower warranty than the previous one. In order to collect, the plaintiff here must prove many of the same elements, such as that this seller sold these goods and made certain representations about them as well as that the injury was the result of the defective goods. In addition however, the plaintiff must show that, as the buyer, he relied on the seller's skill or judgment in selecting these particular goods to perform these specific tasks. It is relatively easy for a plaintiff to show that he has less knowledge about the goods and their suitability than the seller and to show that he relied on the seller's expertise and superior knowledge; this, however, is an issue for the jury to decide. These warranties may be specifically disclaimed—another reason to read all contracts carefully and completely. The UCC provisions regarding warranties and their possible waivers are bolstered by federal legislation.[58]

The UCC provides remedies for the breach of contracts. Generally, although the UCC distinguishes between solvent and insolvent buyers, the seller may withhold the goods, stop delivery, and sue for the price of the goods. The seller may sue for the price of the goods (§ 2-709) and for incidental damages (§ 2-710), for the difference between the contract price and the resale price of the goods (§ 2-706), for damages (§ 2-708), or for the cancellation of the contract. The usual formula for computing the seller's damages if the buyer fails to pay is the difference between the market price at the time of performance and the contract price plus the costs incurred in mitigating the damage minus any expenses saved as a result of the buyer's breach.[59] The buyer's remedies for breach are also provided. If the goods do not conform to the contract, the buyer may reject the goods and advise the seller in a timely fashion.[60] If the buyer keeps the goods, the usual formula is the difference between the value of the goods as they are and the value of the goods had they conformed to the contract (§ 2-711). The buyer is also entitled to incidental and consequential costs (§ 2-715) and to the costs of obtaining substitute goods (§ 2-712) or to specific performance if the goods have unique qualities (§ 2-716). The buyer may also deduct damages from the unpaid portion of the price for the goods.[61]

The UCC is another attempt to add stability to commercial transactions. In our mobile society, uniformity of laws among the various jurisdictions greatly facilitates that goal. In addition, the codification of these provisions into one statute, rather than having the principles scattered throughout legislative enactments and court decisions, allows merchants, consumers, and lawyers to more easily identify the rules and obligations governing such transactions.

CONSUMER LAW

Since the 1960s, legislatures and court decisions have expanded and then contracted protections for consumers. Consumer law is not actually a separate field; rather, it is composed of a conglomeration of elements from torts, contracts, the UCC, usury and bankruptcy, and other areas of law. Heightened awareness on the part of citizens, nurtured by consumer advocates, has resulted in major changes in the legal system's approach to the consumer. No longer is the purchaser of goods or services left to fend for himself or herself; instead, because of the inherent imbalance between a single consumer and a large corporation, legislatures and courts have stepped in to enhance the fairness of the marketplace. That benefit is offset by the volume of government regulation to which businesses must adhere, and for many people the benefits for individuals greatly outweigh the burden of regulation.

The Constitution gives Congress the power to "regulate Commerce" and to "provide for ... general Welfare."[62] The government has taken seriously that charge to regulate for the safety and well-being of the American people. Scores of Supreme Court cases deal with monopolies, labor and employment laws, and other aspects of commerce. Administrative agencies regulate the sale of securities under the Securities and Exchange Commission (SEC), the safety of the skies under the Federal Aviation Administration (FAA), and new medications and food items under the Food and Drug Administration (FDA). Corporate America is accustomed to government regulation of entire industries, but the expectation that they will answer directly to individual consumers for problems with contracts and faulty goods really bloomed in the last half of the twentieth century. The process was furthered by the willingness of the courts to entertain such large class-action suits as the tobacco or pharmaceutical cases. New statutory remedies were fashioned to offer the consumer additional protection against the corporations and merchants of goods.

All agree that some government oversight of commerce is acceptable and necessary, but the ongoing question is the extent of that oversight. Both the executive and the legislative branches have acted to reduce the number of regulations to which businesses are exposed. Nevertheless, businesses of all sizes and types continue to complain about overzealous regulatory agencies and burgeoning court judgments. Some argue that the lack of oversight of such matters as the dubious accounting practices at large corporations harms individuals and society as a whole or comes at the expense of everyday consumers because of the dilution of consumer protection statutes by forbidding certain causes of action, by changing the rules of vicarious liability, and by limiting recoveries, especially punitive damages. Others view these changes simply as necessary course adjustments to keep the economy healthy and a move toward a more balanced equilibrium between business, government, and consumers.

Deceptive trade practices statutes that have been enacted on both the state and the national levels exemplify legislative reform. Merchants are forbidden to include in advertisements misleading statements about, for example, the geographic origin or condition of goods. A grocer cannot advertise Florida oranges when, in fact, they are California oranges. The "bait and switch" tactic of advertising a piece of merchandise for a low price in order to draw customers in and then substituting another in its place is barred.[63] In addition to the implied warranties in the UCC, many deceptive trade practices acts require truthfulness in statements about the condition of goods and allow the consumer to recover damages, attorney's fees, and court costs as damages. In order to allow the recovery of additional damages, suits under the deceptive trade practices acts may be filed in conjunction with other types of suits, such as those for violations of tort law, breach of contract, or violations of the UCC.

Other laws protect people in their financial dealings as, for example, statutes providing protection from overbearing salespeople in home-solicitation sales[64] and requiring, among other consumer credit protections, that debtors be advised of all finance charges, figured annually, and expressed at the annual percentage rate.[65] The increasing concern over identity theft and privacy led Congress to create a bill of rights for identity theft victims, to mandate that consumers be able to obtain a copy of their credit report each year without charge, and to shield medical information available in the financial system.[66] Another substantial credit card reform was enacted in 2009 in the midst of the economic meltdown; the provisions included, among other things, banning credit cards for people under the age of 21 unless they have adult co-signers or show proof that they have the means to repay the debts and requiring card issuers to discuss how long it will take to pay off the balance if only the minimal payments are made as well as the total cost to pay the debt if one makes only the minimal payments. The Credit Card Accountability, Responsibility, and Disclosure Act (Credit CARD Act) also mandated that gift cards and gift certificates are good for five years.[67]

UCC § 2-302 provides that *unconscionable contracts* are unenforceable, although the concept of unconscionability is not limited to cases brought under the UCC. It has generally been invoked in cases in which the seller has taken advantage of the buyer and relates to fairness.

> Does any principle in our law have more universal application than the doctrine that courts will not enforce transactions in which the relative positions of the parties are such that one has unconscionably taken advantage of the necessities of the other?[68]

The party asking for relief must show an absence of meaningful choice on the part of one party or lack of knowledge of the terms of the contract, substantial inequality in bargaining power between the parties, and unreasonably favorable terms for the party with the superior bargaining power.[69] Because courts are so reluctant to overturn contracts, they hesitate to state that a contract is unconscionable, and they infrequently do so when two merchants are involved in the transaction. This clause is used most often to benefit consumers, particularly those who are poor and uneducated. Courts have voided contracts that contained exorbitant prices for consumer goods or clauses waiving all warranties when the implied warranty of fitness existed. As discussed earlier, fraud and duress may cause a court to nullify a contract.

Many of the adopted statutes have been weakened, in part because of the efforts of business-oriented incumbent policymakers who favor few restrictions on the right to contract. Yet, the imbalance between large corporations and consumers is not as lopsided as it once was because many of the revisions and policies remain a vibrant part of consumer law.

BUSINESS RELATIONSHIPS

As most contracts involve transactions with or among business entities, it is appropriate at this point to briefly discuss various types of organizations. The focus is on relationships established to carry out business activities for profit. Nonprofit organizations, such as various charities, universities, and social clubs, may exhibit the same structural characteristics but are outside the scope of this discussion.

Sole Proprietorships

The most basic business structure is the *sole proprietorship*. Sole proprietorships are found in myriad forms, from the artisan selling her works from her studio to a college student conducting a snow-removal business to professionals in solo practice. As the name implies, there is a single owner of the business who alone profits from the business but who alone suffers any loss as well. Liability for all debts or torts is passed directly to the sole proprietor. There is no legal barrier for the sole proprietor from business debts, and her personal assets are subject to all business claims. She would claim all income and all business deductions on her personal income tax form (possibly at a lower rate than the corporate rate).[70]

Partnerships

A *partnership* has many characteristics of the sole proprietorship, with one salient difference. There must be two or more people and/or corporations involved to create a partnership. Partnership agreements generally outline the arrangements for managing the business and providing for possible indemnification among the partners as well as providing for the dissolution of the partnership and division of the assets. The common law rules relating to partnerships have been substantially altered by such statutes as the Uniform Partnership Act and the Uniform Limited Partnership Act (2001); however, one aspect remains unchanged. Partners, like sole proprietors, must report their share of the profits or losses on their personal income tax return (even though the partnership files an informational tax return).

In a general partnership, partners may all participate in business decisions, or they may appoint a managing partner who is responsible for day-to-day operations. Some may be silent partners whose names do not appear on the door and are not otherwise identified as having an ownership interest. Each partner shares individual and joint liability for all debts and torts of the general partnership, and each, when acting with proper authority under the partnership agreement or under statute, may bind the partnership in regard to business transactions or tort liability. In contrast, in a limited partnership, the limited partners are responsible only to the extent of their investment. Under older statutes, the limited partners are not entitled to participate in the management of the business; in essence, they may be viewed as investors only, and if they opt for an active role in management they lose their protected status. Newer statutes abolish that restriction. There must be at least one general partner who faces all the risks and responsibilities.[71]

Limited Liability Companies

The initial statute providing for this organizational structure was adopted by Wyoming in 1977. Although there are pattern statutes, the Uniform Limited Liability Company Act and its revision, only a few states have adopted it, so there is a great variety of statutory schemes. The benefits for the owners are the advantageous tax treatment of partnerships coupled with the limited liability available in the corporate structure. This is the format of choice for many professional service organizations (such as the practices of lawyers or physicians) but may not be appropriate for businesses that will last for generations or that have long-term lending arrangements such as real-estate investments.

Corporations

Corporations are the most complex form of business organization and must be chartered by the state in accordance with statutory provisions. The primary difference between corporations and other types of business organizations is that corporations generally shield owners (the shareholders) from individual liability; that is, the corporation itself and its assets, not those of the individual stockholder, are the source of compensation for debts and torts. Corporations come in all sizes, from immense multinational conglomerates to small, closely held corporations in which all the stock is held by one individual or by a small group, often family members, who share management responsibilities for the family ranch, for example, and the stock is not publicly traded. This mixture of management and ownership is one of the distinguishing features of a closely held corporation. Another variation is the professional corporation or association. The business of these entities is the practice of one of the learned professions such as law, accounting, or medicine. Profits are shared among the members, while liability is generally limited to one's own malpractice and generally does not extend to the malpractice of the other partners, although it will vary from state to state. Small corporations (100 shareholders or fewer) may elect under Subchapter S of the Internal Revenue Code (26 U.S.C. § 1361 *et seq.*) to have the profits passed through to its members on a pro rata basis and taxed as ordinary income rather than paying tax twice: once on the corporate income and once on the profits distributed to the individuals. Losses are also passed through to the individual shareholder under a Subchapter S election.

Corporations, other than professional or closely held corporations, offer the benefit to investors of limited liability and limited management responsibility. Another advantage is that the investment may be made in relatively small amounts of money—the cost of the share and brokers' fees, if any—at any one time, and the investment is usually easy to liquidate if the shares are sold over the counter or listed on one of the stock exchanges. The disadvantage is that the shareholder has limited chance for profit as well. Of course, if the stock price skyrockets, the shareholder may profit handsomely by selling the stock; conversely, if the stock drops in price, the person may lose money. While holding the stock, there is also the chance for profits if the company pays a cash dividend or declares a stock split that increases the number of shares held without additional investment. Only the individual shareholder's profit or loss from sale of the stock or income from dividends or stock splits is reported on his or her income tax form. Common shares are the basic type of stock, and owners are entitled to a pro rata portion of the profits, rights of management, and assets if the corporation is dissolved based on the number of shares held. Preferred stock carries certain rights and benefits such as priority over other types of stock in regard to dividends.

As legal entities, corporations are entitled to own property and assets, and it is to those assets that creditors generally must look for compensation rather than to the property of individual shareholders. While it was once rare for courts to allow the "piercing of the corporate veil" to go behind the corporation and its assets to the directors, the management, or the shareholders, it is not uncommon in light of the accounting scandals and demise of huge, multinational corporations during the first years of the twenty-first century. Directors of corporations, a position once regarded as a sinecure, are coming under frequent legal attacks, both civilly and criminally. The directors are elected by the stockholders, and they are responsible for managing the stockholders' enterprise. Traditionally, many boards met only to ratify management decisions and not to play an active role in guiding the corporation. However, in various lawsuits, directors have had to defend their actions and have actually been held civilly and criminally responsible for corporate policies and activities as well as mismanagement. New corporate responsibility laws double the maximum sentence for violations of securities laws to 20 years and increase the maximum criminal penalty for an individual to $5 million and for a company to $25 million as well as expanding the definition of obstruction of justice and creating a new felony for the destruction of audit work papers.[72] The effect has been a chilling one; people no longer readily accept positions as a director for either profit or nonprofit corporations without a guarantee of indemnity or some type of malpractice insurance, and those aspiring to the position of chief executive officer (CEO) are rethinking their goals.

The selection of the appropriate type of organization to carry out commercial enterprises is a complex one, dependent on a number of variables, because most businesses could be viable as any of the four—sole proprietorships, partnerships, limited liability companies, or corporations. The first factor is the number of people who own the business or share in its profits or losses; that is, whether it is a very large retail store owned by one person, whether it is a closely held family farm, or whether it is a multinational corporation with subsidiaries in foreign countries. The second factor is the desire of the owners to limit their risks in terms of both funds and legal liability. For example, limited partnerships in real estate or mineral exploration may allow investors to reap profits without large investments (or large losses) and without the burden of management. The third aspect (and one that is often determinative) is the tax consequences of the selection for the individuals involved as well as the respective tax rates for individuals and corporations. The owners of the business must carefully weigh the various factors in deciding the form of the business.[73]

CONCLUSION

In this chapter we have discussed the formation of contracts, outlining the required elements of multiple parties, mutual assent as evidenced by the offer and acceptance, and consideration. The courts and legislatures have created certain tools, such as the parol evidence rule and the Statute of Frauds, to help resolve disputes concerning the creation and interpretation of contracts. Breach, or failure to perform one's obligations under a contract, may result in the aggrieved party's collecting damages or in an order for specific performance issued against the nonperforming party. The UCC codifies many of the provisions of the common law in regard to contracts, but its coverage is limited. Elements of various branches of law, including contract law and tort law, have been combined with the UCC to create new areas of protection for consumers, exemplifying a shift from a policy of unswerving sanctity of contracts to recognition of individual rights and concerns.

The overall purpose of contract law and its subsidiaries is to ensure stability in commercial and private transactions. As Justice Noah Swayne wrote:

> A compact lies at the foundation of all national life. Contracts mark the progress of communities in civilization and prosperity. They guard, as far as is possible, against the fluctuations of human affairs. They seek to give stability to the present and certainty to the future. They gauge the confidence of man in the truthfulness and integrity of his fellow man. They are the springs of business, trade, and commerce. Without them society could not go on.[74]

NOTES

1. Samuel Williston as quoted in Joseph M. Perillo, *Calamari and Perillo on Contracts*, 5th edn (St. Paul, MN: Thomson/West, 2003), p. 1.
2. 17A Am. Jur.2d *Contracts* § 12.
3. 17A Am. Jur.2d *Contracts* §§ 7–8.
4. 17A Am. Jur.2d *Contracts* § 5.
5. 17A Am. Jur.2d *Contracts* § 10.
6. 17A Am. Jur.2d *Contracts* § 6.
7. *Dartmouth College v. Woodward*, 4 Wheat. 518 (1819).
8. *Fletcher v. Peck*, 6 Cranch 87 (1810).
9. *Dartmouth College v. Woodward*, 4 Wheat. 518 (1819).
10. *Davis v. Concordia*, 9 How. 280 (1850).

11. *Lessee of Tucker v. Moreland*, 10 Pet. 58 (1836).
12. 42 Am. Jur.2d *Infants* §§ 48, 68–80, 93.
13. *Board of Regents of Univ. of Tex. v. Yarbrough*, 470 S.W.2d 86 (Tex. App.–Waco, 1971).
14. Perillo, p. 307.
15. 17A Am. Jur.2d *Contracts* § 30.
16. *Hotchkiss v. National City Bank of New York*, 200 F. 287 (S.D.N.Y. 1911), at 293.
17. Steven Brill, "Building Castles in the Clouds," *Newsweek*, July 29, 2002, pp. 44–45.
18. "Silverstein Prevails in Second World Trade Center Coverage Trial: All Nine Insurers Found Liable for Two 9/11 Occurrences," *National Underwriter Property & Casualty*, December 13, 2004, p. 6.
19. John Bacon, "700 Katrina Victims Sue Insurance Firm," *USA Today*, May 10, 2006.
20. 17A Am. Jur. 2d *Contracts* § 218.
21. 17A Am. Jur. 2d *Contracts* § 221.
22. "Groucho Marx Case Closes in Confusion as Jury Backs Bank," *New York Times*, March 31, 1983.
23. Serge F. Kovaleski and Alexandra Alter, "Another Drama in Harper Lee's Hometown," *New York Times*, August 23, 2015.
24. 17A Am. Jur.2d *Contracts* § 214.
25. 17A Am. Jur. 2d *Contracts* § 202.
26. 17A Am. Jur.2d *Contracts* § 52.
27. Arthur Linton Corbin, *Corbin on Contracts* (St. Paul, MN: West, 1952), pp. 141–142.
28. 17A Am. Jur.2d *Contracts* §§ 91–98.
29. *German Alliance Insurance Co. v. Home Water Supply* Co., 226 U.S. 220 (1912).
30. *Gary Safe Co. v. A. C. Andrews* Co., 568 S.W.2d 166 (Tex. App.–Dallas, 1978).
31. Perillo, pp. 171–226.
32. 6 Am. Jur.2d *Assignment* §§ 1, 17, 21.
33. 17A Am. Jur.2d *Contracts* §§ 672, 688–689.
34. Corbin, pp. 553–556.
35. *Rossi v. Douglas,* 203 Md. 190, 100 A.2d 3 (Md. 1953), at 7.
36. *ProCD Inc. v. Zeidenberg,* 86 F.3d 1447 (7th Cir. 1996).
37. *Hill v. Gateway 2000 Inc.*, 105 F.3d 1147 (7th Cir. 1997), *cert. denied*, 522 U.S. 808 (1997), at 1148.
38. See, for example, *Klocek v. Gateway*, 104 F. Supp. 2d 1332 (D. Kan. 2000) and *Licitra v. Gateway*, 189 Misc.2d 721, 734 N.Y.S.2d 389 (N.Y. Civ. Ct. 2001).
39. 17A Am. Jur.2d *Contracts* § 214.
40. Perillo, pp. 313–329, 336–360.
41. Ibid., pp. 560–567.
42. *Hadley v. Baxendale*, 156 Eng. Rep. 145 (1854), at 151.
43. Perillo, pp. 584–587.
44. Ibid., pp. 253–273.
45. Ibid., pp. 632–642.
46. Ibid., pp. 735–802; UCC § 2-201.
47. Electronic Signatures in Global and National Commerce Act, 15 U.S.C. §§ 7001–7006; Uniform Electronic Transactions Act, http://uniformlaws.org/ActSummary.aspx?title=Electronic%20Transactions%20Act (visited December 22, 2015).
48. Corbin, pp. 534–537.
49. Perillo, pp. 149–170.
50. *Haslund v. Simon Property Group, Inc.*, 378 F.3d 653 (7th Cir. 2004), at 655.

51. United Nations Convention on Contracts for International Sale of Goods, http://www.cisg.law.pace.edu/cisg/text/treaty.html (visited December 22, 2015).
52. UCC § 1-103.
53. Summary Revised Article 9, Uniform Commercial Code, http://uniformlaws.org/ActSummary.aspx?title=UCC%20Article%209,%20Secured%20Transactions%20%281998%29 (visited December 22, 2015).
54. David Eliot Brody, *The American Legal System: Concepts and Principles* (Lexington, MA: Heath, 1978), p. 188.
55. UCC § 2-312.
56. UCC § 2-314.
57. UCC § 2-315.
58. 15 U.S.C. §§ 2301–2302.
59. UCC § 2-709.
60. UCC §§ 2-601–2-603.
61. UCC § 2-717.
62. U.S. Constitution, Art. I, § 8.
63. 16 CFR § 238.
64. 16 CFR § 429.
65. 15 U.S.C. §§ 1601–1691.
66. Fair and Accurate Credit Transactions Act of 2003, P.L. 108–159, 117 Stat. 1952.
67. Credit Card Accountability Responsibility and Disclosure Act of 2009, P.L. 111–24, 123 Stat.1734.
68. *United States v. Bethlehem Steel Corp.*, 315 U.S. 289 (1942), at 326.
69. Martin A. Frey and Phyllis Hurley Frey, *Essentials of Contract Law* (Albany, NY: West Legal Studies, 2001), p. 164.
70. "Sole Proprietorship," Cornell Legal Information Institute, https://www.law.cornell.edu/wex/sole_proprietorship (visited December 23, 2015).
71. "Partnership," Cornell Legal Information Institute, https://www.law.cornell.edu/wex/Partnership (visited December 23, 2015).
72. Sarbanes-Oakley Act of 2002, P.L. 107–204, 116 Stat. 745.
73. John E. Moye, *Law of Business Organizations*, 6th edn (Clifton Park, NY: Thomson/Delmar Learning, 2005), pp. 14–191.
74. *Farrington v. Tennessee*, 5 Otto 679 (1878).

Property

Of all legal subfields, property law is perhaps the area in which the principles and terminology of the past are most dominant. The concepts and language used today to create and describe property interests originated during the feudal era of England and have remained virtually unchanged.

> The imprint of the past is still discernible in the present. In this branch of the law more than any other perhaps, we can time and time again profitably invoke the often quoted statement of Mr. Justice Holmes: "Upon this point a page of history is worth a volume of logic."[1]

One of the most basic principles of our system of government is private ownership of assets, and its preservation is secured by constitutional provisions: "No person shall ... be deprived of life, liberty, or *property*, without due process of law" (emphasis added).[2] We must not overlook the fact that there is public ownership of certain government assets, such as battleships and parks, that theoretically belong to all of us; however, most of the means of production and capital in the United States are held by private investors.

If you were asked whether you own property, what would be your response? Perhaps you would say no, based on the fact that you do not own land. That answer is likely to be incorrect. You own clothes, a cellphone, and school supplies; you probably have money in your pocket or bank account. These items are your possessions, and title to them has been legally vested in you. Technically, the word *property* means "an aggregate of rights" or "that dominion or indefinite right of use or disposition which one may lawfully exercise over particular things or subjects."[3] Thus, the legal definition of property is one of dominion and control over certain items, whether tangible or intangible. In common parlance, property usually means a thing that is owned or possessed, and judges and lawyers also use the word in that sense.

Two dominant methods are used to classify property. The first is to distinguish between real property and personal property. Real property, or *realty,* is legally interpreted as the land itself and the appurtenances thereto, such as structures constructed on the tract or the trees growing on it, or a possessory interest such as a time share in a condominium along the Maine coast. In addition, items of personal property that have been securely affixed to the structures or to the land are also considered real property. For example, huge pieces of machinery that are permanently installed in factories lose their character as personal property and assume that of realty. Personal property, or *personalty,* is everything other than realty and includes those items of real property that can be severed without injury to the realty, such as minerals or cultivated crops. It includes such diverse items as cash, baseball memorabilia, goodwill for a professional such as an attorney, collections of Waterford crystal, computers of all ilks such as wristwatches, eyeglasses, and tablets, and stocks and bonds.[4]

The second method of classification is to designate property as being tangible or intangible. *Tangible property* includes land and other material items that can be touched, such as paintings and automobiles. Items of *intangible property* are those things that cannot be perceived by touch. For example, debts are intangible, even though the promissory note that is the legal acknowledgment of such debt is tangible. A patent or copyright is another illustration of intangible property, although, again, inventors may be given written documentation of their claims.

ESTATES

The Anglo-American notion of estates is based on the concept of ownership measured in terms of time. The duration of ownership determines both the legal rights of the owner and the manner in which he or she may dispose of the item. A *fee simple estate* is the maximum estate; it may potentially last through infinity because one is permitted to pass it on to one's heirs. The owner of a fee simple may divide it into smaller estates and into nonfreehold estates. The concepts and terms of property ownership are mired in the traditions of the past, particularly the feudal era.

Feudalism

The word *feudalism* is used by historians to describe the social characteristics of Western Europe from the eighth to the fourteenth century. It describes a complicated social hierarchy of reciprocal obligations. For example, a tenant may have owed certain military services to his lord in exchange for the lord's protection against attack. Feudalism developed partly because of the dissolution of the Roman Empire caused by the barbarian invaders. Chaos replaced the order and rule of law imposed by the Romans. It became necessary for private individuals to obtain higher levels of protection than they could provide by themselves. They were willing to give up some degree of personal independence and private ownership of land in order to secure the protection offered by the great lords. The effect was to convert Europe from a place where individuals owned land absolutely in prefeudal days to a place where individual and communal ownership of land was destroyed.

Feudalism existed in England before the Norman Conquest, but it was the doctrines and rules of William the Conqueror and his followers that came to dominate English land law. In 1066, William defeated the Saxon King Harold at the Battle of Hastings and confirmed his somewhat shaky claim to succession from Edward the Confessor by his victory on the battlefield. William's attitude was that because the English landowners had disputed his claim to the throne and required him to assert it by force and because he was justly affirmed as monarch, the Saxon landowners who opposed him should forfeit their land. The King himself became the true owner of every acre of land by right of conquest. As a reward for loyalty and as a tool for maintaining order, William granted dominion over certain manors and castles to his followers with the reservation of ultimate ownership in himself in most cases. In exchange for being granted these properties and their revenues, the holders agreed to provide certain services or funds to the King.

A complex structure of reciprocal obligations eventually developed to deal with various social needs. A lord might hold several manors in widely separated areas of the country, and he would have tenants who owed him services for use and occupancy of an estate. This system of holding land in subordination to some superior was known as the *tenure* system; the king was considered to hold the dominion of the soil, while the tenant held the possessory title and the right to the use and profits of the soil, *seisin*. Thus, C might hold of B, who held of A, who held of the king. As more tenancies were created it eventually became quite bewildering, and in 1290 the *Statute Quai Emptores* was passed. This statute recognized the right of freemen to dispose of their land, but the new holder was obligated to the same person for the same services as the prior holder. In other words, it substituted the new owner for the old in terms of services rather than creating a new level of services. The services due from tenants varied considerably in nature, importance, and duration depending on one's social status.

The tenure system of holding land has continued in England for centuries, although it was substantially altered by the Tenures Abolition Act in 1660 that converted most obligations into a simple rent payment. Major land reform legislation was enacted by Parliament in the first quarter of the twentieth century, and while some land is still theoretically held in tenure and not owned absolutely, it is essentially an empty concept.[5] In the American colonies, land was initially held in tenure. William Penn, for example, was obligated to render two beaver skins annually for his grant.[6] Although lands in the United States were originally held under the feudal concepts of tenure, it is, as a practical matter, not pertinent to landownership today. Despite the fact that tenure itself is no longer important, the theories it generated are the basis of modern property law.

Freehold Estates

There are three types of freehold estates: estates in fee simple, estates in fee tail, and life estates. Each has its own unique characteristics. A fee simple estate is the most durable of all estates and connotes the maximum of legal ownership.

The holder has the right to possession of the property and the right to dispose of it at will. The title remains fixed in the owner until some affirmative divestment occurs, and title may be passed to heirs. This power of the holder to alienate or transfer the land evolved slowly from the feudal system, in which the lord controlled any changes. By the thirteenth century however, it was established that the holder could transfer the interest and that, if the holder had conveyed the title with a warranty for both himself and his heirs, the heirs could not overturn the transfer. Today, land conveyances often include the same language, to the effect that the **grantor** and his or her heirs give up all claims of ownership and warrant good title to the purchaser; in addition, land transferred as a fee simple estate is frequently given "to the purchaser and his or her heirs," although this does not give the heirs a present interest in the property.[7]

Another vestige of feudal law is the **estate in fee tail**. The purpose of the fee tail is to preserve large estates and to keep the property within the family. A fee tail conveys property to a person and the *heirs of his or her body*; that is, descendants of the **grantee**. The effect is to prevent transfer of the property by sale or inheritance outside the family. Like all property transfers, the fee tail may be created by a conveyance of property or by a will. The fee tail, coupled with the system of **primogeniture,** kept many of the major landholdings in England intact and safe from the ravages of dissolute heirs. The grantor could convey the property to a person and the heirs of the body by a particular spouse or limit the lineal descent through either the female line (**fee tail female**) or the male line (**fee tail male**). Such an arrangement may pose difficulties for families if there are adopted children or if the family wishes to sell the property. Fee tails are disfavored by the law, and many courts will dissolve the fee tail so that land may be transferred and then create an equitable trust from the proceeds from the sale. In our egalitarian society, fee tails are relatively rare.[8]

The **life estate** is of limited duration, during the life of the holder or some other person. If the estate is for the duration of the life of a third party it is known as an **estate pur autre vie**. A daughter's will might read "to Mother during her life and then to my children." The purpose is to provide for the mother's welfare during her lifetime and to ensure that the property will ultimately pass to the grandchildren. Life tenants have the right to possession of the property and the right to receive any income and profits from it. They are under an affirmative duty to refrain from any act that would diminish the value of the property and are required to perform ordinary maintenance and repairs. Although a life interest may be transferred, there is often not a market for such limited estates. Life estates may be created by statute in the case of surviving spouses who have a life interest in the property owned by their spouse at the time of death.[9]

Modern conveyances of property employ the same terminology as ancient land deeds in identifying the type of estate created in the grantee. It is ultimately the grantee's responsibility to ensure that the grantor has good title to the property that he or she is conveying, although the grantor usually warrants that the title is clear. Most buyers delegate the duty of checking the title to trained professionals, such as title companies or attorneys, who examine the records to determine whether there is any cloud on the title. This is done by checking the records at the local land office (typically, the courthouse in the county where the land is situated) for any documents affecting land titles such as deeds, mortgages, wills, liens, and judgments. It is the responsibility of those dealing with the land to actually peruse the records; the government merely provides a method of locating the appropriate documents through the indexes and recording of the instruments.[10]

Many purchases of land involve real-estate agents, and their responsibilities and charges should be clarified early in the relationship. Realtors traditionally represent the seller's interest, and today, real-estate agents are frequently required to provide written disclosure of that fact to both potential buyers and potential sellers. Many states now allow that pattern to be altered and the realtor to act on behalf of the buyer alone or of both parties with full written disclosure and after obtaining full consent of all parties to the transaction.[11] Ethical realtors will be completely open and honest about all fees, closing costs, and real-estate prospects in an area. Lending institutions are frequently involved in real-estate transactions; in exchange for lending the money to purchase the property, the institution takes a mortgage or puts a lien on the property. If that loan is not repaid in a timely fashion the institution may force the sale of the asset. The financial institution from which a loan is taken should be selected carefully. All documents involved in the transaction should be studied, and questions should be asked without hesitation because these are important commitments.

Nonfreehold Estates

Nonfreehold estates are leasehold estates that frequently involve periodic payments from a tenant to a landlord; that is, the owner of the fee simple estate carves out a smaller and temporary estate and keeps the reversion interest in herself. There are three main types of leasehold estates: an estate for years, a periodic estate, and an estate at will. The estate for years, which is expressed in terms of a multiple or fraction of a year, has a definite termination date and ends with the expiration of that time or by surrender. The periodic estate resembles the estate for years in that it endures for a year or a fraction thereof and for successive periods of that length until terminated by proper notice by either party. The estate at will has no specified period of termination. It continues at the will of the *lessor* and the *lessee*.

The basis of these arrangements is the *lease*, which is "neither fish nor fowl"; that is, it is neither wholly a contract nor wholly a property conveyance. It is based on a series of covenants or promises made by the parties to the lease and is tailored to suit the particular transaction. Typically, the lessor promises the tenant the right of "quiet enjoyment" of the premises; in addition, the landlord may agree to furnish certain services or to maintain the premises in reasonably good repair. In exchange, the lessee agrees to pay rent; to use the premises in the specified manner, such as for residential and not business purposes; to refrain from subleasing or assigning the lease without the landlord's permission;

and to refrain from causing any damage beyond the normal wear and tear on the premises.[12]

Leases may be either oral or written. Leases for residential property are often standard forms and are frequently much less complicated than are commercial leases. The lessor, as the person with the largest estate, was favored by the common law if a dispute arose, but statutory enactments now offer the residential tenant much more protection than was previously available. State laws and municipal ordinances vary regarding the landlord's responsibilities, but typically, the lessor must maintain the premises in a safe and habitable condition. Failure of either party to comply with the terms of the lease may result in litigation. If a tenant causes excessive deterioration to the property or fails to make timely rent payments, the landlord may evict the tenant under the state's statutory scheme, which may include court action. On the other hand, if lessors do not live up to their part of the bargain, tenants may also sue and punitive damages may be involved. Those who rent property should become familiar with their state and city laws regarding the landlord–tenant relationship. In addition, before a lease is signed, it should be *read*. For the tenant's protection, any pre-existing damage, such as stains on the rug, should be listed on the lease itself, and the landlord or its agent should initial it. In addition, any and all provisions relating to the rental of the property should be included in the written lease, and there should be no oral modifications as to the tenant's obligations.

Concurrent Ownership

There are a number of schemes for owning property in common with other people. One of the most frequent is the marital estate. Marital property comes in two varieties: the ***community property*** system and the so-called common law system. In community property states both spouses each own an undivided half of the marital estate. Property that was owned by either of them before marriage or that is received as a gift or by inheritance is considered to be separate property.[13] In common law states, each spouse has an individual estate; one partner's salary belongs to him or her alone, although the couple may create cotenancies by mutually contributing money to buy an asset, such as a home. These tenancies are usually treated as tenancies in common.

Tenancies in common are interests in property that are concurrently held by two or more parties. Each has the right to use and enjoy the entire property; that is, each has a possessory interest. The separate and distinct ownership interests may be created at different times in different instruments, and the rights thereunder pass to the owner's heirs.[14] In contrast, joint tenancies carry a right of survivorship; that is, the surviving co-owner will inherit the interest. ***Joint tenancies*** are created by one instrument, the interests commence at the same time, and all the owners have the same right to possess and enjoy the property. Joint tenancies terminate with the death of one owner, with divorce if it is a marital estate, or by a ***suit to partition*** land, a lawsuit requesting the court to divide the property into separate and distinct segments and to assign it to the owners individually.[15]

Limitations on Ownership Interests

The traditional rule is that the holder of the fee simple estate owns not only the surface of the land but also the area below it to the center of the earth and the area above it into the skies.[16] Today however, the perceptions of ownership are more limited. One such restriction is an *easement*, namely a right to use some or all of the property of another, and may be created by custom, agreement, statute, or court order. Typical easements include a right-of-way to reach one's land that is surrounded by another's property and easements to prevent the blocking of light, air, and the flow of water.[17] A second development is recognition of limits on the owner's authority over air space above the land; a landowner cannot, for instance, prevent a satellite from being stationed in outer space above his or her land.

A third limitation is the effect of formally separating the property into surface and subsurface estates. The usual reason for severing the two is to allow for the exploration and production of minerals, often oil and gas. Once severance has taken place, often the mineral interest is the dominant one, and its owner has the right to develop that interest even if the surface is damaged. The surface owner may not collect for damage done to his or her interest that is "reasonable" in light of the current industry practices; in other words, the type of injury sustained would have to be unusual or malicious in order for the surface owner to receive compensation.[18]

An interesting corollary is *riparian* or water rights. "Water in its natural state is a part of the land, and therefore real property. Water may be converted into personal property, however, by segregation from the natural stream or body."[19] The characteristics of the body of the water such as navigable or non-navigable, surface or subterranean, and natural or artificial determine the rights to access and use the water and the beach or riverbed. In this area of law as with others, it is critical to examine the statutes of the individual states to ascertain the rules; however, there are several principles that are generally applicable. Government has the right to regulate the use of natural streams and bodies of water in the public interests, and the national government, under the Commerce Clause, may regulate and improve navigable waters.[20] Both non-navigable surface and subterranean rivers and streams (waters flowing in known channels and courses) may be diverted for use by the owner of the land through which the water flows in most jurisdictions, although the allocation between upstream and downstream owners becomes problematic. Dependent on which theory the individual state has accepted, extraction of percolating waters or from artesian basins may be done freely and without consideration of anyone else's rights by the owner of the land who is acting without malice under the English or common law rule; however, under the American rule, the owner's interest is limited to a reasonable and beneficial use of the shared water.[21]

A fourth limitation is the power of the government over private owners of land. Government has the power of *eminent domain* or "the power to take private property for public use."[22] This allows government to seize land to construct new housing projects, sports arenas, highways, or other public facilities even over the owner's objections; however, the Fifth Amendment guarantees that "private property [shall not] be taken for public use, without just compensation." Those owners who are dissatisfied with the price offered by the government may file suit and ask for a jury determination as to the fair value of the property.

The U.S. Supreme Court's decision, *Kelo v. City of New London*, thrust eminent domain to the forefront of the public agenda.[23] The city council of New London and the New London Economic Corporation (NLEC) filed suit under the Connecticut statute permitting eminent domain for economic development purposes to acquire title to land and to subsequently sell or lease it to private developers in an effort to rejuvenate part of the City of New London. There were no allegations that the seized property was blighted or rundown, but the property was appropriated only because of its location. The lower courts supported the City and the NLEC, and the U.S. Supreme Court agreed that economic development is a valid governmental interest and deferred to the local authorities that had approved the project. In reaction, a number of states passed constitutional amendments and statutes restricting the use of eminent domain for economic development.

In addition, local governments frequently restrict the use and occupation of property through zoning ordinances. Zoning determines the type of activity that may be conducted on the property. Typical of such schemes would be delineated areas that are designated for single residences, multiparty residences, commercial purposes, or heavy industry, and landowners are required to match the use of the land to the appropriate zone and would be barred, for example, from placing a retail shop legally selling marijuana or a large factory with the resulting traffic in the middle of a residential district and across the street from a school.

Aesthetic objectives are a legitimate goal for zoning provisions and may contain specific "nuisance prevention" provisions such as specifications for the size and height of signs as well as requirements that eliminate nonconforming uses such as junkyards and adult bookstores. One such case involved Wal-Mart Stores and the Town of North Elba, New York, a resort community noted for its rustic nature and striking scenery. North Elba had established a "scenic preservation overlay" to protect the view of nearby Whiteface Mountain, a view that would be obstructed by the store and its parking lot. The Planning Board rejected Wal-Mart's building permit after reviewing computer simulations of the proposed development. Wal-Mart sued, but the courts sustained the town's protection of its view.[24]

Government may also restrict an owner's use of the property because of historic preservation. Cities or other governmental units may create historic districts and impose various regulations such as controlling the changes to exterior architectural features visible from the street, but a state statute and local ordinance for the district are a prerequisite for this type of control. In 1935, Congress decreed that "it is a national policy to preserve for public use historic sites, buildings, and objects of national significance for the inspiration and benefit of the people of the United States."[25] Thirty-one years later, at the behest of the U.S. Conference of Mayors and others, Congress passed "a remarkable cluster of conservation-minded legislation, intended to fight environmental degradation, suburban sprawl, and urban renewal, those triple shocks to the foundation of national memory"[26] including the creation of the National Historic Preservation Act. This Act initiated the National Register of Historic Places, a listing of sites that meet the criteria of being associated with American history, architecture, archeology, engineering, or culture. The breadth of this description encompasses natural landscapes such as the Grand Canyon and some parts of Yellowstone; historic buildings and sites such as the Alamo and the Empire State Building; and quirky reflections of American culture such as a gas station designed by Frank Lloyd Wright, Elvis Presley's Graceland, and various highways (e.g., the 1940 Pasadena Freeway).

Unless there is federal involvement, a listing on the National Register does not itself prohibit under federal law or regulations any actions that may otherwise be taken by the private property owner.[27] There is no obligation to open the property to the public or even to maintain it. "Listed sites frequently fall into disrepair, burn down, or end up surrounded by concrete."[28] Designation of the property on the National Register does make the owner eligible for federal grants-in-aid and loan guaranties as well as certain breaks on income tax.

The owner's freedom to use the land as he or she sees fit may also be hampered for environmental reasons, for historical preservation, or for aesthetic purposes, such as landscape ordinances. The justification for all these land controls is in the government's power to protect the general welfare.[29] Speaking for the U.S. Supreme Court, Justice William O. Douglas stated:

> The concept of the public welfare is broad and inclusive. The values it represents are spiritual as well as monetary. It is within the power of the legislature to determine the community should be beautiful as well as healthy, spacious as well as clean, well-balanced as well as carefully patrolled.[30]

INCEPTION OF TITLE AND LIENS

Title to property may be acquired in a variety of ways—by property division on divorce, by award of damages in litigation, by foreclosure for nonpayment of debt, by adverse possession, by inheritance or gift, or by deed. We have previously discussed substantive areas of the law—torts and contracts—that involve transfer of property (usually money) from the wrongdoer to the victim when damages are awarded as compensation. Inheritance and gifts will be covered later in this chapter.

Adverse Possession

Adverse possession is "a method of acquisition of title by possession for a statutory period under certain conditions."[31] Under this legal doctrine, a person (natural or artificial) who openly uses another's property may wrest the title from the original landowner and cause it to vest in himself. Assume, for example, that Jennifer wishes to add a swimming pool to enhance the value of her home, so she fences the backyard and constructs the pool. Several years later, when a survey is done of the property pending sale, she is told that one-half of her pool is sitting on the property of her neighbor, Jessica. Through her open and continuous use of Jessica's property, Jennifer may have converted the property to her own depending on the length of the adverse possession and the state's statutory time requirements.

Some jurisdictions require that adverse possession must occur under "color of title." That is, Jennifer would be required to show that her deed to the property indicated that she owned the area of the swimming pool before she could prevail, and the mere use of the land would not suffice to change the title. Other states permit the transformation with or without "color of title" but require those who are not acting under color of title to use the land for a longer period of time. The key to adverse possession is always the open, notorious, and continuous use of the land. Paying taxes on the property in question may be a very helpful piece of evidence in such lawsuits, and it is through litigation that such issues are generally resolved.[32]

Deeds

The most common method of conveying property interests is by deed for real property and by various documents of title—bills of sale, certificates of title, receipts, or registration—for personal property. There are three common types of deeds: (1) warranty deeds, (2) special warranty deeds, and (3) quitclaim deeds. Deeds contain certain essential information about the transaction: the legal description of the property, the grantor and the extent of his or her interest, the grantee, and the consideration for the transfer, which need not be money (e.g., "for the love and affection which I bear my daughter, Mary Sue"). *Warranty deeds* are those in which the grantor of the land guarantees or warrants that he will defend the grantee and his heirs and assigns against title claims and will compensate them for any loss arising from such claims. Such deeds usually encompass a warranty on the part of the grantor that the title is unblemished and that there are no unrevealed encumbrances on the property. The grantor who gives a *special warranty deed* is stating only that she did not cloud the title herself but is making no guarantees about the state of the title before her ownership and that she will not defend the grantee's title from prior claims. A *quitclaim deed* contains no warranties about the title at all and effectively puts the grantee on notice that some flaw may exist in the chain of title. Quitclaim deeds should be avoided because they convey only the grantor's interest in the property and not the property itself, and purchasers should be particularly wary if the seller offers a quitclaim deed during the transaction or if a quitclaim deed pops up during the title examination.[33]

As you know from our prior discussions, the Statute of Frauds mandates that contracts for sale of land must be in writing to be effective. Deeds must also be in writing and signed by the grantor. Many states require that the signatures on the deeds be acknowledged before a notary public. It is imperative that the instruments be recorded, because, in effect, title does not pass until the deed, which gives public notice of the transaction, is registered at the courthouse. Not registering the deed does not affect the interests between the parties, but it does affect the rights of third parties such as subsequent purchasers. Missing deeds in the chain of title may cause the transaction to fail.

Purchasers of real property are concerned that they receive marketable title. A marketable title is one that is free from encumbrances or liens and free from doubts as to its validity or concerns about flaws.[34] It is the role of the title examiner or title insurance company to examine the title and determine its validity. The examiner will look at the documents on file to see if there are any unexplained gaps in the chain of title or if any of the deeds hint at some cloud on the title (e.g., a quitclaim deed) and if there are any recorded easements or encumbrances.

Liens

Much of the property in this country, both personal and real, is held subject to a *lien* which indicates that a creditor has a protected interest in the property. The liens on real property may result from a variety of transactions: a mortgage for the purchase money, a contractor's lien for home improvements, a judgment lien for failure to pay a court-ordered judgment, or a tax lien for failure to pay taxes. Liens on personal property are generally covered by Article 9 of the Uniform Commercial Code which covers both tangible and intangible property. Liens on both personal and real property have the same effects and requirements. The creditor who has accepted a security interest in the collateral (be it a home, merchandise, or equipment) may act to foreclose and assume ownership of the property if the debtor defaults on loan payments. For example, Xavier, a college student, entered into a rent-to-buy agreement for a large-screen television but did not remit the monthly fees. The company could seize the television for nonpayment. Indication of the debt must be in writing, and in order for the creditor to assume priority over other creditors, the instrument must be properly recorded.[35]

Real-estate ownership, both commercial and residential, is often contingent on payments to a financial institution that loaned money for the purchase. Most homeowners cannot afford to purchase a home outright, or they may choose not to do so because of the tax advantage in being able to deduct mortgage payments on one's income tax return (as long as Congress allows that exemption). In addition, there is a certain advantage to using someone else's money rather than one's own, particularly in commercial ventures. Assume that Creighton and Marion choose to buy a home, but they only have the money for a down payment and must borrow the rest from a financial institution, although various government programs may guarantee the loan or insure a lower interest rate. There are typically three instruments involved in such a transaction. First, Creighton and Marion, as purchasers of the home, will receive a warranty deed from the seller transferring ownership to them. Second, as debtors, they will execute a promissory note to the lender for the amount of the loan, using the home as collateral. Third, the lending institution will record an instrument indicating its security interest in the public records as notice to other creditors of its preferred status as a creditor.

Property ownership, whether of a fee simple estate or a leasehold, vests certain rights of use, enjoyment, and transferability of interests in the owner. Ownership may be acquired through diverse methods such as adverse possession, deed, by virtue of court order, or foreclosure for nonpayment of debt. Recording the indicia of title or security interest in public records is critical for the protection of one's property rights.

PROBATE AND SUCCESSION

The old adage "You can't take it with you" succinctly frames the legal problem of what happens to a person's property after death. The law, like nature, abhors a vacuum, and a vast and complicated system of laws has evolved to deal with the troublesome issue. Many of the terms and concepts regarding inheritances are borrowed from property law. For instance, statutes may provide for different distributions of the descendant's property depending on whether it is realty or personalty. A person who is foresighted enough to prepare a *will* in accordance with the legal requisites is described as dying testate, whereas a person who dies without a will is considered to have died *intestate*. In the latter instance, the state will allocate the property in compliance with the intestacy statute. The *testator,* or person making the will, can control "from beyond the grave" who gets the property; otherwise, the state will make that decision.

Provisions relating to succession were a natural outgrowth of individual property ownership. Intestate succession, based on familial or clan relationships, probably preceded testamentary provisions, but the Egyptians were designating their beneficiaries in writing as early as 2548 BCE. The Book of Genesis contains references to testamentary distributions, and the rules governing succession were included in the codes of both Jewish and Islamic religions. The Greeks, during the height of their civilization, had limited testamentary powers, but it was the Romans who fully developed the concept. The Roman traditions were incorporated into English law through the ecclesiastical courts that retained dominion over matters of inheritance until the mid-nineteenth century. As discussed in the previous section, laws such as the estate in fee tail and primogeniture were designed to ensure succession within families and therefore to preserve the family's base of power. Although American laws regarding succession to property are founded in English principles, there are numerous differences. One of the most obvious is the failure to adopt the system of primogeniture and instead to adhere to the Roman principle that the children inherit equally from a parent regardless of birth order or gender.[36]

Intestate Succession

The laws of descent and distribution determine the manner in which a decedent's property will be distributed if he dies without making a will, if the will is invalid, or if it does not cover the entire estate. In effect, the law makes wills for those who do not make their own. The statutes disburse the property by fixed formulations based on consanguinity and affinity rather than on dependency, age, household connections, need, affection, or other factors. The two key elements in most of the intestacy statutes are the structure of the decedent's family and the categorization of property as realty or personalty. Such laws are blind to the individual needs or equities in a particular family because they are drafted to provide certainty and stability in a wide variety of situations. For instance, if you were deciding how your assets would be allocated after your death, you may wish to provide for an aged parent or a handicapped sibling; however, the statute may assign all your property to your minor children with a reservation of a life estate in your spouse.

The rules governing descent and distribution vary from state to state, but there are patterns in the various schemes. First, surviving spouses and descendants receive favored treatment over all other blood relatives. The decedent's children, natural and adopted, inherit the property subject to the interest, if any, of the decedent's spouse. The children are given equal shares without regard to age or sex, and the children of any of the decedent's predeceased children receive the share that their parent would have received if still living. If the decedent leaves no surviving spouse or descendants, the property often goes to the parents, to the siblings, to the children of the siblings, and then to the descendants of the decedent's grandparents, in successive steps. The presence of heirs at any of those levels would stop the process. If there are no *heirs,* then the property will escheat to the state.[37]

Second, every state has some protection for surviving spouses. In community property states the spouse already owns half of the marital estate, and the succession laws may omit the spouse entirely in favor of those related by consanguinity. A surviving spouse may wind up owning his or her undivided half of the marital home, with the other half being owned by the deceased spouse's children from a previous marriage or by other family members who may have disapproved of the union (which can be a most uncomfortable situation). The Uniform Probate Code provides that the spouse receive all the estate if all the decedent's surviving children are also the children of the spouse; otherwise, there is a reduction in the spouse's share in favor of the children.[38] A traditional statutory provision is to allow the surviving spouse to take one-half, one-third, or some other fractional share of the estate or a life estate if the decedent left children; if there is no issue, then the spouse may inherit the entire estate.[39]

To iterate, each state has a different statutory scheme regarding intestacy and the guardianship of minor children. Disposition of the children can be predetermined by a testator, but without testamentary provisions the state will decide the guardianship of the children. Many of the problems common to intestate succession rear their heads here. You may wish for your best friends to have custody of your children instead of your aged parents or your disreputable sibling, but the law gives preference to relatives. The court will base its decision on the objective standard of the best interest of the children in a contested case, but blood relatives are often the preferred choices.

Testate Succession

A person who drafts a will determines the fate of his or her family and disposes of any assets rather than leaving such important issues to the sometimes cold and unfeeling state. No one has a better understanding of a person's wishes in this regard than the person himself or herself, and despite what clairvoyants and mediums proclaim, the law is skeptical of communications "from beyond the grave" and will not give effect to any post-death property dispositions. Drafting a will is really quite simple, but the process does demand that the testator carefully assess the situation and his or her own emotions and then make preparations based on that assessment. Many people are quite uncomfortable with the notion of their own deaths and are hesitant to reveal the needed information about their personal lives and finances to the attorney drafting the document.

Most of us think of a written instrument that has been executed with certain formalities when we hear the term *will*. However, there are other types of wills—holographic and nuncupative—that may be recognized by the law. A *holographic will* is one written entirely in the testator's handwriting and signed by him or her.[40] A *nuncupative will* is an oral will. Oral wills are not favored by the law because of the inherent difficulties in a will contest of determining the exact intent of the testator and the disposition of the property due to the fleeting nature of the will. Typically, statutes governing nuncupative wills set out stringent requirements for validity and may include such provisions as the following: (1) that the testator was aware of impending death; (2) that the witnesses cannot claim under the will; and (3) that only title to personalty such as cash or automobiles, and not realty, may be affected; for example, Kirstie's nuncupative will could pass title to her collection of Nike shoes but not title to her ranch.[41] Not all states accept holographic and nuncupative wills, and, as previously noted, the validity of the will is determined by the laws of the domicile of the testator. Louisiana, in particular, has unique provisions relating to succession, both testate and intestate, because of its civil law heritage.

A testator executing a will—of whatever kind—must have *testamentary capacity*, which is defined as being of "sound mind" or understanding "the nature and extent of his property, the persons who are the natural objects of his bounty, and the disposition he is making of his property," and the nexus between all of these.[42] The moment at which the will is executed is the pivotal time, and the fact that one's mental capabilities fade in and out is not determinative of one's capacity. The testamentary capacity needed to make a will is not tantamount to the legal ability to contract. A somewhat related issue is the question of voluntariness. The will is void if the testator was acting involuntarily or under duress, or if there was fraud or undue influence involved. However, disinheriting one's family members, supposedly the natural objects of one's bounty, in favor of someone else does not automatically cast doubt on the validity of one's capacity.[43]

Other formalities must be observed in executing a written will. It is patent that the testator must sign the will for it to be effective. It must be signed in front of competent witnesses whose number and competency, usually age, are determined by state law, and it is axiomatic that someone taking under the will must not sign as a witness. The witnesses must be advised as to the nature of the ceremony they are observing, although they do not read the will and often do not know the testamentary provisions (unless the witness is the attorney who drafted the will or the assistant who prepared it). The witnesses sign the will after the testator but in his or her presence. The will should be stored in a safe place until it is needed.[44]

Wills must be updated periodically as life circumstances alter. People marry, divorce, have children, and see those children become independent while once independent parents become dependent. One method of changing one's will is to add a *codicil*, a formal modification or addition to the existing instrument. A second method is to execute a new will, in which case the old one should be revoked through language in the new document or, even better, by destruction of the original, or both. A change of circumstances such as a divorce or annulment usually triggers a revocation of provisions favoring the former spouse.[45]

It is relatively inexpensive to have a simple will prepared by an attorney, although it is not absolutely necessary to do so. We heartily recommend avoiding self-help methods or popular "how-to" books or websites. It is true that one might follow these guides with no particular problems, but on the other hand, disaster can strike if one fails to understand all the ramifications. Remember, too, that each state has a different testamentary scheme and requirements for validity. A corollary issue is that of the "living will" that allows you and your family freedom of choice in regard to medical treatment for the terminally ill. Some states mandate a particular format and language in order for the will to be effective; therefore, if you are interested in executing such a document, be sure that you are aware of the law in your state and do not assume that a standard form will suffice. Similarly, state law may provide for a power of attorney for health purposes, such as a document allows you to specify who would make medical decisions on your behalf if you become incapacitated. Federal legislation mandates that hospitals receiving funds under either Medicare or Medicaid (in effect, almost all hospitals) advise patients of the right to refuse medical treatment and to determine if the patient has either a living will or a durable power of attorney for health purposes and to include either in the patient's records.[46] Hospitals often require patients entering the facility to create such a document if one does not already exist.

Probate

The purpose of probate proceedings is to ensure that the heirs and beneficiaries receive good title to the property they receive. Probate is conducted in accordance with the laws of the domicile of the decedent or with the laws of the state where realty is located.[47] Probate is generally much simpler (and often cheaper) if there is a will appointing an executor or administrator of the estate; otherwise, the court will appoint someone to carry out these responsibilities. It is this person's duty to gather the assets, prepare the inventory for the court's approval, pay the debts, prepare the estate tax return, if any, and disburse the assets to the beneficiaries or heirs.[48] Creditors of the decedent have priority over the heirs or beneficiaries, although state laws provide some protection for the surviving spouse and minor children. Again, this is not the ideal time to employ self-help methods or to ignore probate if one wishes to have legal title to any property one inherits.

"HOW SHARPER THAN A SERPENT'S TOOTH IT IS TO HAVE A THANKLESS CHILD!"[49]

The wealth and social status of the Astor family is legendary in American history. The fortune's founder was John Jacob Astor, who migrated to the United States in 1784, and became the nation's first multimillionaire whose adjusted net worth would have been $138 billion in 2014, making him one of the richest Americans ever.[50] Among his great-grandsons was Vincent Astor, who inherited more than $87 million when his father died on the *Titanic* in 1912 and whose third wife was Brooke Russell Marshall, a noted philanthropist who donated approximately $200 million during her lifetime. At the time of Vincent's death in 1959, Vincent's half-brother accused Mrs. Astor of conspiring to drain the estate, challenging the credibility of the witnesses, and claiming that Vincent did not have the mental capacity to execute the will. The court battle was a "headline-grabbing sensation."[51] However, 50 years later, with the replication of a court challenge to the management of Mrs. Astor's estate, that scrutiny was wholly eclipsed by the intensive media coverage.

In July 2006, one of Mrs. Astor's grandsons, Philip Marshall, petitioned the court alleging that Anthony Marshall, his father and Mrs. Astor's only child, was neglecting her care and was enriching himself with her fortune and asking that Anthony "Tony" Marshall be removed as administrator. The case was settled with an agreement that Tony and his wife would resign as co-administrators of her estate valued at more than $132 million as well as a trust of over $60 million and that JPMorgan Chase & Company and Brooke's close friend, Annette de la Renta, assume guardianship over the 104-year-old recluse and her financial affairs.[52]

Upon her death in 2007, allegations that her son and her attorney had unduly influenced Mrs. Astor to change her will and that perhaps the signatures were forged on three key codicils in favor of Tony became the focus of both civil and criminal proceedings. In 31 wills and seven amendments executed over a period of 50 years, Tony was the recipient of the residuary of the estate that would remain after the substantial bequests to a significant number of charities, but, in some of those documents he was given the money outright, while in others he was given only the income from a trust, with the bulk of the fortune going to charities following his death.[53] Two years after Mrs. Astor's death and following a five-month trial, both Tony, then aged 85 and in very poor health, and the attorney were convicted on 13 counts and sentenced to one to three years in prison. Tony served three months of his sentence in 2013 before being released because of his health from Fishkill Correctional Facility which has a medical unit like a skilled nursing center and died the following year at age 90.[54]

Although dying testate is obviously meritorious, it is no guarantee that everything will be copacetic following a person's demise. Those who are omitted may be disgruntled, and the dispositions can generate enmity among relatives. Nevertheless, a prudent and considerate person protects those he or she cares for by preparing a will and engaging in estate planning. This includes maintaining an up-to-date list of all assets and debts, of the location of important documents, and of current advisors such as accountants, insurance agents, stockbrokers, and attorneys. The existence of this list and its whereabouts should be made known to family members. While many of us think of only the elderly as needing wills, it is perhaps more critical for younger people with dependent children to have a will in order to specify the guardianship of those children if something happened to the parent.

TRUSTS AND GIFTS

The laws relating to succession are designed to ensure the preservation of property. Another way to do so is through a *trust*, a transfer of property from the *trustor* or settlor to the *trustee* as trustee to manage the property for the benefit of the settlor or a third party, known as the beneficiary.[55] Trusts may be either created in a will—a testamentary trust—or during the lifetime of the settlor—an *inter vivos* trust.[56] Trusts are created for a variety of reasons. There may be certain tax advantages to this type of property transfer. The trustor may wish to transfer the problems of managing the trust assets to a financial institution while reserving the right to withdraw any or all of the money whenever it is needed. Perhaps the most common reason for creating a trust is to place the management of assets in the hands of an impartial party as a form of protection for spouses, children, or grandchildren. Such appointment may be desirable because the person is a spendthrift and the assets can be protected from creditors, or because the trustor wishes to guarantee the beneficiary an income long after the trustor is gone.[57]

The provisions of the trust may be tailored to suit the trustor's wishes, and while it does allow for extended control "from beyond the grave," all trusts must eventually terminate and none can last more than 21 years past the lives of the persons living and specified at the time of creating the trust. This is known as the **Rule Against Perpetuities**.[58] For example, a wealthy widow might establish trusts that are not to "extend beyond a period of twenty-one years (21 years) after the death of the last to die of those descendants of my father-in-law who were in being at the time of my death"—a class of 30 people. A frequent testamentary arrangement is for the surviving spouse to receive the income from the trust, and after the spouse's death the children or grandchildren would receive the *corpus* or the principal. This provides the spouse with an income and at the same time prevents him or her from wasting the children's inheritance or conveying it to a second spouse. Trustors have been quite creative in the restrictions and control they have exerted.

The trustee has the responsibility to manage the trust assets, protect the corpus, and comply with the directions of the trust instrument. The trustee may be either a natural person or a corporation such as a bank or trust company.

Many settlors opt to have a financial institution serve as trustee because a natural person may not survive as long as the trust, and the corporation does not have such a limited lifespan and because of the expertise of the institutions in managing money. Another factor that settlors must consider in deciding on who is to be named trustee is the size of the management fee that the trustee would receive. In addition, many financial institutions will not accept small trusts, as, for example, those with assets below $100,000.

The obligations of the trustee are mandated by the trust instrument, by statutes such as a Trust Code, and by the common law. The trustee is legally required to manage the assets with the same skill and diligence as a reasonably prudent person would, and any breach of that fiduciary relationship may lead to both civil and criminal liability on the part of the trustee. The trustee has the duty to invest and manage the property in a productive manner and not to waste the assets by not properly caring for the property or by investing in extraordinarily risky business ventures. The extent of the trustee's powers will be determined by reference to the instrument or to the state's trust laws. Trustees may be removed by court order or by meeting provisions of the trust agreement that allow substitution of trustees.[59]

In contrast, gifts come with "no strings attached." *Gifts* are voluntary transfers of property to the recipient. The *donee* receives full legal title to the property and has full management of it. These are gratuitous transfers; that is, there is no exchange of consideration.[60] An estate planner may recommend a plan of annual gifts to reduce a person's estate below the state or federal inheritance tax levels. Gifts are tax-free to the donee. In other words, substantial gifts to individuals and to charities not only warm the *donors*' hearts but may also provide tax advantages to them, although the tax advantages of charitable contributions are limited.

INTELLECTUAL PROPERTY

Intellectual property is an "umbrella term" that describes "proprietary interests in creations of the mind"[61] and is really an amalgamation of traditional property, tort, and contract law principles. Its roots are based in antiquity, and it is enshrined in this country's Constitution among the enumerated powers of Congress "to promote the progress of science and useful arts, by securing for limited times to authors and inventors the exclusive right to their respective writings and discoveries."[62] The second Congress passed the first patent statute in 1790, barely a year after the Constitution was adopted.[63] However, in today's environment of personal computers and digitized information that is readily available through global communications, more people are questioning the basic concept of exclusive ownership of ideas and the products they generate.[64] They are essentially arguing a return to ancient law that did not recognize a "property" right in intellectual property but instead conceived the matters of plagiarism and intellectual theft as matters of honor, credit, or fame.

Before the concept of intellectual property could develop, two prerequisites were necessary. The first was a clear understanding that invention or ideas could indeed be the product of human intellect rather than the random gift of the gods or, in the Judeo-Christian Era, of God. The second which depended from the first was a recognition that the product of the intellect in its intangible form could also have commercial value.[65]

The Greeks and Romans readily accepted the first prerequisite but not the second. The seeds of intellectual property are often attributed to the guilds of the Middle Ages and their proprietary attitudes toward craft knowledge. Particularly noteworthy in this respect were the Renaissance glassmakers of Venice, who recognized that the craft knowledge of the guild and the particular families within the guild had intrinsic commercial worth, separate and apart from the actual glass, and sought to limit the spread of information about the production process in order to achieve control over the industry and to preserve the value of their knowledge.

Then, as today, governments were encouraging economic development by providing financial incentives, granting favorable tax treatment, and awarding exclusive privileges to individuals as well as to groups to introduce and develop new industries and crafts.[66] This practice of granting these monopolies originated in Italy, probably in Venice but perhaps in Florence, early in the fifteenth century, and by 1474 the practice was so ingrained that Venice enacted the first patent statute. It provided for the protection of newly invented works as well as processes and products not previously known within the realm; however, the work or device had to be sufficiently developed so as to actually be used and operated. There was a temporal limitation on exclusivity for ten years, during which time anyone violating the monopoly would be fined, although the patentee could license the work to someone else. The statute is the earliest known version of patent by registration; that is, conforming to set administrative regulations to protect one's property interests.[67] Other nations quickly followed to adopt similar provisions, and patent laws were adopted in France, England, Germany, and especially the Netherlands, where the most advanced and prolific patent custom developed. There the applicant had the burden of clearly delineating the subject matter of the patent, usually accompanied by a drawing or model in case of later litigation. The review was by committee with the relevant technical knowledge to determine whether the invention was indeed so novel as to merit patent protection. In France, for example, this task was assigned in 1699 to the Royal Academy of Science.[68]

The development and practices of patent law in England closely followed the pattern established on the continent—the growth of guilds and the increasing role of the government in encouraging financial development through grants of patents and monopolies. In fact, the practice became so prevalent under Elizabeth I that it became the battleground for an epic constitutional issue: the power of the monarch versus that of Parliament. Patents and monopolies were issued at the discretion of the monarch as a matter of royal grace. Elizabeth I granted so many monopolies and patents to various courtiers that it has been described as a "system of plunder"[69] with the net effects of "hindrance to trade and manufacture, high prices, inferior goods, and unemployment."[70] In November 1601, Parliament debated the subject of royal powers and prerogatives in the guise of "An Act for the Explanation of the Common Law in Certain Cases of Letters Patents." There were actually two facets to the argument: the power of the monarch and the right of Englishmen to freely engage in trade and industry. Elizabeth I won by admitting that there might have been errors in granting some patents and that future disputes would be submitted to the common law courts if the bill were dropped. She temporarily avoided a parliamentary discussion of her powers by compromising, but the problem remained for her successors.[71] In 1602, monopolies were declared to be against the common law in the famous case of *Darcy v. Allin*, also known as *The Case on Monopolies*,[72] which concerned the monopoly on the manufacture, importation, and sale of playing cards. That principle was iterated in the 1623 Statute of Monopolies, but there was a key exception, namely for letters patent issued to the "first and true" inventors for a period of 14 years or fewer.[73] This law was the sole statute governing patents in England for more than 200 years, and it was still a matter of "privilege" rather than a "property" right.[74]

The basic theoretical conflict—monopoly versus property right—was transported to the United States, and the owners of patents more frequently than not were the losers in the U.S. courts. Those seeking to limit competition in business—by trademark protection, copyright, or patents—are subjected to close scrutiny, since the open market is strongly favored as policy and by law.[75] In *Jungerson v. Ostby & Barton Co.*, Justice Robert H. Jackson, in his dissent, noted that seemingly the only valid patent was one that had not come before the Court.[76] However, as stated earlier, one of the first major pieces of legislation passed by Congress dealt with the issues of intellectual property despite this hostility. The legal framework basically incorporates three general substantive areas—*patents, copyrights,* and *trademarks*—to protect the originality of works and to prevent unfair competition.[77]

Patents may be one of three different types: utility, design, and plant patents. Inventors may obtain patents for processes, machines, manufactures, and compositions of matter that are useful, new, and novel. An invention is judged as useful if it is minimally operable toward some practical purpose. The invention also must not be wholly anticipated by the so-called "prior art" or public domain materials such as publications and other patents. The non-obviousness requirement is met if the invention is beyond the ordinary abilities of a skilled artisan knowledgeable in the appropriate field.[78]

Utility patents are those covering machines, industrial processes, compositions of matter, and articles of manufacture; that is, the products and processes that we normally think of as subject to patent.[79] However, the field of patentable subject matter has been expanded to include items such as some facets of computer software, business methods, methods of medical treatment, biotechnological products including genetically engineered organisms, a golf putt, methods of instruction, techniques of psychological analysis, and even the shoes and stage anchors used for creating the anti-gravity illusion that entertainer Michael Jackson patented.[80] Laws of nature, physical phenomena, and abstract ideas are not patentable subject matter. Inventors are granted property rights for 20 years from the time the application is filed, with some limited exceptions.[81]

Design patents are those protecting ornamental features on some manufactured article (e.g., the swoosh on Nike shoes) rather than function. Plant patents are those dealing with the asexual reproduction of new and distinct plants through grafting, budding, or similar techniques.[82]

Applications for patents are made to the Patent and Trademark Office, and the processing of such patents is often arduous, time consuming, and expensive. The application must contain the short title of the invention, identify the inventors, and contain the specifications and/or drawings for the process or item.[83] Once filed, a patent office examiner reviews the patent to determine whether the subject matter is both "objectively novel and unobvious to those familiar with relevant technology."[84] Patents allow the inventor to prevent someone from making or copying the subject but not from seeking to improve or change the process. The right to a patent may be assigned or licensed and have the attributes of personal property. If the inventor's application is denied, the first appeal is to the Patent Trial and Appeal Board and then to the Court of Appeals for the Federal Circuit or by civil action in the United States District Court for the Eastern District of Virginia.[85]

FLASH OF GENIUS

The 2008 film *Flash of Genius* chronicles the saga of Dr. Bob Kearns and his legal fight to protect his patent rights from infringement. Dr. Kearns' "flash of genius" was to come up with the idea and then to invent the intermittent windshield wiper system. In a stirring David versus Goliath tradition, Kearns took on the Ford Motor Company and the Chrysler Corporation for stealing his idea. His eventual triumph illustrates how one person can stand up to powerful corporations and how important it is to receive recognition for one's creative achievements.

If infringement does occur and other methods of resolution fail, litigation must be filed in federal court.[86] Appeal is to the Court of Appeals for the Federal Circuit, subject to infrequent granting of review by the Supreme Court. Recent decisions of the court indicate an increased willingness to support the validity of patents against infringement. Obtaining multinational patent protection is difficult and must be done in accordance with the laws of each nation; however, under the Paris Convention for the Protection of Industrial Property, the inventor may obtain a priority date by filing an initial application with any of the signatory nations (including the United States) and then filing with other signatory nations within 12 months.[87]

Copyrights protect original authorship in literary works, musical works, dramatic works, pantomimes and choreographic works, pieces of visual art (sculpture, pictures, and graphics), audiovisual works such as movies, sound recordings, architectural works including compilations and derivative works, and some aspects of computer software programs. It does not cover such items as various blank forms, works prepared by U.S. government, fonts and typefaces, titles and short phrases (although these may be protected under unfair competition law or trademarks), facts, ideas, systems, methods of operation, or computer-integrated circuits that are governed by a separate statute, namely the Semiconductor Chip Protection Act.[88] The requirements for the work to be protected by copyright include the following: (1) originality, that is, the work must be an independent creation (not copied from a pre-existing source); (2) a minimal degree of creativity; and (3) fixation in a tangible means of expression.[89]

One issue within copyright law is whether the work is done by a full-time employee; if so, it is done "for hire" and the employer owns both the work and the copyright. On the other hand, if it is completed before being sold, the author owns the copyright unless it is separately conveyed. The issue can become quite sticky, as in the case of, for example, university professors who produce literary or artistic works. For example, consider the graphic arts professor who invents the "better mousetrap" or writes the great American novel, both of which are clearly outside the scope of her teaching responsibilities, and the same professor who produces the piece that is heralded as the greatest graphics masterpiece of this century but that was produced on her own time in her own studio. The statute provides that a work specially ordered or commissioned shall also be considered a work for hire if the parties explicitly agree in writing to that effect, and the work is a contribution to a collective work such as a volume of poetry, a part of an audiovisual work, a translation, a supplementary work, a compilation, an instructional text, as a test or an answer material for a test, or an atlas.[90]

The distinction is important in the duration of the copyright. Generally, copyrights for works created in 1978 or later last for the lifetime of the authors plus 70 years, but those for works for hire or anonymous works last for a flat period of 95 years from the date of publication or 120 years from their creation; for works created before 1978, the length of the copyright is determined by prior statutes.[91] The extension of the copyright protection by two decades in 1998 through legislation commonly known as the Mickey Mouse Preservation Act (Disney's copyright on Mickey was close to expiration) drew challenges because it retroactively enlarged copyrights and gave the creators unexpected profits.[92] Copyrights may be challenged; the most popular song in English, "Happy Birthday to You," was the subject of litigation in which a federal judge examined the history of the song and found that the lyrics were not protected by copyright, although the melody was.[93]

Protection under the copyright laws is no longer dependent on "notice," although registration is required before initiating an action for infringement; that is, the famous © is not required in order to trigger the protection. Registration of copyrights, as contrasted with patents, is very routine and inexpensive, and essentially consists of depositing copies with the Copyright Office and paying the fees. Infringement of copyright, even for sharing files, is punishable in federal courts as both a civil and a criminal matter as well as in state courts under either statutory or common law theories. The chief defense is "fair use," in which the purpose and amount of copying pose little chance of injury and are

POW! WHAM! BAM! KAPOW!

Jack Kirby, alone or with partners, created some of the most famous superheroes: Captain America, the Fantastic Four, Incredible Hulk, Mighty Thor, Spider-Man, Avengers, and the X-Men. His heirs initiated action to regain the copyrights to these characters and others. At stake were not only the original works but the rights to characters that are now reappearing in hit movies that earn hundreds of millions of dollars, as action toys, and in theme parks. Marvel, the original publisher, and Disney, as purchaser of Marvel, countered that Kirby's work was "for hire," while the family claimed that he worked at home as a freelance artist. The family and the companies settled the case for an undisclosed amount on Friday before the United States Supreme Court's conference about accepting the case on Monday. This suit was labeled as the "tip of the iceberg" for the film, music, and book industries—given their penchant for basing new works and franchises on older creations—as more works reach the threshold of expiring copyrights.

Sources: Mark Evanier and Steve Sherman, "Biography of Jack Kirby," Jack Kirby Museum & Research Center (visited December 20, 2015); Brooks Barnes, "Marvel Settles With Family of Comics Artist Jack Kirby," *New York Times,* September 26, 2014.

justified on policy grounds. This includes, for example, photocopying articles for use in your research for a class paper; however, reproducing a thousand copies for sale clearly goes beyond fair use.[94]

Changing technology has created new challenges in the area of copyright law with electronic books and unauthorized copying of music, films, games, and other media by downloading them or through streaming video. Government is struggling to balance the rights of the public to have access to great pieces of literature (for example, through the Internet) and the efforts of commercial enterprises such as movie and music studios to control distribution in order to continue receiving the profits for their efforts and who view those who digitally download material as thieves. The Digital Millennium Copyright Act of 1998 was designed to "provide adequate and effective protection against circumvention of technological measures used by copyright owners to protect their works."[95] The Act contained a measure which prohibits circumventing technology that prevents unauthorized access to copyrighted material. However, copying the same material is not necessarily barred because of the fair use doctrine.[96]

Another work product that inventors and corporations may wish to protect is trade secrets. Two former National Football League coaches, Buddy Ryan and Ernie Zampesie, successfully settled lawsuits against two websites that were offering stolen playbooks for sale; the basis of their litigation was that the information was a trade secret.[97] Similarly, three former employees of Coca-Cola were indicted in 2006 for attempting to sell highly classified information about a new product to PepsiCo; to their credit, PepsiCo advised the Coca-Cola Company of the threat.[98] Protection of trade secrets originated under the common law and is governed primarily by state law, although federal copyright law may also be involved. This area is particularly ambiguous regarding the type and nature of violations, especially in light of the maxim, "Information leaks." Information obtained by tortious or criminal methods is clearly actionable. The criminal law may provide the only protections offered by some states. Information submitted by outsiders seems to be governed by contract law with dependence on the trade custom and the professional status of the person submitting the innovation. Trade secrets are of potentially limited duration because secrecy is undercut both by the practical limitations of keeping information secret and by what constitutes misappropriation.[99]

Intellectual property also encompasses the notion of "unfair competition" under both the common law and the Lanham Act, 15 U.S.C.A. §§ 1051–1127. Included in the Lanham Act are prohibitions against a number of unfair trade practices, including provisions relating to source misrepresentation and protections of trademarks and service marks. The chief issue about trademarks is what devices or symbols are so distinctive or so well recognized that they deserve protection. "The courts and the Patent and Trademark Office have authorized for use as a mark a particular shape (of a Coca-Cola bottle), a particular sound (of NBC's three chimes), and even a particular scent (of plumeria blossoms on sewing thread)," colors,[100] and even phrases such as "you might be a redneck" when supported by the creation of marketable goods such as books, albums, and comedy tours employing that phrase.[101] One of the most litigious companies seeking protection for its signature trademarks—"a pentagon surrounding a childlike drawing of a seagull in flight" and two horses pulling on a pair of jeans—is Levi Strauss. Over the last decades, the company has filed more than 100 lawsuits against competitors, including foreign brands, both in the United States and the European Union.[102]

Public personas may also be protected by either state or federal law. For example, the blocks of stamps honoring Marilyn Monroe who died in 1962 in the Legends of Hollywood stamp series bore the notation "All rights reserved. Signature of Marilyn Monroe™, MARILYN™, NORMA JEANE™, and the name, image, voice, and likeness of Marilyn Monroe are properties of the estate of Marilyn Monroe. © 1995 U.S. Postal Service." This right of publicity obviously survives the death of the individual, while the tort right to privacy does not.

Common names of products, trademarks already used by others, or functional aspects (e.g., car freshener) do not qualify for trademark protection. A trademark is "a brand name—the designation for a particular type or style of goods or services that come from a particular producer and have consistent attributes each time you buy them ... Almost any identifying symbol that can be conjured by the human imagination can be used as a trademark."[103] "It can act as a symbol."[104] It does not prevent the use of words or symbols in the customary way. Registration of the term *Apple* as a brand of computers cannot prevent fruit growers from advertising their product as apples. Trademarks may be registered under both federal and state laws. Trademarks have no value without the underlying business, although they can be assigned and licensed. The holder of the trademark has the burden to prosecute any infringement and may obtain injunctive relief as well as damages.[105]

"BRAVES ON THE WARPATH!"©

Trademarks of the National Football League's Washington Redskins that depict a Native American were found to be disparaging of Native Americans in violation of the Lanham Act by the Trademark Trial and Appeal Board and therefore ineligible for registration. A federal district court agreed. Among other arguments, the judge noted that as early as 1868, *Webster's Collegiate Dictionary* defined the term "redskin" as contemptuous and found that of the six trademark registrations at question (1967, 1974, 1978, and 1990) disparaged a composite number of Native Americans as even the Redskins' own linguistics expert conceded that the team name "certainly might be offensive."

To lose the monopoly over merchandizing because of the loss of registration would have a significant financial impact, even for a team worth $2.4 billion in 2014; brand management alone was valued at $214 million. Because the team belongs to a consortium of 31 NFL teams (all except the Dallas Cowboys) that share the merchandizing revenue, other teams would also forfeit the profit. In addition, the value of official sponsorships would be devalued. However, under the court order, the team may continue to control merchandize with the trademarks until all appeals are exhausted and, even then, the team could rely on state laws for protection.

Sources: Pro-Football, Inc. v. Blackhorse, Cause No.1:14-cv-01043-GBL.IDD (N.D.Va. 2015); Ian Shapira, "Federal Judge Orders Cancellation of Redskins' Trademark Registrations," *Washington Post*, July 8, 2015; Darren Rovell, "Patent Office: Redskins 'Disparaging,'" *ESPN*, June 18, 2014, http://espn.go.com/nfl/story/_/id/11102096/us-patent-office-cancels-washington-redskins-trademark (visited December 21, 2015).

Despite the long-standing legal framework for the protection of intellectual property, today it faces renewed challenges. The first comes as the United States becomes more entangled with the global economy via new treaty provisions that sometimes override long-term policy and law within this nation. There is no global intellectual property system in place, and instead protections are established through a variety of agreements and treaties. For example, the Berne Convention of 1886 as revised is the primary international copyright treaty, but it is flawed in that there is no authority to enforce judgments of violations. The Madrid Agreement simplifies the procedure for those seeking international trademark protection, namely filing one trademark application at his or her own national or regional trademark office and designating specific nations for registration rather than filing in each of the signatory nations. The Agreement of Trade-Related Aspects of Intellectual Property Rights (TRIPS Agreement) under the auspices of the World Trade Organization covers copyrights, trademarks, geographic indications such as origin, industrial designs, patents, layout designs of integrated circuits, computer programs, data compilations, and trade secrets in the international setting and provides enforcement techniques.[106]

A second challenge is rulings by courts, including the U.S. Supreme Court, that states are essentially immune from patent infringement lawsuits.[107] These holdings immediately sent chilling reverberations throughout the intellectual property community. Numerous groups from various economic sectors were appalled and vowed to continue the fight, as many "believe it gives states carte blanche to run wild with others' intellectual property."[108] Imagine, for example, the states of Oklahoma, South Carolina, or Texas having the freedom to copy software onto every government computer and not reimbursing the authors and producers.

The third challenge is to the notion of knowledge as "property." It is based on the premise that because of technology, knowledge is more accessible than it has ever been and that it is increasingly more difficult to hoard. One commentator employs the analogy of the "futile struggle of the boy with his finger in the dike" to describe the issue.

Laws and theories written to protect books, radio and television broadcasts, and phonograph records are outmoded, insufficient, and likely to stay behind the technological advances, some argue.[109] Society should recognize that "most of humankind's heritage is in some sense a 'commons,'" and the argument is that perhaps we are applying the "wrong verb" to the "wrong noun" in the "protecting" of "intellectual property."[110] With the onslaught of new advances, the underlying philosophy of intellectual property is indeed open for debate, and perhaps a return to the ancient doctrines of no legal protection will occur.

CONCLUSION

The maintenance of a system of private property has been of paramount importance in this country from its earliest days. It is entrenched in social policy to preserve wealth in the hands of individuals, and the laws reflect that commitment. Americans look askance at those who attempt to limit the use of their property, especially land, and some only grudgingly comply with various zoning and building codes and with corporate regulation. They view these as interference with their God-given right to own and control their property as they see fit.

This chapter conforms to the traditional approach to property law. It discusses the creation of property rights, the traditional classifications, the means of preserving such interests, and the methods of transferring the property from one person through another. The nature of this work precludes an in-depth discussion of the complexity of landlord–tenant relations, financing land purchases, or tax issues related to property. The cursory treatment is not intended to minimize the importance of any of these issues, however.

Although we opted for the traditional approach, you should be aware of emerging trends in property law. Real property is no longer the dominant form of wealth in the United States; instead, billions of dollars are invested in pension and profit-sharing plans, mutual funds, stock markets, and government-backed securities. The result is that the government and courts are directing more attention toward these forms of wealth and toward civil and individual rights than was the case in the past. This focus is producing shifts in American law. First, the courts are employing a balancing test of the owner's right to unfettered use of his or her land versus the interests of the other party.[111] In First Amendment and other cases, there is no longer an automatic reaction to rule in favor of the landowner, and the proprietor's use and enjoyment of the land are being circumscribed through zoning, environmental regulation, historic preservation, and other mandates. Second, the concept of property is being expanded. Courts have held that one's means of livelihood, income, or career are defined as property for due process purposes, which means that certain procedural requirements must be met before a person is deprived of his property interest.[112] Third, in the area of intellectual property, the challenge is to achieve "a balance between the encouragement of labors that lead to creative expression on one hand, and insuring that a sufficient amount of these products of the mind remain freely available as building blocks for the future, on the other."[113] Thus, as society evolves, even the ancient law of property changes.

NOTES

1. Cornelius J. Moynihan and Sheldon F. Kurtz, *Introduction to the Law of Real Property*, 4th edn (St. Paul, MN: Thomson/West, 2005).
2. U.S. Constitution, Amendment V; see also Amendment XIV.
3. Henry C. Black, *Black's Law Dictionary*, 4th edn (St. Paul, MN: West, 1968), p. 1382.
4. 63C Am. Jur.2d *Property* §§ 8–23.
5. G.C. Cheshire, *The Modern Law of Real Property*, 9th edn (London: Butterworths, 1962), pp. 8–15, 27–28.
6. Moynihan and Kurtz, p. 24.
7. Ibid., pp. 33–36.
8. Ibid., pp. 50–60.
9. Ibid., pp. 64–79.
10. Ibid., pp. 222–227.
11. Interview with Richard A. Jackson, real-estate broker; 12 Am. Jur.2d *Brokers* §§ 88–89.
12. Ibid., pp. 78–127.
13. Raymond J. Werner, *Real Estate Law*, 11th edn (Cincinnati, OH: South-Western/ Thomson, 2002), pp. 230–231.
14. Moynihan and Kurtz, pp. 281–285.
15. Werner, pp. 217–223; ibid., pp. 274–280.
16. 63 Am. Jur.2d *Property* § 12.
17. Cheshire, p. 446.
18. 38 Am. Jur.2d *Gas and Oil* § 121; 53A Am. Jur.2d *Mines and Minerals* § 340.
19. 78 Am. Jur.2d *Waters* § 1.
20. 78 Am. Jur.2d *Waters* § 136.
21. 78 Am. Jur.2d *Waters* §§ 213–215.
22. Black, p. 616.
23. *Kelo v. City of New London*, 545 U.S. 469 (2005).
24. *Wal-Mart Stores, Inc. v. Planning Bd. of North Elba*, 238 A.D.2d 93, 668 N.Y.S.2d 774 (N.Y. App. 1998).
25. Historic Sites, Buildings, and Antiquities Act, 16 U.S.C. § 461.
26. Anne Matthews, "Making the List," *Preservation* 50, 4 (July–August 1998): 65–66.
27. 36 C.F.R. § 65.2(b).
28. Matthews, pp. 68–69.

29. *Village of Euclid v. Ambler Realty Co.*, 272 U.S. 365 (1926).
30. *Berman v. Parker*, 348 U.S. 26 (1954), at 33.
31. Black, p. 73.
32. 3 Am. Jur.2d *Adverse Possession* §§ 11, 62, 147.
33. 23 Am. Jur.2d *Deeds* § 223; 20 Am. Jur.2d *Covenants* §§ 58–62.
34. 77 Am. Jur.2d *Vendor and Purchaser* § 103.
35. UCC, ch. 9.
36. Thomas E. Atkinson, *Handbook of the Law of Wills*, 2nd edn (St. Paul, MN: West, 1953), pp. 7–30.
37. William M. McGovern, Jr. and Sheldon F. Kurtz, *Wills, Trusts and Estates*, 3rd edn (St. Paul, MN: Thomson/West, 2004), pp. 50–60.
38. Uniform Probate Code, §§ 2–102 and 2–102A http://www.law.upenn.edu/bll/ulc/upc/final2005.htm (visited August 7, 2006).
39. McGovern and Kurtz, pp. 48–49.
40. Ibid., pp. 196–200.
41. Ibid., pp. 200–201. See, for example, Ohio. Rev. Code § 2107.60 and Tex. Prob. Code § 65.
42. Atkinson, p. 232.
43. Ibid., pp. 255–270.
44. Ibid., pp. 291–354.
45. McGovern and Kurtz, pp. 235–247.
46. Ibid., pp. 644–645.
47. *In re Barrie's Estate*, 240 Iowa 431, 35 N.W.2d 658 (1949).
48. McGovern and Kurtz, pp. 500–501.
49. William Shakespeare, *King Lear*, Act I, Scene IV, lines 310–311, pp. 990–991; Harden Craig, ed., *The Complete Works of Shakespeare* (Glenview, IL: Scott, Foresman and Company, 1961).
50. Steve Hargreaves, "The Richest Americans in History," *CNN Money*, http://money.cnn.com/gallery/luxury/2014/06/01/richest-americans-in-history/3.html (visited December 19, 2015).
51. John Elig on, "Fight for Astor Estate Mirrors Battle 50 Years Ago," *New York Times*, April 25, 2009.
52. Barbara Whitaker, "Brooke Astor's Guardians and Son Battle Over Estate," *New York Times*," August 23, 2007.
53. John Eligon, "Astor Trial is Told of Changes to Her Will," *New York Times*, June 3, 2009.
54. Robert D. McFadden, "Anthony D. Marshall, Astor Son Who Was Convicted in Swindle, Dies at 90," *New York Times*, December 1, 2014.
55. George T. Bogert, *Trusts*, 6th edn (St. Paul, MN: West, 1987), p. 1.
56. 76 Am. Jur.2d *Trusts* § 18.
57. Bogert, pp. 148–160.
58. McGovern and Kurtz, pp. 449–450.
59. Bogert, pp. 91–100, 317–351.
60. Black, p. 817.
61. Roger E. Schechter and John R. Thomas, *Intellectual Property: The Law of Copyrights, Patents, and Trademarks* (St. Paul, MN: Thomson/West, 2003), pp. 1, 4.
62. U.S. Constitution, Art. I, § 8.
63. Edward C. Walterscheid, "The Early Evolution of the United States Patent Law: Antecedents (Part I)," *Journal of the Patent and Trademark Office Society* 76 (September 1994), pp. 697–715.

64. Harlan Cleveland, "How Can 'Intellectual Property' Be 'Protected'?," *Change* 21 (May/June 1989), pp. 10–11; Schechter and Thomas, p. 9.

65. Walterscheid, "The Early Evolution (Part I)," pp. 702–703.

66. Ibid., pp. 706–708.

67. Ibid., pp. 708–710.

68. Ibid., pp. 712–714.

69. W. Hyde Price, *The English Patents of Monopoly,* as cited in Edward C. Walterscheid, "The Early Evolution of the United States Patent Law (Part II)," *Journal of the Patent and Trademark Office Society* 76 (November 1994), p. 864.

70. Walterscheid, "The Early Evolution (Part II)," p. 864.

71. Ibid., pp. 855–872.

72. *Darcy v. Allin*, 72 Eng. Rep. 830 (Moore 671), 74 Eng. Rep. 1131 (Noy 173), 11 Coke Rep. 86 (King's Bench 1602).

73. 21 James I § 6, VII Statutes at Large 255 § 6.

74. Walterscheid, "The Early Evolution (Part II)," p. 875.

75. Thomas G. Field, Jr., "Intellectual Property: Some Practical and Legal Fundamentals," *Idea: The Journal of Law and Technology* 35 (1994), p. 79.

76. *Jungerson v. Ostby & Barton Co.*, 335 U.S. 560 (1949) (Jackson, J., dissenting), at 572.

77. Field, pp. 79–128.

78. Schechter and Thomas, p. 282.

79. 35 U.S.C.A. § 101.

80. Schechter and Thomas, pp. 292–310; Michael Jackson, Michael Bush, and Dennis Tompkins, Patent US5255452 (October 26, 1993).

81. 35 U.S.C.A. § 154(a)(2).

82. 35 U.S.C.A. §§ 161–164, 171–173; Schechter and Thomas, p. 312. The Plant Variety Protection Act, 7 U.S.C. § 2321, applies to sexually reproduced plants and plants found in uncultivated areas and is administered by the Department of Agriculture.

83. Field, pp. 86–96.

84. Ibid., p. 81.

85. 35 U.S.C. § 141 and § 145.

86. Field, pp. 88–89, 96–97.

87. 35 U.S.C.A. § 119; Schechter and Thomas, pp. 454–455.

88. 17 U.S.C.A. §§ 102(a)–103; Semiconductor Chip Protection Act, 17 U.S.C.A. §§ 901–914; Schechter and Thomas, pp. 38–74.

89. Schechter and Thomas, pp. 20–31.

90. 17 U.S.C.A. § 101.

91. 17 U.S.C.A. § 302.

92. Sonny Bono Term Extension Act, P.L. 105–298, 112 Stat. 2827; Damien Cave, "Mickey Mouse vs. the People," http://www.salon.com/2002/02/21/web_copyright/ (visited December 20, 2015); Steven Levy, "Glitterati vs. Geeks," *Newsweek* CXL, 16, October 14, 2002, pp. 40–43.

93. Ben Sisario, "'Happy Birthday' Copyright Invalidated by Judge," *New York Times*, September 22, 2015.

94. Field, pp. 97–106.

95. U.S. Copyright Office Summary, "Digital Millennium Copyright Act of 1998," http://www.copyright.gov/legislation/dmca.pdf. (visited December 21, 2015), p. 3.

96. Ibid., pp. 3–4.

97. "Inadmissible: No Playin," *Texas Lawyer,* September 17, 2001, p. 3; North American Free Trade Agreement, P.L. 103–465, 108 Stat. 2057 (1993).

98. Brenda Goodman, "Agents Arrest 3 in Plot to Sell Coca-Cola Secrets to PepsiCo," *New York Times*, July 6, 2006, p. C-2.
99. Field, p. 111.
100. *Qualitex Co. v. Jacobson Products Co.*, 514 U.S. 159 (1995), at 162.
101. *Foxworthy v. Custom Tees*, 879 F. Supp. 1200 (N.D. Ga. 1995).
102. Michael Barbaro and Julie Creswell, "Levi's Turns to Suing its Rivals," *New York Times*, January 29, 2007; *Levi Strauss & Co. v. Evisu International S.R.L.*, Cause 3:2010cv01292 (N.D. Ca. 2010) as cited at Justia.com Dockets and Filings, http://dockets.justia.com/docket/california/candce/3:2010cv01292/225794/ (visited December 21, 2015); *Levi Strauss & Co. v. Tesco Stores Ltd.*, Case C-415/99, 2001 E.C.R. 1-8691.
103. Schechter and Thomas, p. 539.
104. *Qualitex Co. v. Jacobson Products Co.*, at 166.
105. Field, pp. 116–126.
106. World Trade Organization, "Overview: The TRIPS Agreement," https://www.wto.org/english/tratop_e/trips_e/intel2_e.htm (visited December 21, 2015).
107. *College Sav. Bank v. Fla. Prepaid Postsecondary Ed. Expense Bd.*, 527 U.S. 666 (1999); *Chavez v. Arte Publico Press*, 139 F.3d 504 (5th Cir. 1998).
108. Nathan Koppel, "Fifth Circuit Says States Are Immune from Copyright Suits," *Texas Lawyer*, May 11, 1998, p. 6.
109. Cleveland, pp. 10–11.
110. Ibid., p. 11.
111. *Amalgamated Food Employees Union Local v. Logan Valley Plaza Inc.*, 391 U.S. 308 (1968).
112. *Goldberg v. Kelly*, 397 U.S. 254 (1970); *Board of Regents of State Colleges v. Roth*, 408 U.S. 564 (1972).
113. Schechter and Thomas, p. 9.

CHAPTER 13

Family Law

Families in this country generate a great deal of litigation. Few lawsuits match the magnitude of the impact on the individuals involved, with the exception of the most serious felony cases. These suits impinge upon the most sensitive and personal of relationships; these are the cases that dissolve marriages and determine the custody of children. Many are decided without blazing courtroom battles (the arguments have usually occurred earlier, behind closed doors). Many family law cases are settled by agreement between the parties, and the courtroom proceedings may seem routine and bland to the detached observer, but the emotional impact on the parties is immeasurable.

Laws that affect familial relationships span many fields, including property law, wills and estates, contracts, torts, and criminal law. This chapter focuses on the creation of the family relationship by marriage or other types of domestic commitments, by paternity suits, and by adoption; on the legal principles governing such relations; and on the dissolution of the spousal and parent–child relationship through various types of court action. State legislatures and courts bear the primary onus of dealing with the sometimes complex, often time-consuming issues of family law. It is rare for the U.S. Supreme Court to consider a case involving these matters, although a few involving constitutional questions, such as equal protection, have reached the Court. It is state courts—often specially created domestic-relation courts—that try and then decide the overwhelming majority of such cases.

ROLE OF THE STATE IN FAMILY RELATIONSHIPS

The role of the state in regulating family relationships is so firmly entrenched in jurisprudence that it is virtually unchallenged by today's litigants. In Rome by the time of Christianity, marriage required only the reciprocal consent of the couple, a precursor of today's informal marriages. During this time, the parties were essentially equal; the husband controlled neither the wife nor her property, although he was obligated to maintain her financially, and either party could end the marriage.[1]

The first formal requirements for obtaining a divorce occurred during the reign of Augustus Caesar in 40 CE. There were two grounds for divorce: mutual divorce or "no fault," in which the spouses agreed to everything, and divorce "for cause," such as adultery. If fault was involved, then the innocent party was favored in the property settlement, and the case was heard by one of the praetors. In the mutual divorce, no judge was involved, and the couple settled the matter between themselves.

For a time, there was complete freedom in matters of marriage and divorce, and they were not justiciable matters unless there was controversy over the property settlement. The precepts of Christianity contravened such attitudes, particularly regarding divorce, because marriage was considered to be permanent and to remain indissoluble until death. The Emperor Justinian, a Christian who codified the Roman laws in the sixth century, confronted these countervailing views and chose the moderate path of compromise. The Codes contained limited grounds for divorce—mutual agreement, amicably without cause imputed to either party, and for cause—but the major change was that an agreement between the parties would no longer suffice for a divorce. That was revoked by Justinian's son who, like most of his subjects, shared neither his father's Christian beliefs nor his concern about divorce. However, Justinian's Code served as the basis for the legal systems of most European countries and for canon, or church, law, and his position that divorce by agreement only should be barred has prevailed in the Western world.[2]

Initially, Christianity had little effect on marriage under Roman law. The major change was in limiting freedom to marry by imposing additional barriers such as age requirements (14 for males and 12 for females) and by forbidding marriages within certain degrees of *consanguinity* (related by blood) or *affinity* (by marriage). Eventually, however, the domination by the Catholic Church in the Middle Ages led to the replacement by canon law of many of the previous legal traditions, but it certainly did not obliterate them, and many remnants linger today. As early as the seventh century, marital laws in England included many of the Church's precepts. Among these was the principle that marriage was of divine origin and the attendant corollary that ecclesiastical courts should have exclusive jurisdiction over marriage, a situation that lasted until the mid-nineteenth century and the passage by Parliament of the Matrimonial Causes Act of 1857. The wife was essentially a chattel, and her property rights were not protected until the equity courts interceded, beginning in the seventeenth century.

Divorce was also regulated by canon law which offered few opportunities to escape from an unhappy marriage. One alternative was to have the marriage dissolved because the husband and wife were related within forbidden degrees of consanguinity. Henry VIII used this strategy to end his marriage to Catherine of Aragon in order to marry Anne Boleyn. The other alternative, available after 1660, was divorce by special parliamentary act on the grounds of adultery. Both alternatives were possible only for the rich and the powerful.

The colonists transported English legal traditions along with their worldly goods to the New World. The rules governing the creation of marital relationships, such as the form of the ceremony and age requirements, remained virtually unchanged. However, the colonies, populated primarily by Protestants following the teachings of Martin Luther and John Calvin, regarded divorce as a legal rather than a religious matter, and most adopted general divorce statutes.[3] As new areas opened up and the population migrated westward, the domestic relations laws in the western states and territories became more liberal, to the point of allowing, for a short time, the practice of polygamy, or having plural spouses at the same time.[4] While proof of fault was initially required in divorce actions, the standard today is some version of marriage breakdown such as irreconcilable differences or incompatibility, although several states have mandated some type of counseling or mediation as part of the proceedings.

The role of the state in regulating family relationships has strong historical roots, and it is therefore virtually uncontroverted today. The rationale for such involvement is succinctly explained in the following excerpt:

> Marriage is more than a personal relation between a man and a woman. It is a status founded on contract and established by law. It constitutes an institution involving the highest interests of society. It is regulated and controlled by law based on principles of public policy affecting the welfare of the people of the state.[5]

Families are perceived not only as social but also as legal entities, and government therefore issues rules governing the creation and dissolution of those relationships. Politicians of all ilks, sociologists, and others continually claim that today's families are under attack and frequently blame all society's ills on the breakdown of the family. Part of the difficulty is in defining "family" in a society marked by diversity in interpersonal relationships. Do people who live together, commingle their assets, and care for each other constitute a family? Are widowed sisters who move in together following the deaths of their respective spouses a family? What about single adult children who live separate and apart from their parents but provide the emotional and physical support for the parent; are they still a family? Do a divorced great-grandmother, her widowed son, his lesbian daughter and her spouse, his never-married 18-year-old son, and the son's 16-month-old daughter qualify as a family unit for purposes of insurance, protection under the Family and Medical Leave Act, and benefits under the tax laws as would the traditional model of father, mother, and children? What about if there are no blood ties in the relationship but all other indicia of a family are there? Should the definition of family encompass emotional, psychological, and financial ties rather than blood relationships? Merely defining "family" and what is the ideal family is a major policy decision with extensive implications for the legal system.

Some argue that government is too intrusive into family life in such things as providing sex education classes in school while also maintaining that government does not go far enough in such matters as imposing a total ban on abortion. This ambivalence has prevented the United States from creating a consistent framework of policy and laws dealing with the family. However, the traditions and laws are so strong and society's interest so important that withdrawal of all government involvement is most unlikely.

MARRIAGE

Marriage is a legal status founded on contract law in American jurisprudence. As such, states have created certain rules and regulations to govern the creation of such status, just as the law establishes certain requirements for the existence of contracts. In both instances, for example, parties must have the legal capacity to enter into the bargain, and there must be a mutual assent in order to establish each. There are two methods for creating a valid marriage relationship: informal, or the so-called common law marriage, and formal, whereby the couple is married by someone authorized to do so by law. In determining the validity of the marriage, it is critical to examine the local laws of the jurisdiction in which the marriage occurred. If the creation of the marital relationship satisfied the local requirements and does not violate the strong public policy of another state, then it is valid everywhere in the United States.[6] Traditionally, each state has control over those who marry within its boundaries; regulating marriage relationships is usually outside the sphere of the national government.[7]

> Marriage, as creating the most important relation in life, as having more to do with the morals and civilization of a people than any other institution, has always been subject to the control of the legislature. That body prescribes the age at which parties may contract to marry, the procedure or form essential to constitute marriage, the duties and obligations it creates, its effects upon the property of both, present and prospective, and the acts which may constitute grounds for its dissolution.[8]

The minimum age requirement for marriage has several bases: biology, as the age is generally related to the time of puberty; tradition, such as the age requirements set by canon law; and contract law, which provides that those entering into a contract must be able to comprehend the event. Beyond the age of majority (18 in most states), couples may freely enter into the relationship; however, for those who are unemancipated minors, permission to marry is required from parents or the courts. In the same vein, those who are mentally incompetent lack the legal capacity to contract, and they are barred from marrying.[9]

An additional restriction that states place on the freedom to marry is the requirement of monogamy or having only one spouse at any given time; this requirement is a remnant of Roman and canon law.[10] In other cultures, such as in some African and Islamic countries, polygamy is legal, and polygyny (living with several wives and their children) is practiced, albeit illegally, by some groups in the United States. Obviously, each jurisdiction has wide authority in governing the marriages within its boundaries. The first major nationwide exception was that states could not prohibit interracial marriages. In 1967, the miscegenation statutes that forbade marriage between blacks and whites in 16 states were struck down by the landmark case of *Loving v. Virginia*.[11] The second major exception was the ratification of same-sex marriage in *Obergefell v. Hodges* in 2015.[12]

Laws also prohibit marriage between those who are related within certain degrees of consanguinity and of affinity. That is, one is barred from marrying one's parents, brothers and sisters (both full-blood and half-blood), children and other descendants, and direct ancestors, such as grandparents or great-grandparents. Individual jurisdictions may add to the list of those who cannot marry because they are related.

Beginning in the 1970s, one of the seemingly basic premises regarding marriage was legally challenged. While earlier efforts to achieve legal recognition of same-sex marriages failed, in May 1993 the Supreme Court of Hawaii handed down the case of *Baehr v. Lewin*, later known as *Baehr v. Miike*.[13] The suit was brought by three same-sex couples challenging the denial of marriage licenses to each couple by the State of Hawaii on the grounds that such action violated the couples' right to privacy, equal protection, and due process under the *Hawaiian* Constitution. The lower court issued judgment for the defendant on the pleadings.

The Hawaiian Supreme Court chose first to examine the question of whether same-sex marriage is a fundamental right by employing the standard tests of identifying such:

> a right ... so rooted in the traditions and collective conscience of our people that failure to recognize it would violate the fundamental principles of liberty and justice that lie at the base of all our civil and political institutions [or so] implicit in the concept of ordered liberty, such that neither liberty nor justice would exist if it were sacrificed.[14]

The court held that same-sex marriage was not a fundamental right included in the state right to privacy. However, the court did find that the Hawaii Marriage Law created a sex-based classification in violation of the state constitution and that the proper standard for testing the constitutionality of such a statute was the strict-scrutiny test. The court remanded the case to the lower court to consider that equal protection argument under the guidelines enunciated by the higher tribunal.

The Hawaiian legislature intervened by enacting a law providing that marriage license laws within the state were to apply only to male and female couples.[15] Eventually, Hawaii voters ratified that position by amending the state constitution, and the Hawaiian Supreme Court held that the marriage amendment removed the matter "out of the ambit of the equal protection clause of the Hawaii Constitution ... insofar as the statute, both on its face and as applied, purported to limit access to the marital status to opposite-sex couples."[16]

That Hawaiian courts gave any credence to the idea of same-sex marriage fueled a national debate.[17] Lawsuits against two other states also received a great deal of public attention. In Alaska, the trial court determined that "the choice of a life partner is personal, intimate, and subject to the protection of privacy," the choice was a fundamental right, and the appropriate standard of review was that of strict scrutiny requiring the state to show a compelling state interest in order to restrict that right.[18] Before the case progressed to the appellate level, Alaska voters adopted a constitutional amendment defining marriage as existing between one man and one woman, effectively derailing the original Alaska lawsuit.[19] Nevertheless, the Alaska Supreme Court later upheld the challenge of same-sex couples regarding discrimination in employee benefits that were tied to marriage in *Alaska Civil Liberties Union ex rel. Carter v. Alaska*.[20]

> The incredible irony of Carter is that the marriage amendment possibly ensured that the court would examine the difference in treatment between same-sex and opposite-sex couples, rather than between married and unmarried ones. Without the marriage amendment, there would not have been an absolute need for the court to treat same-sex couples as their own class. This is so because, as unmarried couples, same-sex couples may still have theoretically possessed the opportunity to marry, and thereby, to avail themselves of spousal benefits. [T]he holding was able to carefully navigate between respect for the state's marriage amendment and recognition that same-sex couples are entitled to equal protection.[21]

In Vermont, the state Supreme Court found that, under the Common Benefits Clause of the state constitution, the plaintiffs were entitled to the same benefits and protections as married opposite-sex couples, but the Court deferred to the legislature the method of accomplishing that goal; that is, either to create an equal institution or to allow same-sex couples to marry.[22] In *Goodridge v. Dep't of Pub. Health*, the Massachusetts Supreme Court squarely addressed the question of whether, under the State's Constitution, the government could deny same-sex couples the right to marry and declared that it could not.[23]

These successful challenges relied on state constitutional provisions while those relying on interpretations of the federal Constitution failed.[24] In response, many state legislatures immediately amended their statutes to limit marriages to opposite-sex couples, while 35 went even further and declared as void and unenforceable marriages of same-sex couples created elsewhere. Voters in a dozen or so states approved constitutional amendments defining marriage as between one man and one woman.[25] On the federal level, the Defense of Marriage Act (DOMA)[26] defined marriage for purposes of federal law, such as receiving benefits, to opposite-sex couples in § 3[27] and provided that states were not "required to give effect to any public act, record, or judicial proceeding of any other State, territory, possession, or tribe respecting a relationship between persons of the same sex that is treated as a marriage under the laws of such other State, territory, possession, or tribe."[28] The Supreme Court rejected the portion of DOMA barring federal benefits to same-sex couples whose marriages were valid under state law because it "violates basic due process and equal protection principles applicable to the Federal Government." The Court noted that "By history and tradition the definition and regulation of marriage ... has been treated as being within the authority and realm of the separate States" and deferred to state laws that authorized same-sex marriage.[29] The controversy continued as each state forged its own uneasy path through the quagmire. Some states and local governments adopted various forms of civil unions. These statutes, often applicable to both same-sex couples and opposite-sex couples, generally required that the parties were at least 18 years of age, residing together, competent to contract, and not violating any state laws against incest before the relationship may be officially registered. In addition, the couples typically affirmed that they were responsible for the welfare of each other and that they were the sole domestic partner of the other. Official termination of the relationship followed only after proper notice. The ordinances varied widely in the degree of legal protection and benefits they provided to the partners, but they did provide the psychological benefit of recognition of the relationship.[30] In these locales, the domestic partnership statutes provided the "only government-sanctioned method of solemnizing committed relationships."[31]

Full recognition (or refusal thereof) of same-sex marriages by a state struck at the heart of federalism. Marriages created in one state were usually recognized in other jurisdictions on the basis of comity;[32] that is, as a matter of deference and respect, although some states enacted marriage validation statutes or adopted the Uniform Marriage and Divorce Act that included a validation provision.[33] If a status such as marriage violated a strong public policy, a state was free to ignore the relationship under comity.[34] In 2015, the United States Supreme Court's landmark decision in *Obergefell v. Hodges*[35] decided the issue that had percolated through the legal system with conflicting results. The Court held that all states must issue marriage licenses to same-sex couples and that all states must recognize valid marriages from other states; the holding effectively legalized same-sex marriage. While Justice Samuel Alito's dissent noted that no nation had recognized same-sex marriages until the Netherlands in 2000 and no state did so until Massachusetts in 2003,[36] 36 states, the District of Columbia, and Guam already issued marriage licenses to same-sex couples on the day the opinion was announced.[37] The case reached the Court because of split decision of the circuit courts of appeals as to the constitutionality of state bans against same-sex marriage. The Sixth Circuit ruled that such prohibitions were constitutional, while the Fourth, Seventh, Ninth, and Tenth Circuits had reached the opposite position, thereby setting up the Supreme Court's likely agreement to hear the matter.

The Court combined litigation from four states—Michigan, Ohio, Kentucky, and Tennessee—and six cases in which the federal district courts had ruled for the same-sex couples and other claimants, but the Sixth Circuit of Appeals had overturned the decisions and sustained the bans. The lead plaintiff was James Obergefell who had married John Arthur in Maryland. Arthur was terminally ill with amyotrophic lateral sclerosis (ALS), and Arthur wished Obergefell to be listed as his spouse on his death certificate in order for Obergefell to be buried in the Arthurs' family plot upon his death; this could not occur unless Obergefell was a spouse or all family members who might have an interest in the plot agreed. Based on their Maryland marriage, the Ohio Registrar agreed to the listing, but the state attorney general's office chose to intervene and defend the state's same-sex marriage ban. Arthur died in 2013, but the case continued. Similarly, David Michener filed a lawsuit when his spouse, William Ives, died suddenly, and Michener could not be listed on the death certificate as spouse.

Other cases addressed the parent–child relationship in same-sex marriages. In the Michigan case of *DeBoer v. Snyder*, a same-sex couple were foster parents who were concerned about the custody of the children if either parent died; one partner, Jayne Rowse, had adopted two of the children and April DeBoer had adopted one because Michigan law limited adoptions to single people or to married couples. Three Ohio same-sex couples who had legally married in other states sought to have both parents included on the birth certificates; they were joined by a New York couple whose son was born in Ohio. One of the Kentucky cases included children as named parties in challenges to have their parents' out-of-state marriages recognized. Additional litigants in Kentucky and Tennessee sought to require clerks to issue marriage licenses to same-sex couples.[38]

Justice Anthony Kennedy authored the 5 to 4 majority opinion that same-sex marriage bans are unconstitutional under both the Fourteenth Amendment's Due Process Clause and Equal Protection Clause and, thus, states must both issue marriage licenses and recognize valid out-of-state marriages. The opinion presented four arguments to support the decision; (1) the right to personal choice in the selection of a life partner is inherent in the concept of individual autonomy and dignity; (2) marriage is a union of commitment unlike any others and should be available to same-sex couples; (3) the protection of parental marriage preserves the status of the children and the families, and marriage is no less meaningful for individuals or couples who cannot or choose not to procreate; and (4) "States have contributed to the fundamental character of marriage by placing it at the center of many facets of the legal and social order. There is no difference between same- and opposite-sex couples with respect to this principle, yet same-sex couples are denied the constellation of benefits that the States have linked to marriage."[39]

The four justices in the minority issued four dissents, each of which was joined by at least one other justice. They argued that the basic core of marriage has been one-man-one-woman throughout history and should not be altered. In addition, they predicted that there would be consequences for religious liberty, that the decision could lead to legalized polygamy, and that it could subject those who opposed the ruling to vilification. Justice Antonin Scalia, true to his originalist beliefs, posited that same-sex marriage was not considered legal at the time of the adoption of the Fourteenth Amendment and should not be so now. However, the dissenters' strongest attacks were against the role of the Court as superlegislature and policymaker; the argument was that the majority had overstepped its bounds, had subverted the democratic process, and that such matters should be left to the people and to the legislatures of the states.[40]

The general public, politicians, and pundits immediately pointed out the weaknesses of both the majority and dissenting opinions. Amidst the explosion of commentary about the outcome, Justice Kennedy was charged with "single-handedly" creating rights in prior cases involving same-sex couples, often in 5 to 4 decisions that were used as precedent in this opinion[41] and with employing reasoning that was "indefensible as a matter of law."[42] Critics of the dissenters noted that they ignored recent precedents such as *United States v. Windsor*, the DOMA case, and that none of the dissenting justices had ever voted to support gay rights.[43]

Obergefell decided the essential question of the legality of same-sex marriage, but left many issues unanswered and ripe for litigation. Will the case open the door for underage marriages, plural marriages, or marriages between family members such as first cousins? Is the decision prospective or retroactive? It is important to determine when the marital relationship began, especially for couples in states that did not recognize the legal marriage, because that date determines eligibility for benefits such as pensions and Social Security. The thicket of uncertainty grows even more densely in community property states or those with common law or informal marriages. The inception date also affects many other matters such as the marital privilege in the rules of evidence.

While the U.S. Department of Labor had previously extended protections under the Family and Medical Leave Act and the Employment Retirement Income Security Act to legally married same-sex couples wherever their domicile, many state laws still permit discrimination in employment, public accommodations, and other situations. *Obergefell* did not address Title VII of the Civil Rights Act that provides protection against discriminatory actions by private employers and universities among others, but the Equal Employment Opportunity Commission has since ruled that workplace discrimination based on sexual orientation is sex discrimination under Title VII and is therefore prohibited under federal law. Court decisions examining the practices of various businesses such as wedding planners, florists, and bakeries to refuse services to same-sex couples have been mixed, depending primarily on whether the states have laws against discrimination based on sexual orientation. Several states have passed statutes that protect clergy in their refusal to perform marriages if the refusal stems from religious beliefs. However, someone who acts in official capacity as an agent of a governmental entity, such as a county clerk, must comply with the law regardless of individual religious views, although accommodations may be made for his or her religious scruples when, for example, an assistant clerk issues a marriage license.[44]

Assuming that the parties have the capacity to marry and are not barred from doing so by statutory provisions, there are two methods of creating a legally binding marriage in the United States. All states have standards for formal marriages, while only a few make provisions for informal marriages, but the validity of a marriage is determined by the local law. *Informal marriages* are sometimes called "common law marriages," a term that may refer to their non-statutory origin. The basis of an informal marriage is the *present* consent or agreement between the parties that they are married. An agreement to marry in the future is not sufficient. Most statutes additionally require cohabitation and a public declaration of marriage.[45] This declaration may consist of sharing a joint bank account, introducing the other party as the spouse, or some other indication that the couple consider themselves married. The fact that the woman keeps her own name is not a determining factor if the elements are otherwise met.

An informal marriage is a valid marriage, requiring divorce for dissolution. A spouse who enters into an informal marriage and later formally marries without first obtaining a divorce may be subject to bigamy charges. Proving the existence of an informal marriage is sometimes difficult; however, it is particularly difficult to prove the element of intent. Spouses may try to disclaim intent in a divorce suit in order to avoid a property settlement, but the requisite intent may be shown indirectly by other evidence. Informal marriages are disfavored in part because there is seldom a record of such relationships, which complicates such legal matters as receipt of insurance or social security benefits if one spouse dies; nevertheless, they are valid marital relationships if all other prerequisites are met.[46] Most states accept only a formal marriage as the method of creating a valid marital relationship in their jurisdictions but recognize valid informal marriages from other states.

The vast majority of couples are joined through ceremonial marriages. Typically, they begin the process by paying a fee and obtaining a license from a public official, often the county clerk. Both parties must generally appear to apply for the license and are required to provide certain basic information, including full names, birth dates, and present marital status. Many states impose a short waiting period, and the licenses generally expire within a given time period. In addition to requiring marriage licenses, statutes specify those with authority to perform marriage ceremonies, including ministers, rabbis, priests, or others authorized by religious organizations as well as certain public officials such as justices of the peace and judges. Once the couple is married the marriage license must be returned to the proper official, whereupon it becomes a matter of public record.[47]

DISSOLUTION OF MARRIAGE

States regulate not only the creation of the marital relationship but also its dissolution. Divorce by consent alone is not allowed in the United States, and some type of judicial action is necessary to dissolve marriages. The adoption of *no-fault* grounds both facilitates obtaining a divorce and reduces the involvement of the judicial system to a minimum. For example, California statutes provide that couples who have been married for fewer than five years, have no minor children and no real property, have debts under $4000 and assets of less than $25,000 worth of community property, and have executed an agreement about the property division that includes a waiver of spousal support may jointly file for summary dissolution. Six months later, on either party's motion, the court can divorce the couple without further ado.[48] In many other instances judicial approval is purely *pro forma,* an acceptance of the parties' agreements in regard to custody of minor children, if any, and to the property division. Couples are often urged to enter into such agreements because, like a plea bargain in criminal law, it removes the issues from the vagaries of a judge or jury and provides for certainty. Courts favor these agreements for two reasons: (1) more cases can be processed through the system in a shorter period of time than would be the case if the judge had to consider the evidence and merits of each situation and (2) courts avoid having to decide complex issues such as child (and pet) custody as well as the tiresome minutiae of which spouse gets the towels and pots and pans.

Annulments

Marriages may be dissolved either by divorce or by **annulment.** Divorces are much more common than annulments because of the extremely limited grounds for annulments. An annulment differs from a divorce in that the legal basis of an annulment is that the marriage was invalid from its inception, whereas a divorce acknowledges the initial validity of the marital relationship. The goal in both cases is to dissolve the legal ties between the spouses.[49] Some statutes distinguish between void and voidable marriages. Voidable marriages are those that do not meet the requirements for a valid marriage and can be dissolved on that basis. For example, Jennifer and Peter were both underage when they wed. If this is considered a voidable marriage, either they could file for annulment based on that ground or they could continue their marriage as if they had met the prerequisites. On the other hand, if Peter were married to Sally at the time that he married Jennifer, the second marriage would be void or totally invalid.

The grounds for annulment are rather limited and vary from jurisdiction to jurisdiction. They are generally directed to the capacity or the intent to marry. Those who are underage or mentally incompetent may lack the necessary understanding to enter into a marriage relationship, much as they lack the capability to enter into a binding contract. Mental incompetency may be an issue for the trier of fact. Those who marry during an involuntary state of intoxication such as persons who have been drugged against their wills generally have grounds for annulment; the key here is that the intoxication is not voluntary. (Those who wish to disclaim their marriage vows because of a nip or two before their wedding are out of luck in qualifying for an annulment.) Couples related to each other within prohibited degrees of consanguinity or affinity may file for annulments; some of these marriages are void, while others are voidable according to state law. In addition, some of the relationships will also fall afoul of such criminal laws as incest statutes. Fraud and duress are other grounds for annulment. *Fraud* involves knowingly making false statements about a material and essential fact in order to induce someone into marriage, such as denying that one is currently married. *Duress* results from employing coercion or force in persuading someone to marry. A facetious example is the reluctant groom who is marrying with the bride's father's loaded shotgun pointed squarely at his back.

Logically, declaring a marriage void from its inception leads to extremely harsh results. Any children born of the marriage are bastardized, and the economic results could be devastating. The effects have been mitigated by laws that legitimize the children and provide for equitable property division; these issues are decided in accordance with the rules that apply in divorce actions.[50] It is important to note that annulments are rather rare because most couples do not meet the statutory grounds for filing such a suit.

MARRY IN HASTE, REPENT AT LEISURE

In a whirlwind courtship, Helen and Donald Jones married after a two-week acquaintance before he deployed overseas during World War II. Helen was concerned about a "home marred by drunkenness," and during their brief engagement, Donald advised her that while he drank beer occasionally, he did not drink hard liquor. But before his departure and after his return, Donald did consume hard liquor and became quite drunk on several occasions. Helen left him and filed for an annulment based on fraud.

Donald admitted that he concealed his drinking habits because he knew that Helen would not marry him if he revealed the truth. The Court noted that "It is to be expected that every suitor will put his best foot forward. It would be contrary to human nature if he did not paint himself in glowing colors, and did not fully utilize all the 'seller's puff,' to borrow a phrase from the law of contracts, which was at his command. Boastfulness and self approbation are as natural and as much to be expected under such circumstances as the strut of the rooster in the barnyard." The annulment was denied on the basis that "Not every fraud, even though it may have been the inducing cause of the particular marriage, is an adequate basis for an annulment." Furthermore, once Donald told Helen that he was a "drinking man," she, as a reasonably prudent person, should have inquired further because, as Donald himself stated, "if you had taken time out to check on my character you would have learned I was quite a heavy drinker."

Source: Jones v. Jones, 189 Misc. 145, 69 N.Y.S.2d 223 (1947).

Divorce

The prevalent method for terminating a marital relationship is divorce. Three issues are generally involved in such suits: (1) the procedural aspects, such as residency and the technical grounds for divorce; (2) the property settlement; and (3) the custody and support of the children, if any. The result of a divorce suit is to dissolve the legal ties between the couple. As a practical matter, parties often remain connected to each other because of the children or mutual property interests, including debts, which frequently cause them to reappear in court as litigants against each other. Some divorce-related issues may drag on for many years; failure to pay spousal support or child support in accordance with the court order are common examples. Divorce rarely resolves all the issues or complaints couples have against each other, which is somewhat deceptive to many people who anticipate otherwise.

Procedural Aspects of Divorce

A court must have jurisdiction to grant a divorce, to enter a property settlement, and to decide custody of the couple's children. This jurisdiction stems from state constitutional and legislative provisions. A typical requirement is that one or both parties meet residency requirements. Nevada is famed for its short residency period of six weeks;[51] Alaska merely requires that one party be a resident of the state,[52] while Texas requires six months' domicile in the state and 90 days in the county preceding the filing of a divorce suit.[53] Venue is generally in the county of residence of the parties. Of course, the spouse must be served with divorce papers even if he or she resides in another state or nation.

Divorce petitions must allege the grounds for the action. Most proceed on no-fault grounds, which merely allege incompatibility, marriage breakdown, living separate and apart for a specified time, or similar circumstances to indicate that the parties are no longer getting along and wish to end the marriage. This greatly simplifies the proof required to obtain a divorce; a simple statement to that effect by one of the parties while on the witness stand usually suffices to prove the grounds for divorce.[54]

The practice of claiming fault as a ground for divorce has fallen into disfavor because of the problems of proof. For example, the party who alleges adultery must introduce evidence and persuade the trier of fact that such activity did occur. This is often an expensive (and somewhat embarrassing) procedure. Typical grounds of fault are adultery, desertion, and cruelty. One reason to allege fault in a divorce petition or to prove fault at trial is to affect child custody or the property division against the wrongdoer. In contested cases, the allegations will generally be brought out in testimony and may be considered by the judge in allocating the marital resources. In uncontested cases, they may be used in negotiations as a bargaining chip. The fact that many couples do not wish their private lives to be revealed to public scrutiny, coupled with the difficulty of proof in fault cases, results in most divorces proceeding under the no-fault provisions of the statute.

A number of couples are opting to pursue collaborative divorces in lieu of extensive (and expensive) litigation. Collaborative law, a form of ADR, is aimed at resolving disputes outside the courtroom in a spirit of cooperation rather than adversarial proceedings, and as the Mark Loring character in the movie *Juno* told his wife, "They call it 'Collaborative Divorce.' It's apparently all the rage right now."[55] The attorneys are hired to assist the parties in negotiating a settlement and if an agreement is not reached, the attorneys must resign, and the parties retain new attorneys for the litigation. The benefits of the process are quicker resolution, lower financial costs, and, more importantly, less harm to the families and greater personal satisfaction to the parties and the lawyers. Often, other neutral professionals such as financial planners and child specialists are actively involved. The approach is that of cooperation, and the goal is to limit the psychological damage, especially for the children, and to expedite the proceedings for both economic and temporal reasons.[56] The agreement between the late actor Robin Williams and his former wife Marsha Garces Williams in their collaborative divorce action that "We will strive to be honest, cooperative and respectful as we work in this process to achieve the future well-being of our families. We commit ourselves to the collaborative law process and agree to seek a positive way to resolve our differences justly and equitably" exemplifies the spirit of this approach.[57]

Property Division

During the existence of the marital relationship, the parties are required to financially support each other. When they decide to divorce, a grant of temporary spousal support or maintenance for a spouse who needs it during the pendency of the divorce is often authorized by state legislatures. Such maintenance orders are entered by the court after adequate notice and the opportunity for a hearing on the matter. Of course, that may be circumvented by agreement between the parties.[58]

At the time of the divorce hearing, the property and the debts are divided between the spouses. This aspect of divorce is often the one that causes the most bitterness and ill will. Spouses may control the property division by entering into a prearranged property settlement that is generally ratified by the court, but few agreements satisfy both parties. Some couples anticipate the possibility of divorce and enter into a *prenuptial agreement* outlining the property division even before they marry. According to the Statute of Frauds, such contracts must be in writing.[59] Prenuptial agreements are frequently employed by wealthy individuals who are concerned about preserving their assets or older couples who are marrying for the second time and who want their children from their first marriage, rather than their second spouse's children, to inherit their property. In either event, the goal of the prenuptial agreement is to predetermine the disposition of assets at the time of divorce or death. The courts scrutinize such arrangements carefully to ensure that no overreaching or coercion was involved. Cohabitation agreements, both express and implied contracts, are enforced by the courts with legal and equitable remedies for opposite-sex and same-sex couples.[60]

Marital property is generally defined as all property acquired by either spouse during the marriage relationship, except for gifts or inheritances. In the eight community-property states (Arizona, California, Idaho, Louisiana, Nevada, New Mexico, Texas, and Washington), community property belongs equally to both spouses, regardless of whose efforts garnered the property, while Wisconsin created the same result by adopting the Uniform Marital Property Act.[61] Each has an undivided interest in the property; the husband's or wife's salary belongs equally to both, and the issue of who holds the title to the property is irrelevant if it is community property. In contrast, property owned before marriage or property one inherited or was given during marriage belongs only to that spouse. In the so-called common law states, the early rule was that the wife had no property rights and that her estate was under the control of her husband.[62] The husband's control was abolished by statutes, known as the

Married Women's Act, that gave married women the right to own and control property and to enter into contracts on their own behalf.[63] In these states, ownership of the property still vests in one of the parties unless specifically created in both; for instance, the wage earner has sole ownership of wages. In other words, "under the common-law system, a housewife who does not also work outside the home has no legal right to any marital asset, unless her husband puts it in her name or adds her to the title as a tenant in common or joint tenant."[64] Upon divorce, the marital property or property acquired during marriage is divided.

In both the community property and common law states, the same factors are typically considered in the property settlement. These factors include age, health, occupation, other assets, and the earning capacity of the respective parties. For example, Mary completed three years of college before marrying John, after which she dropped out of school and worked as a bank teller to pay for his undergraduate and dental training. During the 25 years that their children attended public schools Mary did not work outside the home. Now Mary and John, both aged 55, are divorcing. He has an annual income of $200,000, while she has no income and no assets other than the marital property. Her age and lack of recent work experience will hinder her efforts to obtain employment, and any job she finds will probably not pay well. On the other hand, John enjoys a relatively secure income that is likely to continue for some time. The court may consider these factors in dividing the property and in setting *spousal support* if permitted by state law. The recognition of a homemaker's financial contributions to the marriage, along with *no-fault divorce*, was an integral part of divorce reform in the last decades.

All states provide that the marital property be divided in a fair and equitable or reasonable manner. This is not tantamount to requiring that property be divided equally between the spouses. In addition to the aforementioned factors, courts may also consider other items, such as the allocation of debts and custody of minor children, in determining the final property division.[65]

Few topics have ignited as much calumny as the subject of spousal support but they remain an integral part of the legal landscape. The U.S. Supreme Court has held that spousal support statutes must be gender-neutral and cases for spousal support for husbands are ever more common.[66] In addition, such orders today are generally for a relatively short period of time to assist the spouse in "making the transition to economic self-sufficiency" or are designed "to compensate the spouse for contributions to the marriage that cannot adequately be covered with property division orders."[67]

Technically, there are differences between orders relating to the division of property and spousal support. Property orders relate to marital property already in existence. Spousal support, on the other hand, is a payment for support and maintenance usually payable from future income, although the court may approve a lump-sum payment; furthermore, spousal support may be founded on the couple's present standard of living as well as on the factors previously discussed in connection with the property settlement. In some instances, installment payments of the property settlement are permitted, but these must be distinguished from spousal support. To illustrate, Pete and Lucy worked together to build a chain of stores now valued at $1,750,000. The court, having considered all the factors and all the couple's assets, orders Lucy to pay Pete $750,000 for his share of the business. Withdrawing that amount of money from the business at one time might well destroy it; therefore, Lucy may be permitted to pay Pete $75,000 plus interest for each of the next ten years. This is not spousal support but instead represents a division of existing assets. In addition to saving her source of income, such installment payments offer certain tax benefits as well.

Differentiating spousal support from property settlements is important for several reasons. Court decrees dividing the property generally cannot be modified at a later date, whereas spousal support orders can be changed on proof of a change in the circumstances of the payer or recipient. Spousal support payments automatically terminate on remarriage in many states, but the obligation to make the installment payments for the property continues. The two are treated differently under federal tax and bankruptcy laws. Division of property orders typically cannot be enforced by civil contempt, but spousal support orders can be. Any court order involving both spousal support and property division should clearly distinguish one from the other.[68]

Equally (and sometimes more) important than the division of the assets is the division of the debts, including tax liabilities. If marital property is the collateral for the debt, then both parties may remain liable for the debt even if the asset is given solely to one party in the divorce action.[69] Valuation of assets such as professional or celebrity goodwill or deferred compensation plans including pensions and stock options is often an incredibly complex task.

Custody and Support of the Children

Deciding the custody of children is often a difficult decision for a judge or jury, who are well aware that however tormenting the decision is for them, it is much worse for the parties, especially the youngsters. Children, even those who have been mistreated, usually feel loyalty and affection toward their parents, and custody battles exact more from them than from anyone else. Custody arguments generally arise through two types of litigation: (1) cases in which the state is alleging that the children should be separated from their parents; and (2) divorce actions. For a fact-finder, it is relatively easy to decide the issue if one spouse is a model parent and the other is not, but that is rarely true in contested cases.

The current standard used in awarding custody—that of the ***best interest of the child*** rather than the old standard of proving the parent unfit for custody—shifts the emphasis from the parent to the child's overall wellbeing.[70] This intentionally vague standard of best interest allows a number of factors to be considered: (1) the parenting skills of the person seeking custody; (2) the physical safety of the child; (3) the stability of the home and parent; (4) the present and future emotional and physical needs of the child; (5) present and future plans for the child; (6) acts or omissions of the parent that would affect parenting performance, and (7) the child's preference that is not binding on the court.

The items on this list indicate that the parent with the highest earning potential or the most assets does not automatically receive custody, although the ability of each contestant to support the child is considered.

The last decades have seen major revisions in custody laws, and a large number of them have come about through the feminist movement. One of these changes is the general abolishment of a sex preference in granting custody. The old common law rule that the father's claim to custody should be paramount was supplanted by a preference for giving custody to the mother, particularly when the case involved girls or children under the age of 6, whereas fathers were generally awarded custody of older sons. Today, most statutes are neutral, and juries are instructed that the sex of the parent is not to be a determinative consideration. More fathers are seeking and obtaining custody today, either by agreement with their spouses or by court order in contested cases.[71] This is partly due to the recognition of three factors: (1) that fathers often have parenting skills equal to or better than those of mothers; (2) that couples share household tasks, including the rearing of children, more equally than in the past; and (3) that both parents are employed in many American families and no longer do mothers automatically stay at home with the children, as was the pattern of upper- and middle-class families until the mid-twentieth century. Economic reality usually dictates that most single parents must work outside the home, and there is essentially no difference in the amount of time that a working parent, male or female, could spend with the children. Thus, women's search for legal equality and fair treatment under the law has reaped an important benefit for men as well.

Custody orders are not immutable; they can be modified. The typical requirement is that there must have been a substantial and material change in the circumstances of either the parent or the child before the court will modify the original order. The requirement is intended to discourage frequent relitigation of custody decrees in order to promote stability in the children's lives. The enactment by the states of the Uniform Child Custody and Enforcement Act that acknowledges the validity of sister states' original orders and promotes compliance with those orders, along with the adoption of the Parental Kidnapping Prevention Act, has strengthened the enforcement of original orders and curbed the tendency to modify orders or issue new ones.[72]

When parents live apart and a court order is entered regarding custody, one parent is granted possession of the child and the right to determine the child's domicile, while the other is granted visitation rights. Typically, visitation is specified for certain weekends, for longer periods during summer school vacation, and for holidays. Visitation rights may be withheld or circumscribed at the court's discretion. An abusive parent or one who has previously snatched the child may be limited to visits with the child in a grandparent's home or in the offices of the state social service agency. There is a growing trend toward providing visitation rights for the grandparents as well. Custody and visitation rights may be tailored to fit the needs of the children and can be rather creative; an example is a decree that allows the children to remain in the family home while the parents move in and out rather than moving the children. Statutes today authorize or even presume joint custody orders that may be joint legal custody, joint physical custody, or both, and even the statutory terminology is changing to parenting plans or decision-making or custodial responsibilities.[73]

Parents are legally obligated to support their unemancipated children, and while courts generally do not intervene to enforce this provision if the parents and children are living together, they frequently do so in suits affecting the parent–child relationship, including parentage suits and divorces. The parties may set the amount of child support by agreement, subject to ratification by the court, or the court will assess the amount after considering the relevant evidence. The following factors are often considered in such decisions: actual and potential earnings and other assets of the parents, especially the obligor; division of property and debts; lifestyles of the parties and the children; the children's ages; health of both the parents and the children; and the cost of living.[74]

Child support orders, like custody orders, may be modified if there are substantial and material changes in the circumstances of the children or the parents. A well-paid executive who has lost her position because of economic depression in a particular industry may seek to decrease her child support, or the custodial parent of a child who develops severe medical problems may seek to increase the support. These are extreme examples, but modification of child support orders may be triggered by increases in the cost of living or by increased demands as children grow older.

Determining the initial amount of support or modifying it is seldom as difficult a legal problem as enforcing the court order. Both visitation and child support orders are enforceable primarily through contempt proceedings and are a fertile source of litigation. Visitation and child support are parallel rights and are not tied to each other. Failure to pay child support on a timely basis does not authorize the custodial parent to withhold visitation as punishment; self-help methods are not favored by the courts in this regard. Both parties in such a situation could be held in contempt of court, which is punishable by fines or by jail sentences, or both, after a hearing that involves adequate notice and the opportunity to present any defense. True inability to pay child support is a valid defense, but courts carefully scrutinize such claims. A parent who claims that he is unable to pay because he lost his job, but who is not looking for work, is unlikely to find favor with the court, nor is the parent who supports his new wife's children but not his own biological children. However, parents who are unable to work because of injury or who are actively seeking work may win a reprieve and time to catch up on the payments at a later date.

Other remedies for nonpayment of support include reducing the amount to judgment and putting a lien on the obligor's property, garnishment of wages, and criminal nonsupport charges. To facilitate collection of child support when the obligor has moved outside the state, states have adopted the Uniform Interstate Family Support Act; in addition, treaties provide for collection across international borders. The lawsuits are initiated in the children's home state in the required format and mailed to the site of the parent's new home. Authorities there file the papers, give legal notice and an opportunity to be heard to the parent, collect the support payments, and remit them to the children, all without forcing any of the parties to incur travel expenses.

Intense concern about the spiraling costs of welfare, along with increasing awareness that nonpayment of child support was reaching epidemic proportions, led Congress to enact P.L. 93–647, the Social Security Amendments of 1974 (42 U.S.C. §§ 651–666). States were mandated to create child support collection programs under threat of withholding federal funds for assistance to poor families. The programs are primarily directed toward the absent parents of children collecting government assistance but are available to assist all in establishing and enforcing child support obligations. The state agencies have access to the parent-locator service and to the national new hire registry to locate absent parents. Penalties for nonpayment of support include interception of tax returns, revocation of driver and professional licenses, and denial of passports to those who are delinquent with child support payments.[75] It is even a federal crime if there is a willful failure to pay for a year or the amount owed is over $5000 and the child resides in another state.[76] States are also being creative in regard to remedies to force parents to support their children; for example, the Supreme Court of Wisconsin upheld a probation order that bars a man convicted of failure to pay child support from having more children until he can prove that he can support all his children and that he is actually doing so. At the time of the decision, David W. Oakley had nine children by four women and owed $25,000 in back support. Failure to comply with the terms of his probation could result in an eight-year prison sentence.[77]

The dissolution of a marriage is an emotion-laden, if not traumatic, event for most people. Many initiate the process hoping that it will be a cathartic experience and are therefore disappointed in the detached and apparently insensitive attitudes of judges and attorneys. The parties often want the courts to allocate blame and to punish the other person for perceived injustices and grievances but that rarely happens. The courts are there only to resolve the legal issues of dissolution, property, custody, and support in accordance with the statutes and legal precepts.

THE PARENT–CHILD RELATIONSHIP

The relationship between parents and children is both biological and legal. The two may not be identical, however. The potential difference arises because of legitimacy statutes, adoption, and, oddly enough, modern medical technology. Legally, the parent–child relationship may be created by operation of law; by contract, as in the case of surrogate parents; and by court order. As used here, the term *parent* refers to the legal, rather than biological, parent. Parents owe certain duties and responsibilities to their minor children including the duty of care, support, and supervision. Whereas the biological relationship lasts as long as the parties live, legal parent–child relationships end. Children who reach the age of majority are no longer legally under the control of their parents. This is true of the mentally handicapped as well; most jurisdictions require the appointment of a guardian, who essentially carries out the parental responsibilities and, in fact, is often the parent. In addition, the relationship can be terminated by court order.

Establishment of the Parent–Child Relationship

Traditionally, illegitimacy, or birth out of wedlock, has been both a social and a legal handicap. For many years, bastards (in the legal sense only) could not claim support or inherit from their natural fathers. Today, illegitimacy no longer makes one a social pariah, nor is it an absolute bar to enforcing legal rights. Children whose biological parents are married to each other at the time of conception or at the child's birth are presumed to be legitimate. Over the years, laws have evolved that grant that status to children whose natural parents subsequently marry.[78] Traditionally, children who are conceived by artificial insemination and born of married women are considered the legitimate children of her husband; in some states, the written prior consent of the husband is required before the procedure is performed. Legitimate children are allowed by the law to claim support from both parents as well as to inherit from them. For centuries, determination of parentage focused solely on the father; however, today, parentage of the mother may also be litigated. To resolve these issues, some states have adopted the Uniform Parentage Act that provides "the child, the mother of the child, a man whose paternity is to be adjudicated, a support-enforcement agency, an authorized adoption agency or licensed child-placing agency, a representative of a deceased, incapacitated or minor person, or an intended parent under a gestational contract have standing" to determine the legal relationship of the parties.[79]

The legalization of same-sex marriages has affected many of the traditional rules about parentage and created instability. For example, the presumption that the spouse is the parent of the child when a couple is married may also be applied to lesbian and gay couples; however, state courts have split on this point.[80] Lawsuits have been filed to force states to list both spouses on new birth certificates or to amend prior certificates.[81] Other potential lawsuits will focus on adoption and gestational agreements. Many same-sex couples have adopted children, either singly or together, if permitted by law. One of the lesbian partners in same-sex marriages has traditionally been required to seek adoption to establish parental rights while the other is listed on the birth certificate as the parent. For married gay men, both partners will still be required to adopt in some states while other states will allow both to become parents upon the birth if the state surrogacy laws permit. Gestational agreements that require the parents to be married will also be impacted by legalization of same-sex marriage. The traditional rules have been unsettled, and it will take some time (and many court decisions) to again create stability.

Relationship of Child to Mother

In the past, the biological mother was considered to be the parent without further action, and the child was considered as her legitimate offspring until the relationship was terminated by court order.[82] However, this has been changed by the development of alternative methods of reproduction through the use of artificial insemination with the contracting father's sperm, *in vitro* fertilization with the implementation of donated eggs in which case the legal mother has no genetic connection to the child, and perhaps, in the future, cloning. While some states bar all surrogacy arrangements, others have statutory provisions that strictly regulate the agreements, especially artificial insemination involving married couples. These arrangements apparently establish parenthood by contract.[83]

Relationship of Child to Father

Establishing the parent–child relationship between a child and the natural father may be more difficult. All states provide a mechanism by which the father may voluntarily acknowledge the relationship. In addition, there are paternity statutes—the bases for judicial determination as to the existence of the relationship. Texas was the last jurisdiction in the United States to incorporate a paternity statute in its laws; wags in the state always claimed that it was to prevent the legislators from being sued, and, in fact, the legislature enacted the law only after the U.S. Supreme Court decided in *Gomez v. Perez*, 409 U.S. 535 (1973) that denial of paternal support to illegitimate children was a violation of the equal protection clause and therefore unconstitutional.[84]

Paternity suits, as do all other suits, require that the putative father be given adequate notice and an opportunity to present a defense. Typical defenses include denying sexual intercourse with the mother at the pertinent time or alleging that she was also having intercourse with other men during that time period. The crucial factor in many paternity suits is the result of sophisticated genetic tests, including DNA. Establishment of paternity invokes rights to visitation or custody and the obligations attached to such relationships, including financial support for the child.[85]

Adoption

Another method of establishing the parent–child relationship is by adoption. *Adoption* is defined in *Black's Law Dictionary* as "the act of one who takes another's child into his own family, treating him as his own, and giving him all the rights and duties of his own child" and as "a juridicial act creating between two persons certain relations, purely civil, of paternity and filiation."[86] As used here, the term refers to formal adoptions that are court-approved, as opposed to merely taking a child into one's home for succor and to adoptions of children rather than adults. The process legally substitutes one set of parents, the adoptive set, for another, the biological set. The chief limitation on the right to adopt is the child's status in regard to his or her biological parents; that is, the child's relationship to his or her genetic parents must have been terminated by court order before adoption may occur.

The criterion used by the court to judge whether to grant an adoption petition is whether the adoption will be in the child's best interest. As previously discussed, the best interest of the child is a nebulous standard that allows judges to exercise a great deal of discretion. The focus in applying the standard is the *fitness* of the proposed parent or parents, another rather vague term. Statutes and case law provide some guidelines, and judges frequently call on neutral social service agencies to investigate the parents and the home environment, and to file a report with the court or even to testify. It is firmly established that, if other prerequisites are met, an adoption cannot be denied solely on the basis of different religious backgrounds or even on the basis of the parents' lack of belief in a Supreme Being.[87] An absolute bar on interracial adoptions is also unconstitutional. In addition, many states now allow single persons to adopt, reflecting the legislatures' awareness that many families in the United States are headed by single parents. Another recent modification is the relaxation of the rule that the adoptive parents must meet certain physical specifications; those who have been deemed unfit by adoption agencies merely because of physical handicaps or obesity have successfully challenged those rejections in court.[88]

The Indian Child Welfare Act of 1978 established the pre-eminence of tribal law and proceedings in foster care, adoptions and termination of parental rights of Native Americans by providing that state courts have no jurisdiction over children residing on their own reservations and by providing for concurrent jurisdiction with tribal courts over children not residing on the reservation.[89] The increasing number of international adoptions led Congress to adopt the Intercountry Adoption Act of 2000 to ensure that the adoption is in the best interest of the child and that all proper procedures have been followed in both nations.[90] Other trends are open adoptions in which the adopted child may continue to have contact with his or her genetic family and the removal of the shroud of secrecy from adoption records; sealed court records are rarely opened, but some statutes authorize the limited opening of adoption records.[91]

Thus, there are two traditional methods of legally establishing the parent–child relationship: by being the genetic parent and having legitimate offspring or by obtaining a court order through parentage suits or adoption. We have seen the emergence of a third method: by contract, in situations of artificial insemination or with surrogate mothers. Accompanying the initiation of such relationships are certain duties and responsibilities.

Parental Rights and Obligations

The obligations and responsibilities of parents, or of those having custody of children, are many and varied. The primary right is to have physical possession of the child and to establish his or her legal domicile without interference by third parties. The state may intercede to assume physical possession if child abuse is suspected or proven, or under other circumstances ordered by the court. Parents also have the power to make legal decisions for the child and to sue and be sued on the child's behalf. They have authority to consent to medical, surgical, and psychiatric treatment for a child and to approve of marriage or military enlistment for minor children.

The primary parental responsibilities toward children are twofold: (1) to provide the basic necessities of food, shelter, and clothing, and (2) to provide care, control, supervision, education, and reasonable discipline. Violation of either of these obligations by the parents may result in the state's intervening in the situation. The parent–child relationship is a privileged one in the eyes of the law, and legislatures and courts hesitate to intervene, as indicated by the following quotation from the U.S. Supreme Court.

> It is cardinal with us that the custody, care, and nurture of the child reside first in the parents ... And it is in recognition of this that these decisions have respected the private realm of family life which the state cannot enter ... But the family itself is not beyond regulation in the public interest.[92]

The law imposes a duty upon parents to supervise children and allows a corollary right of discipline. Failure to adequately supervise children may lead to either civil or criminal liability on the parents' part as well as removal of the children from the home by the state. The duty to control one's children is offset by restrictions limiting the punishment a parent may dole out to children. Statutes generally employ such language as "reasonable" discipline. Locking children in closets for days, withholding food or water, and burning them with cigarettes do not fall within this category. Corporal punishment is permitted, but it must not be excessive, an issue that sometimes becomes a fact question at child abuse trials.

Parents are also obligated to financially support their children and to provide the basics of life, including food, shelter, and clothing.[93] Generally, the standard of living within each home is outside the state's sphere, but if there is a complaint that children are being neglected, the family will be investigated by representatives of the state social service agency. A destitute family may be offered emergency or long-term assistance from private or public sources. If the neglect is intentional however, a suit may be filed to remove the children from the home and to place them under the care of the state, either temporarily or permanently.

The societal goal is the protection and best interest of the children, but balancing that against the parents' interest is often difficult, even when there is common agreement on what constitutes the best interest of the children. Those instances in which a parent severely injures a child demand that the child be protected. Where is the line to be drawn, though, between spanking a child for disciplinary purposes and physically abusing the child? Parents are given the primary responsibility for the moral and religious instruction of children, but there is a public interest in seeing that children are educated.[94] A growing number of parents are teaching their children at home because of dissatisfaction with public schools or for religious reasons. If the parents are prosecuted for violation of school attendance laws, then the court must attempt to balance the competing interests. Such complex and weighty matters are politically sensitive issues for legislators and judges, as are issues of medical treatment over parental objection.

Termination of Parental Rights

The parent–child relationship may be ended by the child's emancipation or by court order. Parents may accede to the termination of parental rights or it may be involuntary. As previously discussed, a child cannot be adopted until the rights of the biological parents have been terminated. Voluntary relinquishment is common among unwed and often young parents in order that the child may be placed for adoption. Generally, the written assent of both natural parents is required even if paternity has not been legally established, and a "cooling-off" period is imposed, often 30 days, during which time the parents may revoke their consent. That the parent who is relinquishing the child is a minor does not invalidate the consent.[95] Voluntary termination also frequently occurs when the non-custodial parent agrees to adoption by the custodial parent's new spouse.

TEXAS MIS-STEP

Texas officials, acting under court order, removed 439 children from the Yearning for Zion Ranch (YFZ), where a polygamist sect of the Fundamentalist Church of Jesus Christ of Latter Day Saints (FLDS) had settled. Several phone calls were made to a local family shelter by a 16-year-old pregnant mother, Sarah Jessop, who stated that she had been physically and sexually abused by her "spiritual" husband who was more than 30 years older than she. During the course of their investigation, child protective officials did identify 20 teenagers with children, some of whom had become pregnant between the ages of 13 and 17, and five pregnant minors who had become pregnant between the ages of 15 and 17. The investigators were thwarted in their attempts to identify individuals and their relationships by the church members, but it was reasonable on the part of the investigators initially to assume that Jessop was among them, although she was not found on the ranch. These findings convinced a district judge to issue the order to remove *all* the children from the ranch on the basis that their physical health and safety were endangered by their caregivers and that there was an urgent need to protect the children that justified their immediate removal. Law enforcement authorities, including SWAT teams, raided the ranch and removed the children under the glare of international media attention.

The Texas Supreme Court held that the state had overreached its authority by removing all the children rather than focusing on specific children who were at risk and discussed alternative legal means that could have been employed to protect them. All the children were subsequently returned to their mothers, and criminal prosecutions against 12 men on charges related to underage marriages at the ranch, including sexual assault of a child, conducting an unlawful marriage ceremony involving a minor, bigamy, and failure to report child abuse, were initiated. This case epitomizes the tightrope that the state walks in this type of case—"the harm caused by the unnecessary removal of hundreds of children who were not in immediate danger of abuse and harm caused by the return of teenage girls who were at risk for sexual abuse on the ranch."

Source: Jessica Dixon Weaver, "The Texas Mis-step: Why the Largest Child Removal in Modern U.S. History Failed," 16 Wm. & Mary J. Women & L. 449 (2010).

Suits to involuntarily terminate a parent's rights are usually generated by the state. These stem from abuse of the child—physically, mentally, or sexually, from neglect of the child, or from failure to properly supervise the child.[96]

Permanently removing the child from the home by the state on these grounds requires a court order, but legislation provides for immediate removal without court approval if there is a serious or life-threatening emergency; in such a case, judicial review must take place as quickly as possible, often within 24 hours. Again, it is necessary to square the rights of the children with those of the parents and also to protect against hasty, ill-considered state action, or excesses on the part of overzealous social service agency representatives, many of whom are under a statutory charge to assist in keeping families together. Child protection agencies are caught in the classic dilemma. If they fail to act and a child is injured or dies, then there is an immense public outcry. If they act and the claims prove false, then the officials are castigated by the public who are highly offended.

Involuntary termination may be initiated by a custodial parent against a divorced spouse. The basis of the suit is often an alleged failure to financially support the child or an allegation that the parent ignored the child and has failed to visit or establish contact. The impetus behind such suits is often to facilitate adoption by the petitioner's new spouse.

The effect of terminating the parent–child relationship is to sever all connections between parent and child. It relieves parents of all duties and obligations toward their children, but it also means that the parents are to have no contact at all with their offspring. It voids the original legal relationship, and in adoption cases the court records are sealed and new birth certificates may be issued.

CONCLUSION

Domestic relations law touches every American because it deals with family issues. It is an area in which the state is reluctant to intrude; yet, for many people, the intrusions are accepted and seldom controverted. Most citizens accept the necessity of meeting certain statutory requirements, such as those of obtaining a marriage license and attending school. They applaud the intervention of the state to protect abused children and battered spouses. They recognize the rationale for accurate government records regarding marriages, births, and dissolutions of marriage. The need for a neutral third party to referee domestic disputes and to render impartial decisions is apparent.

The topics discussed in this chapter, including marriage and the parent–child relationship, are only a sampling of the issues involved in family law. For example, juvenile laws are often contained in family codes, and cases involving alleged delinquency are routinely decided by family law judges. Family litigation often seems interminable because of various modification and enforcement orders. It is the area of law in which many have their only contact as parties with the legal system. Decisions made in these lawsuits have immeasurable and permanent effects on the lives of the spouses and their children. Family law is intensely personal in many ways, while in others it is the most public area of law. National debate centers around the family, its configuration, and its role in society as a whole. It is a most troublesome area for policymakers who have thus far failed to set coherent family policies because of the diverse nature of these relationships and the deeply rooted social and religious attitudes of the American people about the sanctity of family and government involvement therein. The legalization of same-sex marriages has created uncertainty and challenges in family law that will not be resolved until the individual cases wend their way to the states' highest courts or state legislatures rewrite their family codes and other laws.

NOTES

1. Homer H. Clark, Jr. and Ann Laquer Estin, *Cases and Problems on Domestic Relations*, 7th edn (St. Paul, MN: Thomson/West, 2005), p. 2.
2. Peter I. Riga, "Are We Copying Ancient Rome on Divorce?," *Texas Lawyer*, December 18, 1985, p. 13.
3. Clark and Estin, pp. 3–9.
4. *Reynolds v. United States*, 98 U.S. 145 (1878).
5. *Fearon v. Treanor*, 272 N.Y. 268 (1936), at 272; 5 N.E.2d 815 (N.Y. 1936), at 816.
6. *Patterson v. Gaines*, 6 How. 550 (1848).
7. *Simms v. Simms*, 175 U.S. 162 (1899).
8. *Maynard v. Hill*, 125 U.S. 190 (1888), at 205.
9. Clark and Estin, p. 114.
10. *Reynolds v. United States*, 98 U.S. 145 (1878).
11. *Loving v. Virginia*, 388 U.S. 1 (1967).
12. *Obergefell v. Hodges*, 576 U.S. _____ (2015).
13. *Baehr v. Lewin*, 852 P.2d 44 (Haw. 1993); *Baehr v. Miike*, 1996 WL 694235 (Haw. Cir. Ct).
14. *Baehr v. Lewin*, p. 57.
15. Noel Myricks and Roger H. Rubin, "Legalizing Gay and Lesbian Marriages: Trends and Implications," *American Journal of Family Law* 9 (1995), pp. 35–44.
16. *Baehr v. Miike*, 92 Haw. 634, 994 P.2d 566 (Haw. 1999).
17. Jeffrey J. Swart, "The Wedding Luau: Who is Invited? Hawaii, Same-Sex Marriage, and Emerging Realities," 43 Emory L.J. 1577 (1994).
18. *Brause v. Bureau of Vital Statistics*, No. 3AN-95-6562-CI (Alaska Super. Ct., 1998).
19. Nancy Maxwell, "Opening Civil Marriage to Same-Gender Couples: A Netherlands-United States Comparison," 18 Ariz. J. Int'l & Comp. L. 141 (2001).
20. *Alaska Civil Liberties Union ex rel. Carter v. Alaska*, 122 P.3d 781 (Alaska, 2005).
21. Eric Lobsinger, "Comment: A National Model for Reconciling Equal Protection for Same-Sex Couples with State Marriage Amendments: Alaska Civil Liberties Union ex rel. Carter v. Alaska," 23 Alaska L. Rev. 117 (2006), at 135–137.
22. *Baker v. State*, 744 A.2d 864 (Vt. 1999).
23. *Goodridge v. Dep't. of Pub. Health*, 798 N.E.2d 941 (Mass. 2003).
24. Maxwell, p. 169.
25. John David Rausch, Jr., *Morality or Locality? The Political Context of Marriage Definition Direct Democracy Voting Outcomes* (Washington, DC: American Political Science Association, 2004); John David Rausch, Jr., *Constitutionally Defining Marriage in a Non-Presidential Election Year: A Study of the Vote in Two States* (Lubbock, TX: Sixth Annual State Politics and Policy Conference, 2006).

26. Defense of Marriage Act, P.L. 104–199.

27. 1 U.S.C. § 7.

28. 28 U.S.C. § 1738C.

29. *United States v. Windsor*, 570 U.S. _____ (2013) (slip opinion).

30. Swart, pp. 1598–1600.

31. Ibid., p. 1599.

32. Habib A. Balian, "Till Death Do Us Part: Granting Full Faith and Credit to Marital Status," 68 S. Cal. L. Rev. 397 (1995).

33. Thomas M. Keane, "Aloha, Marriage? Constitutional and Choice of Law Arguments for Recognition of Same-Sex Marriages," 47 Stan. L. Rev. 499 (1995).

34. Balian, pp. 398–399.

35. *Obergefell v. Hodges*, 576 U.S. _____ (2015).

36. Ibid. (Alito dissent).

37. Lyle Denniston, "*Opinion Analysis: Marriage Now Open to Same-sex Couples,*" *SCOTUSblog*, http://www.scotusblog.com/2015/06/opinion-analysis-marriage-now-open-to-same-sex-couples (visited June 26, 2015).

38. *Obergefell v. Hodges*, 576 U.S. _____ (2015); "John Arthur, Man who Challenged Ohio's Gay Marriage Ban, Dies at 48," *New York Daily News*, October 22, 2013.

39. *Obergefell v. Hodges*.

40. Ibid. (Roberts dissent, joined by Scalia and Thomas; Thomas dissent joined by Scalia; Scalia dissent jointed by Thomas; and Alito dissent joined by Scalia and Thomas).

41. Adam Lamparello, "Justice Kennedy's Decision in Obergefell: A Sad Day for the Judiciary," 6 Hous. L. Rev.: Off the Record 45 (Fall 2015).

42. *Obergefell v. Hodges*, 576 U.S. _____ (2015) (Roberts dissent).

43. Richard Lempert, "Obergefell v. Hodges: Same Sex Marriage & Cultural Jousting at the Supreme Court," Brookings Institute FIXGOV, June 29, 2015, http://www.brookings.edu/blogs/fixgov/posts/2015/06/29-obergefell-same-sex-marriage-lempert (visited December 16, 2015).

44. Elizabeth Brenner, "Marriage for All," 78 Tex.B.J. 622 (September 2015).

45. *In re Estate of Fisher*, 176 N.W.2d 801 (Iowa, 1970).

46. Clark and Estin, pp. 105–106.

47. Ibid., pp. 89–90.

48. Cal. Fam. Code §§ 2400–2403.

49. *Perlstein v. Perlstein*, 152 Conn. 152, 204 A.2d 909 (1964).

50. *Sefton v. Sefton*, 45 Cal.2d 272, 291 P.2d 439 (1955).

51. Nev. Rev. Stat. § 125.020.

52. Alaska Stat. § 25.24.080.

53. Tex. Fam. Code § 6.301.

54. Riane Tennenhaus Eisler, *Dissolution* (New York: McGraw-Hill, 1977), pp. 12–13.

55. *Juno*. Screenplay by Diablo Cody. Director Jason Reitman, 2007. 20th Century Fox.

56. Patrick Foran, "Adoption of the Uniform Collaborative Law Act in Oregon: The Right Time and the Right Reasons," 13 Lewis & Clark L. Rev. 787 (2009).

57. J. Benjamin Stevens, "The 'Respectful Divorce,'" *South Carolina Family Law Blog*, May 12, 2008, http://www.scfamilylaw.com/the-respectful-divorce/ (visited December 16, 2015).

58. Clark and Estin, p. 765.

59. Joseph M. Perillo, *Calamari and Perillo on Contracts*, 5th edn (St. Paul, MN: Thomson/West, 2003), pp. 756–757.

60. *Marvin v. Marvin,* 18 Cal.3d 66, 134 Cal. Rptr. 815, 557 P.2d 106 (Cal. 1976); *Gormley v. Robertson,* 120 Wash. App. 31, 83 P.3d 1042 (Wash. Ct. App. 2004).
61. Clark and Estin, p. 614.
62. Jean A. Stuntz, *Hers, His, & Theirs: Community Property Law in Spain & Early Texas* (Lubbock, TX: Texas Tech University Press, 2006), pp. 101–102.
63. Eisler, pp. 32–34.
64. Ibid., p. 33.
65. Ibid., pp. 34–40.
66. *Orr v. Orr,* 440 U.S. 268 (1979).
67. Clark and Estin, p. 765.
68. Ibid., p. 764.
69. Ibid., pp. 716–717.
70. Eisler, p. 56.
71. Ibid., pp. 55–56.
72. Uniform Child Custody and Enforcement Act, http://www.uniformlaws.org/ActSummary.aspx?title=Child+Custody+Jurisdiction+and+Enforcement+Act (visited December 16, 2015); Parental Kidnapping Prevention Act, 28 U.S.C. § 1738A.
73. Clark and Estin, p. 959.
74. Robin Green, *Divorce Without Defeat* (Amarillo, TX: Cimarron Press, 1982), p. 152.
75. Susan Coleman and Franci Smith, *Child Support Enforcement in Texas* (Austin, TX: League of Women Voters of Texas, 1982); Health and Human Services, *Child Support Handbook,* https://www.acf.hhs.gov/sites/default/files/programs/css/child_support_handbook_with_toc.pdf (visited December 16, 2015).
76. Child Support Recovery Act, 18 U.S.C.A. § 228.
77. *State v. Oakley,* 629 N.W.2d 200 (Wis., 2001).
78. Eisler, p. 122.
79. Uniform Parentage Act, http://www.uniformlaws.org/ActSummary.aspx?title=Parentage%20Act (visited December 16, 2015).
80. Brenner, p. 622.
81. David Adams, "Birth Certificates Latest Battleground in Florida's Gay Marriage Fight," Reuters, August 13, 2015; Chris Johnson, "Arkansas High Court Halts Birth Certificates for Same-Sex Parents," *Washington Blade,* December 11, 2015.
82. *Barnardo v. McHugh,* as cited in Sophonisba P. Breckinridge, *The Family and the State* (Chicago, IL: University of Chicago Press, 1934), pp. 444–446.
83. Clark and Estin, pp. 408–424.
84. John J. Sampson, "Texas Family Code Symposium, Chapter 13, Determination of Paternity," 13 Tex. Tech L. Rev. 838 (1982).
85. *Stanley v. Illinois,* 405 U.S. 645 (1972).
86. Henry C. Black, *Black's Law Dictionary,* 4th edn (St. Paul, MN: West Publishing Company, 1968), p. 70.
87. *In re Adoption of "E,"* 59 N.J. 36, 279 A.2d 785 (1971).
88. Clark and Estin, pp. 362–366, 376–378, 382.
89. Indian Child Welfare Act, P.L. 95–608 (1978), 25 U.S.C. §§1911 *et seq.*
90. Intercountry Adoption Act of 2000, P.L. 106–279 (2000), 42 U.S.C. §§14901 *et seq.*
91. Clark and Estin, pp. 389–390.
92. *Prince v. Massachusetts,* 321 U.S. 158 (1944), at 171. See also *Troxel v. Granville,* 530 U.S. 57 (2000).

93. *Hunt v. Thompson*, as cited in Sophonisba P. Breckinridge, *The Family and the State* (Chicago, IL: University of Chicago Press, 1934), p. 242.
94. *Wisconsin v. Yoder*, 406 U.S. 205 (1972).
95. *Johnson v. Cupp*, 274 N.E.2d 411 (Ind. App. 1971).
96. Eisler, pp. 59–60; Clark and Estin, p. 320.

Conclusion

We began this book by observing that anyone who wishes to understand the American legal system must first understand the meaning of law. We noted that law may be defined in terms of the functions it performs in a society, the sources of law, and the different kinds of law. This book has attempted to acquaint the reader with the many facets of law in our society. Viewing law may be compared to the pleasant pastime of cloud gazing. Most of us at one time or another have looked up at the sky and described what we thought we saw in the various cloud formations above—a kind of heavenly Rorschach test. If accompanied by others, we soon discover that there are differences of opinion about the pictures formed by the various combinations of clouds. We also discover that unless it is an unusually calm day, the cloud formations begin to change, drawing new pictures across the sky. An image we once thought to be clear and distinct is soon misshapen. What is formed by the clouds is a function of time, space, and the perceptions of the viewer.

In a sense, looking at the law is like looking at cloud formations. Law has the same elusive qualities as a cloud. Like a cloud, the law has a real presence, and yet our understanding of it may evaporate in an instant. Like a cloud, the law is constantly changing, but often at a rate so slow that it is almost imperceptible. Like a cloud, the law may appear to be different to different people at various points in time. In this chapter, we will try to bring together some of the facets of the law that have been described either explicitly or implicitly in previous chapters. We will try to pull together the loose ends we have left untied. In so doing, however, we will remind the reader that others have spent a lifetime trying to define and explain the concept of law. The reader may conclude, as we have after years of studying it, that law, like beauty, is in the eye of the beholder.

LAW AS PROTECTOR AND OPPRESSOR

Abraham Lincoln once used the example of the shepherd, the wolf, and the sheep to illustrate the potential variety of perceptions of government. The sheep looks to the shepherd for protection from those who would prey upon and even kill him. The wolf, on the other hand, sees the shepherd as an oppressor. After all, a wolf, like all living things, needs food to survive, and it is hardly his fault that nature made him carnivorous. To the wolf, the shepherd is an enemy who keeps him from the food he so desperately needs for survival. Lincoln's point was that government, like the shepherd, represents different things to different people. To some, government is the guardian of liberty and the protector of the weak from the strong. To others, government is a source of oppression that interferes with their "pursuit of happiness." To some extent, neither view is entirely incorrect. Government is indeed capable of being both protector and oppressor, as history certainly confirms.

Like the shepherd and government, the law may be viewed as a source of both protection and oppression. For example, consider how the divorced parents of a minor child might view child support laws. To the custodial parent, the state's child support laws may seem like the protector of the child's rights. Most children need the financial support of both parents. The law provides the custodial parent with the means (albeit often inadequate) to force the recalcitrant former spouse to pay a fair share of the financial burden of childrearing. On the other hand, the noncustodial spouse may see the state's child support laws as a burden, particularly if there is any controversy about how the funds are spent. Forced to maintain a separate household, the noncustodial spouse has living expenses that may make child support payments an onerous burden. If the noncustodial spouse remarries, he or she is often drained by the job of trying to support two families emotionally and financially. Although he or she clearly has a legal and moral obligation to provide financial support for the child, he or she cannot help but feel that the law has created an intolerable burden. One more example should help clarify the view of law as protector and oppressor. In Chapter 11, we discussed contract law. A common form of contract is a rental agreement or lease. To the landlord, such agreements are designed to protect the rights of the property owner against abuses by renters. That is, the law serves as the protector of property rights. To the renter, the typical lease gives the landlord unfair advantages, especially if the renter is desperate to find a place to live. Although the law assumes that the two parties entered into the rental contract as equals, the renter often feels that he or she has no choice but to accept the terms set out in the lease. That the lease gives the landlord an advantage seems to the renter patently unfair. In the eyes of the law however, the renter was not forced to sign the lease and consents to the terms of his or her free will.

More examples could be cited, and the reader can doubtless think of others. It is not our place to say who is right or wrong on these issues. Like most questions of law, there are two sides to every story. We will allow readers to decide for themselves which party is the wolf and which is the sheep in the examples we have cited. Suffice it to say that there will always be those who will use the law to their advantage or to exploit others. As we noted in Chapter 1, law is a function of the society that creates it. Consequently, law is only as good or as bad as the people who make it.

LAW AND POLITICS

It is almost impossible to escape the conclusion that law and politics are inseparable. The legal profession has a vastly disproportionate amount of influence on both our legal and political institutions. A few examples will illustrate this point. At any given time, approximately half the members of Congress are lawyers. Compared to their percentage of the American population as a whole, lawyers are vastly overrepresented. Although there may be good reasons for this overrepresentation, the fact remains that lawyers have disproportionate influence over the making of national laws. The same is true, but to a lesser extent, at the state level. One authority on state government has noted that lawyers, farmers, and business owners are heavily represented in state legislatures.[1] Similarly, lawyers almost completely dominate the judicial branch of government. Although there is no constitutional requirement that a president's choice for the Supreme Court be a lawyer, the likelihood of a non-lawyer being approved by the lawyer-dominated Senate Judiciary Committee is remote. At the state level, the possession of a law license is a requirement for appointment or election to most judicial offices. In addition, as noted in Chapter 3, the selection of judges at the state and federal levels is a highly politicized process. It makes little difference whether judges are elected, appointed, or chosen by merit; politics will always play a role. Different selection methods do nothing more than change the level of politics involved. As long as judges make political decisions, politics will enter into the selection process. It appears that the close relationship between law and politics will continue. Political science majors still constitute the largest single group of students taking the Law School Admission Test (LSAT).

The dominance of the legal profession in our political institutions is not the only way that law and politics interact. Courtrooms are increasingly becoming the battlegrounds for causes won or lost in the political arena. Americans have a tendency to turn to courts to resolve the most controversial issues of our society. As noted in Chapter 6, the issues of same-sex marriage, abortion, gun control, and capital punishment are perennial issues before the courts of the nation. Civil rights, environmental, women's, and other special interest groups often turn to courts to win the results they have failed to achieve in other political arenas. A loss today is a mere temporary setback for most groups because they know that in time the makeup of the courts could change in their favor. Today's loss is tomorrow's victory. They know that, with perseverance, they can eventually achieve the desired results. Law, then, becomes a never-ending battle between the status quo and the forces of change.

LAW AND SOCIETY

We noted in Chapter 1 that law is a function of the society that creates it, and we have already observed in this chapter that law is only as good or as bad as those who make it. Law reflects the values of the lawmaker and the dominant political and economic forces in a society. In Chapter 7, we discussed this relationship in the area of criminal law. Just what kind of behavior society deems unacceptable is manifested by the acts it prohibits by its criminal law. Just how serious society deems that behavior to be is reflected in the vigor with which the law is enforced and the severity with which it is punished. Let us take littering as an example. While it is true that most American cities have ordinances prohibiting littering, it is equally true that these ordinances are infrequently enforced and that the punishment is a relatively small fine. What this fact seems to indicate is that while littering may be universally condemned and prohibited, it is generally not viewed as a serious offense in our society.

Other, more serious, examples could be cited to reflect on the relationship of law to society. For most of our nation's history, the tobacco industry has been relatively immune from legal process and political opposition. Because of the political clout of the industry, governmental regulation has been limited to taxing tobacco products. The industry was also successful in defending itself against lawsuits from injured smokers. Most people viewed smoking as the personal choice of the individual who was expected to accept the consequences (often unknown to those who began to smoke decades ago) of the decision to smoke. Under the leadership of several aggressive state attorneys general, society began to demand greater accountability from the tobacco industry for the health consequences of their products. States, realizing the public health costs of treating indigent and elderly victims of smoking-related diseases, have successfully sued tobacco companies. Where smoking was once seen as a fashionable custom, today's society views it as both dangerous and costly. In the process, the once-invincible and heavily subsidized tobacco industry has found itself beleaguered on all sides. Similarly, until such time as problems like dignity in death, sexual harassment, and abuse of the elderly are viewed as serious by our society, the law will continue to treat them as relatively minor offenses.

We also noted in Chapter 7 that law reflects a society's attitude toward the law-breaker. Critics of American criminal justice argue that our legal system is overly concerned with the rights of those accused of crime and almost totally unconcerned about the rights of the victims of crime. Our purpose here is not to reopen that debate. Suffice it to say that our Founding Fathers, themselves branded as "outlaws" by the British government, were sensitive to the ability of government to use its coercive power against the individual. Whether they "overreacted" by placing so many safeguards into the Constitution is also open to discussion. The point is that we, as a society, are divided over the proper balance between the rights of the accused and the rights of society. Consequently, there is a constant struggle among law enforcers, civil libertarians, and the public at large over what is the proper balance. The likelihood of reaching a consensus on this issue seems remote.

Finally, we would like to reiterate the evolutionary nature of the law. Law, like the clouds we discussed earlier, changes over time as our society changes. Our ideas and ideals about decency, justice, and due process evolve over time. As noted in Chapter 7, we have narrowed the range of offenses for which a person can be put to death. Crimes that once resulted in hanging, such as horse stealing and bank robbery, are treated today like any other theft of property. It is true that there are still those in our society who would like to see harsher penalties imposed. Generally, however, we have reached a consensus on those offenses that merit the ultimate punishment. Perhaps someday we will reach a similar consensus on the decriminalization of a range of other activities, including gambling and marijuana use.

LAW AND ECONOMICS

One frequently overlooked facet of law is the relationship between law and economics. As previously noted, landlords have historically used the law of contracts to their economic advantage. In addition, landlords have used local city ordinances or state laws to evict tenants who failed to pay their rent on time. Disputes typically arose over the failure of the landlord to effect some needed repairs, and the tenant withheld the rent only to discover that the law favored the landlord. Fortunately, that situation is a thing of the past in most jurisdictions. Laws have been changed to guarantee the tenant the right to live in a habitable dwelling, and informal as well as formal methods have been devised to mediate landlord–tenant disputes.

The use of eviction laws was just one way in which an economic group used the law to gain an advantage over another. During the early struggle between labor unions and management, the latter would use court injunctions as a weapon against striking workers. If an owner were able to convince a judge that a labor strike caused him "irreparable damage," the judge would issue an injunction ordering an end to the strike. Stripped of their principal weapon, the workers were fired and replaced by other workers desperately in need of employment. In this manner, employers were permitted to keep wages low, hours long, working conditions unsafe, and workers insecure. The use of the injunction as a strike-breaker also illustrates the importance placed on property rights in our legal system. Judges, often sympathetic to the views of the owners, placed property rights above the workers' rights to decent wages and working conditions. It is fascinating to read accounts of state and national efforts to enact laws to protect the rights of workers only to have those laws ruled unconstitutional by the courts.[2] In a sense, the law was a battleground in an economic class war.

The modern era can provide similar examples of the influence of economics on the law. Tax law is frequently cited as an example of how laws are written to benefit a particular economic class. Laws that provide tax breaks and tax incentives for wealthy investors in municipal bonds and other tax shelters are widely known. A common complaint of the average American is that the tax code gives unfair advantages to those in our society who are already wealthy. Whether this accusation is actually true or not is seldom questioned. The fact is that most Americans believe it to be true. Another example of the relationship of economics and law is in the area of criminal law. Until the 1963 *Gideon v. Wainwright*[3] decision, indigent persons accused of noncapital offenses were forced in most states either to defend themselves at trial or to plead guilty. Until the *Gideon* decision ruled that states must provide counsel for indigent defendants, those who were economically disadvantaged were also legally disadvantaged.

One final example of the relationship of law and economics is in order. The medical profession has been plagued by an increase in both the number of malpractice suits and the amount of damages awarded to successful plaintiffs. The response to the crisis has been twofold. First, the cost of medical malpractice insurance premiums has skyrocketed to the point that the costs are nearly prohibitive for many physicians. Second, pressure has increased from both the medical profession and the insurance industry to put a ceiling on the amount of damages that can be awarded in a malpractice suit. In fact, many states have enacted such limits. These two groups have sought legislation in various states under the general label of "tort reform." Physicians and insurance companies have been opposed in their efforts to win tort reform by segments of the legal profession. Lawyers, especially those who represent plaintiffs, argue that the problem has been grossly exaggerated. Physicians argue that lawyers may not be totally neutral parties because they are often working on a contingency fee basis. Consequently, physicians argue that lawyers have a financial interest in maintaining a system that encourages large awards. Lawyers counter that large awards are given only in cases of extreme or gross negligence, that they are usually justified, and that the jury system serves as a check on any abuses. Although strong arguments can be made on both sides, our point is that physicians, lawyers, plaintiffs, and insurance companies all seek to use the law to promote some economic self-interest. Despite disclaimers to the contrary, economics is central to this controversy.

We are not prepared to say, as perhaps an economic determinist would, that economics is the only or even the major force behind the enactment of every law. We are, however, prepared to say that the economic impact of the law is a powerful influence on the way in which law in our society is shaped.

FINAL REFLECTIONS

We will conclude with a few final reflections on law in American society. As we noted at the beginning of this chapter, law is perceived differently by different people. In a sense, then, our perceptions about the nature and meaning of law have colored the contents of this book. What we have chosen to emphasize or to ignore is a function of our own individual biases. The fact that hundreds of books have been written on law is a testimony both to its complexity and to the fascination with which law is viewed.

What is this fascination with the law? Part of it is because of the need for humans to have an ultimate answer. There is finality in law that is comforting to most people. Even those who have lost a lawsuit are sometimes comforted by the fact that they did everything possible to prevail. Even in defeat, they know that they will never have to wonder what would have happened if they had not pursued their case to the fullest extent of the law. A losing litigant may analyze what went wrong and what may have been done differently, but in the final analysis there is the realization that the issue has at least been resolved.

Another reason for our fascination with the law is the feeling of righteousness that often accompanies our involvement with it. One usually hears the relative of a murder victim express satisfaction that "justice was finally done" upon learning of the killer's conviction. Despite the efforts of religion and philosophy to persuade us to rise above our human failings, the fact remains that the need for retribution is powerful in most humans. The old saying "Don't get mad—get even" appeals to many. Law provides us with a civilized way to exact revenge, because even if the individual victim is forgiving, society, in its role as avenger, is not. The same is true for litigants in civil cases. Although we would not entirely rule out avarice as a motivator, litigants in civil suits frequently disavow the desire for money as their reason for suing. Instead, they cite "the principle involved." Given the expense in time and money and the uncertainty of success, principle probably does play a major role in most lawsuits. Law, then, helps fulfill the basic human need for justice.

Finally, law is a source of comfort to most of us. In a world described by Thomas Hobbes as "solitary, poor, nasty, brutish, and short,"[4] it is comforting to realize that we have risen above the law of the jungle, where the strong prey on the weak. As previously noted, the law really does serve as the sheep's protector. People want a hero who will protect them from the injustices of life and the wrath of their enemies. To many, the law is such a hero—a great equalizer ready to come to our assistance if needed.

We hope this book has made its readers think about the law in a variety of ways. Regardless of whether the reader accepts or rejects the ideas presented herein, we will have succeeded if each reader has reflected on the nature and purpose of the law and perhaps has even grown to understand the law a little better.

NOTES

1. Murray S. Stedman, Jr., *State and Local Governments* (Boston, MA: Little, Brown, 1982), p. 118.
2. See, for example, *Lochner v. New York*, 198 U.S. 45 (1905); *Hammer v. Dagenhart*, 247 U.S. 251 (1918); *Bailey v. Drexel Furniture Co.*, 259 U.S. 20 (1922); *Adkins v. Children's Hospital*, 261 U.S. 525 (1923).
3. *Gideon v. Wainwright*, 372 U.S. 335 (1963).
4. Thomas Hobbes, *Leviathan*, ed. Michael Oakeshott (New York: Collier Books, 1962), p. 100.

APPENDIX

Legal Research

"It is a matter of deep study to be exact in the law."[1] Fortunately, those who seek to be "exact in the law" have available to them a highly organized and widely indexed knowledge base because "that which is law to-day is none to-morrow."[2] Law evolves and changes with each legislative enactment and court decision. The legal researcher must be aware of what the law was yesterday (*stare decisis*), what it is today, and often what it will be tomorrow. The chief tools available for such research include both the traditional configuration of books and printed case reports and the newer mode of computers and networks of sophisticated databases in law, business, and social science literature as well as others.

Because this country follows common law principles, the chief lawgivers are the legislative bodies and courts at all levels. The primary sources in legal research include the national and state constitutions, legislative enactments (or those adopted by the people through initiative), the written decisions of the courts, administrative regulations, rules of procedures, and any constitutional or statutory provisions accepting or receiving the common law of England. All jurisdictions, except Louisiana, which relies heavily on civil or code law, have adopted English common law as the basis of their jurisprudence. The effects of these statutory or constitutional provisions adopting English common law have been diluted by the development of uniquely American jurisprudence since the establishment of the colonies over 400 years ago. Today's legal precepts, while founded on English common law principles, are more the product of American jurisprudence than English. One factor contributing to the lessened dependence on English law is the federal system, which permits each state to incorporate its own values and mores into law, thereby weakening uniformity.[3]

The secondary sources in legal research include various legal encyclopedias, learned treatises, legal periodicals, and computer research databases such as Westlaw® and LexisNexis® as well as scholarly literature in fields other than law. Judges do not limit themselves only to law in arriving at their conclusions but draw upon information from a variety of other fields, including medicine, engineering, and social science studies. The openness of courts to information from a variety of sources mandates that researchers must also be flexible. For example, judges often integrate history into their opinions. Two very different cases by the same justice in the 1971 and 1972 terms of the U.S. Supreme Court illustrate that point. In *Flood v. Kuhn* (a case dealing with whether antitrust laws apply to baseball as they do to other professional sports), Justice Harry A. Blackmun, writing for the majority, began the opinion by tracing the history of professional baseball from its beginnings over a century earlier.[4] For *Roe v. Wade*, Justice Blackmun was described as having "immersed himself in research in the huge Mayo Clinic medical library," while other justices also pursued their own independent research into the medical and philosophical issues surrounding abortion.[5] The result is that *Roe v. Wade* contains not only a lengthy discussion of attitudes toward abortion from ancient times up until the present but also a discussion of medical procedures and philosophy.[6]

Extensive use of statistics and materials from the social sciences has been debated by those on the bench and by legal scholars; nevertheless, such studies are rather routinely accepted in various cases alleging discrimination. In *Craig v. Boren*,[7] the Court mentioned several statistical surveys about youthful drivers and alcohol while considering Oklahoma's discriminatory gender-based traffic safety laws. In *McCleskey v. Kemp*, Warren McCleskey, an African American, employed as his primary defense a sophisticated statistical study that revealed significant disparities in sentencing of blacks and whites to the death penalty in Georgia. The Court, with some discussion, accepted the statistics but eventually decided that McCleskey had not shown that discrimination actually existed in his case.[8] Just as judges themselves go outside the narrow confines of "legal" materials, the legal researcher, particularly those drafting appellate briefs, may find himself or herself doing research in areas other than law.

THE STAGES OF RESEARCH

The basis of any scholarly inquiry is a clear understanding of the goal of research—drafting a document, preparing for trial, writing an appellate brief or a legal memorandum for a supervising attorney, or counseling a client on her legal business—before one begins. The initial step is assembling the facts, evaluating their relevancy to the legal issue, and determining the legal problems to be researched. The factors to be considered in that determination include some of the following: (1) relevant characteristics of the parties, such as age in contract cases or level of expertise in malpractice suits; (2) the events (a car accident) or the subject matter (a professional athlete's employment contract); (3) cause of action (a child custody suit) or ground of defense (consent in a sexual assault case); and (4) the remedy sought such as injunction or monetary damages.[9]

The second step is to plan the research and choose the logical starting point. Technology and the internet have transformed traditional research processes. Anyone with a smartphone may pose a query and obtain an answer—even verbally—to factual questions such as a list of authors' books or what years the Dallas Cowboys won the Superbowl. Search engines allow ready access to vast banks of data on a myriad of subjects, and indeed, many lawyers now begin their legal research by turning to free research databases such as Google or Cornell University's Legal Information Institute. The younger the attorney, the more likely he or she is to turn first to electronic sources rather than print.[10] While the delivery mode now is often electronic, the traditional methods and tools of legal research endure.

A researcher who is unfamiliar with the issue may begin with one of the general legal encyclopedias that are arranged (like other encyclopedias) by topic. Searches involving statutory interpretation might start with an annotated code that would identify related cases and where to locate the legislative history, that is, the committee reports and debates that accompanied the enactment of the statute. A researcher with a case name in hand might begin with the digests that are listings of cases arranged by subject matter or with an index. The type of problem and type of research lead will determine where the researcher begins.

The third step is to actually conduct the research. Legal research is rarely done only in one type or set of research materials. An annotated code of statutes would steer one to case reporters, to legal periodicals on the topic, to legislative histories, and to sources that indicate whether the case was appealed and what happened during the appeal. As law does change and evolve, it is necessary for the researcher to always be aware of the most current developments in the law. Obviously, reference may be made to nonlegal news periodicals or daily newspapers that cover important cases and the various Internet sources that provide almost instantaneous access to court rulings and changes in statutes. Bound volumes of statutes and the legal encyclopedias are often updated through means of "pocket parts" inserted at the back. It is the investigator's responsibility to check these updates when doing research.

The fourth step is to actually compile the research and present it in the appropriate form—as argument at trial, as communications to courts or attorneys, or as documents for clients.[11] Obviously, legal research has become much more complex than in the days when the relatively few copies of William Blackstone's *Commentaries on the Laws of England* circulating in the colonies were the chief source of the law, but those undertaking legal research today are very fortunate that basic legal materials are, for the most part, readily available and even more fortunate that the law is highly organized and easily cross-referenced whether the researcher is using a computer or doing things the old-fashioned way, namely looking things up in books.

TOOLS OF RESEARCH

Mandatory and Persuasive Authority

The foundation of a common law system is the decisions of juries and judges at both the trial and appellate levels. This is because of the doctrine of *stare decisis* which dictates that courts follow precedent; however, judges are bound only by decisions of superior courts in their jurisdiction, that is, judges in Michigan are bound by Michigan appellate decisions and not by Utah law. The same is true on the national level; federal trial courts in the Eleventh Circuit are obligated to follow decisions of that Court of Appeals and not those of the First Circuit. In certain instances, such as interpretation of the U.S. Constitution, federally enacted law is also binding on state courts, but not all federal statutes are binding on state courts. Similarly, federal courts must apply the state law of the state where they are situated in certain types of cases.

Authority that must be followed is termed **mandatory authority** and may come from constitutions, cases, or statutory enactments. Mandatory authorities are primary sources, and such things as law review articles, decisions from other states, and learned treatises are nonbinding in nature and are deemed to be **persuasive authority.** For a case to be mandatory authority or to be binding precedent, it must be "on point," which means that there must be sufficient similarity between the key facts in the two cases and between the rule of law that was interpreted in the first case and the rule of law to be applied in this case. When these similarities do not exist, the case is not mandatory authority.[12]

In addition, lower courts are not bound by plurality opinions that are of "limited" precedential value. A majority opinion is one in which a majority (e.g., five out of nine) of the judges agree on both the holding and the reasoning of the opinion. In contrast, a plurality opinion is one that receives "more votes than any other opinion supporting the outcome on which a majority of the judges have agreed."[13] As the late Chief Justice William Rehnquist stated, discussion in a plurality opinion is the "considered" opinion of several of the judges and provides guidance for later cases, but it is not "binding precedent."[14]

Similarly, *obiter dictum* must be distinguished from the *ratio decidendi* of the case. *Ratio decidendi* is the ground for a decision, while *dicta* are gratuitous comments by a judge about a solution to a question that is not necessarily involved in the case at hand or essential to its determination.[15] *Dicta* are not binding as precedent.

Case Law

Collections of court opinions are gathered and published in sets of volumes called reporters or reports. Originally, these reports were prepared and published by individuals, and private publication is still the general rule, although official reports are published by various governments. Cases are cited in a fairly consistent manner that facilitates locating the case. Despite the American Bar Association's call a decade or so ago, there is not a single authority that establishes a uniform system. The standard reference work for citing legal materials remains *The Bluebook: A Uniform System of Citation*, despite the emerging use of the *ALSD Citation Manual* of the Association of Legal Writing Directors in law schools.[16] Not only are there different rules for writing for different audiences such law reviews and courts, but there is some degree of variance because of federal or state court preferences; these differences can be determined by examining the reported cases, court rules, and state bar journals. In addition, citations in various commercial databases may be tailored to promote the particular publishers' products.[17]

The following are examples of the meaning of the citations. It is important for the researcher to know if the case has been appealed, and if so, what happened on appeal—whether the case was upheld or reversed. The subsequent history of the case should also be included in the citation. For example, someone seeing a citation to *Telex Corp. v. International Business Machines Corp.*, 367 F. Supp. 258 (N.D. Okla. 1975), 510 F.2d 894 (10th cir. 1975), *cert. denied*, 423 U.S. 802 (1975) can track the history of the case and determine its status. It began in a federal district court in the Northern District of Oklahoma, was appealed to the Tenth Circuit, and then to the U.S. Supreme Court, although the Supreme Court declined to accept the case. To determine the fate of the case and to locate any other cases that refer to it, one goes to *Shepard's Case Citations*, now a part of LexisNexis, or a similar tool such as Westlaw's Key Cite that are published for both state and federal levels and include not only cases but also statutes, constitutions, and administrative regulations. The practice of reviewing a case to determine if it has been overturned, reaffirmed, questioned, or cited by later cases is commonly known as Shepardizing even if the actual tool is another product.

At the state level, decisions of trial courts are rarely published, whereas appellate court decisions are generally collected and published in either an official reporter by the state or, more commonly, the National Reporter System, originally published by West, now a subsidiary of Thomson Reuters. The company compiles the court cases and prints them in various regional reporters and online. The state and level of court is included in the citation because several states are included in the regional reporters as are at least two levels of courts in each state. For instance, seeing only this information, *Bristol Telephone Co. v. Weaver*, 243 S.W. 299 (1921) and *Oder v. Commonwealth*, 243 S.W. 877 (1922), the reader would not know that the former was decided by the Tennessee Supreme Court while the latter was a product of the Court of Appeals of Kentucky. It is therefore very important to include all the information in the case citations.

At the national level, the cases are reported by the level or type of court, as for example, district court cases or tax court cases. Supreme Court cases are officially published by the government in the United States Supreme Court Reporter (U.S.), by Thomson West in the Supreme Court Reporter® (S.Ct.), and by Michie (a part of LexisNexis®) in the United States Supreme Court Reports, Lawyer's Edition (L.Ed.). Publication by the three companies leads to the triple citation format often used for Supreme Court cases—*Reynolds v. Sims*, 377 U.S. 533, 84 S.Ct. 1362, 12 L.Ed.2d 506 (1964)—which allows the researcher to readily access whichever set is available. At the intermediate appellate level, the cases are published in the set known as the *Federal Reporter*, and the case citations must indicate which circuit actually issued the opinion—*Knafel v. Pepsi-Cola Bottlers of Akron, Inc.*, 899 F.2d 1473 (6th Cir. 1990)—allowing the researcher to determine at a glance whether it is mandatory or persuasive authority. Federal district court cases are generally self-reported and, when published, are found in the *Federal Supplement Reporter*. The district, if there is more than one in a state, is indicated in the citation. An example is *Banks v. Havener*, 234 F. Supp. 27 (E.D. Va. 1964).

Recent decisions are published in the form of advance sheets or slip opinions, which are paperback or online collections of newer decisions or individual case opinions. In addition, private companies also publish various loose-leaf services that are updated monthly or even weekly. For example, current U.S. Supreme Court decisions may be found in *United States Law Week* (U.S.L.W.), published by Bloomberg BNA. There are also numerous electronic databases—both official and unofficial—that provide almost instantaneous access to opinions as they are read from the bench. Reporters on specialized subjects (e.g., Media Law Reporter® or Chemical Regulation Reporter®) are also available.

A secondary source that may be used to assist with locating relevant cases is the *Digest*. The *American Digest System,* published by West, is a subject classification system that brings together cases on a similar point of law on the federal level, state and regional levels, as well as subject digests such as bankruptcy and military justice. Under each subject heading is included a very abbreviated summary of each case on the point of law. The topics are subdivided, and points of law are assigned unique key numbers. These key numbers facilitate movement among the digests, cases, statutes, and other West publications. There are other helpful features of the *Digests*, including the *Descriptive Word Index* and *Table of Cases*. Like *Shepard's Case Citations*, the *Digests* are indexes—research tools only—and should never be cited as a source.[18]

Constitutions, Statutes, and Administrative Regulations

Constitutions, statutes, ordinances (passed by local governmental units), and administrative regulations are also published both by the government and by the private companies in annotated form. The annotations often include summaries of cases interpreting the provision, citations to legislative histories, mentions of pertinent articles in legal periodicals, and references for accessing the computer databases. If the research problem involves a statute, an annotated code can be an extremely useful research tool.

Neither state legislatures nor Congress pass laws in any sort of organized manner, that is, one law may deal with financing the space program while the next may deal with the type of nets required for commercial fishing. Each law as it is passed is published in the form of a slip law—an individual printing of each bill. These are then collected and published in chronological order of passage without reference to subject matter nor any effort to correlate amendments with the original legislation. On the national level, the collection is known as the *Statutes at Large,* whereas state collections are generally referred to as session laws. These are helpful if one knows the session and year of passage, but as the volumes are organized chronologically and not topically and are published yearly or after each session, they are not overly helpful for tracing the development of a point of law or ensuring that one has the most current information.

That need has been met through codification on both the state and national level. Codes are arranged topically, which simplifies the task of working with statutes. They are also updated and contain amendments to the statute. It is very important to check the pocket part of these volumes to access more recent information. The official edition of the national laws is the *United States Code* (U.S.C.), published by the national government, and there are annotated versions such as the *United States Code Annotated*® (U.S.C.A.) and the *United States Code Service* (U.S.C.S.), published by private companies. A national statute that has not yet been codified would be cited to the *Statutes at Large* or, if it has been codified, to the U.S.C. or one of the annotated versions. On the state level, the same holds true. A state statute would be cited to the sessions laws—*Acts and Joint Resolutions, South Carolina*—or to a state code, if one exists—*Code of Laws of South Carolina*. Most sets of codes also contain conversion tables in order that one may move from the session laws to the codes as well as a *Popular Names Table*. The latter identifies cases by the popular name, such as the Selective Service Act, and provides the citation for it.

Locating the legislative history or what is said during various committee hearings and floor debates may be critical when dealing with statutory ambiguity. While legislative history is not actually law and is therefore persuasive authority only, it is valuable because it provides information about the intent of the legislators. In cases involving statutory interpretation, courts frequently rely on this type of information to divine the actual intent of those writing the law. Legislative history may be found in transcripts of committee hearings, committee reports, and reports of debates on both the state and national level.[19]

Administrative regulations are promulgated by governmental agencies under their rulemaking authority. The public is often invited to comment on proposed regulations, and these (if federal in nature), along with adopted regulations and other matters such as executive orders, are available electronically and in printed form in the *Federal Register*, a daily publication. The *Code of Federal Regulations* (C.F.R.) is the compilation of the administrative regulations by subject matter and, through a rotation basis, is entirely revised each year and is updated daily through the unofficial e-CFR.[20] Generally, agencies with decision-making authority, such as the Internal Revenue Service or the National Labor Relations Board, must make their decisions available to the public. This is done through either official or private publication, often in the form of loose-leaf and electronic services, which are easily updated. On the state level, similar publications exist along with publication of the state *Attorney General's Opinions* that indicate his or her opinion of the legality of state and local officials' activities or interpretations of state law.

Legal Encyclopedias, Annotations, and Treatises

When the researcher needs to begin with a general overview of the topic and legal principles, the best source is one of the legal encyclopedias. Two extensive and widely accepted legal encyclopedias are *American Jurisprudence 2d* (Am. Jur.2d) and *Corpus Juris Secundum* (C.J.S.). Both are topically arranged and present succinct but thorough narrative discussions of general legal rules with extensive cross-references to other types of materials, such as cases, statutes, and law review articles. Courts often cite both works in their opinions, although local practice will dictate whether Am. Jur.2d or C.J.S., rather than cases, is acceptable for trial or appellate arguments, especially formal appellate briefs.

Local reference encyclopedias are available for some states, such as *California Jurisprudence 3d* or *Encyclopedia of Mississippi Law*. In addition, single-focus encyclopedias are also published. Examples of these are *Corbin on Contracts* or *Wigmore on Evidence*. These encyclopedias are distinguishable from learned treatises in that the encyclopedias merely summarize the law, whereas treatises also interpret and evaluate the law. Some treatises are multi-volume sets, while others are single volumes.

The topical organization of legal encyclopedias is similar to that employed in the *American Law Report*® (A.L.R.) series. Annotations of appellate cases include historical analysis of the legal doctrine, current law in those jurisdictions that have considered the matter, and probable future developments. It is the annotation, and not the case itself, to which one refers when using this source. Like Am. Jur.2d and C.J.S., A.L.R.® is frequently cited by judges in their opinions, but researchers should use caution in relying on it in court, as it is secondary authority and therefore not binding.

Legal Dictionaries

One of the most basic of all research aids, regardless of type of research, is the dictionary. Specialized law dictionaries are available that contain definitions of legal terms drawn from cases and that assist with pronunciation of the words. Three of the most commonly used and more traditional dictionaries are *Black's Law Dictionary*, *Ballentine's Law Dictionary*, and *Bouvier's Law Dictionary*. Legal thesauri and glossaries are available as well.

Legal Periodicals

Legal periodicals, also persuasive authority, contain commentaries and analyses of the law and include not only law reviews but other law-related journals as well. Law reviews are journals published by law schools with scholarly articles on legal issues by law professors, outstanding students, attorneys, and judges. Most law reviews contain articles on a potpourri of subjects, although some are topical in which all articles relate to a single topic; as, for example, the *Journal of Biosecurity, Biosafety, and Biodefense Law* published by Texas Tech School of Law. Law review articles are particularly helpful in critical analysis of court decisions and in identifying trends in the law; they frequently contain extensive case and statutory citations that can assist the researcher.

Computer-Assisted Research

Law with its entrenched reliance on history and precedent is not always forward-looking, and its practitioners are sometimes recalcitrant and somewhat leery of changing established patterns of behavior and operation. However, the legal profession has joined the computer age, albeit with varying degrees of reluctance. Computers, tablets, and cell phones are ubiquitous—in lawyers' offices, on the floors of various legislative bodies, in judges' chambers, and in courtrooms as well. Lawyers today communicate with their clients via e-mail, instant messaging, or texting; establish a home page on the web and social media to advise other firms and clients of their specializations; convene a meeting among participants who may be in a distant location with both audio and video transmissions; and file court documents online. Seminars with the nation's leading experts are available through commercial services on the Internet. Legal encyclopedias, indexes to legal and other periodicals and databases, and the various reporters are readily available online. Software packages designed especially for attorneys allow them to internally administer the firm's business, including billing and tracking clients' cases, to draft and modify various legal instruments quickly, to manage complex cases that involve literally thousands of exhibits, and to access pleadings, briefs, and court opinions for research. A plethora of individual courts as well as states and the national government maintain websites that allow almost instantaneous access to a multitude of legal information. For example, the staff of the U.S. Supreme Court annually update their list of "Where to Obtain Supreme Court Opinions" on the Supreme Court's website that includes paper, electronic, official, and unofficial publications

Today there are many commercial legal databases, but in the beginning there were only two—LEXIS (now LexisNexis®, a division of Reed Elsevier) and Westlaw® (Thomson Reuters). Initially, these interactive networks, available only on a contract basis with time-related and/or transaction-related fees, were relatively expensive. However, like so many other computer-related products and services, they have declined in price and broadened the richness of their coverage as others have joined the field. Whether dealing with the specialized legal databases or other research services, the researcher should carefully hone the research problem to avoid being inundated with irrelevant material. Identifying the problem with the descriptive words is a critical part of formulating the research plan when using computer-assisted research. The databases are somewhat chequered, in that older cases, especially state court decisions, and other materials are not always available. Even given the limitations and the expense of computer-based research, many law firms and researchers feel that the advantages of speed, thoroughness, scope, and flexibility are worth the investment.

Technology is affecting not only the retrieval of information but also its storage. As Justice Joseph Story bemoaned, "The mass of law is, to be sure, accumulating with an almost incredible rapidity ... It is impossible not to look without some discouragement upon the ponderous volumes, which the next half century will add to the groaning shelves of our jurists." The date of his complaint? 1821.[21] Professor Thomas Baker pointed out that the growth rate has been accelerating. Using the *Federal Reporter, Second Series* as an example, he noted that the total volumes reached "100 in 1939 (14 years); 200 in 1953 (14 years); 300 in 1962 (9 years); 400 in 1969 (7 years); 500 in 1975 (6 years); 600 in 1979 (4 years); 700 in 1983 (4 years); 800 in 1987 (4 years); 900 in 1990 (3 years); and 999 in 1993 (3 years)."[19] The proliferation of volumes poses problems of storage for all libraries with limited shelf space. Technology has relieved the severity of the problem. Many government records—statutes, administrative rulings, court opinions, and others—were placed on microfilm and microfiche that require very little storage space or are scanned directly into electronic databases that researchers may use on their personal computers— both those on the office desk and the smaller notebooks or tablets that travel with the attorney to court, to depositions, and elsewhere. This tool effectively provides the attorney with a portable library that is instantaneously available, possibly the advantage needed to win the case.

CONCLUSION

A legal system which is founded on precedent requires that practitioners be able to locate that precedent in order to sway judges and juries at trial and to adequately perform their responsibilities to clients. The findings of the research form the basis for advising the client and acting as advocate. Because the task is so important, researchers are blessed in that the rich body of knowledge encompassed in the law is very organized, widely indexed, and widely circulated.

Researchers are further favored in that there is no single correct approach to initiating or designing the research. A variety of research media is available whether the researcher has only the sketchiest of information or is an expert in the field. Cases and statutory materials are the primary sources of the law and may be found in case reporters, session laws, or annotated codes. Other secondary sources (for example, legal periodicals and encyclopedias) are also readily obtainable and provide theories, philosophies, and summaries that are persuasive to judges and helpful in ascertaining the status of the law in order that we "may be exact in the law."

NOTES

1. Gilbert Burnet, *History of His Own Times*, as cited in Simon James and Chantal Stebbings, comps., *A Dictionary of Legal Quotations* (New York: Macmillan, 1987), p. 88.
2. Robert Burton, *The Anatomy of Melancholy*, as cited in James and Stebbings, p. 88.

3. Martin Weinstein, *Summary of American Law* (Rochester, NY: Lawyers Co-operative, 1988), pp. 100–101.
4. *Flood v. Kuhn*, 407 U.S. 258 (1972).
5. Bob Woodward and Scott Armstrong, *The Brethren* (New York: Simon & Schuster, 1979), p. 229.
6. *Roe v. Wade*, 410 U.S. 113 (1973).
7. *Craig v. Boren*, 429 U.S. 190 (1976).
8. *McCleskey v. Kemp*, 481 U.S. 29 (1987).
9. J. Myron Jacobstein and Roy M. Mersky, *Fundamentals of Legal Research*, 8th edn (Westbury, NY: The Foundation Press, 2002), pp. 14–20.
10. Joshua Poje, "Legal Research," *ABA TechReport 2014*, http://www.americanbar.org/publications/techreport/2014/legal-research.html. Visited November 12, 2015.
11. Larry L. Teply, *Legal Research and Citation*, 5th edn (St. Paul, MN: West Group, 1999), pp. 75–84.
12. William P. Statsky and R. John Wernet, Jr., *Case Analysis and Fundamentals of Legal Writing*, 4th edn (St. Paul, MN: West, 1995), pp. 154, 170.
13. George E. Dix, "A Plea for Clarity," *Texas Lawyer*, October 12, 1992, p. 10.
14. *Texas v. Brown*, 460 U.S. 730 (1983).
15. Henry C. Black, *Black's Law Dictionary*, 4th edn (St. Paul, MN: West, 1968), pp. 541, 1429.
16. Association of Legal Writing Directors/Legal Writing Institute, *ALWD/LWI 2014 Survey Report*, http://www.alwd.org/wp-content/uploads/2014/07/2014-Survey-Report-Final.pdf, p. vii. Visited November 12, 2015.
17. Peter W. Martin, "Introduction to Basic Legal Citation (online ed. 2015)," Cornell School of Law, https://www.law.cornell.edu/citation/. Visited November 12, 2015.
18. Jacobstein and Mersky, pp. 81–114; Teply, pp. 293–300.
19. Teply, pp. 340–415.
20. Code of Federal Regulations, http://www.gpo.gov/help/index.html#about_code_of_federal_regulations.htm.; Electronic Code of Federal Regulations, http://www.ecfr.gov/cgi-bin/ECFR?page=browse. Visited November 12, 2015.
21. Justice Joseph Story, as quoted in Thomas E. Baker, "The Third Millennium of Federal Reporter," *Texas Lawyer*, January 17, 1994, p. 18.
22. Baker, p. 18.

GLOSSARY

Acceptance. In contract law, the offeree's compliance with the terms of an offer and the manifestation of such compliance.

Accessory. A person who contributes to or aids in the commission of a crime.

Accessory after the fact. A person who receives, relieves, comforts, or assists another, knowing that he or she has committed a felony.

Actus reus. The "guilty act"; the forbidden act or omission that is an element of a crime.

Adjudication. The resolution or settlement of a dispute between two parties by a third party.

Administrative law. The law that governs the actions of administrative agencies.

Adoption. The act of voluntarily assuming the rights and obligations of a parent over a child.

Adverse possession. A method of acquiring title to land by possession.

Adverse witness. Also called a hostile witness, an adverse witness is one who provides prejudicial information against the party conducting the examination.

Affinity. Related by marriage, such as a mother-in-law and son-in-law or stepchildren or stepbrothers.

Age of majority. The age set by statute at which one loses the disabilities of minority and becomes able to enter legally binding contracts.

Annulment. Dissolution of a marriage that was invalid from its inception through judicial action.

Answer. The defendant's response to allegations made by the plaintiff in the latter's complaint.

Appellant. The party, usually the losing one, that seeks to overturn the decision of a trial court by appealing to a higher court.

Appellate court. A court that hears appeals on points of law from trial courts.

Appellee. The party, usually the winning one, against whom a case is appealed.

Arbitration. The submission of an argument to a neutral party for resolution under an agreement by the parties to be bound by the decision or under a court order.

Arraignment. The stage of the criminal justice process in which the defendant is formally informed of the charges and allowed to enter a plea.

Arrest warrant. A court order that allows the police to take a person accused of a crime into custody.

Artificial person. A corporation that is given certain human attributes by legal fiction in order that it may sue and be sued.

Assault. The apprehension of an offensive or unwanted contact from another person.

Assignment. The transfer of a present contractual interest to a third party.

Battery. Harmful or offensive contact with another person.

Bench trial. A trial conducted without a jury in which the judge serves as the trier of fact.

Best interest of a child. An objective standard used by the courts in determining custody of a child in contested cases or in adoption cases.

Bilateral contract. A contract in which the parties exchange promises to do some future act.

Bond. Something of value, either money or property, posted by a criminal defendant to ensure the defendant's appearance in court.

Bound over. If, at the preliminary hearing, the judge believes that sufficient probable cause exists to hold a criminal defendant, the accused is said to be bound over for trial.

Breach of contract. Failure to perform any aspect of a contract.

Brief. A legal document in which an attorney outlines the facts, alleged errors, and precedents in a case appealed to a higher court.

Canon law. A system of church law.

Capacity. The ability of an individual who is not under some legal disqualification, such as infancy or insanity, to enter into legally binding agreements.

Case law. A law that develops through the interpretation of previous cases, statutes, constitutions, treaties, and other forms of written law.

Caveat emptor. Literally, "let the buyer beware." At common law, the doctrine that purchasers of goods must inspect them to avoid being cheated by merchants.

Certification. One method of appealing to the U.S. Supreme Court by which the lower court formally identifies questions of law for decision.

Challenge for cause. One method of striking a potential juror because of specified reasons such as bias or prejudgment.

Charge to the jury. The instructions given to the jury by the judge in which the judge outlines what the jury must find in order to rule for the plaintiff and what they must find to rule for the defendant.

Chattel. An item of tangible property other than realty.

Choice-of-law question. In conflict of laws, determining which state law will be applied when some or all

the operative elements occurred in a jurisdiction other than the forum state.

Circumstantial evidence. An indirect method of proving the material facts of the case. Testimony that is not based on the witness's personal observation of the material events.

Civil action. A civil lawsuit brought by one person or corporation against another.

Civil disobedience. The theory that a person may disobey human laws that conflict with natural law or God's law.

Civil law. A system of law, both criminal and non-criminal, in which the legislature is the ultimate law-maker and that relies on codes rather than court precedent as the basis of decisions; the dominant world legal system.

Closing statement. The address made by an attorney at the end of the presentation of evidence in which the attorney summarizes the case for the jury.

Codicil. A formal modification of the terms of a will.

Comity. In conflict of laws, a willingness to accept judgments of foreign courts as a matter of courtesy or respect.

Common law. Laws developed, mainly in England, by judges who made legal decisions in the absence of written law. Such decisions served as precedents and became "common" to all of England.

Community property. Property gained during marriage that belongs to each spouse equally unless it is a gift or inheritance as defined by the marital property laws in community property states.

Comparative negligence. A theory that allocates negligence between the plaintiff and the defendant and that allows the plaintiff to recover, even if he or she contributed to his or her own injury.

Complaining witness. In criminal law, the person, often the victim, who swears out a complaint against another, leading to an arrest warrant being issued against the latter.

Complaint. In civil law, a legal document in which the plaintiff makes certain allegations of injury and liability against the defendant. In criminal law, the written accusation of a criminal act against a criminal defendant.

Concurring opinion. An opinion by an appellate court judge in which the judge agrees with the decision of the majority but not for the same reasons given in the majority opinion.

Consanguinity. Related by blood such as parents and children, siblings, or cousins.

Consideration. The inducement to contract that may include money, mutual exchange of promises, or the agreement of parties to do or refrain from doing some act.

Constitutional court. A type of federal court created by Congress under its power under Article III of the Constitution to create courts inferior to the Supreme Court.

Constitutional law. Law that consists of court decisions that interpret and expand the meaning of a written constitution.

Contingency fee. The normal fee arrangement in a civil suit in which the attorney receives a percentage of any award won by the plaintiff.

Contributory negligence. A legal theory that totally bars the plaintiff who contributed, even slightly, to his or her own injury from recovering damages.

Conversion. The deprivation of an owner of possession of tangible property.

Copyright. Exclusive legal right to sell, reproduce, or publish a literary, artistic, or musical work.

Corporation. A business organization in which the owners are the stockholders who have limited liability and management responsibilities based on the pro rata share of ownership.

Corpus. The principal of a trust as opposed to the interest or income.

Court of general jurisdiction. Trial court responsible for major criminal and civil cases.

Court of last resort. At the state level, the highest court with jurisdiction over a particular case. At the national level, the U.S. Supreme Court.

Court of limited jurisdiction. Lower-level state court, such as a justice of the peace court, whose jurisdiction is limited to minor civil disputes or misdemeanors.

Court of record. A court in which a record of the proceedings is kept, usually in the form of a transcript made by a court reporter.

Criminal law. Laws passed by government that define and prohibit antisocial behavior.

Cross-examination. At trial, the questions of one attorney put to a witness called by the opposing attorney.

Culpability. In law, a person who is blameworthy or responsible in whole or in part for the commission of a crime or injury.

Damages. Pecuniary or monetary compensation paid by the wrongdoer in a civil case.

Defamation. The injury to one's reputation in the community by defamatory comments.

Default judgment. A judgment awarded to the plaintiff because the defendant has failed to answer the complaint.

Defendant. The person against whom a lawsuit is brought.

Delegation. In administrative law, the theory that allows a legislative body to delegate its law-making power to administrative agencies.

Delegatus non potest delegare. Literally, "a delegate cannot delegate." A person who has been empowered by another to do something may not redelegate that power to another.

Demurrer. A motion by the defendant asking for dismissal of a case on the grounds that the plaintiff has insufficient grounds to proceed.

Deposition. A form of discovery that involves taking the sworn testimony of a witness outside open court.

Determinate sentencing. A sentencing structure in which a flat or straight sentence is imposed, generally without possibility of parole.

Direct causation. The causing or bringing about of an effect without the interference of an intervening variable or factor.

Direct evidence. Evidence derived from one or more of the five senses.

Direct examination. At trial, the questions asked of a witness by the attorney who called the witness to the stand.

Directed verdict. An order from a judge to the jury ordering the latter to decide the case in favor of one of the parties for failure of the other party to prove its case.

Discovery. A pretrial procedure in which parties to a lawsuit ask for and receive information such as testimony, records, or other evidence from each other.

Dissenting opinion. A written opinion of an appellate court judge in which the judge states his or her reasons for disagreeing with the decision of the majority.

Diversity of citizenship suit. A specific type of federal lawsuit between citizens of two different states in which the amount in controversy exceeds $75,000.

Divine right of kings. The medieval theory that the king was chosen by God to rule, thereby establishing the king's legitimacy.

Divorce. Dissolution of the marital relationship through judicial action.

Domicile. A person's legal home.

Donee. One who receives a gift.

Donor. One who gives a gift.

Due process of law. A term used in the Fifth and Fourteenth Amendments to refer to the process that is due before government may deprive a person of life, liberty, or property.

Easement. The right to use someone else's property.

Emancipation. The removal of one's legal disability of being a minor, either by reaching the age of majority or by other statutory methods such as marriage or by court order.

Eminent domain. The power of the government to take private property for public use.

En banc. A situation in which all the members of an appellate court participate in the disposition of a case.

Environmental law. Field of law that emphasizes the protection of wildlife and the environment in the public interest.

Equity. A branch of law that provides for remedies other than damages and is therefore more flexible than common law.

Estate in fee tail. A freehold estate that limits the succession to the "heirs of the body" or descendants of the donee or devisee.

Estate pur autre vie. An estate that is held during the lifetime of another.

Exclusionary rule. A judicially created rule which holds that evidence obtained through violations of the constitutional rights of the criminal defendant must be excluded from the trial.

Executed contract. A contract in which all the terms have been met or all action completed.

Executive privilege. The doctrine that permits the president to withhold information sought by Congress or the courts.

Executory contract. A contract in which some or all the terms remain to be completed.

Exhaustion of administrative remedies doctrine. In administrative law, the doctrine that requires persons aggrieved to avail themselves of all administrative remedies before seeking judicial relief.

Express contract. An oral or written contract that explicitly states the contract terms.

Express warranty. An explicit statement or promise that a certain fact in relation to the subject of the contract is true or accurate.

Federal question. A question of law over which a federal court exercises jurisdiction, including interpretations of the Constitution, treaties, and federal statutes.

Federalism. A political system in which governmental powers are divided between a central government and regional and/or state governments.

Fee simple estate. An absolute interest in property; the fullest amount of control over property possible.

Fee tail female. An estate in fee tail that may only pass through the female line.

Fee tail male. An estate in fee tail that may only pass through the male line.

Feudalism. The social system of the Middle Ages that involved a series of reciprocal responsibilities from the king through the lords to the serfs.

Forum non conveniens. A legal doctrine that allows a court to refuse to accept jurisdiction over a case.

Foundation. Also known as "laying a predicate." Preliminary questions that establish the relevancy and admissibility of evidence.

Garnishment. Process whereby money owed to one person as a result of a court judgment may be withheld from the wages of another person known as the garnishee.

General damages. Damages, such as payment of medical bills, awarded to the plaintiff to restore him or her to the condition the person was in before he or she was injured by the defendant.

General verdict. A verdict in which the jury finds the defendant liable and awards the plaintiff the monetary damages sought, less than what was sought, or more than what was sought.

Gift. A voluntary transfer of property without consideration.

Grand jury. A group of citizens who decide whether persons accused of crimes should be indicted (true billed) or not (no billed).

Grantee. The person to whom property is being conveyed.

Grantor. The person who is conveying property.

Habeas corpus. Literally, "you have the body." In criminal law, a judicial writ ordering a law enforcement official to bring a person before the court and show cause as to why the person is being detained.

Harmless error. An error made during a trial that an appellate court feels is insufficient grounds for reversing a judgment.

Hearsay. An out-of-court assertion or statement made by someone other than the testifying witness that is being offered to prove the truth of the matter stated. Hearsay evidence is excluded from trials unless it falls within one of the recognized exceptions.

Heir. Generally, one who inherits property under a will or by intestate succession; technically, a person who receives a property interest through intestate succession.

Holographic will. A will that is written entirely in the handwriting of the testator.

Hung jury. A jury that is unable to reach a verdict, especially significant in criminal trials if a unanimous verdict is required.

Impanelled. After jurors are sworn in, the jury is said to be impanelled and in a criminal case the defendant is placed in "jeopardy."

Implied contract. A contract that is inferred from the conduct of the parties.

Implied Warranty of Merchantibility. The warranty imposed upon merchants that the goods are merchantible as defined in the UCC; the warranty is imposed even though the merchants do not actually make such claims.

Incorporation Theory. The theory that the Bill of Rights has been incorporated or absorbed into the due process clause of the Fourteenth Amendment, thereby making it applicable to the states.

Indictment. A formal accusation handed down by a grand jury of a criminal offense made against a person.

In forma pauperis. Literally, "in the manner of a pauper." A request for permission of the court for a poor person to seek judicial relief without having to pay the usual court fees.

Informal marriage. A type of legally recognized marriage created by informal means, also known as common law marriage.

Information. A formal accusation charging someone with the commission of a crime, signed by a prosecuting attorney, that has the effect of bringing the person to trial.

Initial appearance. During the initial appearance, the accused is informed of the charges against him or her, given his or her constitutional rights, informed of the amount of bail, and given a date for a preliminary hearing.

Injunction. A court order directing a person to refrain from doing certain acts or carrying out certain activities.

In personum jurisdiction. Jurisdiction of a court to enter a personal judgment or decree against the person.

In rem jurisdiction. Jurisdiction of a court to enter a decree affecting property interests.

Intangible property. Those items of property that are not capable of being touched such as debts owed to someone.

Interpretivism. The doctrine that judges should decide new constitutional issues in light of the underlying constitutional principles as well as the literal meaning of the written provisions.

Interrogatory. A form of discovery in which written questions about a lawsuit are submitted to one party by the other party.

Inter vivos. During life.

Intestate. To die without a will.

Invitee. In tort law, a business visitor on one's premises.

Jeopardy. The point in the criminal justice process where the accused is in danger of criminal liability. Once in jeopardy, the accused must be either acquitted or convicted and may not be placed again in jeopardy for the same offense.

Joint tenancy. Concurrent ownership of property in which the survivor inherits the entire property.

Judicial conduct board. An official body whose function it is to investigate allegations of misconduct made against judges.

Judicial gatekeeping. Term used to describe how judges control access to the judicial system by either opening or closing the judicial "gates" to certain kinds of controversies.

Judicial notice. A method of providing trial evidence which allows the court to accept facts that are commonly known or verifiable without formal proof.

Judicial review. The power of a court to declare acts of governmental bodies contrary to the Constitution null and void.

Jurisdiction. The power and authority of courts to render a binding decision in a case.

Laying a predicate. Also known as "laying a foundation." Preliminary questions that establish the relevancy and admissibility of evidence.

Leading question. A question by which an attorney attempts to put words into the mouth of a witness; that is, a question which states the information to which the attorney wishes the witness to testify.

Lease. An agreement, oral or written, that governs the rental of property.

Legislative address. A method of judicial removal used in some states that allows the state legislature to remove a state judge, usually by a two-thirds vote.

Legislative courts. A type of federal court created by Congress under one of its legislative powers; for example, military and territorial courts.

Lessee. Also known as the tenant; the person who is in possession of the property under a lease.

Lessor. Also known as the landlord; the person who owns the fee simple estate and carves out a small estate for a tenant.

Libel. Defamation that is preserved in some permanent form.

Licensee. In tort law, a social guest on one's property.

Lien. An encumbrance on property that is the result of a security interest held by the creditor.

Life estate. An estate in land that is held only during one's lifetime or during the life of another.

Long-arm statute. A legislative enactment that extends a court's jurisdiction to nonresident parties as long as there are "minimum contacts"

between the litigant and the state, a requirement of due process.

Majority opinion. The opinion of a majority of appellate court judges in which the decision of the court and its reasons for that decision are given.

Malum in se. Literally, "wrong in itself." In criminal law, something that is made illegal because it is inherently or morally wrong.

Malum prohibitum. In criminal law, something, such as gambling, that is made illegal because government has deemed it undesirable, thereby prohibiting it.

Mandatory authority. Prior court cases, constitutional provisions, legislative enactments, court rules, or administrative regulations that are binding on courts in rendering decisions.

Mandatory release. Automatic release from prison when the calendar time and good time served equal the maximum time for which the inmate was sentenced.

Marriage. A legally recognized special relationship between two people that is founded in contract.

Mediation. The process whereby a neutral third person intervenes in a controversy to assist the parties in achieving a resolution.

Mens rea. Literally, "the guilty mind." The wrongful purpose that is an element of a crime.

Missouri Plan. The name given to a method of judicial selection that combines merit selection and popular control in retention elections.

Mootness. A term used to describe a case that has become a dead issue because the controversy that gave rise to the case was resolved before a final judicial decision could be made.

Motion *in limine*. A motion that bars prejudicial questions and statements on specified topics.

Municipal court. A court whose jurisdiction is limited to the geographic area of a municipality or incorporated area. Cases are limited to minor offenses and violations of municipal ordinances.

Natural law. The theory that human law must conform to the laws of God and nature, just as the physical world must conform to the laws of physics.

Negligence. A theory of tort recovery involving a legal duty, a breach of duty, proximate cause, and injury.

Negligence per se. A method of establishing the defendant's negligence by proving a violation of a safety statute or regulation.

No bill. A term used to describe the decision of a grand jury not to indict a person for a crime.

No-fault divorce. A divorce in which neither party must allege or prove fault (adultery, cruelty, etc.). In order to dissolve the marriage, the grounds are generally incompatibility or failure of the marriage.

Nolo contendere. Literally, "I will not contest it." A plea, tantamount to a guilty plea, in which the accused refuses to admit culpability but accepts the punishment of the court.

Non-interpretivism. The doctrine that the Constitution should be interpreted according to evolving standards of decency and justice and not frozen in time or meaning.

Nuisance. The use of the defendant's land in such a way that it interferes with the plaintiff's use or enjoyment of the plaintiff's land.

Nuncupative will. An oral will.

Obiter dictum. Also known as *dicta;* statements in a judicial opinion that were not essential to the resolution of the case and are not binding precedent.

Offer. A proposal to enter into a contract.

Offeree. The person to whom an offer is made.

Offeror. The person making an offer.

Opening statement. Address made by attorneys for both parties at the beginning of a trial in which they outline for the jury what they intend to prove in their case.

Oral argument. The part of the appellate court decision-making process in which lawyers for both parties plead their cases in person before the court.

Oral testimony. A form of evidence that is given by the witness on the stand in open court or in a deposition under oath.

Ordinance power. The power of cities and other local government units to enact regulations binding on citizens within their jurisdiction.

Original intention. The doctrine which holds that judges should interpret the Constitution in accordance with the intent of the Framers.

Panel. A group of appellate judges, less than the full membership of the court, assigned to review a case on appeal.

Parol evidence rule. A rule of contract construction that prevents modification of written contracts by any oral statements.

Parole. Punishment for a crime that involves release from incarceration on the condition of good behavior.

Partnership. A business organization in which ownership is shared by two or more people and/or legal entities.

Party. One of the principals, either the plaintiff or the defendant, in a lawsuit.

Patent. Exclusive legal monopoly granted by the government to sell, use, or assign the right to use or sell a product or process that one has invented, created, or discovered.

Peremptory challenge. A method used to strike a potential juror from the jury without specifying the reason for doing so.

Personal service. A notice to a party of pending litigation, or providing a copy of a subpoena to a witness, that is personally delivered.

Personalty. All property except realty or those items that cannot be severed from the realty without damage to it.

Persuasive authority. Secondary sources or materials from other jurisdictions by which courts are not bound but upon which they may rely in deciding cases.

Physical taking. The taking of property under eminent domain by which the government takes physical possession of one's property.

Plaintiff. The person or party who initiates a lawsuit.

Plea bargain. An arrangement whereby the accused agrees to exchange a plea of guilty for a lesser sentence, a reduction of charges, or some other consideration by the court.

Plurality opinion. Any written opinion of an appellate court in which the majority agree on the outcome but not the rationale for the decision.

Political question. The doctrine that courts will not decide cases which involve issues for which a final decision is clearly left to one of the political branches of government by the Constitution.

Positive law. The theory that law is merely a reflection of the will of the strongest in a society.

Precedent. A case previously decided that serves as a legal guide for the resolution of subsequent cases.

Preliminary hearing. Either a pretrial hearing at which motions are considered or, in criminal law, a pretrial hearing to determine whether there is probable cause to hold the accused for an indictment.

Prenuptial agreements. Also known as antenuptial agreements; these are contracts entered into before marriage by the spouses that outline certain conditions such as the division of property in case of divorce.

Preponderance of the evidence. In civil law, the standard of proof required to prevail at trial. To win, a plaintiff must show that the greater weight, or preponderance of the evidence, supports his or her version of the facts.

Pretrial publicity. Prejudicial information, often inadmissible at trial, which is circulated by the news media before a trial and which may reduce the accused's chances of a trial before an impartial jury.

***Prima facie* case.** The plaintiff's version of the facts, which if taken at first glance or "first face" seems to substantiate the plaintiff's allegations against the defendant.

Primary jurisdiction doctrine. In administrative law, the doctrine that requires litigants to take a dispute to the administrative agency with primary responsibility for handling the dispute before seeking judicial relief.

Primogeniture. A legal doctrine whereby the oldest son alone inherits the property of his ancestors.

Principal. In criminal law, a chief actor who participates in the crime or who recruits an innocent agent to participate.

Principal brief. A brief filed by an appellant that includes the issues and legal arguments to be appealed.

Prior restraint. The censoring of material by the government before it is published rather than penalizing the publisher after publication.

Private nuisance. A common law tort which forbids the use of one's property in a way that is offensive or obnoxious to one's neighbors.

Privilege. In evidence, a recognized right to keep certain communications confidential or private.

Probable cause. Standard used to determine whether a crime has been committed and whether there is sufficient evidence to believe that a specific individual committed it.

Probation. Punishment for a crime that allows the offender to remain in the community without incarceration but subject to certain court-established conditions.

Procedural due process. A theory of due process which stresses "by-the-book" adherence to predetermined rules of behavior that government must observe.

Procedural law. Law which outlines the legal procedures or process that government is obliged to follow.

Product liability. A theory of tort recovery that imposes liability on the manufacturer, seller, or distributor of dangerous products for injuries sustained by consumers and bystanders who use the product.

Promissory estoppel. A contract remedy that is employed where one party has changed positions in reliance of the other party's gratuitous promise.

Property. The legal right to use or dispose of particular things or subjects.

Proximate cause. The theory that the injury sustained by the plaintiff and the defendant's action were so closely connected that the defendant's act caused the injury and there were no intervening causes.

Public nuisance. The use of one's property in a way that offends the health, safety, or morals of the general public.

Punitive damages. Money beyond actual damages awarded against a defendant whose conduct was so wanton, reckless, or reprehensible as to justify additional punishment.

Quasi-in-rem jurisdiction. The power and authority of courts to enter a judgment affecting property interests to satisfy the owner's personal obligations, even though the owner is not otherwise subject to the court's jurisdiction.

Quitclaim deed. A written instrument conveying the grantor's interest in property, not the title to the property itself.

Ratio decidendi. Those statements in a judicial opinion that are essential to the resolution of the case and are binding precedent.

Realty. Also known as real property; land and the appurtenances thereto.

Reasonably prudent person. A mythical person created by the courts who is used as the objective standard by which the party's conduct is measured.

Recall. A method used in some states to remove judges from office. Recall elections allow the voters directly to remove judges from the bench.

Recognizance. A term used to describe the release of an accused person from custody without requiring a property or money bond.

Re-cross-examination. The questions asked of a witness after direct examination, cross-examination, and redirect examination. Essentially, a second series of questions asked of a witness called by the opposing attorney.

Redirect examination. The follow-up questions asked of his or her own witness by the attorney who originally called the witness to the stand.

Regulatory law. The rules and regulations promulgated by administrative agencies that are just as binding as statutes passed by legislatures.

Regulatory taking. A taking under eminent domain that does not involve the actual possession of the property by the government, such as zoning regulations.

Remittitur. The process by which a jury verdict of money damages is reduced because the amount is excessive.

Renvoi. A legal theory applicable where there is a choice-of-law question and the forum state adopts the entire law of the sister state.

Reply brief. The brief filed by the appellee that attempts to rebut the appellant's grounds for the appeal.

Repudiation. The contract remedy excusing one party from performance of the contract terms based on the other party's statements of prospective nonperformance.

Res ipsa loquitur. A method of showing the defendant's tort liability by proving that all the instrumentalities were under the defendant's control and that the accident is of a kind that would not have occurred without negligence.

Respondeat superior. A theory of vicarious liability in which the employer or master is financially responsible for the torts of employees or servants.

Reversible error. An error made at trial serious enough to warrant a new trial.

Riparian rights. A landowner's right to extract, divert, control, or use water.

Ripeness. The doctrine that an appellate court will not review the decision of a lower court until all remedies have been exhausted. Courts will not decide an issue before the need to do so.

Roman law. A system of laws created by the Romans and codified in the *Code of Justinian.*

Rule against perpetuities. The rule that interests in property must vest not later than 21 years after the lives of the persons specified at the time that the interests were created.

Rule enforcement. The power of an administrative agency to enforce rules promulgated by the agency under its rulemaking authority.

Rulemaking. The power of an administrative agency to promulgate rules and regulations concerning matters that fall within its jurisdiction. Rules promulgated by administrative agencies have the force of law.

Rule of four. The requirement that four Supreme Court justices must agree to

hear a case before the Court will grant a writ of *certiorari.*

Scienter. An element of a crime that requires special knowledge or awareness.

Seisin. Possession of land under a claim of a freehold estate, very akin to absolute ownership of land.

Selective incorporation. As opposed to total incorporation, the doctrine that only those parts of the Bill of Rights deemed "fundamental" are incorporated into the Due Process Clause of the Fourteenth Amendment.

Senatorial courtesy. The custom in the U.S. Senate that requires the president to clear judicial appointments with the senators of the state wherein the appointment occurs when the senators are of the president's party.

Separation of powers. The constitutional arrangement whereby legislative, executive, and judicial powers are exercised by three separate and distinct branches of government.

Sequestered. A jury is sequestered when its members are isolated from the community until it has reached a final verdict.

Service. The process of formally delivering the complaint or a subpoena to the defendant or a witness in a lawsuit.

Shield law. A law that allows a newspaper or other reporter to refuse to disclose the source of his or her information in a criminal case. Shield laws are a type of privilege.

Slander. Defamation that is spoken or not preserved in permanent form.

Small claims court. A lower-level state court whose jurisdiction is limited to a specified dollar amount; for example, that damages may not exceed $1500.

Sociological theory of law. The theory that law is a function of the society that makes it and that law changes as society changes.

Sole proprietorship. A business organization in which ownership is vested in a single individual who receives all profits but who also bears all liability.

Special issues verdict. A verdict in which the jury answers a series of questions rather than merely entering a general finding.

Special warranty deed. A written deed conveying all property interests held by, through, or under the grantor.

Specific relief. Equitable remedies that are directed to the defendant personally and obligate him or her to do or refrain from doing some activity.

Spousal support. Court-ordered support payments from one spouse to the other during or following the dissolution of marriage.

Standing. The doctrine requiring that a party bringing suit before a court must have a legal right to do so.

Stare decisis. The policy of courts to follow the rules laid down in previous cases and not to disturb settled points of law.

Statutes of limitations. Statutes that prescribe the time periods in which lawsuits must be filed.

Statutory law. Laws, called statutes, passed by legislative bodies that bestow benefits, impose obligations, or prohibit antisocial behavior.

Subpoena. An order from a court directing a person to appear before the court and to give testimony about a cause of action pending before it.

Subpoena duces tecum. An order from a court directing a person to appear before the court with specified documents that the court deems relevant in a matter pending before it.

Substantial evidence rule. Rule that says a finding of fact by an administrative agency is to be final if there is substantial evidence to support the agency's conclusion.

Substantive due process of law. A theory of due process that emphasizes judging the content of a law by a subjective standard of fundamental fairness.

Substantive law. Law that deals with the content or substance of the law; for example, the legal grounds for divorce.

Substituted service. A notice of pending litigation or other legal matters that is not personally delivered to the person; for example, publication of such a notice in the newspapers.

Substitutionary relief. The award of money damages as compensation for legally recognized losses.

Suit to partition land. A lawsuit dividing land held by co-owners or joint tenants into separate and distinct parts.

Summary judgment. Decision by a judge to rule in favor of one party because the opposing party failed to meet a standard of proof. For example, if a plaintiff fails to present a *prima facie* case, the judge may enter a summary judgment in favor of the defendant.

Summons. A court order directing the defendant to appear in court at a specified time and place, either in person or by filing a written answer to the plaintiff's complaint.

Suspect classification. Classification of persons, such as by race, to which the Supreme Court applies strict judicial scrutiny and for which government must offer compelling reasons to justify its use.

Suspended sentence. Punishment for a crime in which either the determination of guilt or the sentence is held in abeyance for good behavior and probable completion of certain court-imposed obligations.

Takings Clause. The clause in the Fifth Amendment to the U.S. Constitution that forbids the taking of private property for public use without just compensation.

Tangible evidence. Any evidence that the trier of fact may touch or observe in the courtroom.

Tangible property. Land and other material items that can be touched.

Taxpayer's suit. A suit brought by a person who claims standing on the basis of his or her status as a taxpayer.

Tenancies in common. Current ownership of property that does not carry a right of survivorship.

Tenure. The system of landholding in the feudal era wherein land was held in subordination to a superior.

Testamentary capacity. The mental ability of an individual to understand the legal consequences of the act of making a will.

Testate. To die with a will.

Testator. The person making a will.

Third-party beneficiary contracts. Contracts intended to benefit a third party; that is, one who is not a party to the contract.

Tort. A private or civil wrong in which the defendant's actions cause injury to the plaintiff or to property, and the usual remedy is money damages.

Tortfeasor. The wrongful actor in a tort suit.

Total incorporation. The doctrine that all of the federal Bill of Rights should be absorbed into the due process clause of the Fourteenth Amendment and made applicable to the states.

Trademark. A distinctive sound, symbol, color, device, or word that is associated with a product or service that identifies its origin and is legally reserved for that product or service.

Trespass to chattel. The damage to another's item of tangible, personal property.

Trespass to land. The injury to another's real property by an unlawful entry.

Trial de novo. Literally, a trial "from the beginning." Cases appealed from courts that have no transcript are reheard in their entirety "from the beginning."

Trier of fact. The trier of fact is responsible for hearing and viewing the evidence at trial and evaluating the veracity of it. The trier of fact may be either the judge or a jury.

True bill. A bill of indictment by a grand jury.

Trust. A right or property held by one person for the benefit of another.

Trustee. The person or institution that is vested, under an express or implied agreement, with property to be used for the benefit of another; also known as a fiduciary.

Trustor. The person creating a trust.

Ultra vires. Literally, "beyond the powers of." In administrative law, the doctrine that an administrative agency has exercised powers beyond those delegated to it by a legislative body.

Unconscionable contract. A contract in which one party imposed an unreasonably favorable contract on the other who lacked a meaningful choice as to the contract terms.

Unenforceable contract. Contracts that cannot be legally enforced because of some missing legal element, such as being notarized or witnessed.

Uniform Commercial Code (UCC). A set of uniform statutes governing commercial transactions that have been enacted by state legislatures with some modifications.

Unilateral contract. A contract in which one of the parties acts immediately in response to an offer.

Venire. A group of citizens from which members of the jury are chosen.

Venireman. A person called for jury duty.

Venue. The geographic location of a trial that is determined by constitutional or statutory provisions.

Vicarious liability. The shifting of liability from the tortfeasor to another party, usually an employer.

Void. Null, ineffective, not able to support the purpose for which it was intended.

Voidable. Something, such as a contract or marriage, that is not void in and of itself but can be voided at the option of the parties.

Voidable contract. A contract that one party may safely disaffirm under certain conditions while the other party is bound by its terms.

Void contract. A contract that is void from its inception.

Voir dire. Literally, "to speak truth." The process by which prospective jurors are questioned by attorneys to ascertain whether there is cause to strike them from jury.

Voluntary assumption of risk. A defense used in tort law that the plaintiff was cognizant of the danger and voluntarily chose to encounter the danger.

Warranty. A covenant or promise that a statement or fact is true.

Warranty deed. A written deed conveying property in which the grantor guarantees title and warrants that he or she will compensate the grantee for any failure of the title.

Will. The legal expression of one's wishes regarding the disposition of one's property that is to be effective after death.

Witness. A person called to the stand to give testimony in a trial.

Writ of *certiorari*. An order from a higher court to a lower court in which the former orders the latter to send up the record of case for review by the higher court.

Writ of execution. A court order allowing a law enforcement official to seize the property or assets of a defendant against whom a civil judgment has been rendered.

TABLE OF CASES

*Note: Page numbers in **bold** indicate references in the text.*

INDEX